X

Dictionary of Literary Biography

Dictionary of Literary Biography Documentary Series

Dictionary of Literary Biography Yearbooks

1980   edited by Karen L. Rood, Jean W. Ross, and Richard Ziegfeld (1981)

1981   edited by Karen L. Rood, Jean W. Ross, and Richard Ziegfeld (1982)

1982   edited by Richard Ziegfeld; associate editors: Jean W. Ross and Lynne C. Zeigler (1983)

1983   edited by Mary Bruccoli and Jean W. Ross; associate editor Richard Ziegfeld (1984)

1984   edited by Jean W. Ross (1985)

1985   edited by Jean W. Ross (1986)

1986   edited by J. M. Brook (1987)

1987   edited by J. M. Brook (1988)

1988   edited by J. M. Brook (1989)

1989   edited by J. M. Brook (1990)

1990   edited by James W. Hipp (1991)

1991   edited by James W. Hipp (1992)

1992   edited by James W. Hipp (1993)

1993   edited by James W. Hipp, contributing editor George Garrett (1994)

1994   edited by James W. Hipp, contributing editor George Garrett (1995)

1995   edited by James W. Hipp, contributing editor George Garrett (1996)

1996   edited by Samuel W. Bruce and L. Kay Webster, contributing editor George Garrett (1997)

1997   edited by Matthew J. Bruccoli and George Garrett, with the assistance of L. Kay Webster (1998)

1998   edited by Matthew J. Bruccoli, contributing editor George Garrett, with the assistance of D. W. Thomas (1999)

1999   edited by Matthew J. Bruccoli, contributing editor George Garrett, with the assistance of D. W. Thomas (2000)

2000   edited by Matthew J. Bruccoli, contributing editor George Garrett, with the assistance of George Parker Anderson (2001)

2001   edited by Matthew J. Bruccoli, contributing editor George Garrett, with the assistance of George Parker Anderson (2002)

2002   edited by Matthew J. Bruccoli and George Garrett; George Parker Anderson, Assistant Editor (2003)

Concise Series

Concise Dictionary of American Literary Biography, 7 volumes (1988–1999): *The New Consciousness, 1941–1968; Colonization to the American Renaissance, 1640–1865; Realism, Naturalism, and Local Color, 1865–1917; The Twenties, 1917–1929; The Age of Maturity, 1929–1941; Broadening Views, 1968–1988; Supplement: Modern Writers, 1900–1998.*

Concise Dictionary of British Literary Biography, 8 volumes (1991–1992): *Writers of the Middle Ages and Renaissance Before 1660; Writers of the Restoration and Eighteenth Century, 1660–1789; Writers of the Romantic Period, 1789–1832; Victorian Writers, 1832–1890; Late-Victorian and Edwardian Writers, 1890–1914; Modern Writers, 1914–1945; Writers After World War II, 1945–1960; Contemporary Writers, 1960 to Present.*

Concise Dictionary of World Literary Biography, 4 volumes (1999–2000): *Ancient Greek and Roman Writers; German Writers; African, Caribbean, and Latin American Writers; South Slavic and Eastern European Writers.*

Dictionary of Literary Biography® • Volume Two Hundred Eighty-Nine

Australian Writers, 1950–1975

Dictionary of Literary Biography® • Volume Two Hundred Eighty-Nine

Australian Writers, 1950–1975

Edited by
Selina Samuels

A Bruccoli Clark Layman Book

GALE®

THOMSON
✳
™
GALE

Detroit • New York • San Diego • San Francisco • Cleveland • New Haven, Conn. • Waterville, Maine • London • Munich

THOMSON
GALE

Dictionary of Literary Biography
Volume 289: Australian Writers, 1950–1975
Selina Samuels

LIBRARY OF CONGRESS CATALOGING-IN-PUBLICATION DATA

Australian writers, 1950-1975 / edited by Selina Samuels.
   p. cm. — (Dictionary of literary biography ; v. 289)
"Bruccoli Clark Layman book."
Includes bibliographical references and index.
   ISBN 0-7876-6826-5 (hardcover)
   1. Australian literature—20th century—Bio-bibliography—Dictionaries.
   2. Authors, Australian—20th century—Biography—Dictionaries.
   3. Australian literature—20th century—Dictionaries.
   4. Australia—In literature—Dictionaries. I. Samuels, Selina. II. Series.

PR9609.6.A973 2004
820.9'994'099409045—dc22   2003018899

Printed in the United States of America
10 9 8 7 6 5 4 3 2 1

Contents

Plan of the Series

The advisory board, the editors, and the publisher of the *Dictionary of Literary Biography* are joined in endorsing Mark Twain's declaration. The literature of a nation provides an inexhaustible resource of permanent worth. Our purpose is to make literature and its creators better understood and more accessible to students and the reading public, while satisfying the needs of teachers and researchers.

To meet these requirements, *literary biography* has been construed in terms of the author's achievement. The most important thing about a writer is his writing. Accordingly, the entries in *DLB* are career biographies, tracing the development of the author's canon and the evolution of his reputation.

The purpose of *DLB* is not only to provide reliable information in a usable format but also to place the figures in the larger perspective of literary history and to offer appraisals of their accomplishments by qualified scholars.

The publication plan for *DLB* resulted from two years of preparation. The project was proposed to Bruccoli Clark by Frederick G. Ruffner, president of the Gale Research Company, in November 1975. After specimen entries were prepared and typeset, an advisory board was formed to refine the entry format and develop the series rationale. In meetings held during 1976, the publisher, series editors, and advisory board approved the scheme for a comprehensive biographical dictionary of persons who contributed to literature. Editorial work on the first volume began in January 1977, and it was published in 1978. In order to make *DLB* more than a dictionary and to compile volumes that individually have claim to status as literary history, it was decided to organize volumes by topic, period, or genre. Each of these freestanding volumes provides a biographical-bibliographical guide and overview for a particular area of literature. We are convinced that this organization—as opposed to a single alphabet method—constitutes a valuable innovation in the presentation of reference material. The volume plan necessarily requires many decisions for the placement and treatment of authors. Certain figures will be included in separate volumes, but with different entries emphasizing the aspect of his career appropriate to each volume. Ernest Hemingway, for example, is represented in *American Writers in Paris, 1920–1939* by an entry focusing on his expatriate apprenticeship; he is also in *American Novelists, 1910–1945* with an entry surveying his entire career, as well as in *American Short-Story Writers, 1910–1945, Second Series* with an entry concentrating on his short fiction. Each volume includes a cumulative index of the subject authors and articles.

Since 1981 the series has been further augmented by the *DLB Yearbooks,* which update published entries, add new entries to keep the *DLB* current with contemporary activity, and provide articles on literary history. There have also been nineteen *DLB Documentary Series* volumes, which provide illustrations, facsimiles, and biographical and critical source materials for figures, works, or groups judged to have particular interest for students. In 1999 the *Documentary Series* was incorporated into the *DLB* volume numbering system beginning with *DLB 210: Ernest Hemingway.*

We define literature as the *intellectual commerce of a nation:* not merely as belles lettres but as that ample and complex process by which ideas are generated, shaped, and transmitted. *DLB* entries are not limited to "creative writers" but extend to other figures who in their time and in their way influenced the mind of a people. Thus the series encompasses historians, journalists, publishers, book collectors, and screenwriters. By this means readers of *DLB* may be aided to perceive literature not as cult scripture in the keeping of intellectual high priests but firmly positioned at the center of a nation's life.

DLB includes the major writers appropriate to each volume and those standing in the ranks behind them. Scholarly and critical counsel has been sought in deciding which minor figures to include and how full their entries should be. Wherever possible, useful references are made to figures who do not warrant separate entries.

Each *DLB* volume has an expert volume editor responsible for planning the volume, selecting the figures for inclusion, and assigning the entries. Volume editors are also responsible for preparing, where appropriate, appendices surveying the major periodicals and literary and intellectual movements for their volumes, as well as lists of further readings. Work on the series as a whole is coordinated at the Bruccoli Clark Layman editorial center in Columbia, South Carolina, where the editorial staff is responsible for accuracy and utility of the published volumes.

One feature that distinguishes *DLB* is the illustration policy–its concern with the iconography of literature. Just as an author is influenced by his surroundings, so is the reader's understanding of the author enhanced by a knowledge of his environment. Therefore *DLB* volumes include not only drawings, paintings, and photographs of authors, often depicting them at various stages in their careers, but also illustrations of their families and places where they lived. Title pages are regularly reproduced in facsimile along with dust jackets for modern authors. The dust jackets are a special feature of *DLB* because they often document better than anything else the way in which an author's work was perceived in its own time. Specimens of the writers' manuscripts and letters are included when feasible.

Samuel Johnson rightly decreed that "The chief glory of every people arises from its authors." The purpose of the *Dictionary of Literary Biography* is to compile literary history in the surest way available to us–by accurate and comprehensive treatment of the lives and work of those who contributed to it.

The *DLB* Advisory Board

Introduction

Dictionary of Literary Biography 289: Australian Writers, 1950–1975 is the third in the *DLB* series on Australian literature and the sequel to *DLB 230: Australian Literature, 1788–1914* and *DLB 260: Australian Writers, 1915–1950*. These volumes, and the one covering the period 1975–2000 that will follow, constitute the first *DLB* series devoted to the literary historiography of Australia and provide a thorough overview of the most prominent and influential Australian writers and of the central literary and cultural movements of the nation.

The post–World War II period in Australia is popularly regarded as one of conservatism and materialism, a period of calm following the upheaval and tragedy of the Great Depression and World War II. Australian factories increased production to satisfy the demand for such goods as refrigerators, stoves, and cars. Shortages in Europe led to demand for Australian wool, wheat, meat, and dairy products, as well as canned and dried fruits. Australia entered into a period of economic boom. Conservatism and loyalty to the British monarch were features of the leadership of Robert Menzies, who led the Liberal Party to victory in the 1949 federal election and remained in power for seventeen years. (He also served as prime minister briefly from 1939 to 1941.) Menzies's strong royalist sentiments fostered a sense that the period was one of continued colonialism, with Australia still considered a colony of Britain, enjoying secondary cultural status.

Postwar Australia was a land of burgeoning suburbia; the "typical Australian family" was the proud owner of a Holden car (a symbol of modern Australia but manufactured by American-owned General Motors), a Hills hoist rotary clothesline, and a Victa motor mower. This society saw itself as racially and culturally homogeneous: homosexuals, political radicals, and intellectuals were all treated with equal distrust and anxiety. While communism was never considered as serious a threat in Australia as it was in the United States, the Menzies government took a concerted anticommunist stance. (The attempt by the government to outlaw the Communist Party was narrowly defeated in the 1951 referendum.) Australia had won international respect for its Anzacs (see the Introduction to *Australian Writers, 1915–1950* for a discussion of the myth of Anzac) after valiant fighting in two world wars and was, in fact, experiencing an increasingly sophisticated literary and artistic environment. But Australians still had a strong sense that "real" culture took place elsewhere, most particularly in Europe.

This national sense of "cultural cringe," a phrase coined by A. A. Phillips in *The Australian Tradition: Studies in a Colonial Culture* (1958), and the overriding conservatism of mainstream culture encouraged expatriation among artists, writers, and academics. Expatriate writers of the period include Sumner Locke Elliott, who left Australia for America in 1948; Barbara Hanrahan, who divided her life between London and Adelaide; and Shirley Hazzard and Peter Porter, both of whom have spent the majority—if not all—of their adult lives outside Australia. While internationalization freed Australian writers, on one hand, from the constant analysis of the Australian identity and place that marks much of the literature of the nineteenth and early twentieth centuries, expatriation and the frequent (and continued) reluctance of Australian critics to accept expatriates as true Australian writers emphasizes the insecurity of Australian literary and cultural identity.

During the 1950s, Australian universities started taking Australian literature seriously as a field of study. The subject was contentious, however, and gave rise to a popular and often heated debate about the ways in which Australian literature should be interpreted and the extent of its value. The introduction of the study of Australian literature into the academy therefore came at a time of particular tension between protestations of national cultural confidence and continued anxiety about Australian cultural identity. Academics interested in Australian literature rather than the more established subjects had to justify their interest with reference to a system of evaluation based on the canon of English literature. This need for justification in turn gave rise to competition between academics, literary journalists, and the writers themselves for "ownership" of the definition and understanding of Australian literature. This atmosphere was, perhaps inevitably, an influence in the development of the literature of the period and in the compilation of literary histories and anthologies. Geoffrey Dutton's introduction to *The Literature of Australia*

(1964) ends with the celebratory, defiant, and faintly uncertain words:

> Literature in Australia has grown strong from its own roots and its own idiom. Without the need any more to be self-consciously "Australian" it can take an individual and mature place in the world-wide literature of the English language.

Despite the dominant atmosphere of conservatism that fostered Cold War anxiety and an overriding desire for security and prosperity, the period covered by this volume was one of cultural flux, particularly in the area of immigration. The basic tenet of the Australian immigration policy for more than a hundred years had been to strengthen "White Australia." Before Federation in 1901 (when what had been many Australian colonies, each administered separately by Britain, united into one federal government with six states and two territories), the colonies introduced anti-Chinese immigration restriction acts as a response to the influx of Chinese during the gold rushes of the 1850s. Federation was accompanied by the 1901 Immigration Restriction Act, better known as the White Australia Policy. Under this legislation, black labor from the Pacific Islands was expelled from Queensland sugar plantations, and Chinese were refused admission as immigrants.

The White Australia Policy created legislation in favor of British migration, and, failing that, a marked preference for immigrants from northern European countries. At the same time, and particularly after the experience of both world wars, the Australian government was conscious of the need to increase immigration to boost the population of the country. The Menzies government was concerned that if Australia continued to be underpopulated and largely empty, it would be vulnerable to the greed of Asian countries keen to colonize and populate Australia themselves. The nation thus must "populate or perish." In the period following World War II–despite the intention of the government to continue the White Australia Policy–refugees and "displaced persons" were allowed to enter the country in order to enable it to reach its immigration targets. The immigration net was cast wider and wider to include southern Europe (Italy and Greece most notably) and the Middle East–until the 1980s, when the Indo-Chinese were the largest ethnic group in the Australian immigration intake. A policy that had initially been planned to develop a homogeneous and racially pure society had, by default, produced one of the most ethnically diverse of all immigration programs, with immigrants from more than a hundred nationalities and ethnic groups. Between 1947 and 1973 immigration contributed nearly 60 percent of the increase in popula-

tion (if the Australian-born children of immigrant parents are included in the calculation). An ideology of assimilationism continued to dominate Australia in the 1950s and 1960s: the ideal immigrant was one who could easily and unproblematically be assimilated into Australian society. The newcomers were expected to fit in, abandon their old languages and customs, and adopt unquestioningly the "Australian way of life," life in "the lucky country."

While the majority of Anglo-Australians and politicians were still aspiring to a homogeneous Australian identity, the increase in non-Anglo or northern European immigrants was substantial, particularly immigrants from Mediterranean and eastern European countries. By June 1959, migrants from Holland, Italy, Greece, and Yugoslavia constituted almost half of the immigrants to have arrived in Australia since June 1947. As the population was changing, so was its literature. Judah Waten, whose family immigrated to Australia from Odessa in the U.S.S.R. in the years before World War I, is an example of a writer who initiated a sufficient change in the definition of "Australian literature" to allow for the possibility of literature by immigrants. Antigone Kefala and Peter Skrzynecki have also been enormously influential in altering perceptions of Australian literature. Their writing both contributes to and benefits from a shift in political attitude toward the place of the immigrant in Australian society–from assimilationism to multiculturalism toward the end of the 1960s and the early 1970s.

Multiculturalism became the officially sanctioned philosophy about the place of immigrants in their new country. In American terms, the movement was from the melting pot, in which cultural differences melted down to ensure that everyone was essentially the same, to the salad bowl, which allowed for cultural differentiation. Al Grassby, minister for immigration during the Gough Whitlam government (1972–1975), favored the concept of "the family of the nation" in order to stress the contribution of immigrants to Australia and to emphasize the need to recognize, rather than dismiss, their distinctiveness. The White Australia Policy was officially abandoned in 1972. Writers such as Waten, Kefala, and Skrzynecki have been extremely influential, not only in the development of literature by immigrants to Australia but also in the reconceptualizing of Australian literary and cultural identity. Significantly, immigrant writers questioned the Australian preoccupation with place, particularly the "empty" center of the country. By writing of Australia as an alien space, the inevitable feeling of the immigrant, they also accentuated the extent to which the space of Australia was alien to the Australian-born writer, reminding Anglo-Australians that all non-Aboriginals are essentially immigrants and that Australian history—at least, Australian-European history—was only two hundred years old.

During the 1950s, while the White Australia Policy was being reconsidered, government policy toward the indigenous population of Australia continued in much the same fashion as had been established earlier in the century. During this decade, with Menzies's secret approval, the British government tested nuclear bombs in the desert near Maralinga in South Australia, home to tribal Aborigines, causing widespread radiation poisoning among the indigenous population in the area. Aboriginal children of mixed race continued to be taken from their parents in various states in Australia to be educated in white mission schools and adopted by white parents (a practice established at the beginning of the twentieth century and responsible for the "Stolen Generation" of Aboriginal children, the subject of a 1997 report by the Human Rights and Equal Opportunity Commission titled *Bringing Them Home*).

Not until 1966 did the Commonwealth Arbitration Commission rule that Aboriginal workers should receive the same wages as whites. In the following year, a national referendum (voted on by white Australians) to recognize Aboriginals as full citizens of Australia and accord them full franchise passed by an overwhelming majority. Activism surrounding the referendum—with a freedom ride in which students accompanied Aboriginal activists to protest the segregation in public facilities in country towns—drew attention to the treatment of the indigenous community from colonization in 1788. Despite the real and symbolic significance of the referendum, the situation of the indigenous population has continued to be a central focus for activists—Aboriginal and otherwise—and at the heart of the literature that has emerged from that community. Oodgeroo of the Tribe Noonuccal (who first published under the name Kath Walker) and Colin Johnson (who has also published under the name Mudrooroo) were at the forefront of the first wave of Aboriginal writers to emerge from the activism and identity politics of the 1960s, establishing a voice for young Aboriginal writers and artists and repositioning the debate surrounding Australian literary and cultural identity. The influence of these early writers can be seen during the second half of the 1980s in the popularity of autobiographical fiction by indigenous writers, particularly by Aboriginal women. While the development of indigenous literature has not been without its controversies, not least because of the contested cultural identity of such writers as Johnson, it has also been an important part of the development of the Australian national literature in the second part of the twentieth century.

The shift from the 1950s to the 1960s is popularly regarded as a movement from conservatism to increased political and social radicalism. This change was evident in the activism surrounding the 1967 referendum for Aboriginal citizenship and in the opposition to Australia's entering the Vietnam War in 1965. By 1967 there were 6,300 Australians fighting in Vietnam; 40 percent of them were conscripts. Australian support of the United States was largely a legacy of the cooperation between Australia and the United States during World War II. Menzies's royalist model of Australian identity seemed to have shifted to a focus on an association with a virile United States, whose anticommunist foreign policy was as attractive to the government as its popular culture was to the Australian people. Despite the popularity of American culture in Australia after World War II, involvement in the Vietnam War brought considerable and vigorous public opposition, which increased as the war continued. The Vietnam War was seen as a foreign war and therefore irrelevant to Australia. A sense of opposition arose, not unlike that voiced by the opponents to both world wars, that insisted that Australia was fighting a battle in a distant country, induced by the sense of child-like loyalty to a neocolonial power. Opposition to the Vietnam War played an important role in the Australian process of self-definition by stimulating a debate about the country's role in international affairs, and it forced politicians and citizens to consider the repercussions of tying themselves to a foreign power.

The spirit of protest of the period was also evident in the rise of the second-generation feminist movement. In 1969 the Women's Liberation Movement was launched in Adelaide. The following year an expatriate academic, Germaine Greer, published *The Female Eunuch*, a groundbreaking and highly influential critique of the place of women in a male-dominated and oppressive society. The groundswell of feminist scholarship inspired two of the most influential books of feminist social history: *Damned Whores and God's Police: The Colonization of Women in Australia* (1975) by Anne Summers and *The Real Matilda: Women and Identity in Australia* (1976) by Miriam Dixon. Both books provide a critical interrogation of the masculinist structure of Australian society and culture. In literature, the legacy of the feminist ideology of such writers as Miles Franklin, Marjorie Barnard, Flora Eldershaw, Katharine Susannah Prichard, and Christina Stead found expression in the work of such writers as Dorothy Hewett. Nevertheless, while Thea Astley was, arguably, one of the first Australian women writers to receive critical acclaim and popular attention, she has always been conscious of the difficulty of her position within a male-dominated culture such as that of Australia. She has often written from a male point of view because she believed, at least early in her career, as she said in a 1992 interview with Rosemary Sorensen for *Australian Book Review,* that it was the only way to produce literature that would be read:

> . . . when I first started writing I kept thinking, well, people talk about women's books, I won't have any credence if I write from a female point of view. . . . And I thought that the only way to have any credibility would be to try to write novels from a male point of view, or make a male your central character. In those days, and I still think this holds, I don't think men liked reading women writers, it's like listening to a woman for three hours. And they don't want to bloody do that!

The women represented in this volume–Hewett, Astley, Hanrahan, Gwen Harwood, and Hazzard–are among the best respected and most critically acclaimed Australian writers. While women writers are in a minority in this volume, the literature of the period was heavily influenced by the political activism of women, their increased role in the public life of the country, and their contribution to the zeitgeist, with its questioning of social traditions and taboos, and its rupturing of convention and form.

In the universities, the radical nationalist criticism of the 1950s–which asserted that the writing of the pivotal 1890s defined such features of the national spirit as optimism, egalitarianism, anti-authoritarianism, and mateship–gave way in the 1960s and 1970s to the New Critics (such as G. A. Wilkes, Leonie Kramer, Harry Heseltine, and Vincent Buckley), who saw within the writing of the same period a spirit of crisis, anxiety, disillusionment, and alienation. The attempts to define and label the features of Australian literature with reference to literature of the past–to devise a foolproof canon–continued while the literature itself was taking on an entirely new character. This volume covers a period of structural experimentation, as the social realism of the 1950s–represented by such writers as Ray Lawler and Judah Waten–was followed by the structural disruption and experimentation of such writers as Frank Moorhouse, Peter Carey, David Ireland, Gerald Murnane, and John Tranter. The young poets who appeared in the late 1960s and early 1970s, known as the "Generation of '68," reacted against the more traditional poetry of such "establishment" poets as A. D. Hope. Livio Dobrez, in *Parnassus Mad Ward: Michael Dransfield and the New Australian Poetry* (1990), has written, "The sixty-eighters *can say it,*" an effective way to describe the rejection, by this generation of poets, of tradition and propriety in favor of immediacy, passion, and structural experimentation. Tranter, Robert Adamson, Thomas W. Shapcott, Rodney Hall, Bruce Beaver, Porter, Bruce Dawe, and Chris Wallace-Crabbe can all be said to represent a revitalization of Australian poetry,

inspired by the possibilities suggested by postmodernism and the influence of American confessional poetry.

The period was also one of innovation in the short story, assisted by rapid circulation of new material through the media and literary "events," inspired by the arts-friendly atmosphere of the early 1970s and the Whitlam Labor Party government. The early work of Carey, Moorhouse, and Michael Wilding reflected the urban, bohemian values of a group of young writers who gathered in inner Sydney and who reflected an internationalist, unconventional approach to Australian identity and to the form of the short story. The paradigmatic collections of this period are Moorhouse's *The Americans, Baby* (1973) and Carey's *The Fat Man in History* (1974), both of which show a fascination with the increased influence of American culture on Australia. These works–particularly Carey's short fiction–also represent a clear movement away from social realism toward an almost surreal or "fabulous" landscape that suggests a developing maturity in Australian literature in its de-emphasis on the construction of Australian identity upon the central trope of the landscape and a willingness of the writers to place themselves and their writing within an international framework.

This volume includes writers who produced at least their first important work before 1975. The date 11 November 1975, the day on which Governor-General, Sir John Kerr, dismissed the prime minister, Gough Whitlam, is pivotal in recent Australian history. In dismissing the prime minister and his government, Kerr invoked a constitutional right that had never before (and has never since) been exercised by the vice-regal representative, and its exercise prompted a constitutional as well as a governmental crisis. The governor-general's decision prompted a public debate surrounding his role and the ties of Australia to a colonial political structure, a debate that has never really gone away. It marked a tumultuous conclusion to a period of great social, political, and cultural change.

The sense of transformation defined by this period in Australian history is reflected in this volume by the enormous diversity of literature and writers represented. Indeed, despite the organizing rationale of the volume, which establishes clear temporal boundaries, the book also covers a large period of time. Each entry moves beyond the 1975 mark and points to the development of the literature at the end of the twentieth century. Hence, the apparent anomaly of having writers such as Judah Waten, Vincent Buckley, Sumner Locke Elliott, John Iggulden, and A. D. Hope alongside much younger writers such as Peter Carey, David Foster, and Rodney Hall is an effective way to represent what was a period of great cultural upheaval. Many of the writers featured in *DLB 289*–Carey, Kefala, Thomas Keneally,

David Malouf, Les Murray, and David Williamson, for example—are still writing prolifically, while many writers featured in the earlier volumes, such as Patrick White and Judith Wright, were reaching their peak during this period. The awarding of the 1973 Nobel Prize in literature to White, the only Australian so far to receive it, gave Australia a sense of having arrived on the international literary scene.

This volume is designed to be read alongside the others in the series to provide a sense of the interconnections and development in Australian literature. The multiple viewpoints offered by the entries in the volume and across the series also provide the reader with a sense of the range of scholarship and the diversity of critical approaches to Australian literature. As is always the case, omissions in this volume have occurred as a result of the constraints of space and time. Readers are encouraged to follow the links between the entries and to consult the Books for Further Reading in order to understand the nature of Australian literature and culture as continually evolving.

—*Selina Samuels*

Acknowledgments

This book was produced by Bruccoli Clark Layman, Inc. Penelope M. Hope was the in-house editor.

Production manager is Philip B. Dematteis.

Administrative support was provided by Ann M. Cheschi and Carol A. Cheschi.

Accountant is Ann-Marie Holland.

Copyediting supervisor is Sally R. Evans. The copyediting staff includes Phyllis A. Avant, Caryl Brown, Leah M. Cutsinger, Melissa D. Hinton, Philip I. Jones, Rebecca Mayo, and Nancy E. Smith.

Editorial associates are Jessica Goudeau, Joshua M. Robinson, and William Mathes Straney.

In-house prevetting is by Catherine M. Polit.

Permissions editor and database manager is Amber L. Coker.

Layout and graphics supervisor is Janet E. Hill. The graphics staff includes Zoe R. Cook and Sydney E. Hammock.

Office manager is Kathy Lawler Merlette.

Photography supervisor is Paul Talbot. Photography editor is Scott Nemzek.

Digital photographic copy work was performed by Joseph M. Bruccoli.

Systems manager is Donald Kevin Starling.

Typesetting supervisor is Kathleen M. Flanagan. The typesetting staff includes Patricia Marie Flanagan, Mark J. McEwan, and Pamela D. Norton.

Walter W. Ross is library researcher. He was assisted by the following librarians at the Thomas Cooper Library of the University of South Carolina: Jo Cottingham, interlibrary loan department; circulation department head Tucker Taylor; reference department head Virginia W. Weathers; reference department staff Laurel Baker, Marilee Birchfield, Kate Boyd, Paul Cammarata, Joshua Garris, Gary Geer, Tom Marcil, Rose Marshall, and Sharon Verba; interlibrary loan department head Marna Hostetler; and interlibrary loan staff Bill Fetty, Nelson Rivera, and Cedric Rose.

Nicholas Pounder of Sydney, Australia, provided books.

Dictionary of Literary Biography® • Volume Two Hundred Eighty-Nine

Australian Writers, 1950–1975

Dictionary of Literary Biography

Robert Adamson
(17 May 1943 –   )

Martin Duwell
University of Queensland

BOOKS: *Canticles on the Skin* (Sydney: Illumination Press, 1970);
The Rumour, Prism Poets (Sydney: New Poetry, 1971);
Swamp Riddles (Sydney: Island Press, 1974);
Zimmer's Essay, by Adamson and Bruce Hanford (Glebe, N.S.W.: Wild & Woolley, 1974);
Theatre I–XIX (Sydney: Pluralist Press, 1976);
Cross the Border (Sydney: New Poetry, 1977);
Selected Poems (Sydney: Angus & Robertson, 1977);
Where I Come From (Sydney: Big-Smoke Books, 1979);
The Law at Heart's Desire (Sydney: Prism Books, 1982);
The Clean Dark (Sydney: Paper Bark Press, 1989);
Selected Poems: 1970–1989 (St. Lucia: University of Queensland Press, 1990);
Wards of the State: An Autobiographical Novella (Pymble, N.S.W.: Angus & Robertson, 1992);
The Brutality of Fact (Applecross, W.A.: Folio, 1993);
Waving to Hart Crane (Pymble, N.S.W.: Angus & Robertson, 1994);
The Language of Oysters: Images and Poems of the Hawkesbury, text by Adamson, photographs by Juno Gemes (Sydney: Craftsman House, 1997);
Meaning (Cambridge: Peter Riley, 1998);
Black Water: Approaching Zukofsky (Rose Bay, N.S.W.: Brandl & Schlesinger, 1999);
Mulberry Leaves: New and Selected Poems, 1970–2001, edited by Chris Edwards (Sydney: Paper Bark Press, 2001).

OTHER: *Australian Writing Now,* edited by Adamson and Manfred Jurgensen (Indooroopilly, Qld.: Outrider, 1988).

Superficially, Robert Adamson's work seems to be about two often contradictory sources of experience:

Robert Adamson (photograph by Juno Gemes; courtesy of the author)

the prison life of his adolescence and early adulthood, and the Hawkesbury River area, north of Sydney, where he grew up and where he has always lived—a kind of spirit home. But the central presence in his poetry is always Adamson's self, conceived with a sensitivity to subtle inner states that is reminiscent of symbolism. His poetic method, with rare exceptions, almost never exploits intense experience for its own sake, preferring to take an angled and often surprising position in relation to that experience.

Adamson was born on 17 May 1943 in Sydney, New South Wales, although many of his books–including *Selected Poems* (1977) and *Selected Poems: 1970–1989* (1990)–give his year of birth as 1944. His parents lived in Neutral Bay and had family connections with fishermen on the Hawkesbury River. In *Wards of the State: An Autobiographical Novella* (1992) Adamson describes initial problems both at school and in later adolescent years when he worked as an apprentice pastry cook. He spent time both in institutions for juveniles and in Maitland Prison. In the latter, according to the partly factual/partly fictional *Zimmer's Essay* (1974), he discovered poetry. After his release he lived in Sydney and became associated with *Poetry Magazine* becoming one of its editors in 1970 and eventually overseeing its transformation to *New Poetry,* perhaps the most important venue for the poets of the New Writing Group, a generation of Sydney and Melbourne writers with interests in avant-garde developments and recent American poetry. An engagement with publishing has continued throughout his career: he was an editor of a series by *New Poetry* called Prism Books and later cofounder of both Big-Smoke Books and Paper Bark Press. He married his first wife, Cheryl, in 1973, but the marriage ended in divorce; he married his second wife, photographer Juno Gemes, in 1988.

The first phase of Adamson's writing career probably consists of his first three books: *Canticles on the Skin* (1970), *The Rumour* (1971), and *Swamp Riddles* (1974), although important biographical material can be found in the prose works *Zimmer's Essay* and *Wards of the State.* In the first three books of poetry, the conjunction of the two strands of his material is at its most jarring. Prison stories and the stance of "rebel angel" exist alongside the world of the Hawkesbury, and the material is screened through an intense interest in symbolist poetics. The prison experiences are never used simply for their confessional value–they are always mediated through a poetics that makes the power of the experience equivocal. Even the most apparently open of the prison experiences, "The Imitator," the first sequence of *Canticles on the Skin,* has, as epigraph, a quotation from Paul's First Letter to the Corinthians: "For though I be free from all men, yet have I made myself servant unto all, that I might gain the more. . . . To them that are without law. . . ." On the surface this work seems no more than a description of a successful survival strategy in a prison farm or prison, but *Zimmer's Essay* warns readers that the fixed roles of a total institution such as a prison enables a profound and creative adjustment of

personality similar to the magical powers craved by the hermetic tradition of symbolism:

> This was a powerful magic he gave his Carol, the magic of changes. A man survives as best he can. Zimmer was a magician in a hard place, a place of stone. How could he have known tenderness was so dangerous? Through his Carol Zimmer was sappho. Zimmer was eagle, Zimmer was fish sounding in the deep Sulu sea. The earth is raddled with burrows of burrowing things, and Zimmer was marmot. . . .

The epigraph from Paul also warns that poetry includes a masking element, a sense of providing voyeuristic readers with intense revelations. Adamson's poetry constantly mocks this quality. "The Imitator" begins with an intense proem combining drugs, prison life, and cars in a powerful but confusing mix:

> Dirty hypodermics rattle in the glove-box: morphine flows
> over the top of your brain. An artery collapses
> and migraine floats out of your eyes–Alright, there'll always
> be glib explanations: cashing in on experience again?
> Don't be distracted now, watch the speedo.
> Plant your foot until the big V8 starts to mainline juice
>
> straight from your cirrhotic liver–Let her go, the most fantastic
> demo ever.

The intensity of this passage–its use of enjambment and internalized commands–recalls the poetry of Francis Webb, a poet of great influence on Adamson's early work. The rest of "The Imitator" is a much quieter depiction of being taken to a prison farm and escaping ("Central Station slides by, I sit here stranded in a window pane. / Trainlights come on with a flutter"), but in the initial publication of the poem in a little magazine, these lines formed the opening. What became the proem was originally an after-lights-out fantasy; moving it to the opening of the book version of the poem emphasizes fantastic aspects of the poetry at the expense of a simple "confessionalism."

Another process of transformation can be seen in "Action Would Kill It / A Gamble," one of the best of the prison poems from the second book, *The Rumour.* It describes a conversation between two men walking along a seashore:

> On that isolated part of the Coast, counting over
> the youngest politicians.
> Huge shoulders of granite grew higher
> as we walked on, cutting us from perspectives.
> . . . .
> He didn't care about himself at all, and the sea
> just licked his blood away.

The conclusion (of walk, talk, and poem) is a memorable one:

> When the beach ended,
> we would have to split up. And as he spoke
> clearly and without emotion
> about the need for action, about killing people,
> I wanted him.

Enough evidence can be found in the poem itself and in *Zimmer's Essay* for this poem to be seen as a transformation of prison experience. The walk takes place in prison, not by the sea. The "huge shoulders of granite" are not mountains cutting off a beach but prison buildings, and the entire experience has been transposed.

The Rumour also includes a long, experimental title poem distinctive because it is not anchored in the physical realities familiar to readers of Adamson's poetry. In fact, it does not seem anchored in any reality at all, though it is a long, self-reflexive poem about poetry itself. Its inspiration, the American poet Robert Duncan, is one of the most important of Adamson's large cast of mentor figures. Although a major work, "The Rumour" was greeted with considerable skepticism, probably born of confusion. In retrospect, it is perhaps best seen as a sequence in which the symbolist impetus, mediated by Duncan, is given freest reign. "The Rumour" is concerned with poetic process, and the title seems to refer to the essential impulse of poetry before its shape is hardened by its articulation in words, a process that can eventually lead to a mere formula:

> And from an endless text surrounding me
> The seraphic Outrider
> Draws his question "All this and you offer
> Me virtuous rhetoric?" His
> Accusation goes
> > > unanswered as rumour
> > > unfolds
> It is Compulsion

The attempt to keep the poem free of existing rhetoric while at the same time not losing meaning is a continuously enacted struggle in the nearly twenty pages of "The Rumour." The poem is referred to as the "open song," and, for all its contemporary references—the list of poets it "discusses" includes (with Percy Bysshe Shelley, Samuel Taylor Coleridge, Arthur Rimbaud, Stéphane Mallarmé, and Edgar Allan Poe) Louis Zukofsky, Duncan, Jack Spicer, and John Ashbery—it retains the hieratic, magian mode of classic symbolism:

> > His song goes
> up nightly   The sequence cut
>
> and shuffled, his doctrine is lifting, his head

Front cover for Adamson's first collection of poems (1970), which includes a sequence about prison experiences (Bruccoli Clark Layman Archives)

> that lifts
> > > the hand of keys
> saying
> > damn you
> > > see the force, take focus
> There: thief, singer

Adamson's third book, *Swamp Riddles,* includes poems that, as the title suggests, are largely set in the Hawkesbury River area, although the second word of the title warns readers that the poems are not always what their surface setting suggests. One of the sequences, "Sonnets to Be Written from Prison," is, however, about prison experience, although it is continuously cast in the subjunctive, and the poems are always concerned about their public stance and whether it is unduly exploitative or whether the self of the poems is unduly slippery. The sonnets are built on patterns of repetition of phrases and themes and thus

A novel by Robert Adamson and Bruce Hanford

ZIMMER'S ESSAY

Dust jacket for the 1974 novel based on Adamson's time in Maitland Prison (Bruccoli Clark Layman Archives)

structurally suggest that the interplay of experience and self-aware poetic performance that they enact is a continuous one.

> I could, once more, go out with pale skin
> from my veritable dank cell—the sufferer, poking fun
> at myself in form, with a slightly twisted tone.
> My stance, ironic—one-out, on the run.

In 1976, two years after *Swamp Riddles* was published, Adamson released *Theatre I–XIX*. Essentially a response to Yves Bonnefoy, it is driven by the symbolist imperatives of Adamson's verse. Reluctant to allow that the muse, "Douve," is a mere construction—"a linguistic device dependent on the French language"—Adamson struggles for ways of asserting the existence of a real muse, a flesh and blood (if variously incarnate) source of inspiration. *Theatre I–XIX* is a fascinating experiment—an attempt to reply to an existing poem

that derives a notion of inspiration from the same source (Mallarmean poetics) but that takes the idea in a direction Adamson finds unacceptable. The poem is not an argument; it must be a way of demonstrating the existence of the muse and of (as the "Argument" of the book says) finding "a possible ingress for her," a place "where my muse could enter and be a completely operative force." The subject of the muse is taken up in a more discursive way in "Lady Faith" from *The Clean Dark* (1989), which describes an era of "serious fads / where the muse gets deconstructed like a toy."

Cross the Border, published in 1977, is a large book in terms of both length and format. The first section is a series of dedications, although their method of composition is unusual. True to the title of the book, they seem to cross the border between one creative mind and another. The result is not parody but a moment in which Adamson seems to share the thematic obsessions of the poets whom he celebrates and with whom he quarrels creatively. These poets include John Tranter (the poem circles around one of the cool females who inhabit Tranter's early verse), Bruce Beaver (the poem echoes the first poem of Beaver's *Lauds and Plaints* [1974] and focuses on paranoia), and Dorothy Hewett. In this long poem, Adamson uses the name of the heroine of a Hewett play, Sally, and images of folktales associated with the Hewett of *Rapunzel in Suburbia* (1975). The book includes four other sections: "Cross the Border," "Charms and Fairy Tales," "The Glorious Lie," and "The Grail Poems." The first and last of these sections are dedicated to the painters Brett Whiteley and Garry Shead and reflect the growing importance of contemporary Australian art in Adamson's work. This interest is reflected in the cover of the book: a diptych reflecting the responses of the two artists to the theme of D. H. Lawrence in Australia. The title poem of the book reflects these paintings and interprets the idea of border-crossing in a specific way:

> The painting is divided and dividing its borders
>
> the diptych becomes a simple device to hold two realms
>
> though the realms are realms apart.
> The border dividing the two sides of the painting is a
>   space
>
> and the inclination to cross it
> becomes a passion that draws me into the blue.

The final section of the book is a group of Grail poems. In them Adamson uses Arthurian myths not so much for social comment as for a mix of complex states and complex personal biography. Of all the characters, Merlin and his female alter ego, Vivian, are the closest to the poet: they have true power. Guinevere is unattainable partly because she operates in a world of "constraining" laws:

> My devotion's borne on the scales of impossible music,
> while she generates in me
> fictions alive with her tactile beings.

Gawain and his eventual killer, Lancelot, are lovers. The complexity of the sequence recalls "The Rumour" in places, and a complexly allegorized roman à clef is possibly at the center of its characters and its limited narrative.

The largest section of the book, "The Glorious Lie," is made up of twenty-three poems that, while a sequence, have radically different settings. Some of the poems are Hawkesbury based ("The Nankeen Kestrels," "The Mullet Run," and "Dead Horse Bay"); some are built around classical mythological references, especially to Artemis; and some are in the high hieratic mode. Of the latter type, perhaps the most extreme (and perhaps the most extreme of any of Adamson's poems) is the central poem, "Evocation." The figure evoked is clearly Duncan:

> Enamored Mage, sculptor of light & transmutator of energies
> > firing opacity through my clear decisions
> your green-flames flickering on the new formed ice.
>
> Has San Francisco crazed your delicate extremeties?
>
> The fugitive evangel's yours in every sense.
> > Though its risky sanctity settles now across your
> reflective faces.
>
> Listening there, in what new Gospel do Merline's prophesies alight?
> > spelling's as shiftful as history synchronous
> with the present and tomorrow.
> Out from the dictionary's burning stream Osiris speaks:
> > > & the Glass
>
> > transforming in the Burning Bush, returning to the vase,
> > again to Yahweh, artful glass-blower.

To find a more extreme example of the hermetic in Australian poetry, even within the work of Christopher Brennan, would be hard. Given that, historically, Australian poetry has been inclined toward the concrete, this poem is brave, risking sounding grotesque. *Cross the Border,* a culmination of the kind of poetry represented by "The Rumour," does give some sense of this important component of Adamson's art and the kind of poetry he is likely to produce.

Adamson's next book, *Where I Come From* (1979), can be seen as a reaction–perhaps even a chastened reaction–to the excesses of *Cross the Border.* It is modestly produced; the poems are rooted in the mundane facts of family, upbringing, and emotional life; and they are written in what seems, initially, to be a remorselessly "unpoetic" style, as though Adamson is experimenting with how far poetry can go in this opposite direction. Even the endpapers of the book–a child's drawing of the Hawkesbury region with handwritten comments such as "Big Jewies Here" and "Griffo's Bream Spot"–suggest its homely content. In fact, the book seems much more accomplished when read on its own and is not out of keeping with the general patterns of Adamson's career. It is about childhood life, a life that is often revisited (as it was later in *Wards of the State*). As such, it is also about the images of the past that lodge in memory and whether or not these images are trustworthy–the title of the first section is "They Say Memory's a Lie." The structure of the poems is fairly simple, often relying on a single turn to form a conclusion. In "My Fishing Boat," for example, the turn is formed by using a symbol. The boy, disturbed by his mother and father's fighting over something he has done, leaves the house and goes fishing in the middle of the night:

> all I catch are catfish here
> and have them sliding
> about in the belly of the boat
>
> they are the most ugly looking things
> in the world.

Also, the final twenty or so poems are set in the present and focus on a broken relationship:

> our life was a bridge
> for you to cross
> . . . .
> I built it knowing all along
> what it would mean
> and look across at you free of me
>
> framed naked in the window
> > –from "Kate"

In the acknowledgments Adamson thanks Hewett, and *Where I Come From* includes much in the manner of Hewett's later books–a simple, denotative style, quick and simple twists to conclude the poems, and a focus on memories of youth and later life.

Adamson's next book, *The Law at Heart's Desire* (1982), while not itself a major work, is important for establishing a style that dominates the rest of Adamson's output. The radical experiments and disjunctions

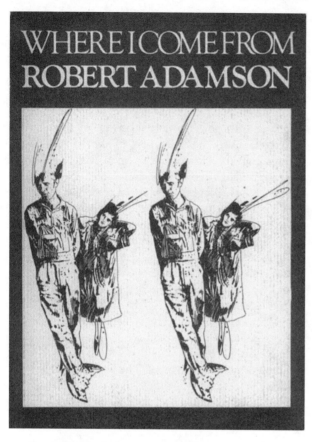

*Paperback cover for Adamson's 1979 collection of poems, about
his childhood in the Hawkesbury River region
(Bruccoli Clark Layman Archives)*

der, "Lovesong from across the Border," which
describes life as moving forward (in an automobile) and
leaving poems behind:

> I drive, so all I have taken in
> revolving here, will be turned about, change
> and drift freely over the border
> and there dissolve;
> . . . .
>   moving—
> only aware of what comes before
> as I plunge through the life I burn.

When the pair have left the last conventional signs of
the human behind them, they are forced to "take bearings" from each other: "all the comfortable signs we
make / signifying our ease with the interior life, / the
privacy of art." The poem concludes with a potent
meditation on signs, language, and the inner life, defining art as it does so:

> So the only permanence is in what we say,
> what we imagine through language, a permanence
> that is neither within nor beyond the pale—
> it is the sole arbiter between the heart and its desire
> the law and love's freedom,
>
> the fine and burning line of art, the fence.

The first section of the book includes poems
about Rimbaud and Webb, continuing the tradition of
Cross the Border in naming and making obeisance to
influences. The second section includes poems about
the breakdown of a relationship (a theme continued in
the final section), but the third and fourth sections
include poems written in the newer style. "Into Forest"
seems to augur the later poems: it is anchored in
domestic discomfort and the search for yet another new
identity. Also, it is set in a house in a forest "among the
spotted gums," though, typically, images of fish and the
Hawkesbury River break through.

The Clean Dark, published in 1989, is, as suggested
by its dedication to Adamson's second wife, "a new
book for a new life." It was probably the first of Adamson's books to receive widespread recognition—beyond
the approval of specialist critics. It won both the New
South Wales and the Victorian Premier Awards as well
as the National Book Council Award. It also marked
the inauguration of Paper Bark Press, publisher of most
of Adamson's subsequent work. The early poem,
"Songs for Juno," begins, "My lies are for you . . ." and,
after a stanza detailing individual items and events of
Hawkesbury life ("Blue-wrens hovering for invisible
insects, a shag / hunched on a wing") concludes with a
reaffirmation of renewal, "The new list begins." In the
final poem of the first section, new love, rather than

of all the previous books seem to have settled into a
middle style. (His interview with Tranter gives some
idea of Adamson's sense of the discreteness of each of
these books.) On the surface, the poems have natural
settings and a fairly simple poetic structure more
aligned with the poems of *Where I Come From* than the
"open song" of "The Rumour" and parts of *Swamp Riddles* and *Cross the Border.* They engage a complex biography and a complex inner life at levels that usually
escape the reader, even though they are clearly present,
and the hieratic and symbolist seem almost entirely
absent. *The Law at Heart's Desire* does, however, begin
with a magnificent poem that is not at all in this style.
"Beyond the Pale" describes a journey (real or imagined) into the desert interior of Australia. The poem is
dedicated to Tim Storrier, and Adamson is accompanied by an artist; the poem describes the signs as the
two move through civilization into areas with only
crude remains of the human. The "pale" is another border, and the structure of the poem makes clear that it is
a companion piece to the opening poem of *Cross the Bor-*

*Dust jacket for Adamson's 1989 collection of poems, which won a National Book Council Award
(Bruccoli Clark Layman Archives)*

being discussed, is anchored in a description of a particular experience:

> On days still when the tide's full, river
> hours with you are momentary fire
>
> in the head, shall not stay memories
> even, so intensely lived. . . .

Two other possible sources contribute to the attractiveness of the book to a wider audience. It includes poems that frankly discuss the act of writing, partly as a way of defending it against the reductive approaches of much critical theory fashionable at the time. One of these poems, "Clear Water Reckoning," is notable for the way it conveys a sense of the poetic process:

> anything is possible here
> I remind myself and begin to hum
> flattening out all the words that were
> impossible to put together today,
> I hum out all the poems I should have
> written, I hum away now also
> the desire to write from memory,
> there is enough sorrow in the present—

> I look out over the in-coming tide, dark racks
> of oysters jut from its ink.

The Clean Dark also includes poems overtly dealing with social issues. "No River, No Death" is a meditation on a potential nuclear apocalypse, and "Canticle for the Bicentennial Dead" is a powerful poem on Aboriginal deaths in custody, remarkable because its unequivocalness is so unlike Adamson's usual stance.

Waving to Hart Crane, published in 1994, consolidated Adamson's wider readership. It was published by Angus and Robertson, an important Australian nonspecialist publisher, but one with strong historical connections to poetry publishing. *Waving to Hart Crane* follows Adamson's general practice of having a first section dense with references to friends and mentor figures: poets Kevin Hart, Kevin Gilbert, Brennan, Webb, and Robert Harris are included (often as dedicatees) as are Brett Whiteley and Piet Mondrian. The initial poem, "Folk Song," ostensibly describes different ways of fishing: the Ibis, "Egyptians blown in / on some cosmic whim," fish by plunging their heads in the silt and finding bloodworms while "we" are devoted to catching the mulloway. The title of the poem indicates that it is not to be read literally, and a deftly included quotation from William Butler Yeats, "There are too // many of us here," warns the reader that this complex poem is about Australian poets and their ways of dealing, in poetry, with the world. The last and penultimate sections of the book are also intriguing. The last is a series of humorously experimental poems based on the figure of a pepper mill. The sequence in *Waving to Hart Crane* is a slightly shortened and lightly revised version of the nine poems published as the pamphlet *The Brutality of Fact* (1993). The penultimate section is a long single poem, "The Sugar Glider," which comically explores the idea and possibilities involved in conceiving poetry as being totemic. As with the first section of the book, this poem constantly engages notions of poetry and the way poetry deals with "presence." The practice of Michael Palmer is juxtaposed with those of Philip Larkin and, especially, Les Murray, and uses animals as potential totemic symbols: these animals include the numbat and the slighter, Australian relative of the aardvark. But the poem opens and concludes with the most delicate animal of all, the "feather-tailed" sugar glider, "limbs flying / in all directions," which "throws itself into the air / above the numbats and glides on mist / towards the sugar."

Between *Waving to Hart Crane* and *Black Water: Approaching Zukofsky* (1999) Adamson published two smaller books, *The Language of Oysters: Images and Poems of the Hawkesbury* (1997) and *Meaning* (1998). *Meaning* includes "The Night Heron," important for its description of the poet "drawing up some endings to make / a few last marks":

> I write down words, they all seem fake,
>
> so I crack them open. A night
> writing letters to the future and the past–

The idea of poems as letters becomes an important part of Adamson's most recent development, embodied in *Black Water* and the new poems from *Mulberry Leaves: New and Selected Poems, 1970–2001* (2001).

Adamson has published three books of selected poems–one published by Angus and Robertson (1977), one by the University of Queensland Press (1990), and one by Paper Bark Press (2001). The differences between these selections are extreme. For the 1977 book of selected poems, Adamson even rewrote most of his early poems or experimented with their lineation. The most recent selection is the most valuable, but, in order to include new poems, it provides only nugatory selec-

tions from early work. Given the character of Adamson's poetry and the sense of a continuous reexamination of the self, perhaps these differences are understandable. At the least they show that Adamson's sense of himself in his poetry is not one of accretion but one of redefinition.

Few figures have been as influential in Australian poetry in the past forty years as Robert Adamson. Although there are not many poets who have shared his obsession with symbolism, many have found his complex and elusive use of autobiographical details challenging. He has also been responsible for encouraging American poets to engage with Australian poetry. And his contribuiton in editing and publishing–beginning with his involvement with *Poetry Magazine* and continuing to Paper Bark Press–has also been extensive. Inevitably it has resulted in a far-flung web of connections in the poetry world and has helped to make him one of the indisputably important figures of Australian literature.

Interviews:

John Tranter, "Robert Adamson," in Martin Duwell, *A Possible Contemporary Poetry* (St. Lucia, Qld.: Makar, 1982), pp. 132–143;

Michael Sharkey, "Robert Adamson and the Persistence of Mallarme: An Interview," *Southerly,* 45 (1985): 308–320.

References:

David Brooks, "Feral Symbolists: Robert Adamson, John Tranter, and the Response to Rimbaud," *Australian Literary Studies,* 16 (May 1994): 280–288;

Martin Duwell, "'Homages and Invocations': The Early Poetry of Robert Adamson," *Australian Literary Studies,* 14 (October 1989): 229–238;

Michael Wilding, "'My Name is Rickeybockey': The Poetry of Robert Adamson and the Spirit of Henry Kendall," *Southerly,* 46 (1986): 25–43.

Papers:

Two extensive collections of Robert Adamson's papers are held by two libraries. The National Library of Australia, Manuscript Section, holds his letters, copies of reviews, and drafts of poems from the mid 1970s. The University Library at the Australian Defence Force Academy is an ongoing collection and includes, as well as letters and manuscripts, material relating to Adamson's role as a publisher.

Thea Astley

(25 August 1925 –)

Susan Lever
University of New South Wales at the Australian Defence Force Academy

BOOKS: *Girl with a Monkey* (Sydney: Angus & Robertson, 1958; London, 1959; Ringwood, Vic. & New York: Penguin, 1987);

A Descant for Gossips (Sydney: Angus & Robertson, 1960; London: Angus & Robertson, 1960; St. Lucia & New York: University of Queensland Press, 1983);

The Well Dressed Explorer (Sydney: Angus & Robertson, 1962; Ringwood, Vic. & New York: Penguin, 1988);

The Slow Natives (Sydney: Angus & Robertson, 1965; London: Angus & Robertson, 1966; New York: M. Evans, 1967);

A Boat Load of Home Folk (Sydney: Angus & Robertson, 1968; London: Angus & Robertson, 1968);

The Acolyte (Sydney: Angus & Robertson, 1972; London: Angus & Robertson, 1972); republished in *Two by Astley: A Kindness Cup & The Acolyte* (New York: Putnam, 1988);

A Kindness Cup (Melbourne: Thomas Nelson, 1974; London: Penguin, 1989; New York: Penguin, 1989); republished in *Two by Astley: A Kindness Cup & The Acolyte* (New York: Putnam, 1988);

Hunting the Wild Pineapple, and Other Related Stories (West Melbourne, Vic.: Thomas Nelson, 1979; New York: Putnam, 1991);

An Item from the Late News (St. Lucia & New York: University of Queensland Press, 1982; Ringwood, Vic. & Harmondsworth, U.K.: Penguin, 1982);

Beachmasters (Ringwood, Vic.: Penguin, 1985; New York: Viking, 1986);

It's Raining in Mango: Pictures from a Family Album (Ringwood, Vic.: Viking, 1987; New York: Putnam, 1987);

Reaching Tin River (Port Melbourne, Vic.: Heinemann, 1990; New York: Putnam, 1990);

Vanishing Points (Port Melbourne, Vic.: Heinemann, 1992; New York: Putnam, 1992; London: Minerva, 1995);

Thea Astley (from the dust jacket for It's Raining in Mango, *1987; Richland County Public Library)*

Coda (Port Melbourne, Vic.: Heinemann, 1994; New York: Putnam, 1994; London: Secker & Warburg, 1995);

The Multiple Effects of Rainshadow (Ringwood, Vic. & New York: Viking, 1996);

Drylands: A Book for the World's Last Reader (Ringwood, Vic. & Harmondsworth, U.K.: Viking, 1999; Ringwood, Vic. & New York: Viking, 1999).

Collection: *Collected Stories* (St. Lucia: University of Queensland Press, 1997).

OTHER: *Coast to Coast: Australian Stories 1969–1970*, edited by Astley (Sydney: Angus & Robertson, 1970).

SELECTED PERIODICAL PUBLICATIONS—
UNCOLLECTED: "The Idiot Question," *Southerly*, 30 (1970): 3–8;

"Being a Queenslander: A Form of Literary and Geographical Conceit," *Southerly*, 36, no. 3 (1976): 252–264;

"Writing in North Queensland," *LiNQ*, 9, no. 1 (1981): 2–10.

Thea Astley's career as a novelist spans the post–World War II decades, with a series of acclaimed novels. Since 1958 she has published a novel every two or three years, working steadily to produce a variety of critical and satirical perspectives on Australian and South Pacific life. She is probably the most awarded Australian writer, with four Miles Franklin Awards, for *The Well Dressed Explorer* (1962), *The Slow Natives* (1965), *The Acolyte* (1972), and *Drylands: A Book for the World's Last Reader* (1999); an Australian Literature Society Gold Medal, for *Beachmasters* (1985); a Patrick White Award (1989); and an Age Book of the Year Award for *The Multiple Effects of Rainshadow* (1996). Although she has won a reputation as one of the most stylish, witty, and acerbic writers of Australia, critics often have responded uneasily to her work, admiring its energy and skill but rarely endorsing it wholeheartedly, partly because her work presents obstinate difficulties to any single critical approach. Astley's early work resisted both the representation of women's experience and any openly feminist position, though her later work sometimes presents feminist opinions in an obvious way. She appears to be a social and cultural conservative, yet she passionately attacks some conservative positions. While her talents appear to be comic and satirical, her novels often confront violent or tragic events. She declares her sympathy for the marginalized and oppressed, but she exposes the failings of her characters with an unforgiving irony. She is a stylist who shifts from one style to another, often within the same novel.

Some of these contradictions may be understood in terms of Astley's personality and her experience of a rapidly changing Australian society. Personally, she can be contrary, even cantankerous, though she also has a great comic gift, expressed in witty self-mockery. In some ways, she is a typical Australian intellectual of her generation, jealously guarding her isolation from major intellectual groups and resisting participation in wider political and social movements. This isolation provides a platform for a sometimes passionate, sometimes wry denunciation of Australian society; it also ensures that she can never be claimed by any single political group or ideology.

Thea Beatrice May Astley was born 25 August 1925 in Brisbane, Queensland, to Cecil and Eileen Lindsay Astley, middle-class Catholics. Her father was a journalist, working mainly on *The Queenslander* and *The Brisbane Courier* (later *The Brisbane Courier-Mail*). Astley was educated at Catholic parish schools and then at All Hallows' School, a convent school, before going to Queensland Teachers' College to qualify as a teacher. During this time she also began evening study for a bachelor of arts degree at the University of Queensland and continued to teach by day and study at night or by correspondence until she finished the degree at the end of 1947. She has admitted that World War II affected her life little; the one upheaval was the evacuation of All Hallows' School to the country town of Warwick in 1942, a move that forced her to become a boarder for her final year. Astley was a religious teenager, and Catholic attitudes and problems turn up time and again in her novels. The division between routine work and intellectual enthusiasms, which she experienced as a schoolteacher and part-time university student, also recurs in the lives of her characters.

In 1948 Astley married Edmund John (Jack) Gregson, an educational administrator, and they moved to Sydney where their son, Edmund, was born in 1955. Astley entered her first novel manuscript in *The Sydney Morning Herald* literary competition, where it was commended and submitted to the publishing company Angus and Robertson, which published it in 1958 as *Girl with a Monkey*. It is an accomplished first novel, breaking with the tradition of social-realist writing practiced by prominent Australian writers of the time, including women such as Dymphna Cusack, Kylie Tennant, and Ruth Park. Patrick White's novels *The Tree of Man* (1956) and *Voss* (1957) had opened up Australian writing to more experimental modernist styles, and with her first novel Astley demonstrated that she, too, could represent Australian experience through a prism of subjective style. The third-person narrative identifies closely with the sensibilities of its central character, Elsie, a woman schoolteacher in a Queensland country town, as, on the day she leaves, she recalls her life there. Like the young Astley, Elsie studies for her university degree and aspires to an intellectual and cultural life beyond the pettiness of the country town (based on Townsville, where Astley taught in the 1940s). She is also sexually timid, and her intellectual aspirations have an edge of snobbishness as she flirts with, then abandons, a laborer who loves her. Astley demonstrates Elsie's cleverness through her own allusive, witty style, but the third-person point of view maintains a distance that prevents complete sympathy with Elsie and leaves a residual ambivalence about whether she is a prude and a snob, or merely someone asserting her right to a richer life and sympathetic companions.

Astley returned to schoolteaching in Sydney in the late 1950s, writing her novels at night and teaching by day. Although her second novel, *A Descant for Gossips* (1960), draws on her earlier experience as a schoolteacher in rural Queensland, its immediate inspiration came from her contact with an outcast child in a Sydney classroom and a story told to her by a fellow teacher about the suicide of a schoolgirl. In the novel two teachers embark on an adulterous love affair in the face of small-town gossip and spite. The major victim, however, is a thirteen-year-old schoolgirl for whom the teachers have represented the key to a world of culture and kindness beyond the vulgarities of the town. While the situation in the novel verges on the melodramatic, Astley conveys the dreariness of the life of the itinerant schoolteacher, living in rented rooms and forced to socialize with a small group of narrow-minded people. At the same time, Astley's barbs against the gossips are double-edged, as she demonstrates her own skill in dissecting her characters.

While Astley sympathizes with the adulterers of *A Descant for Gossips,* her next novel portrays the career of a Don Juan, a journalist named George Brewster. *The Well Dressed Explorer* almost qualifies the sexual tolerance of the earlier novel by demonstrating that adulterers may also be selfish buffoons. Bruce Clunies Ross—in "'Words Wrenched out of Amusement and Pain': Thea Astley's Musical Style," in *New Studies in Australian Literature* (1996)—sees this novel as "an ironical study of style as vanity," in which the ironic style of the novel, with its complex insights into George's self-regard and his effect on other characters, provides a degree of understanding of George's weakness while exposing the insincerity of his life.

Astley's ambivalence about unconventional sex may be attributed partly to her Catholic upbringing, but it also seems to come from her experience as a woman in the years immediately after the war, when women were encouraged to identify themselves with purity and faithful marriage. Nevertheless, adulterous sex features in most of her novels as she worries about its moral and social implications. In *The Well Dressed Explorer,* George Brewster belongs to an older generation, that of Astley's journalist father, and she gives him the pomposities and patronizing attitudes toward women of that generation. She also provides a plausible and sympathetic psychological explanation for George's sexual obsessions—his idyllic adolescent romance with a girl met on holidays. Once George embarks on his own career as a sexual predator, however, Astley maintains her critical distance, not only from George but also from all the characters of the

Dust jacket for Astley's 1962 novel, winner of the Miles Franklin Award, about a journalist who is a compulsive adulterer (Bruccoli Clark Layman Archives)

novel, including Alice, George's long-suffering wife. The novel becomes not so much overtly comic as bitterly ironic—a stance found in much of Astley's later work.

During the late 1950s, Astley developed a friendship with the novelist Patrick White—which ended abruptly, as reported in David Marr's biography of White. She continued to admire White's writing and acknowledges that he influenced all her work. This influence is most apparent in *The Slow Natives,* which adopts the strategy White used in his *Riders in the Chariot* (1961) of observing a group of contemporary Australians whose lives overlap in various ways. Like White, Astley examines the spiritual state of these Australians, who are entrapped in dreary suburban or country-town lives. Yet Astley's Catholicism seems to direct her attention to sin and guilt, rather than to the transcendent understanding that lifts White's protagonists out of their mundane existences. The fear of sexual sin—particularly adultery and unruly desire—dominates the lives of her characters. On the one hand, she creates a group of pure characters, such as the teenage Keith Leverson and the nun Sister Matthew, who find themselves submissive to the more corrupt authority of par-

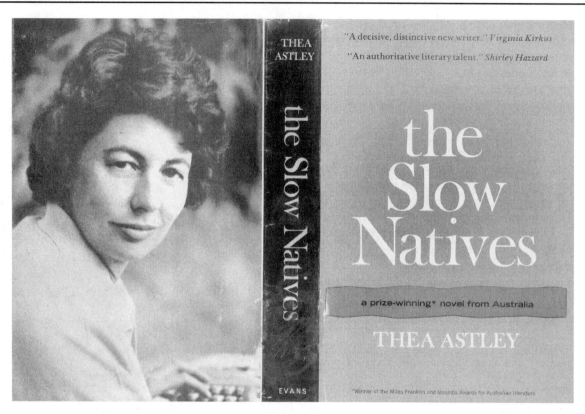

Dust jacket for the U.S. edition (1967) of Astley's 1965 novel about troubled suburban and small-town
Australians whose lives overlap (Richland County Public Library)

ents and church. On the other hand, her adulterous suburban parents, homosexual teachers, or sexually frustrated spinsters are driven more by boredom than by passion. While Keith shoplifts and worries about the consequences of sin, his mother conducts a rather forced affair with a neighbor. As a music examiner, Keith's father visits Condamine (based on Warwick), where Sister Matthew makes him the victim of a sexually accusing letter and where another music teacher, Miss Trumper, attempts to seduce him. At the climax of the novel Keith runs away, meeting a boy from Condamine who believes himself to have raped Miss Trumper, and the novel ends with a car accident that kills the boy and maims Keith.

For the first time, Astley focuses her attention on several religious characters—the three priests living together in a presbytery at Condamine and the nuns running the convent school—and through them examines the difficulty of Christian charity within a celibate life. Perhaps because she respects the idealism behind the choice of a religious life, Astley appears to treat these characters more sympathetically than she does her suburban husbands and wives. This novel draws out her comic skills and her detailed knowledge of Catholic parish life, convent schools, and the absurd ritual of the visiting music examiner. The scenes in which

Sister Matthew attempts to put more feeling into her performance of Johann Sebastian Bach and Fathers Lingard and Lake make cocoa for their crabby monsignor represent high points in Astley's comic, yet pathetic, vision of Australian life. While Astley's characters speak a consistently witty dialogue and many scenes are overtly funny, the novel does not become comedy. Its narrative pattern remains that of sin, guilt, and confession—followed by a kind of retribution in the car accident at its end.

Characters from *The Slow Natives* turn up in several of Astley's later novels. In *A Boat Load of Home Folk* (1968) Father Lake has become a missionary priest on an island in the Pacific to the north of Australia, and by strange coincidence Gerald Seabrook (the Leversons' adulterous neighbor), his wife, Miss Trumper, and her friend Verna Paradise also find themselves together on this island. While the island setting, researched on a two-week visit to what were then called the New Hebrides, promises a more political dimension to Astley's fiction, this perspective never eventuates. Once again, Astley examines sexual temptation and sin as Father Lake is caught making advances to his servant boy; the Seabrooks' marriage deteriorates; and Miss Trumper faces the ultimate disintegration of her body. Given Astley's later interest in white colonial mistreatment of Aborigines and Pacific Islanders, this novel is curious for its blindness to cultural and racial politics. It ends in total destruction as a hurricane sweeps the island, wreaking a kind of retribution on the sinners of the novel. Astley frequently adopts this pattern of violent physical breakdown as the natural world, or the bodies of individual characters, mirror the disintegration of the narrative.

If *The Slow Natives* echoes Patrick White's *Riders in the Chariot*, then *The Acolyte* answers his *The Vivisector* (1970), as Astley told Ray Willbanks for *Australian Voices: Writers and Their Work* (1991). Whereas White examines the life of the genius artist in suburban Australia, Astley chooses to view the artist through the eyes of his devoted assistant. The blindness of her artist-musician, Jack Holberg, intensifies his self-absorption, and Astley presents his art form as peculiarly apart from social and political interests and more a matter of "gift" than the consciously acquired crafts of painting and writing. Holberg's music, then, engages less with the world around him than does the painting of White's Hurtle Duffield, and Paul Vesper, the acolyte, narrates the novel as a jaundiced retrospective on his own devotion. This device solves some of the difficulties in Astley's earlier novels, in which the narrative voice was opinionated, allusive, and dense without being declared as a character in its own right. In *The Acolyte* the skips of logic, the opinions, the puns, and the metaphoric density can be ascribed to Paul's character as he records his own domestic failures and subservience to the artist. Paul's experience of middle-class life in Brisbane and the Queensland country town of Grogbusters during World War II and his postwar career as an engineer in Northern Queensland form the narrative—experiences clearly based on Astley's own early life. While Paul remains peripheral to the social world around Holberg, he represents Astley's own art form, writing, as he records the lives affected by the composer. The novel may be read as a comment on the parasitic, voyeuristic nature of writing compared with the purer art form of music, though Bruce Ross insists that it follows the patterns of musical composition. Paul seems to be commenting on Astley's own fragmented style when he writes,

> Look, I lump all these things together—slob art. Whack this at the canvas, or that, or tack on a bit of jam-can label, the bicycle pump, an empty can of beans. Framed, the whole thing will give you some sort of an impression and that's all I can offer, for being affixed myself between gobbets of Pammastic [paint], I can hardly evaluate the totality.

In *The Acolyte* Astley makes her habitual ironic refusal of sentiment part of her characterization of Paul. While Holberg is physically maimed by blindness, Paul

is emotionally maimed, and he is left catapulting rocks through the glass expanses of Holberg's house. Some critics have found the elaborately metaphoric narrative style of *The Acolyte* a barrier to reading; yet, the novel appears to be about art as a barrier to, rather than as a source of, communication. While Astley's engagement with White's depiction of the artist is apparent, she was also influenced by what she calls in her interview with Willbanks the "outrageously ornamented sickly imagistic style" of Hal Porter, and Paul Vesper prefigures the ironic detachment of the Porter persona in his *The Extra* (1975). Readers might see in it an acceptance of a lesser role for the artist than the spiritually transcendent aspirations of White's artists and his art.

From 1967 to 1980 Astley worked as a tutor in English at Macquarie University in Sydney. Her writing grew steadily less reliant on her own early experience as she sought out and researched subjects that interested her. She gave Commonwealth Literary Fund lectures in rural Queensland in the late 1960s and served on the Literature Board of the Australia Council from 1978 to 1982.

During this time, Astley made frequent visits to Queensland and, from 1970, spent every summer there, first in a cottage at Ball Bay near Mackay and later near Kuranda in the ranges outside Cairns. At Ball Bay she found the central idea for her next novel, *A Kindness Cup* (1974), in the massacres of Aborigines in that area during the late nineteenth century. This novel represents one of the first postwar fictional acknowledgments of the hidden history of the murder of Aborigines behind the colonizing of the North by white Australia, and Astley describes the treatment of the Aborigines in horrifying detail. She, nevertheless, passes over the broader political implications of this injustice in order to dissect her favorite subject—the guilt and hypocrisy of a small group of white Australians. In "A Life of Its Own: A Deconstructive Reading of Astley's *A Kindness Cup*," published in *Hecate* in 1985, Elizabeth Perkins has examined Astley's disconcerting failure in the novel to address this history in a consistent way and argues that it inscribes the contradictions of a white civilization that has promoted masculine violence. While Astley's narrative voice appears to endorse the values of education, particularly an education in the classic European texts, the action of the novel demonstrates that this education cannot prevent inhumanity. Perkins notes that the novel is undermined by the characters' participation in cultural traditions that the novel demonstrates are impotent. Astley returned to the subject of white mistreatment of Aborigines in *It's Raining in Mango: Pictures from a Family Album* (1987) with a firm comic perspective and a much greater understanding of the contemporary implications of white injustice to Aborigines.

*Dust jacket for the U.S. edition (1991) of Astley's 1979
collection of stories narrated by Keith Leverson, a
character from* The Slow Natives *(Richland
County Public Library)*

vant life in North Queensland. The incidents that form the basis of his stories are sometimes his own experiences, sometimes second- or third-hand accounts of the experiences of others. They offer the familiar Astley preoccupation with failed marriages, uncharitable clerics, and the sexual desperation, boredom, and selfishness of middle-class lives. A new element is the introduction of a group of hippie characters, who are lambasted for their irresponsibility and selfishness in "Write Me, Son, Write Me." Most of the stories ride on Keith's wit and comic perspective on human frailty, but "The Curate Breaker" drops the first-person voice to tell a story of sectarianism and selfishness between the Catholic parish priest and his Anglican counterpart. Father Rassini practices a form of domestic cruelty on his own father, but Astley gives him all the witty lines, so there can be no doubt which religion retains her loyalty. Only one story, "A Northern Belle," offers a thoroughly sympathetic character, in the Aborigine Willy Fourcorners, but Keith retells Willy's story in Astley's habitually ironic tone. The title story observes the manipulative competitiveness of a couple living on a pineapple plantation, while "Petals from Blown Roses" conveys the drunken heartiness of middle-aged Australians who have lost direction. Astley's recurrent depiction of women as unwanted bodies, in stories such as "Ladies Need Only Apply," may be justified in this one under the cover of Keith's misogyny and his hatred of his own mutilated body.

By the late 1970s, though, Astley was being read by feminists who questioned her choice of male narrators and male protagonists for her stories. Astley told Candida Baker in 1985—for *Yacker: Australian Writers Talk about Their Work* (1986)—that she felt that she had been "neutered" by her upbringing, and admitted that she made the narrator of *An Item from the Late News* (1982) a woman in order to experiment with the female voice. This comment has led to speculation that the masculine qualities in Astley's writing were somehow forced upon her by patriarchal social and cultural circumstances, particularly by her Catholicism and her career as a university teacher. The "neutering" idea may be traced to J. M. Couper's 1967 comment, in an article for *Meanjin,* that Astley creates at least three sexes in her novels, but Astley has repeated the phrase in interviews and novels. Her perspective on middle-aged women is particularly confronting; she portrays innocence in children, Aborigines, and islanders, but her adult worlds are always corrupt, with women bearing signs of this corruption in their deteriorating bodies.

If the comedy in *Hunting the Wild Pineapple* has a bitter edge, *An Item from the Late News* is unrelievedly bleak. The device of using a woman narrator repre-

Astley's next book, *Hunting the Wild Pineapple, and Other Related Stories* (1979), is a collection of short stories narrated by an adult Keith Leverson, the troubled adolescent of *The Slow Natives*. Astley's summers in North Queensland provided rich material for this collection, and her eye for the bizarre elements in Australian life have served her well. Astley claims that she finds the short story a more difficult form than the novel, but her books that can be variously read as collections of short stories or discontinuous novels—*Hunting the Wild Pineapple, It's Raining in Mango,* and *Drylands*—represent the major achievements of her career.

In *Hunting the Wild Pineapple,* Keith Leverson shows some of the qualities of Paul Vesper in *The Acolyte*. His one-legged state indicates a kind of withdrawal from sexual life, though, like Paul, he declares his heterosexuality in bitter references to passing affairs with women. Keith is without family; he is a failed musician and a failed motel manager, living a bored but obser-

sents no softening of Astley's voice as a divorced woman tells the story of North Queensland small-town malice against a harmless dropout preparing to survive a nuclear war. Whereas the image of Sadie Klein naked on her knees in the mud at the end of "Ladies Need Only Apply" exemplifies Astley's vision of the middle-aged sexual woman, in *An Item from the Late News* she invents a male New Year's ritual in which two characters wearing bullock horns maul each other. This incident appears to be Astley's statement on primitive male aggression—the approaching nuclear calamity writ small in country-town barbarism. Like *A Kindness Cup,* the novel *An Item from the Late News* has disturbed critics because Astley appears thoroughly misanthropic and devoid of any hope for the future.

When she retired as fellow in English at Macquarie University in 1979, Astley, with her husband, began to spend the whole year at Kuranda. She was at last in a position to write full-time, and she researched her next book by returning to the Pacific islands. Though clearly based on the political situation in Vanuatu (formerly the New Hebrides)—mixed-race political leader Jimmy Stevens is the model for her Tommy Narota—*Beachmasters* returns to the kind of island colony of *A Boat Load of Home Folk,* this time with an awareness of native subjectivities and concerns. Though her white characters form a typical Astley social group of schoolteacher, doctor, British Resident Commissioner, and their wives, this novel gives to the islanders the power to disrupt their existences, driving the whites away in an attempted coup. While the conversations of Astley's middle-class characters bristle with wit, she takes issue with the language of colonization, contrasting the self-satisfied competition between French- and English-speaking colonizers with the pidgin language granted to the colonized. For this novel, Astley not only chose a simpler style to convey the perspective of the mixed-race and island people, but she also managed to employ a language combining English and the "island" speech, rich enough to convey an intelligent perspective on the world, simple enough to be credible. Paul Sharrad has noted, in "The Well-Dressed Pacific Explorer: Thea Astley's *Beachmasters,* a Study in Displacement" for *Ariel* (1990), that in this novel, Astley's shifting styles reflect the inherent contradictions in the position of Australians sympathetic to postcolonial movements.

Astley was disappointed with the reception of *Beachmasters,* a novel that in many ways answered the critics of her earlier novels through its disciplined style, its political astuteness, and its more sympathetic range of characters. But the exercise stood her in good stead for her next work, *It's Raining in Mango,* which draws together her range of interests and her strengths as a writer. *It's Raining in Mango* won the inaugural Steele

Rudd Award for a collection of short stories though it is clearly conceived as a novel. Astley offers the image of the photograph album to connect her stories about a pioneering white family in the north of Queensland. The novel operates as a sustained satire on the celebratory Australian family saga, with the members of the Laffey family functioning as outcasts, derelicts, eccentrics, and dropouts. Astley also manages to address the history of Aboriginal oppression in terms of the present position of Aborigines on the fringe of Queensland society. The story of Astley's own grandfather, a Canadian-born journalist who abandoned her grandmother and his children, forms the basis for the Laffey patriarch, Cornelius. Through the generations the fictional female Laffeys are driven to pub keeping and prostitution, while the men endure the hopelessness of small farming and the miseries of World War II. Their lives are intertwined with those of members of the Mumbler family, Aborigines who survive nineteenth-century massacre and twentieth-century interference by the law. While Astley's wit flashes as usual, in this novel she directs her criticisms firmly at the authorities of church and state rather than at the failings of her individual characters. Readers may want to applaud grandmother Jessica Olive's attack on Father Madigan for the attitude of Catholicism toward women, anachronistic and incredible though her action may be: "That terrified obedience you and your brothers in Christ exact is directed largely at women. Women. You've neutered us. Made us nonhuman."

It's Raining in Mango, published in 1987, appeared in time to take issue with the Bicentennial Celebrations of 1988. While other novels published about that time, such as Peter Carey's *Oscar and Lucinda* (1988) or Kate Grenville's *Joan Makes History* (1988), address the meaning of Australian history and white relations with the Aborigines, Astley manages both to debunk public history and to celebrate the survival of ordinary Australians. After years of lamenting Australian failure and guilt, Astley turns this material to sustained comic use. The retributive rain carries a brothel full of singing prostitutes gloriously out to sea and death. Billy Mumbler is jailed for tax evasion but expresses a shoulder-shrugging acceptance of white paradox. The failures of individuals appear to be at the hands of God or the legal system, not some sign of their own guilt-ridden weakness. This perspective allows Astley to break through to a pure comedy, unbounded by self-hatred or remorse. *It's Raining in Mango* probably represents her most accomplished and most generous achievement.

Reaching Tin River, published in 1990, carries on this vital comedy. In a self-conscious postmodern style, Belle, the narrator, offers the reader several alternative novel openings before settling on the strategy of photo-

chpt opening

(*handwritten*) ... for it is impossible to understand this point at all h.

In the waters of these islands there is a certain fish whose eyes, like the eyes of the chameleon, are able to look in opposite directions at the same time.

Like aeland Kristi.

Kristi last winter and the summer before that, while the wind off the Channel was munched by the wooden teeth of the shutters.

Like man Kristi——man bush or man solwata.

Like the colons and the British ex-patriates and the rag dolls District Agent Cordingley with his wife Belle and French District Agent Boutin and Madame Boutin and Planter Salway and his grandson Gavi and Gavi's maman, Lucie Ela, and Madame Guichet and Chloe of the Dancing Bears and a beach bum from the big land, man blong Australia, whose real name was never known, with a lifetime of small riots behind and more in his blood like bubbles.

And, too, oh in this litany, pray, your eyes east-west, pray for Hedmaeta Woodful, now and at the hour of the changing, and for the Bonsers, mechanics of more than boat engines, for Planter Duchard and family, and above all, for the big man, the yeremanu, Tommy Narota, part Kristi, part Tongan, part Devon, who has taken on his new native name, abandoning that of his sea-faring adventurer daddy, along with his ceremonial dress of pipi fringed table cloth and lace antimacassar loin-wrapper. Send your prayers east-west or north-south for the wanikoro to pluck up with its swoop of a beak.

And pray in three tongues: in Seaspeak, in English, in French; for there are three ways of praying.

The eyes move two ways. The voice moves three. Two-eyed. Triple-tongued. While the wind is eaten by the shutters and the

Corrected typescript page for Astley's 1985 novel Beachmasters, *in which Pacific islanders drive off white colonizers (from Candida Baker,* Yacker: Australian Writers Talk about Their Work, *1986; Paterno Library, Pennsylvania State University)*

graph notes, similar to the photograph album of *It's Raining in Mango*. Like that novel, *Reaching Tin River* interweaves family history and the present, with Belle increasingly obsessed by a desire literally to reach the past. The novel takes an overtly feminist stance and sometimes slips into anachronistic feminist jargon–as in Belle's declaration that "my gender is meat." Feminism finds comic expression in an ongoing joke about the relationship of women to music. Belle's mother and aunt abandon rural slavery to form a dance band, which has moderate success until a genuinely talented woman saxophonist joins them. The first part of the novel moves at a fast pace, as Belle dazzles the reader with a parade of comic characters and wit. The final sections, though, follow Belle's search for a nineteenth-century character encountered in the archives and her attempt to leap into his life. She becomes an Alice trying to step through the looking glass, from real life into the world of fantasy and story. Belle is a reader rather than an artist, but her quest for a center "outside the perimeter" suggests that Astley is commenting on the relationship between fiction and life. Belle says, "I can write only about what I see or think I see"–invention and experience are of the same order.

In 1985 Astley surrendered to the heat of the North Queensland summer and moved with her husband to Cambewarra in the hills outside Nowra on the New South Wales South Coast. Though closer to Sydney, Cambewarra is nevertheless isolated from city culture, and Astley's imagination continued to find versions of Queensland the most congenial setting for fiction. Both *Vanishing Points* (1992) and *Coda* (1994) develop minor characters that first appeared in *Hunting the Wild Pineapple*. *Vanishing Points* consists of two novellas, "The Genteel Poverty Bus Company" and "Inventing the Weather." In the first of these, Mac, one of Leverson's friends, wages a one-man war on the music and technology of the present age by answering the music from the tourist resort on a nearby island with loud classical music. Through him, Astley expresses her frequently voiced hatred of pop music and tourist developments. Mac's music war, though, seems more like intolerance gone mad than like the battle between pure art and the tawdriness of contemporary culture. In the second story, the estranged wife of the tourist-resort developer in the first story embarks on a quest for revenge. A group of nuns living in isolation among Aborigines on the far North Queensland coast inspire Julie with an ideal of purity, apart from the trials of family life. Astley's heroine is not so much neutered by men, society, or religion as actively seeking the "neutered" life found by the nuns, apart from sexuality. After all the years of working her way from the constricted Catholic attitudes to the sexuality of her youth,

Astley has returned in this novella to the Catholic ideal of the nonsexual adult woman.

In *Coda*, Astley moves beyond sexuality to examine the life of a kind of comic female Lear–Kathleen Hackendorf, the elderly mother of "Brain," the failed developer and lost singer of "Petals from Blown Roses." Kathleen recalls her life as wife and mother to a dead friend, Daisy, as she finds her loss of memory and increasing incontinence relegate her to being a burden on her children and society. Familiar Astley scenarios appear in the novel: Kathleen lives for a time in the New Hebrides; her children live the suburban life in Brisbane and North Queensland; her daughter is married to a politician and developer; and Brain leaves his wife for Mrs. Waterman of the earlier story. For all her raging against men, Kathleen can hardly be called likable or just. She has lived the middle-class life of relative comfort, which Astley seems to acknowledge by providing some of Daisy's more working-class experiences as ammunition for Kathleen's anger. Perhaps the most poignant element of the story, though, is the decline of Kathleen's body; she is not simply the sexually rejected middle-aged woman, such as Miss Trumper or Sadie Klein, but the physically deteriorating old woman swamped in her own urine. *Coda* may remind the reader of Patrick White's last novel, *Memoirs of Many in One* (1986), in which a dying woman recalls her experiences in various roles as she confronts the ultimate decay of her body. White's need in this novel, and in his earlier novels, to present the failure of the physical through women's bodies may be seen as colluding with conventional Western attitudes toward the female body as the symbol of mortality. Astley's similar attitude may be more disturbing, though Kathleen's rage against men, just as Julie's in "Inventing the Weather," can be read as a rage against being female. Some critics find an aggressive feminism in this late work by Astley, but it remains a doubtful feminism, playing with simple reversals of male and female roles.

While *Coda* appeared to be a last, bitter statement about female mortality, Astley returned with renewed vigor to broader social interests in *The Multiple Effects of Rainshadow*. Like *It's Raining in Mango*, this novel confronts the darker history of North Australia, using as a base an incident on the Aboriginal reserve of Palm Island in 1930 when the white superintendent ran amok, killing his own children before being shot by an Aborigine. In the novel a variety of narrators report their perspectives on this incident, examining it for its complex meanings about the nature of white colonization. Astley gives several of these narrators a sharp wit and brilliant turn of phrase–Mrs. Curthoys, the manager of the staff boardinghouse, provides a brisk and clever account of the island, and her daughter, Leonie,

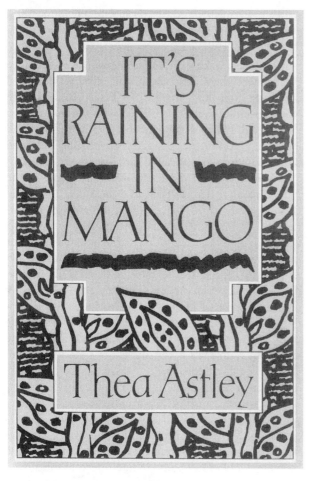

Dust jacket for the U.S. edition of Astley's 1987 novel about the intertwined lives of a white family and an Aboriginal family (Richland County Public Library)

continues the narrative through the years of World War II. As she did in *Beachmasters* and *It's Raining in Mango,* Astley also risks an indigenous voice, accessing Manny Cooktown's thoughts on the incident and its implications for him. The first part of the novel, which circles around the murders, exemplifies Astley's writing at its most controlled and dramatic, but the latter part follows the lives of white participants into the familiar territory of marriage boredom, adultery, and the school system. The contradiction—which is relevant to the problem of race relations in Australia—is the failure of civilized and educated whites to improve the position of native peoples. Mrs. Curthoys, Mr. Vine, and Dr. Quigley—in spite of all their intelligence, education, and goodwill—are too weak to help when Captain Brodie goes mad and kills his children, and the Aborigines must act and suffer for the whites' weaknesses. The last part of the novel is set mainly in a boarding school to which one of the Aboriginal boys has been sent. Astley clearly believes in the power of education and the civi-

lizing effects of art: all of her sympathetic narrators demonstrate their commitment to Western high culture. Yet, educated and cultured people consistently fail to achieve anything in her novels, apart from the act of storytelling itself; indeed, their failures often open the way for more active and brutal elements of colonial society. Leigh Dale, in his article "Colonial History and Post-Colonial Fiction: The Writing of Thea Astley" for *Australian Literary Studies* (1999), argues that *The Multiple Effects of Rainshadow* criticizes the nature of narrative, particularly historical narrative, for its inability to give due weight to the consequences of lived history. The novel itself is, of course, a kind of history and so signals its own sense of failure.

In this despairing vein, *Drylands* seems to announce an end of things through its subtitle—*A Book for the World's Last Reader*. Janet Deakin, the owner of a country-town news agency, settles down to write a novel. Literacy becomes its passion, and those excluded from it, such as the teenager devoted to video games, are most likely to act immorally. Janet proudly describes how she taught her husband to read, and the novel does not question her conviction that this feat is a moral triumph. In the town of Drylands, the women uphold civilization—through reading and art—while the men spend their lives in the pub watching sports on satellite television. Outside the pub, these men can be brutal or selfish—beating and bullying their wives and even raping a defenseless woman. The few sensitive men in the town also become victims of abuse and cruelty, including Randler, whose retirement project of building a boat ends in flames, and Benny Shoforth, the part Aborigine (who has already suffered removal from his mother), who is removed from his house on the edge of the town. In this novel the educated women help those weaker than themselves, but there is something rather wish fulfilling in the faith of such acts to teach and nurture. Eventually, all these characters leave the town, a symbol of the decline of this kind of small-town life and the decay of white Australian culture.

Despite its depiction of social decay, the novel is written with a surprising energy, fueled by Astley's apparent anger at the decline of culture, particularly literacy, in Australia. The novel seems to revel in the destruction of Drylands, abandoned by every character with any sensitivity or self-awareness.

Perkins has argued that the key to understanding Astley's work lies in dissociating the author and the text. Perkins's reading of *A Kindness Cup* elucidates the way that Astley, against the grain of her apparent intentions, identifies a crisis in Western society. Debra Adelaide, in "Thea Astley—'completely neutered': Gender, Reception and Reputation" (*Southerly,* 1997), adds that the preponderance of published interviews with the author over critical readings of the novels has restricted understanding of their complexity by focusing too insistently on the novelist rather than her art. Yet, the most consistent element of Astley's fiction may be the personality of the novelist herself, as she keeps up the jokes and the anger in the guise of one or more narrative voices, in fiction after fiction. The contradictions in this personality, with its concern for social justice and humanity and corresponding distaste for the crassness of Australian society and individual humans, provide a creative friction, so that the decadence of Australian society stimulates an artistic response. Thea Astley may be read as the kind of satirist who, rather than offering a consistent reformist program or set of values, inhabits her own fictions with a comic energy and shifting anger.

Interviews:

Graeme Kinross-Smith, "Thea Astley," *Kunapipi,* 4 (1982): 20–37;

Candida Baker, "Thea Astley," in *Yacker: Australian Writers Talk about Their Work* (Sydney: Picador, 1986), pp. 29–53;

Jennifer Ellison, "Thea Astley," in *Rooms of Their Own,* edited by Ellison (Ringwood, Vic.: Penguin, 1986), pp. 50–69;

Robert Ross, "An Interview with Thea Astley," *World Literature Written in English,* 26 (1986): 264–269;

Ray Willbanks, "Thea Astley," in *Australian Voices: Writers and Their Work* (Austin: University of Texas, 1991), pp. 26–42.

References:

Debra Adelaide, "Thea Astley–'completely neutered': Gender, Reception and Reputation," *Southerly,* 57 (1997): 182–190;

Laurie Clancy, "The Fiction of Thea Astley," *Meridian,* 5 (May 1986): 43–52;

J. M. Couper, "The Novels of Thea Astley," *Meanjin,* 26 (1967): 332–337;

Leigh Dale, "Colonial History and Post-Colonial Fiction: The Writing of Thea Astley," *Australian Literary Studies,* 19 (1999): 21–31;

Pam Gilbert, "Thea Astley," in *Coming Out from Under: Contemporary Australian Women Writers* (North Sydney: Pandora, 1988), pp. 109–128;

Kerry Goldsworthy, "Thea Astley's Writing: Magnetic North," *Meanjin,* 42 (1983): 478–485;

Goldsworthy, "Voices in Time: *A Kindness Cup* and *Miss Peabody's Inheritance,*" *Australian Literary Studies,* 12 (October 1986): 471–481;

Anthony Hassall, "The Deserted Village? Thea Astley's *Drylands,*" in *Unemployed at Last: Essays on Australian Literature to 2002,* edited by Ken Stewart and Shirley Walker (Armidale: Centre for Australian Studies, 2003), pp. 147–160;

Roslynn Haynes, "'Shelter from the Holocaust': Thea Astley's *An Item from the Late News,*" *Southerly,* 48 (June 1988): 138–151;

Susan Lever, "Changing Times, Changing Stories: Thirty-Six Years of Thea Astley's Fiction," *Australian Studies* (U.K.), 10 (1996): 50–60;

Brian Matthews, "'Life in the Eye of the Hurricane': The Novels of Thea Astley," *Southern Review,* 6 (1973): 148–173;

Elizabeth Perkins, "A Life of Its Own: A Deconstructive Reading of Astley's *A Kindness Cup,*" *Hecate,* 11 (1985): 11–17;

Bruce Clunies Ross, "'Words Wrenched out of Amusement and Pain': Thea Astley's Musical Style," in *New Studies in Australian Literature,* edited by Irmtraud Petersson and Martin Duwell (St. Lucia: University of Queensland Press, 1996), pp. 151–163;

Robert Ross, "The Shape of Language in Thea Astley's Work," *World Literature Written in English,* 28 (1988): 260–265;

Ross, "Thea Astley," in *International Literature in English: Essays on the Major Writers* (New York: Garland, 1991), pp. 593–602;

Selina Samuels, "Queensland Baroque: Thea Astley's Stories," *Heat,* 10 (1998): 186–191;

Paul Sharrad, "The Well-Dressed Pacific Explorer: Thea Astley's *Beachmasters,* a Study in Displacement," *Ariel,* 21 (1990): 101–117.

Papers:

The major collection of Thea Astley's papers, including novel manuscripts, correspondence, and research material, is in the Fryer Library, University of Queensland. The National Library of Australia holds manuscript drafts of *The Well Dressed Explorer* and *The Acolyte.*

Bruce Beaver

(14 February 1928 –   )

Felicity Plunkett
University of New England

BOOKS: *Under the Bridge* (Sydney: Beaujon Press, 1961);

The Hot Summer (Sydney: Horwitz, 1963);

Seawall and Shoreline (Sydney: South Head Press, 1964);

The Hot Men (Sydney: Horwitz, 1965);

The Hot Spring (Sydney: Horwitz, 1965);

You Can't Come Back (London: Angus & Robertson, 1966; Adelaide: Rigby, 1966);

Open at Random (Sydney: South Head Press, 1967);

Letters to Live Poets (Sydney: South Head Press, 1969);

Lauds and Plaints: Poems 1968–1972 (Sydney: South Head Press, 1974);

Odes and Days (Sydney: South Head Press, 1975);

Death's Directives, Prism Books (Sydney: New Poetry, 1978);

As It Was (St. Lucia: University of Queensland Press, 1979);

Selected Poems (London & Sydney: Angus & Robertson, 1979);

Headlands: Prose Sketches (St. Lucia & New York: University of Queensland Press, 1986);

Charmed Lives (St. Lucia, New York & Manchester, N.H.: University of Queensland Press, 1988);

New and Selected Poems 1960–1990 (St. Lucia & Portland, Ore.: University of Queensland Press, 1991);

Anima and Other Poems (St. Lucia & Portland, Ore.: University of Queensland Press, 1994);

Poets and Others (Rose Bay, N.S.W.: Brandl & Schlesinger, 1999).

OTHER: *King Tide Running: Australian One Act Plays: Book Three,* by Beaver and Barbara Vernon, edited by Musgrave Horner (Adelaide: Rigby, 1967), pp. 22–51.

Bruce Beaver has been publishing poetry for more than forty years, straddling the "before" and "after" phases of the poetry of 1968, the year imagined as bringing the reinvigoration of Australian poetry. Much of his work is in the confessional mode and reiterates a thematic of exploring the inner life and the

Bruce Beaver, 1983 (photograph by A. T. Bolton; used by permission of the National Library of Australia)

emotional and mental challenges faced by the sensitive person. Writing in 1982, in *The American Model,* Thomas Shapcott argued that "Of Australian poets, I think only Bruce Beaver has been able to discover the vulnerability that leads to an opening up of creative range, not a withdrawal into self-pity or personal pleading." Beaver's first major work was *Letters to Live Poets* (1969), in which his experiments with confessionalism are foregrounded. Among the honors Beaver has received are the Patrick White Award (1982), the Federation of Australian Writers' Christopher Brennan Award (1983), and the Order of Australia (1991) for his contribution to Australian literature.

Bruce Victor Beaver was born in the Sydney seaside suburb of Manly on 14 February 1928 to Victor

Beaver (a salesman) and Thelma Jenman Beaver (a clerk). His autobiographical collection about his childhood and adolescence, *As It Was* (1979), in the poem "Dying," describes an unhappy childhood and adolescence spent in Manly, amid family conflicts, his father's alcoholism, and the development of a personality "born middle-aged." Beaver's poems in *As It Was* examine the ways in which immersion in popular culture provided solace for him. His "early tutors," he writes in "Raisons d'etre," were "the abominable, the magnificent media of the comic book, the radio, the film." Later, after these early "bright, unsubtle panaceas," came the seduction of poetry. Beaver was educated at Balgowlah Public School, near Manly, and later at Sydney Boys' High School, a selective state school in central Sydney, which he left after a year, "in disgrace." Gaining entry to the latter school was, Beaver suggests in "Flying," something of a fluke, though this self-disparaging remark says more about the tone and attitude of his self-scrutiny in his autobiographical writing than it does about his intellectual ability.

During his late adolescence, from the age of seventeen, he began to suffer from mental illness, diagnosed as bipolar disorder. In "Crises" Beaver details his botched suicide attempts and his subsequent hospitalization in the Prince Alfred Hospital, where he underwent shock therapy. Later, he was sent to Broughton Hall in Rozelle, next door to, and later amalgamated with, the more notorious psychiatric asylum Callan Park. During these periods of hospitalization, Beaver came to embrace poetry, identifying with lonely figures such as Australian poet Christopher Brennan's protagonist in *The Wanderer* (series collected in *Poems [1913]*, 1914) and relishing work by the Imagists, the Georgians, and modernists such as W. H. Auden. Beaver's poems also refer to his identification with the alienated characters played by German Jewish actor Conrad Veidt in movies such as *Jew Suss* (1934) and *The Wandering Jew* (Parts 1 and 2, 1933). At the end of "Crises," Beaver articulates his new orientation toward life: with the focal point of "verses to be written," life seems less meaningless. "Breakthroughs" in *As It Was* describes a decision to accept willingly a "life sentence in the quarry of words."

In 1961, not long after the childhood and adolescent period *As It Was* charts, Beaver's first book, *Under the Bridge,* was published. In the intervening period prior to this publication, Beaver's late adolescence and early adulthood were spent in literal and figurative mobility. During this period he spent time working in different parts of New South Wales in jobs as diverse as farming, arranging radio programs, fruit picking, and working as a railway surveyor laborer. He also traveled, lived on Norfolk Island in 1958, and in New

Zealand from 1958 until 1962, where he worked as a proofreader for *The New Zealand Herald* from 1960 through 1962. In the early 1960s he returned to Manly, where he has remained, with his wife, Brenda (the former Kathleen Brenda Bellam, whom he married in 1963), living in a house built on the site where his childhood home once stood.

By 1961 he had come to focus more on writing and was making a living from freelance journalism while seeking publication in literary journals and newspapers. *Under the Bridge* includes poems that had been published in such key literary journals as *Australian Poetry, Meanjin, Overland,* and *Southerly.* He had also had poems published in such newspapers and magazines as *The Sydney Morning Herald* and *The Sydney Bulletin.* Many of the poems in his first collection take as their subjects an acutely observed outside world of nature and humanity. Subjects such as a park, a musician on a ferry, and children at a kindergarten are delineated in crystalline imagery. Much of this imagery is unexpected, as when the children in "Kindergarten" are described as being like "hard boiled / Lollies being sticky together / Or splintering against and apart." Similarly, a ferry musician ("To a Ferry Musician") becomes, as the ferry moves out of the heads and braves the rolling waves (as it does on a rough, rainy day on its journey from Circular Quay to Manly), a salvific figure, allaying the fear of other passengers.

Allusions to T. S. Eliot and Australian poet John Blight show something of the influences on the poems. Although most of the poems are carefully structured and mannered, some, in their experiments with free verse and eccentric lineation, suggest the influence of modernist poetry, in which Beaver had earlier been immersed. Set amid these vignette-like poems, with their acute yet often detached observations, are other poems that show inklings of the confessional mode, wherein Beaver later found a voice. Love poems such as "Reasons," "Waiting for the Word," and "Spell" best exemplify the confessional focus. An "I" and a "you" come to the fore, along with an emotional force, as in "Discovery," in which "I paused unnoticed for the moment, / Taking your warmth as a drowned man takes the sun."

Beaver's next two collections, *Seawall and Shoreline* (1964) and *Open at Random* (1967), continue in this vein, juxtaposing poems in which the world is observed from a distance with those that are more overtly located within a first-person perspective. Poet and critic Robert D. FitzGerald, reviewing *Open at Random* in the context of the first two volumes, saw in the three collections a unifying theme of "an understanding–though a bitter one at times–of the universal composite nature of life, realized within individual experience" (*Meanjin*, 1969).

Bruce Beaver

OPEN AT RANDOM

*Dust jacket for Beaver's 1967 collection, which, in addition to
some experimental verse, includes poems of self-examination
and reflection (Bruccoli Clark Layman Archives)*

FitzGerald opened his review with the comment that "There are no Australian poets of his generation, and few of any other, whose work I have been willing to give such diligent attention to as that of Bruce Beaver." In a review of *Open at Random* in *Southerly* (1969) Don Anderson praised Beaver's "intellectual control" and "very real wit," as well as his "acute sense of the value of the pun." Each critic, however, had reservations about Beaver's work. Anderson found that the title poem of *Open at Random* "smacks of over-defensiveness about poetry and against critics and readers." FitzGerald perceived at times "an uncertainty about what the poet actually wants to say," resulting, at its worst, in "a feeling of vacancy where meaning is not doubtful so much as tipped out altogether." FitzGerald also noted some problems of mannerism, finding no compelling reason for the dropping of punctuation and other departures from conventional grammar.

While Anderson and FitzGerald found aspects of Beaver's work laudable, an unsympathetic review of *Open at Random* by Max Richards in *Meanjin* (1969) illustrates a more conservative reaction to Beaver's experiments. Richards wrote archly that Beaver "often writes in Contemporary Diction"; Richards also objected to a "vulgar allusion" to the Crucifixion and remarks on "a remarkable aural insensitivity" in some poems.

The emphasis of these critics on wordplay and experimentation as either positive traits or deficiencies belies that often the lyric poems about love are some of the most striking in the volumes. In the more intimate and emotional poems, a theme of self-scrutiny and evaluation emerges, which is fed by Beaver's reading of such American poets as Frank O'Hara and Walt Whitman.

This motif of self-examination and intimate reflection culminated in the 1969 publication of the book considered Beaver's first major collection, *Letters to Live Poets,* which established his reputation. Geoffrey Lehmann, reviewing the collection, called it "the first fully confessional book of verse to be produced" in Australia" (*The Bulletin,* 30 May 1970). Lehmann commented that "this is poetry which hurts and abrades with its rawness" and that Beaver "has never been a poet to dress his subject up," preferring "a vigorous untidiness to smooth articulated surfaces." The book won many awards, including the Poetry Society of Australia Prize, third prize in the Captain Cook Bicentennial Prize for Poetry (1970), and the Grace Leven Prize for Poetry (1970).

The collection shows Beaver exploring the possibilities of the confessional mode. It marks a watershed in his career in terms of the acknowledgment of his work and a loosening of form in the work itself, from which flows an intimate scrutiny of the inner life. In particular, the collection returns to an assessment of the "big crass statement of pain," which is described as "Maybe the most intimate / experience we're capable of." Like Robert Lowell's *Life Studies* (1959), as well as the works of Sylvia Plath and Anne Sexton, Beaver's confessional poems include analyses of the experience and treatment of mental illness. His work contests the barbarism and futility of much of this treatment, and locates its origins in pain—"the assaults of the mind." The portrait of a condescending science graduate with whom the speaker shares a hospital room in "XXVI" exposes the human cruelties that underlie psychological pain, as the student greets his father "begging without a word to be embraced." Like the father's cold and limited response (he mutters, embarrassed, "Control yourself") the collection continually touches on the covert and socially condoned violences that rip at lives, and it offers radical views on mental and emotional illness.

Despite the generally positive reception of the book, some contemporary critics reacted with discomfort to this unflinching access to the central consciousness and emotional experience of the poems. Writing in *Meanjin,* John M. Wright described *Letters to Live Poets* as "almost obsessive in its sense of self and . . . therefore seldom able to get far beyond a more or less agonising consciousness focusing on itself." Wright preferred to praise the poems in which this self retreats a little, those in which, according to Wright, Beaver was able to "employ a narrative technique without distraction and without intrusive self-consciousness" (*Meanjin,* 1974). James McAuley reacted to what he saw as poems that "read a little too much like wordy improvisations, impromptus," though this assessment was tempered by the acknowledgment that they "have force and truth in them." Only slightly later, considering the volume in *Meanjin* in 1976, R. D. FitzGerald said that the "somewhat youthful experimentalist had stepped straight into maturity" (*Meanjin,* 1976). Calling the book a "masterpiece," FitzGerald saw as its strength the centrality of self by which Wright was so unsettled: "an innate ability to see very intently whatever is straight in front of him." In more recent years, FitzGerald's view has predominated, suggesting perhaps that readers have become acclimatized to the directness that was so striking and pioneering in the early confessional poets.

Certainly the degree of emotional openness in the collection was new in Australian poetry at the time. Yet, the collection is not solipsistic; Beaver has situated his poems overtly where they can address and intersect with those of other poets. He signals this arrangement in the title, with its allusion to Austrian poet Rainer Maria Rilke's *Letters to a Young Poet* (1929; translated, 1934), in which Rilke considers the role and meaning of the poet while responding to the letters of an aspiring poet, Franz Kappus. While Rilke stresses the need for solitude and exploring deep within one's own thoughts, his letters are an exercise in mentorship and generosity, and a similar paradox marks Beaver's collection. In it, the speaker refers to being "more conscious of the community / world-wide of live, mortal poets." Dedicated to Australian poet and doctor Grace Perry, the poems address named and unnamed poets and allude to the work of a spectrum of poets that includes William Blake, Dylan Thomas, and Jonathan Swift. In the last stanza of the final poem of the collection, the definition of *poet* is extended from the literal to the figurative, as the book is given to "the live poets of my knowing, / not all writers, yet all conscious / of the gift of the living word." References to the Vietnam War place the collection in its time, while allusions to Callan Park Psychiatric Hospital, Rushcutter's Bay Park in Sydney, and meter maids "glabrous in gold bikinis" at Surfers' Para-

dise place the poems geographically within urban Australia. Yet, through engaging with literature, Beaver evokes a wider sphere.

The collection is significantly placed in terms of the development of Australian poetry. Beaver was, by this stage, older than most of the poets of the generation John Tranter called "the generation of '68"–a generation credited with having revolutionized and revivified Australian poetry. Yet, his poetry and his work as a contributing editor to the journal *Poetry Australia* attest to his importance as part of this year when the "New Australian Poetry" emerged. *Letters to Live Poets* prefigures the energy and innovation with which the New Australian Poetry is associated.

Lauds and Plaints (1974) was produced more slowly than *Letters to Live Poets* and in many ways complements it. Although thematically more outward-looking than its predecessor, it is also stylistically experimental. Whereas *Letters to Live Poets* exemplifies a loosening of form, *Lauds and Plaints* displays other experiments. Alongside the dropping of punctuation, Beaver develops his own patterns of lineation and indentation. The rhythms of the poems are reflected by their shape on the page, and the forms shift toward the prose-poetry hybrid that Beaver later explores more fully. Several of the poems have epigraphs, which draw on popular cultural sources–Simon and Garfunkel and news broadcasts–as well as more traditional literary sources, such as works of Rilke and Ezra Pound. These poems are more buoyant than those in *Letters to Live Poets,* perhaps paradoxically, considering the acclaim that followed the more serious and intense earlier volume.

In 1975 Beaver published *Odes and Days,* comprised of poems published in Australian and New Zealand journals. The first section, "Odes," includes fifteen poems that, Beaver explains in an introductory note to the collection, were written while he was "staying at Dr. Grace Perry's 140-year-old residence at Berrima." Beaver's explanation for the return to more formal structures ("neo-classical forms") is described as a response to the environment. The note goes on to define the ode and to sketch the shape of the section, wherein eight odes addressed to "the self and the house" are "bisected" by seven biographical sketches of poets and composers whose work had affected and influenced Beaver. Written in the form of addresses to them, these sketches are of Rilke, Friedrich Holderlin, Ludwig van Beethoven, Christopher Brennan, Gustav Mahler, Rilke, Frederick Delius, and Hermann Hesse. The "Days" section was so named because, according to the prefatory note, "they were written during a period of weeks prior to, during, and overlapping the composition of the odes." Beaver describes them as a

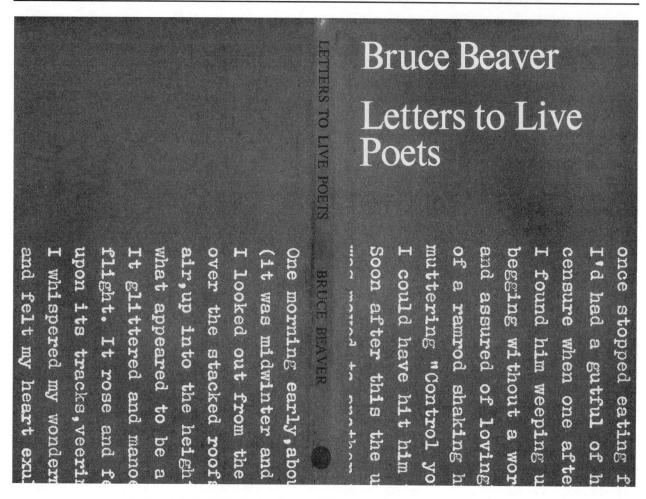

*Dust jacket for the 1969 collection of raw, confessional poetry that won awards and established
Beaver's reputation (Bruccoli Clark Layman Archives)*

"verse journal." These impressionistic poems are addressed to friends and family, or alight on observations about the events of the day. Trying to write while listening to the evening news through a closed door, talking to a loved one on the telephone, hearing a child's swing creaking, and even something as small as "the nowness of eating an apple" attract the poet's attention. This careful evocation of the textures of everyday living exquisitely registers the sensory, emotional, and imaginative experiences of a series of days. While these days may be uneventful in any large sense, they are lived fully, in the way Rilke advocates in his *Letters to a Young Poet,* in which he writes of being "poet enough to call forth" the riches of everyday living.

In 1978 Beaver published *Death's Directives,* which he dedicated to David Malouf. This sequence of twenty poems has an overarching theme of mortality. The speaker experiences the visitations of an animated death, who offers advice on living and who provides an often wry commentary on the speaker and his existence. The speaker of the poems muses on death, but with self-deprecating wit and a sense of playfulness. Death, he recalls, in "XX," originally visited the speaker "while I was at my inward role of hermes psychopompos." In that poem, as the speaker foresees his own end, he imagines death as almost dapper, if slightly passé, sporting "an off-white safari suit, almost the latest style." The effect of all this dialoguing with death has been that the speaker feels himself to be "on almost friendly terms with death." Recognizing the human tendency to ignore the existence of death, the speaker feels that conversation with and contemplation of death assist in enabling it "to assume a less minatory / aspect without in any way distracting from / the pallid grandeur of its ceremonial presence."

The poems range across meditations with death and on death. The confessional poets' fascination with death—"the [death] we wore on our skinny breasts," as

Anne Sexton wrote in "Sylvia's Death"—is considered in "XVIII." The speaker thinks about Sexton's early death and challenges death, saying that she should have been allowed to live longer "and move in the calms / of after-love." Death responds that "she had begun / to live beyond life." Death's relationship to poetry, a theme at the heart of confessional poetry—as Adrienne Rich described it, "speaking the unspeakable"—recurs as a motif throughout the collection, but always leavened by the somewhat bizarre and ludicrous mannerisms of death and the self-lacerating perspective of the speaker. Death, despite being seen as "much too otherwise / for that Doppelganger kind of thing," is nevertheless described overtly as a projection in "V," where it is physically similar to the speaker: "short of stature, pot bellied, grey haired, weak eyed." The "embarrassing possibility" that the speaker draws is that his conversations with death may be construed as his talking to himself. The genial self-effacement of the speaker illuminates the sequence, in which a levity emerges that the title and subject belie.

Beaver's next work, *As It Was,* was a further experiment in prose-poetry and an exploration of autobiographical experience. The allusion to Catullus in "The Dilemma" is at the heart of this collection: "odi et amo [I love and I hate] / overlapping, frustrating and alienating," as Beaver explores ambivalence in childhood and adolescence. Describing the more overt bullying of the school playground in "The Happiest Days etc.," the speaker comments that all these school memories are "discolored by the omnipresent tint of fear." This idea resonates in other subjects in the collection, such as the sometimes more covert violences of home and, later, the treatment for mental illness that Beaver experienced at Prince Alfred Hospital and Broughton Hall. The collection is divided into three parts. "Beginnings" includes pieces, mostly prose-poem hybrids—about early childhood, family, and adolescence—and culminates with descriptions of being treated for mental illness, deciding to refuse further similar treatment, and an embarkation on the journey of becoming a poet. The second section, "The Poems," includes a single long poem about poetry and about the relationship between the poet and his poems. The final section, "Bucolics," describes rural experiences. This structure reinforces something of the overarching theme of ambivalence in the collection, since the explicit focus on poetry is sandwiched between the opposing experiences of urban and rural lives.

Following the publication of *As It Was,* Beaver experienced a phase during which he found writing difficult. Although *Selected Poems* (1979) was published during this period, new writing was slow and inspiration elusive. Reflecting on this period later, in an essay writ-

Dust jacket for Beaver's 1975 collection, which includes odes to the environment and poems about writers who have influenced him (Bruccoli Clark Layman Archives)

ten for the literary journal *Meanjin,* Beaver considers the reasons for the blockage and suggests that he was inhibited either by the fear of hurting others through what he might write or by lack of a suitable theme. He also mentions the logistical difficulty of interruptions forced by the need to work at occupations other than writing.

Early in the essay, Beaver writes of poetry as a demonic experience. He touches on notions of haunting and writes a piece about Rilke, with whom he had long been fascinated. As Beaver describes the process of overcoming the block in his writing, the portrait of Rilke emerges, and Beaver's meditation on Rilke functions as something of a talisman. While writing about the exercises he set himself to combat his feeling of being blocked—short versicles written on a daily basis as a discipline, short pieces about Rilke, and drafts of work on the subject of Tiresias—Beaver considers the nature of Rilke's career. In a sense, Beaver situates himself as Kappus (the "young poet" to whom Rilke writes in *Letters to a Young Poet*), drawing from Rilke solace and encouragement, as many poets have done and continue to do. He seems to put himself through a new apprenticeship, mindful of Rilke's advice to "be patient toward all that in unsolved in your heart" and to "try to love the *questions themselves* like locked rooms and like books that are written in a very foreign tongue." Yet, Beaver describes the years between 1977 and 1985 as involving not writing but journalism.

Despite this slowing of inspiration, some work by Beaver was published during this period. *Headlands: Prose Sketches,* published in 1986, was six years in the making. The spell was broken by 1988, when Beaver published *Charmed Lives,* which opens with a verse biography of Rilke, shifts to two sections of shorter poems, "Silhouettes" and "Solos," then concludes with a series called "Tiresias Sees." In the Rilke series, the description of the poet's childhood touches on themes close to those explored in the "Beginnings" section of *As It Was.* This echoing creates a sense of Rilke's life as a lens through which Beaver revisits his own, as well as a means by which to scrutinize more broadly themes of the formation of the poet and the poet's life. Poems about Rilke's sexual and romantic initiation, similarly, may be read alongside those poems pertaining to Beaver's own in *As It Was.* Beaver presents intense portraits of the key phases of Rilke's life, all the while considering the poet's themes and the rhythms and rigors of creativity. The Tiresias sequence opens with the epigraph of T. S. Eliot's comment in the notes to *The Waste Land* (1922) that "What Tiresias *sees* is, in fact, the substance of the poem." Just as Eliot's Tiresias watches wearily the anodyne encounter between the young woman and her carbuncular lover in "The Fire Sermon," so Beaver's Tiresias is a seer beset with ennui, moving between blindness and second sight. Beaver explores the Tiresias myth as an allegory for the poet's role. Dorothy Porter describes the voice in the Tiresias series as a "gossipy, esoteric, androgynous voice that enthralled me," and the sequence as a "hot poem" (*Southerly,* 1995).

Following the publication of *New and Selected Poems* in 1991, Beaver published *Anima and Other Poems* (1994), which is divided into four sections, the final and eponymous one of which describes Beaver's relationship with his wife, Brenda. Critics have commented on Beaver's return to more-formal structures in his later poems, and the use of formal structures is apparent in this collection. In his most recent collection, *Poets and Others* (1999), Beaver juxtaposes his various signature styles. A series of carefully made sonnets sits alongside lyric and confessional poems to his wife, experimentation and play, and allusions to a range of other poets and their work (for example, Rich, Robert Duncan, and Vivian Smith).

The gentleness of the vision in these most recent two collections, evidenced in homages to Paul Celan and love poems for Brenda, shows the generosity and wisdom that typify Beaver's work. The simple faces of many of these poems belie their depth and emotional complexity. This contradiction renders Beaver's work compelling and is one that he articulates when he writes, in the February 1989 issue of *Meanjin,* that "Trying to fly with or without wings is the prerogative of poets, epileptics and angels' fledglings. Perhaps poets should also learn to walk and sit within an area of one life at a time. Their own, if possible, making do with words and a vocation."

References:

Livio Dobrez, *Parnassus Mad Ward: Michael Dransfield and the New Australian Poetry* (St. Lucia: University of Queensland Press, 1990);

Joan Kirkby, ed., *The American Model: Influence and Independence in Australian Poetry* (Sydney: Hale & Iremonger, 1982);

James McAuley, *A Map of Australian Verse: The Twentieth Century* (Melbourne: Oxford University Press, 1975);

Rainer Maria Rilke, *Briefe an einen jungen Dichter* (Leipzig: Insel, 1929); translated by M. H. D. Herter Norton as *Letters to a Young Poet* (New York: Norton, 1934; revised, 1993).

Papers:

The State Library of New South Wales holds papers of Bruce Beaver.

Vincent Buckley

(8 July 1925 – 12 November 1988)

Chris Wallace-Crabbe
University of Melbourne

BOOKS: *The World's Flesh* (Melbourne: Cheshire, 1954);

Essays in Poetry: Mainly Australian (Carlton, Vic.: Melbourne University Press, 1957);

Poetry and Morality: Studies on the Criticism of Matthew Arnold, T. S. Eliot, and F. R. Leavis (London: Chatto & Windus, 1959);

Henry Handel Richardson (Melbourne: Lansdowne Press, 1961; Melbourne: Oxford University Press, 1961);

Masters in Israel (Sydney: Angus & Robertson, 1961);

Arcady and Other Places (Melbourne: Melbourne University Press, 1966; London & New York: Cambridge University Press, 1966);

Poetry and the Sacred (London: Chatto & Windus, 1968; New York: Barnes & Noble, 1968);

Golden Builders and Other Poems (Sydney: Angus & Robertson, 1976; London: Angus & Robertson, 1976);

The Pattern (Dublin & Atlantic Highlands, N.J.: Dolmen Press / Melbourne: Oxford University Press, 1979);

Late Winter Child (Dublin: Dolmen Press / Melbourne: Oxford University Press, 1979);

Selected Poems (London & Sydney: Angus & Robertson, 1981);

Cutting Green Hay: Friendships, Movements and Cultural Conflicts in Australia's Great Decades (Melbourne: Allen Lane / Penguin, 1983);

Memory Ireland: Insights into the Contemporary Irish Condition (Melbourne: McPhee Gribble, 1985; Ringwood, Vic. & New York: Penguin, 1985);

Last Poems (Ringwood, Vic.: McPhee Gribble, 1991).

OTHER: *The Incarnation in the University: Studies in the University Apostolate,* edited by Buckley (London: Chapman, 1957);

Australian Poetry 1968, edited by Buckley (Sydney: Angus & Robertson, 1958);

Leonard French, *The Campion Paintings,* edited by Buckley (Melbourne: Grayflower, 1962);

Vincent Buckley, 1984 (photograph by A.T. Bolton; by permission of the National Library of Australia)

The Faber Book of Modern Australian Verse, edited by Buckley (London & Boston: Faber & Faber, 1991).

Vincent Buckley was a poet with a wonderfully good ear, perhaps the finest in Australian poetry. From early in his maturity he was a remarkably influential critic, coming on the scene just as Australian poetry—indeed, Australian literature—began to become visible to the Anglophile universities in Australia. He was the first serious critic to pay close attention to poets A. D. Hope, Judith Wright, and James McAuley, whom he already saw fit to set beside Kenneth Slessor in an unfolding canon. Buckley's work was prophetic back in the 1950s.

Buckley's own poetry started more slowly and may indeed have reached its peak in the posthumous *Last Poems* (1991), poems that look back over a life, clustered around Australian landscapes and university life, and the continuing troubles of Ireland. Somewhere behind all the adult phenomena lies his country childhood, whether in the disabling heat of summer or in a haunting wind:

> I see Romsey through a hole in the wind
> as I used to in late autumn, in the southern gales,
> just there, not vibrating with changes
> but like a model that has grown to its full height.

Vincent Thomas Buckley, poet and critic, was born near the township of Romsey, Victoria, on 8 July 1925. His father was Patrick Buckley, variously a farm laborer, a salesman, and a postman; his mother was Frances Condon Buckley. The area of his childhood was a part of south-central Victoria given over to small farming, often in the hands of Irish Australians. Buckley celebrated this shaping environment in his autobiography, *Cutting Green Hay: Friendships, Movements and Cultural Conflicts in Australia's Great Decades* (1983).

Sent to board in the city, Buckley was educated by the Jesuit fathers at St. Patrick's College, the cathedral school in Melbourne. His later reflection on his early life was to say, with his characteristically oblique irony, "There's nothing like a boy of poor family given a Jesuit education. They're very faithful but uncomfortable colleagues." After all, his childhood had straddled the Great Depression and his father's recurrent unemployment. The upside is that he was "dux" (top student) of the school.

His forebears—Scanlons, Condons, and Buckleys—came to Australia from Cork and Tipperary, victims of what the poet has called "the great emptying of Munster." A century later the young Buckley still felt that "the population was divided into Catholics and others, and the others never actually seemed to do anything, except play football with us in our Young Christian Worker teams under assumed names." Small in stature, Buckley played football as a rover, before ill health put an end to his playing sports. Illness haunted him, indeed, throughout his adult life and may have played its part in rendering such acute responses to physical pressure and sensation in his poetry.

Leaving school in the middle of World War II, Buckley enlisted in the Royal Australian Air Force but was soon invalided out and sent to convalesce in a hospital. He revisited this period late in his life with the sequence of poems "Hospital Summer: Western Suburbs," which appears in *Last Poems*. This period was a time of enforced reflection; he was alone in a strange city—Sydney (a city whose poets were always reluctant to respond to his work or to his values).

Buckley returned to Melbourne, where he completed a bachelor of arts degree in English, philosophy, and economics at the University of Melbourne. Completing his honors year at the end of 1950, he began teaching in the English department, where he remained until his early retirement in 1987. His teaching experience is recorded in the poem "Late Tutorial" and sardonically at the end of his career in such poems as "Nightmare of a Chair Search Committee" and the hilarious "Teaching German Literature." The intersection of academic teaching and managerial bureaucracy continually drove him to distraction.

Appearing in some of the same journals that published the work of young avant-gardists of Angry Penguins descent (a group of modernist poets), Buckley immediately impressed readers with an idiom of his own, lofty and even hieratic, yet marked by the voices of modernism—William Butler Yeats and Dylan Thomas, mollified here and there by the verbal delicacy of John Crowe Ransom. Buckley's first collection, *Masters in Israel* (1961), now seems a curious work, as Buckley himself realized as he moved into easier idioms—a development reflected in his later essay "Ease of American Diction." *Masters in Israel* was a book that attracted one hostile review, by a local devotee of Ezra Pound, who complained of Buckley's frequent catachreses.

Among its few clear successes, poems that escaped the Brennanish elevation of rhetoric, are "Country Town," "Autumn Landscape," and the strong kinetic development of "Winter Gales"—all lyrics, significantly, that hark back to the poet's country childhood. A stranger poem, "The Points of the Sea," is indebted to Hart Crane for its splendid linguistic excesses and its memorable tropes.

After three years as a senior tutor in English at the University of Melbourne, Buckley traveled to Cambridge University in England on an Archbishop Mannix Travelling Scholarship to work on the moral criticism of Matthew Arnold, F. R. Leavis, and T. S. Eliot. Buckley was at Cambridge at the same time as Ted Hughes, Sylvia Plath, A. S. Byatt, and Richard Weber, Weber becoming a poetic ally. During this period, 1954–1956, Buckley made his first trips to the Ireland that loomed so large in his antipodean imagination. Returning to Melbourne, he was appointed the first Lockie Fellow in Australian literature and creative writing, thus initiating the study of Australian writers at the University of Melbourne. Indeed, he was one of the pioneers of this field anywhere in the country, since the literature of Australia was treated with scornful neglect by its universities for a long time.

In contrast to the uncertainty of his poetry of the 1950s, the persuasive eloquence of Buckley's critical prose came early. The pieces gathered in *Essays in Poetry:*

Dust jacket for Buckley's first book, published in 1954 (Bruccoli Clark Layman Archives)

Mainly Australian (1957) comprise some of the most beautiful critical writing to have appeared in Australia. He spoke memorably of Hope as "a heavy almost brooding mind consciously detaching itself in the act of poetry from what most exercises and torments it" and of Slessor, about whom he said, "For all his occasional joy, there runs throughout his poetry a faint ground-bass of disgust with life." These eloquent essays also worked to establish a canon of modern poets, chief among them Slessor, Hope, Wright, and McAuley. Such canon formation became unfashionable twenty years later, but it was absolutely essential then if Australian writing was to be studied in a systematic way.

Buckley did not employ the same degree of style in his poetry until *Arcady and Other Places* (1966), which wedded his already firmly established sense of presence with new kinds of attachment to the solid world—to the sturdy, or even frail, natural objects and human artifacts that make up the geography of Australians' lives. His earlier poetry, however eloquent, was curiously remote from what R. P. Blackmur described as "behav-

iour." In *Arcady and Other Places,* however, the trees of Buckley's childhood had become more substantial, while the poetry was harnessed with two fields of behavior, love and politics. The love poems in this 1966 volume were, no doubt, connected with Buckley's coming to know the woman who became his second wife, Penelope Jane Curtis (he and his first wife, Edna, had divorced); but they are presented as "Versions from Catullus." The persona leaves Buckley free to write such lines as "When I, torment, feel my whole body / Lapse out at the first sight of you. / My mouth is drained of voice, my tongue / Stopped." Sappho via Catullus is the double frame here, while the lapsing out comes from D. H. Lawrence, a writer whose passion Buckley admired. Of the two other sequences in *Arcady and Other Places,* "Eleven Political Poems" is a group of angry satires against Stalinism and the shilly-shallying of "fellow travellers." These poems were written in the wake of the fiercely divisive Disarmament Conferences of the angry 1950s. The last two lyrics in Buckley's suite swerve away from politics to the "sweeter work" of his art, as his career did in time. Stronger, deeper, and more sustained is the opening sequence, "Stroke." This passionate work traces his father's final illness and his passage toward death. Like many modernist poets, Buckley was enamored of the suite, or sequence. A mode that has Pindaric origins, the sequence was much practiced in later times by Yeats, W. H. Auden, and Francis Webb, the latter a friend and poetic crony of Buckley. The peculiar advantage of the sequence is that it retains the immediacy of lyric, while wedding it to middle-distance stamina and to extension of theme and attitude—or attitudes.

From his return to Australia in the late 1950s, Buckley had been deeply involved in politics, especially in the areas in which the religious and the ideological overlap or come together. To use a phrase from later times, he became one of the leading "public intellectuals" of the country. His schooling, followed by his membership in the university Newman Society, forged his Catholicism but also gave it a debater's combative edge. Australian Catholicism after World War II was often conservative, many of his elders actually having favored General Francisco Franco in the Spanish Civil War; another face of that religious culture, however, was deeply involved with traditional Labor politics. In the mid 1950s a major split occurred in the Labor Party, its Catholic right wing—strongly anticommunist—breaking off to form the DLP, or Democratic Labor Party; it was short-lived, but destructive to the Left. Buckley remained in the thick of such politics, balancing his fervent hatred of communism with his continuing support of organized labor and its social policies.

As he wrote much later,

There, where the committee voted, there's a proverb on
    the wall,
at this shining oval table, there's a message for us all,
an old message, about Newness, how it withers up and
    dies
unless we use old tricks to tease it, tricks of style, disasters,
    lies.

This voice is surely that of a man who has sat on committees, made motions, decided about splinter groups, formed policies, and developed plans of action. Politics was surely in his blood from his campus days in the Lay Apostolate to his founding of the Committee for Civil Rights in Ireland.

In 1967 Buckley was appointed to a personal chair in the University of Melbourne, an appointment that gave recognition not only to his qualities as poet, critic, and scholar but also to his broader intellectual influence in Australia. In the same year, he was awarded the Myer Prize for Poetry. Like Hope, his friend and mentor, Buckley had become a distinguished

example of that new kind of figure, the poet-professor, one whose criticism could be seen as deeply rooted in his practice. Thirty years later, such a doubled career became common as the universities anxiously Americanized themselves. In the title poem of *Golden Builders and Other Poems* (1976), Buckley paid tribute to the formative meanings of his home city, Melbourne. He entered that overdetermined city powerfully but indirectly, by way of William Blake's visionary London, Buckley's epigraph coming from Jerusalem and including the question "What are those Golden Builders doing?" Republishing the sequence five years later, Buckley dropped the epigraph, replacing it with a dedication to the painter Leonard French; Buckley had published a book on French's "Campion Paintings," canvases whose symbolic authority he greatly admired. "Golden Builders" comprises twenty-seven longish sections, three of them in quatrains, the rest in free verse. The impulse is frequently imagistic, and the loose narrative partly autobiographical; the poems reach back to early manhood in the inner city and forward to the frailty of the middle years, ending with a religious-toned drive back to "my timber birthplace / and the wilderness of flies." Rural Victoria is recalled as salvific: perhaps all seminatural landscapes are, green lungs that offer a contrast to "the long cough / of crushed cities." As with Robert Lowell's "Colloquy in Black Rock" (and Lowell was surely a major influence on Buckley), the cruel juddering of jackhammers opens the poem, ushering in Buckley's golden construction sites:

The hammers of iron glow down Faraday.
Lygon and Drummond shift under their resonance.
saws and hammers drawn across the bending air
shuttling like a bow; the saw trembles
the hammers are molten, they flow with quick light
striking; the flush spreads and deepens on the stone.

Characteristically, the life of the verse is kinetic: all is in movement; even the air is felt to be "bending." The sequence is a string bag, capacious enough and flexible enough to hold a whole variety of themes. Within a city as forbidding as those of Eliot and Charles Baudelaire, battered signs of God's presence are everywhere, sweet smells indeed of his immanence. The city holds the suffering of emigrants from Europe or Southeast Asia, one of whom has recently burned herself to death; abortions; echoes of the war in Vietnam; traces of relatives; the intensities of a love affair; baying animals in a microbiology lab; a near-fatal accident; the recurrent pain of the body; and, unsurprisingly, the poet's dying father, who takes the reader back to the "Stroke" sequence in his dazed, mute suffering. "Golden Builders" took on the task of doing for the city of Melbourne what Slessor's poems had done for Sydney. The inner urban life it both celebrates and anatomizes is graphic, tangible, and eloquent. Its moments of *haecceitas* (thisness; what distinguishes one individual from another) can be beautiful, for all the tension out of which they rise. "The smudged bricks / get back their flush of red," and the poet returning from overseas notices the mixed smell "of stone corners planted among / shrubs and flowers, was it / rosemary or simple air? The smell of space." Even heavy industry is made pictorial in this visionary sequence, a factory "mashing out its lengthening / masks of smoke / sulphurous Breughel-red swirlings in air." The volume also includes poems springing from Buckley's short residence in Edmonton, Alberta–a diversion from the usual shuttling of his imagination between Australia and Ireland.

Relations with the Church became more idiosyncratic as Buckley's career burgeoned. He always remained part of a distinctive culture, that ardently sustained by Australians of Irish descent; yet, he grew less and less satisfied with what the hierarchy had to offer. On one social occasion he was ambushed by a post-Protestant atheist, who asked what he thought of the Pope's reconfirmed ruling against contraception. "Silly old bugger panicked," was his gruff reply. For six years from 1958 Buckley was editor of the political journal *Prospect,* many of whose contributors came from the Catholic mid-Left. Later he became poetry editor of the old, conservative Sydney weekly, *The Bulletin,* but his role there was apolitical, as far as that is ever possible in the arts. Certainly, by his later years he was bitterly suspicious of the ways in which politics can debauch literature. One of Buckley's most fascinating pieces of prose was a 1970 essay titled "The Strange Personality of Christ." Like Harold Bloom's reading of the Hebrew Scriptures, Buckley's account laid emphasis on irony, absurdity, and intellectual challenge. His Christ was oddly like the poet himself in seeking to make any question more difficult, and any answer more paradoxical in his quest for an adequate response. Buckley's Jesus "shocks us into a kind of stillness not by what we recognize as his rightness but by what we recognize as his strangeness." Near the end of his life, in a short prose self-portrait, Buckley followed an admission of following sports on television "as much as ever" and other such reflections with a comment from Henry James: "It is as impossible to avoid religion as to avoid morals." Buckley could not do so, but he steadily refined religion away to a subtle metaphysics.

Buckley's third substantial volume of criticism was *Poetry and the Sacred* (1968). In the essays gathered together in this book the poet-critic suggests a mini-canon of writers in whom the romantic impulse drives language toward mystery or transcendence. Of the critics in Australia whom John Docker characterized

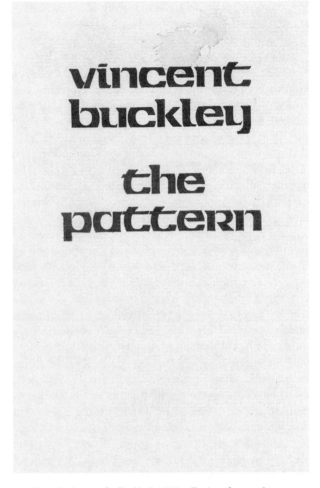

Paperback cover for Buckley's 1979 collection of pastoral poems about Ireland (Bruccoli Clark Layman Archives)

(negatively) as "metaphysical," Buckley was perhaps the most romantic: indeed, as Australian Leavisism split, many of its company veering into Marxism, he clearly emerged as the leader of the other party, standing out in his final decade as a fiercely satirical opponent of literary "theory." His heroes in this 1968 volume included Thomas Wyatt, John Donne, William Wordsworth, Emily Brontë, Herman Melville, and–reluctantly, at the behest of his junior colleagues in the art of poetry–Auden. Buckley sought to retain "the sacred" as a living concept, even as his relation to formal religion became more and more diluted. Plainly, ancestral landscapes and meanings were always tugging at the poetry.

Buckley's Ireland was far more than the romantic projection of an antipodean "Celt." He visited or lived in that country on many occasions between the mid 1950s and 1986, haunted and often disappointed by its anthology of suggestions. He was seriously disturbed, for instance, by what he saw as the "virtual avoidance of play" in Ireland and by its general aimlessness; this period was before the economic rise of Ireland and the rise of the Celtic Tiger (strong Irish economy).

Moreover, Buckley was appalled by the drug culture found in the Dublin estates. For him this nation seemed to have lost its memory, a loss that he struggled with in his late prose work *Memory Ireland: Insights into the Contemporary Irish Condition* (1985). He was deeply pleased to be awarded the Dublin Prize for Arts and Letters in 1977: it attached him to Ireland by another long thread. His first, baroque response to that fabled country was the poem "Walking in Ireland"; his most profound was the posthumously collected "Hunger-Strike," which has been described by John Montague in conversation as the finest of all poetic accounts of that dark time of violence and self-punishment in Northern Ireland. Indeed, many lyrics in *Last Poems* are Ireland-based. One whole collection of poems treats of the Republic, its landscapes, and its ways of life. *The Pattern* was simultaneously published in Dublin and Melbourne in 1979, the same year in which *Late Winter Child* was published. This twin publication represented Buckley's attempt, Janus-headed, to take the Irish landscape at his nerve ends at the same time as he was recording his second wife's pregnancy and the impending birth of a daughter. After the birth itself, he wrote, "Every day, now, she's born again. / With her head back, she rides / breathless on your hip." Buckley was always fond of punctuation as precise musical timing. Avoiding it on occasion, he employed spacing in its stead, as he did so effectively in "Origins" and "Orangemen," two neighboring poems linked by the sound of their titles. They represent the strong pastoral, revenant impulses in *The Pattern*. Both these volumes are made up of medium-short lyrics, or sequences of poems of the same length.

Late Winter Child is unusual in the poetry of Australia for its capacity to celebrate, responsively, a woman's body. In a time of pregnancy, the mother-to-be is seen and felt as intimately as his own body so often was in that poetry of vulnerability. The achievement is delicate, sensuous, altogether remarkable. It is an inner experience, in balanced contrast to the political anthropology of *The Pattern*. An extended, discursive treatment of Buckley's relations with the Old World is found in *Memory Ireland*. The book is full of disappointments. The reality of the lived-in Republic distorts or effaces an Australian dream of Gaeltacht (the western areas of Ireland where Irish is spoken as a community language) and ancestral voices. Reality presses in too hard; yet, witness still has to be borne to it. Such is the nature and fine character of a poet's

task. Just as Wordsworth had borne witness to an England of beggars and crippled former servicemen, so Buckley wrote of a mundane, diurnal Ireland and its inhabitants, however prosaic. As he wrote in a later poem, "At dusk the sluttish children / Wandered down the Grand Canal. Where the soft lights lean over dark. / Who'll catch them when they fall?" This reality was not the same belatedly recalled in a poem titled "Hear how the Irish speak pentameters."

Buckley's last years as a professor were marked by continual illness, profound disillusion with universities ("The new broom may sweep cleanest, but what will clean the broom?"), and several further visits to Ireland. The poems were gathering in folders, and he looked forward to a published entity titled "A Poetry without Attitudes"; yet, anxiety and dread trod close on his heels now. In 1985 he won the inaugural Red Earth Prize for Literature, but he was ever looking to his retirement from academic life and to the new imaginative freedom that it would allow him. As Peter Steele wrote about Buckley in a newspaper obituary a week after his death, "He regarded poetry as the greatest mediator or interpreter between the solitudes of the self and the bulking realities of the world."

Retiring at the end of 1987, Buckley had less than a year to live. He was working still on "A Poetry without Attitudes," both a provisional title and a strongly held point of view, betokening the kinds of freedom that had been enjoyed by William Carlos Williams and Galway Kinnell, away across the Pacific. He developed his new anthology, *The Faber Book of Modern Australian Verse* (1991), in the teeth of his rapidly failing health. He never completed the introduction to that book; it was assembled by his widow, as best she could from the diverse manilla palimpsest, but it included the characteristic plaint, a specimen of what his peer A. F. Davies had called Small Country Blues:

> All Australian poets are disadvantaged by the same comparative neglect. They are all, except for a favoured few, disadvantaged by the international system of publication and distribution. They read poets who will never get a chance to read them.

As he wrote, amid a prose self-portrait, about a billabong near his suburban home, "How muddy life is, you think. Birds will come back to anything, if they're allowed. Still the same curves of the river. Who cares if I am dying if the banks are green."

Buckley died in 1988, two hundred years after the founding of European Australia. Curiously, he found the questions raised by the Aboriginal peoples too hard to contemplate, let alone answer, in this limited lifetime: perhaps Ireland occluded them, with its many centuries of colonial subjugation. The works in his *Last Poems* were winnowed out from his sheaves of remaining verse. It is a book that put its stamp on him as one of the most impressive poets of Australia, but his death has helped to blur his reputation. This volume weaves together what might have been three collections or so: one looking back over Ireland and its subjectively historical meanings; one treating of the aging process and its pains; a third, more satirical, even larrikin-like, mocking the putative stability of managerial institutions. It was his abiding dream as a real poet that he spoke to "a people no-one has seen in public / ancient as lampreys in their wet darkness." The Vincent Buckley Prize for Poetry, which alternates between Irish and Australian poets, was first awarded in 1993. Much of Buckley's prose writing, especially, awaits collection and publication.

Interview:

Henry Rosenbloom, "An Interview with Vincent Buckley," *Meanjin,* 28 (1969): 317–325.

References:

Elizabeth Booth, "Vincent Buckley, an Interview," *Quadrant,* 20, no. 8 (1976): 27–32;

David Carter, "Critics, Writers, Intellectuals: Australian Literature and its Criticism," in *The Cambridge Companion to Australian Literature,* edited by Elizabeth Webby (Cambridge: Cambridge University Press, 2000), pp. 258–293;

Carter, "The Death of Satan and the Persistence of Romanticism," *Literary Criterion,* 5, nos. 3–4 (1980): 65–69;

John Colmer, "The Quest for Roots: Vincent Buckley and Sally Morgan," in his *Australian Autobiography: A Personal Quest* (Melbourne: Oxford University Press, 1989), pp. 98–116;

Jim Davidson, "Vincent Buckley," in his *Sideways from the Page* (Melbourne: Fontana, 1983), pp. 209–229;

Paul Kavanagh and Peter Kuch, "Scored for the Voice: An Interview with Vincent Buckley," *Southerly,* 47, no. 3 (1990): 249–266;

Helen O'Shea, "A Poet's Place," *Mattoid,* 19 (1984): 31–33;

Vincent O'Sullivan, "Singing Mastery: The Poetics of Vincent Buckley," *Westerly,* 34, no. 2 (1989): 50–57;

Peter Steele, "Vincent Buckley as Critic," *Meanjin,* 28 (1969): 309–316;

Andrew Taylor, "Irrationality Individuality Drug Poetry Romanticism–Where We Are Today," *Meanjin,* 31 (1972): 373–384;

A. K. Thompson, "The Poetry of Vincent Buckley: An Essay in Interpretation," *Meanjin,* 38 (1969): 293–308;

C. B. Thornton-Smith, "Catholic Revolutionaries: A Reply to Patrick O'Brien," *Quadrant,* 16, no. 2 (1972): 63–65;

Chris Wallace-Crabbe, *Falling into Language* (Melbourne: Oxford University Press, 1990): 85–96.

Papers:

The National Library of Australia in Canberra holds letters and manuscripts of Vincent Buckley. The Australian Defence Force Academy Library in Canberra also holds some of his papers.

Joanne Burns

(5 December 1945 –   )

Margaret Bradstock
University of New South Wales

BOOKS: *Snatch* (London: Strange Faeces Press, 1972);

Ratz, Saturday Centre Poets' Series, no. 2 (Cammeray, N.S.W.: Saturday Centre, 1973);

Alphabatics (Cammeray, N.S.W.: Saturday Centre, 1976);

Adrenalin Flicknife (Cammeray, N.S.W.: Saturday Centre, 1976);

Radio City 2am, by Burns, Stefanie Bennett, and Ruth K. Fordham (North Ward, Qld.: Cochon International Press, 1976);

Correspondences, by Burns and Pamela Brown (North Sydney, N.S.W.: Red Press, 1979);

ventriloquy (Glebe, N.S.W.: Sea Cruise, 1981);

blowing bubbles in the 7th lane: Small Stories, introduction by Brown (Broadway, N.S.W.: Fab Press, 1988);

on a clear day (St. Lucia, Qld. & Portland, Ore.: University of Queensland Press, 1992);

penelope's knees (St. Lucia, Qld. & Portland, Ore.: University of Queensland Press, 1996);

aerial photography (Wollongong University, N.S.W.: Five Islands Press, 1999);

people like that, Wagtail-1 (Warner's Bay: Picaro Press, 2001).

OTHER: "Death on a Polka Dot," in *Cheeries and Quartermasters,* edited by John Jenkins (Carlton, N.S.W.: Paper Castle, 1975), pp. 58–63;

"the next hiroshima" and "language lesson," in *Minute to Midnight,* edited by Anna Couani, Christopher Kelen, Carmel Kelly, and Mark Roberts (Sydney: Red Spark Books, 1985), pp. 27–28;

"mixed metaphor," in *Writers in the Park: The Book 1985/6,* edited by Carol Christie and Kim O'Brien (Surry Hills, Sydney: Fab Press, 1986), pp. 76–77;

"space dust," in *Poetry and Gender,* edited by David Brooks and Brenda Walker (St. Lucia: University of Queensland Press, 1989), pp. 28–29;

"bilingualism," in *Body Lines: A Women's Anthology* (Broadway, N.S.W.: Women's Redress Press, 1991), pp. 137–139;

"album," in *Second Degree Tampering* (Melbourne: Sybylla Feminist Press, 1992), pp. 153–155;

"loitering," in *The Book of Poets on the Heath,* edited by Kerry Leves and Ellyn Lewis (Katoomba, N.S.W.: Window Ledge Publications, 1993), pp. 44–47.

SELECTED PERIODICAL PUBLICATIONS–UNCOLLECTED:

POETRY

"reading the newspapers: themes," *Blast,* no. 10 (Winter 1989): 17;

"fireworks," *Blast,* no. 11 (Summer 1989–1990): 14–15;

"epistemology and the stickybeak," *Voices,* 1, no. 3 (Spring 1991): 63–66;

"grace," *Southerly,* 52, no. 3 (1992): 194–196;

"singing" and "bare feet," *Scarp,* no. 20 (May 1992): 34, 57;

"original sin," *Hermes,* 8 (1992): 60–64;

"aristotle's thongs," *Scarp,* no. 23 (October 1993): 27–30;

"better than one: for the occasional traveller," *International Quarterly* (USA), 6, no. 2 (1993): 125–129;

"poem is in the prose," *Australian English Teacher* (May 1994): 19–20;

"butterfly blues," *Ulitarra,* no. 7 (1995): 15–16;

"chip on the shoulder" and "the egg," *Meanjin,* 36, no. 3 (Spring 1997): 380–382;

"market forces," *Tinfish* (USA), no. 5 (1997): 42;

"shelf life" and "truce: the humid handshake," *Cordite: Poetry and Poetics Review,* no. 4 (1998): 4, 19;

excerpt from "footnotes on a hammock," *Island,* no. 76 (Spring 1998): 27–30;

"trade winds," *Westerly,* 43, no. 2 (Winter 1998): 68–69;

"postcards from lounge lizard isle," *HOBO Poetry Magazine,* no. 19 (December 1998): 54;

"wind in the willows," *Heat,* no. 8 (1998): 159;

"witness proof," *Verse* (USA), 15, no. 3 (1998): 53;

"ampersand," *Verse* (USA), 16, no. 1 (1998): 54;

"queue jumping," "industrial relations," "cut-up prose– a collector's item," "intermission in the global vil-

Joanne Burns (photograph by Loma Bridge; courtesy of the author)

lage," and "chip," *Overland,* no. 157 (Summer 1999): 38–39;

"tabloid," *Atlanta Review,* 6, no. 2 (Spring/Summer 2000): 54;

"ghost" and "so soon," *Island,* no. 84 (Spring/Summer 2000–2001): 29–30;

"chubby," "how to sneeze in peace," and "peerage," *Heat 2,* new series (Summer 2001): 158–160;

"mardi gras" and "flat chat," *Tinfish* (USA), no. 10 (2001): 39–40.

NONFICTION

"The Poetics of Anger," *Australian Author,* 22, no. 4 (Summer 1991): 16–17;

"Mouthing Off," *Scarp,* no. 23 (October 1993): 24–26;

"Over the Page," *Australian Book Review,* no. 176 (November 1995): 36–39;

"Writing from Life," *Southerly,* 56, no. 4 (Summer 1996–1997): 78–82.

Joanne Burns is one of the best-known names in contemporary poetry. Writing in both line-break and prose-poem format, she has perfected the art of compression in revealing meaning and significance. Her targets are hypocrisy and falseness in society, but at the same time she is able to evoke as she says in "space

dust," "the mystery in the mundane; to see both sides of the coin" (*Poetry and Gender,* 1989). Challenging in both technique and subject matter, Burns's work can range from humor to biting satire. Her self-consciously aware and lucid statements of her own poetics provide an invaluable aid to understanding and evaluating the extent of her achievement.

Joanne Burns was born in Vaucluse, Sydney, on 5 December 1945, the only child of Sheila Dorothy (née Partridge) Burns and Charles Malcolm Burns. She grew up in the eastern suburbs, at Rose Bay and Dover Heights, close to both Sydney Harbour and the cliffs and ocean at Dover Heights, with Bondi Beach not far away. She recalls with pleasure her parents' garden with its various secret places. Although the physical landscape of her childhood was a halcyon one, she was made well aware of cruelty, injustice, and the suffering of others: from infancy she was surrounded by Jewish neighbors and friends who had either fled Nazi Germany in the 1930s or come to Australia after surviving the Holocaust. From the ages of five to eight she attended Our Lady of Mercy College, Rose Bay, and then went on to St. Vincent's College at Potts Point, completing the Leaving Certificate in 1962 with honors in Latin and ancient history.

She spent the years from 1963 to 1965 at Sydney University, studying for a B.A., majoring in English and history with philosophy and psychology as her other subjects. Germaine Greer was a tutor in the English department at that time, and Burns valued her outspokenness, her verbal clarity, wit, and dramatic incisiveness. Being in Greer's tutorials in 1964 at the age of eighteen was, she says, "a mental blast—and an awakening to the powers of rhetoric." In 1966 Burns completed her Diploma of Education at Sydney Teachers' College, in English and history teaching methods. Since then she has worked mainly as a teacher, on a casual basis since the end of 1975 in order to devote time to writing. ("If I taught full time I fear that I would never write more than an intermittent dribble, and that would be like a slow death. My life would feel empty," she says in *Heroines* [1991].) She also taught swimming with the Department of Education Programs from 1977 through 1984, an experience reflected in some of her poems, in particular "blowing bubbles in the 7th lane."

Burns early developed a love of reading, devouring the works of D. H. Lawrence at the age of fifteen and infatuated with the wit of Oscar Wilde—a major influence on her own writing. Poetic influences at school included "Ulysses" by Alfred, Lord Tennyson, and "Ode to the West Wind" by Percy Bysshe Shelley. The influence of Albert Camus emerged later, at university, as well as that of Jean Paul Sartre, the Existentialists, and the Absurdists. Other early satiric and ironic interests included works of Alexander Pope and Jonathan Swift, the monologues of Robert Browning, and the novels of Evelyn Waugh. Burns began writing, from 1963 onward, what she refers to as "unpublishable poems—ludicrous juvenilia." "By thrashing around, trying to imitate the poetry of the past," she says in *The New Writer's Survival Guide* (1989), "I was in fact writing in a foreign language, a foreign voice." Her first poems were published in 1966 in *Drylight,* the journal of the Sydney Teachers' College. In the late 1960s she became interested in contemporary poetry, in particular that of Miroslav Holub and Günter Grass, with their "matter-of-factness" and "downplayed lyrics," and the American Beat poets. From then until the 1970s, she became more interested in theater and drama, did several acting courses, and was involved in a variety of theater activities, including acting. The early Edna Everage shows of Barry Humphries provided a satirical model from popular culture.

In the 1970s Burns began writing "seriously." She traveled to Europe, spending time in Greece, then moved on to London. Her stay in London was interrupted by a three-month visit to Portugal, where, living at the edge of a Portuguese fishing village, she began to write poetry with a view to publi-

cation. At that time she also developed a passion for the novels of Patrick White, whose writing she considers a firm and continuing influence. In London, Burns taught and wrote, stimulated by the many poetry readings and performances she attended and by the atmosphere of the bookshops. She especially remembers the Turret Bookshop in Kensington Church Walk, where she went looking for recently published poetry books and little magazines. Listening to the poets of her own time, the rhythms of speech and contemporary language, she found her own voice. During her time in London she saw the "Pop" poets Roger McGough, Adrian Henri, and Brian Patten perform. Other performances included ones by Patti Smith, Pablo Neruda, and Robert Lowell, as well as those by poets included in the Penguin anthology *The Children of Albion—Poetry of the "Underground" in Britain* (1969). The verbal energy, humor, and wit of such poets fueled her writing.

Burns's poems were published in the underground magazine *Strange Faeces,* edited by Opal and Ellen Nations, and her first collection, *Snatch,* was put out by the Strange Faeces Press in 1972. *Snatch* is a photocopied foolscap production with no ISBN, unevenly typed on Burns's idiosyncratic typewriter (the *a*'s all dropped below the line) and hand-illustrated by Opal L. Nations. The poems play with rhyme, nursery rhymes, and language, and, while easily dismissed as juvenilia, some display the quirky sense of humor and social conscience that have become her trademark. The pithy style of "the grammarian's prophecy" is likewise a forerunner of later works: "if you have a tense past your future will be perfect." Burns's first public poetry reading took place in the Troubadour Coffee Shop in Earl's Court, and she soon developed a "powerful voice, a talent for mimicry and a good sense of timing" (Geoff Page, *A Reader's Guide to Contemporary Australian Poetry,* 1995) that have brought her fame as a performance poet.

In mid 1972 Burns returned to Sydney and became involved with the Saturday Centre, a new press for publishing poetry run by Patricia and Kenneth Laird. Burns did some editing for their magazine, *The Saturday Club Book of Poetry (SCOP),* and her next collection, *Ratz* (1973), was published by the Saturday Centre. *Ratz* includes many poems from *Snatch,* such as "she had more friends . . . ," "i would never have called . . . ," "he'd had a sleepless night," and "you want my words." This volume also includes the hard-hitting "and you say yr not an easy rider," later anthologized in *The Oxford Book of Australian Love Poems* (1993):

and you say yr not an easy rider
that's why yr bed
            is jam packed
            with a dozen dangling feet
            rubbing callouses
            that's why you hitch hike
            from one mattress to another
            thumbs up all the way

The evolution of the poet's voice in a little more than a year is noteworthy. Humor and irony are continuing elements, but now they are expressed with a sense of authority and an awareness of established technique. The development of the epigrammatic last line becomes a particular hallmark.

Alphabatics, a collection of children's stories, and *Adrenalin Flicknife* were published in 1976, also by the Saturday Centre. Satirizing institutionalized religion and other icons, *Adrenalin Flicknife* is a strong collection, the tone increasingly confident, the style more poetically imagistic. Burns herself tends to see it as "more direct, immediate in its expression of anger" and part of "the upfront postures of the 1970s" ("The Poetics of Anger," 1991). Poems such as "mea culpa?" and "good friday and who's yr daddy" are both confronting and technically sound, however, and stand the test of time. *Radio City 2am* (written with Stefanie Bennett and Ruth K. Fordham) came out in 1976 with Cochon International Press, which had earlier published Judith Wright and Thomas Shapcott. In this collection, Burns continues to play with line breaks, punctuation, and the presence of the poem on the page, and to work with almost violently juxtaposed similes. Both *Adrenalin Flicknife* and *Radio City 2am* demonstrate an acknowledged influence of the dramatic, disturbing, and lyrical verse of Sylvia Plath.

Throughout the 1970s Burns was active in the new-poetry performance scene in Sydney and made frequent visits to Melbourne readings. She was also involved in the many feminist and women's readings of the 1970s. In 1977 Burns was a founding member of the Lean Sisters with comedian Julie Macrossin, Netta Perrett, Pamela Brown, Loma Bridge, and others—an anarchist theater group that performed at the Tin Sheds, undermining societal power structures and sacred cows. According to Pamela Brown in the introduction to *blowing bubbles in the 7th lane: Short Stories* (1988),

> Throughout 1977 the *Lean Sisters* performed their madcap political theater to packed houses; and a number of women artists, writers, filmmakers, lawyers, singers, journalists, academics and actors became members of the group during that time. Joanne's particular propensity for satire was a lynch-pin in the development and presentation of these performances.

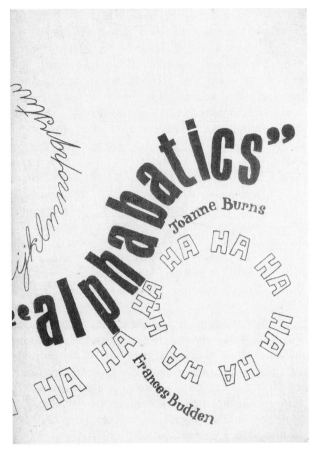

Paperback cover for Burns's 1976 collection of children's stories (Bruccoli Clark Layman Archives)

The Tin Sheds (literally tin sheds), on the fringe of the Sydney University campus, on City Road, were a busy center of radical art production at the time. In the 1980s, the Tin Sheds Contemporary Arts Gallery was built adjacent to the original Tin Sheds. The name Lean Sisters grew out of the women's having fun together, lampooning society, and supporting each other in doing so. The performers all had "Lean" names—Burns's was "Staggerlene."

Burns was a member of the Poets' Union, newly formed in 1977, and an original member of the Sydney Women Writers' Workshop, formed in 1978, which became known as the No Regrets Group. The group included such writers as Susan Hampton, Anna Couani, Barbara Brooks, Pamela Brown, and Lee Cataldi as inaugural members. Burns remained a member of the Poets' Union for many years, until the Union sold its papers, including the minutes of meetings, to the Australian Defence Forces Academy (ADFA) Library. As she did not believe a military institution was an appropriate repository for literary material, she did not renew her membership for many years but eventually rejoined the Poets' Union in the late 1990s.

In the late 1970s, Burns began teaching poetry workshops in schools. She also began writing in prose-poem form and creating satiric monologues—many of which became performance scripts. *Correspondences* (written with Brown), published by Red Press in 1979, shows the development of the prose-poem, although "the house where you used to / live" demonstrates that, for Burns, the generic division is never entirely clear-cut. In her own words, one of the features of the prose-poem that is particularly invigorating is "that it involves the trans-generic, the blurring of the genres of poetry and prose, challenges rigid notions of textual identities and boundaries" ("poem is in the prose," 1994). *ventriloquy* (1981) exemplifies the technique of satiric monologue, since developed further by Burns, the prose-poem acting as a satiric comment on the speaker-persona.

Since the late 1970s Burns has traveled to India, Thailand, and Indonesia, with subsequent influences on her writing. Her journeys promoted a scrutiny of the spiritual quest and cultural travel—with some irony, especially evident in the poems in *on a clear day* (1992). Throughout the 1980s she continued to write mainly prose-poems and monologues, and she began to teach creative writing more extensively—in schools, at the tertiary level, and in the community. In the early to mid 1980s she was for a time part of the editorial team of *Compass* magazine, with Chris Mansell and Dorothy Porter. In 1985 the short-lived Women Writers' Guild presented a trilogy of Burns's monologues, "Karma Pyjama," at the Performance Space (directed by Finola Moorhead, the performers including Kathleen Mary Fallon). During the same year, she was a member of the Four Poets Reading Tour of the United States and Canada with John A. Scott, Pi O, and Geoff Page—a tour organized and led by Lyn Tranter and funded by the Australia Council and Cultural Department of Foreign Affairs. The tour members read in some eighteen venues along the East and West Coasts of America, including Honolulu, and also in Toronto, Canada. Reading venues included the University of Georgetown, Washington, D.C.; Wesleyan College, Connecticut; St. Marks in the Bowery, New York; the University of Oregon, Eugene; the California Institute of Arts; Stanford University; and The Harbourfront, Toronto.

When *blowing bubbles in the 7th lane* was published in 1988, it was a culmination of the technique of prose-poetry. The sequence that gives the book its title, deriving from Burns's experience teaching children to swim, was broadcast on Radio Helicon in July 1988, produced by Jane Howard as a radio play, and rebroadcast many times since; other pieces were read

on the *Coming Out Show* and *2SER*. Many of the "small stories" had already appeared in journals, newspapers, and anthologies. In them, Burns's early cynicism becomes deeply satirical, the materialism and absurdity of Australian everyday life her main targets. She concerns herself with a failure to transcend, and by means of humor, requires readers to see beyond the mediocre and mundane.

Burns was Writer-in-Residence in the School of Creative Arts, Wollongong University, in 1990 and 1993, where she also lectured part-time in fiction- and poetry-writing. In 1991 and 1996 she held Australia Council Fellowships for poetry and fiction/monologues. During the 1990s, and up to the present, Burns has returned to writing in line-break poetic form as well as in the prose-poem format, although she continues to champion the liberating effect of the prose-poem and its "de-iconisation or secularisation of the often facilely claimed sacred territory or space of the poem on the page" ("poem is in the prose"). A book now used for schools under the ETT imprint, *on a clear day* (1992)—consisting mainly of prose-poems or "small stories" and some half a dozen poems that can be categorized as such—is an example of this generic fluidity. "autobiography," reflecting the paradox of the supremacy of everyday triumphs over more world-shattering events in people's lives, is reminiscent in its message of W. H. Auden's "Musée des Beaux Arts." Other pieces—such as "how," on the anomalies of recycling; "corners"; "tradition"; and "background"—lay bare some of the absurdities of modern living and require the reader to question conventional "wisdom." *on a clear day* was short-listed for the National Book Council's Poetry Award in 1992 and selected as a Higher School Certificate (New South Wales School Leaving Certificate) English text for 1995–1998.

In 1996 Burns was a joint winner of the inaugural La Mama Poetica Prose Poem Competition, and in the same year she published *penelope's knees* with the University of Queensland Press. *penelope's knees* again demonstrates the generic fluidity of poetry, prose-poetry, and fiction, stretching the boundaries of traditional definition. The mythologies of literature and everyday life are undercut and, with recognizable humor, the poet speaks ironically of the reading and writing process:

> see that pile of books sprawled across the bed like an odalisque. You are forced to sleep on the shelf.

The title piece from the book *penelope's knees* is "a kind of parodic, ambulatory odyssey . . . moving into the realm of the playfully mythic" ("Writing from Life," 1996–1997). Like Leopold Bloom's odyssey in James Joyce's *Ulysses* (1922), Penelope's is both ordinary and extraordinary as she comes full circle through her day to her home in Ithaca Road, "clips her toenails onto the week's program lift out" or "unscrews the mentholatum, anoints her knees."

An Australia Council Writer's Fellowship for 1996 allowed Burns the time to write many of the poems for her next book, *aerial photography* (1999), hailed by critics as her "best collection yet." *aerial photography* targets modern living with all its "conveniences" and idiosyncrasies, from refrigerators and microwave ovens to mobile phone behavior and designer face masks, suggesting an overwhelming absurdity and failure to connect, as she shows in "mere anarchy":

> the day wakes to the metaphysics
> of garbage men deconstructing silence;
> limbs wrangle with worn black sheets
> too lethargic to secure a dream from
> the dawn's intrusions, they'd really
> prefer a good wash; birdsong chirps and
> bubbles through the air like a choir of
> dame joans at a monarchists' breakfast;
> the day wanders through the hallway not
> knowing where to start

Many poems included in the volume had already been published in journals such as *Southerly, Meanjin,* and *Ulitarra;* and "napkin" was used as part of Artransit, the Poetry on the Buses Project.

From 1998 to 2001 Burns was a tutor in Five Islands Press New Poets Residential Workshops at the University of Wollongong. She has also read many of her monologues and poems on ABC Radio. A second collection of monologues (longer than most of those in *ventriloquy*)–"epistemology and the stickybeak," on the subject of obsession–is as yet unpublished in book form, but several of the individual pieces have been published in magazines and journals ("epistemology and the stickybeak," "aristotle's thongs," "bare feet," and "bilingualism"). "bare feet" and "ergo sum" were produced as a radio drama for the ABC program *Soundstage* under the title "missionary positions," broadcast in August 1999. As well, an unpublished collection of future fictions titled "a stab in the dark" includes a novella, "australia who," and several pieces published in magazines and anthologies ("original sin," "album," "loitering," and "better than one").

Many of Burns's monologues and other writings have been performed by theater groups, and a theater performance using Burns's various shopping pieces was presented by the University of Western Sydney Theatre and Dance Students in the mid 1990s. In 2000 the poem "empyrean" from *on a clear day* was adapted by composer Stephen Adams and presented as a piece for choir and orchestra at the Seventy-Fifth Anniver-

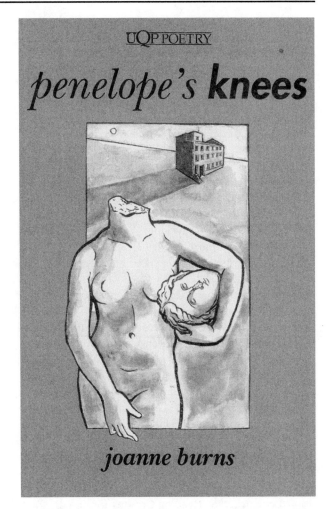

Paperback cover for Burns's 1996 collection, the title poem of which follows the heroine through a daylong journey down Ithaca Road, similar to Leopold Bloom's wanderings around Dublin in Ulysses *(Bruccoli Clark Layman Archives)*

sary Musical Celebration of the Queenwood School for Girls.

Joanne Burns currently lives in Elizabeth Bay, Sydney, with her partner of twenty years, artist Loma Bridge. Burns's writing is of considerable critical importance, being both innovative and "cutting edge" in its subject matter and style.

Interviews:
Rae Desmond Jones, "Another Kind of Feminism," *Makar,* 13, no. 3 (June 1978): 4–9;
Andrew Banks, honors thesis, University of New South Wales, 1993.

References:
Adam Aitken, Review of *penelope's knees, Heat,* no. 2 (1996): 206–207;

Dianne Bates, *The New Writer's Survival Guide* (Ringwood, Vic.: Penguin, 1989), pp. 71–72;

Margaret Berg, *Joanne Burns–Get Smart Study Guide* (Marrickville, N.S.W.: Science Press, 1996);

Paola Bilborough, Review of *aerial photography, Heat,* no. 13 (1999): 260–263;

Kelly Burke, "Suddenly, it's cool to doff your caps," *Sydney Morning Herald,* 18 October 1995;

Heather Cam, "Marathon Efforts Extend the Territory," *Sydney Morning Herald,* 19 September 1992, p. 42;

Cam, "Upper Case Protagonists," *Australian Book Review,* no. 180 (May 1996): 46–47;

Janet Chimonyo, "Travelling, Whittling, Bubbling," *Age* (25 February 1989): 12;

Catherine Colebourne, Review of *on a clear day, Antithesis,* 6, no. 1 (1992): 120–123;

Glen Hooper, "Zen Anarchism in the poetry of Joanne Burns," *mETAphor,* no. 3 (1997);

Rosemary Huisman, "'Bow to Your Partner': Social Conventions of Genre in Contemporary Australian Poetry," in *Reconnoitres: Essays in Australian Literature in Honour of G. A. Wilkes,* edited by Margaret Harris and Elizabeth Webby (South Melbourne: Sydney University Press in association with Oxford University Press, 1992), pp. 214–225;

John W. Knight, "Verse in Review: Two Hands, Clapping," *Social Alternatives,* 18, no. 3 (July 1999): 81–82;

John Leonard, "No Reading Lessons Required," *Social Alternatives,* 11, no. 2 (July 1992): 63–64;

Kerry Leves, "Routines & Revelations: New Poetry," *Overland,* no. 157 (Summer 1999): 109–111;

Ian McBryde, "A Summer Feast," *Island,* no. 80/81 (Spring/Summer 1999–2000): 203–208;

Geoff Page, "Australian Women Poets," *American Book Review,* 18, no. 4 (May–June 1997): 6;

Page, "A Month on the U.S. Poetry Circuit," *Island,* no. 25/26 (Summer/Winter 1986): 22–23;

Page, "Plugged into the Collective Madness," *Canberra Times,* 11 September 1999, p. 24;

Page, "Praise for Poetry Highly Deserved," *Canberra Times,* 27 May 1989, p. B4;

Page, *A Reader's Guide to Contemporary Australian Poetry* (St. Lucia, Qld.: University of Queensland Press, 1995), pp. 35–36;

Rob Riel, "Living in the Age of Feuilleton," *LiNQ,* 26, no. 1 (May 1999): 89–90;

Graham Rowlands, "Confusion and Clarity," *Makar,* 9, no. 3 (February 1974): 48–50;

Darlene Sourile, "Variety Is the Spice," *Social Alternatives,* 8, no. 2 (July 1989): 72–73;

Louise Wakeling, "Straight through the page: Margaret Bradstock's Award-Winning *The Pomela Tree* and Joanne Burns's *aerial photography* as Supplementary Texts for Changing Self/Worlds/Perspectives," *mETAphor,* 2 (April 2002): 28–34;

Alan Wearne, "Let's Not Be Averse to a Verse," *Sydney Morning Herald,* 17 July 1999, p. 8;

Michael Wiley, "A Plethora of Poetry Appears," *Antipodes,* 11, no. 1 (June 1997): 67–68;

Warwick Wynne, "Travellers," *Five Bells,* 3, no. 6 (July 1996): 11.

Alex Buzo
(23 July 1944 –   )

Tom Burvill
Macquarie University

BOOKS: *Norm & Ahmed* (Clayton, Vic.: Monash University Press, 1968);

Macquarie (Sydney & London: Currency Playtexts, 1971);

Three Plays: Norm and Ahmed, Rooted, The Roy Murphy Show (Sydney & London: Currency Press, 1973);

Coralie Lansdowne Says No (Sydney & London: Currency Methuen Drama, 1974);

Tom (Sydney: Angus & Robertson, 1975);

Martello Towers (Sydney & London: Currency, 1976);

Makassar Reef (Sydney: Currency, 1979);

Tautology (I don't want to sound incredulous but I can't believe it) (Ringwood, Vic. & New York: Penguin, 1980);

Meet the New Class (Sydney: Angus & Robertson, 1981);

Tautology Too (Ringwood, Vic.: Penguin, 1982);

Big River: The Marginal Farm (Sydney: Currency, 1985);

The Search for Harry Allway (North Ryde, N.S.W.: Angus & Robertson, 1985);

Glancing Blows: Life and Language in Australia (Ringwood, Vic. & New York: Viking / Penguin, 1987);

The Young Person's Guide to the Theatre and Almost Everything Else (Ringwood, Vic.: Penguin, 1988);

Prue Flies North (Port Melbourne: Mandarin, 1991);

Kiwese: A Guide, A Ductionary, A Shearing of Unsights (Port Melbourne: Mandarin, 1994);

Pacific Union: The Story of the San Francisco Forty-Fivers (Sydney: Currency in association with Playbox Theatre Centre, 1995);

A Dictionary of the Almost Obvious (Melbourne: Text, 1998).

PLAY PRODUCTIONS: *Norm and Ahmed,* Sydney, Old Tote Theatre, 9 April 1968;

Rooted, Canberra, Childers Street Hall, and Sydney, Jane Street Theatre, 14 August 1969; Hartford, Connecticut, Hartford Stage Company, January 1972; Hampstead, London, Hampstead Theatre Club, 1973;

The Front Room Boys, Sydney, Australian Arts Laboratory, 9 October 1969;

Alex Buzo (photograph by Bliss Swift; from John McCallum, Buzo, *1987)*

The Roy Murphy Show, Sydney, Nimrod Theatre, 1 July 1971;

Macquarie, Melbourne, Melbourne Theatre Company, 2 May 1972;

43

Tom, Melbourne, Melbourne Theatre Company, 21 November 1972; Washington, D.C., Arena Stage Theatre, 19 December 1973;

Rooted, Hampstead, Hampstead Theatre Club, 5 March 1973;

Batman's Beach-Head (adaptation of Henrik Ibsen's *An Enemy of the People*), Melbourne, Comedy Theatre, 13 September 1973;

Ploys Town, Sydney, Actor's Company, 1974;

Coralie Lansdowne Says No, Adelaide, Nimrod Theatre at Theatre 62, 9 March 1974;

Martello Towers, Sydney, Nimrod Theatre, 30 April 1976;

Vicki Madison Clocks Out, Adelaide, State Theatre Company of South Australia, 1976; Louisville, Kentucky, The Actors' Theatre of Louisville, 1980;

Makassar Reef, Melbourne, Melbourne Theatre Company, 23 March 1978; Seattle, Washington, A Contemporary Theatre Company, 31 August 1978;

Big River, Adelaide, Melbourne Theatre Company, Arts Theatre, 7 March 1980;

The Marginal Farm, Melbourne, Melbourne Theatre Company, 2 November 1983;

Stingray, Sydney, Stables Theatre, 28 October 1987;

Shellcove Road, Sydney, Marian Street Theatre, 16 September 1989;

Pacific Union: The Story of the San Francisco Forty-Fivers, Melbourne, Playbox Theatre Centre, 19 September 1995.

PRODUCED SCRIPTS: *Rod,* motion picture, Brevis Productions, 1972;

File on Rod, radio, Australian Broadcasting Commission (ABC), 1972;

Duff, radio, ABC, 21 June 1981;

In Search of the New Class, radio, ABC, 1982;

East of Singapore, radio, ABC, 1986.

OTHER: *The Front Room Boys,* in *Plays,* edited by Graeme Blundell (Ringwood, Vic.: Penguin, 1970);

The Longest Game: A Collection of the Best Cricket Writing from Alexander to Zavos, from the Gabba to the Yabba, edited by Buzo and Jamie Grant (Port Melbourne: Heinemann, 1990).

SELECTED PERIODICAL PUBLICATIONS—UNCOLLECTED: *Ploys Town, Southerly,* 41, no. 2 (June 1981): 123–125;

"Cremorne: Peninsular of Gentility," *Overland,* 107 (June 1987): 28–30.

Alex Buzo had an unusual and notorious start to his career with police prosecution of his first play *Norm and Ahmed* (9 April 1968). This one-act midnight dialogue between an archetypal Aussie and a Pakistani student ends with Norm violently assaulting Ahmed with the words "Fuckin' boong." The actor playing Norm was prosecuted in Queensland for obscenity, and a series of celebrated court proceedings and instances of police scrutiny of productions followed. Today one might notice in the play not so much the alleged obscenity as the careful differentiation and exploration of the two characters through their characteristic uses of language and the way the racial theme is embedded in a context of associated insights into the contradictory make-up of this "typical Aussie bloke."

A series of subsequent plays produced in quick succession during the 1970s and 1980s helped Buzo to become recognized as one of the creators of the Australian "new wave" of nationalist or definitively local playwriting, bringing the Australian voice and idiom, and in particular the speech peculiarities of a middle-class variety of the so-called okker male, onto the stage in stylishly patterned comic scenarios. His work up to the mid 1970s earned him a reputation as a satirist and comic observer of manners, and in particular of the language of young male Australians, which in his plays becomes an index of spiritual shallowness and at times a descent into a mime of communication masking profound alienation. This interest in language as an index of cultural health and what he sees as the impoverishment of thought and literary art by fashionable intellectual and artistic trends may be seen as one of the continuing themes in his work. Buzo's success as a dramatist continued into the 1980s; in the 1980s and 1990s he also became well-known as an occasional satirical journalist and social commentator, particularly on the language of what he called "the new class" and on the prevalence of tautology in the speech of everyday life.

Alexander Buzo was born on 23 July 1944 in Sydney, the son of Zihni Jusef Buzo and Elaine Johnson Buzo. His father was an American-educated civil engineer of Albanian background, and his mother an Australian-born teacher. Buzo was educated in the important rural center and university city of Armidale in northern New South Wales and at Ecolint, the International School of Geneva, Switzerland. He has described this period of his education in the autobiographical piece "Hot Runnings" (*Sydney Morning Herald,* 4 January 2001). Although the school was serious about education and was no "finishing school," his fellow students were the sons and daughters of the international jet set and United Nations diplomats. After returning from Switzerland, Buzo graduated with a B.A. from the University of New South Wales, Sydney, in 1965, having studied English literature, Scientific Thought, and History Honours. His interest and training in history showed up again particularly in the plays *Macquarie*

Scene from the 1976 Melbourne Theatre Company production of Buzo's Martello Towers, *a comedy in which three couples meet, each thinking it has a holiday house to itself (photograph by David Parker; from John McCallum,* Buzo, *1987)*

(1971; first performed, 1972), *Big River* (1985; first performed, 1980), and *Pacific Union: The Story of the San Francisco Forty-Fivers* (first performed, 1995). On 21 December 1968 (the same year as the first production of *Norm and Ahmed*) Buzo married Merelyn Johnson, a teacher. They have three children–Emma Jane (born 22 December 1972), Laura Clare (29 January 1978), and Genevieve Lee (27 October 1989).

At the New Theatre in Sydney as a recent graduate, in 1966–1967, while also working as a waiter, Buzo received his first practical theater experience, in writing as well as in acting and working backstage. The play Buzo calls his "apprentice piece," *The Revolt,* had a workshop production in November 1967 at the New Theatre, the originally socialist semiprofessional theater company that has pioneered many radical theater works during its history in Sydney. These plays include Jean-Claude van Itallie's *America Hurrah* (first performed, 1966), which was also at the center of a censorship storm in 1968, at the height of the political struggles over the Vietnam War and conscription. Involving himself with the New was an adventurous choice for Buzo, given his family background. He records in his short autobiographical piece "Cremorne: Peninsular of Gentility" (*Overland,* June 1987) that in the context of his parents' conservatism "my intention to

write plays in the rationalist/anti-colonialist style was definitely not sympatico." Katherine Brisbane comments (in "Points of Reference," the introduction to the first publication of three of Buzo's plays by Currency Press in 1973) that "Among contemporary playwrights he is in a minority in having grown up in middle-class security; and while he involved himself as closely as any of them in the problems of Australian urban society and the study of the Australian character, Buzo is alone in viewing them not from the centre of the imbroglio but from his chosen observation post."

Buzo had an unusual entry to public notice with the prosecution of *Norm and Ahmed.* The play is written in one continuous scene consisting of a dialogue set on a city street at midnight between Norm, a middle-aged storeman who describes himself as "almost a white collar worker," and Ahmed, a young Pakistani overseas student studying history at the university. The play ends when the white man suddenly and viciously attacks Ahmed both physically and with the words "fuckin' boong." According to the "Glossary of Australian English" appended to the Currency Press edition of *Three Plays: Norm and Ahmed, Rooted, The Roy Murphy Show* (1973), the colloquial word *boong* is "a perjorative term for aboriginals [sic] [and] by extension any black or coloured person." During the play, Norm's combination of an insistent overassertion of egalitarianism with an abject respect for established authority and privilege is revealed through his linguistically formulaic and clichéd responses to both Ahmed's more formal English and to his antihierarchical sentiments and hopes for progressive social change in his home country. Norm's distinctively contradictory attitude toward hierarchy is revealed in passages such as the following, responding to Ahmed's story about his and his schoolmates' irreverent and anarchic response to the public humiliation of a group of "Establishment" dignitaries visiting their school in Pakistan:

> NORM . . . I mean, you know, I'd be the last bloke to start defending the bloody dignitaries, and I don't go much on pomp and circumstance and all that sort of garbage, but still, all in all, and looking at both sides of the question, I'd be a bit inclined to say that the blokes who get into these official positions, well, they're pretty important blokes, and I'd say they deserve a little bit of respect from the general public. I mean, I'd be the last one to start putting them up on a pedestal, and if they ever bung on side with me, mate, they know what they can expect. I don't take no crap from no one. But, by the same token, and taking all things into consideration, I reckon that if a bloke's in an official capacity, like those blokes who came to your school, well, it's only fair that he should earn a little bit of respect.

Norm and Ahmed remains one of Buzo's best-known plays. It is widely studied in high school and university courses, was filmed by Film Australia in 1988, and has been translated, performed, and published in Japan.

Buzo's next play, *Rooted* (first performed, 1969), produced simultaneously in Sydney and Canberra in 1972, is a dark satirical comedy in three acts. It concerns the apparently inevitable decline of the outrageously put-upon character Bentley, a middle-class public servant in his mid twenties. According to the glossary of the Currency Press edition, "rooted" means "to be ruined, trapped, without resource." Bentley is driven out of his home by his self-absorbed and ruthless wife, Sandy, so that she can comfortably continue her affair with the character Simmo, who, although never seen, is idolized by all. Simmo moves in, and Bentley is forced to move out. Bentley ends up in a rented room from which he is also driven out by the owner of the house, his "good mate" Gary, in order to make room for a party for Simmo. Bentley begins as an insecure materialist consumer of status goods, constantly referring to the excellence of his modern home unit, and at the end of the play he exits as a homeless and jobless loser. Constant references to the Australian sacred cow of "mateship" (male loyalty, solidarity, comradeship) are shown as shallow and meaningless verbal gestures. All the characters around Bentley, both male and female, appear to be ready to do anything to curry favor with the always absent but always dominant character Simmo. One also sees in this play Buzo's characteristic concern with language. As Peter Fitzpatrick puts it, "The primary interest is in the patterns of cliché which deform all relationships; . . . in *Rooted* (1969) Pinteresque litanies of triteness . . . are tokens of emptiness, and of the impenetrability of surfaces." Fitzpatrick quotes the following typically highly patterned section of dialogue:

> Richard. You've got no charisma.
> Diane. You've got a complex.
> Richard. You need a rest.
> Diane. A complete break.
> Richard. Rejuvenation.
> Diane. Regeneration.
> Richard. Wake up to yourself.
> Diane. Wake up and live.
> Richard. You'll be all right.
> Diane. You see what we mean?
> Bentley. Yes.
> Richard. Take the bull by the horns.
> Diane. Grab the nettle.
> Richard. Face the facts.
> Diane. You'll be all right.
> Bentley. Yes, I'll be all right. I'll take action.

In both *Rooted* and *The Roy Murphy Show* (first performed, 1971), and indeed also in *The Front Room Boys* (first performed, 1969), female characters are assigned limited roles as either inhumanely cruel and dominant and at the same time sexually promiscuous and amoral (Sandy in *Rooted*), or as glamorous and empty-headed (Pammy in *The Front Room Boys*), or as flirtatious and exploitable (the League Maid in *The Roy Murphy Show*). This belief appears to be part of Buzo's satirical picture of the world, particularly of younger middle-class males, with their obsessions with sex and cars, in particular the "B," or MGB sports car, the driving of which seems to be the iconic status symbol in this milieu.

Buzo's time in the 1960s as a junior clerk in a stockbroker's office and in the New South Wales Public Service informed his portrayal of office work and its social rituals in *The Front Room Boys*. This play shows a group of minor clerical officers in a large corporation, whose job is to process documents, which are endlessly passed down to them by the "backroom boys." Like the unseen but dominant Simmo (and Davo and Hammo) in *Rooted,* the backroom boys dominate from offstage and only once appear physically, in the character of Hendo.

Director Grahame Blundell refers to the style of this play (and Jack Hibberd's *White with Wire Wheels* [published in *Plays,* edited by Graeme Blundell, 1970]) in an oft-cited phrase as "quasi-naturalistic with absurd-

Barbara Tarbuck as Wendy and Denis Arndt as Weeks in a scene from the 1978 Seattle ACT production of
Buzo's Makassar Reef, *in which the main characters withdraw from the acquisitiveness of society*
(photograph by Chris Bennion; from John McCallum, Buzo, *1987)*

ist overtones." Buzo discusses the influence of both Samuel Beckett and Harold Pinter in an interview with Geoffrey Sirmai (*Southerly,* March 1986)—in particular, how Beckett enabled the breaking of the "rule" of never having a major character remain offstage. *The Front Room Boys* has a nonrealistic structure consisting of twelve scenes (following the twelve months of the calendar year) without a conventional narrative plot. The emphasis is on the powerlessness of the "front room boys" to control their working lives, with the constant reference to deadlines set by one boss or another in the "backroom," the fatalism with which this pattern is accepted, and the internal intolerance and conformism among the front room boys themselves. Two scenes show surreal attempts at celebration. One of these scenes is the annual office party, involving slapstick and cross-dressing. In the other scene, the characters stop work for a few minutes to listen to the annual Melbourne Cup horse race. This almost sacred observance is interrupted as the race is about to end by backroom

boy Hendo's abruptly turning off the portable radio. On a series of occasions the "front room boys" show their subservience to authority and indeed their hatred of those individuals who might disturb the established order. They throw rubbish on the heads of demonstrators in the street below and are shocked at the demonstrators' antiboss slogans. The one character who dares to make an antihierarchical comment is rejected by the others and loses his job by the end of the play. Buzo comments on "the sad and baffling fatalism of the silent and subservient majority. These people resist every challenge to the imagination, . . . [and] support a hypocritical and discredited elite who in turn exploit them and pervert their spontaneous expressions. Above all, *The Front Room Boys* attempts to probe this problem and draw attention to it" ("Authors Note," *Plays*–Buzo, Hibberd, and John Romeril).

Buzo's next play, *The Roy Murphy Show,* is a farcical parody of a television sports show, with an array of stereotyped characters, including commentators; a stupid young Rugby League player; and a young woman, Sharon, in the sexist role of a decorative "League Maid." Roy, the incumbent host, battles for survival but is eventually replaced by a well-connected English newcomer. The play also includes an extravagant parody of the language of sporting commentary with its legendary heroes, nicknames for players, and rivalry between the various experts. The play approaches genuine farce in its increasing confusions and comic violence as parts of the television stage set appear to be in danger of destruction. Buzo lists watching the Rugby League as one of his personal interests, so the parody of sports language is perhaps more affectionate than critical.

Buzo was resident playwright at the Melbourne Theatre Company during 1972–1973, and the final script for his next play, *Macquarie,* was developed in the Melbourne Theatre Company Workshop under the direction of George Ogilvie. *Macquarie* is a serious historical drama, the central character for which is an early governor of the British colony of New South Wales. The characters are based on historical originals and real events from the period 1810–1822. *Macquarie* departs both in structure and content from the urban middle-class satires to date. Buzo dramatizes the period as a struggle between the liberal humanism of Macquarie, his belief in treating all human beings equally, regardless of race or social standing, and his desire to reform the excesses of colonial rule (arbitrary and extreme punishment of convicts, slave labor, and the neglect of Aboriginal welfare) and the greed and savagery of the opponents of reform. These opponents, who eventually defeat Macquarie, include the Rev. Samuel Marsden, portrayed as both savagely moralistic and punitive as a magistrate, and self-seeking and greedy in his own interests. Buzo creates characters who, while they represent distinct value positions, are not comically conceived stereotypes. An "offstage" figure holds the power to determine the outcome of the hero's projects. This character is the British colonial secretary, Lord Bathurst, who remains in London and to whom prejudiced reports about Macquarie flow. The theatrical staging most clearly departs from that of earlier plays, as the Colonial Office is, in fact, simultaneously onstage with a variety of locations in colonial Sydney and with the university office of modern-day academic specialist in Australian history, Dr. Polski. This double-time/triple-place structure enables a series of contrapuntal effects. Not only is Lord Bathurst seen reading reports and issuing decrees that will affect Governor Macquarie, but Dr. Polski is shown reading aloud sections of student essays, a practice that functions as a direct source of information for the audience. At times a literal counterpoint of voices are played simultaneously and interleaved as passages of dialogue in the three locations.

Dr. Polski also serves another function in *Macquarie,* as, in John McCallum's words, "an embodiment of an ineffectual form of modern liberalism which is continually compared in the play with Macquarie's more active version." As McCallum points out in *Buzo* (1987), the dilemmas of a liberal reformer with (for his time) unconventional ideas, who is also seen by some as autocratic, gained an extra contemporary resonance with the rise and fall of the reforming E. G. Whitlam Labor government (1972–1975). McCallum records in *Buzo* that when Buzo rewrote *Macquarie* in 1985, "the Polski sequences were rewritten specifically to incorporate the sacking of the Whitlam government in November 1975." Buzo was awarded the inaugural Gold Medal of the Australian Literature Society in 1973 for *Macquarie* and his play *Tom* (first performed, 1972).

Buzo turned to history for material once again in *Batman's Beach-Head,* adapted for the Melbourne Theatre Company in September 1973 from Henrik Ibsen's *An Enemy of the People* (1882). The play has an environmental theme and is set in the fictional Victorian resort town of Batman's Beach. Buzo returns to history as fictional location and to the accompanying adoption of a more documentary, realist style in later plays.

In 1972, however, Buzo also had his play *Tom* produced by the Melbourne Theatre Company. The characters are three middle-class couples in their late twenties. All of the male characters work for the same corporation, a shadowy organization called Stallion. Stallion spies on its own employees and is generally ruthless and heartlessly internally competitive. Tom is a mysterious troubleshooter who becomes involved in the ascension to the vice presidency of the company by his friend Stephen. In the first of several scenarios in which a female character is central, Tom's wife, Susan, occupies the stage for longer than any other character. The play is set in the domestic space of their "sparsely and tastefully furnished modern Harbourside flat" in Sydney, and although much discussion about the crises and machinations of the Stallion company takes place, the focus is equally on personal relationships within and between the couples. Tom himself is often monosyllabic, except when he is chatting up Carol, the wife of his colleague Ken, or attacking Susan. The character of Stephen continues the theme of ruthless competition among mates. Stephen is a public relations (PR) man for the firm and continually spouts the kind of pretentious and allegedly fashionable pseudointellectual jargon that Buzo later attacked as the mark of the "new class."

In *Buzo,* McCallum sees *Tom* as the last of the plays that focus on an alienating society that crushes

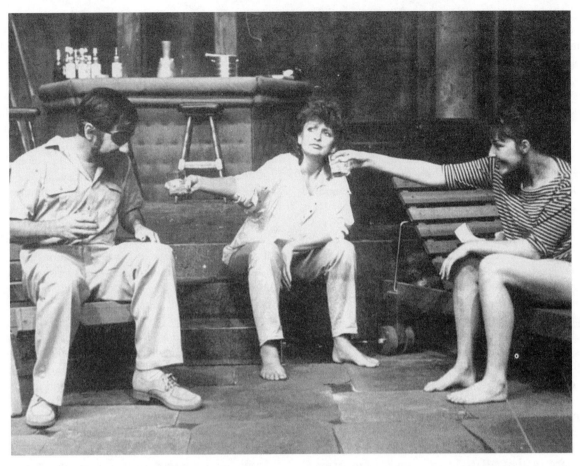

Scene from the 1984 production by Ensemble Studios in Sydney of Buzo's Coralie Lansdowne Says No *(1974),*
a comedy about a strong woman who chooses among three suitors (from John McCallum, Buzo, *1987)*

more-sensitive individuals—in this case, Susan, who, like Bentley in *Rooted,* is destroyed essentially because of her "niceness." As McCallum writes, "in this play the humanism which underlies all Buzo's writing is expressed in negative terms of outrage and loathing for an anti-humanist society." In an interview with Kirsten Blanch in 1978, Buzo commented that looking back, "The early plays were more negative than I would write now, more pessimistic. They were humanist protests against what seemed wrong. Now I am more interested in a humanistic rescue of what seems good." Buzo defines humanism in the same interview as "organised niceness."

In his next play, *Coralie Lansdowne Says No* (first performed, 1974), the centrality of the female character is crucial. Coralie is portrayed as a strong, independent, and rather tall woman who during the course of the play has several suitors. Initial indications are that she will say no to all, as she has said no to a conventional career, but in the end she says yes to Stuart, described as a poet and public servant and clearly not only much shorter but less original and energetic than she. Buzo

has made clear that he does not regard her refusals and independence as feminist, as he sees feminism as a form of ideological commitment, while Coralie is an individual. In this play the action takes place in an affluent middle-class setting, a modern holiday house above one of the northern beaches of Sydney. Two features of the set are a bar, to which the characters frequently resort, and a live tree, which grows through the room and up through the roof. The impression is of a milieu of leisure, hedonism, and affluence, but for Coralie, who is house-sitting, the house is only a temporary home. Coralie's toughness is counterpointed in the play by the suicide of another female character, offstage in the surf. In this play characterization and language are not developed in the satirical and often surreal mode of the first three plays. Coralie is a strong and even flamboyant character, and the dialogue is often a contest of wits, but this play is a comedy in which the heroine's decision is meant to be taken seriously.

Buzo's next play, *Martello Towers* (first performed, 1976), reverses initial audience expectations by being more serious toward its characters than it first appears it will be. The set is the living room of a well-appointed holiday house on an island in Pittwater, just north of Sydney. The set has entrances from the front door through a short hall, exits to two bedrooms, and glass doors to a sundeck overlooking the sea. This arrangement allows for the expectation of the classic farce structure of coincidence and surprise meetings as one after another of three interconnected couples arrives, each thinking they have the cottage to themselves for a romantic weekend. Edward Martello, retired although only in his early thirties, has already arrived with his weekend partner, Francesca. His recently separated wife, Jennifer, unexpectedly arrives with Lonnie Randall, a "radical radio disc jockey" and spouter of new-class culture-babble. His speech is the antithesis of Edward's. Soon afterward, Edward's younger sister, Vivien, also shows up, with Edward's old friend "Ice" Berg. During the course of the action Jennifer's mother, Marian, and Edward's father, Anthony, also appear. After the initial surprises about who should be there or not, the action settles down to a series of verbal parryings. Edward is particularly scornful of Lonnie Randall, who eventually confesses his real name is John Mackenzie; he is a failed stage hypnotist and many-times loser. The dialogue, especially the wit of Edward Martello, exemplifies Buzo's version of the Wildean comedy of manners and mock-self-deprecating middle-class irony. A serious theme, however, underlies the seeming inconsequence of the surface. After Lonnie's "alternative" credentials are smashed (confirming Edward's good judgment) and Francesca leaves, realizing that the romantic weekend she was expecting is not to be, the tone shifts to a more sensitive level, unveiling the relationships between Edward and his father and between Edward and Jennifer. The elder Martello's offer to establish a substantial trust for the first child born who will carry on the family name leads to the revelation that Jennifer is childless because she is infertile and to the reuniting of Jennifer and Edward, who, in Edward's words, realize that "their separation is a failure." Although as two mature, self-possessed, and witty individuals in a comedy, they do not fall into each other's arms immediately, clearly they will reunite shortly. Edward appears to have rediscovered that Jennifer is an individual with "taste, sensitivity and intelligence," essential humanist qualities that are equally unfashionable in the business world from which Edward has retreated and in the alternative radical cultural sector. Being an "individual" becomes affirmed as "an ideal of grace."

Buzo's next play, *Makassar Reef* (1979; first performed in 1978), continues in some ways the exploration of the problems of being an intelligent "individual" in a complex, even ambiguous, world. Buzo uses the device of a story of romance and some intrigue in a tropical island setting in Makassar, the capital of the Celebes (Sulawesi) Islands in Indonesia. The town is not pictured as a popular tourist destination. The play explores the theme of withdrawal from everyday society, paralleling the withdrawal from the values of an acquisitive society, a move that Edward Martello initially attempted and with which Coralie Lansdowne's story began. Buzo creates a romantic setting in an exotic location with elements of both the colonial expatriate adventure and the detective story, and he shows a group of variously alienated Western characters and some locals and go-betweens, the Westerners dallying with each other at various levels, delaying an inevitable return to the "real world." Once again the drama focuses on characters in relative isolation from everyday society, who probe each other's trustworthiness as they seek to make human contact while protecting precarious values and identities that they feel may be at risk. No character is totally admirable (at least one is involved in amateur drug smuggling); all are edgy and temporary acquaintants; all are capable of some level of infidelity, except for the teenage daughter, Camilla Ostrov, whose idealism is perhaps the foil to the worldweariness of not only her mother Wendy but also Weeks Brown, a brilliant and alcoholic economist hiding out apparently from the decision to take a big job with the World Bank. This play represents perhaps Buzo's most nuanced writing, using the implicit reference to the glamour of motion pictures such as *Casablanca* (1942) to create a new style of wit.

Buzo's play *Big River* is set on a property on the banks of the river Murray in southern New South Wales near the town of Albury, around the years 1900–1909. The play is an historical family drama with hints of Anton Chekhov, as the property is in financial trouble, and the action begins as the family returns from the funeral of the father, whose various entrepreneurial attempts have sustained them until now, but only barely. The family consists of three daughters and one son, and the play conveys an atmosphere of provincial isolation. It also includes a sense of struggle for economic survival and in particular for the retention of the family mansion, Wombelano, and the family fortune. Various alternatives are represented by local men with sometimes obscure intentions and claims. Although the son, Charles, attempts to take the place of the father, Charles is injured and crippled. The crucial decision making initially falls to the mother, Ivy; in some ways, however, the action centers on the fate of the most precocious daughter, Adela, who has returned from the city a young widow. She is attracted to her sister Monica's intended, a young man named Hugh, but in the end marries a man from a lower class, Leo Mulcahy.

Ian Spence as Sludge and James Laurie as Bentley in a scene from the 1985 Australian Broadcasting Corporation
television adaptation of Buzo's Rooted (1969), about a middle-class public
servant (from John McCallum, Buzo, 1987)

Mulcahy has practical survival plans for the property, especially through the cultivation of grapes. At the end of the play, Adela is pregnant, sitting on the veranda with her brother, looking over the big river, and eating grapes from the property. She may be isolated and away from the city where she has spent much of her life, but her decision to "make do" with Mulcahy seems to have created a scene of stability and contentment, as well as the renunciation of some more glamourous aspirations. The action continues through the period of Australian Federation and involves discussions of possible futures for rural Australia. The focus is domestic, however, and associated with working through various levels of loyalty and choices in response to change.

In *Big River* the majority of the central characters are women. In the next play, *The Marginal Farm* (first performed, 1983), a centrally important character, and one who is in some ways parallel to such characters as Adela and Coralie, is the young woman Elspeth, nicknamed Toby, who has left Australia to take up a position as a governess to two teenage children living in a sugar-growing area of the islands of Fiji during the 1950s and 1960s, when the power of the Colonial Sugar Refining (CSR) Company administration paralleled that of the Australian colonial government. Toby

comes to the home of Marshal, a CSR field officer—a benevolent colonial patriarch and a sahib who controls the lives of the people of the district. Toby is courted ineffectually by James, a thirty-something English aircraft pilot with a dashing manner. She is also courted by Illy, a local Indian Fijian with a reputation for seducing tourist and expatriate ladies. Toby, who is warned against Illy by Marshal, not only enters into an ongoing affair with Illy but also defies convention by not attempting to keep it secret. Although she is initially determined not to end up as the somewhat eccentric expatriate lady owning a small shop, Toby does have to accept a somewhat ambiguous position both in Illy's life and in the community. She is not, however, spiritually defeated. She is another example of an intelligent and sensitive middle-class woman with limited practical options, who with some courage attempts to find an individual path of life against both the implicit and explicit warnings of conventional society.

Buzo's *Pacific Union: The Story of the San Francisco Forty-Fivers* was produced in 1995. This thoroughly researched and intricately detailed historical drama is about the negotiations and machinations at the United Nations Conference on International Organisation that met in San Francisco for nine weeks beginning 25 April 1945 and that led to the formation of the United Nations (UN). The Australian foreign minister at the time, Herbert Evatt, played a leading role in the formation and the writing of the constitutional provisions of the UN. *Pacific Union* is the story of his struggles to have key principles and procedures adopted. Evatt played a leading intellectual role, particularly in issues of independence and self-government for former colonies and on the veto powers of the major powers that eventually made up the UN Security Council. He did not always win, and the backward White Australia policy of his own Australian Labor Party is shown as not only embarrassing but also a political liability for a man who wished to advance the cause of less powerful nations. The play combines the detailed story of these negotiations and discussions with a backdrop of Australian electoral politics and an acknowledgment of Evatt's personal failings. Evatt is shown as a principled, strong-willed, and determined individual, who loves the "slog" of the detailed drafting of documents and who also wishes to carry through certain principles derived both from his Labor Party background and from his personal vision for the way in which all countries can be empowered to contribute to global problem solving in the post–World War II world.

In addition to his substantial contribution to Australian theater, Alexander Buzo has written comic novels and volumes of satirical commentary and has worked in other media, including animation and adaptation. He continues to contribute occasional specialist journalistic pieces on the loss of precision and elegance in writing and speaking (and thinking) involved in the use of fashionable pseudointellectual jargon, the language of "the new class," a phrase he has successfully bequeathed to Australian English. He also targets clichés (and especially tautologies) in media and everyday speech, and the denial of regional variation in Australian English. He has, in addition, written on what he calls the "narrowing" of Australian theater by the rising visibility, during the 1990s in particular, of new Australian work voicing the concerns of particular social groups and by the production of overseas texts, whose

appeal (according to him) is their reference to currently fashionable political issues rather than to the excellence of their writing. He writes from the position of what he calls "humanism," a nonideological belief in human decency; he advocates, moreover, the use of informed and impartial intelligence. As a dramatist, Buzo will always be seen as a key figure of the Australian New Wave and as a writer whose vision matured from the satiric quasi-theater of the absurd of the early plays into explorations of the educated middle-class, baby-boomer generation, of which he is a part, as they experienced coming into responsible adulthood in the 1980s.

Interviews:

Kirsten Blanch, "Organised Niceness," *Theatre Australia,* 2, no. 11 (June 1978): 16–17;

Geoffrey Sirmai, "An Interview with Alexander Buzo," *Southerly,* 46, no. 1 (March 1986): 80–91;

Ron Verburgt, "'Middle-Class Dissenter': An Interview with Alexander Buzo," *Australasian Drama Studies Journal,* no. 22 (April 1993): 33–52.

References:

Peter Fitzpatrick, "Mythmaking in Modern Drama," in *The Penguin New Literary History of Australia,* edited by Laurie Hergenhan (Ringwood, Vic.: Penguin, 1988);

John McCallum, "Alex Buzo," in *Companion to Theatre in Australia,* edited by Philip Parsons and Victoria Chance (Sydney: Currency Press in association with Cambridge University Press, 1995);

McCallum, *Buzo,* Australian Playwrights Series (Sydney: Methuen, 1987);

Leslie Rees, *A History of Australian Drama* (North Ryde, N.S.W.: Angus & Robertson, 1987);

Terry Sturm, "Drama," in *The Oxford History of Australian Literature,* edited by Leonie Kramer (Melbourne: Oxford University Press, 1981).

Papers:

A collection of Alex Buzo's correspondence is in the Australian National Library, and some play manuscripts are held in the Fryer Library, University of Queensland.

Peter Carey
(7 May 1943 –)

Anthony J. Hassall
James Cook University

BOOKS: *The Fat Man in History* (St. Lucia: University of Queensland Press, 1974);

War Crimes (St. Lucia: University of Queensland Press, 1979);

The Fat Man in History (London: Faber & Faber, 1980; New York: Random House, 1980; St. Lucia: University of Queensland Press, 1990); republished as *Exotic Pleasures* (London: Picador, 1981)—comprises stories selected from the 1974 edition of *The Fat Man in History* and from *War Crimes;*

Bliss (St. Lucia: University of Queensland Press, 1981; London: Faber & Faber, 1981; New York: Harper & Row, 1981);

Bliss: The Film (London: Faber & Faber, 1985);

Illywhacker (St. Lucia: University of Queensland Press, 1985; London: Faber & Faber, 1985; New York: Harper & Row, 1985);

Bliss: The Screenplay, by Carey and Ray Lawrence (St. Lucia: University of Queensland Press, 1986);

Oscar and Lucinda (St. Lucia: University of Queensland Press, 1988; London: Faber & Faber, 1988; New York: Harper & Row, 1988);

The Tax Inspector (St. Lucia: University of Queensland Press, 1991; London: Faber & Faber, 1991; New York: Knopf, 1991);

The Unusual Life of Tristan Smith (St. Lucia: University of Queensland Press, 1994; London: Faber & Faber, 1994; New York: Knopf, 1995);

A Letter to Our Son (St. Lucia: University of Queensland Press, 1994);

Collected Stories (St. Lucia: University of Queensland Press, 1994; London: Faber & Faber, 1995)—includes the previously uncollected "Joe," "Concerning the Greek Tyrant," and "A Million Dollars Worth of Amphetamines";

The Big Bazoohley (New York: Holt, 1995; St. Lucia: University of Queensland Press, 1995; London: Faber & Faber, 1995);

Jack Maggs (St. Lucia: University of Queensland Press, 1997; London: Faber & Faber, 1997; New York: Knopf, 1998);

Peter Carey (photograph by Marion Ettlinger; from the dust jacket for Jack Maggs, *1997; Richland County Public Library)*

American Dreams (Pymble, N.S.W.: HarperCollins, 1997);

True History of the Kelly Gang (St. Lucia: University of Queensland Press, 2000; London: Faber & Faber, 2000; New York: Knopf, 2000);

30 Days in Sydney: A Wildly Distorted Account (London: Bloomsbury, 2001; New York: Bloomsbury, 2001);

My Life as a Fake (New York: Knopf, 2003).

PRODUCED SCRIPT: *Bliss,* motion picture, by Carey and Ray Lawrence, New South Wales Film Corp., 1985.

SELECTED PERIODICAL PUBLICATIONS–UNCOLLECTED: "From an Alien to His Second Son," *HQ Magazine* (Autumn 1993): 96–99;

"Home and Away," *Sunday Age Agenda,* 29 January 1995, p. 5;

"A Small Memorial," *New Yorker* (25 September 1995): 54–63.

Peter Carey is widely acknowledged as one of the most accomplished and successful Australian novelists of recent decades and is one of a handful–along with Thomas Keneally, David Malouf, and Tim Winton–who command an international reputation. Carey's novels and short-story collections have won virtually every major literary award in Australia, on many occasions, and his international reputation was confirmed when he won a second Booker Prize in 2001 (the first was in 1988), a feat equaled only by the South African J. M. Coetzee. Though he has lived in New York since 1989, Carey describes himself as an Australian writer, and his books continue to explore Australian history and culture.

Carey is an ambitious and adventurous novelist whose work is consistently risk taking and original. His early stories were influenced by science fiction and his early novels by the modernist fiction of William Faulkner and the magic realism of Gabriel García Márquez. Carey's more recent work has explored real and imagined episodes from Australian history, and mythology from a variety of revisionist perspectives, while maintaining a strong sympathy for, and identification with, the victims rather than the victors of history. For a writer who does not simply exploit traditional genres or cater to conventional expectations, Carey's books have sold extremely well in Australia, England, and the United States and have been widely translated.

Peter Philip Carey was born on 7 May 1943 in the provincial town of Bacchus Marsh in Victoria, where his parents, Percival Stanley Carey and Helen Jean Warriner Carey, operated the local General Motors dealership. His paternal grandfather, R. Graham Carey, flew the first airmail in South Australia and barnstormed in a Bleriot monoplane now restored and displayed in the Powerhouse Museum in Sydney. The youngest of three children, Peter was educated at Bacchus Marsh and Geelong Grammar School. In 1961 he began a science degree at Monash University but abandoned it in 1962 to work as an advertising copywriter in Melbourne. He married Leigh Weetman in 1964.

From 1967 to 1970 Carey lived in London and traveled extensively in Europe. Between 1964 and 1970 he wrote three novels that were not published and had his first short stories published. From 1970 to 1973 he worked in advertising in Melbourne and wrote in his spare time, completing a fourth novel, which was accepted for publication but withdrawn by the author. After these uncertain beginnings, Carey's career accelerated dramatically. *The Fat Man in History,* his first book of short stories, was published by the University of Queensland Press in 1974 and won him an enthusiastic public and something of a cult following. Having separated from his wife in 1973, he moved in 1974 from Melbourne to Sydney in order to take a senior advertising position.

The short story occupies a distinguished position in Australian literary history, but Carey was not writing within that tradition but at a point of fracture in its history when a long-dominant social realism was being assailed by postmodern and other experiments. His stories do not reflect a commonly agreed upon sense of what constitutes reality, either in fictional or in extrafictional experience. Pointillist narrative fragments of problematic status and varying degrees of self-consciousness, they include a heady mixture of nightmare, fantasy, and science fiction but remain linked in eerie and disturbing ways to the more commonplace cultural fictions of the twentieth and early twenty-first centuries. The voice they articulate was a new one when Carey first began publishing, unlike anything previously heard in Australian fiction.

The inhabitants of Carey's stories are typically victims, losers trapped in a disintegrating society that denies them any fulfillment or self-expression. They are also trapped in surreal psychological dungeons and the machinations of a technology going terribly wrong. Like the stories of Franz Kafka, Milan Kundera, and J. G. Ballard, Carey's parables of imprisonment and metamorphosis destabilize traditional constructions of fictional reality, leaving the reader with a suggestive and beckoning array of alternative interpretations but no ultimate certainty. The frequent shifts between a nightmarish yet recognizable present and an all-too-imaginable yet frighteningly distorted and out-of-control future, combined with the transgressions of the familiar boundaries of fiction, taste, and propriety, challenge the reader's expectations of what is appropriate or even permissible in fictional writing.

In 1977 Carey moved from Sydney to an alternative community near Yandina in southern Queensland with his artist partner, Margot Hutcheson, commuting back to Sydney for one week each month to work in advertising. Most of the stories in his next collection were written in Yandina. As the second book from an exciting young writer, *War Crimes* (1979) attracted favorable critical attention and won Carey his first literary prize, the 1980 New South Wales Premier's Award for fiction. In a memorable phrase in *The Sydney Morning Herald* (13 October 1979), Jill Neville described reading these stories as "like being shot by a firing squad of angels," and most reviewers welcomed *War Crimes* as further, unmistakable evidence that a new and compelling talent had arrived on the Australian literary scene.

This second book continued Carey's movement away from the social realism of the traditional Australian short story toward satiric fantasy and science fiction, Latin American–style magic realism, stomach-turning Zolaesque physicality, and Kafkaesque nightmares of terror and imprisonment, all of which are used to defamiliarize the horrors that readers had almost come to accept as the routine narratives of the final decades of the twentieth century. The novella-length stories in *War Crimes* allow more sustained and more sophisticated development of themes and situations, a wider range of characterization, and less concentration on losers. In place of the single-minded, despairing hostility directed at the incompetence and indifference of "those in charge" in *The Fat Man in History*, *War Crimes* is a more even-handed critique of both middle-class, radical-chic leftism and Neanderthal, new-right brutality. As a result, the political analyses in stories such as "The Puzzling Nature of Blue" and "War Crimes" are searching and subtle.

Carey is alert to the pervasive influence of the political on the personal, but he is ultimately more concerned with personal morality and the individual human fate, as is evident in "The Chance" and "War Crimes," his own favorite stories from *War Crimes*. The grim, baffled, nightmare world of *The Fat Man in History* has expanded in *War Crimes* to encompass a wider segment of contemporary society. The nightmare is lightened by a more overt sympathy for the dreamers locked in its embrace, but it remains a scarifying vision of powerlessness and corruption. *War Crimes* widened Carey's readership substantially, attracting both popular and discerning literary audiences.

His next book, also written at Yandina, was the novel *Bliss* (1981). Expecting more short stories, some reviewers were disconcerted by the change of genre, unaware that *Bliss* was the fifth novel Carey had written and that his ambition had always been to succeed as a novelist. But as he said in an interview with Craig Munro in *Makar* (June 1976), "I thought if you're going to do anything you're going to write a novel. A story wasn't really a serious thing. A novel was." More typical, however, of the enthusiasm with which reviewers greeted the book was Francis King's accolade in the *Spectator* (12 December 1981): "Not since Patrick

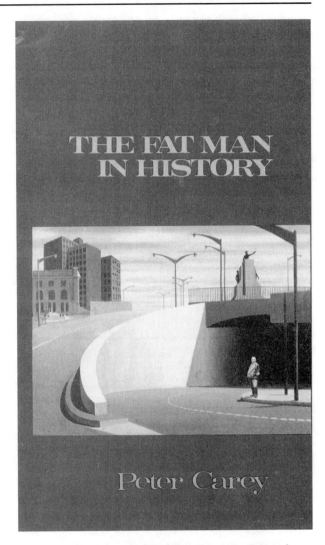

Paperback cover for Carey's first book, a 1974 collection of disturbing short stories that mix nightmare, fantasy, and science fiction (Bruccoli Clark Layman Archives)

White's *The Aunt's Story* has a novel so much convinced me of the emergence of a potentially major talent." *Bliss* consolidated Carey's growing Australian and international reputation as one of the most exciting and imaginative of contemporary writers of fiction. It won three major literary awards and was made into a multi-award-winning Australian motion picture.

Bliss is a novel about writing copy and writing novels, about different kinds of stories and storytelling. It portrays advertising as a dangerously addictive art form that colonizes and usurps the social roles of storytelling and mythmaking. The wider scope of the novel allowed Carey to enlarge on the themes of art and its deceptions that he had explored in such short stories as "Report on the Shadow Industry" and "American Dreams," and he continued his fiercely satiric depiction of contemporary Australian society. *Bliss* does, how-

*Dust jacket for the 1986 U.S. reprint of Carey's 1981 novel about
an advertising copywriter, which won three major literary prizes
(including the Miles Franklin Award), was made into an
award-winning 1985 movie, and brought Carey an
international reputation (Richland
County Public Library)*

ever, move away from the stark, monochromatic confrontations of the early stories toward a more sophisticated analysis of late-twentieth-century mores. Elements of fantasy and caricature remain, but the hauntingly accurate depiction of a recognizably familiar world is inescapable.

The larger canvas of the novel also allows the depiction of more-complex and compelling characters, such as Harry Joy, who is both a loser and a winner. Harry begins as a licensed clown, a "Good Bloke" who was "suckled on stories" and who went on to tell approved lies about Krappe Chemicals for a living. Like many of his predecessors, Harry undergoes an arbitrary metamorphosis—in his case "dying"—and experiences, also like them, the nightmares of being unemployed, solitary, imprisoned, and powerless. But Harry's ending is different: he is the first of Carey's victims to break out of the trap, to escape from the prisons

of city and family, to metamorphose positively from telling the lies of advertising to telling the ritual, life-enhancing stories of the forest.

This ultimate change in Harry's fortunes also represents a turning point in Carey's career. While he remained aware of the postmodern sophistication about stories and their problematic status, as *Illywhacker* (1985) demonstrates, he also celebrates in *Bliss* the functions that good and well-told stories serve, particularly in a half-formed, postcolonial culture hungry for its own enabling myths, for native stories to displace imported stories. The story of Harry Joy addresses the ambitious task of substituting an Australian mythology for a colonial mythology, whether English, American, or Japanese.

In 1980 Carey moved from Yandina back to Sydney, joining Bani McSpedden to form the advertising company McSpedden Carey, for which Carey continued to work part-time. In 1981 he moved again with Hutcheson to Gleniffer in northern New South Wales, where he wrote his next novel, *Illywhacker*. The novel was greeted in 1985 with enthusiasm by the critics and was a popular success. It was the first indication that Carey was passionate about Australian nationalism, which had not figured prominently in his earlier work. It won more literary awards in Australia than any previous Carey book and was short-listed for the 1985 Booker Prize.

The narrator of *Illywhacker* introduces himself to the reader in the first sentence of the book and makes clear that he, Herbert Badgery, is going to be telling the stories in this book. Carey retrieved the title *Illywhacker* from obscurity as an upmarket synonym for the ubiquitous Australianism "bullshit artist" to alert the reader that this narrator is a trickster or spieler. As Badgery says of himself, "I am a terrible liar and I have always been a liar. I say that early to set things straight. *Caveat emptor* [Let the buyer beware]." Readers are thus warned to approach Herbert's narrative of his life and times with some caution. Alternatively, they can accept his advice not "to try to pull apart the strands of lies and truth, but to relax and enjoy the show." And what a show it is—sad and funny, a towering, three-decker, six-hundred-page family saga. Carey's imaginative power and creative energy are as dazzling as ever, but a new breadth of comic vision and a more detailed documentation of character give *Illywhacker* a range, a richness, and a substance that delight and astonish the reader.

In the course of revisiting what Mark Twain called the "beautiful lies" of Australian history, Carey laments the continuing Australian failure to shake off its industrial cringing to successive colonial masters—British, American, and Japanese—and to believe and

I. *My name is Herbert Badgery. I am*
~~Badgery, something~~ 140 years old and something of a celebrity. They
come and look at me and wonder how I do it. They wonder why I don't
die and there are weeks when I wonder the same, whole stretches of
terrible time. It is hard to believe you can feel so bad and still
not die.

I am a terrible liar. I have always been a liar. I say that early
to set things straight and also to tell you that my age is one of
the few facts you'll be able to rely on. This is autheticated. It
is signed and witnessed by indepedent experts. They have poked me and
proded me and scraped around my foul smelling mouth.

They have measured my ankles and looked at my legs. I don't care
about my legs any more. When they photographed me I did not care that
my dick looked as scabby and scaley as a horse's, even though there
was a time when I was a vain man and would not have permitted the
type of photographs they the chose to take. Apart from this (and
it is all there, written on a chart not three feet from where I lie)
I have also been written up in the papers. Don't think this is any
novelty for me. Being written up has been one of my weaknesses, so
I don't state this to impress, but rather to make the point that I
am not lying about my age.

But for the rest of it, you may as well know, I intend to lie now
and then. There are few stories that can't be improved with a

bit of lying. It's a great relief for me to acknowedge all this.
It's taken me long enough, Christ knows. Now I feel no more ashamed
of this than farting or burping (I rip forth a beauty to underline
the point). There will be complaints, of course. (There are complaints
now, about the farting. My apologies, fellow sufferers). But don't
waste your time going through all this with a red pen looking for
the lies, because you'll only come a gutser. When you think I must be
lying I'll be telling the truth. And vice-versa.

I think I'm growing tits like Horace. They stuck their calipers in
me an measured them. It'd be one for the books if I turned into a
woman at this stage of life. It's probably the curiosity that keeps
me alive, to see what my dirty old body will do next.

~~I am disgusting to look at.~~ You can see them flinch when they ~~come~~ *look at*
to me. ~~They look at me~~ *the* like some disgusting old fish decaying on the

beach and they could not guess that there is anything inside my head
but cruel, brain soup sloshing around in a basin. My voice is gone,
so how can they know what changes have taken place inside me. I no
longer hate. No, no, that's not true. But I hate less. I am a nicer
person entirely. I may even have become kind, which would please me
if it was true. It has been an ambition.

Revised typescript page for Carey's 1985 novel Illywhacker *(from Candida Baker,* Yacker: Australian Writers
Talk about Their Work, *1986; Paterno Library, Pennsylvania State University)*

invest in its own talent. He also challenges received histories of Australia, portraying the country instead as initially stolen from its original inhabitants and then sold out to a succession of international carpetbaggers who exported minerals, inventions, and native fauna, and pacified the locals with enough to eat and a comfortable cage in the best pet shop in the world. The climactic image in the book—of Australia as a human zoo, a theme park, and a penal colony of the Japanese tourist industry—is the most powerful example of the linked prison and animal images that run throughout *Illywhacker* and connect the public imprisonment of the country with the private incarceration of its inhabitants (in family and sexual narratives of loss and of love betrayed into hatred). The pet shop graphically visualizes the bleak sense of powerlessness and imprisonment that continues to haunt the European Australian consciousness, and it offers little hope for a genuinely postprison and postcolonial future.

In 1984 Carey met theater director Alison Margaret Summers and moved to Sydney to live with her. They married 16 March 1985, and their first son, Sam, was born in 1986. *Oscar and Lucinda,* which was written in Sydney and published in 1988, again won Carey a shower of awards. Like *Illywhacker,* it was short-listed for the Booker Prize, but this time Carey's book won. Achieving such prestigious recognition for two consecutive books confirmed Carey's status in the front rank of novelists writing in English and ensured that his work would reach an even wider audience.

Oscar and Lucinda is another historical novel, but it is not at all like *Illywhacker.* The title suggests a love story, and the depiction of the chaste and tender love of two gentle and generous nineteenth-century innocents is in striking contrast to the hyperactive, exploitative, and frequently violent sexual behavior that pervades much of Carey's earlier fiction and surrounds the central couple even in this book. Carey generates a powerful imaginative sympathy with Oscar and Lucinda, a sympathy that their oddness and eccentricity only enhance, and one that is warmer and more genial than that accorded to the harder-edged characters in Carey's earlier books. The tone of *Oscar and Lucinda* is less satiric than that of *Bliss,* and the picaresque detachment of *Illywhacker* is replaced by an intense engagement. The tragic ending of *Oscar and Lucinda* is pervaded by a poignant emotional intensity that leaves scenes reverberating unforgettably in the reader's memory.

In 1989 Carey moved to Greenwich Village in New York, where his second son, Charley, was born in 1990. *The Tax Inspector,* begun in Sydney and completed in New York, was published in 1991. Carey does not repeat himself, but no one would have expected the sequel to *Oscar and Lucinda* to be a violent and confronting psychothriller. *The Tax Inspector* sets a grimly detailed account of three generations of incest in the Catchprice family against a broader account of public venality and corruption in Sydney. The sexual abuse of children by parents, which was once a taboo subject, has received media attention in recent years; but it remains a sensitive subject, and part of the negative reaction to the book in Australia resulted from the public's dislike of the deliberate breaking into this particular silence, and of the suggestion that this private indecency was symptomatic of a wider social decay in Sydney, a theme revisited in *30 Days in Sydney: A Wildly Distorted Account* (2001).

Carey himself experienced doubts about incest as a subject: "Every day it was hard to write. Without being too melodramatic, there were dark corridors one had to make oneself walk to the end of, even though it was repulsive or frightening. I asked myself every day whether the book was worth writing" (*The Age,* 25 July 1992). Part of the difficulty some readers had with the portrayal of violence and sexual deviance in *The Tax Inspector* was the result of the way they are both limited and not limited in the narrative. Joseph Conrad set the heart of darkness in the middle of the alien continent of Africa, which is reached after a long preparatory journey. He further limits the horror by narrating the story from a setting in London, at the center of civilization, though that center is itself tainted with darkness at the end. Carey uses no such framing, distancing devices in *The Tax Inspector.* The heroine, Maria Takis, is flawed, and the authority beyond her is worse. Order is in the hands of a corrupt, self-serving elite. The emergency rescue squad may come at the end, but they will not rescue anyone from the real dilemmas of the book. Carey has imprisoned many characters in his fiction, but the reader is the one who is trapped in the text at the end of *The Tax Inspector.*

The Unusual Life of Tristan Smith (1994), the first of Carey's novels to be written wholly in New York, is his most extensive exploration of the complex love-hate relationship between the culture of his native Australia and that of the United States. The theme is familiar from his short stories and *Bliss,* but the form is a departure from that of his earlier works. *The Unusual Life of Tristan Smith* is an allegory about two imaginary countries, Efica and Voorstand, which bear some resemblance to Australia and the United States. Efica is a small, formerly colonial nation struggling to establish a political and cultural identity distinct from that imposed on it by its great and powerful ally Voorstand. Tristan Smith, a native Efican deformed and disfigured at birth, challenges the political and cultural hegemony of Voorstand, and his adventures in the two countries take the reader on a picaresque roller-coaster ride through contemporary neocolonial cultural politics.

Dust jacket for the U.S. edition of Carey's 1988 novel, a tragic love story of two nineteenth-century eccentrics, that won the 1988 Booker Prize (Richland County Public Library)

At the center of the allegorical world of the books, which is fantastically defamiliarized and yet hauntingly familiar, is the image of the Voorstand Sirkus. This Sirkus, which is the centerpiece of Voorstand culture, is a dazzlingly imagined variation on the Disney/Hollywood/multimedia entertainment circus, and even in faraway Efica the early life of Tristan Smith is dominated by it. The Sirkus and the Voorstand Intelligence Agency (VIA) are the vehicles of Voorstand's oppression of Efica. The Sirkus desensitizes the hearts and minds of Voorstanders and Eficans alike, and it facilitates their political subservience by purveying homogenized global infotainment on a platform of seductive technology. For its part, the VIA murders Tristan Smith's mother, Felicity, a native of Voorstand who has become an ardent Efican nationalist and has left her agitprop theatrical company to become a popular candidate for an anti-Voorstand political party, which seems likely to win an election.

Despite his terrible physical handicaps, Tristan is partly successful in his subsequent campaign of revenge against Voorstand. When he arrives in its capital, Saar-lim, clearly the Voorstand empire is vulnerable to subversion, and in an unexpectedly upbeat ending to the book, Tristan wreaks a humiliating revenge on the bungling VIA. He uses both the mythology and the technology of the Sirkus with exquisite appropriateness to expose and humiliate the decaying culture of Voorstand. His revenge, like Carey's book, takes the form of a subversive narrative, and its unlikely extravagance reflects the disempowerment of the colonized and their desire for a fantasy revenge on the powers that gave Tristan a body as inadequate as the oppressed body politic of his native Efica. Like its immediate predecessor, *The Tax Inspector,* Carey's *The Unusual Life of Tristan Smith* was received less enthusiastically by the reading public than his earlier novels, perhaps because the physical deformities of its protagonist were as confronting in their way as the moral deformities of the Catchprice family. Reviewers, however, were more enthusiastic, many of them rating it Carey's best, most imaginative and inventive book.

Moving from adult fiction to children's fiction represented something of a gamble for an author of

Dust jacket for the U.S. edition (1998) of Carey's 1997 reworking of Charles Dickens's novel Great Expectations
(1860–1861), in which the convict Abel Magwitch is shown in a more sympathetic light and Dickens
himself appears as a character (Richland County Public Library)

Peter Carey's stature, but the reception of his first children's book, *The Big Bazoohley,* published in 1995, suggested that the gamble paid off. *The Big Bazoohley* was a runner-up for the 1996 Children's Book Council of Australia Children's Book of the Year in the "Younger Readers" category and was included in the United States *Publishers Weekly* 1995 Children's Fiction List.

Carey's critique of American culture and his love-hate relationship with Hollywood/Disney are continued in *The Big Bazoohley,* in which the young protagonist, Sam Kellow, chances his luck in the Perfecto Kiddo Competition, a classic Hollywood combination of excruciating banality and a disturbing misconception of what is natural and admirable in children. Like Tristan Smith, Sam Kellow plays the game and wins, despite his seeming lack of qualifications. But unlike Tristan, Sam wins by gambling on life, not art. His victory marks an interesting new stage in the battle between the two in Carey's fiction and the parallel battle between optimism and pessimism in his endings.

Optimism wins out, somewhat unexpectedly, in his next adult novel, *Jack Maggs* (1997), in which Carey gambles his reputation against the greatest of English novelists, Charles Dickens.

Jack Maggs is a rewriting of the story of Abel Magwitch, the convict in Dickens's *Great Expectations* (1860–1861), switching the center of interest from Pip to Magwitch, renamed Jack Maggs, and to Dickens himself, characterized in the book as Tobias Oates. In an unpublished speech given at the University of Queensland Press when the novel was published, Carey explained why he was drawn to the subject:

> Dickens's Magwitch is foul and dark, frightening, murderous. Dickens encourages us to think of him as "other" but . . . Magwitch was my ancestor. . . . I needed to write his story. I wanted to reinvent him, to possess him. I did not want to diminish his "darkness" or his danger but I wanted to give him all the love and tender sympathy that Dickens's first-person narrative provides his English hero Pip.

In *Jack Maggs,* Carey subverts the nineteenth-century cultural hegemony of England and its greatest writer over colonial Australia, as he had subverted the late-twentieth-century cultural hegemony of the United States in *The Unusual Life of Tristan Smith.*

Carey's characters typically struggle with little success to escape from the social and psychological prisons in which they find themselves. Jack, however, who starts off with almost nothing in his favor, escapes from both his man-made and his self-made prisons—not, like Dickens's Pip, into some uneasy middle-class Victorian status, with an ambivalent and rewritten ending to his unrequited passion for Estella, but to the place of a respected citizen surrounded by a loving family in New South Wales. The contrast is clearly in favor of Australia.

The critical reception of *Jack Maggs* was markedly more enthusiastic than the reception of *The Unusual Life of Tristan Smith:* several reviewers compared its achievement to that of *Oscar and Lucinda,* Frank Kermode even suggesting in the *London Review of Books* (16 October 1997) that it was so impressive an achievement that future reprints of *Oscar and Lucinda* may well bear the legend "by the author of *Jack Maggs.*" Like *Oscar and Lucinda, Jack Maggs* draws on nineteenth-century English writing as it intersects with the beginnings of European Australia, but the tone is more optimistic and more overtly compassionate. In *Oscar and Lucinda,* Boat Harbour in 1866 is an ugly, brutal outpost of an arrogant, racist empire, the sustaining ideology of which has been mortally wounded by the double failure of the established church to controvert Charles Darwin's theory of evolution, and to establish a strong foundation in New South Wales. While the Wingham where Jack Maggs and his family settle some thirty years earlier is geographically close to Boat Harbour, it is altogether more benign. In London, Jack Maggs was offered no life but a criminal's, and his wife Mercy Larkin no life but a prostitute's: Wingham, however, readily accommodates them and recognizes their fundamental decency. This outcome is in stark contrast to the bleak and despairing ending of *Oscar and Lucinda* and more optimistic than that of any Carey novel since *Bliss.*

The tragic mood returned in Carey's next book, *True History of the Kelly Gang* (2000), in which Carey created a fictional autobiography of one of the most celebrated folk heroes of Australia. Legends have continued to surround Ned Kelly himself, his gang of four, and the story of the Kelly uprising in northern Victoria from 1877 to 1880. On the one hand, Kelly has been celebrated as the archetypal Australian, courageously rebelling against an oppressive and inept colonial authority, and on the other, he has been condemned as a common thief and murderer deservedly

Dust jacket for Carey's 2000 fictional autobiography of the nineteenth-century Australian outlaw and folk hero Ned Kelly. The work won the 2001 Booker Prize (Richland County Public Library).

hanged in 1880. A minor literary industry has been devoted to these conflicting legends, and Sidney Nolan mythologized him in his Kelly series of paintings.

Carey's sympathy for, and identification with, losers, whom Australians once called battlers, drew him to the Kelly story. Kelly's own apologia for his career was the 8,300-word "Jerilderie Letter," written with gang member Joe Byrne and left behind in the hope of publication when the gang robbed the Jerilderie Bank in 1879. Carey has said that he was so moved by this letter that he carried a copy of it for years. The final impetus for the book was a New York exhibition of Nolan's Kelly paintings, in some of which Kelly is depicted wearing the headpiece of his armor with the vacant slit where his eyes should be. Carey wanted to fill in that vacancy, to flesh out the "Jerilderie Letter" into a book-length document by creatively imagining the man concealed behind the armor and the accompanying legend.

The book purports to be thirteen parcels of papers written by Ned Kelly in the manner, voice, and language of the "Jerilderie Letter." The title *True History of the Kelly Gang* is both the fictional Kelly's assertion that he is correcting the public record, in which he believes he has been grossly misrepresented, and Carey's transparently playful but nonetheless serious assertion that the truth about Kelly and his gang will finally be revealed. While he otherwise stays close to the historical record, Carey gives Kelly a fictional daughter, who escaped with her mother to America before his capture and to whom his self-justification is addressed. Apart from this invented family, Carey's major addition to the historical record is his psychological portrait of the outlaw, which explains his response to his family's persecution by the police; his devotion to his widowed mother, Ellen; and his passionate sense of injustice. While judgment on the Kelly legend may well remain divided, Carey's account of it, ventriloquised into the voice and language of Ned Kelly himself, was favorably received: *True History of the Kelly Gang* was a runaway best-seller and won Carey another shower of awards, including his fourth Miles Franklin Award and his second Booker Prize.

30 Days in Sydney was another departure for Carey, a contribution to a series in which celebrated writers describe the cities they know best. The subtitle, "A wildly distorted account," and Carey's statement that, despite its appearance of recording a thirty-day visit he made to Sydney, some of the book was invented and written in New York, alert the reader that this account will be more fictional than conventional. Carey has Sydney characters tell their personal stories of what he and they see as representative experiences of the elemental, social, and political forces that contribute to the texture of the city. These are embedded in a commentary that reflects on the physical and elemental forces, and the historical experiences that have shaped the ethos of the city. The selection and sequencing of the characters' stories is masterful, rising to a complex and emotionally powerful climax. In the process Carey captures the look, the feel, the history, and the spirit of the city more searchingly and more completely than any travelogue could.

Throughout his career Peter Carey has fictionalized Australia from a variety of perspectives and historical and allegorical removes. The mirror he holds up to late-twentieth-century Australian society and culture, and its international context, never simply reflects. It distorts, like those mirrors in the amusement parks that recur in his work, and it is designed to defamiliarize the object and to allow Carey's readers to see it for the first time. A decade and a half of living in New York has not diminished Carey's fascination with his homeland or the quality of the stories with which it inspires him.

Interviews:

Craig Munro, "Building the Fabulist Extensions," *Makar,* 12 (June 1976): 3–12;

Candida Baker, *Yacker: Australian Writers Talk about Their Work* (Sydney: Pan, 1986), pp. 54–77.

References:

Anthony J. Hassall, *Dancing on Hot Macadam: Peter Carey's Fiction,* third edition (St. Lucia: University of Queensland Press, 1998);

Graham Huggan, *Peter Carey* (Melbourne: Oxford University Press, 1996);

Karen Lamb, *Peter Carey: The Genesis of Fame* (Pymble, N.S.W.: Angus & Robertson, 1992);

Bruce Woodcock, *Peter Carey* (Manchester & New York: Manchester University Press, 1996).

Papers:

Manuscripts for most of Peter Carey's works are in the Fryer Library at the University of Queensland. Some early manuscripts are in the National Library of Australia, and the manuscripts for *True History of the Kelly Gang* and related correspondence are in the State Library of Victoria.

Bruce Dawe

(15 February 1930 –   )

Carmel Bendon Davis
Macquarie University

BOOKS: *No Fixed Address: Poems* (Melbourne: Cheshire, 1962);

A Need of Similar Name (Melbourne: Cheshire, 1965);

An Eye for a Tooth (Melbourne & Canberra: Cheshire, 1968);

Beyond the Subdivisions (Melbourne: Cheshire, 1969);

Heat-Wave: Poems (Bulleen, Vic.: Sweeney Reed, 1970);

Condolences of the Season: Selected Poems (Melbourne: Cheshire, 1971);

Just a Dugong at Twilight: Mainly Light Verse (Melbourne: Cheshire, 1975);

Sometimes Gladness: Collected Poems 1954–1978 (Melbourne: Longman Cheshire, 1978); enlarged as *Sometimes Gladness: Collected Poems 1954–1982* (Melbourne: Longman Cheshire, 1982); enlarged as *Sometimes Gladness: Collected Poems 1954–1987* (Melbourne: Longman Cheshire, 1987); enlarged as *Sometimes Gladness: Collected Poems 1954–1992* (Melbourne: Longman Cheshire, 1992); enlarged as *Sometimes Gladness: Collected Poems 1954–1997* (Melbourne: Longman, 1997);

Five Modern Comic Writers (Toowoomba, Qld.: Dept. of External & Continuing Education, Darling Downs Institute of Advanced Education, 1980);

Over Here, Harv! and Other Stories (Melbourne: Penguin, 1983);

The Wicked Laughing Crow and Other Stories (Edinburgh: Published by the author, 1984);

Towards Sunrise: Poems 1979–1986 (Melbourne: Longman Cheshire, 1986);

This Side of Silence: Poems, 1987–1990 (Melbourne: Longman Cheshire, 1990);

Bruce Dawe: Essays and Opinions, edited by Ken Goodwin (Melbourne: Longman Cheshire, 1990);

The Writer and the Community (Toowoomba, Qld.: University College of Southern Queensland, 1990);

Tributary Streams: Some Sources of Social and Political Concerns in Modern Australian Poetry, The John Murtagh Macrossan Memorial Lecture 1991 (St. Lucia: University of Queensland Press, 1992; Portland, Ore.: University of Queensland Press, 1992);

Bruce Dawe (from the University of Southern Queensland, www.usq.edu.au/faculty/arts/dhis/images/dawe.jpg)

Mortal Instruments: Poems 1990–1995 (Melbourne: Longman, 1995);

A Poet's People (South Melbourne: Addison Wesley Longman, 1999);

The Chewing-Gum Kid (Camberwell, Vic.: Puffin, 2002);

No Cat—and That's That! (Camberwell, Vic.: Puffin, 2002);

Towards a War: Twelve Reflections (Warners Bay, N.S.W., 2002);

*The Headlong Traffic: A Collection of Poems and Prose Mono-
    logues, 1997–2002* (Melbourne: Longman, 2003);
Show and Tell (Camberwell, Vic.: Penguin, 2003).

RECORDINGS: *Bruce Dawe Reads from His Own Work,*
    read by Dawe, St. Lucia, Poets on Record Series,
    University of Queensland Press, 1971;
Some Poems of Bruce Dawe; Selected and Read by the Poet,
    read by Dawe, Sydney, Australian Broadcasting
    Commission, 1978;
Bruce Dawe Reads His Poetry, read by Dawe, Melbourne,
    Longman Cheshire, 1983.

OTHER: *Dimensions,* edited by Dawe (Sydney:
    McGraw-Hill, 1974);
Speaking in Parables, edited by Dawe (Melbourne: Long-
    man Cheshire, 1987);
Foreword, in *Turns of Phrase: Young Queensland Writers,*
    edited by Lawrie Ryan and Ross Clark (St. Lucia:
    University of Queensland Press, 1988).

Bruce Dawe is one of the most successful and
prolific contemporary poets of Australia. In a writing
career that, to date, has spanned five decades, more
than five hundred of Dawe's poems have been published individually and in anthologies. Dawe's poetry
reflects the Australian way of life, representing it in a
language that captures the Australian idiom with its frequently satirical tone, distinctive cadence, and tendency
to understatement. The wide-ranging subject matter of
Dawe's work embodies the ordinary, everyday experiences of urban dwellers as well as displaying the poet's
commitment to social, political, and religious issues.
While some commentators have noted the stylistic
influences of Dylan Thomas, William Butler Yeats, and
W. H. Auden in particular, Dawe draws on multiple
styles, sometimes using them as vehicles of parody to
achieve, overall, a distinctive voice in all his work.

Donald Bruce Dawe was born in Geelong, Victoria, on 15 February 1930, the fourth (and youngest)
child of Alfred James Dawe and Mary Ann Matilda
Hamilton Dawe. Dawe's siblings—Violet, Ethel, and
George—were more than twenty years his senior, and
his father, an unskilled laborer, was often absent from
home looking for work, and so Dawe was thrown onto
his own imaginative resources from an early age, beginning to write poetry at Marshall Primary School (near
Geelong), where he started his education in 1935. At
ten or eleven years of age, he moved to Lee Street Primary School (North Carlton) and at twelve, commenced his high-school education at North Fitzroy
Central School. The transfer to Northcote High School
in 1944 gave impetus to Dawe's interest in poetry. His
English teacher there, George Stirling, encouraged him

to read widely and to aim for publication of his poems.
For this early enterprise Dawe used the pseudonym
Llewellyn Rhys, and several poems under this name
appeared until 1950 in such periodical publications as
The Jindyworobak Anthology and *Junior Age.* In 1945 Dawe
successfully gained his Victorian Intermediate Certificate, but his indifference to all subjects except English—
at which he excelled—prompted him to leave school in
the middle of 1946. Although he found employment as
an office boy for a firm of Melbourne solicitors, Dawe
showed little aptitude or interest in the legal profession,
and he moved on to work in a succession of jobs in
both Melbourne and rural Victoria, which included
stints as an office boy, newspaper copyboy, laborer,
farmhand, and fruit picker.

In 1953 Dawe returned to study for his matriculation at night school in Melbourne. He was successful,
and his results earned him a scholarship to attend Melbourne Secondary Teachers College and the University
of Melbourne.

University life suited Dawe, giving him the intellectual and social stimulation he had been seeking and
the opportunity to contribute poems and stories to various university publications. In the late 1950s and early
1960s Dawe wrote more than twenty short stories,
some of them unpublished at the time, others appearing
in the Melbourne University magazine, *M.U.M.,* the
student newspaper, *Farrago,* and the periodicals *Compass,
Twentieth Century,* and *Today.* These early stories, though
not published until 1983, under the title *Over Here,
Harv! and Other Stories,* presage the thematic concerns
and idiomatic structure of Dawe's poetry. Most obviously, Dawe's interest in ordinary characters and everyday experience is encapsulated in the main protagonists
of the stories, Joey Cassidy and his cohorts. Nothing
about them is heroic, and as Ken Goodwin comments
in his 1988 biography *Adjacent Worlds: A Literary Life of
Bruce Dawe,* "In *Over Here, Harv!* incompetence, inatten-
tion, and bad luck by characters combine to effect wist-
ful or pathetic endings." The stories are an early
indication of Dawe's proclivity to champion the underdog. In addition, the stories exhibit Dawe's early appreciation of the Australian idiom. Joey's manner of
speaking echoes the Australia of an earlier time, and in
the Author's Note to the 1983 edition, Dawe explains
that the stories "reflect the interest I had in the vernacular based on my years of working as a labourer in the
late 1940s and early 1950s. They also reflect the debt I
owe to those writers in the vernacular whose work I
had read and admired: Tim Burstall, Frank Kellaway,
and Frank Sargeson."

At about this time, Dawe's interest in religion and
politics was peaking, and in his first year at the university, he converted to Roman Catholicism. The two

interests converge to underpin much of Dawe's subsequent poetry, imbuing it with the voice of a strong social conscience, a concern for the individual, and the sense of a spiritual reality beyond the everyday struggles. Though university life supported Dawe's ideals, he did not apply himself wholeheartedly to his studies and consequently failed two out of four subjects in his final examination. A return to the unskilled jobs of his youth followed.

In 1959 Dawe enlisted in the Royal Australian Air Force (RAAF), eventually finding his way into the education section, where he remained until he left the service in 1968. His situation in the RAAF enabled him to continue writing poetry, and in 1962 his first collection, *No Fixed Address: Poems*, was published. This collection features forty-seven poems that were written in the period 1954–1962.

The collection received favorable reviews. Dulcie Hall, writing in *Poetry Magazine* (1963), was impressed by the "sharp and penetrating humour" of the poems. David Martin, writing in *The Sydney Bulletin* (1 December 1962), considered that Dawe's poetry accomplished "what poetry alone can do but all too rarely achieves: it touches [the reader] with surprise." Not everyone was as enthusiastic, however, particularly with regard to Dawe's subject matter. Peter Kuch reports in his 1995 critical biography, *Bruce Dawe,* for the Australian Writers series of Oxford University Press, that the critic T. H. Jones, for example, was concerned that Dawe had "caught the current English fashion for 'tough' urban poems deriving their themes from mass culture." In consideration of this opinion, Kuch observes that "Of all the criticisms, this is the most interesting because it points to a number of fundamental issues underlying those poems about contemporary Australian society that have helped to establish Dawe's reputation"–that is, though Jones had suggested that Dawe was emulating the "English fashion," the collection, instead, establishes Dawe's concern with authentically Australian experience. Dawe was not interested in perpetuating the mythical notion of a population of bush characters at a time when the majority of Australians lived in the cities and suburbs. Dawe's focus was on depicting the ordinary and genuine Australian character and experience, and in the 1960s, mass culture was as much a part of life in Australia as it was in other Western nations. Dawe's awareness of this trend is shown to strong effect in "Enter Without so Much as Knocking." Narrative in structure and satirical in tone, the poem charts the life cycle of an individual born into an Australia that is newly enamored of consumerism, the television, the car, and the power of advertising. The poem weaves a clever course between snippets of conversations, the repeated onomatopoeic "beep," and other visual warn-

Dawe and Gloria Blain on their wedding day, 27 January 1964 (from Ken Goodwin, Adjacent Worlds, *1988; Hayden Library, Arizona State University)*

ing signs of modern life and catchy advertising jargon. It became one of Dawe's best-known poems, and the generally positive reception of the volume encouraged Dawe to continue writing when, in 1963, he was transferred for RAAF service to Toowoomba, Queensland. There he met Gloria Blain, whom he married on 27 January 1964 in St. Joseph's Chapel, Toowoomba; in December of the same year the couple's first child, Brian, was born.

In November 1965 Dawe's second collection, *A Need of Similar Name,* was published. Dedicated to his wife, Gloria, this volume features poems that reflect Dawe's recent experience of married life and fatherhood, as well as his continuing interest in politics, religion, and the effects of rising consumerism on the Australian way of life. These latter concerns are melded to satiric effect in such poems as "First Corinthians at the Crossroads," in which Dawe parodies St. Paul's famous letter with the opening lines "When I was a blonde I / walked as a blonde I / talked as a blonde"; and in "Song for the New Americas," in which the cadence of each line mimics that of the American national anthem in a biting satire on the "business as usual" and "fast-talking buck" expedients of "the old

U.S.A." This collection was awarded the prestigious Myer Poetry Prize in 1966.

Dawe received news of the prize while on a six-month posting for the RAAF at Butterworth, Malaysia. In 1966, too, Dawe's twins, Jamie and Katrina, were born, and shortly after, the family returned to Australia, where Dawe assumed a position in the library of Headquarters Support Command in Melbourne. In March 1967 Dawe received the Ampol Arts Award in creative literature, and further success followed in 1969 when he again was awarded the Myer Poetry Prize for his third volume of poetry, *An Eye for a Tooth,* which was published in 1968. The subject matter for the poems of this volume focuses on personal and topical issues. "Katrina," for example, poignantly expresses the parent-poet's feelings of powerlessness as his baby daughter fights for life in a hospital ward. The poem includes finely balanced images–the description of the child's uncertain situation standing as the literal complement to the poet's emotional uncertainty. As the child lies "suspended between earth and sky," the parent-poet finds that he, too, hovers between hope and despair for her recovery. No such emotional ambivalence is present in the four poems that deal with the death of Ronald Ryan, the last person to be legally executed before the abolition of capital punishment in Australia. Discussing these particular poems in his biography of Dawe, Goodwin observes that the poet sides "with the criminal underdog against the sordid trappings of State justice," a position that Dawe consistently assumes in his work. Equally definite stances are evident in the short but bitingly satirical "On the Conferring of an Honorary Doctorate of Law on a Politician" and "For Inscription on a Statue Facing Eastwards" (both from the collection *An Eye for a Tooth*). Poems such as "In the New Landscape" and "The Not-So-Good Earth" (also in *An Eye for a Tooth*) reiterate Dawe's interest in the depersonalizing effects of the new consumerism, particularly society's growing obsession with the car and the television.

In June 1968, at the conclusion of his nine-year contract with the RAAF, Dawe completed, as an external student, the requirements for the award of a B.A. degree from the University of Queensland. In the year of his graduation, 1969, Dawe's fourth child, Melissa, was born, and the family returned to Queensland, settling in Toowoomba where Dawe took up a teaching position at Downlands College, a Catholic high school. Prior to that appointment, the family had had some difficult and unsettled years, so the move to Toowoomba was prompted by Dawe's dismal employment prospects in Melbourne, not by choice. Because Dawe's fourth collection, *Beyond the Subdivisions,* was published at the end of 1969, Dawe's biographer, Goodwin, cognizant of Dawe's personal difficulties at the time, states the belief that the collection ". . . hints at something of a crisis in Dawe's outlook on life and on poetry." Goodwin further considers that the collection includes "poems with awkward loose ends, poems too generalized to be readily comprehensible–perhaps generalized away from embarrassing specificity–and poems with odd changes of linguistic level. More poems than in any other volume are about the practice of writing poetry, as if Dawe were questioning or seeking to justify his profession." The public reaction to the collection, however, was generally positive, and the general-specific nexus was seen by some critics as indicative of Dawe's empathy with the "common people." Alan Riddell, for example, in his review for *The Sydney Morning Herald* of 7 November 1970 comments on the "panache and freshness" of the collection, achieved, in part, by Dawe's ability to reach "out from the private pain towards a common denominator of shared experience." Truth probably rests in both Goodwin's and Riddell's views of the collection, the experience of those difficult years acting as both a spur and an impediment to the creative process. What is more certain, however, is that with the improvement in the family's financial situation as a result of Dawe's permanent teaching position, Dawe entered one of his most productive and successful phases.

In 1970, *Heat-Wave: Poems,* a pamphlet of seven poems, was published. It was followed in 1971 with the publication of Dawe's first retrospective collection, *Condolences of the Season: Selected Poems.* As Goodwin points out, this volume "had an initial print run of 5000, but it was so successful that a further run of 10 000 was required in 1972." Philip Roberts, writing in *The Sydney Morning Herald* of 20 May 1972, considers that this "publication of 85 of [Dawe's] poems from earlier collections, together with 19 new ones . . . presents the best of this very seminal poet and . . . shows how (in what way) Dawe has influenced so many other Australian poets." This collection, with its topical concerns and accessible Australian idiomatic language, made the collection eminently suitable for general English study at the high-school level, and part of Dawe's success is attributable to the increasing interest in his poetry shown by the education departments of several Australian states. *Condolences of the Season* was awarded the Dame Mary Gilmore Medal of the Australian Literature Society in 1973.

In 1972 Dawe had taken up a position as lecturer in literature at the Darling Downs Institute of Advanced Education, Toowoomba, and his teaching and work on two research degrees vied for attention with his poetry writing. He graduated with a Bachelor of Letters (B.Litt.) from the University of New England (in northern New South Wales) in 1973. In 1974 the

*Dawe with his wife and children, Melissa (front), Katrina, Brian and Jamie (standing), at Melissa's confirmation,
Holy Name Parish School, Toowoomba, 1974 (from Ken Goodwin,* Adjacent Worlds,
1988; Hayden Library, Arizona State University)

Dimensions volume was published, and in 1975 Dawe was awarded a Master of Arts from the University of Queensland. In 1975 the collection *Just a Dugong at Twilight: Mainly Light Verse* was published. All the poems in this collection had appeared first in the Toowoomba newspaper, *The Chronicle,* as comments and reflections on current news items. The opening poem, from which the collection takes its title, is introduced with the comment that "A television set has been installed in the gorillas' cage at Frankfurt Zoo to stop them getting bored. The zoo's director says their favorites are scenes, weight-lifting and motor-racing." The poem that follows is a humorous look into the world of caged gorillas, from the gorillas' point of view. The majority of the poems in the volume deal with other light-hearted news topics, such as the popularity of nudity in stage plays, pigeons on the town hall roof, and the demise of newspaper as gift-wrapping paper. The success of this volume speaks both for Dawe's facility for drawing poetic inspiration from the most ordinary

sources and the public's acceptance of poetry in general.

Several of these popular and topical poems became part of Dawe's next published volume, *Sometimes Gladness: Collected Poems 1954–1978.* Published in 1978 with a clear view to the high-school study market, this collection was well received, not only by the general public but also by other poets. Fellow poet Les Murray, reviewing the collection in the "Good Weekend" supplement of *The Sydney Morning Herald* on 3 February 1979, notes that Dawe's work shows a "wonderfully modulated command of vernacular language and concerns" and that the poems "reflect, and reflect widely on, the common experience of urban and suburban Australia . . . [and] are often genuinely in touch, and more open to a participatory compassion and acceptance than most recent Australian writing," though Murray laments that "few of the best Dawe poems [of the volume] are recent." Of the recent poems in the volume, "Teaching the Syllabus" is representative of Dawe's personal experience in the 1970s. The poem compares the imposition of a strict teaching syllabus on students to training animals to perform tricks. The strict rhythm and rhyming pattern of the poem, together with the repetition of the word *teaching* as the leading word in all but the last six lines of the poem, recreates the atmosphere of the classroom "drill" and builds to a somewhat plaintive ending, in which the poet begs "to teach them one thing more, / the thing that in the process they've forgotten: / Dogs, to bark again; lions to roar . . . ," that is, to be themselves. Other new additions to the collection highlighted Dawe's continuing interest in politics, particularly issues affecting Queensland in that period and his support of the rights of the individual within the state. Geoffrey Dutton, writing in *The Sydney Bulletin* on 16 January 1979, considers that "Dawe has emerged as the most eloquent and deadly of the opponents of the law-and-order arrangements of [Premier] Joh Bjelke-Petersen." *Sometimes Gladness* was awarded the Grace Leven Poetry Prize in 1978 and was declared the Braille Book of the Year in 1979. In 1980 Dawe received the Patrick White Literary Award. In the same year he graduated with a Ph.D. from the University of Queensland and took up the position of senior lecturer in literature in the School of Arts at the Darling Downs Institute of Advanced Education. By 1983 Dawe had earned the position of senior teaching fellow at the institute, and the continuing interest in the *Sometimes Gladness* volume resulted in its being revised, expanded, and republished as *Sometimes Gladness: Collected Poems 1954–1982*. This new volume coincided with the publication of Dawe's short-story collection *Over Here, Harv! and Other Stories,* which was named one of the Ten Best Australian Books of the Decade in 1984. Further success followed in the same year when Dawe received the Christopher Brennan Award for poetry.

In 1985 Dawe accepted a position as senior lecturer in the School of Arts at the University of South Queensland, and in 1986 *Towards Sunrise: Poems 1979–1986* was published. This volume featured twenty-seven poems from *Sometimes Gladness* and forty-two new poems. Many of the new additions reassert Dawe's political concerns. The monologue "Las Desaparacidas" dramatizes an extremist's view as he seeks to justify the political torture of dissenters in Guatemala. On a lighter political note, the satirical "New Readers, Begin Here . . ." caricatures both the appearances and public personas of the Australian prime ministers Malcolm Fraser (1975–1983) and Bob Hawke (1983–1991). "At a Literature Board Gathering" is another satirical, often scathing, observation about the posturing of some of the more arrogant board members and the more sycophantic contenders for literary grants. This poem is

reflective of Dawe's own experience, as are other works, such as "Physiotherapy Psalm" and "Writer-in-Residence, U. of Q." Judith Rodriguez, writing in *The Sydney Morning Herald* on 14 March 1987, praises this volume for its "particularly strong and varied final line-up [that] spans Dawe's range, from the bite on grit to the lighted place of love and concern."

Always present in Dawe's range is his strong religious conviction, and it has been the foundation for many of his poems over the years. In 1986 and 1987 Dawe wrote many poems on religious themes for publication in such newspapers as the *Catholic Worker,* and in 1987 his volume based on the parables of the New Testament, *Speaking in Parables,* was published. In 1987 *Sometimes Gladness: Collected Poems 1954–1987* was published. This third edition of the popular title included poems from *Towards Sunrise* and some of Dawe's religious poems of the mid 1980s. One poem in the collection from this period is "Mary and the Angel," in which Dawe draws a parallel between the Virgin Mary's reception of the angel Gabriel's news of her impending pregnancy and the situation of a fifteen-year-old girl being taken by her mother to a gynecologist for a tubal ligation. The analogy pivots on questions of the morality of medical and social intervention in the fertility and pregnancy process, juxtaposing the contemporary desire for "an all-round future beautifully planned" and the acceptance of the inevitable vicissitudes of life with an evocation of the Virgin Mary as the model of acceptance. This poem is indicative of Dawe's willingness to engage with topical matters and to take a definite (and sometimes unpopular) stance on controversial issues.

Political and social comment form the foundation for many of the poems in Dawe's 1990 collection, *This Side of Silence: Poems, 1987–1990.* A strong criticism undercut with pathos is found in "On the Shadow of a Japanese Child Blasted upon a Wall after the Dropping of an Atomic Bomb in 1945." This poem is a powerful sketch of the pain suffered by the parents of the "child" of the poem, their initial hopes for her young life to be full of "the usual things: / the time of toys, of dolls with black fringed hair, / and pull-along wooden ducks" dashed when everything becomes "suddenly phantasmal, / including you, our beloved daughter." This somber poem finds its opposite reflection in the jubilant and personal "Katrina's Wedding," in which proud father Dawe remembers and rejoices in his daughter's achievements as he walks her down the aisle.

In 1992, the fourth edition of *Sometimes Gladness: Collected Poems* was published. Dawe's own considerable achievements were honored publicly in 1992 when he was made an officer of the Order of Australia (OA) for his services to literature. Further recognition of Dawe's achievements was demonstrated in 1993 when he

Dust jacket for Dawe's 1969 collection, including several poems about writing poetry
(Bruccoli Clark Layman Archives)

retired from his position of associate professor of literature at the University of South Queensland and was made an honorary professor.

Another collection, *Mortal Instruments: Poems 1990–1995,* was published in 1995. Dedicated to Dawe's earlier biographer, Ken Goodwin, it includes many works that had appeared first in a variety of newspapers and poetry journals, and it features the well-established and wide-ranging interests of the poet, from the cutting irony of "Revelations Revisited" to the lighthearted "To My Moustache." Heather Cam, reviewing the collection for *The Sydney Morning Herald* of 30 September 1995, describes it as "poetry for Everyman, immensely satisfying to read . . . [and with a] voice [that] is clear, measured, cadenced and artfully natural with a wry sense of goodnatured humour [that] alerts [us] to the human fallibilities flesh is prone to." This ability to appeal to all strata of society culminated, in 1997, in the award to Dawe of the inaugural Philip Hodgins Memorial Medal for Literary Excellence.

Dawe's *A Poet's People,* published in 1999, is a collection of both new poems and poems from previous publications. Though featuring Dawe's particular mix of humor, satire, and social comment, this volume

offers some poems of an extremely personal nature. Dedicated to his recently deceased wife, Gloria, the final two poems of the volume, "For Gloria, In Her Final Illness" and "In Retrospect," in particular, sum up many of Dawe's concerns throughout his literary career. The movingly expressed emotions of mingled love, grief, and acceptance of death in these final poems work toward consolidating the undercurrents of philosophical and religious interests of this and the poems of other volumes. In the final words of the last poem of the volume, "In Retrospect," the poet marvels at his wife's courage and reflects that

> You had no fear of what would come, as though you had
> Forseen that Calvary—this, I find
> Most wonderful and most difficult to bear,
> And Heaven—a state I never gave much heed
> —Now that it holds you, seems more real than Earth.

In this poem Dawe muses on the joy and the pain inherent in everyday experience and marvels at the strength of the human character in the face of adversity; he juxtaposes the "ordinary" with the "extraordinary" in an expression of faith in the coexistence of the secular and the sacred. Other poems in the collection deal with a broad range of social and personal concerns and exhibit the same sharp insight and complexity of tone that have become Dawe's trademarks. Contemporary fears, such as "stranger danger," for example, are addressed in such poems as "Ceremonies of Innocence," in which the poet mourns the loss of freedom for modern generations of children and their preclusion from discovering "possibly wonderful strangers" because of adults' fears of children discovering "that other sort" of stranger. While Dawe is not dismissing the danger, he reminds his readers that "(the terrible is not a contemporary invention, however we conjugate fear)," and he is, perhaps, reflecting on the diverse range of characters who, over the years, have helped form the fabric of his poetry.

Bruce Dawe lives in Queensland's Sunshine Coast area with his second wife, Elizabeth Qualtrough, whom he married 9 October 1999. In 1999 he endowed the Bruce Dawe National Poetry Prize. This prize, held in trust by the University of Southern Queensland, offers an annual $1,000 award "to encourage emerging poets throughout Australia." It is an appropriate endowment that encapsulates Dawe's enormous contribution and abiding commitment to the development and continuance of an authentically Australian poetry.

Interviews:

Roger McDonald, "Bruce Dawe: An Interview with Roger McDonald," *Australian Writers on Tape* (St. Lucia: University of Queensland Press, 1973);

Paul Kavanagh and Peter Kuch, "'The Fire i' the Flint': An Interview with Bruce Dawe," *Southerly,* 43, no. 1 (1983);

Suzanne Hayes, "Conversations," Audio Tape Series, tapes 28 and 29, Adelaide, Media Unit, Adelaide College of TAFE, 1988.

Bibliographies:

Robert L. Ross, *Australian Literary Criticism–1945–1988. An Annotated Bibliography* (New York & London: Garland, 1989);

Martin Duwell, Marianne Ehrhardt, and Carol Hetherington, *The* ALS *Guide to Australian Writers. A Bibliography 1963–1995,* second edition (St. Lucia: University of Queensland Press, 1997).

Biographies:

Basil Shaw, *Times and Seasons: An Introduction to Bruce Dawe* (Melbourne: Cheshire, 1974);

Ken Goodwin, *Adjacent Worlds: A Literary Life of Bruce Dawe* (Melbourne: Longman Cheshire, 1988).

References:

Dennis Haskell, *Attuned to Alien Moonlight: The Poetry of Bruce Dawe* (St. Lucia: University of Queensland Press, 2002);

Peter Kuch, *Australian Writers: Bruce Dawe* (Melbourne: Oxford University Press, 1995).

Papers:

The Australian National Library, Canberra, and the Fryer Library, University of Queensland, St. Lucia, hold collections of Bruce Dawe's papers.

Sumner Locke Elliott

(17 October 1917 – 24 June 1991)

Sharon Clarke
Boston University Sydney Internship Program

BOOKS: *Interval: A Play in Three Acts* (Melbourne & London: Melbourne University Press in association with Oxford University Press, 1942);

Buy Me Blue Ribbons, Comedy in Three Acts (New York: Dramatists Play Service, 1952);

Careful, He Might Hear You (New York: Harper & Row, 1963; London: Gollancz, 1963);

Some Doves and Pythons (New York: Harper & Row, 1966; London: Gollancz, 1966);

Edens Lost (New York: Harper & Row, 1969; London: Joseph, 1970; Melbourne: Sun Books, 1980);

The Man Who Got Away (New York: Harper & Row, 1972; London: Joseph, 1973);

Going (New York: Harper & Row, 1975; London: W. H. Allen, 1975; South Melbourne, Vic.: Macmillan, 1975);

Water under the Bridge (New York: Simon & Schuster, 1977; South Melbourne, Vic.: Macmillan, 1977; London: Hamilton, 1978);

Rusty Bugles [revised edition] (Sydney: Currency Press, 1980);

Signs of Life (New Haven, Conn.: Ticknor & Fields, 1981; Ringwood, Vic. & Harmondsworth, U.K.: Penguin, 1982);

About Tilly Beamis (New York: Watts, 1984; London: Pavanne, 1985);

Waiting for Childhood (New York: Harper & Row, 1987; Sydney: Pan, 1988);

Fairyland (New York: Harper & Row, 1990; Sydney: Pan, 1991);

Radio Days, edited by Sharon Clarke (Sydney: Angus & Robertson, 1993).

PLAY PRODUCTIONS: *The Cow Jumped over the Moon,* Sydney, Independent Theatre, 1937; Hollywood, The Call Board Theatre, 1938;

Interval, Sydney, Independent Theatre, 1939;

Little Sheep Run Fast, Sydney, Independent Theatre, 1941;

Goodbye to the Music, Sydney, Independent Theatre, 1942;

Sumner Locke Elliott (from Sharon Clarke, Sumner Locke Elliott, *1996; Robert W. Woodruff Library, Emory University)*

Your Obedient Servant, Sydney, Independent Theatre, 1943;

Invisible Circus, Sydney, Independent Theatre, 1946;

Rusty Bugles, Sydney, Independent Theatre, 1948;

Buy Me Blue Ribbons, New York, The Empire Theatre, Broadway, 1951;

John Murray Anderson's Almanac, New York, Imperial Theatre, 1953.

PRODUCED SCRIPTS: *When Dawson Died,* radio, 2SM (Sydney), 1935;

1937–1945

David and Dawn and the Sea Fairies, radio, 2UW;

The Laughing Man, radio, 2UW;

The Blind Man's House, radio, 2UW;

Girl of the Ballet, Two Destinies, and *Tales of Hollywood,*
    radio, 2UW;
Following Father's Footsteps, radio, 2UW;
The Crazy Family, radio, 2UW;
Trademen's Entrance, radio, 2UW;
Jezebel's Daughter, radio, 2UW;
Scarlet Rhapsody, radio, 2UW;
Man in the Dark, radio, 2UW;
Wicked Is the Vine, television, *Kraft,* NBC, 1949;
The Crater, television, *Lights Out,* NBC, 1949;
Pengallen's Bell, television, *Lights Out,* NBC, 1949;
Of Human Bondage, television, *Studio One,* CBS, 1949;
Jane Eyre, television, *Studio One,* CBS, 1950;
The Willow Cabin, television, *Studio One,* CBS, 1950;
Little Women, television, *Studio One,* CBS, 1951;
Old Jim's Other Woman, television, *The Web,* CBS, 1951;
Dusty Portrait, television, *Philco,* NBC, 1952;
We Were Children, television, *Philco,* NBC, 1952;
The Thin Air, television, *Philco,* NBC, 1952;
Wish on the Moon, television, *Philco,* NBC, 1953;
Fade Out, television, *Philco,* NBC, 1953;
The Girl with the Stopwatch, television, *Philco,* NBC, 1953;
Buy Me Blue Ribbons, television, *Philco,* NBC, 1954;
The King and Mrs. Candle, television, *Philco,* NBC, 1954;
Friday the Thirteenth, television, *Philco,* NBC, 1954;
Run, Girl, Run, television, *Philco,* NBC, 1955;
Beloved Stranger, television, *Philco,* NBC, 1955;
Peter Pan, television, *Producer's Showcase,* NBC, 1955;
Daisy, Daisy, television, *Playwrights 56,* NBC, 1956;
You and Me and the Gatepost, television, *Playwrights 56,* NBC, 1956;
Keyhole, television, *Playwrights 56,* NBC, 1956;
Love at Fourth Sight, television, *Studio One,* CBS, 1957;
Whereabouts Unknown, television, *Kaiser,* NBC, 1957;
Babe in the Woods, television, *Studio One,* CBS, 1957;
Mrs. Gilling and the Skyscraper, television, *Alcoa,* NBC, 1957;
The Laughing Willow, television, *Studio One,* NBC, 1958;
Wish on the Moon, television, *U.S. Steel Hour,* CBS, 1959;
The Grey Nurse Said Nothing, television, *Playhouse 90,* CBS, 1959;
Hedda Hopper's Hollywood, television, *Special,* NBC, 1959;
I Heard You Calling Me, television, *Way Out,* CBS, 1961.

OTHER: "The Cracked Lens," *Harper's* (December 1960);
Rusty Bugles, in *Khaki, Bush and Bigotry: Three Australian Plays,* edited by Eunice Hanger (St. Lucia: University of Queensland Press, 1968; Minneapolis: University of Minnesota Press, 1968), pp. 24–26;
"Where are all my books?" *Australian Author* (Spring 1974);
"The Man of 1000 Voices," *Bulletin* (22 July 1980): 56–62;
"Against Nostalgia," *Writer* (Boston) (February 1988).

Sumner Locke Elliott was an expatriate Australian novelist and former radio, television, and stage dramatist, whose birth in Kogarah, a southern suburb of Sydney, on 17 October 1917, resulted in the death of his mother the following day. The responsibility he carried, both as child and adult, from his knowledge of this consequence–coupled with his father's almost immediate formal abandonment of him–directed the course of much of Elliott's life and writing.

The search for both mother and self dominates Elliott's work, particularly his novels, the realist form of which provided him with a sense of control over the temporal and spatial boundaries of his life: Elliott never diverted from the exploration of self and family as his canvas, nor did he cease exploring the distortion of time, place, and circumstance to produce a shifting in outcome, a testing of apparent truth. While frequently declaring himself a great believer in "Fate," Elliott's continual remapping of his own and his family's life through his writing seems to challenge its finality. His stories consider the other narrative possibilities Fate might have taken. In this sense many of his novels, in particular, are fictional autobiographies. "I think autobiography happens automatically for me," Elliott observed. "Memory is the strongest power I have; it is my lifeline to the truth" (Jeremy Eccles, "Careful He Remembers," *Sydney Morning Herald,* 27 February 1989). With the exception of *Careful, He Might Hear You* (1963), which is a thinly veiled account of his own boyhood, Elliott rarely confines his autobiographical inscription to one character or one gender; rather, the author's own life informs several characters, often of different genders, within the same story.

While Elliott was writing seriously from the age of fourteen, not until the publication of his first novel, *Careful, He Might Hear You,* when he was in his forties, did he gain worldwide recognition from both critics and the reading public. The book sold ten million copies worldwide in the first ten years of publication. Even in his native Australia, where early reception of *Careful, He Might Hear You* was somewhat indifferent, Elliott was praised for his debunking of the myth that Australia was a classless society, and he received the prestigious Miles Franklin Award for Literature in 1963. In this first novel his detailed evocation of 1930s Sydney and his innovative narrative form–a complex weave of stream of consciousness and free indirect discourse in which he inventively juxtaposed scene and point of view–brought praise from contemporary reviewers. Elliott's fine ear for dialogue and the cinematic quality of his prose–where the encoded landscape is experienced through character rather than described by narrator–owe much to the author's earlier writing for other media. Elliott was a playwright and dramatist who evolved into a novelist.

In Australia during the 1930s and 1940s Elliott established himself as a playwright for the Independent Theatre in Sydney–run by the first great mentor of his life, Doris Fitton–and a radio dramatist for the George Edwards' Studios, the largest operation of its kind in the Southern Hemisphere. He earned success in both arenas: his radio serial scripts were broadcast nationally when he was only nineteen years old, and one of his stage plays, *The Cow Jumped over the Moon* (1937), was produced in both Sydney and Hollywood before Elliott turned twenty-one. His minor celebrity status in both fields continued throughout his young adulthood.

Elliott had returned to Sydney after World War II, when he did military service in the Northern Territory, to discover that both it and broader Australia had become a conservative and repressive society. As a covert homosexual Elliott found the homophobic environment of his native land intolerable and moved to New York in 1948, breaking into what was then the new medium of television, for which he wrote hour-long screenplays for almost fifteen years. Elliott rose to be counted among the top seven television dramatists in a country still generally acknowledged to be the television mecca of the world. The group was described as "the golden seven" by *The New York Herald Tribune* in 1958. During this same period he also wrote for the Broadway stage–*Buy Me Blue Ribbons* (1951)–and theater always remained his preferred medium. However, the prose fiction form of the novel was the means through which he discovered his real voice: his heart was the play, but his mind was the novel. Of his eleven books, seven have an Australian focus, exploring fictionally the uneasy relationship which the exiled author had with himself, his family, and his homeland.

As the only child of the deceased Australian novelist, poet, and playwright Helena Sumner Locke (1881–1917) and the journalist, sometime accountant, Henry Logan Elliott (1880–1939), who was serving with Australian troops in France at the time of his son's birth–the infant Sumner was placed in the joint legal guardianship of two of his maternal aunts, Lily Locke Burns, married but childless and then aged forty-eight, and her younger unmarried sister, Jessie Locke, who was then thirty-eight years old and living as companion to a wealthy cousin in England. The latter returned home to Australia when her nephew was three and triggered a family dispute over his custody that eventually led the warring sisters to the Supreme Court of New South Wales. This incident was the impetus for Elliott's first novel, *Careful, He Might Hear You,* in which Lily appears as Lila Baines and Jessie as Vanessa Scott.

Elliott's rendering of this part of his life takes place during a symbolic nine-month period, as P.S. (the author's fictional counterpart), who has been so named

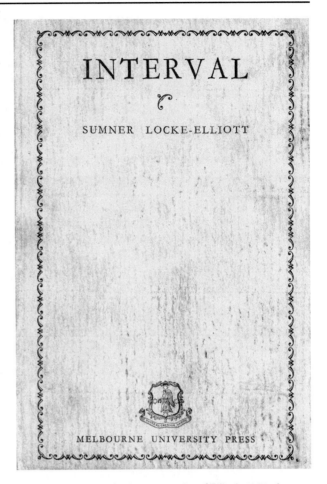

Paperback cover for the 1942 version of Elliott's 1939 play (Bruccoli Clark Layman Archives)

because he is a postscript to his writer-mother's "ridiculous life," travels through a rebirthing and reaches a metamorphosis as "Bill," a seven-year-old boy who proclaims a new identity. In reality, this period of Elliott's life was closer to nine years, as the infant, child, and then adolescent was emotionally and physically torn apart, living a life divided between two aunts and two houses–at one point spending half a week in each–and in the process traversing the jarring divide of the distinctly upper and lower classes of Australian society. Sharon Clarke in her 1996 biography of Elliott quotes him as commenting, "At my Aunt Jessie's we did have a cook and a maid and it was up in Vaucluse, in a very superior part of Sydney. And there was of course a dramatic difference for a child to adjust to a tiny suburban cottage in Carlton where I lived with my aunt Lily . . . [and where] they were always broke."

By the time of the New South Wales Supreme Court case over his custody, Elliott was almost twelve years old. The judge ruled that the child be placed in a boarding school rather than in the care of either aunt. Not until Jessie Locke's sudden death from a heart attack

Elliott on his thirty-fourth birthday, 17 October 1951, in New York City for the premiere of his first play produced on Broadway (from Sharon Clarke, Sumner Locke Elliott, *1996; Robert W. Woodruff Library, Emory University)*

a year later–not from the ferry accident drawn from history that the author used so convincingly to portray her demise in *Careful, He Might Hear You*–was Elliott, who found life as a boarder at Cranbrook School in Sydney to be totally repugnant, reunited with his aunt Lily and uncle George. His aunt Jessie inspired many of the cold-hearted and aloof women characters he later wrote about, usually cast as attractive and superficially polished but emotionally stunted figures: Eve in *Edens Lost* (1969) and Mother VanZandt in *About Tilly Beamis* (1984) present less obvious examples.

During his boyhood years of torment Elliott had often wished Jessie dead–"the thought occurs to me occasionally that it was deliberate homicide," he once wrote in *Waiting for Childhood* (1987), and her death recurs with startling regularity in his books and screenplays. Through Elliott's rewriting of the past, Jessie Locke is given many chances to redeem herself, but falling short, she is most often killed off in the end.

Several other of Elliott's maternal aunts are also prominent fictional characters in his novels. Lily, in particular, appears in his books–as the heroic homemaker and "real" mother figure in *Careful, He Might Hear You, Waiting for Childhood,* and *Fairyland* (1990). His aunt Agnes Locke, usually retaining her own name–as the misunderstood but misguided outcast and sometimes religiously fanatic character–appears in *Careful, He Might Hear You*

and *Waiting for Childhood.* His aunt Blanche Locke, who, as the wild bohemian, retains a freshness as Vere in *Careful, He Might Hear You,* also appears as Mig in *Waiting for Childhood* but is martyred by ersatz motherhood in *Water under the Bridge* (1977). Yet, as Elliott signaled by dedicating his first novel "For H.S.L." (Helena Sumner Locke), his unknown mother was the person whom he endeavored to retrieve through his writing. She is a strong presence in many of his novels and inspired the characters of Sinden in *Careful, He Might Hear You,* who dies after the birth of her son, P.S.; Victoria in *Edens Lost,* whose death leaves her young son, Angus, in the care of an aunt; "little Uke" in *Water under the Bridge,* who, along with her husband, dies during the flu epidemic that struck Sydney in the 1920s, leaving her infant son, Neil, in the care of an old vaudeville friend; Sidney Lord in *Waiting for Childhood,* who dies shortly after giving birth to a son who also dies; and Hope Daly, the "little Soldier Woman" in *Fairyland,* who pines so for her dead husband that she dies, leaving her infant son, Seaton, to be raised by a close cousin.

The experience of his childhood and adolescence is central to most of Elliott's writing. His acute sense of otherness–resulting from his family situation and his developing awareness, as a young boy of ten, of his alternate sexual orientation and of imminent abandonment, as a result of his mother's death and his alcoholic father's defection—left psychological scars on Elliott that only his writing could heal. Because of the unusual circumstances of Elliott's childhood, he was dissuaded from calling anyone "Mother."

Themes of entrapment and escape and the character of the outsider are prevalent not only in the psychodramas of his novels but also in many of his television plays—*Keyhole* (1956), *Mrs. Gilling and the Skyscraper* (1957), and *Whereabouts Unknown* (1957) stand as examples—as well as in his most celebrated stage play, *Rusty Bugles* (first performed, 1948). While his homosexuality—not publicly acknowledged by him until he was in his seventies when his final full-length novel *Fairyland* was published—and his concomitant self-loathing, which plagued him throughout his young and middle adult years, informs such themes and character studies, his childhood experience of difference provided his earliest insights. As Elliott once declared, according to Clarke's biography, "It isn't only homosexuals who are outsiders." In his novels many of Elliott's autobiographical characters reflect his own anguished need to escape the pains of his childhood situation and are transformed by a new landscape: Angus in *Edens Lost* ventures to the Blue Mountains; Neil in *Water under the Bridge* sheds the shackles of responsibility by leaving Australia for England; and Tilly in *About Tilly Beamis* reinvents herself as Tanya Bond in America. Other characters, such as Virginia Green in *Going* (1975), "escape" through death, as the author always thought his mother had done. One of Elliott's American novels, moreover, is called *The Man Who Got Away* (1972) and is about a character who regresses through his life to arrive back at his own infancy, in much the same way as the older Elliott continued to do through his writing.

In 1948 Elliott arranged his own physical escape from the expectations of his family—none of whom could have accepted his homosexuality—and from the conservatism of Australia, by gaining entry to live and work in America. His youthful success in Sydney theater and radio had faded after the war: he was approaching his thirty-first birthday and no longer could consider himself "the boy playwright." During the time he was waiting to be demobilized from the army and waiting for authority to move to America, he had written *Rusty Bugles*—his most celebrated and controversial stage play—based on his time serving at an ordnance depot in Mataranka in the Northern Territory of Australia during World War II. This play depicted the genuine but markedly different heroism of those men with whom he served in the back blocks of the war, where the "enemy" was boredom, heat, illness, and depression. The play was written in the words and nuances of the raw Australian language and accent (and was initially banned because of its ripe language before enjoying a two-year season nationally and causing a revision of Australian censorship laws). How-

Paperback cover for the 1988 edition of Elliott's 1987 novel, in which the character Sidney, who dies in childbirth, is based on Elliott's mother (Bruccoli Clark Layman Archives)

ever, even Fitton and the Independent Theatre showed little interest, as the feeling was that audiences were sick of the war. *Rusty Bugles* became a hit after the author had left Australia, and he never saw a production of the two-year season. The success of the play was seven years in advance of Ray Lawler's *Summer of the Seventeenth Doll* (first performed 1955), which is usually heralded as the first play to portray Australian accents on stage.

Following his arrival in New York in August 1948, Elliott spent several anxious months, reliant on friends and living almost a hand-to-mouth existence, before he began to establish himself in the fledgling medium of television with the CBS network. In 1951 he wrote a play for Broadway, *Buy Me Blue Ribbons*, which, as he later commented, in an interview with Gwen Plumb in 1974, "was the last flop to play the beautiful Empire Theatre,

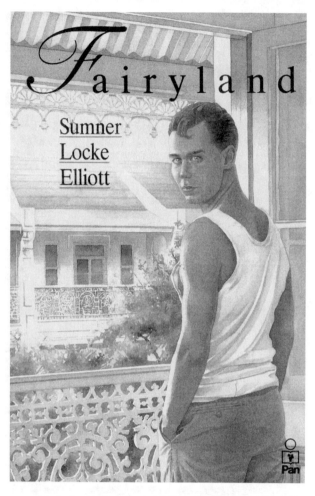

Paperback cover for Elliott's 1990 novel, about the loneliness of homosexuals (Bruccoli Clark Layman Archives)

now torn down." Yet, this Broadway foray, unsuccessful largely because of the inexperience of the young producer, Jay Robinson, who was also the lead actor, failed to diminish Elliott's desire to write for the stage. Even while working on his last, unfinished novel, *Radio Days* (1993), he was talking of "doing a play next." Most of his novels, in fact, continued to unfold in scenes and parts rather than chapters.

If Broadway proved a disappointment, Elliott's television career was flourishing, especially, in 1952, when he moved to the National Broadcasting Company (NBC) and met the second mentor of his artist life, Fred Coe. The hour-long original screenplays Elliott wrote under Coe's guidance for the NBC *Philco Television Playhouse,* which later alternated with *The Goodyear Theatre,* established Elliott as a leading writer in the medium. His 1952 script *The Thin Air* was studied in the drama course at Dartmouth College; his script *Keyhole* was a self-reflexive piece and one of the earliest explorations of the medium of television, revealing its ability to manipu-

late facts and details; and his script *Mrs. Gilling and the Skyscraper,* while making pertinent social comment on the architectural loss of old New York, also acquired an Emmy Award for Helen Hayes as best dramatic actress. Elliott's enthusiasm for the medium did not wane until the television industry began to move from New York to the West Coast.

After a disastrous Hollywood television assignment in 1959, *Hedda Hopper's Hollywood,* Elliott realized he could never live in California, and to survive in New York he needed to find a new career path. Years later, according to Jane Nicholls, he remembered that he tried writing prose for the first time: "I stepped into it and it was just as if I'd learned to skate."

Committing to his first novel in 1960 meant Elliott had to decline the offer of another Broadway play. Yet, his description of the moment as reported by Clarke suggests little regret: "I was sitting in the Palm Court of the Plaza Hotel being offered a Broadway musical to star Ray Bolger . . . But I got up and was slightly surprised to hear myself say: 'No . . . thank you. I'm not available. I'm going to write a novel.'" While finishing his last scripts for Fred Coe between 1960 and 1962, he wrote *Careful, He Might Hear You,* which was released to worldwide acclaim, particularly in the United States, where it was bought by *Reader's Digest,* which agreed to produce three million copies. Elliott was given a fifteen-minute television spot on the *Today Show* at NBC, his old network. Print reviews from well-regarded literary critics, such as Jean Stafford in *Cosmopolitan* (April 1963), were glowing. Around the world the reception was the same: only in Australia was there indifference, a response that confirmed Elliott's long-held belief that his home country offered only begrudging praise to its own artists.

In the decades that followed, Elliott continued to produce a novel every two to three years: his second, *Some Doves and Pythons* (1966), suffered by comparison with *Careful, He Might Hear You.* This was one of Elliott's four American novels, which, with the exception of *Going,* failed to match the success of those books for which he used Australia as his landscape of imagination. In her 1993 thesis Clarke quotes Elliott as saying just before his death: "It's *my* time: the thirties and forties in Australia. It's a place not in existence anymore. But I can see the Sydney tram coming round the corner now." Elliott's detailed recall of "his time" breathes life into the period setting of Sydney and allows the city to emerge as one of the main characters in many of his novels. While he frequently declared that each novel would be his "last Australian book," he was, it appears, involuntarily drawn back to his native land, his family, and the time of his youth to find his wellspring of inspiration: *Careful, He Might Hear You, Edens Lost, Water under the Bridge, About*

Tilly Beamis, Waiting for Childhood, Fairyland, and *Radio Days* all stand as evidence.

Throughout most of his life Elliott had remained without a significant and permanent partner, although he had established a wide circle of friends and a substitute family among Fred Coe and his NBC colleagues. One of this "family," Tad Mosel, remembers Elliott as a lonely man: "Sometimes I'd bump into him at a restaurant, where he'd be having supper alone, reading a book." Elliott inscribed his personal loneliness onto the characters of his television plays and novels, but his writing did little to exorcise his own sense of isolation. This pattern changed in 1977 when Elliott met Whitfield Cook, a former Hitchcock writer, playwright, and novelist. Their lasting relationship, in which the men shared an apartment in New York and a summer house in New Hampshire, provided Elliott with the security and sense of belonging he had never known before. In this environment he continued to flourish, both personally and professionally, until his death from cancer in New York on 24 June 1991.

Largely due to his decision to become an American citizen in 1955, Sumner Locke Elliott has never received the critical recognition from his homeland due his body of work. This fact was cited in 1978 by Patrick White, Australia's only Nobel Prize–winning author, when he awarded Elliott the Patrick White Prize for Literature. According to Bruce Beresford, White considered Elliott to be the finest living Australian novelist, apart from himself. *Careful, He Might Hear You,* however, remains one of the best-loved books in Australia and is still in print, almost forty years after its poor reception on its initial publication.

Elliott in 1991, a few months before his death (photograph by Bob Cato)

Interviews:

Gwen Plumb, "An Interview with Sumner Locke Elliott," *Gwen Plumb Show,* Sydney Radio 2UW, 1974;

Jenny Palmer, "PS: We Hear You–Sumner Locke Elliott: An Interview in New York" *Bulletin* (27 December 1983);

Candida Baker, *Yacker 2: Australian Writers Talk about Their Work* (1987), pp. 42–70.

Biography:

Sharon Clarke, *Sumner Locke Elliott: Writing Life: A Biography* (St. Leonards, N.S.W.: Allen & Unwin, 1996).

References:

Piers Akerman, "Prize for a Prodigal Who Didn't Come Back," *Age* (Melbourne), 28 November 1977;

Bruce Beresford, "Obituary Notice: Sumner Locke Elliott (1917–1991)," *London Independent,* 29 June 1991;

Sharon Clarke, "The Search for Self-identity: A Critical Analysis of Sumner Locke Elliott's Novel *Careful, He Might Hear You,*" Honors English thesis, University of Wollongong, Australia, 1989;

Doris Fitton, *Not without Dust and Heat* (Sydney: Harper & Row, 1981);

Jane Nicholls, "Signs of Living: About Sumner Locke Elliott," *FOLLOW me* (Sydney) (June 1988): 132–135;

Clyde Packer, *No Return Ticket* (Sydney: Angus & Robertson, 1984);

Max Wilk, *The Golden Age of Television: Notes from the Survivors* (New York: Delacorte, 1976).

Papers:

The Sumner Locke Elliott Collection is held in the Special Collections Branch of Mugar Memorial Library, Boston University, Boston, Massachusetts. Other pertinent material is located in the Mitchell Library and State Library of New South Wales, Sydney, Australia.

David Foster

(14 May 1944 –   )

Susan Lever
University of New South Wales at the Australian Defence Force Academy

BOOKS: *North South West: Three Novellas* (South Melbourne, Vic.: Macmillan, 1973);

The Pure Land (South Melbourne, Vic.: Macmillan, 1974);

The Fleeing Atalanta (Adelaide: Maximus, 1975);

Escape to Reality (South Melbourne, Vic. & London: Macmillan, 1977);

The Empathy Experiment, by Foster and D. K. Lyall (Sydney: Wild & Woolley, 1977);

Moonlite (South Melbourne, Vic.: Macmillan, 1981; London: Picador, 1982; Ringwood, Vic. & New York: Penguin, 1987);

Plumbum (Ringwood, Vic. & New York: Penguin, 1983; Ringwood, Vic. & Harmondsworth, U.K.: Penguin, 1983);

Dog Rock: A Postal Pastoral (Ringwood, Vic. & New York: Penguin, 1985); republished with *The Pale Blue Crochet Coathanger Cover* as *Dog Rock* (Milson's Point, N.S.W.: Vintage, 1996);

The Adventures of Christian Rosy Cross (Ringwood, Vic. & Harmondsworth, U.K.: Penguin, 1985; Ringwood, Vic. & New York: Penguin, 1986);

Testostero: A Comic Novel (Ringwood, Vic. & New York: Penguin, 1987);

The Pale Blue Crochet Coathanger Cover (Ringwood, Vic.: Penguin, 1988); republished with *Dog Rock: A Postal Pastoral* as *Dog Rock* (Milson's Point, N.S.W.: Vintage, 1996);

Hitting the Wall: Two Novellas (Ringwood, Vic. & New York: Penguin, 1989)—comprises *Eye of the Bull* and *The Job;*

Mates of Mars (Ringwood, Vic. & New York: Penguin, 1991);

A Slab of Foster's: Excerpts from the Novels (Darlinghurst, N.S.W.: Yellow Press, 1994)—includes "Essay on Satire," by Foster, and introduction by Andrew Riemer;

The Glade Within the Grove (London: Fourth Estate, 1996; Sydney: Random House, 1996; Milson's Point, N.S.W. & New York: Vintage, 1996);

David Foster (photograph by Samantha Foster; from the back cover for Moonlite, *1987; Bruccoli Clark Layman Archives)*

The Ballad of Erinungerah (Milson's Point, N.S.W.: Vintage, 1997);

In the New Country (London: Fourth Estate, 1999);

Studs and Nogs: Essays and Polemics 1987–98 (Milson's Point, N.S.W. & New York: Vintage, 1999);

The Land Where Stories End as Narrated by the Angel Depicted in "Madonna con Bambino e due angeli" by Filippo Lippi (Pott's Point, N.S.W.: Duffy & Snellgrove, 2001; Dingle, Ireland & London: Brandon, 2003);

A Year of Slow Food: Four Seasons of Growing and Making Your Own Food in the Australian Countryside, by Foster and Gerda Foster (Pott's Point, N.S.W.: Duffy & Snellgrove, 2001).

OTHER: *Self Portraits,* edited by Foster (Canberra: National Library of Australia, 1991).

SELECTED PERIODICAL PUBLICATIONS–
UNCOLLECTED: "Like Spinoza the Philosopher," in
Toads: Australian Writers: Other Work, Other Lives,
edited by Andrew Sant (Sydney: Allen & Unwin,
1992), pp. 72–84;
"My Country Childhood," edited by Annabel Frost,
Country Style (March 1995): 18–20.

David Foster has established himself as the most
ferocious literary satirist in Australia. Idiosyncratic and
intellectually adventurous, Foster writes novels that
express a despair with the state of Australian, and all
Western, civilization. While he stands apart from his
contemporaries, he nevertheless writes in a recognizably Australian satiric and comic tradition evident in
the novels of Joseph Furphy, Xavier Herbert, Peter
Mathers, and David Ireland before him. Foster has
been the most consistently experimental Australian
writer of his generation, seeking out lost satiric forms
and mixing genres and vocabularies in novels that challenge the limits of fictional structure. Yet, his political
and social stance appears conservative, as he challenges
many of the assumptions of contemporary liberalism.

Foster's satire seeks out paradox and duality, but
a desire for some kind of spiritual consolation lies not
far beneath the surface of his mockery of the material
world. While his novels have won prizes, including the
1981 National Book Council Award, for *Moonlite*
(1981), and the 1997 Miles Franklin Award, for *The
Glade Within the Grove* (1996), his work creates too much
discomfort for popular admiration. Those readers who
appreciate Foster's digressive and unaccommodating
style generally agree that *Moonlite, Mates of Mars* (1991),
The Glade Within the Grove, and possibly *Plumbum* (1983)
are major achievements.

David Manning Foster was born on 14 May 1944
to George Foster and Hazel Manning Foster, vaudeville
and radio performers. Foster's parents separated before
his birth. He spent his early childhood living at
Katoomba in the Blue Mountains of New South Wales
with his maternal grandparents and his mother. When
he was six years old, Foster suffered from poliomyelitis
and spent months bedridden, doing lessons by correspondence. He claims that the experience made him a
writer. His mother married again, this time to a bank
officer, whose job entailed regular moves around the
tablelands of New South Wales. As a teenager in Armidale and Orange, Foster learned to play the drums and
developed his passion for modern jazz.

Foster graduated with the 1967 University Medal
in chemistry from the University of Sydney. He had
married Robin Bowers in 1964 while still an undergraduate, and over the next ten years they had three children: Natalie (born 9 March 1968), Samantha (born 6

January 1969), and Seth (born 14 October 1973). Foster
completed a Ph.D. at the Australian National University in 1970, spending the following year as a fellow of
the National Institute of Health at the University of
Pennsylvania and writing the stories later published in
North South West: Three Novellas (1973). In 1972 he left
his job as senior research officer in the Department of
Medicine at the University of Sydney in order to write.
He has given various accounts of his decision to leave
science–from his lack of inspiration as a chemist and
the recurrence of a duodenal ulcer, to the time wasted
in commuting to Sydney from his home at Hazelbrook
in the Blue Mountains. He first took work as a pool
foreman and has since worked from time to time as a
truck driver, postman, fisherman, mover, or jazz drum-
mer. He divorced his first wife in 1975 and married his
second wife, Gerda Busch, in the same year. They
moved to Bundanoon in the Southern Highlands of
New South Wales, where they manage a degree of subsistence farming and have raised their combined family
of eight children, including three born to them: Antigone (born 17 June 1975), Levi (born 10 October 1976),
and Zoe (born 28 July 1980).

In the title story of *North South West,* an obsessive
narrator treks around the suburbs of inner Sydney,
detailing the stations along the railway line between
Redfern and Strathfield, and digressing on the meaning
of each suburb. In "Mobil Medley," another narrator
introduces a series of stories told by three companions
traveling to a country town called Mobil. "Time's
Arrow" follows a scientist's fascination with entropy to
the point where the text itself breaks down. These
novellas all indicate some of the preoccupations and
techniques in Foster's later novels–particularly, his frustration with Australian cultural mediocrity in "North
South West," his interest in doubles in "Mobil Medley," and his exploration of scientific models as a guide
for art in "Time's Arrow." With the publication of this
book, Foster was acknowledged as one of the new
voices of the 1970s, and he was awarded an Australia
Council Fellowship for 1974. Foster told Geoffrey Dutton that he spent the early months of his fellowship
playing music, smoking hashish, and reading the hermetic and alchemical texts that have remained an influence on his writing and thinking. His first book of
poems, *The Fleeing Atalanta* (1975), is steeped in alchemical imagery.

Foster's first novel, *The Pure Land* (1974), uses
some of his family background and his experiences in
the United States as the basis for a quest for cultural
and spiritual meaning from Australia to the United
States and back. Foster's love of contradiction and
antithesis emerges in the contrasts between Katoomba
and Bondi, Australia, and the United States, and

Dust jacket for David Foster's 1974 novel, which examinies cultural contrasts between Australia and the United States (Bruccoli Clark Layman Archives)

between rational science and intuitive spiritualism. In the first section of the novel Manwaring, a Katoomba postcard photographer, is lured to a career in pornography in America. There, his daughter Jean has a son, Danny, by a vaudeville star. Danny becomes a scientist, but his disillusion with the hypocrisies of science and the corruption of the United States leads him to travel back to Sydney in search of spiritual enlightenment. Foster's own defection from science and his commitment to Australia are reflected in Danny's frustration with the limitations of rationality and his quest for meaning in the backwardness of Australian life.

Escape to Reality (1977) collects a range of Foster's short stories and novellas. These pieces work over Foster's particular territory of masculine irresponsibility and excess, showing the clear influence of such American writers as William S. Burroughs. Drug-taking jazz musicians feature in some of them ("Green Changes" and "The Hat"), while others observe the feminized and closed nature of Australian domestic life ("The Salt

Man") or the illogical ironies of double lives ("The Job"). A spirit of adolescent experiment dominates *The Empathy Experiment* (1977), which Foster wrote with a scientific colleague, D. K. Lyall. In it the two scientist- writers play with the idea of a paranoid, empathic psychologist working in a dystopian institute in Canberra, where scientists murder people to test their brains.

In 1978 Foster was awarded a Marten Bequest for Prose, enabling him to travel to Scotland, where he researched his satire on British colonialism, *Moonlite*, published in 1981. Foster sets the first part of this novel on Hiphoray, a tiny island based on St. Kilda, an outlier of the Outer Hebrides, where the people live a bare subsistence life, secure in the belief that their lives participate in a spiritually meaningful universe. Two highland exiles begin the process of disrupting the islanders' lives with rationality and the beginnings of Christianity. Eventually, a Christian parson converts the island, pulling down their primitive blackhouses and building a stone church and cottages. Tourism follows Christianity, corrupting the people with disease and the prospect of easy money, until they are finally cleared from the island completely.

Finbar MacDuffie (Moonlite), gifted with night sight, grows up on this island to understand that the mysterious Sidhe spirit is merely an unrecognized bird, and his experience of the optical illusion of "the glory" leads him to Christianity. After a period in the wilderness, Moonlite makes his way to an English university, where he encounters the snobberies of the British class system while devoting himself in turn to science, specifically mathematics and optics. By this point, Foster is in full satirical flight, calling on eighteenth- and nineteenth-century English picaresque satirical traditions, flavored with an Australian vernacular. Moonlite's mathematical rationality relentlessly reveals the flaws in belief systems, including his own Christianity, thus making way for his career on the goldfields of the New West Highlands, by this time identifiably Australia. The novel charts the movement from an indigenous pagan life through Christianity to science as a preparation for the driving, secular greed of capitalism. The pattern acted out on the islanders is the archetypal pattern of colonization, specifically in its British form, and the parallels between the fate of the islanders and the Australian Aborigines become explicit in the final section of the novel.

The novel also operates at an intellectual level, interrogating the way that Christianity, by challenging the irrationality of the islanders' faith in the Sidhe, paves the way for the scientific mind that ultimately rejects all spiritualism in favor of an utterly material existence. Foster makes quantum theory into a metaphor for the possibility of holding two contradictory beliefs at the same time; scientific rationalism and intuitive spirituality may not be mutually exclusive. At the end of the novel Moonlite loses his soul in an encounter with Aboriginal spirituality. Without a soul, he can become a politician, and the narrative voice ends the novel with a despair that seems close to Foster's own attitude toward Australia: "Climb or Let Go! Thou hast had Time Enough, and the patience of Thy Father is exhausted."

Part of the strength of *Moonlite* as a novel is its careful scientific observation of the natural world on Hiphoray; the descriptions of the vegetation and patterns of existence on the island are minutely detailed. The novel shifts from detail to broad comic satire and becomes the first of Foster's novels to acknowledge his commitment to satire. Stephen Harris, in *Westerly* (Autumn 1997), has argued that the brilliance of the novel lies in the way it opposes, through rancorous satire, the established colonial discourse of history as progress with a "counter-discursive colonial myth." In Foster's hands, history is not a narrative of progress but of degeneration, as the islanders move from a difficult but spiritually satisfying subsistence life, to a disease-ridden and corrupted Christian community, and finally to clearance from their home so that they can become the secular colonists of the New West Highlands. For many readers, *Moonlite* remained Foster's strongest novel, at least until the publication of *The Glade Within the Grove* in 1996. In her *Liars* (1988) Helen Daniel declares it "one of the most important novels ever written in Australia," and in *The Australian's Review of Books* (June 1997) Kerryn Goldsworthy called it "the most extraordinary feat of imagination in the history of Australian writing."

Foster used his experience as a jazz musician to write *Plumbum,* a satire on the rock industry, in which a group of Canberra musicians sell their souls to a Mephistophelian manager in order to achieve international fame and access to "all the money in the world." In this work Foster displays the range of his technical virtuosity and originality—writing parodic rock songs for the band, verbal equivalents for the musical obscenity of their songs, and gradually simulating the kaleidoscopic, hallucinatory effects of their heavy-metal music as they build themselves into frenetic concert performers. The novel begins slowly, with various riffs on the names of Canberra streets and digressions on the lives of the band members. It mimics the boredom of gigs at country RSL clubs (Returned Services League clubs, places for former servicemen to socialize) and describes the squalor of their lives in inner Sydney. In order to achieve success, the band goes to Bangkok, then follows their manager to Calcutta. Amid the frenetic confusion of Calcutta, the central dualities of Foster's vision become fully apparent: the fair and good-looking Jason Blackman is drawn to a passive spirituality, walking the

streets as a sightless Buddhist monk until he actually becomes blind. His half brother Pete, dark and misanthropic, is driven by anger to devote himself to changing material conditions for the people on the streets. The band's singer, Sharon, joins the Ananda Margi (members of an Indian sociospiritual cult), following a path of sensual indulgence as a means to enlightenment. Felix works as a rickshaw puller, while Rollo finds his natural home in the Indian public service. The Indian section of the novel is fundamental to the sources of the band's brilliance and corruption, and in it Foster expresses moral outrage and disgust at the poverty of Calcutta, the "anti-Canberra."

In the final section of the novel, the band plays in Utrecht, but the novel begins to move at a rapid pace, with the text breaking down as the musicians, their music, and their minds disintegrate. In the last pages, Foster mocks his musicians with the normality of Dutch family life, braking the hectic pace of the novel, and leaving readers with an enigmatic conclusion.

Foster's next novel, *Dog Rock: A Postal Pastoral* (1985), shifts to a more comic and benign view of community, and Foster poured all his small-town experiences of Bundanoon into it. For the first time a Foster novel was entirely narrated by a character, in this case a postman called D'Arcy D'Oliveres, a British migrant who delivers the mail in an Australian country town and runs the telephone exchange by night. The narrative proceeds as a murder mystery, with D'Arcy pursuing a serial killer manifest in the town, though this plot also serves as an excuse for Foster to digress on aspects of Australian country-town behavior. D'Arcy, maintaining a conversational tone throughout the novel, invites the reader to accept the role of confidante and occasional collaborator in his plans.

Dog Rock is full of nostalgia for the passing of the small rural community in Australia. The telephone exchange will soon close, and productive agricultural work is declining as city dreamers take over good land to play at farming. D'Arcy hints that he is himself a renegade British aristocrat suffering the dual commitments to home and the mock-British Australian life. At the same time, *Dog Rock* offers plenty of Foster's lists of detail, particularly those minutiae from the nature of working life—the daily life of the town baker, or the operations of a manual telephone exchange. The novel celebrates the small-scale obsessions of ordinary people, in contrast to the larger historical and spiritual perspectives of the previous two novels. While *Dog Rock* reveals Foster's ability to write a lighter comic and more controlled fiction, it also marks the appearance of his most developed character, D'Arcy D'Oliveres. D'Arcy offers a voice to express Foster's interests without implicating the author in his absurdities and opinions.

Paperback cover for the 1987 edition of Foster's 1981 novel, a satire of colonialism in which the innocent paganism of Outer Hebrides islanders is corrupted by Christianity, modern science, and capitalism (Bruccoli Clark Layman Archives)

With *The Adventures of Christian Rosy Cross* (1985) Foster returns to historical satiric subject matter based on the Rosicrucian movement of the seventeenth century and drawing on A. E. Waite's translations of Rosicrucian tracts on alchemy. Foster explains in his introduction to the novel that he was attracted by the evidence of a continuing Gnostic tradition in the West, suppressed by Christianity. He apparently began writing this novel in 1973, and his reference to Michael Maier's *Atalanta fugiens* (1617) for the title of his first book of poetry, *The Fleeing Atalanta* (1975), and later for the chapter images of *The Land Where Stories End as Narrated by the Angel Depicted in "Madonna con Bambino e due angeli" by Filippo Lippi* (2001) suggests an ongoing inspiration from these alchemical sources.

At the same time, *The Adventures of Christian Rosy Cross* is a burlesque of history in which Christian travels from Western Europe to the Middle East, suffering physical and mental humiliations in his search for the alchemic stone. The drug jokes and farcical situations refer to attitudes of the 1970s, in accordance with Foster's statement in the introduction that the present age is at a point of decline and change, like that of Christian Rosy Cross. The novel may hold most interest as a measure of Foster's fascination with duality, his awareness that satire can bear spiritual meanings, and his support for the irrational and mind-expanding. It also shows Foster's long-standing interest in counters to Christianity, whether Rosicrucian subversion, the paganism of the Scottish islanders in *Moonlite,* the mysticism of India in *Plumbum,* or the classical pre-Christian mythology of *The Glade Within the Grove.*

In 1984 Foster and his wife spent a month at the Venice studio of the Australia Council, and Foster's next novel, *Testostero: A Comic Novel* (1987), invoked Italian farcical models, particularly Carlo Goldoni's *The Venetian Twins* (1748). Foster creates a set of twins, separated at birth–Leon Hunnybun and Noel Horniman–to examine his fascination with duality. Leon, a homosexual British scientist, meets Noel, a working-class Australian poet, while Noel is writer-in-residence in Venice with his wife, the green feminist Judy Rankenfile. The twins exchange places so that Leon can learn the life of a Sydney pool attendant while Noel addresses the failures of statistical method in a London laboratory. The novel mixes styles and genres, scientific speculation and vulgar humor, before building to a Carnivale climax in Venice and the unveiling of a third sibling (the twins are triplets).

Once again, Foster consciously explores various forms of satire and comedy, using traditional models as a base for his own experiments. In his 1987 *Southerly* article on Foster's work, Andrew Riemer thought that *Testostero* was Foster's "in many ways most successful and accessible novel" because of the combination of its irreverent attitude toward high cultural themes and its concern for cultural identity.

The Pale Blue Crochet Coathanger Cover (1988) returned to D'Arcy D'Oliveres and life in Dog Rock. Indeed, in 1996 the two Dog Rock novels were reprinted in one volume as *Dog Rock.* Once again, murder has occurred (or appears to have occurred), and D'Arcy is both suspect and sleuth. This time D'Arcy addresses the reader as the dog found wearing a pale blue crochet coathanger cover around his neck after a strange accident near the African Mission Opportunity shop. Foster offers a clever subversion of the detective novel through the device of the dog-reader-listener (found to be wired by the detective Purvis), and the final revelation of the murderers quirkily allows an animal perspective on human activity. In her 1997 survey of Foster's work in *Meanjin,* Marilla North recognizes this novel as a version of an animal fable, crossed with the crime novel and the pastoral comedy.

In 1989 Foster published *Hitting the Wall: Two Novellas,* including *Eye of the Bull* and reprinting *The Job,* which had been published earlier in *Escape to Reality. Eye of the Bull,* written in 1986, expresses a masculine malaise through its protagonist's obsession with running and his abandonment of domestic responsibilities. It lacks the element of comic self-mockery that pervades most of Foster's writing on the subject, especially *Mates of Mars.*

Mates of Mars, published in 1991, represents Foster's comment on the Australian Bicentennial flurry of 1988, offering a satiric counter to the celebrations of white Australian settlement. In his introduction Foster declares that the premise of the novel is that Australians are both members of a declining and decrepit Western Christian civilization and "barbarian" members of a rising Sinic Mahayan Buddhist civilization "in its Westernised Japanese/Korean/Colonial Chinese branch." In this work Foster finds a promising satirical paradox: he measures the state of a civilization by the prowess of its warriors, its culture by its savagery. To illuminate this premise, Foster creates a group of Australians dedicated to the Tae Kwon Do form of martial arts, in which Foster holds a second-degree black belt—an Aborigine, a Jewish Australian, a Singapore Chinese Australian, a Swedish Australian, a paraplegic working-class Australian, and a woman. After detailing the individual lives of this disparate group, the novel takes them to the homeland of the Aborigine in the Northern Territory for a training camp with the locals. There the mates experience violence and terrifying spiritualism, some of them escaping by fishing boat to the open sea.

The novel draws on Foster's experiences as a martial-arts devotee, as a fisherman on his son-in-law's prawn trawler, and his visits to his eldest son in the Northern Territory. The bridging section from Sydney to the Northern Territory is a comic monologue by a corrupt Aboriginal politician. Foster mocks the rise of feminism but gives his woman character the voice of sanity when the men are most irresponsible. Yet, the principal target of the satire is the failure of Australians, both black and white, to create a vibrant civilization for the country.

Mates of Mars addresses a multicultural contemporary Australia in which Asian culture is as important as European or indigenous elements. Foster examines the philosophical basis for Australian society in millennial terms: Western Christian civilization has promoted the rise of a rational science that has wiped away the kind of tribal spiritualism that gave men a role in courageously defending their communities. His martial artists cling to that role, despite the evidence that a woman can join them and that they are no match for modern weaponry. The outlandish situations of the novel provide opportunities for discussions of a range of Foster's favorite topics: the invalidity of statistical scientific method, war as a method of genetic selection and population control, biological determinism and the effects of testosterone, and the destruction of the environment by grasping development.

While the novel challenges most liberal-minded readers on one ground or another (its mockery of feminism, its portrayal of Aborigines, or its attacks on the Japanese), it addresses the topical subject of men's culture in contemporary Australia and scorns the national failure to come to terms with the place of Australia in the world. Though most reviewers admired this novel as both an important statement about the direction of contemporary Australia and a brilliantly witty account of Australian men's culture, its lack of "political correctness" caused some nervousness in its reception.

In 1991 Foster was awarded a Creative Fellowship by the Australian government. He used the time to research his next novel, reading Latin classics in their original language and studying in detail Sir James George Frazer's *The Golden Bough* (1890) and the histories of Arnold Joseph Toynbee and Edward Gibbon. The resulting novel, published in 1996, *The Glade Within the Grove,* demonstrates the full range of Foster's talents and obsessions. It was narrated by a rather more obviously learned D'Arcy D'Oliveres, now retired from Dog Rock and working as a relief postman at Obliqua Creek in an imagined New South Wales corner of Gippsland. D'Arcy has found the manuscript of a poem in an old mailbag and proceeds to tell the story surrounding the poem. A group of 1960s dropouts has been lost in a secret valley near Obliqua Creek and cut off from civilization for a generation. D'Arcy tells how they got into the valley and the nature of their lives in Sydney before it was cut off, but he never manages to complete the story, digressing so much about the customs of Obliqua Creek and the nature of civilization that by the end of the novel lung cancer has overtaken him, and he dies before its conclusion.

While the secrets of the novel lie within the valley, it reaches its comic heights in D'Arcy's account of the lives of the MacAnaspie family, who have lived on the mountain above it for generations. These men are archetypal male Australians—timber-cutters and lorry drivers—and their dialogues resound with vernacular wit. The youngest son, Attis, was mysteriously found as a baby in a woodchip sawmill and is drawn to the valley and its cult, becoming the link with the people in the valley.

Behind all its comic energy the novel offers a serious examination of the state of post-Christian Australia.

by hand, was a chore the settler put off as long as possible, so that the fields, despite an appearance suggesting the recent passage through a sawmill of a large meteorite, are already fenced, with post and rail, and sown down to pasture.

Two houses, each, in its way, a precursor of things to come, can be seen in this early photograph: one, set amid stumps, and standing roughly where Fitzgibbon's greyhound kennel stands roughly today, is a shoddily erected stringybark slab hut, built on the lines of a Gaelic blackhouse, but with an external chimney, owing to the highly combustible nature of its bark roof; the other, within twenty two yards of the railway line and later to be demolished to make way for the platform, is a neat sandstone cottage, built to resemble a gatekeeper's lodge on a manor house in the Gloustershire Cotswolds, but with a roof of galvanised iron to nullify the insulating properties of its walls of Hawkesbury Sandstone, which, unlike the highly refined Cotswold limestone, cannot readily be split into roof shingles.

The descendents and contemporary equivalents of these two archetypes house the present day population: if only the genius who conceived the stump jump plough had been born to bake bread on a fuel stove in a blackhouse with an iron roof; and what contemporary Snowshill or could sneer at a village built wholly of petrified sand, and roofed in stringybark shingles? We observe Dog Rock as it is, and not as it might have been, for nothing is more certain than that it might have been even worse than it is; a Barren Grounds, for instance, or a Cow Flat. A cigarette dangling from his lower lip, under a mysterious sky full of strange and lavish constellations, the names of which only retired master mariner of has ever known, and he's forgotten, Irving Tibbet, railway engineman, gazes over the tumbledown fence at the house of his next-door neighbour and cousin, Maurie Tibbet, Renee's husband, landless farmer, or fencing contractor, to give him the usual.

A fibro cottage the colour of a postman's shirt with garage to

Page from the revised typescript for Foster's 1985 comic murder-mystery, Dog Rock *(from Candida Baker,* Yacker: Australian Writers Talk about Their Work, *1986; Paterno Library, Pennsylvania State University)*

Consistent with Foster's analyses in *Moonlite* and *Mates of Mars,* he proposes that Christianity has deformed human civilization, leading it away from any spiritual link with the natural world and ultimately to a secular materialism that offers no hope for the future. The problem is exacerbated in Australia, where Europeans have found no spiritual bond with the native trees, destroying them in the battle for survival. The novel seems to advocate a return to a pre-Christian paganism, founded on the Phrygian cult of Cybele or Brigid, in which men sacrifice their sexuality to achieve spiritual enlightenment. Attis, it seems, eventually makes such a sacrifice and turns into a tree.

The eucalypts provide another element of paradox for the novel. While Foster eulogizes the beauty of the old-growth forest, he recognizes the powerful colonizing habits of the eucalypts that invite the fire that destroys their rivals. Australians are clearing the native forest at a rapid rate, but D'Arcy suggests that only when the forest is gone can a civilization, such as that in the deforested Mediterranean, begin.

Foster probes the sacred mysteries through a detailed and rambling observation of the patterns of Australian life—whether a description of the contents of Horrie MacAnaspie's shed or an extended contemplation of the Southeastern Forest with all its varieties of plant life. In these descriptions, the influence of the Latin models are clear, and Foster finds a way to link his scientific interest in the precise detail of the variety of life-forms to an artistic mode that reaches toward spiritual enlightenment. At times the rhythmic cadences of the prose suggest that words themselves carry the weight of spiritual meaning.

While *The Glade Within the Grove* has baffled some readers, it won the kind of recognition previously denied to Foster, with publication by Fourth Estate in London and a Miles Franklin Award in 1996. Some controversy arose when Foster produced as a separate book of poems yet another element to the novel—*The Ballad of Erinungerah* (1997), the manuscript D'Arcy found in the mailbag. This poem is the work of "Orion," Timothy Papadimitriou, a child of the valley who survived the strange mysteries that took place there. The ballad is the sacred heart of the novel, the spiritual mystery that Foster must disguise in a lyrical poetic form in opposition to the digressive and satirical novel. While critics disagree about the quality of the poetry, *The Ballad of Erinungerah* provides further evidence that Foster invests words themselves with the possibility of sacred revelation.

After its publication, Foster claimed that his essay "Castration," first published in *Heat* magazine in 1997 and republished in his collection of essays, *Studs and Nogs* (1999), should be read with *The Glade Within the Grove*

and *The Ballad of Erinungerah* as part of a trilogy. Once again, he blurred the boundaries between genres and between his own persona and his fictional creations. The elaborate forms of the novel and poem, with their layers of narrators and mix of vocabularies, enact Foster's exploration of the mythical and spiritual meaning beneath the banality of contemporary Australian society. *The Glade Within the Grove* attempts, and for some critics achieves, the long-standing ambition of Australian literature to reconcile vulgar Australian life with the great and universal mythologies of human civilization.

With *In the New Country* (1999), however, Foster returned to rural comedy, set in a declining wool town on the western slopes of New South Wales. Foster's experiences in his local bushfire brigade and regular participation in the annual Sydney City to Surf running race contribute some of the comic background to the novel. It begins with a "gorilla" winning the City to Surf, then follows the mystery of the winning athlete back to the town of Knocklofty and the antics of its bushfire brigade. Foster even includes a reference to the singer-songwriter Peter Allen, once a member of Foster's high-school band, in the expatriate singer Dud Leahey. The novel links the Irish and the Aboriginal backgrounds of this part of Australia, with two Irishmen working to rebuild the old Catholic church, Fane of St. Fiacre, and genealogical searches revealing that one of the local families has claims to Aboriginality. The novel follows more-traditional comedic patterns than Foster's earlier work, with sex-change confusion and culmination in a party. The main comic voice of the novel is that of the deputy mayor of the local council, Ad Hock, whose commitment to a commercial future contends with the complacent somnolence of his community.

The Land Where Stories End, published in 2001, approaches the division between the world of the flesh and the world of the spirit through the genre of the fairy story. Inspired by Foster's trip to Ireland as part of his James Joyce Suspended Sentence Prize in 1997, the tales in this book recall the alchemical interests evident in *Moonlite, The Fleeing Atalanta,* and *The Adventures of Christian Rosy Cross.* The narrator of the book claims to be the cheeky angel depicted in Filippo Lippi's "Madonna con Bambino e due angeli" (reproduced on the cover of the Australian edition), but no attempt is made to place the voice in the context of the Italian Christianity of the painting. Instead, the story of the woodcutter who goes in search of the Land Where Stories End evokes an Irish-Celtic setting clearly reminiscent of *Moonlite.* The woodcutter encounters witches and ogres, and saints and kings, on a journey that ends by stepping outside the world of human understanding. Foster, once again, seems to propose a kind of alternative Christianity that denies sexuality to those who want to achieve eternal life. At the same time the story is told in relatively simple language, interspersed with an infantile vulgarity that some reviewers have found jarring. While the book returns to metaphysical speculation, it does not attempt to match the richness and complexity of *The Glade Within the Grove.*

In the past David Foster has declared several times that he will write no more novels—each time returning to publication with a surprising new approach to the genre. His latest book, written with his wife, Gerda, is ostensibly a cookbook, *A Year of Slow Food: Four Seasons of Growing and Making Your Own Food in the Australian Countryside* (2001). Its essays about their life in Bundanoon through the changing seasons offer a pattern of the kind of idyllic rural existence sought by the valley communards in *The Glade Within the Grove. A Year of Slow Food* suggests that Foster may live out an ideal of self-sufficiency and understanding of nature that his novels lament as impossible. Despite his frequent declarations of pessimism about Australian culture, there is a recurrent idealism in his work that suggests a continuing creative friction.

Interviews:

Candida Baker, "David Foster," in *Yacker: Australian Writers Talk about Their Work* (Sydney: Pan, 1986), pp. 104–126;

E. A. Travers, "On the Philosophical: An Interview with David Foster," *Westerly,* 37, no. 1 (Autumn 1992): 71–78.

Biography:

Geoffrey Dutton, "David Foster: The Early Years," *Southerly,* 65, no. 1 (Autumn 1996): 23–48.

References:

D. R. Burns, "The Coming of the 'Contained Account,' *Moonlite,* David Foster's Landmark Novel," *Overland,* 129 (1992): 62–67;

Helen Daniel, "The Alchemy of the Lie: David Foster," in her *Liars: Australian New Novelists* (Melbourne: Penguin, 1988), pp. 77–104;

Ken Gelder, "The 'Self-Contradictory' Fiction of David Foster," in *Aspects of Australian Fiction,* edited by Alan Brissenden (Perth: University of Western Australia Press, 1990), pp. 149–159;

Stephen Harris, "David Foster's *Moonlite:* Re-viewing History as Satirical Fable–Towards a Post-Colonial Past," *Westerly,* 42, no. 1 (Autumn 1997): 71–88;

Susan Lever, "David Foster's *Decline and Fall,*" *Southerly,* 65, no. 1 (Autumn 1996): 41–48;

Lever, "A Masculine Crisis: David Foster's *Mates of Mars,*" in her *Real Relations: The Feminist Politics of Form in Australian Fiction* (Sydney: Halstead, 2000), pp. 120–130;

Marilla North, "Postman's Knock: Is David Foster a Clever Dick–or What?" *Meanjin,* 56, nos. 3/4 (1997): 686–696;

Andrew Riemer, "Bare Breech'ed Brethren: The novels of David Foster," *Southerly,* 47, no. 2 (June 1987): 126–144;

Narelle Shaw, "It's a Small Martial Arts World: *Mates of Mars* and the Foster Novels," *LiNQ,* 21, no. 2 (October 1994): 63–70;

Shaw, "The Postman's Grand Narrative: Postmodernism and David Foster's *The Glade within the Grove,*" *Journal of Commonwealth Literature,* 34, no. 1 (1999): 45–64.

Papers:

The major collection of David Foster's notebooks and manuscript drafts is held in the Australian Defence Force Academy Library (MS160). The collection is partly restricted. The Geoffrey Dutton papers (MS7285) at the National Library of Australia include correspondence between Dutton and Foster. This collection is restricted until 2010.

Rodney Hall

(18 November 1935 –   )

Veronica Brady
University of Western Australia

BOOKS: *Penniless till Doomsday* (Dulwich Village, U.K.: Outposts, 1962);

Statues and Lovers, in *Four Poets: David Malouf, Don Maynard, Judith Green, Rodney Hall* (Melbourne: Cheshire, 1962);

Forty Beads on a Hangman's Rope: Fragments of Memory (Newnham, Tasmania: Wattle Grove Press, 1963);

The High Priest, Coifi, with paintings by Andrew Sibley, Australian Artists and Poets Booklets, no. 10, (Adelaide: Australian Letters, 1963);

Social Services for Aborigines, written and edited by Hall and Shirley Andrews (Melbourne: Federal Council for Aboriginal Advancement, 1963);

Eyewitness: Poems (Sydney: South Head Press, 1967);

The Autobiography of a Gorgon, and Other Poems (Melbourne & Canberra: Cheshire, 1968);

The Law of Karma: A Progression of Poems (Canberra: Australian National University Press, 1968);

Focus on Andrew Sibley (St. Lucia: University of Queensland Press, 1968);

Heaven, in a Way (St. Lucia: University of Queensland Press, 1970);

The Ship on the Coin: A Fable of the Bourgeoisie, Paperback Prose, no. 2 (St. Lucia: University of Queensland Press, 1972);

A Soapbox Omnibus, Paperback Poets, no. 16 (St. Lucia: University of Queensland Press, 1973);

A Place among People (St. Lucia: University of Queensland Press, 1975; St. Lucia & New York: University of Queensland Press, 1984);

Selected Poems (St. Lucia: University of Queensland Press, 1975);

Black Bagatelles (St. Lucia: University of Queensland Press, 1978);

J. S. Manifold: An Introduction to the Man and His Work (St. Lucia: University of Queensland Press, 1978);

The Most Beautiful World: Fictions and Sermons (St. Lucia & New York: University of Queensland Press, 1981);

Rodney Hall (from the dust jacket for The Second Bridegroom, *1991; Richland County Public Library)*

Just Relations (Ringwood, Vic. & New York: Penguin, 1982; London: Allen Lane, 1983);

Australia: Image of a Nation 1850–1950, by Hall and David Moore (Sydney & London: Collins, 1983);

Kisses of the Enemy (Ringwood, Vic. & New York: Penguin, 1987; London: Faber & Faber, 1987);

Captivity Captive (New York: Farrar, Straus & Giroux, 1988; Melbourne: McPhee Gribble, 1988; London: Faber & Faber, 1988);

Journey Through Australia (Richmond, Vic.: Heinemann, 1988; London: Murray, 1988);

An Australian Place: The Upper Hunter Valley, text by Hall, photographs by David Moore (McMahon's Point, N.S.W.: Chapter & Verse, 1991);

The Second Bridegroom (Melbourne: McPhee Gribble, 1991; New York: Farrar, Straus & Giroux, 1991; London & Boston: Faber & Faber, 1991);

The Grisly Wife (Chippendale, N.S.W.: Macmillan, 1993; London: Faber & Faber, 1993; New York: Farrar, Straus & Giroux, 1993);

Sydney Harbour, text by Hall, illustrated by David Moore (McMahon's Point, N.S.W.: Chapter & Verse / Mullumbimby, N.S.W.: State Library of New South Wales Press, 1993);

A Dream More Luminous Than Love: The Yandilli Trilogy (Sydney: Picador, 1994); republished as *The Yandilli Trilogy* (London: Faber & Faber, 1994; New York: Noonday Press, 1995)—comprises *The Second Bridegroom, The Grisly Wife,* and *Captivity Captive;*

The Writer and the World of the Imagination, Sir Robert Madgwick Lecture for 1995 (Armidale: University of New England, 1995);

The Island in the Mind (Sydney: Macmillan, 1996; London: Granta, 2000);

Abolish the States!: Australia's Future and a $30 Billion Answer to Our Tax Problem (Sydney: Pan Macmillan, 1998);

A Return to the Brink (Sydney: Currency Press in association with Playbox Theatre Centre, Monash University, Melbourne, 1999);

The Day We Had Hitler Home (Chippendale, N.S.W.: Picador, 2000; London: Granta, 2001);

The Owner of My Face: New & Selected Poems, edited by John Kinsella (St. Leonards, N.S.W.: Paper Bark Press, 2002).

RECORDING: *Romulus and Remus,* with music by Richard Mills, St. Lucia, University of Queensland Press, Poets on Record 1, 1970.

OTHER: *New Impulses in Australian Poetry,* edited by Hall and Thomas Shapcott (St. Lucia: University of Queensland Press, 1968);

Australian Poetry, edited by Hall (Sydney & London: Angus & Robertson, 1970);

Jack Murray and others, *Poems from Prison,* edited by Hall (St. Lucia: University of Queensland Press, 1973);

Australians Aware: Poems and Paintings of Today, selected and edited by Hall (Sydney: Ure Smith, 1975);

Michael Dransfield, *The Second Month of Spring,* edited by Hall (St. Lucia: University of Queensland Press, 1980);

The Collins Book of Australian Poetry, edited by Hall (Sydney & London: Collins, 1981);

Dransfield, *Michael Dransfield: Collected Poems,* edited by Hall (St. Lucia: University of Queensland Press, 1987);

"Being Shaped by the Stories We Choose from Our History," in *The Deakin Lectures: The Future of Civil Society* (Sydney: ABC Books, 2001).

SELECTED PERIODICAL PUBLICATIONS—UNCOLLECTED: "Columbus' Flagship," *A.B.C. Weekly,* 21, no. 3 (1959);

"The Poetry of Judith Wright," *Outposts,* no. 63 (Winter 1964);

"The Birdcage Man," *Meanjin Quarterly,* no. 3 (1968): 336–342;

"Poetry for the Converted," *Australian,* 9 August 1969;

"Australian Literature," *Times of India,* 17 January 1970;

"Attitudes to Contemporary Australian Poetry," *Poetry Australia,* 32, no. 1 (1970): 44–45.

Rodney Hall is one of a group of writers, painters, and musicians who came to prominence in Brisbane in the 1960s. In a sense he began his career outside the literary mainstream, which was then located in Sydney and Melbourne. He is unusual in the breadth of his artistic concerns, since he is also an accomplished musician and is deeply interested in the visual arts. Cosmopolitan in his interests, he was one of the first writers of his generation to become aware of the significance of new movements occurring internationally in the arts and culture generally.

In his introduction to the most recent collection of Hall's poetry, John Kinsella, now a significant poet himself, writes of the influence Hall had on him:

> I was sixteen and searching for . . . a voice that was both Australian and international. . . . Rodney Hall's [poetry] opened a territory I had not encountered before. I realised that fragments could be built into a whole, and that one could have a political consciousness and still be lyrical. . . . It was cultural poetry but not just polite gesturing. It had guts it was really saying something.

As chairman of the Australia Council from 1991 to 1994 Hall had a substantial influence on cultural politics. He has also been involved in Aboriginal and environmental issues.

Beginning his career as a poet, Hall turned to fiction in mid career, transferring and extending his poetic concerns with the creative and critical power of language in the direction of "magical realism" without losing the ability to tackle social and even political questions. His interest in myth, empowered by his knowledge of non-Western cultures, also enables him, according to Kinsella, to deal with "the big questions about the place of inspiration and spirituality in terms of the materiality of language, of text," opening up new "corridors of imagination." The winner of several prestigious literary prizes in Australia, Hall has also gained an international reputation.

Born in Solihull, Warwickshire, England, on 18 November 1935, six months before the death of his father, Percy Edgar Hall, Rodney was the youngest of three children. The Great Depression was then at its height, so even though his father had been a businessman, he did not leave much money, and Hall recalls himself as brought up "in a sort of impoverished middle class household." His mother, born Doris Emma Buckland, to whom he owed his love of music, had been born in Australia but had come to England to make a career as an opera singer. She was determined that her children would have a good education. So Rodney was sent to the City of Bath School.

When World War II broke out, the family were living in Stroud in Gloucestershire, which was not far from Swansea, a frequent target for German bombers, who, on their way home, often tried to gain height by releasing their remaining bombs over the surrounding countryside. When the sirens sounded, the family would take shelter under the keyboard of their mother's upright piano. To take their minds off the falling bombs, she would show them photographs of Kangaroo Valley on the south coast of New South Wales, where she had grown up. Photographs of pioneering life, of settlers posing beside tall gum trees or standing outside rough huts in a clearing in the bush–the kind of landscape in which Hall later set the novels of his Yandilli trilogy–they set up for the boy, according to a conversation with Veronica Brady in 2002, the "enticement of Australia," which became "the secret land" of his imagination. Hall's interest was reinforced by the food parcels that arrived from "Aunty This" or "Uncle That" in Australia.

The years immediately after the end of the war were bleak in England. Consequently, his mother decided to return to Australia, in her son's words "a courageous decision," since she had "no money and no prospects." Berths were scarce since returning servicemen and other migrants were ahead of them in the queue, and it was four years before they set sail. The long voyage made a profound impression on the boy. He was fascinated by the sights, sounds, smells, and vibrant life of the ports at which they called along the

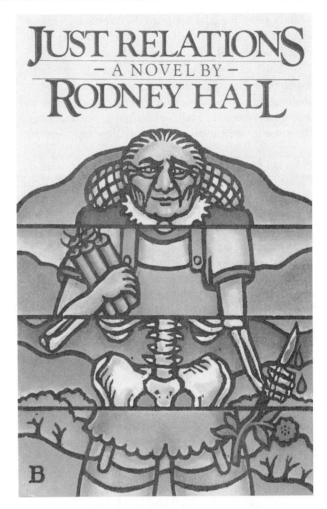

Dust jacket for the 1983 London edition of Hall's 1982 novel, about life in a decaying former Australian gold-rush town (Bruccoli Clark Layman Archives)

way–Port Said, Aden, and Colombo–before making landfall in Australia at Fremantle.

Brisbane, where they settled to be near his mother's family, was something of an anticlimax since, after the excitements of World War II when it had been the headquarters of the war in the Pacific during its final stages, it had reverted to the easygoing tropical city it had been. First of all, Hall had to endure "the tedium and brutality" of boarding school, Brisbane Boys' College. Lack of money gave him his release at the age of sixteen, he told Brady, "before it [school] did me any permanent damage." Then followed a "stiff dose of tropical suburbia" and "stints drudging as a junior clerk and delivery boy." But music opened a way into a different world.

Having already become proficient in the clarinet, Hall was looking for somewhere to play when he heard of John Manifold, who had a reputation as a musician, poet, and folklorist. Manifold had been born into a wealthy pioneering family from the Western District of Victoria but had returned from World War II a convinced radical and joined the Communist Party.

Unable to settle down in Victoria, Manifold retreated north to Brisbane to pursue his interests in poetry, music, folklore, and radical politics. To the seventeen-year-old Hall, Manifold's weatherboard house on its stilts in the suburb of Wynnum, resounding with music and good talk and "creaking with plurality," Hall says in his 1978 book on Manifold, seemed a center of vitality in the midst of a society otherwise "luxuriating in a state of suspended animation." He still vividly recalls train journeys through "the heat and humidity" to the weekly evenings of music there.

Manifold was "very much a man of the present," and his interest in Australian folklore gave Hall a feeling for the vernacular culture. Manifold was also an admirer of eighteenth-century music, philosophy, and literature, and he introduced Hall to the works of John Wilmot, Earl of Rochester; William Fielding; Johnathan Swift; Alexander Pope; and to a range of nineteenth-century European writers from Francois Rabelais and Molière (Jean-Baptiste Poquelin) to Guy de Maupassant, Leo Tolstoy, and Fyodor Dostoevsky. But Manifold's influence was political also. As a Communist, Manifold was an internationalist, and through him Hall was made aware of the campaign opposing the execution of the Rosenbergs as Communist spies in the United States and of Senator Joseph McCarthy's persecution of the Left. In Australia, too, the defection of Russian diplomats, the Petrovs (Vladimir and Evdokia, husband and wife), had fanned anti-Communist feeling, and the group gathered at Manifold's house lived in fear of police raids. One recent migrant Hall knew lost his job for refusing to become a part-time informer reporting on the proceedings of the Brisbane Realist Writers Group, of which Manifold was president.

Through this group Hall came to meet such writers as Vance and Nettie Palmer, Dymphna Cusack, and Alan Marshall. At one of their meetings, Hall met the Aboriginal poet and activist Kath Walker (later Oodgeroo), and through her he became involved in the Aboriginal struggle for justice, becoming the editor of the newsletter of the Queensland Council for the Advancement of Aboriginal and Torres Strait Islanders.

Until then, Hall had seen himself as a poet. But he proved to be an effective journalist, writing simply and directly for an Aboriginal readership—supplying contact, news, and advice on civil rights and employment conditions, but, because of the strict supervision of missions and state reserves, copies had to be smuggled in—by members of the Railway Workers' Union and the Seamen's Union. Responses from its readers provided shocking evidence of widespread abuse of the rights of Aboriginal and Islander peoples, and attempts were made to silence them. Hall was vilified in the conservative press, and he recalls one occasion when a man sat all night in the street opposite his house with a gun across his knees.

By now, however, Hall was committed to working for Aboriginal and Islander advancement. In 1963 with Shirley Andrews he wrote and edited a user handbook, *Social Services for Aborigines,* published by the Federal Council for Aboriginal Advancement, and in the years that followed, he worked for a yes vote in the referendum held in 1967 to recognize Aboriginal peoples as citizens. The campaign was successful and resulted also in the Australian federal government being given a more significant role in Aboriginal affairs. For the rest of his career, Hall, whose first images of Australia had been the photographs of white pioneers in the bush, explored this other, Aboriginal side of Australian history and culture.

In the meantime, Hall was also studying for an arts degree at the University of Queensland, supporting himself as a freelance radio actor and scriptwriter for the Australian Broadcasting Commission (ABC). At the University of Queensland he got to know the already established poet Judith Wright, who was also a friend of Walker and a champion of the Aboriginal cause. The friendship was enduring, as Wright and Hall shared many other environmental concerns (Hall was a dedicated bush walker)—opposition to nuclear power, for example. (When much later on Wright went to the World Poetry Conference, part of Expo '67 in Montreal, Canada, Hall and his wife looked after Wright's teenage daughter, Meredith.)

At the University of Queensland, Hall majored in music, a study that also had an effect on him as a writer. In his research for an essay on opera, for instance, he came across a proposition of one of the founders of opera, Galileo Galilei, father of the famous scientist, that opera is not so much a drama set to music as a drama of the hidden passions revealed through music.

This idea had a profound influence on Hall when he began to write novels. But his study of music also gave him an entrée into professional music. On one occasion, for example, he was called on by the Sydney Symphony Orchestra under Richard Divall to play the recorder obbligato to Yvonne Kenny's initial solo aria in her triumphant appearance in George Frideric Handel's *Xerxes* (composed circa 1738). At a more academic level, Hall, through his study of the history of music, founded and directed the Australian Summer School of Early Music, first at the University of New England, then in Canberra.

He also studied English and Indian philosophy, and this study revived his interest in Asia and the Middle East that had begun with the voyage to Australia in 1949. Consequently, in 1958, not long after his graduation, with the £100 he had managed to save, he decided to travel. At the time, a trip overseas had become a rite of passage for many young Australians who felt their own culture limited and limiting and were looking for something more. Many of them, such as Clive James and Peter Porter, did not return and made a reputation in London. Hall, however, did return.

Onboard ship on the way to England, he met a young Indian, Satinder Gupta Chaudhary, who introduced him to the teachings of Swami Vivekanand, which became an important influence in his life at that age. Hall did not stay long in England but soon made for Europe, carrying a backpack and walking much of the way through southern France into Spain, where he hoped to meet poet Robert Graves, whose book *The White Goddess* (1948) he had just read. Graves lived on the island of Majorca, and Hall made his way there; finding Graves's address in Palma, Hall sat down outside the apartment, intending to waylay the poet. He waited several days in vain; one of the residents finally took pity on him, telling him that Graves spent most of his time in a village some twenty miles away. Hall shouldered his backpack, walked there, and finally managed to speak to Graves and show him some of his work. Graves was impressed, saying that there was nothing he could teach the young poet about poetry, but he generously spent two hours talking to Hall and offering advice on writing prose. Graves's argument that the reader should be seen as cocreator of a work of literature impressed Hall.

When Hall returned from the Continent to London, he found work with Thomas Cook's travel agency, where he found time to work on a novel, *The Ship on the Coin: A Fable of the Bourgeoisie* (published later, in 1972), a parable in which American tourists buy a ticket to slavery and row their own *quinquereme* (galley with five benches) around the Mediterranean. He also arranged for the publication of his first book of poems, *Penniless till Doomsday,* which appeared in London in 1962. By then he had returned to Australia, and not long after his return in 1962 married Maureen Elizabeth McPhail, the "Bet" to whom several of his works are dedicated and with whom he had three daughters–Imogen (born 1963), Delia (born 1963), and Cressida (born 1966).

In 1963 Hall and his wife set out again for Europe, spending much of their time in Greece, where they met and made friends with the expatriate Australian writers George Johnston and Charmian Clift. In one of the poems written at the time and dedicated to

Dust jacket for Hall's 1988 novel, the first volume of a trilogy set in the Yandilli area (Bruccoli Clark Layman Archives)

Johnston and Clift, "Evolution: Pass and Repass," Hall suggests the importance of this time in Greece, a place in which the ancient myths still retained their power:

> To seek a barbarous age
> some need to quit their own,
> discover clans and customs,
> towns that still engage
> in the model Marathon;
>
> their audacity is such
> they hope to decompound
> legend, myth and dream:
> lay bare the frame in which
> occurrences are bound.

Increasingly assured technically as well as intellectually, Hall was beginning to make a name for himself and was represented in every volume of the annual *Australian Poetry* between 1963 and 1969 and in other major anthologies, such as *Poetry Australia* and *An Overland Muster*. His work also appeared in *New Voices of the Commonwealth,* published in London in 1961, and he published seven collections of his poetry between 1963 and 1973. One of these, *The High Priest, Coifi,* published in 1963 as one of the series of booklets on Australian artists and poets (with paintings by Andrew Sibley, on whose work Hall wrote a monograph published in 1968, *Focus on Andrew Sibley*), also reflects his growing interest in the interrelationship between the arts, and the publication of *Selected Poems* in 1975 established him as a poet of some stature.

But Hall was also contributing to critical discussion. With Thomas Shapcott he put together an anthology, *New Impulses in Australian Poetry* (1968), highlighting the work of younger and more adventurous poets. But his interests extended beyond the literary mainstream. He edited *Poems from Prison* (1973) by Jack Murray and others, and at the other end of the scale, in 1968 he edited *Prometheus,* the journal of the Australian National University Students' Association. As poetry editor of the national newspaper *The Australian* between 1967 and 1978, Hall introduced readers to the work of such young Australian poets as Michael Dransfield, Geoff Page, and Roger Macdonald but also secured first rights to poems by such international figures as the American poet Galway Kinnel and the English poet whose work he had long admired, Robert Graves.

Hall was interested in experiment, in the ways in which the arts reflected the radical search in the late 1960s and early 1970s for new modes of consciousness. After the untimely death of Dransfield, Hall saw to the publication of a hitherto unpublished collection of Dransfield's poems, *The Second Month of Spring* (1980), and later *Michael Dransfield: Collected Poems* (1987). In his own work, too, Hall was experimenting with new forms, particularly with the interplay between music and poetry. In 1970 he organized a performance of his poetic sequence *Romulus and Remus,* with music by Richard Mills, a work that was published as a record. The poems explore such issues as schizophrenia and the search for identity, the passion for power, the loss of confidence in history, and the search for alternative forms of consciousness that preoccupied many at the time.

Even in Brisbane, where Hall still lived, this sense of crisis was strong, intensified perhaps by the way in which the conservative premier Johannes Bjelke-Petersen cracked down harshly on protestors. In the late 1960s Hall had been involved in the struggle led by Judith Wright to save the Great Barrier Reef from commercial exploitation. But like many of his generation, Hall was also opposed to the war in Vietnam. The opposition was gaining momentum. As he recalled it in his 2002 conversation with Brady, even conservatives were "beginning to fall victim to an unspeakable horror," the suspicion that the carnage in Vietnam, which

the Australian government supported, was impossible to justify. The Aboriginal struggle continued with a new emphasis to which Bjelke-Petersen was implacably opposed. When the Springboks, the South African rugby team touring Australia, came to Brisbane, Hall joined in the street protests. But he and his friend Judith Wright devised a protest of their own against apartheid; they invited Kath Walker and the Aboriginal pastor Jim Brady to dinner with them at the motel at which the Springboks were staying, confronting them with the spectacle of blacks and whites kissing each other in greeting and dining together as friends.

A Place among People, set in Brisbane and written in 1970 but not published until 1975, reflects these political concerns and won third place in the Captain Cook Literary Award competition. But Hall was increasingly turning his attention to the novel. *The Ship on the Coin,* which he had begun in London in the 1950s, was published in 1972, the first in a succession of novels about the abuses of power and the ways in which present and future are burdened with the treacheries of the past.

The political climate was changing, however, as the election of the Edward Gough Whitlam government in 1972 put an end to the long reign of the Conservatives in federal politics, and Hall was beginning to be drawn into cultural politics. In 1970 he was asked by the Australian Department of Foreign Affairs to join a cultural delegation to India to meet Indian writers, visit some Indian universities, and take part in a five-day seminar on Australian literature in New Delhi. The delegation was made up of writers and academics, with Professors Leonie Kramer and George Russell from the universities and James McAuley, Judith Wright (who brought her daughter with her at her own expense), and Rodney Hall as the writers.

Hall and Wright were delighted by the sights, sounds, and smells and by the rich variety of cultures of a society that, as Hall put it in a letter to Wright (Wright Collection, National Library of Australia), seemed "paved with people," and these experiences were reflected in the growing interest of his work in the fantastic and the fabulous. He and Wright were used to traveling the hard way, so whenever they could, they escaped from their position of privilege. On one occasion, arriving at the train station before the rest of their party and finding a special carriage reserved for them, they removed the notice reserving the carriage for them, and people streamed in—eating, feeding their babies, talking, and laughing around them for the rest of the journey. This visit also led Hall to reflect on his British inheritance and question its imperial assumptions.

With the election of the Whitlam government, which promised significant political change, Hall began to think of moving south. He had lectured on the recorder at the Canberra School of Music from 1961 to 1971 and in 1968 had been the first writer appointed to a Creative Arts Fellowship at the Australian National University in Canberra, so he already had a foothold there. The Halls decided to leave Brisbane. But before they did so, Hall, Bet, and their daughters traveled overseas again–to London first, then to Eastern Europe and on to Greece to the island of Hydra, where George Johnston and Charmian Clift lived. There the Halls looked after the house for some months while Johnston and Clift were away.

On their return to Australia the Halls began looking for a place in the bush where they could live cheaply and Hall would be able to spend more time writing, thinking at first to settle somewhere in the Blue Mountains not far from Sydney. In the end, however, they chose the South Coast, seven acres of bushland not far from the little town of Bermagui on a headland looking out across a "vast expanse of ocean in the direction, roughly speaking, of Alaska." The country reminded Hall of his mother's photographs of the bush that had fascinated him as a child. More practically, it was not far from Canberra and Sydney. This area became the "Yandilli," a countryside haunted by its Aboriginal past and by the violence and eccentricities of pioneering days that figured in his subsequent novels as a legendary place rather like William Faulkner's Yoknapatawpha County.

In 1974 Hall was awarded a fellowship from the Literature Board of the Australia Council, which had been set up by the Whitlam government, and this fellowship and a part-time tutorship at the Canberra School of Music from 1978 to 1983 enabled him to settle down to work on the novel *Just Relations* (1982). Set in the former gold-rush town of Whitey's Falls, now largely populated by aged eccentrics living in a state of suspended animation as they contentedly watch themselves and the town fall into decay, and six years in the writing, it won the Miles Franklin Prize for the best Australian novel of the year when it appeared. But the dedication to his redoubtable grandmother Edith Buckland, his godmother Vera Bridgstock-Choat, who had taken in a boarder, Freddie Bowcher, a retired bank manager, suggests that the novel draws also on Hall's childhood memory, and this fact contributes to the affectionate richness of the novel.

Just Relations also interrogates the myth of progress and development taking hold in the 1980s in Australia, making a foray into the marvelous and fantastic and contesting the disenchantment of the world, which is the other side of the preoccupation with money making, having, and spending, and in this way continues Hall's search for alternative forms of con-

Dust jacket for the U.S. edition of Hall's 1991 novel, the second volume in a trilogy exploring early life in Australia (Richland County Public Library)

sciousness. For him the act of naming often distorted the experience, and the artist's task is to put names to new uses.

For the next two years, 1983 and 1984, Hall spent a good deal of time lecturing on Australian literature in Europe for the Australian Department of Foreign Affairs. An awareness of the larger world and of the interplay of political and economic power is evident in his next novel, *Kisses of the Enemy,* published in 1987. The most directly political of his novels, it is about the attempt by international economic interests to establish a dictatorship in Australia. The dictator, Bernard Buchanan, is a grotesque figure who "would take nobody's word that the future so much as existed until he might tramp in its wreckage for himself." But clearly his power also rests on a society addicted to "a vocabulary of the future too deeply known in our secret selves to be opposed." The only force to oppose this tyranny, the novel suggests, is music, represented by Dorina–a pianist, but also Buchanan's wife–in whose presence even workmen on a building site begin to whistle. For Hall, music is the language of the secret self that he sees as the heart of civilization and the great enemy of the "econocentric world" represented by Buchanan and his cronies.

Hall's concern for the direction in which Australia seemed to be moving was continued in *Captivity Captive,* which appeared in 1988, the year of the bicentenary of European settlement of Australia, a year in which many were beginning to rethink the story of settlement to take into account the history of the settlers' relations with the Aboriginal inhabitants. As Hall said later in his Alfred Deakin lecture in 2001, one of a series to commemorate the centenary of Federation, if Australians were to develop an authentic sense of themselves as a people, "the first thing is to give up our falsified and laundered view of what has happened since 1788."

Captivity Captive is the first of a trilogy set in the Yandilli area that attempts to fulfill this idea. Concerned with the meaning of freedom and captivity, it turns on a brutal nineteenth-century murder that involves a family of poor Irish settlers. But significantly, it concludes with an ambiguous deathbed confession and in this way touches on the question of guilt, which Hall found not only a "deeply interesting phenomenon" but also "deeply demanding," as he told Felicity Plunkett. Despite or perhaps because of its ethical concerns, the novel was a critical and financial success, especially in the United States, where the legendary radio personality Studs Terkel did a long and sympathetic interview with him.

The next volume in the trilogy, *The Second Bridegroom* (1991), continues the reworking of the "authorized version" of Australian history. But it moves further back in history than the 1890s, in which *Captivity Captive* was set, to the first days of settlement on the South Coast in the 1830s, to the estate of a wealthy farmer and the arrival of a ship bringing supplies and convicts to work for him. One of these, an apprentice printer convicted of forgery, is a victim of attempted rape by a fellow convict and escapes, shortly after his arrival, into the bush, where he is taken in by the Aborigines. The central character and main narrator, he is a man caught between two worlds; he is able for this reason to see what is really happening, the "age-old story of ownership," the clash between the newcomers and the Aboriginal people whose land has been invaded and whose culture is threatened with destruction. When the settler's house is burned down, the young escapee watches with "terrified joy" the destruction of the colonial dream of property and possessions, a "frail idea" that "will remain forever beyond reach." In this way the novel explores what Hall has called "the dark

secret haunting the Australian heart . . . the knowledge that we stole what we have" from its first peoples.

Hall decided at this stage that the pair of novels should be expanded to a trilogy, introducing a woman's narrative, operatic in language and form that would be able to express the innermost passions involved. Just at that moment, however, Hall was approached to accept a four-year appointment as chairman of the Australia Council. He was aware that the council was in a difficult position politically and was facing substantial cuts in funding. He also realized that if he accepted, he would have little time to write. Nevertheless, he decided to accept the appointment, since, as he explained later to Plunkett, he believed in the council and thought "that it has transformed our lives in this country, it's certainly transformed *my* life."

He felt that he should put something back into it. His decision was helped by the fact that when he met the treasurer, Paul Keating, who had been one of the strongest critics of the council and soon became prime minister, they hit it off personally. Keating became a strong supporter of the council, while Hall came to admire the prime minister, especially for his strong support for Aboriginal land rights. Hall expressed this admiration in the dedication of his novel *The Day We Had Hitler Home* (2000), in which he praised "the magnificent achievement" of the Native Title Act, which Keating pushed through Parliament.

In the brief time between the announcement of his appointment to the council and taking up his duties as chairman—knowing how little time he would have to write—Hall said in his interview with Plunkett that he "dashed off a draft" of the novel that became *The Grisly Wife* (1993) "very quickly, three weeks or something." He thus had something to work on whenever his duties at the council allowed it. It was not an easy time. But when his term of office ended in 1994, Hall had the satisfaction of leaving the council in a better position financially than it had been when he took over.

The Grisly Wife appeared not long before his appointment ended. About a religious commune, a group of women gathered around a charismatic preacher who came from England to Yandilli in the late nineteenth century to establish a community that "claimed direct access to the divinity," it won the Miles Franklin Prize for 1994. But what most satisfied Hall was that he felt that in it he had solved the technical problems that had been troubling him and was able to give each of the characters an appropriate voice, thus enabling him to investigate the process of "re-making Australia into a new Britain" from a range of different angles. But this technique meant that the novel made significant demands on its readers, asking them to take the characters on his or her own terms, many of which seemed difficult to credit—a confident belief in miracles, for instance. This collision between the documentary and the fantastic was by now central to Hall's work, though in this novel it is particularly powerful, since Hall is writing about a closed community of women gathered around a dominant but ultimately ineffectual male. The description of the gradual disintegration of this community into a group of complex and often confused individuals, however, makes its own comment on the society and history Hall is exploring.

His next novel, *The Island in the Mind* (1996), moves further into the world of fantasy; it is set in an unnamed European court of the seventeenth century, "an age of intrigue and bloodshed, religious upheavals, the rise of atheism and overt homosexuality," as the dust jacket of the book describes it. Operatic in style and form, its tone is polyphonic, as characters within and without the pale of power and influence appear and disappear, circling around the image of a vast unknown island that could be regarded as an image of Australia, the "Great South Land" of European imagination. The book did not, however, attract much attention except in England.

In the meantime, Hall continued his contribution to public life. In 1997 he was appointed to the Australia-Korea Foundation, an advisory body to what had now become the Department of Foreign Affairs and Trade, and in the same year he was a participant in the Centenary of Federation Convention held at the South Australian Parliament in Adelaide. In 1998, in a pamphlet, *Abolish the States!: Australia's Future and a $30 Billion Answer to Our Tax Problem,* he called for a new constitution, and his play *A Return to the Brink* (published in 1999), which dealt with Aboriginal Australians' claims for justice, was produced for the Melbourne International Festival of 1998.

The next novel, *The Day We Had Hitler Home,* reflected his political concerns more directly than *The Island in the Mind* had done. It was dedicated not only to the former prime minister, Keating, whose work for Aboriginal land rights had been admired by Hall, but also to Wolfgang Borchet, described in the dedication as a German "who dared to say no to Nazism at a time when it seemed impossible to stop." Hall was troubled by the direction in which he believed Australian politics was moving under Prime Minister John Howard, and *The Day We Had Hitler Home* reflects Hall's concerns.

Combining fantasy with history, the novel begins with a bureaucratic bungle at the end of World War I that brings the young Corporal Adolf Hitler, who has been temporarily blinded by gas, to the little town of Cuttajo, the port for the Yandilli district, on the same ship on which the surviving Australian soldiers from the district are returning home. But the real story con-

Dust jacket for the U.S. edition of Hall's 1993 novel, about a nineteenth-century commune (Richland County Public Library)

cerns the history of Germany in the 1920s and 1930s as experienced by the young woman Audrey McNeil, stepdaughter of the richest man in the Yandilli district. Intrigued by the mysterious stranger, she manages to smuggle Hitler back to Germany and stays on to become a moviemaker there, living through the collapse of the Weimar Republic and Hitler's rise to power. As a young woman in Yandilli, she had been a mere spectator of history. But in Germany she is drawn into the growing murder and mayhem when her Jewish lover is murdered by Nazi thugs, and she risks her life to smuggle his daughter to safety in England. In this way the novel makes its comment on what in Hall's Deakin lecture the following year he identified as the "heart of what is unsatisfactory in Australia," the failure to "embrace the *uncomfortable* things" and find "the grace and the largeness to take into ourselves the monstrous in us."

As his career draws to its close then, Rodney Hall continues to ask large questions, even as he remains committed to the belief that art can be the means to an independent existence. His "lifelong quest," as he said in the Deakin lecture, has been "the search to uncover Truth," which he sees as "affecting everybody." But this truth is complex and complicated, "to be found in bits and pieces in the hidden places and passions of the self and in the ambiguities of daily life and of history." He is convinced that it is a quest of special importance for Australians, who must bridge the gap between the image and the reality of the colonial legacy by giving up what he sees as a "falsified and laundered version of history, 'our comfort zone'" to search instead for "the story at the heart of experience, at the heart of our knowledge and confusion, the story of our loves and disappointments, our grief and our happiness." It is this story, he believes, which "governs whom we trust, how we behave, and what we do with our lives."

Interview:

Felicity Plunkett, "All Those Layered and Clotted Images: An Interview with Rodney Hall," *Australian and New Zealand Studies in Canada,* 11 (1994): 1–12.

Papers:

Many of Rodney Hall's manuscripts and some correspondence are held by the National Library of Australia, Canberra.

Barbara Hanrahan

(6 September 1939 – 1 December 1991)

Elaine Lindsay

BOOKS: *The Scent of Eucalyptus* (London: Chatto & Windus, 1973; Sydney: Fontana/Collins, 1980);

Sea Green (London: Chatto & Windus, 1974; Sydney: Fontana/Collins, 1980);

The Albatross Muff (London: Chatto & Windus, 1977);

Where the Queens All Strayed (St. Lucia: University of Queensland Press, 1978);

The Peach Groves (St. Lucia: University of Queensland Press, 1979; London: Chatto & Windus, 1980);

The Frangipani Gardens (St. Lucia: University of Queensland Press, 1980; St. Lucia & New York: University of Queensland Press, 1984);

Dove (St. Lucia: University of Queensland Press, 1982; St. Lucia & London: University of Queensland Press, 1982);

Kewpie Doll (London: Chatto & Windus, 1984);

Annie Magdalene (London: Chatto & Windus, 1985; New York: Beaufort, 1986);

Dream People (London: Grafton, 1987);

A Chelsea Girl (London & Sydney: Grafton, 1988);

Flawless Jade (St. Lucia: University of Queensland Press, 1989);

Iris in Her Garden: Eight Stories (Deakin, A.C.T.: Officina Brindabella, 1991);

Good Night, Mr Moon (St. Lucia: University of Queensland Press, 1992);

Michael and Me and the Sun (St. Lucia: University of Queensland Press, 1992);

The Diaries of Barbara Hanrahan, edited by Elaine Lindsay (St. Lucia: University of Queensland Press, 1998).

OTHER: Untitled contribution, in *Why Children?* edited by Stephanie Dowrick and Sibyl Grundberg (London: The Women's Press, 1980), pp. 43–53;

Shaw Neilson, *Some Poems of Shaw Neilson,* foreword and illustrations by Hanrahan (Deakin, A.C.T.: Brindabella Press, 1984);

"A Red and Purple Rain," in *Unsettled Areas: Recent Short Fiction,* edited by Andrew Taylor (Netley, S.A.: Wakefield Press, 1986), pp. 43–46;

Barbara Hanrahan (photograph by Michael Kluvanek; from the dust jacket for the 1988 London edition of A Chelsea Girl; *Bruccoli Clark Layman Archives)*

"Piles," in *Expressway,* edited by Helen Daniel (Ringwood, Vic.: Penguin, 1989), pp. 215–217;

"Butterfly," in *Moments of Desire, Sex and Sensuality by Australian Feminist Writers,* edited by Susan Hawthorne and Jenny Pausacker (Ringwood, Vic.: Penguin, 1989), pp. 7–10;

"Sleeping Beauties," in *First Loves,* edited by John Malone (Sydney: Collins Australia, 1989), pp. 81–85;

"Earthworm Small," in *Inner Cities: Australian Women's Memory of Place,* edited by Drusilla Modjeska (Ringwood, Vic.: Penguin, 1989), pp. 143–152;

"Weird Adelaide," in *Eight Voices of the Eighties: Stories, Journalism and Criticism by Australian Women Writers,* edited by Gillian Whitlock (St. Lucia: University of Queensland Press, 1989), pp. 73–80;

Twelve Linocuts: A Suite of Prints (Canberra: Officina Brindabella, 1990);

"Rambling Rose," in *Heroines: A Contemporary Anthology of Australian Women Writers,* edited by Dale Spender (Ringwood, Vic.: Penguin, 1991), pp. 144–154;

"Some Girls," in *Wilder Shores: Women's Travel Stories of Australia and Beyond,* edited by Robin Lucas and Clare Forster (St. Lucia: University of Queensland Press, 1992), pp. 148–151.

SELECTED PERIODICAL PUBLICATIONS– UNCOLLECTED:
FICTION
"Mac," *Meanjin,* 39, no. 4 (1980): 578;
"Joy and the Bikies," *Antipodes,* 1, no. 1 (1987): 15–16.
NONFICTION
"Snapshot," *Words and Visions,* 15 (1984): 6;
"Miracle Nite," *Otis Rush,* 2 (1988): 44–50.

Barbara Hanrahan is known for her celebration of the lives of working-class women and men in the first half of the twentieth century, her compulsive recording of her suburban Adelaide childhood in the 1940s and 1950s, and her exploration, in a series of Gothic or fantastic fictions, of the interplay between good and evil. Similar concerns are evinced in her prints and paintings.

Hanrahan's life and work were shaped by an intense, idiosyncratic spirituality, clearly evident in her diaries but also hinted at in interviews and articles. At the age of twenty she pondered whether God's creations were fulfilled through human creativity; this thought process firmed to a belief that her talents were God-given and that it would be sinful if she were to fail to complete the creative task she had been set. She dedicated her life to revealing, through her art and writing, the presence of God's goodness in the world. For Hanrahan, art was a religious quest and writing was her religion.

Barbara Janice Hanrahan was born at St. Ives Hospital, Adelaide, South Australia, to Ronda (Goodridge) and William Maurice "Bob" Hanrahan on 6 September 1939. Her father, Barbara recorded in her diary on 14 August 1970, "was born into a Catholic Australian Irish family on the up-and-up." Grandfather Hanrahan may have worked as a blacksmith's striker, but Grandmother Hanrahan and her daughter "were bent on improving their social standing which they eventually did."

Bob Hanrahan worked at the machine shop at Holden's car factory. He died of tuberculosis and pneumonia at the age of twenty-six, when Barbara was one year old. His premature death affected Barbara deeply, as recorded in her memoir, *The Scent of Eucalyptus* (1973), and in later autobiographical stories. In her diaries she wrote of having to take up the responsibility of fulfilling the promise of his life through her art and writing.

Hanrahan was raised by her mother; her maternal grandmother, Iris Goodridge; and her grandmother's sister, Reece Nobes. The latter had been born with Down's syndrome and had been cared for by Iris Goodridge virtually from childhood. To support the family, Ronda Hanrahan worked as a commercial artist at John Martin's Emporium in Adelaide while Goodridge ran the household at 58A Rose Street, Thebarton. The three women and their inner-city working-class suburb feature repeatedly in Hanrahan's memoirs, diaries, and prints.

Barbara attended the Thebarton Primary and Technical Schools. She wanted to study languages and art subjects, but her family thought she would be better fitted for life as a wife and mother if she learned dressmaking and commercial skills. Despite her artistic talents, she was lonely and unhappy, having little in common with her fellow students, either in upbringing or aspirations.

In 1954 Ronda Hanrahan remarried, and the following year she and her family moved to 31 Pemberton Street, Oaklands Park, with Wal Wiseby and his two daughters. Barbara could not adjust to sharing her mother with another family and sought refuge in her artwork and diaries.

In 1957 Hanrahan started at Adelaide Teachers College and the South Australian School of Art. She took English I at the University of Adelaide before deciding to concentrate on art. Despite her shyness, she seemed to thrive at the college, designing posters for the student magazine and social functions, participating in the art club, publishing stories and drawings in the college magazine, attending Student Christian Movement devotions, and selling artwork at the Adelaide *Advertiser* Open Air Art Exhibition. In 1960 she began teaching art and music at Strathmont and Elizabeth Girls' Technical High Schools, having achieved her diploma in art teaching and winning the H. P. Gill Memorial Medal and the School Council Prize for Art Teaching. At night she took classes at the School of Art with Udo Sellbach and Karin Schepers and exhibited her work, attracting positive critical attention. In 1961 she was appointed assistant lecturer in art at Western Teachers' College in Adelaide and was awarded the Cornell Prize for Painting. At home, however, she continued to find life with her stepfather and stepsisters difficult, and in 1963 she sailed to England to study printmaking at the London County

Council Central School of Arts and Crafts. In *Michael and Me and the Sun* (1992) Hanrahan recorded her first exposure to American pop art and her discovery that she could use the sexual imagery then rampant in early-1960s London to bring together and sharpen the images of prettiness and torment that typified her early Adelaide prints.

When her money ran out in mid 1964, Hanrahan returned to Australia. She taught at the South Australian School of Art, exhibited her prints, and met Jo Steele. On 31 August 1965 Hanrahan again set off for London, in company with another Adelaide artist, Barbara Harvey. Fictionalized episodes of their voyage on the *Fairstar* appeared in Hanrahan's second book, *Sea Green* (1974), and caused an enduring rift between Hanrahan and Harvey.

Hanrahan resumed her studies at the Central School of Arts and Crafts. In November 1965 she had a brief affair, became pregnant, and, in the absence of family or financial support, had an abortion. This decision troubled her for the rest of her life. Early in 1966 Hanrahan reencountered Steele, who had preceded her to London and was working as an engineer and inventor. In June 1966 she moved to Fulham to be with him. They had an intensely close and complementary relationship for the rest of her life. They never married.

No diaries exist for the years 1962–1966. Hanrahan admitted to burning a diary relating to her first stay in London, but apparently she also refrained from diary writing for several years. In January 1967 she returned to her diary, hoping, as she noted on 4 January, to "find" herself and to "banish all the beastliness and wickedness and sin that have been in me lately." Her 1967 diary records mood swings, depression, fits of temper, feelings of isolation, love for Jo, worry that her part-time work as an art teacher would end, memories of Adelaide, and frustration that she was not getting anywhere with her prints. In one form or another, these concerns reappear throughout her diaries, which offer insights into her psychological state and, in particular, her sense of being two people—one hungering for critical recognition and commercial success and the other desperate to live apart from the world, creating work that was true to her talents.

Her diaries also reveal that she sometimes longed for a child, even though she and Jo had consciously decided against children, in order to dedicate themselves to their creative activities. In an article written for publication in *Why Children?* (1980), she explains how, as an artist, she had come to terms with this longing, saying that "a real child for me could be more truly created by making contact, spiritually, with

Dust jacket for Hanrahan's first novel (1973), based on memories of her childhood (Bruccoli Clark Layman Archives)

the child I once was." By re-creating herself in her writing, she "created a child that was more truly my own that [sic] any other might have been. . . ." This child, she believed, was "the source of all my creativity." In her autobiographical and Gothic fictions she often employed a child-like perspective, a technique that freed her to present the strangeness and mystery of things as if seen for the first time, seemingly unaffected by adult reticence, shame, or judgment.

In January 1968 Hanrahan's grandmother Iris died. Hoping to overcome the emotional distance between England and Australia, Hanrahan started recording her memories of childhood. These writings became the basis of her first book, *The Scent of Eucalyptus*, formally begun in 1971 and published in London in 1973. The book secured mixed reviews in England and Australia: Geoffrey Dutton, in a review for *The Bulletin*, described *The Scent of Eucalyptus* as "the most evocative account of growing up in suburbia that exists in Australian literature," while Carl Harrison-

Ford wrote in *The Australian* that Hanrahan had "written one of the gooiest and most precious accounts of that magic garden known as childhood I've ever had the misfortune to read." Throughout her literary career critics and readers were polarized by Hanrahan's highly polished writing style, her earthy subject matter, and her belief in the spiritual world that "lies behind and all about the small everyday existence," as she described it to Elsebeth Gabel Austin in 1985.

Even before *The Scent of Eucalyptus* had been published, Hanrahan had attempted two further books and was close to completing the manuscript of *Sea Green,* a blend of fiction and fact about a young Adelaide artist who travels to London to study art in the mid 1960s, becomes pregnant, has an abortion, and begins a long-term relationship with a character called "Black Jem," a thinly disguised Jo Steele. Hanrahan later judged this book to be her worst and instructed that it should not be reprinted.

Hanrahan's published books fall into three categories: autobiographical fictions or memoirs—*The Scent of Eucalyptus, Sea Green, Kewpie Doll* (1984), *Iris in Her Garden: Eight Stories* (1991), and *Michael and Me and the Sun;* Gothic novels—*The Albatross Muff* (1977), *Where the Queens All Strayed* (1978), *The Peach Groves* (1979), *The Frangipani Gardens* (1980), and *Dove* (1982); and biographical fictions based on the lives of people known to her—*Annie Magdalene* (1985), *Dream People* (1987), *A Chelsea Girl* (1988), *Flawless Jade* (1989), and *Good Night, Mr Moon* (1992). The autobiographical fictions cover her life up to the publication of her first book: in their repetitiveness they suggest the importance Hanrahan placed on that time when her imagination ran free and when she started to see art as a means of accessing the transcendent within her conventional suburban self. The best source about her later years is her diaries, published posthumously (*The Diaries of Barbara Hanrahan,* 1998).

The Albatross Muff, Hanrahan's first excursion into Gothic fiction, was triggered by the purchase (from an old circus shop in London) of a plastic bag full of letters, dating back to 1809, covering the lives of the Hodge family. Hanrahan started work on the manuscript in 1972, forwarding it to Chatto and Windus in December 1975, by which time she was planning *Where the Queens All Strayed.* These books, and the three that followed, are conscious attempts to move away from autobiographical writing, even though they grew out of Hanrahan's late-adolescent reading of her great-grandmother's books, as recalled in *Why Children?:*

Bits of bridesmaid's fern pressed to tissue-paper frailty fell out as I turned the *Girl's Own Annual*'s pages.

Inside covers like that I found a world that suited me exactly. The juxtaposition of the concrete and the immaterial was fascinating; under the whimsicalities and Willy-wetleg pieties was a harshness I could relate to, a cruelty—little white girl is constantly threatened. Surrounded by pressure from the people I loved to lead the conventional life they'd failed at themselves, I was saved by a fantastic world. Art and poetry came out of the book's inconsistencies. I liked my angels weighed down in marble; I relished the marvelous absurdities, the hypocrisies, the terrible extremes.

While the English reviews of *The Albatross Muff* (set in England) were positive, the remaining Gothic novels were first published in Australia. Admittedly, *Where the Queens All Strayed, The Frangipani Gardens,* and *Dove* were set in Adelaide, and *The Peach Groves* in New Zealand (in homage to Katherine Mansfield), but their melodramatic style may have been too much for English sensibilities: Hanrahan's English editor, poet D. J. Enright, who had encouraged her early writing, rejected *The Frangipani Gardens* on the grounds, as reported by Hanrahan in her diary on 22 January 1980, that "it is squalid 'very Hanrahanesque, but gone rancid.'" The subsequent, relatively restrained, biographical fictions (*Kewpie Doll, Annie Magdalene, Dream People,* and *A Chelsea Girl*) were first published by English publishing houses.

Hanrahan returned to Adelaide for two months in 1973, and again in 1974 to take up a yearlong teaching position in 1975 at the South Australian School of Art. Research undertaken during these visits fed her Gothic novels, which were set between the 1850s and the early 1930s. Steele, meantime, undertook a B.A. (honors) in fine art at the Central School of Art, majoring in sculpture. In 1978, prompted by her intense homesickness, Steele and Hanrahan bought an old house and shop in Adelaide, at 48 Esmond Street, Hyde Park. From then until Hanrahan's health prevented it, they divided their time between Australia and England.

Despite her desire for a life apart from the "newspaper world," Hanrahan was pleased that her talents were being recognized at home, with exhibitions and teaching positions, purchase of her prints by the state galleries, invitations to writers' festivals, and writing grants from the South Australian government and the Australia Council. She was frustrated, however, that her books failed to win literary awards or interest North American publishers.

Hanrahan's fascination with questions of morality and with the nonmaterial world is most obvious in her Gothic fictions, in which she explores what happens when evil, carnality, and greed run unchecked in insular societies. Taken as a whole, these books read as commentaries on moral and spiritual matters, including the individual's search for wholeness, the deadening effects of a society on its members, the hypocrisy that lurks behind religious display, the healing powers of nature, the mystery of the spirit, and the potential of art to transcend the mundane.

Dove, the last book in the series, written during 1980–1981, focuses on the "grim underworld" that sustains respectable society. In the novel, set in South Australia between the 1870s and 1932, corruption pervades all levels of the population: the self-styled aristocrats, the working class, and the unemployed.

At the apex of society is the wealthy but witchlike widow, Mrs. Arden, and her adopted son, Valentine. She collects little girls like playthings, returning them to the orphanage when she tires of them. After her (possibly suspicious) death, Valentine installs himself in an Adelaide mansion, a "picture-book place" full of treasures and exotic birds with clipped wings. Like a vampire, he feeds on the living, collecting an entire family for his amusement, starting with Dove Thorn, whose spirit he consumes, and then her sisters, Rosa and Crystal, their husbands, and, finally, Dove's daughter, Clare. He rewards and punishes, stirs up trouble between them, and blackmails them with shameful memories from their past.

Hanrahan's working class is ready enough to sell its soul for the sake of trifles. In the main, the men are weak, and the women are in thrall to romantic fictions that promise loving marriages, wealth, and social advancement. For such rewards they lie about their past, emasculate their husbands, and abandon their children. They lose themselves and any happiness they might already enjoy.

The rich patronize the working class, but they underestimate the anger of the unemployed. Even though Hanrahan uses the unemployed to bring down Valentine and the materialistic society he represents, she has no illusions about their revolutionary ideals. The starving rabble, descending on Arden House as Adelaide's upper class entertain (and ridicule) the local workers and their families, is driven by thoughts of despoliation: like everyone else, they have sold their souls to greed. Little wonder that Hanrahan ends the book with a grand and beautiful conflagration, sparked by a wax candle in a silver candlestick. People cling together as they try to escape—whether or not they do is of little consequence. The final image is of the burning house, as it seems to tremble: "It was a magic thing, all ruffled. It was a splendid flowering."

Dove, like the other fantastic fictions, reads like a fairy tale, with its child-like narratorial voice, which unwittingly reveals the intentions of its characters, its cast of grotesques, with their heightened emotions, its startling images, its feverish pace prohibiting pause for conversation or reflection, and its air of corruption and perverted sexuality. Like the other novels, it does not offer a conventionally "happy" ending, but instead offers a form of moral consolation, demonstrating that unchecked corruption brings about its own collapse. These novels, more than any others, demonstrate the singularity of Hanrahan's voice within Australian literature: no other writer has produced such a concentrated study of good and evil so far removed from twentieth-century realism, yet still speaking directly to a society built on consumerism and Hollywood fantasies. Hanrahan's bonfire of the vanities completes her examination of the more negative aspects of life; the biographical fictions that follow celebrate the hidden spirituality of ordinary people who are at peace with the world.

In July 1981 Hanrahan and Steele, on their way back to London, made their first visit to America, hiring a car in Albuquerque and driving to Taos to pay homage at the shrine of D. H. Lawrence. They went on to Mexico, as Hanrahan was keen to write a book about Frida Kahlo. While Hanrahan reveled in the strangeness of Mexico, she was exhausted by the noise, humidity, dirt, and unfamiliar food. The book on Mexico never eventuated, despite several attempts to bring the material together. More pleasing was a visit to Flannery O'Connor sites in Milledgeville, Georgia.

In London, on Christmas Day 1981, Hanrahan began writing *Kewpie Doll,* another autobiographical fiction covering her life up to 1963. She decided that she could only write of Australia, and she and Steele returned to Adelaide in September 1982, via the American South and pilgrimages to D. H. Lawrence's ranch and Willa Cather's childhood home in Red Cloud, Nebraska. On 11 April 1983 Hanrahan recorded in her diary that *Kewpie Doll* had been accepted by Chatto and Windus, provided that some of the "pees, snots, blackheads" were removed.

May 1983 marked a new direction in Hanrahan's writing, when she started taping the memoirs of an elderly Adelaide neighbor, Anne McGeoch, sensing in it a "sacred thing." This book was the first of the biographical fictions. In these narratives and short stories Hanrahan offers Australians—long used to celebrating explorers, sportsmen, and soldiers—an alternative, a collection of modest suburban heroes, noted for their courage in enduring everyday life. She described her intentions in an interview with John Stevens, published in *The Age:*

Dust jacket for Hanrahan's 1977 novel, her first attempt at Gothic fiction (Bruccoli Clark Layman Archives)

If I can get close to one woman in Thebarton and record all the small things important to her it's the same as writing a Greek myth. The woman starts to loom large.

In Greek myths the characters are like great big archetypes, sort of cut-out designs, and if you can do one tiny woman in Thebarton well enough she becomes a pattern.

In her autobiographical fictions Hanrahan wrote of her need to escape the constrictions of Adelaide; in *Annie Magdalene* she uncovered the richness and adventure of a life lived from childhood in a single suburb. In all of the biographical fictions she sought to preserve the texture and integrity of working-class lives that were ignored by historians.

Annie Magdalene is a monologue, with the reader acting as an invisible auditor. It starts with Annie Magdalene's account of her grandparents and ends with her in her garden, aged in her seventies, feeding the birds and burying dead bees in order to save them from being eaten by the ants: images that call to mind Hanrahan's "Earth Mother" prints.

Annie Magdalene's strength lies in her ability to cope. She does not daydream about lives she might have led had she married or continued her education past the age of fourteen. She is kind to others but emotionally self-contained, to the extent that events, whether sad or pleasurable, scarcely seem to touch her. She sounds as if she is recalling the past by rote, rather than reliving it. If she is proud, it is because she lives independently, without burdening others.

Annie Magdalene's self-confidence, however, brings with it a lack of curiosity in, or involvement with, what is happening in the outside world. For her, World War I is processions and sock knitting; the Depression causes her to lower her prices for dressmaking; and World War II sends her to work in an aircraft-parts factory. Domestic events and relationships are more important than wars and politics, as epitomized in her attitude toward the media: she turns on her television every six months to see if it is working, listens to the radio for the time calls, and gives up buying the newspaper "because it was only full of other people's troubles; if you'd known the people you might have sympathized or gone and helped them, but when you didn't I couldn't see any sense in reading about them."

Hanrahan captures in this work, as in her other biographical fictions, a character representative of those generations who were taught not to complain about circumstances, not to question authority, not to regret the past, and not to dwell on their own feelings. Annie Magdalene values honesty, practicality, modesty, equanimity, and a sense of responsibility. To a more cynical world, she appears naive and limited, but she has a unified sense of self and remains open to enjoy whatever life brings her. Significantly, the biographical fictions have generated the warmest reception from reviewers. Phyllis Fairie Edelson, writing in *Antipodes* (March 1987), speaks for many women when she sees Annie Magdalene as "successful in living her life to the fullest in the narrow space which history and fate have allotted her. . . . This slim novel reflects both the unrealized potential and the private, as opposed to public, achievements of generations of women."

In February 1983, while preparing prints for an exhibition, Hanrahan felt as though she were having to drag her body about but blamed it on Adelaide's summer heat. She experienced increasing discomfort in her back and received a variety of diagnoses but no relief. In March 1984 she was hit by a car, suffering a broken collarbone. By June the pain in her spine was so intense she saw a neurologist, who found a lump at the base of her spinal cord. She was operated on immediately, and a malignant sarcoma was removed. Her prognosis was poor.

Prior to Hanrahan's beginning radiotherapy, Hanrahan and Steele went to Melbourne to see Ainslie Meares, a doctor who, through meditation, had enabled some people to achieve remission of terminal cancer. For the rest of her life, with relatively few lapses, Hanrahan meditated four times each day, an hour at a time, and followed a strict dietary regime. She withdrew from public life and concentrated on her creative work. Between 1984 and 1991 her output was prodigious: seven books completed and a book of linocuts published, as well as multiple art exhibitions in Adelaide, Melbourne, Brisbane, and Canberra.

Against the odds, Hanrahan's cancer went into remission, although she was never free of the pain caused by damage to the nerves from the operation. Gradually she was drawn back into literary and artistic life. In April 1985 she and Steele returned to London, where she interviewed Annie McKewen for the biographical fiction *A Chelsea Girl*, and Terry Currell, a former fellow student at the Central School of Art,

for what became her final memoir, *Michael and Me and the Sun*. They returned to Adelaide in August 1985, and she worked with Alison Carroll, selecting prints for the book *Barbara Hanrahan, Printmaker* (1986). In October she completed her collection of biographical narratives, *Dream People*. In June–July 1986 she represented Australia at literary conferences in Austria and Scotland, using the time in England to research *A Chelsea Girl* and to visit D. H. Lawrence's birthplace. In September 1986 she was in Darwin for a writers' workshop; a side visit to Broome resulted in the essay "Miracle Nite" (1988). In April 1987 Hanrahan started interviewing Victoria West for the book that became *Good Night, Mr Moon;* in May she began working on *Flawless Jade,* based on the life of her friend Winnie Wong; in June she was writer-in-residence at the University of Adelaide; in August she visited Melbourne and Sydney to promote *Dream People;* and in September she read at the Brisbane Writers' Week, then took up a residency at Rollins College in Florida, returning to Australia in early December.

In January 1988 the sarcoma recurred at the base of her spine. She returned to Melbourne for meditation sessions and again renounced public life and ambition. She and Steele took a flat in Melbourne, and Steele (who had become disillusioned with the art world) gave up his sculpture to care for her full-time. In September she read at the Spoleto (Melbourne) writers' festival; a week later she was advised that the tumor had grown slightly. She remained optimistic, joining the Victorian Print Workshop in October so she could continue printmaking in Melbourne.

The progress of the tumor could not be halted, and from early 1989 she experienced increasing pain and numbness. Nevertheless, she worked on stories of great tenderness about her family for the collection *Iris in Her Garden* while continuing with *Good Night, Mr Moon* and starting research for a book based on the South Australian township of Moonta. By February 1990 she found sitting in a car for any length of time difficult; the pain was attributed to a hemorrhage of the nerves in her back, damaged by the radiotherapy. By 23 September she was having trouble walking and sitting and spent much of her time in bed, but could still write in her diary that day: "I do have faith, and I don't feel low, but very light and gay inside. My spirit part is all right and feels as if it flies. And I know that my body will heal." In October she started chemotherapy in Adelaide and continued to write and to color her prints.

In January 1991 Hanrahan started writing *Michael and Me and the Sun*. The pain increased to such an extent that she had a morphine pump fitted in Feb-

ruary. She was constantly nauseous. She went to Melbourne for more meditation sessions in June but within a few days was returned to the hospital in Adelaide by air ambulance, suffering from meningitis. At this stage she was unable to walk and agreed to a further operation on her spine to try to remove the sarcoma. The operation, as was expected, left her a paraplegic. Her creative urge was undiminished, however, and in August she visited the public library in her wheelchair to research material for *Michael and Me and the Sun*. She commenced radiotherapy at the Memorial Hospital in September, and in late September the nurse noted that her hands were slipping off the keys of her typewriter. Steele put her notes for *Michael and Me and the Sun* together for typing in October and November. Her last diary entry, on 5 November, records a brain scan the previous day and her doctor's fear that there could be a new sarcoma.

She felt she needed new glasses and ended, "Help me find me, dear God."

In fact, she had a brain tumor and was going blind. Her last words to Steele before she slipped into a coma in late November were "I'm happier now than I've ever been, and I don't want anyone to pity me." She died peacefully on 1 December 1991.

Hanrahan's death was noted in Australian newspapers and literary and art journals, but she stood outside of mainstream Australian literature. She belonged to the generation of Australians who sought artistic freedom in London, and she was little known in Australia when her first three books were published. She did not partake fully of literary life in Australia, avoiding book reviewing and awards judging, public commentary, and literary committees. Her writing style was idiosyncratic, and while most of her books were set in South Australia, they dealt with past, not current, events. She ignored literary and critical trends and took inspiration from the Elizabethan poets, D. H. Lawrence, Virginia Woolf, Katherine Mansfield, William Blake, and later, Flannery O'Connor, Eudora Welty, and William Faulkner. She envied the success of contemporary Australian novelists but was not prepared to compromise herself by emulating their style of writing: she felt she could only write successfully from her own "insides." After her death the South Australian government established the Barbara Hanrahan Fellowship for writers of poetry and creative prose, and a wing of the University of South Australia's City West Campus was named after her.

One book-length study of Hanrahan's work has been published–*Woman and Herself* (1998), by Annette M. Stewart, who offers a psychoanalytical reading of Hanrahan's art, writing, and life, stressing its "unusual," "weird," and contradictory nature. Stewart comments positively on the "visionary quality" of Hanrahan's art, observing that "little work of this kind has been done in our country, especially not by women."

Hanrahan's books were reviewed in London, the United States, and Australia, but few reviewers asked what she was attempting to achieve in her work. The most sympathetic reviews and articles have been written by women who have responded to the moral and spiritual dimensions of Hanrahan's work, particularly in the Gothic fictions, and who have appreciated the sensuality of her writing. The least-sympathetic reviews have been written by men objecting to the "sweet decadence" of her writing style; to her treatment of the past as "day-dream stuff"; to her insistent reworking of autobiographical material; and, as Laurie Clancy wrote in "The full circle before the world" for the *Australian Book Review* (August 1984), to her fixation with "physical ugliness and maiming, sexual perversion and obsession, the processes of the body and the grotesquerie of various kinds." The biographical fictions have generated the most positive responses, with reviewers recognizing Hanrahan's intention of making unacknowledged lives sacred.

Barbara Hanrahan insisted that she wrote for ordinary readers, not for academics, but her work invites a range of critical approaches, including humanist, poststructuralist, feminist, postcolonial, psychoanalytical, and theological. While she stood apart from the literary mainstream, the intensely personal nature of her work and her insistence on creativity as a religious vocation have enriched Australian literature and ensured that she remains, as she wished, "an original."

Interviews:

Hazel De Berg, 13 October 1982, tape 1261, Australian National Library, Canberra;

Jennifer Palmer, *Bulletin*, 103, no. 5345 (21–28 December 1982): 203–206;

Julie Mott, *Australian Literary Studies*, 11, no. 1 (1983): 38–46;

Suzanne Hayes, March 1984, audiocassette released by CALS (Media Unit), Adelaide College of Technical and Further Education;

Elsebeth Gabel Austin, *Kunapipi*, 7, nos. 2–3 (1985): 152–162;

John Stevens, "An author who finds little joy in her task of writing," *Age* (Melbourne), 15 June 1985, p. 15;

Candida Baker, *Yacker 2: Australian Writers Talk about Their Work* (Woollahra, N.S.W.: Pan, 1987), pp. 72–92.

Bibliography:

Barbara Hanrahan, Austlit <http://www.austlit.edu.au>.

References:

Ian Adam, "Margin? Center? The Polychromagic Realism of *The Frangipani Gardens*," *Antipodes*, 5, no. 1 (1991): 47–50;

Elsebeth Gabel Austin, "An Australian Eve: A Study of Barbara Hanrahan's Novels," thesis, Copenhagen University, 1989;

Barbara Hanrahan: A Retrospective Exhibition of Prints, catalogue of Adelaide exhibition, 6 December 1992;

Carmel Bird, "Generosity," in *The Eleven Saving Virtues*, edited by Ross Fitzgerald (Port Melbourne, Vic.: Minerva, 1995), pp. 193–212;

Pearl Bowman, "Barbara Hanrahan–'for writing and for art,'" *Antipodes*, 6, no. 2 (1992): 103–106;

Diana Brydon, "Barbara Hanrahan's Fantastic Fiction," *Westerly*, 27, no. 3 (1982): 41–49;

Giovanna Capone, "Barbara Hanrahan and *The Albatross Muff*," in *Percorsi Immaginati: Journey, Metaphor and Model, in Anglophone Writers from Africa, Asia, America and Australia* (Bologna: Cooperativa Libraria Universitaria Editrice Bologna, 1993), pp. 163–178;

Alison Carroll, *Barbara Hanrahan, Printmaker* (Netley, S.A.: Wakefield Press, 1986);

Pam Gilbert, "Barbara Hanrahan," in *Coming Out From Under: Contemporary Australian Women Writers* (Sydney: Pandora, 1988), pp. 66–86;

Kerryn Goldsworthy, "'Your Only Entry Into the World': Barbara Hanrahan's Adelaide," in *Southwords: Essays on Australian Writing*, edited by Philip Butterss (Kent Town, S.A.: Wakefield Press, 1995), pp. 144–159;

Joan Kirkby, "Daisy Miller Down Under: The Old World/New World Paradigm in Barbara Hanrahan," *Kunapipi*, 8, no. 3 (1986): 10–27;

Elaine Lindsay, "Barbara Hanrahan: Caught in the Eye of God," in *Rewriting God: Spirituality in Contemporary Australian Women's Fiction* (Amsterdam & Atlanta, Ga.: Rodopi, 2000), pp. 213–276;

Lindsay, "Barbara Hanrahan: Eyeing God," *Australian Religious Studies Review*, 6, no. 1 (1993): 1–6;

Lindsay, "'From the Earth is Risse a Sun': The Later Diaries of Barbara Hanrahan," in *A Talent(ed) Digger: Creations, Cameos, and Essays in Honour of Anna Rutherford*, edited by Hena Maes-Jelinek, Gordon Collier, and Geoffrey V. Davis (Amsterdam & Atlanta, Ga.: Rodopi, 1996), pp. 171–177;

Lindsay, "A Mystic in Her Garden: Spirituality and the Fiction of Barbara Hanrahan," in *Claiming Our Rites: Studies in Religion by Australian Women Scholars*, edited by Morny Joy and Penelope Magee (Adelaide: AASR, 1994), pp. 19–35;

Lindsay, "Spiritual Subversions," in *Australian Feminist Studies*, 14, no. 3 (1999): 357–366;

Lindsay, "Women Rising: Spirituality in the Writings of Barbara Hanrahan," *Kunapipi*, 16, no. 1 (1994): 13–21;

Kate Llewellyn, "A Torch Held by a Malevolent Stranger," review of *The Diaries of Barbara Hanrahan*, edited by Lindsay, *Southerly*, 58, no. 3 (1998): 246–250;

Carol Merli and Paul Salzman, "Barbara Hanrahan's *Annie Magdalene*: The Inside Story," *Southerly*, 52, no. 4 (1992): 105–118;

Maryvonne Nedeljkovic, "Flawless Jade," *Commonwealth Essays and Studies*, 13, no. 1 (1990): 87–94;

Bruce A. Clunies Ross, "On Not Meeting Barbara Hanrahan in the Adelaide Suburbs: A Colonial Rhapsody," in *A Talent(ed) Digger: Creations, Cameos, and Essays in Honour of Anna Rutherford,* edited by Maes-Jelinek, Collier, and Davis (Amsterdam & Atlanta, Ga.: Rodopi, 1996), pp. 178–183;

Annette M. Stewart, "Barbara Hanrahan's Grotesquerie," *Quadrant,* 32, nos. 1–2 (1988): 59–65;

Stewart, *Woman and Herself: A Critical Study of the Works of Barbara Hanrahan* (St. Lucia: University of Queensland Press, 1998);

Alrene Sykes, "Barbara Hanrahan's Novels," *Australian Literary Studies,* 11, no. 1 (1983): 47–57;

Sykes, "*The Scent of Eucalyptus:* Gothic Autobiography," *Australian Literary Studies,* 14, no. 3 (1990): 306–315;

Sue Thomas, "Writing the Self: Barbara Hanrahan's *The Scent of Eucalyptus,*" *Kunapipi,* 11, no. 3 (1989): 53–66;

Brenda Walker, "Tea-Rose and The Confetti-Dot Goddess: Images of the Woman Artist in Barbara Hanrahan's Novels," in *Who Is She?: Images of Women in Australian Fiction,* edited by Shirley Walker (St. Lucia: University of Queensland Press, 1983), pp. 204–219.

Papers:

Barbara Hanrahan's diaries and some manuscripts are held by the National Library of Australia, Canberra (Barbara Hanrahan papers, 7754). The manuscript of *The Scent of Eucalyptus* and some memorabilia are held by the Mortlock Library, Adelaide. Hanrahan's prints and paintings are held by all the major art galleries in Australia and by private collectors; the National Gallery of Australia in Canberra has a virtually complete collection of her printed works.

Gwen Harwood
(8 June 1920 – 5 December 1995)

Jennifer Strauss
Monash University

BOOKS: *Poems* (Sydney: Angus & Robertson, 1963);
Poems: Volume Two (Sydney: Angus & Robertson, 1968);
Selected Poems (Sydney: Angus & Robertson, 1975; revised, Sydney & London: Angus & Robertson, 1985; revised again, North Ryde, N.S.W.: Collins/ Angus & Robertson, 1990);
In Plato's Cave, Broadsheet no. 25 (Canberra: Open Door Press, 1977);
The Lion's Bride (Sydney: Angus & Robertson, 1981; London: Angus & Robertson, 1981);
Bone Scan (North Ryde, N.S.W.: Angus & Robertson, 1988);
Collected Poems (Oxford & New York: Oxford University Press, 1991);
Night Thoughts, Pamphlet Poets, series 2, no. 1 (Canberra: National Library of Australia, 1992);
Freely They Stood Who Stood, and Fell Who Fell, The Tasmanian Peace Trust 1993 Lecture (Hobart, Tas.: Tasmanian Peace Trust, 1993);
The Present Tense, edited by Alison Hoddinott (Pott's Point, N.S.W.: Imprint, 1995).
Collections: *Selected Poems: A New Edition,* edited by Gregory Kratzmann (Victor Harbor, S.A.: Halcyon, 2001);
Gwen Harwood: Collected Poems 1943–1995, edited by Alison Hoddinott and Kratzmann (St. Lucia: University of Queensland, 2003).

OTHER: *Lenz,* music by Larry Sitsky, libretto by Harwood (Canberra: Canberra School of Music, 1970);
The Fall of the House of Usher, music by Sitsky, libretto by Harwood (Sydney: Ricordi, 1974);
Voices in Limbo, music by Sitsky, libretto by Harwood (Broadway, N.S.W.: Australian Music Centre, 1977);
De profundis, music by Sitsky, libretto by Harwood (Broadway, N.S.W.: Australian Music Centre, 1980);
Fiery Tales, music by Sitsky, libretto by Harwood (New York: Seesaw Music, 1992);

Gwen Harwood (Graeme Kinross Smith Collection; from Peter Pierce, Australian Melodramas, *1995; Thomas Cooper Library, University of South Carolina)*

The Golem: Grand Opera in Three Acts, music by Sitsky, libretto by Harwood (Sydney: Pellinor, 1993);
Southland: A Cantata for Baritone, Two Choirs and Orchestra, music by James Penberthy, words by Penberthy and Harwood (Yamba, N.S.W.: Southland Music Publishing, 1995);

Northward the Strait, music by Don Kay, words by Harwood (Broadway, N.S.W.: Australian Music Centre, 1999);

Eight Songs of Eve, music by Penberthy, words by Harwood (Grosvenor Place, N.S.W.: Australian Music Centre, 1999).

SELECTED PERIODICAL PUBLICATIONS–
UNCOLLECTED: "A Note on Noel Stock's Note on Wittgenstein's *Tractatus,*" *Poetry Australia,* 67 (1978): 79;

"Statement of Poetics," *Meanjin,* 39 (1980): 453;

"Lamplit Presences," *Southerly,* 40 (1980): 247–254;

"Words and Music," *Southerly,* 46 (1986): 367–376.

No one was likely to have predicted that Gwendoline Nessie Foster, the child born on 8 June 1920 in semirural Taringa, part of the city of Brisbane, would become one of Australia's major poets. In retrospect, however, as she told Stephen Edgar, one of several interviewers who sought her out in the 1980s, she could see that "everything I needed [to become a writer] was present in my childhood: my grandfather's library, literate and lively-minded adults, teachers with a passion for good grammar and no interest at all in self-expression from those whose parsing was less than perfect." This somewhat dry prescription for the making of a poet is dramatized in her depiction of a much-loved teacher, Fred Bennett, during the verse address she delivered on receiving an honorary D.Litt. from the University of Tasmania in 1988:

For Fred, if poetry existed,
it wasn't there to give us joy.
When parts of speech were duly listed
we were instructed to employ
our time in numbering and scanning[.]
("Syntax of the Mind," *The Present Tense,* 1995)

The childhood that preceded her school days presaged the different kind of poet she became. In 1988 Harwood said to another interviewer, Anne Lear: "I am a Romantic. I am a great Romantic with all the capitals that you care to give me. An upper-case Romantic. . . ." One thing that clearly links Harwood to Wordsworthian Romanticism is her account in "Alla Siciliana" (*Poems,* 1963) of her childhood experience of landscape as numinous, of a natural world where "earth in its own radiance turned / always from nightmare-dark to morning." The remembered radiance of childhood informs Harwood's later experience, and "light" becomes a central term in her poetic lexicon. But, as in the passage from "Alla Siciliana," radiance is not a simple state; rather, its powerful significance comes from its contiguity with its opposite,

the "nightmare-dark." Again and again Harwood's poems are set in morning or evening light, at moments when light and darkness meet and yet remain distinct, even as earth and sea touch and yet remain distinct in the littoral region that is such an important literal and metaphorical presence in her work.

Certainly, some shadows existed in her early childhood years. Her father, Joseph Richard Foster, had served in World War I before coming home in 1919 to a salesman's job and marriage to a young school teacher, Agnes Maud Jaggard. From part-heard and half-understood stories, the children of this postwar generation "knew about atrocities" ("The Secret Life of Frogs," collected in *The Lion's Bride,* 1981). When a small brother arrived in the family, his older sister was not exempt from the malice of sibling jealousy, recalled in "The Wasps" in *The Lion's Bride.* Against such shadows, however, reassurance came from the love of the parents later memorialized as "lamplit presences" in "The Violets" (*Selected Poems,* 1975).

In 1925 Gwen Foster was claimed by the world of school, an event she represents in a letter of 1 March 1943 (*Blessed City: The Letters of Gwen Harwood to Thomas Riddell, January to September 1943,* 1990) as disrupting an idyllic existence:

It was an unhappy day for me when I had to go to school. I would much rather have stayed under the orange trees and I'm sure it would have been much better for me in the long run. I'm sure you can't realise the dreariness of a Queensland State school.

Nonetheless, as an intelligent, even precocious, child, she had little trouble coping with schoolwork, either at Michelton or Toowong School, which she attended after the family moved to the Brisbane suburb of Auchenflower in 1927.

In 1933 Foster entered Brisbane Girls' Grammar School and encountered a new influence in Vera Cottew. Described in "Memoirs of a Dutiful Librettist" as an "inspired teacher of art," Cottew taught her to understand the paradox that the "unfading light" ("Giorgio Morandi," *Poems,* 1963) illuminating true art comes only from acknowledging that "light speaks always of *now*" ("Nightfall To the memory of Vera Cottew," *Poems: Volume Two,* 1968). But while art became an abiding poetic theme and led to friendships such as the one she enjoyed with painter and engineer Edward Tanner, it was not a prime preoccupation.

Admirers of Harwood's poetry, knowing how major a part music plays, not only in its themes but also in its metrical craftsmanship and complex tonality, will not be surprised that she stated to Edgar that "music was, is and always will be my first love." Music was part of the family life, and Foster, who began piano lessons early, completed her Associate in Music Australia (performance) in 1936 while still at school before studying under the George Frideric Handel scholar Robert Dalley-Scarlett. Although she gained her music-teaching diploma with distinction in 1939, she was aware that she would never become a concert pianist. "Suburban Sonnet" (in *Poems: Volume Two,* 1968), written some thirty years later, recalls the moment of truth when she was taken to play before Arthur Rubinstein, who was in Brisbane to give a recital: "Once she played / for Rubinstein, who yawned."

Foster did, however, become assistant organist, and later organist, at All Saints', Brisbane's oldest Anglo-Catholic Church. There she met Peter Bennie, a theological graduate of Melbourne University and her first love. Later public declarations of this romance tend to be marked by the insouciance with which Harwood told Vincent Buckley about it in a letter of 20 September 1961:

> I was a natural target in those far-off days for musicians, but my heart was set on a curate (C of E) who read Francis Thompson . . . in the pulpit; I gave the curate free piano lessons so that I could hold his hand but he got a stomach ulcer from the rectory cooking and married his nurse (Vincent Buckley Papers, National Library of Australia).

The next step in Foster's life was undoubtedly influenced by the religious environment of All Saints' if not by disappointed love. In August 1941 she entered the Anglican convent of the Poor Clares. After only six months of the novitiate, however, she decided that she lacked a vocation. Leaving the convent, she went to work at the War Damage Commission, a compulsory insurance agency set up by the Commonwealth. While there, if the 1943 letters to Thomas Riddell published in *Blessed City* are any indication, she positively reveled in her lack of vocation for the role of public servant, expressing astonishment at fellow workers who could be serious about a foolproof system for sorting bundles of cards:

> It may have been fool-proof, but it wasn't Gwen-proof and I found some lovely names on the cards, such as Mrs Herodias Smith, Mr Archelangelo Piccolo and William Ewart Gladstone somebody. And then the sight of twenty people all sorting cards frantically and seriously under electric light at long tables, and wearing those funny eye-shades, struck me as being so ludicrous that I started to laugh and they looked at me suspiciously and resentfully.

Gwen and Bill Harwood with their son John, 1950 (from Gregory Kratzmann, ed., A Steady Storm of Correspondence, *2001; Mississippi State University Libraries)*

Her fascination with comic names and with inventive pseudonyms was lifelong, as was a mischievous sense of the ludicrous, which was not always well received.

The recipient of the letters in *Blessed City,* however, shared Foster's sense of humor as well as her love of music. Riddell was a young World War II naval lieutenant who came to Brisbane in 1942. He was introduced to the Foster household by Bennie and formed a lifelong friendship with Foster, nurtured in the correspondence they exchanged when he was posted to Darwin. When the letters written by Foster to him during 1943 were published in *Blessed City* in 1990, they revealed that she was a scintillating letter writer, deft in framing an anecdote or sketching a character, and able to move with confidence from witty word games to the great questions. The talent was probably innate, but her affinity with Riddell offered an ideal opportunity to develop it and to discover the pleasures of writing for an appreciative audience.

She did not seem, however, to be anxious to extend the scope of that audience by seeking publication of the satiric and parodic verse she had been writing for some time. She did send one poem, "The Rite of Spring," to the recently created journal *Meanjin,* but by the time it appeared in 1944 her life was taking a whole new direction.

When Riddell returned to Brisbane in September 1943, he introduced to the Foster household a fellow naval officer, Frank William (Bill) Harwood. Two years later, in September 1945, Gwen Foster married Harwood, and they settled in Hobart, where he had been appointed to a lectureship in linguistics at the University of Tasmania. Although she came in time to love Tasmania's softer light and cloud-shifting skies, Harwood's initial reaction to them was to yearn for Brisbane's warmth and brilliant sunlight. The poem "1945," published in *Bone Scan* (1988), sharply evokes her sense of exile, but the poem nonetheless ends on a forward-looking note: "In my husband's luggage the *Tractatus* waits / with the world that was the case already fading." The *Tractatus Logico-Philosophicus* (1922) is the earlier of the two major works of the philosopher Ludwig Wittgenstein. The reference of the last line of "1945" is to the first proposition of the *Tractatus:* "The world is everything that is the case."

The value that Harwood placed on the stimulus that Wittgenstein gave to her writing is clear in this statement to Edgar:

> After we were married and we unpacked [my husband's] luggage I came across the *Tractatus* and in the lonely winter afternoons began to read this. I was enchanted. I didn't understand it at all. When I came to the end I felt like someone who'd come upon a new religion . . . when I read in Wittgenstein "Not how the world is, is the mystical, but that it is" I took my first step towards being a poet.

Even allowing for Harwood's inclination to hyperbolic exuberance in acknowledging indebtedness to people, places, and experiences that influenced her, she obviously found in Wittgenstein congenial food for thought on two of her major preoccupations: the nature of being and the nature of language. So "Heidegger" in *Bone Scan* begins, "Like Wittgenstein, he found much cause to wonder // 'that there are things in being.' / Searching for roots, he thought all words were names."

Besides Wittgenstein, other influences, both intellectual and personal, affected Harwood's 1945 "lonely afternoons" and laid the foundations of her later poetry. She now resumed seriously the study of German begun in defiance of the jingoistic and anti-intellectual atmosphere of the War Damage Commission. The poets Johann Wolfgang von Goethe, Friedrich Hölderlin, Heinrich Heine, Rainer Maria Rilke, and Georg Trakl added their voices to those of the German *Lieder* (songs) that she had long admired. Other, more immediate demands, however, must have claimed much of her attention. On 16 August 1946 her first child, John, was born, followed in 1947 by a

stillborn daughter, of whom she later wrote movingly in "Dialogue" (*The Lion's Bride*). A second son, Christopher, was born on 2 April 1950 and twins, Mary and Peter, on 3 August 1952. Harwood was immersed in the world of motherhood, which she celebrates variously in "An Impromptu for Ann Jennings" as "squalling disorder" and a "beautiful tyrannic kingdom" *(Selected Poems).* A stroke of good fortune allowed Harwood to find, in the outer suburb of Fern Tree, a friend who shared not only motherhood but also her intellectual and musical interests, so that they could push their prams "exchanging views on diet, or Aristotle, / discussing Dr Spock or Wittgenstein."

The idea that Harwood's relative poetic silence during the 1950s typified the havoc maternity wreaks on the woman artist was understandably taken up by late-1960s feminism, but Harwood resisted it strenuously. At the heart of the argument was the possible autobiographical nature of the popular sonnet "In the Park," collected in *Poems.* There, the mother, embarrassed by an encounter with a previous lover who is clearly unconvinced by her clichéd praise of motherhood, finally declares of her three children, "They have eaten Me alive." Harwood does not, in fact, subscribe to the idea that the "I" of a poem is necessarily a persona; indeed, she insists in her interview with Lear that poems to close friends—and in particular the poem "Mother Who Gave Me Life" (*The Lion's Bride*)— should be read "as spoken from my heart, my heart and nobody else's. Nevertheless," she adds, "I'm a notorious trickster-prankster writer under pseudonyms and comic disguises, and I am often amused to see the 'I' of other poems read as Mrs Harwood of 18 Pine Street, West Hobart." In the case of "In the Park," she protested that the poem was in the third person, which indicated its non-autobiographical status, and under persistent questioning at a seminar at Monash University added indignantly, "her clothes are out of date, and *I* am never dowdy."

Nonetheless, during the 1988 interview with Barbara Williams she stated, "I gave myself wholeheartedly to my children. They need a wholehearted mother, not a half-hearted poet, in the house"; she later added, "I kept all that out of the way; a secret vice. . . . I had my poems in odd places. Late at night, I'd take them out, or early in the morning, just in my head." This description connects with the depiction of the frustrated poet of "Burning Sappho," published in *Poems: Volume Two* but excluded from *Selected Poems* because, Harwood said, "it was too cruel." In general, Harwood's poetry has been resolutely discreet about her life with her husband and children; a poem such as "Iris" (in *The Lion's Bride*), which explicitly acknowledges and resolves the tensions in being "husband and wife so long we have forgotten / all singularity," is a rarity.

Not until the mid 1950s was Harwood ready for publication. "Death of a Painter" and "Daybreak" appeared in 1956 in *Meanjin.* This magazine became, with

The Bulletin, her major publishing outlet, and she was awarded the short-lived *Meanjin* Poetry Prize in both 1959 and 1960. Indeed, as the 1950s turned into the 1960s, she was entering the publishing field with a rush that was obscured from readers—and even editors—by the curious history of her pseudonymous publishing. Between 1960 and 1962 three "new" poets made a considerable impression on the literary scene: Francis Geyer and Walter Lehmann in 1960 and Miriam Stone in 1962. All these poets were Gwen Harwood, as was the T. F. Kline who published some dozen poems in a variety of venues between 1968 and 1970.

Lehmann's unmasking followed publication under "his" name of a pair of sonnets, in *The Bulletin* of 5 August 1961. The acrostic message of "Eloisa to Abelard" bade a frivolous farewell to *The Bulletin,* while that of "Abelard to Eloisa"—Fuck All Editors—was positively scandalous. *The Bulletin* editor, Donald Horne, was furious and set about discovering what was already known to at least some among the circle of literary friends that Harwood was beginning to acquire. One of these was Melbourne poet and academic Buckley, who was encouraging and assisting Harwood to put together a collection in her own right. Since Lehmann's identity had been revealed, Harwood was free to claim "his" poems for this first collection, *Poems,* published by Angus and Robertson in 1963. Not, however, until *Poems: Volume Two* appeared in 1968 were the identities of Stone and Geyer claimed, although they had ceased publishing in 1963 and 1964 respectively.

The reasons for the extensive pseudonymous life seem neither simple nor single. Alison Hoddinott has suggested that the male pseudonyms were intended to circumvent editorial prejudice against "lady-poets." Thomas Shapcott attributed the use of pseudonyms to the nature of her creative drive: "Play is a natural extension of her understanding, and the creation of poets a natural extension of her play." This explanation seems closer to Harwood's own stance at the time, which represented the whole thing as a high-spirited literary prank, but later, in a 1972 interview recorded at the Canberra School of Music, she offered the thoroughly pragmatic explanation that she had so much material available that it seemed that sharing it among pseudonyms would ensure more acceptances in the limited and hotly contested field of poetry publishing.

Acceptances and recognition in her own right were not a problem after the reception of *Poems.* Critics admired her capacity to play variations on the "fugue of love and loss" ("Group from Tartarus") that has remained central to all her work, but they particularly admired the group of poems that embodied a striking critique of a certain kind of intellect in the figure of Professor Eisenbart, "who prized his dry / indifference to love and luck." In *Poems: Volume Two,* however, Eisenbart is displaced by the quite different Professor Kröte, who holds Harwood's interest up

to *The Lion's Bride* by his vulnerability to these very forces—and, of course, to music, since the redemption of this clownish, sad European exile lies in the fidelity he shares (as in "A Scattering of Ashes") with Harwood to "Music, my joy, my full-scale God."

In 1975, *Selected Poems,* which added some thirty new poems to a selection from the two earlier volumes, was awarded the Grace Leven Poetry Prize. A series of major awards followed. In 1977, the Fellowship of Australian Writers awarded her the Robert Frost Award for sustained poetic excellence. This honor was followed by the Patrick White Award in 1978 and in 1988 an honorary doctorate from the University of Tasmania (La Trobe University bestowed the same degree in 1994). *Bone Scan* won the Premier's Literary Award for Poetry in both Victoria and South Australia in 1989, the year in which she was made an Officer of the Order of Australia (OA). In 1990 *Blessed City* won *The Age* Book of the Year Award. From *The Oxford Book of Australian Poetry* (1965), edited by Judith Wright, onward, Harwood was represented in every anthology of Australian poetry and was one of only three Australians to appear in *The Faber Book of Twentieth Century Women Poets* (1987), edited by Fleur Adcock.

Harwood, however, was not a particularly prolific poet. While the 1975 edition of *Selected Poems* was supplemented by some thirty uncollected poems, not until 1981 did a new collection, *The Lion's Bride,* appear, which was not followed until 1988 by *Bone Scan.* One reason for the scarcity of poems, apart from her having returned in 1963 to the workforce as a medical receptionist, was that she was pursuing a parallel artistic career, that of librettist. In 1962 she had struck up a friendship with pianist Rex Hobcroft, who in 1963 introduced her to a visiting pianist and composer who had come to Hobart to take part in New Music, a seminar performance of contemporary music. Harwood's "New Music" *(Poems: Volume Two)* is a tribute to the influence Larry Sitsky had on her poetry; her meeting with him also offered a new scope for combining writing with music. For thirty-five years from 1963 she worked as his librettist; the two exchanged ideas for the coordination of music and words for the most part by letters.

The first product of their collaboration was *The Fall of the House of Usher* (published 1974), performed at the Theatre Royal in August 1965. A projected opera based on Kafka's *The Trial* had to be abandoned when copyright was refused, but work began in 1969 on *Lenz,* an operatic version (published in 1970) of Georg Büchner's fragment of a novel, *Lenz* (1850; translated into English, 1860), although the first performance of the opera by Harwood and Sitsky, in the Sydney Opera House, did not take place until 1974. The linear history of the collaboration of Harwood and Sitsky is confused by the vagaries of performance and of musical publication. For example, publication of *Lenz* preceded not only its performance but

BLESSED CITY

Letters to
Thomas Riddell 1943

GWEN HARWOOD

IMPRINT

Paperback cover for the collection of letters Harwood wrote to
a young naval lieutenant during World War II, published
in 1990 (Bruccoli Clark Layman Archives)

also the publication of its predecessor, *The Fall of the House of Usher*. The biographical sections of *A Steady Storm of Correspondence: Selected Letters of Gwen Harwood, 1943–1955* (2001), Gregory Kratzmann's comprehensive edition of her letters, indicate Harwood was already working in 1973 on the libretto of *The Golem*, which was only performed, after several revisions, in 1993 (also published in 1993).

Music thus remained a major part of Harwood's life. A shared passion for music, for instance, brought about her friendship with James McAuley, although she had little affinity with his political views and had been critical of his aesthetic judgment as poetry editor of *Quadrant*. While several of the poems in *The Lion's Bride* commemorate episodes involving McAuley, it is only in "Three Poems for Margaret Diesendorf" that Harwood reveals that the title poem had its source in hilarity shared with McAuley over an inept translation of Robert Schumann's "Die Löwenbraut" (The Lion's Bride, 1840).

One more major poetic stimulus to Harwood's poetry came when in 1975 Bill Harwood resigned from

the university for health reasons, and they moved to the rural community of Oyster Cove on the d'Entrecasteaux Channel. Apart from several fishing poems, Oyster Cove inspired Harwood's complex pastoral mode in which she weds something of Wordsworth's romantic sense of the independent voice of nature and of wild and solitary things to something of a classical affection for a serene landscape inhabited by human beings and domestic animals.

These pastorals, which form the final section of *Bone Scan* (1988), caught reviewers' attention less than two other components of the collection. One was the sequence "Class of 1927," in which Harwood recalls a classroom that is not "dreary," but a vividly detailed site of primary, if only partly understood, education in the complexities of light and dark in human nature: the class bully is defeated not by cleverness but by an instinctive assertion of goodness ("Slate"); ambition overrides generosity, but the fruits of victory taste sour ("The Spelling Bee"); exacted charity is disconcerted by the pride of the poor ("The Twins").

The other component was a new onset of the "nightmare-dark," confronted in the bravura performance wherein a monster Crab sings his aria in one of her more spectacular dream-poems, "Night and Dreams." In 1985, a few months after the move back to Hobart, Harwood was diagnosed with breast cancer. She recovered well from surgery and was able to make the experience part of this last, and successful, collection. After *Bone Scan,* however, her creative drive slackened, although she continued to be an energetic presence at writers' festivals, conferences, and other public occasions. For these she could still produce highly accomplished occasional verse, such as "Six Odes for Public Occasions," collected along with several of her prose autobiographical recollections and some entertaining self-parodies in *The Present Tense,* published in 1995 and edited by her old friend Hoddinott. The title poem, however, is the last of a long line of memorable elegies and marks the death of Buckley in 1988.

One of the self-referential or "Late Texts" of *The Present Tense* is "The Owl and the Pussycat Baudelaire Rock," which takes readers back to the striking "Night Thoughts: Baby and Demon" from *Selected Poems* (1975). The final poem in the collection, it ends "Baby, baby, the night is falling." Although Harwood lived to see the book published in September 1995, in January she had been diagnosed with untreatable renal cancer. On 5 December Gwen Harwood died in St. Helen's Hospital, and, according to her wishes, her ashes were scattered over the Brisbane River. Her reputation survives, and the fabric of Australian literature continues to be enriched by the wit, intelligence, and tenderness embodied in the distinctive musicality of her poetry.

Letters:

Alison Hoddinott, ed., *Blessed City: The Letters of Gwen Harwood to Thomas Riddell, January to September 1943* (North Ryde, N.S.W.: Angus & Robertson, 1990);

Gregory Kratzmann, ed., *A Steady Storm of Correspondence: Selected Letters of Gwen Harwood, 1943–1955* (St. Lucia: University of Queensland Press, 2001).

Interviews:

Stephen Edgar, "An Interview with Gwen Harwood," *Island Magazine,* 25–26 (1986): 74–76;

Anne Lear, "Interview with Gwen Harwood," *SPAN,* 26 (1988): 1–11;

Barbara Williams, "Interview with Gwen Harwood," *Westerly,* 33, no. 4 (1988): 53–58;

Candida Baker, "Gwen Harwood," in *Yacker 3: Australian Writers Talk About Their Work* (Chippendale, N.S.W.: Pan, 1989), pp. 130–157;

Jenny Digby, "The Evanescent Things," in *A Woman's Voice: Conversations with Australian Poets* (St. Lucia: University of Queensland Press, 1996), pp. 44–66.

Bibliographies:

Robert Sellick, "Gwen Harwood: A Checklist," in *Gwen Harwood,* edited by Sellick (Adelaide: Flinders University of South Australia Centre for Research in the New Literatures in English, 1987), pp. 93–103;

Jennifer Strauss, "Bibliography," in *Boundary Conditions: The Poetry of Gwen Harwood* (St. Lucia: University of Queensland Press, 1992; revised and enlarged, 1996), pp. 231–242;

Kath McLean, *Gwen Harwood: An Annotated Bibliography* (Canberra: ALIA Press, 1993);

The ALS Guide to Australian Writers: A Bibliography 1963–1995, edited by Martin Duwell, Marianne Ehrhardt, and Carol Hetherington, second edition (St. Lucia: University of Queensland Press, 1997), pp. 154–157.

References:

Alison Hoddinott, *Gwen Harwood: The Real and the Imagined World* (North Ryde, N.S.W.: Imprint-Collins/ Angus & Robertson, 1991);

A. D. Hope, "Gwen Harwood and the Professors," *Australian Literary Studies,* 5 (1972): 227–232; republished in *Native Companions* (Sydney: Angus & Robertson, 1974), pp. 197–203;

Elizabeth Lawson, *The Poetry of Gwen Harwood* (South Melbourne: Sydney University Press in association with Oxford University Press, 1991);

Lawson, "'They trust me with the axe': The Poetry of Gwen Harwood," in *Poetry and Gender: Statements and Essays in Australian Women's Poetry and Poetics,* edited by David Brooks and Brenda Walker (St. Lucia: University of Queensland Press, 1989), pp. 145–164;

Lyn McCredden, "Gwen Harwood: Poetry and Theology," in *Bridgings: Readings in Australian Women's Poetry,* edited by Rose Lucas and McCredden (South Melbourne: Oxford University Press, 1996), pp. 43–54;

Robert Sellick, ed., *Gwen Harwood* (Adelaide: Flinders University of South Australia Centre for Research in the New Literatures in English, 1987);

Thomas Shapcott, "The Faces of Gwen Harwood," in *Biting the Bullet: A Literary Memoir* (Brookvale, N.S.W.: Simon & Schuster, 1990), pp. 109–115;

Glenda Smith, *The Poetry of Gwen Harwood* (Glebe, N.S.W.: Pascal Press, 2000);

Jennifer Strauss, *Boundary Conditions: The Poetry of Gwen Harwood* (St. Lucia: University of Queensland Press, 1992; revised and enlarged, 1996);

Strauss, "Playing in Time: The Poetry of Gwen Harwood," *Critical Survey,* 6 (1994): 81–87;

Strauss, "She / I / You / It: Constructing Mothers and Motherhood in the Writing of Gwen Harwood," *Southerly,* 52 (1992): 1–19;

Andrew Taylor, "Gwen Harwood: The Golden Child Aloft on Discourse," in his *Readings in Australian Poetry* (St. Lucia: University of Queensland Press, 1987), pp. 112–125;

Stephanie Trigg, *Gwen Harwood* (Melbourne: Oxford University Press, 1994);

Chris Wallace-Crabbe, "My Ghost, My Self: The Poetry of Gwen Harwood," *Meanjin,* 28 (1969): 264–267; republished in *Melbourne or the Bush* (Sydney: Angus & Robertson, 1974), pp. 127–130.

Papers:

The major repository of Gwen Harwood's papers is the National Library of Australia (Canberra), which holds her papers (MS 3189) and correspondence 1954–1960 (MS 3657), while further material is to be found in the Papers of Vincent Buckley (MS 7289), of Larry Sitsky (MS 5630), and of Thomas Shapcott (MSS 3822, 5577). The National Library also holds a recording of an interview and several readings in its Tape Recording Collection. The Fryer Library of the University of Queensland holds some manuscript letters in MS 45 of its Australian Authors Collection.

Shirley Hazzard

(30 January 1931 –   )

Brigitta Olubas
University of New South Wales

See also the Hazzard entry in *DLB Yearbook: 1982.*

BOOKS: *Cliffs of Fall and Other Stories* (New York: Knopf, 1963; London: Macmillan, 1963);

The Evening of the Holiday (New York: Knopf, 1966; London: Macmillan, 1966);

People in Glass Houses: Portraits of Organization Life (New York: Knopf, 1967; London & Melbourne: Macmillan, 1967);

The Bay of Noon (London: Macmillan, 1970; Boston: Little, Brown, 1970; Ringwood, Vic.: Penguin, 1982);

Defeat of an Ideal: A Study of the Self-Destruction of the United Nations (Boston: Little, Brown, 1973; London: Macmillan, 1973);

The Transit of Venus (London: Macmillan, 1980; New York: Viking, 1980; Ringwood, Vic.: Penguin, 1981);

Coming of Age in Australia: 1984 Boyer Lectures (Sydney: ABC Enterprises for Australian Broadcasting Corporation, 1985);

Countenance of Truth: The United Nations and the Waldheim Case (New York: Viking, 1990; London: Chatto & Windus, 1991);

Greene on Capri: A Memoir (London: Virago, 2000; New York: Farrar, Straus & Giroux, 2000);

The Great Fire (New York: Farrar, Straus & Giroux, 2003).

RECORDING: *Shirley Hazzard Reading from Her Work,* read by Hazzard, Madison, Wis. (LM113), 1983 – comprises selections from *Transit of Venus.*

Shirley Hazzard's fiction is known and admired for its complexly bourgeois pleasures and interests, its internal personal and symbolic dynamics and complexities. However, also important to Hazzard are what she calls, according to Peter Fuller (*The Canberra Times,* 31 May 1992), "public themes," most evident in her non-fiction, but also resonating through her novels and stories. In addition to her ongoing critique of the United Nations (UN), her work canvasses a range of aesthetic issues and an abiding commitment to humanist values and the perceived need for writers and artists to ensure the retention of these beliefs in the modern world. The fiction, drawing on her own vast familiarity with European culture, poetry in particular, is thus demanding of its readers: as John Colmer has noted, "Shirley Hazzard writes for an audience sensitive to the slightest nuances of speech and alert to every literary allusion." The writing is also noted for its self-reflective delicacy of phrasing, its wit and irony, its intensely personal resonances, and the finely realized sense of place it evokes.

Shirley Hazzard was born 30 January 1931 in Sydney and grew up in upper-middle-class Mosman. She was the daughter of Reginald Hazzard, of Welsh background, and Catherine Stein Hazzard, whose background was Scottish. Her parents had met in Sydney while working for the British firm that built the Sydney Harbour Bridge in the 1920s, and they remained in Sydney after marrying. During the war years, Reginald Hazzard worked for the Australian government in the munitions industry, and at the end of the war, he moved into the Australian Foreign Service. The account Hazzard has given of her early life stresses the cultural aridity of this period in Australia as formative, in negative terms, of the broad cultural and imaginative values espoused and defended in her work.

A further intensely negative impact of this period was the 1930s Great Depression, of which she recalls primarily the broadly experienced humiliation, writing that "I was lucky that my family did not actively suffer during the Depression, which was terrible in Australia. It's not something a child lives through and ever forgets. It becomes a yardstick really for human experience when you've seen an entire populace humiliated, compounded by the penury of veterans of the First World War" (Gordan and Pasca). Her first *New Yorker* publication, the uncollected story "Woollahra Road" (8 April 1961), provides a first-person narrative focalized through a four-year-old girl's self-centered but expanding consciousness of her mother's identification with

114

another woman across the delineations of class, in just such a context of humiliation and lack.

Hazzard attended Queenwood College in Sydney. During World War II, with fears of a Japanese invasion of Sydney running high, her school was evacuated to the countryside–as dramatized in the Australian sections of *The Transit of Venus* (1980). Hazzard cites encountering Italian prisoners of war there as a significant moment in terms of her humanistic education: "In Australia, in wartime, Italy and Italians were a theme of derision to us–yet, here were these prisoners, recognizable in simple human terms" (Gordan and Pasca). Against this humanity sits her experience of rural Australia:

> Anywhere in the country then was desolate. There was a feeling you might be forgotten there, and at night the silence was the silence of a convent. There was a farm on the property, and I was sent down to get the milking can one evening. The sun was dying, there was the smell of cows, and I thought, Oh, to be more sad than this would hardly be possible. It was like a scene out of Thomas Hardy. It felt hopeless. (Wyndham)

Hazzard also writes and speaks of the effects of reading poetry, beginning as a child with Robert Browning, and describes herself as somewhat isolated as a consequence of these interests. According to Desmond O'Grady in an article in *The Sydney Morning Herald, Spectrum* (15 January 2000), Hazzard said, "In childhood, I lived much in books, and imagination, where one discovers affinities." Rather than remain at school as a boarder, on her parents' departure in 1947 to Hong Kong where her father had been posted as Australian trade commissioner, she chose to take up what, according to O'Grady, she saw as the "fortunate, formative" experience of overseas travel. In Hong Kong she began working for British Combined Services Intelligence. (Her *New Yorker* essay "Canton More Far" [16 December 1967] expounds with typical understated irony an incident from this period.) Her stay also provided material for her fourth novel, *The Great Fire,* released in 2003 following the publication of two extracts in *The New Yorker* in 1987 and 1990. While in Hong Kong, according to Jan Garrett, Hazzard visited Hiroshima "not many months after the bomb had been dropped," an experience accorded as formative to Ted Tice in *The Transit of Venus.* Hazzard remained in Hong Kong for two years, then traveled with her family to Wellington, New Zealand, for two years, then on via London to New York, where her father was appointed Australian trade commissioner in 1950.

Hazzard's years in New Zealand clearly mirrored earlier experiences in Australia; however, in New Zealand she was able to contrast Anglo lifestyles with more-vital cultures: "I was eighteen; I'd arrived from a dramatic, exotic, eventful place and now found myself in an extremely subdued, ingrown, and conventional society–everyone in bed by 7 pm" (Gordan and Pasca). This experience was tempered by her growing confidence in the existence of broader contexts for her life through reading. While living in Wellington, she was introduced to the translated poetry of Giocomo Leopardi, a discovery that led her to take up the study of Italian.

In 1951, on the marital separation of her parents and their subsequent departure from New York, Hazzard elected to remain there, taking up a position with the UN, where she remained for ten years. "I was 20 and I was part of that feeling of hope that came into the world with the end of the war. I went, like many other people then, to apply to the United Nations in a spirit of idealism, little dreaming indeed that idealism was the last thing that was wanted there" (Garrett). She was employed at a rather menial level–"I typed"–and she has written trenchantly about the organization's continuing lack of recognition of the skills of its female employees. In cultural and imaginative terms, too, this time was a period of lack: "I lived an obscure and penurious life in New York for several years, working at the UN . . . a very deprived life . . . a starvation diet" (Garrett).

She first visited Italy with the UN, in 1956, spending a year with the international mission to supply the peacekeeping force set up to send equipment to the UN army stationed in the Suez during the Suez crisis. During this year in Naples, she became friendly with an Italian family, and after her term there was up, she continued to visit them frequently at their home in Siena. She has described how, under their influence, she began to embrace, or to return to, humanistic rather than survival values. The experience, referred to both in interviews and in her fiction, was transformative in its effects on her aesthetic, ethical, and imaginative life: "From the first day (in Naples), everything changed. I was restored to life and power and thought" (Wyndham). The significance of Italy for Hazzard goes well beyond the personal. She has noted that "in Italy, the mysteries remain important: the accidental quality of existence, the poetry of memory, the impassioned life that is animated by awareness of eventual death. There is still synthesis, rather than formula. There is still expressive language" (O'Grady).

During this period she began to write, and her first story was accepted by *The New Yorker* magazine. *New Yorker* fiction editor William Maxwell has commented that Hazzard's early stories were received with some

Dust jacket for the London edition of Shirley Hazzard's 1967 collection of stories about working for the United Nations,
first published in The New Yorker *(Bruccoli Clark Layman Archives)*

astonishment, for they required almost no revision or editorial work, appearing to be "the work of a finished literary artist about whom they [we] knew nothing whatever" (Wyndham). She continued to write and publish with *The New Yorker* with such regularity that in 1962 she was able to resign her position with the UN and support herself solely by her writing.

In 1963 ten of Hazzard's *New Yorker* stories were collected and published in *Cliffs of Fall*. Central in them is Hazzard's preoccupation with questions of love and loss, aesthetics, and moral distinction, within the world of the personal relationships of the European and Anglo-American middle classes. The source of the title of the collection in Gerard Manley Hopkins's "O the mind, mind has mountains; cliffs of fall / Frightful, sheer, no-man-fathomed. Hold them cheap / May who ne'er dwelled there" encapsulates the concern of these narratives with the persistence of poetic insight in the inner drama of individual lives and relationships.

In January 1963 Hazzard met the man who became her husband—eminent literary translator and biographer Francis Steegmuller, twenty-four years her senior—at a party given by their mutual friend, writer Muriel Spark, in New York. Hazzard recollects the meeting in terms familiar from her fiction: "I noticed Francis, whom I'd never met, as he entered the room. He was, and is, very tall; he was very serious, even austere; and he was wearing a fawn-coloured greatcoat, a sort of British Warm, which he has to this day. . . . It was a singular moment: *colpo di fulmine*—a lightning bolt. In any case we sat down in a corner together and stayed there. When we came out of that corner, you might say, we went and got married" (Gordan and Pasca). The intensity of this narrative, the pleasures it recounts of good clothes and discreet settings, the social context of intense privacy, the literate and literary modalities of the experience as well as the recounting are all features of Hazzard's writing, sustained across her writing career. Hazzard and Steegmuller married on 22 December 1963.

The Evening of the Holiday, which had been published the previous year as a long short story in *The New Yorker,* was published in book form in 1966. This novella, a restrained work proceeding from the conventions of the Anglo-Italian romances of E. M. Forster and Henry James (though without overt reference to either of these writers), charts an unlikely romance between Anglo-Italian Sophie and Tancredi, a middle-aged Italian architect whose wife has left him. They meet in Siena, where Sophie is visiting her aunt; Tancredi, older, has separated from his wife. The textures of Italian life and culture are bound up with the romance. As Anatole Broyard points out in *The New York Book Review* (13 June 1982), "They are attracted to each other's complications, as seen against the larger complications of Italian art and life." When they part at the conclusion of the novel, the narrator comments, "It seemed to him that they were doing an obscure, outmoded thing in parting from each other." In this spirit, the novel engages broad cultural, aesthetic, and imaginative contexts, bringing them to bear on contemporary lives and modernity more generally.

In 1967 Hazzard's *New Yorker* stories set in the UN (although the institution is never named) were collected and published as *People in Glass Houses: Portraits of Organization Life.* The satirical stories trace the lives of individuals from across the globe as they are caught up in the institutional machinery, playing off idealism against disillusion and irony against self-interest.

The Bay of Noon, published in 1970, takes again the conventions of Anglo-Italian experience as a point of departure, drawing once more on Hazzard's own life in Italy. Jenny, the narrator, traces the events of one year she spent working at a NATO office in Naples, after a displaced wartime childhood spent in Africa, and escaping an obliquely dysfunctional family. Recounting these events, she reflects on humans' habitual severing of the past from current and contemporary life, the conventional status of the past as a sign of completed existence. Against this background, Jenny's experience of the city of Naples is testimony to the interrelatedness of past, present, and future, a place where the chaos and confusion of daily life are inextricably bound up with the legacy of past centuries and where human experience is part of a vast continuum in time. In the course of the narrative, Jenny tries to untangle the threads of a series of relationships—with her Neapolitan friend Giaconda; Giaconda's lover Gianni, with whom Jenny also has a brief romance; and Justin, a Scottish scientist with

whom Jenny sustains a flirtation and who runs off with Giaconda after the briefest of meetings. In the process, Jenny develops a familiarity with the patternings of love and loss that enables her to leave this site of discovery and to return to it years later, taken up differently with the experience of love. The core of the novella is its account of the determinations of love and its engagement with questions of memory and their relation to experience, the sense of self, and narrative. As Jenny reflects, "It's all wrong, what I've told you . . . but I can come no closer to it."

In 1973 Hazzard published her first major work of nonfiction, *Defeat of an Ideal: A Study of the Self-Destruction of the United Nations,* a critique of the UN establishment. She argues that the effects of McCarthyism in the United States left indelible effects on the UN structure, thus proscribing the UN from reaching its potential in relation to international human rights.

The publication of Hazzard's most substantial novel, *The Transit of Venus,* secured her reputation internationally as a significant and distinctive writer. Enormously popular and critically acclaimed (winning the United States National Book Critics Award for best novel of 1980), it is a vast and allusive, cosmopolitan and contemporary work that is yet "radically old-fashioned" (Peter Pierce) in its commitment to humanistic values and modes of articulation. Intricately plotted and densely symbolic, drawing on the elegant prose and characterization of her earlier fiction, the novel is yet memorable, perhaps, for its carefully controlled exploration of the expanding possibilities of the novel form. In it Hazzard's finely articulated bourgeois sensibilities are fully realized by being located in a more critically precise cultural and historical field, with events (and characters) self-consciously recalling specific novels—most explicitly Charles Dickens's *Great Expectations* (1860–1861)—as well as broader patterns and traditions of romance, fairy tale, melodrama, history, and myth.

The novel charts the social, sexual, and emotional fates of a group of characters—Caro, Grace, Ted, and Paul and their families, spouses, and workmates. It traces the details and diversions of their romantic fates from their individual childhoods through mature contacts and relationships as they move through a recognizably contemporary world, from Australia to Britain and the United States. Secondary characters divert much of the interest and energy of the novel toward unexpected and marginal experiences. This characteristic has the effect, as does the proleptic structure of the novel, of diverting the readers' attention from the satisfactions of traditional narrative and toward a sense of the centrality of the

Dust jacket for the U.S. edition of Hazzard's 1970 novel, based on her experiences while working in Italy during 1956 (Richland County Public Library)

nality, a structured world, and the importance of human volition in fate and faith. Some critics have read this investment in tradition as linked to, indeed bound by, the bourgeois values also inscribed in these works; however, for the most part, the novel was read enthusiastically within the context of postmodernist self-consciousness, as outlined by Nina Baym: "Its conspicuous passion for literary art makes it as serious and self-aware as the most radical experimental novel—makes it, in some extraordinary fashion, a radical experiment itself."

In 1984 Hazzard returned to Australia to present the Australian Broadcasting Corporation (ABC) Radio Boyer Lectures, *Coming of Age in Australia: 1984 Boyer Lectures* (published in book form in 1985), addressing the contrast she had noted between the Australia of her childhood and the country as it appeared to her during return visits to Sydney in 1977 and 1984. She wrote of the changes she perceived in Australian political, cultural, and public life generally. From the aridity of the 1930s and immediate postwar years, expressed in violent misogyny and xenophobic nationalism, she traced a growing tolerance and openness to pleasure and culture dating from the 1970s. The lectures, drafted before Hazzard left New York, were substantially reworked on her arrival, as she remarked dramatic and significant changes in Australian lifestyle, culture, and outlook in the more affluent 1980s. The series was criticized by some commentators as not providing an accurate or viable portrait of contemporary Australia because it neglected to reference Australian thought and letters.

In 1980 she had begun publishing articles documenting her case that the former UN secretary general, Kurt Waldheim, had concealed his past as an officer in Adolf Hitler's army and that UN member governments, including the United States, had assisted him in the cover-up. Her critique was eventually taken up by other writers and her claims borne out by the exposure of his background on his election as Austrian president. Her 1990 book, *Countenance of Truth: The United Nations and the Waldheim Case,* originally written as an article for *The New Yorker,* argued that the structure of the UN facilitated the rise of such a figure. This work was finished quickly during a period when she felt too distracted to write fiction, drawing on her extensive research, clippings files, and collection of documents relating to these issues at the UN. Hazzard has described herself during this period as torn between what she felt to be her duty as a witness and her duty as a novelist; this conflict is captured in the title, a quotation from Milton, who was criticized for writing essays against corruption in the Church, describing as the "bright countenance of

unexpected. Thus, Caro Bell's experiences in love and loss are explicitly compared to those of explorer James Cook throughout the novel and without irony: "The calculations were hopelessly out. . . . Calculations about Venus often are." Against this undecided point, the lives and movements of all the characters are linked throughout to the movement of the planets, to an overarching sense of what Hazzard elsewhere terms "destiny, things fulfilling themselves . . . a sort of wholeness really" (Garrett). Ultimately, the persistence of scientist Ted Tice's love for Caro, the "child of Venus," structures the narrative and the moral vision of the novel, along with the repudiation of what amounts to the self-interest of lesser characters, such as Paul Ivory and Angus Dance, both of whom betray the love of the Bell sisters.

Hazzard's writing derives self-consciously from the European humanist traditions of beliefs in ratio-

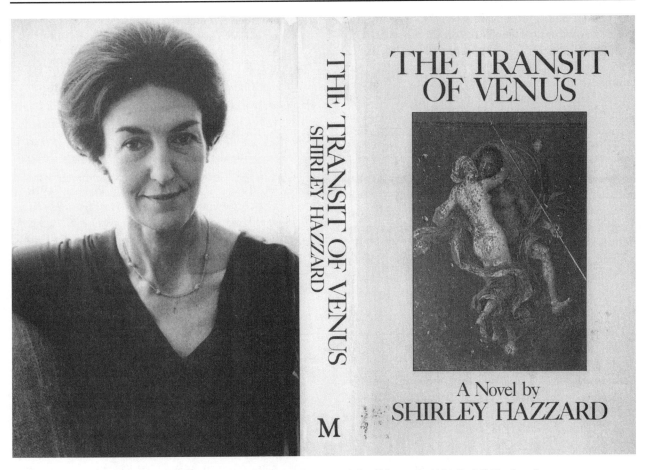

Dust jacket for the London edition of Hazzard's 1980 novel, which won the 1980 Book Critics Award
in the United States (Bruccoli Clark Layman Archives)

truth" his work as a poet, from which he must turn away because of his obligation to criticize corruption.

Hazzard and Steegmuller shared a seventeenth-floor apartment in the Upper East Side of Manhattan and apartments in Naples and Capri from the time of their marriage until Steegmuller's death in October 1994 from heart failure at the age of eighty-eight. The intensity of their shared literary lives characterizes, and even determines, much of the published biographical information about Hazzard. Steegmuller's influence can be seen to have taken the form of shared literary passions—references to writers on whom he was a specialist also proliferate through Hazzard's writing and conversation. Their participation in and contributions to the literary and cultural establishments of New York was sustained through this period, from the early 1960s until Steegmuller's death. Hazzard's own literary output through the 1990s, including a speech delivered in 1997 to the Sydney Institute, evidences her continuing investment and participation in an international literary and cultural life, with a continuing interest in Australian

issues. After Steegmuller's death, Hazzard commented in an article by Alan Attwood in *The Sydney Morning Herald,* 8 September 1997, that her work became even more the center of her life: "when I work I feel it's more like the life I had with him." The writing and revising of her new novel has occupied most of the 1980s and 1990s, with two extracts published so far in *The New Yorker,* in 1987 and 1990.

Her most recent work, *Greene on Capri: A Memoir* (2000), had its genesis in a request from Graham Greene's biographer, Norman Sherry, for details about Greene's life on Capri, which he first visited in 1948 and where he later became friends with Hazzard and Steegmuller. Hazzard's recollection of that period outgrew the few paragraphs originally planned for Sherry and resulted in the memoir, which has been hailed as both a vital account of Greene and an exemplar of the literary memoir form.

Hazzard does not reject her designation as an Australian writer but insists "my temperament is not a very national one" (Trish Evans). One impact of this view has been on her citizenship; she only took out United States citizenship twenty-five years after she began living in New York, on the resignation of Richard Nixon. Eschewing nationalistic identifications, she argues that it is "a privilege–to be at home in more than one place" (Gordan and Pasca). Further, "it wouldn't occur to me to consider myself an expatriate. I'm not even sure which country I'd be an expatriate of" (Gordan and Pasca). However, her novels are full of what might be termed an "expat." sensibility–peopled with displaced Anglos in Hong Kong, Italy, and the antipodean colonies, or displaced Australians in London and New York. She writes of the particular displacements of international bourgeois lifestyles and cultures, underpinned by colonial histories and continuities. As Caro explains in *The Transit of Venus*: "London is our achievement. Our career for the time being," and later, "Going to Europe, someone had written, was about as final as going to heaven. A mystical passage from which no one returned the same."

Interviews:

Catherine Rainwater and William J. Scheick, "An Interview with Shirley Hazzard (Summer 1982)," *Texas Studies in Language and Literature: A Journal of the Humanities,* 25 (1983): 213–221;

Lucy Latané Gordan and T. M. Pasca, "Shirley Hazzard: Back to Basics," *Wilson Library Bulletin,* 65, no. 3 (November 1990): 45–48.

Bibliographies:

John B. Beston, "A Bibliography of Shirley Hazzard," *World Literature Written in English,* 20 (1981): 236–254;

William J. Scheick, "A Bibliography of Writings by Shirley Hazzard," *Texas Studies in Literature and Language,* 25 (1983): 249–253.

References:

Nina Baym, "Artifice and Romance in Shirley Hazzard's Fiction," *Texas Studies in Literature and Language,* 25 (1983): 222–248;

Delys Bird, "Text Production and Reception: Shirley Hazzard's *The Transit of Venus,*" *Westerly,* 1 (March 1985): 39–51;

Giovanna Capone, "Shirley Hazzard: *Transit* and *The Bay of Noon,*" *Australian Literary Studies,* 13, no. 2 (1987): 172–183;

John Colmer, "Patterns and Preoccupations of Love: The Novels of Shirley Hazzard," *Meanjin,* 29 (1970): 461–467;

Colmer, "Shirley Hazzard's *The Transit of Venus,*" *Journal of Commonwealth Literature,* 19, no. 1 (1984): 10–21;

Trish Evans, "Shirley's 'Transit' is a rare event," *Weekend Australian,* 29–30 November 1980, p. 13;

Jan Garrett, "The Transits of Hazzard," *Look and Listen,* 1, no. 4 (November 1984): 36–39, 96;

Geoffrey Lehmann, "The Novels of Shirley Hazzard: An Affirmation of Venus," *Quadrant* (March 1981): 33–36;

Bronwen Levy, "Constructing the Woman Writer: The Reviewing Reception of Hazzard's *The Transit of Venus,*" in *Gender, Politics and Fiction: Twentieth-Century Australian Women's Novels,* edited by Carole Ferrier (St. Lucia: University of Queensland Press, 1985), pp. 179–199;

Russell McDougall, "Beyond Humanism? The Black Drop of Shirley Hazzard's *The Transit of Venus,*" *Journal of Commonwealth Literature,* 30, no. 2 (1995): 119–133;

E. B. Moon, "Fate, Individual Action and the Shape of Life in Shirley Hazzard's *The Transit of Venus,*" *Southerly: A Review of Australian Literature,* 43 (1983): 332–344;

Moon, "Indispensable Humanity: Saviours and Destroyers and Major and Minor Characters in Shirley Hazzard's *The Transit of Venus,*" *Southerly: A Review of Australian Literature,* 44, no. 1 (1985): 94–108;

Susan Moore, "Meaning and Value in Shirley Hazzard's *Transit of Venus,*" *Quadrant,* 28, no. 5 (May 1984): 75–79;

Brigitta Olubas, "Rewriting the Past: Exploration and Discovery in *The Transit of Venus,*" *Australian Literary Studies,* 15, no. 3 (May 1992): 155–164;

Peter Pierce, "Conventions of Presence," *Meanjin,* 40, no. 1 (1981): 106–113;

Anna Rutherford, "Mars Versus Venus: The Dialectics of Power in Shirley Hazzard's *The Transit of Venus,*" *Kunapipi,* 18, nos. 2–3 (1996): 309–327;

Robert Sellick, "Shirley Hazzard: Dislocation and Community," *Australian Literary Studies,* 9 (October 1979): 182–188;

K. M. Twidale, "Discontinuous Narrative and Aspects of Love in Shirley Hazzard's Short Stories," *Journal of Commonwealth Literature,* 26, no. 1 (1991): 101–116;

James Wieland, "'Antipodean Eyes': Ways of Seeing in Shirley Hazzard's *The Transit of Venus,*" *Kunapipi,* 5 (1983): 36–49;

Susan Wyndham, "Hazzard Ahead," *Weekend Australian,* 17–18 July 1993, pp. 26–32.

Dorothy Hewett

(21 May 1923 – 25 August 2002)

Bruce Bennett
University of New South Wales

BOOKS: *Bobbin Up* (Melbourne: Australasian Book Society, 1959; London: Virago, 1985; New York: Penguin, 1987);

What About the People! by Hewett and Merv Lilley (Sydney: Realist Writers, 1963);

Windmill Country (Melbourne: Overland in conjunction with Peter Leyden Publishing, 1968);

The Chapel Perilous (Sydney: Currency Press, 1972);

Rapunzel in Suburbia (Sydney: Prism, 1975);

Bon-Bons and Roses for Dolly and The Tatty Hollow Story: Two Plays (Sydney: Currency Press, 1976);

This Old Man Comes Rolling Home (Sydney: Currency Press / London: Eyre Methuen, 1976);

The Man from Mukinupin: A Musical Play in Two Acts (Perth: Fremantle Arts Centre Press / Sydney: Currency Press, 1979; revised, Perth: Fremantle Arts Centre Press, 1980);

Greenhouse (Sydney: Big Smoke, 1979);

Susannah's Dreaming; The Golden Oldies (Sydney: Currency Press, 1981);

Christina's World, music by Ross Edwards, libretto by Hewett (London: Universal, 1984);

Joan, music by Patrick Flynn, text by Hewett (Montmorency, Vic.: Yackandandah Playscripts, 1984);

Golden Valley; The Song of the Seals (Sydney: Currency Press, 1985);

Alice in Wormland (Paddington, N.S.W.: Paper Bark Press, 1987);

A Tremendous World in Her Head: Selected Poems (Sydney: Dangaroo Press, 1989);

Alice in Wormland: Selected Poems, edited by Edna Longley (Newcastle upon Tyne: Bloodaxe, 1990);

Wild Card: An Autobiography, 1923–1958 (South Yarra, Vic.: McPhee Gribble/Penguin, 1990; London: Virago, 1990; revised, South Yarra, Vic.: McPhee Gribble/Penguin, 1991);

Selected Poems (South Fremantle, W.A.: Fremantle Arts Centre Press, 1991);

Collected Plays, Volume 1 (Sydney: Currency Press, 1992)–includes *This Old Man Comes Rolling Home,*

1986 (from Candida Baker, Yacker, *1986; Paterno Library, Pennsylvania State University)*

Mrs Porter and the Angel, The Chapel Perilous, and *The Tatty Hollow Story;*

The Toucher (Ringwood, Vic.: McPhee Gribble / New York: Penguin, 1993);

Zimmer: A Mock Opera in Two Acts, by Hewett and Robert Adamson (Montmorency, Vic.: Yackandandah Playscripts, 1993);

Peninsula (South Fremantle, W.A.: Fremantle Arts Centre Press, 1994);

Collected Poems, 1940–1995, edited by William Grono (South Fremantle, W.A.: Fremantle Arts Centre Press, 1995);

Neap Tide (Ringwood, Vic. & New York: Penguin, 1999);

Wheatlands, by Hewett and John Kinsella (Fremantle, W.A.: Fremantle Arts Centre Press, 2000);

Halfway Up the Mountain (North Fremantle, W.A.: Fremantle Arts Centre Press, 2001);

A Baker's Dozen (Ringwood, Vic.: Penguin, 2001);

Nowhere (Strawberry Hills, N.S.W.: Currency Press, 2001).

PLAY PRODUCTIONS: *The Chapel Perilous,* Perth, New Fortune Theatre, 1971;

Catspaw: A Rock Musical, Perth, New Fortune Theatre, 1974;

Joan, Canberra, Canberra Repertory Society, 1975;

Miss Hewett's Shenanigans, Canberra, Canberra Playhouse, 1975;

The Golden Oldies, Melbourne, 1977;

Pandora's Cross, Sydney, Paris Theatre, Sydney Opera House, Theatre Australia, 1978;

The Man from Mukinupin, Perth, Playhouse Theatre, 1979;

The Fields of Heaven, Sydney, Sydney Opera House, 1982;

Zimmer, by Hewett and Robert Adamson, Wollongong, N.S.W., Wollongong College of the Arts, 1983;

Christina's World, Sydney, Seymour Centre, University of Sydney, 1983;

Zoo, by Hewett and Adamson, New South Wales Youth Centre, 1984;

Me and the Man in the Moon, by Hewett and Robert Page, Rivcol, 1986;

The Rising of Pete Marsh, Perth, New Fortune Theatre, 1987.

PRODUCED SCRIPTS: *Journey among Women,* motion picture, by Hewett, Tom Cowan, and John Weiley, Ko Ann Film Productions, 1977;

The Planter of Malata, motion picture, by Hewett and Cecil Holmes, 1981;

Crossing the Border, motion picture, by Hewett and Robert Adamson;

The Delinquents, motion picture, by Hewett and Lex Marinos, 1988;

Frost at Midnight, radio, Perth, Australian Broadcasting Corporation (ABC);

Chrissie and Jules, radio, ABC, Sydney, 2000.

OTHER: *Sandgropers: A Western Australian Anthology,* edited by Hewett (Nedlands, W.A.: University of Western Australia Press, 1973);

Journeys, edited by Fay Zwicky (Carlton South, Vic.: Sisters, 1982)–includes poems by Hewett.

SELECTED PERIODICAL PUBLICATIONS–UNCOLLECTED: "Excess of Love: The Irreconcilable in Katharine Susannah Prichard," *Overland* (Summer 1969–1970): 27–31;

"Creating Heroines in Australian Plays," *Hecate,* 5, no. 2 (1979): 73–79.

Dorothy Hewett is an Australian poet, playwright, novelist, short-fiction writer, and autobiographer whose published work spans a period from the early 1940s to the early twenty-first century. Often described as a "romantic"–a term endorsed by the writer herself–Hewett, like the British Romantic poet George Gordon, Lord Byron, is frequently perceived in terms of a mythicized, larger-than-life projection of her life through her writings and responses to them. While the dramatis personae of her writings across a variety of genres often bear a relationship to herself and to people she has known, she should also be recognized for her powers of invention and the literariness of her work.

Dorothy Hewett was born in Perth, Western Australia, on 21 May 1923, the older of the two daughters of Tom and René (née Coade) Hewett. Dorothy and her sister, Lesley, who became a doctor of medicine, grew up on a three-thousand-acre wheat and sheep farm, Lambton Downs, at Malyalling via Wickepin in the Great Southern region of Western Australia. Place, in its sensuous and metaphoric aspects, plays a large part in Hewett's work. The childhood homestead, its surroundings, the family history, and the community gossip of the Great Southern region all contribute to Hewett's composite picture of what American Southern writer Eudora Welty called "the heart's country."

Hewett's early poem "Testament" (1945) recalls aspects of the writer's secluded childhood on the farm, which she did not leave until she was twelve. The poem evokes a characteristic nostalgic scenario of a real and mythological garden:

> And I have loved
> An old house lying silent in the summer,
> Haunted by children, flowers and orchards,
> Days that seemed a dim and golden
> Heritage of dream. . . .

In some of Hewett's later imagery used to describe gardens, this lyrical and nostalgic note of innocence and simplicity is complicated and troubled by notions of a darkening experience, as in poet William Blake's dialectic of innocence and experience that recognizes a worm in the bud. In *Wild Card: An Autobiography, 1923–1958*

(1990) Hewett writes in the historic present tense of the farm as a garden and of its metaphoric significance: "The farm is the centre of our existence, our Garden of Eden, but I always know that under bridal creeper and the ivy geraniums, the black snakes wait and slide."

Hewett's poetry and plays, especially, have been influenced by stories and images of her parents and grandparents. Her paternal grandparents, Ephraim and Alice Hewett, followed their sons from Victoria to Western Australia after World War I, from which their son Tom, who had been awarded the DCM and Croix de Guerre, had emerged as a war hero. In *Wild Card,* Hewett emphasizes her father's rural working-class background, along with a streak of Protestant fanaticism, against which she defines her desire for a rebellious, bohemian lifestyle. Yet, he is the parent who first takes Dorothy to the theater and to her first interview for a job as a journalist, and she idealizes him in a late poem, "Inheritance," collected in *Halfway Up the Mountain* (2001), as "the handsome father haloed in sparks." Tom Hewett, known as "the Black Prince," is presented by his daughter as a quiet and withdrawn man on the farm at Wickepin—an image of the classical outsider. By contrast, the meeting of Hewett's parents-to-be, Tom Hewett and René Coade, in postwar Corrigin, where René was postmistress, is presented in *Wild Card* in theatrical and romantic terms. Tom dashes off with his girl in a sulky drawn by a black horse—but takes her through Kunjin to a family prayer meeting at Vale Farm. A romantic impulse for freedom continually clashes with Protestant and Puritan restrictions in Hewett's autobiographical and fictional scenes.

While Hewett portrays her paternal grandparents as inheritors of the constraints and distorted energies of Puritanism, she presents her mother's parents, Mary and Ted Coade, as capitalists. They own houses, land, a shop in the country, and the Regal Theatre in Subiaco, a suburb of Perth, where Hewett's theatrical imagination grew. Hewett identified with the volatile Ted Coade, who had blonde hair like her own, and with whom she shared "a natural joyousness," when she could forget "the black blood of the Hewett clan." The dynamics of her emotional relationships with grandparents, as well as her parents and sister, in an extended family of readers and storytellers, helped to shape Hewett's nascent storytelling abilities.

Until she was twelve, Hewett and her sister, Lesley (nicknamed Dessie), were educated on the farm, with their mother's assistance, through correspondence classes supplied by the Education Department of Western Australia. Perhaps Hewett's difficult relationship with her mother began in this context. Sets of work had to be sent in every fortnight. Hewett's skills were verbal and not mathematical. But for the most part the sisters

Paperback cover for Hewett's 1979 comedy, which critic Katharine Brisbane called "a marriage feast in which the journey of life is celebrated" (Bruccoli Clark Layman Archives)

led what Dorothy later called in an interview with Jim Davidson "a very free life"—drifting around the farm, "riding horses and wandering up and down creeks." Hewett developed there a strong sense of place, and her father inculcated environmental values.

Hewett's play *The Fields of Heaven* (first performed, 1982) includes a characterization of a farmer, like her father, who cares for the land, warns of the dangers of salt erosion, and proposes the planting of trees, but is ignored by those in authority. Hewett's musical plays for children, *Golden Valley* and *Song of the Seals* (1985), reinforce respect for creatures and conservationist ethics. The collection *Wheatlands* (2000), which she wrote with John Kinsella, brings together many of Hewett's poems and prose pieces that as a whole reveal the strong influence of the physical environment of her early years on her memory and imagination. To describe the three-thousand-acre farm near Wickepin as the seedbed of Hewett's creative fiction is no exaggeration. Recalling in *Wild Card* her departure from the farm to attend school in the city, Hewett wrote, "I have given my heart once and for all and I know I will never have another real home in the world again." But her pact with her father that she would return when she grew up and start a studhorse farm there was never realized.

After a brief false start at Perth Girls' High School, Hewett completed her secondary schooling from 1936 to 1940 at Perth College, an Anglican private school, at which some of the teachers were nuns. Hewett's experiences at Perth College provided a partial basis for her most controversial play, *The Chapel Perilous* (first performed, 1971; first published, 1972). Margaret Williams, in her monograph *Dorothy Hewett: The Feminine as Subversion* (1992), summarizes the divided views of audiences and readers about the protagonist of this play, Sally Banner:

> To some Sally is still [at the end of the play] merely an arrogant and selfish "nuisance," but many people still identify strongly with her rebellion against false authority, her insistence on her right to sexual freedom, and her quest for full independence as a person.

While clearly Sally Banner has an autobiographical dimension that has led some readers and viewers of the play to equate her with the author, the irony directed at Sally's banner-waving excesses and her tendency to theatrical exaggeration, distance the forty-eight-year-old author to some extent from her adolescent character. But Hewett—middle-aged, old, or young—throve on excess: "the road of excess leads to the palace of wisdom," she would quote from William Blake, and neither her life nor her work reveal a pattern of conventional or "graceful" aging.

The dramatic conflicts in *The Chapel Perilous* reflect those in much of Hewett's life and work. They show, in particular, a clash between abstract ideals and the demands of the body. At the end of her final year at Perth College, Hewett played the Virgin Mary in the school pageant. Sally Banner's theatrical journey toward purity and simplicity of purpose parallels this path, but it reveals a characteristic predicament. Hewett's women frequently seek singleness and purity while knowing they are sexually and mentally promiscuous. The barrier that Sally Banner crashes through in parochial Western Australian society is a conspiracy of silence around these matters. In her preface to *Sandgropers: A Western Australian Anthology* (1973), Hewett wrote of a "brutal innocence" in her state of origin. Against this, Sally Banner defiantly chooses to "walk naked through the world." Her exploits, affairs, and alliances

during and after her school years flagrantly flout not only her mother's "bourgeois" values but also those of the society's conventional authorities. Yet, Hewett makes a retrospective comment in "Creating Heroines in Australian Plays" (1979) that Sally/Hewett's most important critic in *The Chapel Perilous* was Judith, the lesbian "love figure," who "stands for intellectual control and a denial of sexual love." Her lack of "intellectual control" is something that Sally laments in act 2 when she confesses, "I wanted to live so completely a dozen lives, to suffer everything."

Hewett commenced a bachelor of arts degree at the University of Western Australia in 1941 and wrote in her diary, as she says in *Wild Card:* "Live wildly today, forget tomorrow." This credo may have contributed to her failure in one of her subjects, French, but her love of literature and drama were undiminished, and she excelled in English and history. In *Wild Card* she recalls Professor of English Allan Edwards, "a disciple of Freud and Leavis" (who appears in a later poem, "Professor Quixote," "torturing his paper clips"), and Alec King, a William Wordsworth specialist, who fed the flames of her romantic worldview by telling students that if they wanted to understand Wordsworth's relationship to nature, "we should go out of the lecture theatre, take off our shoes, and feel the grass springing under the soles of our bare feet."

While she was at the university, Hewett espoused pacifist views. She joined the staff of the communist *Workers' Star* newspaper in Perth, where, Justina Williams recalls in a review of *Wild Card* (*Westerly,* December 1990), Hewett's nickname was "Toddy," and her edition of the university literary magazine, *Black Swan,* became known as the "Red Swan." Hewett was living at home with her parents in South Perth at this time. Keeping a diary proved costly when Hewett's mother discovered an entry for March 1941, which referred to a secret lover, and berated her. So deeply influenced was Hewett's outlook by British Romanticism that she gave her lover a copy of Emily Brontë's novel *Wuthering Heights* (1847) and inscribed it, "To my Heathcliff / from your Cathy." When her secret lover turned eighteen and joined the air force, Hewett says (in *Wild Card*) that she felt she had been jilted and decided "to be a whore." She set about playing that role flamboyantly.

When Hewett was required to discontinue her university studies because of her failure in French, she took up a short-term position in a bookshop, from which she says she was dismissed for reading the books. She contemplated another avenue of work for a time when she enrolled at Kindergarten Teachers' Training College in 1943, but she did not complete the year. Her idea at this time, according to her interview with Lynne Hunt in *Claremont Cameos* (2002), was that "I was going to be a famous writer and a famous actress, and teaching was regarded by me as something that you had to do if you had to make a living."

Hewett stopped attending Communist Party meetings but continued her life of sexual promiscuity (she says in *Wild Card*) as a means of "revenge on my parents, revenge on my idealised concept of the perfect love—Heathcliff and Cathy, and the sentimental love songs on the radio. . . ." At about this time (Hewett recalls in *Wild Card*) she became conscious of a divided self: "There is the girl who moves and talks and rages and loves and there is the writer who watches and writes it down, who even in her most passionate moments is saying, 'Remember this.'" She continued to be a recorder of such moments.

Although Hewett was distant from the battle-fields, she was deeply affected by the atmosphere and circumstances of the war on the homefront. Following the departure of her air force lover, in 1945 Hewett poisoned herself with Lysol, a toxic household antiseptic, and was rushed to the hospital. One of the consequences of this highly publicized event was that a left-wing friend from university days, law student Lloyd Davies, who had joined the army and was based in Darwin and Fremantle, visited Hewett regularly while she was in the hospital. Davies wrote in *In Defence of My Family* (1987) that, "on her discharge from hospital we had a whirlwind romance and, within a month, we married. It was one of those wartime marriages!" Hewett recalls that she "pushed him into this marriage" in 1945, more quickly than Davies intended.

The marriage between Hewett and Davies lasted for approximately three years. Their son, Clancy, was born in September 1947. Aspects of Hewett's relationship with Davies, their marriage, and its aftermath seem to be adverted to in some of her poems and plays, and she writes about these matters in *Wild Card*. Later, in the mid 1970s, Davies issued writs for libel against Hewett and her publishers for allegedly defamatory references to him and members of his family. From Davies's perspective in *In Defence of My Family,* he and Hewett had "lived together happily" for the years of their marriage. Hewett's account, in contrast, indicates a continuing restlessness as she tried to juggle mothering, a social life, part-time study at the university, editing *Black Swan,* and producing Clifford Odets's play *Waiting for Lefty* (1935). A highlight of their life together was perhaps their visit to Port Hedland in Western Australia in the summer of 1946–1947 in support of three jailed leaders of a strike by Aboriginal shearers and stockmen in the Pilbara region. Hewett's well-known ballad "Clancy and Dooley and Don McLeod" mythologizes the jailed strike leaders as heroes in the struggle for equality of black Australians. According to

The paperback cover for Hewett's 1987 semi-autobiographical novel features a photograph of the author in costume (Bruccoli Clark Layman Archives)

Davies, Hewett became pregnant with their son, Clancy, during this time in Port Hedland.

Hewett left Davies and their son in April 1949 to live with Les Flood, a Sydney boilermaker and member of the Communist Party of Australia. Hewett described in *Wild Card* her tendency to hero worship: the fair-haired Flood seemed to her "the personification of the working-class hero." Davies suggests in *In Defence of My Family* that Hewett's infatuation was partly with "the bright lights of Sydney—particularly the theatre lights." He adds that when Hewett and Flood moved to Sydney, she wrote in November 1949, during a temporary separation from Flood, to ask Davies for a reconciliation—a proposition that Davies denied. Later, Hewett says, Davies changed his mind and wanted her to return to Perth, but by then she and Flood were together again. Hewett's volatile state was exacerbated by the news from Perth that Clancy had been diagnosed with leukemia in May 1950. He died in October

1950, Hewett having managed to spend some time with her son when he was sent to Melbourne for treatment. Divorce proceedings between Hewett and Davies were concluded in 1951. These and subsequent events led Hewett to remark in later years that she would never again leave a child of hers for a man.

Hewett lived with Flood in the Sydney working-class suburbs of Redfern, Rosebery, and Rockdale from 1949 to 1958 and bore him three sons—Joe, Michael, and Tom. Flood obtained shift work on the Sydney waterfront. The Cold War was at its height in Australia at this time. Prime Minister Robert Menzies introduced the Communist Party Dissolution Bill to the Australian Parliament in 1950, but a proposal to ban the Communist Party was defeated in the referendum of 1951. Hewett took part in many Communist Party activities at this time, held several short-term positions in it, and worked in the Alexandria textile mills for about a year. This latter experience provided a basis for her first novel, *Bobbin Up* (1959), which academic critic Stephen Knight says "stands up with remarkable success against other major examples of the international working-class novel" (*Dorothy Hewett: Selected Critical Essays*, 1995). Her first play, *This Old Man Comes Rolling Home* (1976), also draws on Hewett's experience of work and family life in Redfern, an inner suburb of Sydney. The play exhibits a mainly realistic narrative and expositional mode with only occasional hints of the Surrealistic and Expressionistic methods of later plays.

Hewett continued to engage in left-wing political and cultural activity through the 1950s and 1960s. She visited Russia and China in 1952 with an Australian delegation that included Flood, Davies, and the latter's new wife, Jo. The visit is recorded in Hewett's poem "Hidden Journey," written after a second visit to the U.S.S.R. and other countries with an antifascist writers' group in 1967. Although Hewett had second thoughts about her membership in the Communist Party after the Soviet invasion of Hungary in 1956 and its treatment of dissident writers, she did not resign from the party until 1968. Fellow writer Frank Hardy had helped to keep alive her sense of independent creative and critical flair within the auspices of the Realist Writers Group, which she had joined in 1956. Something of the drama of Hewett's thwarted ideals and expectations of communism can be seen in her essay in *Overland* (Summer 1969–1970) following the death in 1969 of fellow West Australian writer and communist Katharine Susannah Prichard. In her newfound independence from the Communist Party, Hewett wrote that Prichard's political beliefs had been "not a living, changing, dialectical force, but a frozen religious dogma."

Hewett's personal and marital dramas during the 1950s and 1960s were no less turbulent than her poli-

tics, and indeed these two aspects of her life remained closely related. A rift opened between Hewett and Flood in the mid 1950s. Physically close at first, their verbal and emotional communications were often at odds, and this conflict degenerated into physical violence. Short periods of separation were followed by reconciliations, work together for the Communist Party, and the increasingly lonely task for Hewett of bringing up her sons. The concluding chapters of *Wild Card* show Hewett's attempts to deal with Flood's violent and erratic behavior following a diagnosis of paranoid schizophrenia. Finally, in 1958, Hewett escaped at night from the house in Rockdale with her three young sons and returned to Perth.

Hewett spent a period in hiding from Flood in Rockingham and at her sister's farm at Kendenup. She and the boys spent a fortnight with her parents at 20 Ridge Street, South Perth, before moving into her sister Lesley's house, "Cathay," at 19 Ridge Street. Hewett resumed studies at the University of Western Australia, where she completed a bachelor of arts degree and was enrolled in a master of arts preliminary program before turning to her own creative writing in a more sustained way. A seaman she had met at Communist Party and writers' events in Sydney, Mervyn Lilley, visited Hewett in Perth in 1959, and this meeting led to what Hewett called "a rip roaring affair." She and Lilley—a Queenslander who had worked as a cane cutter, drover, and miner before going to sea—were married at a registry office in 1960. They lived in Queensland—first at Yeppoon, then at Moreton Bay, and finally at Brisbane—from late 1961 to late 1962, before returning to Perth, where their two daughters, Katherine (Katie) and Rozanna (Rosie), were born.

The tall, muscular sailor and his blonde wife became a focal point for parties of writers, students, and literati at their home in Forrest Street, South Perth, in what Lilley called "the backyards of the bourgeoisie." (Their house was built on the tennis court of Hewett's parents' property.) Teacher and poet William Grono was one of those who took part in writing workshops at the home of Hewett and Lilley in the mid 1960s; he subsequently edited Hewett's *Collected Poems* (1995). Other writers who attended Hewett's parties and workshops included Peter Jeffery, Malcolm Levene, Griff Watkins, Frank Smith, Peter Bibby, and Tony Thomas. Hal Colebatch, Peter Cowan, Randolph Stow, and Mary Durack also visited the house. Hewett's influence on other writers extended beyond the University of Western Australia, where she taught part-time and then full-time for ten years, from 1963 to 1973. At the same time, her teaching—especially of the Romantic poets and drama—influenced her own writing, and she was intrigued in her later years there by the challenges of the New Fortune Theatre in the courtyard outside her office window at the university.

Hewett's first book of poems, *What About the People!* (1963), was written with Lilley and published by the Realist Writers Group in Sydney with a foreword by Frank Hardy, in which he wrote, "With other Communist poets like John Manifold and Denis Kevans, Dorothy Hewett and Merv Lilley stand as living proof that communism and creative writing go hand in hand, and that poetry with a purpose can be artistic." Hewett's first collection that she wrote alone, *Windmill Country* (1968), published by *Overland,* includes thirteen poems from the first collection together with twenty "new" poems (four of which had been written in the 1940s). The personal, lyrical note in some of the poems celebrates childhood, idealism, and young love, but an angry, critical voice often intervenes to attack social injustice. One poem, "My Fortieth Year," celebrates marriage and a broader, more inclusive view of the journey ahead, a "second coming."

Hewett's second coming as a writer in the 1970s occurred as both playwright and poet. Her third and most popular play to that time, *The Chapel Perilous,* was directed by Aarne Neeme in the New Fortune Theatre at the University of Western Australia in 1971. Hewett described Neeme as "the first and best director" of the play. The various controversies generated by different productions of *The Chapel Perilous*—whose form was influenced by both Bertolt Brecht and the Elizabethans—tended to focus on the question of why Sally bows to the altar at the end of the play. In this most autobiographical of Hewett's plays, written early in "second wave" feminism in Australia, does her protagonist succumb to the authority figures of her society? In a postscript to the revised 1977 edition of the play, Hewett observed that her "female *doppelganger's*" bow was not a surrender but "a gesture to the exigencies of life" and that the way that the bow is made is important: "There is nothing craven nor defeated about it. It is an inclination of the head, a bow to the forces of life and death, the limitations of our own humanness . . .". Hewett's interpretation seemed to suggest an acceptance of responsibility, though not necessarily to temporal authorities.

In 1974 a three-year funding grant from the Literature Board of the Australian Council of the Arts enabled Hewett and her family to move to Sydney, where theatrical and poetic opportunities beckoned. At first they lived in leafy Woollahra, a far cry from working-class, inner-suburban Redfern, where she and Flood had moved in her previous migration to Sydney. Nearby were former West Australians Katharine Brisbane and Philip Parsons (who had founded Currency Press in 1971), both of whom contributed enormously to the renaissance of Australian drama in the 1970s by publishing and promoting work by Hewett and others.

As they had done in South Perth, Hewett and Lilley hosted parties and readings at 49 Jersey Road, Woollahra, and Hewett became close to members of the "New Poetry" group, especially Robert Adamson. Sometimes described as "neo-romantics," Adamson and such fellow poets as John Tranter, Tim Thorne, and Eric Beach tried to keep themselves and readers abreast of contemporary American developments in poetic form and content. Influenced in part by her new milieu, Hewett produced her poems for *Rapunzel in Suburbia* (1975), which was published by Adamson's Prism Books but was then withdrawn when Davies sued for libel. As a whole, the volume shows Hewett at a vigorous, experimental moment in her development in an era that included "confessional" American writers such as John Berryman, Robert Creeley, and Frank O'Hara. Behind the experimentation was Hewett's old, dual impulse—to tell the truth, and to sing. In "Let Candid Speech at Last . . . ," echoing William Butler Yeats, she wrote in *Rapunzel in Suburbia:* "Let candid speech at last fall from my gaping mouth." Despite the libel suits undertaken by Davies—which led to out-of-court settlements by Hewett and publishers of her work, including the literary magazine *Westerly,* which published a review that included part of the poem "Uninvited Guest"—Hewett's work continued its quest for candor and clarity in a variety of literary forms.

The late 1970s and 1980s were Hewett's most active years as a playwright. Hewett's *Joan* (published in 1984) was produced by the Canberra Repertory Society in 1975, and *Miss Hewett's Shenanigans* was produced at the Canberra Playhouse as part of the Australia '75 Festival. *The Golden Oldies* (published, 1981) was used in a workshop in Canberra in 1976 and performed in Melbourne in 1977. *Pandora's Cross* was performed in the Paris Theatre at the Sydney Opera House in 1978 but closed after a week following negative publicity and poor houses. The play is interesting for its theatrical mythologizing of a place, King's Cross in Sydney; and like *The Fields of Heaven,* which gives dramatic presence to the West Australian wheat fields, the play is likely to have a life beyond its early productions. Despite further legal maneuvers by Davies in 1978, which threatened action over *The Chapel Perilous* and *The Tatty Hollow Story* (published in 1976) and led to an agreement that these plays would not be published or produced in Western Australia, Hewett returned to her home state for the production of her successful comedy, *The Man from Mukinupin: A Musical Play in Two Acts* (published, 1979), at Perth's Playhouse Theatre in 1979.

The Man from Mukinupin was written for the sesquicentenary celebrations in Western Australia and was

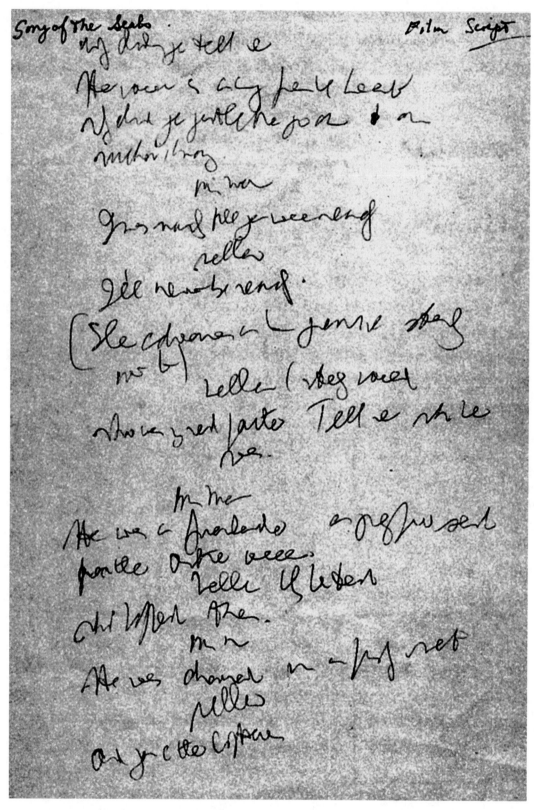

Page from a draft for one of Hewett's musical plays for children (from Candida Baker, Yacker: Australian Writers
Talk about Their Work, *1986; Paterno Library, Pennsylvania State University)*

published jointly by Fremantle Arts Centre Press in Perth and Currency Press in Sydney. It is dedicated to "Joe, Michael and Tom Flood, who, like their mother, grew up in the West." While the play is localized in terms of geography, speech idioms, and small country town characteristics, it makes many references to popular and classic works. Paramount among these are William Shakespeare's *The Tempest* (given at court, 1611) and *A Midsummer Night's Dream* (printed, 1600). In a preface to the published edition, Katharine Brisbane remarks that *The Man from Mukinupin* dramatizes "a sense of community" in the form of "an epithalamion, a marriage feast in which the journey of life is celebrated." It shows a triumph of love over bitterness and division in Hewett's visionary West.

The vantage points from which Hewett has written have provided both local color and symbolism for her work. When she and Lilley moved after eight years in Woollahra to 195 Bourke Street, Darlinghurst, in 1983, they forsook settled suburbia for the challenges of inner-city Sydney. In her early sixties and suffering from osteoarthritis in her knees, Hewett found herself in a semidetached house with busy traffic outside, a noisy brothel next door, and a small Anglican church opposite. Hewett enjoyed the contrast, color, and energy of her surroundings but, as she said in a 1985 interview with Candida Baker for *Yacker* (1986), found the prostitution depressing: "most of the girls are about fifteen . . . they've come from the country and they're nearly all on smack, which is what they're working to buy." This description was not the lighthearted, bohemian King's Cross that Hewett had created in *Pandora's Cross* but a harsher milieu that found its way into certain poems in *Alice in Wormland: Selected Poems* (1990), linking sex and mortality. Jennifer Strauss commented of this book in an essay in *Dorothy Hewett: Selected Critical Essays:* "Death is much more of a taboo subject than sex nowadays, and its treatment is one of the most original and creative features of *Alice in Wormland*."

Alice in Wormland offers a conscious mythologizing of aspects of the author's life in a fairy-tale format. The love interest in this book is represented in the figure Nim, a boy-man with a beautiful face and a wicked heart. In this figure, as in Billy Crowe, the charming villain in Hewett's second novel, *The Toucher* (1993), may be seen the presence of Robert Adamson, the neo-Romantic, Sydney-based poet with a criminal record, who was twenty years younger than Hewett and who fascinated and charmed her. The tortured relationship of an older woman with a younger man—another taboo subject that Hewett was ahead of her time in exploring—may be glimpsed in the poems but is more fully delineated in the novel. Set on the south coast of Western Australia, a coastline near Albany that Hewett

remembered from holidays from the Wickepin farm when she was a girl—and to which she periodically returned—*The Toucher* poetically evokes a garden world beside the open sea, toward which the sixty-seven-year-old protagonist is drawn, as if toward death. The expansiveness and tranquility of this setting contrasts with the protagonist's memories of Sydney, and especially of the semidetached terrace house in Darlinghurst: "that house with the back-breaking stairs, crammed from floor to ceiling with dusty manuscripts; the scream of police sirens; the click of the prostitutes' heels at midnight, coming to work in the brothel next door."

Seaside settings predominate in much of Hewett's later work. Significant poems in *Peninsula* (1994) refer to the Mornington Peninsula near Sorrento in Victoria, where Hewett stayed several times in the early 1990s, including one period when she was recovering from a hysterectomy. In a state of physical weakness and virtual immobility, Hewett was thrown back on her most precious resources, observation and memory. The section headings in *Peninsula* are indicative: instead of the "wild world" evoked in *Rapunzel in Suburbia,* the quiet peninsula dominates as place and metaphor. The peninsula sequences that open and close the volume offer some fine and graceful lyrics, but Hewett's way is also to undercut facile romanticizing of her situation with the painful details of bodily decrepitude. A sequence of "upside-down sonnets" defies any static tonality with reminders of grotesque, violent, or tragic encounters in the past.

Hewett's third novel, *Neap Tide* (1999), draws on visits by the author in the late 1980s and early 1990s to the New South Wales south coast near Bermagui where writer Rodney Hall and other writers and artists lived. Hewett and Lilley considered living there themselves. Hewett's female protagonist in this novel, as in her others, is a recognizable alter ego, though details such as age, physical build, and some attitudes differ from the author's. Jessica Sorenson, in her mid fifties, rents a cottage by the sea, where she is haunted by dreams of lost love, which she focuses in the image of a legendary and mysterious romantic poet of the region named Oliver Shine. Shine is a mesmerizing, bewitching figure. The remaking of Jessica's life involves her working through her obsession with Shine and his death-dealing romanticism. One of the achievements of this novel is its interpolation of ghosts from the past with present realities. Music, the Moon Festival, and the neap tide—when people are at their most vulnerable—provide an atmosphere in which imagined worlds become real.

In 1994 Hewett and Lilley left Darlinghurst and moved to a rustic house in Faulconbridge at 496 Great Western Highway in the Blue Mountains outside Sydney. The house had been a Cobb and Company coach house in the nineteenth century, and ghosts were said to

Dust jacket for Hewett's 1994 collection of poems, some of which are set on the Mornington Peninsula near Sorrento, Victoria (Bruccoli Clark Layman Archives)

inhabit it. Hewett found there a connection with her rural past as well as her magnetic city, which she could never wholly escape, as semitrailers plied their noisy way up or down the mountain. Her latest volume of poems, *Halfway Up the Mountain,* dramatizes this in-between state. From the bed to which she had been largely confined with severe arthritis since the early 1990s, Hewett's literary imagination and sympathies remained remarkably fertile, evoking places, people, and communities with clarity and force. She remained a rebel in spirit, regretting her physical inability, for example, to take up an invitation by left-wing Indonesian poet W. S. Rendra to join him in protests and revolutionary activity ("An Invitation from Rendra"). Hewett in this volume celebrates wind and rain, the scent of flowers and trees, and the sound of birds. She returns often to the child-self, as a sense of mortality presses upon her. The poems have the distilled candor and immediacy of diary entries. The title poem "Halfway Up the Mountain" offers a two-finger salute at death. In 1994 Lilley bought a black funeral car from

an undertaker in Wagga Wagga—large enough for the massive frames of Hewett and her husband: "now we drive it sleek black shining / like death or America up and down the mountains." In her infirmity, Hewett's defiant gestures threaten to outface the authority of death.

Hewett wrestled with the idea of a "straight" autobiography before she was commissioned by Virago of London in 1982 to write one. The basis of her difficulty was outlined in the poem "Creeley in Sydney" (*Greenhouse,* 1979) in which she wrote,

I can't write autobiography   because there is no me
Me is not a stable reality / the collective
Me in the changing world no propped up statue
in the square for pigeons to shit on turning green.

She struggled with her autobiography, nevertheless, through the 1980s, and *Wild Card,* covering the first thirty-five years of her life, was published, first in London with Virago and then in Australia by McPhee Gribble/ Penguin in 1990.

Wild Card sold about twenty thousand copies (author's estimate, in interview with Bruce Bennett) and was a critical success. An indication of Hewett's public esteem was that the premier of Western Australia, Carmen Lawrence, launched *Wild Card* in Perth and reviewed the book in *Westerly* (December 1990), including the following remarks: "Dorothy was born a romantic, free spirit before her time. She made her own way, tackling misunderstanding and prejudice head on, seeking her own solutions—and painstakingly finding them." As a left-wing cultural nationalist with powerfully individual impulses, Hewett swam against the prevailing social and political tides. In 1998, two years after John Howard's Liberal and National Party Coalition won government, she criticized "the whole conservative backlash we're going through." Following the publication of *Wild Card,* Hewett worked intermittently on a second volume of autobiography with the provisional title "The Empty Room."

Dorothy Hewett died 25 August 2002 in Springwood, New South Wales. Readers, lovers, friends, and critics have envisioned many different Dorothy Hewetts. Nevertheless, a consensus has emerged that Hewett was one of the major women of letters in Australia in the second half of the twentieth century. She won many awards, including the Western Australian and Victorian Premiers' Awards for *Wild Card* in 1991, the Western Australian Premier's Award for her *Collected Poems* in 1996, and the New South Wales Premier's Special Literary Award in 2000. She held eight fellowships from the Australia Council and was awarded a lifetime Emeritus Fellowship from the Literature Board in 1988. She was an invited writing fellow at eight Australian universities and Rollins College, Florida. Hewett was elected a Member of the Order of Australia (AM) in 1986 for her service to literature. In 1996 she was made an honorary doctor of letters by the University of Western Australia. Most significantly, perhaps, her late plays in the Jarrabin trilogy are in production, and her reputation as a poet, following publication of her *Collected Poems* in 1995 and subsequent volumes, has continued to grow.

Interviews:

Jim Davidson, "Interview: Dorothy Hewett," *Meanjin,* 38 (1979): 350–367;

Candida Baker, "Dorothy Hewett," in *Yacker: Australian Writers Talk about Their Work* (Sydney: Pan/Picador, 1986), pp. 184–209;

Lynne Hunt, "Dorothy Hewett Talks to Lynne Hunt," in *Claremont Cameos: Women Teachers and the Building of Social Capital in Australia,* edited by Hunt and Janina Trotman (Churchlands, W.A.: Edith Cowan University, 2002), pp. 138–150.

References:

Bruce Bennett, ed., *Dorothy Hewett: Selected Critical Essays* (South Fremantle, W.A.: Fremantle Arts Centre Press, 1995);

Lloyd Davies, *In Defence of My Family* (Peppermint Grove: Peppy Gully Press, 1987);

Margaret Williams, *Dorothy Hewett: The Feminine as Subversion* (Sydney: Currency Press, 1992).

Papers:

The papers of Dorothy Hewett, 1934–1975, are held by the National Library of Australia in Canberra.

Jack Hibberd
(12 April 1940 –   )

Paul McGillick

BOOKS: *A Stretch of the Imagination: A Play* (Sydney: Currency Press, 1973; London: Eyre Methuen, 1973);

Dimboola: A Wedding Reception Play (Harmondsworth, U.K.: Penguin, 1974; Ringwood, Vic.: Penguin, 1974);

Three Popular Plays, text by Hibberd, music by Lorraine Milne (Collingwood, Vic.: Outback Press, 1976)—includes *One of Nature's Gentlemen, A Toast to Melba,* and *The Les Darcy Show;*

The Overcoat; Sin: Two Pieces of Music Theatre, text by Hibberd, music by Martin Friedel (Sydney: Currency Press, 1981);

Peggy Sue; or The Power of Romance (Montmorency, Vic.: Yackandandah Playscripts, 1982);

Goodbye Ted, by Hibberd and John Timlin (Montmorency, Vic.: Yackandandah Playscripts, 1983);

The Barracker's Bible: A Dictionary of Sporting Slang, by Hibberd and Garrie Hutchinson (Melbourne: McPhee Gribble, 1983);

A Country Quinella: Two Celebration Plays (Ringwood, Vic.: Penguin, 1984; Harmondsworth, U.K.: Penguin, 1984)—comprises *Dimboola* and *Liquid Amber;*

Squibs: A Collection of Short Plays by Jack Hibberd (Brisbane: Phoenix, 1984)—comprises *Three Old Friends, Just Before the Honeymoon, O!, This Great Gap of Time, No Time Like the Present, A Knotty Problem, A League of Nations, Asian Oranges, Commitment, The Three Sisters, Death of a Traveller, A Modest Proposal, Breakfast at the Windsor, See You Tomorrow at Maxim's, The Common Touch,* and *Below the Belt;*

Captain Midnight V.C. (Montmorency, Vic.: Yackandandah Playscripts, 1984);

Performing Arts in Australia (Parkville, Vic.: University of Melbourne, 1984);

Duets: Two Plays by Jack Hibberd (Montmorency, Vic.: Yackandandah Playscripts, 1989)—comprises *Old School Tie* and *Glycerine Tears;*

Memoirs of an Old Bastard–Being a Portrait of a City, An Epicurean Chronicle, Fantasia and Search: A Novel (Melbourne: McPhee Gribble, 1989);

Jack Hibberd (photograph by Virginia Wallace-Crabbe; by permission of National Library of Australia)

The Life of Riley: A Novel (Port Melbourne: Heinemann, 1991);

Perdita: A Novel (Ringwood, Vic.: McPhee Gribble, 1992; Harmondsworth, U.K.: Penguin, 1992);

The Great Allergy Detective Book: A Guide to the Mystery Illness (Melbourne: Bookman Press, 1995);

Slam Dunk (Sydney: Currency Press in association with La Mama Theatre Melbourne, 1996);

The Genius of Human Imperfection: Poems (North Fitzroy, Vic.: Black Pepper, 1998);

Selected Plays (Sydney: Currency Press, 2000)–comprises *White with Wire Wheels, Dimboola,* and *A Stretch of the Imagination;*

Insouciance [by Barry Dickins]. The Prodigal Son [by Jack Hibberd] (Sydney: Currency Press in association with Playbox Theatre, Melbourne, 2001).

PLAY PRODUCTIONS: *Three Old Friends,* Carlton, La Mama Theatre, July 1967;

Brainrot–An Evening of Pathology and Violence, Love and Friendship, Carlton, La Mama Theatre, 1967;

White with Wire Wheels, Melbourne, Melbourne University Drama Society, September 1967;

Dimboola: A Wedding Reception Play, Carlton, La Mama Theatre, July 1969;

Marvellous Melbourne, Melbourne, Pram Factory, 1970;

Klag, Melbourne, 1970;

Customs and Excise, Carlton, 1970; produced again as *Proud Flesh,* 1972;

Aorta, Melbourne, 1971;

Flesh, Carlton, 1972;

A Stretch of the Imagination, Carlton, 8 March 1972;

Captain Midnight V.C., Carlton, 1973;

The Les Darcy Show, Adelaide, Australia, 1973;

Peggy Sue, Carlton, 1974;

A Toast to Melba, Adelaide, 1976;

The Overcoat (adaptation of a story by Nikolai Vasil'evich Gogol), Carlton, 1976;

Mothballs, Melbourne, 1981;

Liquid Amber, Melbourne, 1984.

OTHER: *White with Wire Wheels and Who?* in *Plays* (Melbourne: Penguin, 1970); republished in *Four Australian Plays,* edited by G. Blundell (Ringwood, Vic.: Penguin, 1973);

Le vin des amants: Poems from Baudelaire, translated by Hibbert (Toorak, Vic.: Gryphon, 1977);

"Stretching the Naturalistic Sinews," introduction to Clem Gorman, *A Night in the Arms of Raeleen, The Harding Women* (Sydney: Currency Press, 1983).

SELECTED PERIODICAL PUBLICATIONS– UNCOLLECTED: *Just Before the Honeymoon, Komos,* 2, no. 1 (May 1969): 16–22;

"A Symposium on the Future of Australian Drama," *Melbourne University Magazine* (1974): 55–61; reprinted as "Meat Pies and Sauce: A Debate on the Future of the New Australian Drama," in *Theatre Quarterly,* 7, no. 26 (1977): 82–86;

The Overcoat, Theatre Australia, 2, no. 1 (May 1977): 34–44;

"After Many a Summer: the 'Doll' Trilogy," *Meanjin,* 36 (1977): 106–109;

"How 'Marvellous Melbourne' Came to Life," *Theatre Australia* (August 1977): 36–37;

Memoirs of a Carlton Bohemian, Meanjin, 36 (1977): 298–305;

Marvellous Melbourne, by Hibberd and John Romeril, *Theatre Australia,* 2, no. 4 (1977): 35–44; 2, no. 5 (1977): 298–305;

Sin, Meanjin, 37, no. 4 (1978): 456–478;

"*Dimboola:* Play into Film," *Theatre Australia* (November 1978): 53–58;

"National Drama as Melodrama," *Westerly,* 23, no. 4 (December 1978): 53–58;

"Proscenium Arch Blues," *Meanjin,* 38, no. 4 (1979): 474–479;

Mothballs, Meanjin, 39, no. 4 (1980): 560–573;

"Pram Factory: The Cradle of Dingo Theatre," *Australian Financial Review* (20 June 1980): 38, 46;

"Playwriting in Australia," *Theatre Australia* (May 1981): 20–21;

Lavender Bags: A Prothalamion, Aspect, 25 (1982): 23–36;

Glycerine Tears, Meanjin, 41, no. 4 (1982): 509–522;

"The Myth of an Australian Theatre," *Island Magazine,* 9/10 (1982): 8–12;

Death Warmed Up: A Melocomedy, Scripsi, 2, no. 4 (June 1984): 203–214;

Odyssey of a Prostitute, Outrider, 2, no. 1 (June 1985): 87–154.

Jack Hibberd's voice is unusual in contemporary Australian literature. Best known as a playwright, his work has been consistently antinaturalistic in a theater culture steeped in naturalism, while his dramatic sources are substantially located in European modernism rather than the "well-made play" of English repertory theater, which has otherwise dominated Australian playwriting. Similarly, Hibberd's poetry and novels go against the local grain and, despite their surface vernacular, also belong in the tradition of European modernism, although the novels pay added homage to the much older and more widespread picaresque inspiration.

Hibberd is a comic writer whose humor is neither parodistic nor situational but generated by a particular epistemology or worldview. That he has had a parallel career as a medical doctor–most of it spent either with alcoholics, drug addicts, the homeless, the working class, or, in recent years, with people afflicted by allergies–goes some way toward explaining his absurdist vision of the world. The earthy realism of the doctor informs all of Hibberd's work, in which the world is a place "gone awry"–as Vladimir Nabokov says of Nikolai Vasil'evich Gogol, a major influence on Hibberd. It defies any form of reasoning in its indifference, arbitrariness, and unfairness. As for the

Paperback cover for the 1976 collection that includes Hibberd's plays based on the lives boxer of Les Darcy and opera singer Dame Nellie Melba (Bruccoli Clark Layman Archives)

social world, it is equally absurd in its pretensions, flimsy social roles, and fragile institutions.

The only response to this state of affairs is a comic one, if readers are not to be crushed by despair. All of Hibberd's characters from his first plays tend to try to deal with the absurdity of life by immersing themselves in rituals that are forever oscillating between those absurdist rituals that endorse the pointlessness of life and those that regenerate, and through which people reinvent themselves.

Hibberd's humor is markedly Rabelaisian in Mikhail Mikhailovich Bakhtin's sense of the word, derived from a medieval culture of laughter, a "grotesque realism" that inverts and subverts social realism. This laughter is bawdy and iconoclastic, anticlerical, anti-authority, obsessed with bodily functions, in love with verbal parody, and ever alert to life as a kind of ridiculous performance. It is a celebration of human fallibility and, if only in this sense, places Hibberd within a Catholic literary tradition, as distinct from a Protestant one with its preoccupation with per-

fectibility. In other words, Hibberd's work is transgressive in a comic way, and his persistent formal, thematic, and linguistic transgression has ensured that he occupies a highly ambivalent position in Australian literature, especially Australian drama.

John "Jack" Hibberd was, in his own words, "conceived in Ararat, born in Warracknabeal, weaned in Kyneton and raised in Bendigo," all towns in northwestern Victoria. His father, James George Hibberd, was a plumber descended from Irish and English stock, while his mother came from Irish and Spanish forebears. The artistic strain comes from his mother's side. His grandmother, apart from being an outstanding tennis player, was also an excellent painter, while his mother, Moira Honora Richardson Hibberd, was a talented singer who appeared in lyric opera. Moira's education was interrupted by the breakup of her parents' marriage. She moved to the rural city of Shepparton, where she worked in a delicatessen, and there she met and married James Hibberd.

Hibberd has recounted that his mother was in labor for several hours before his two-week premature birth, during which she read Elizabeth Cleghorn Gaskell's *Round the Sofa* (1858). His early life was marked by ill health, especially respiratory problems, which dogged him until he finally left the city in 1985 to live in the countryside, where he continues to live.

He began his education at St. Mary's Sisters of Mercy Convent in Bendigo, moving three years later to the Marist Brothers College. He attributes the awakening of his interest in literature, art, music, and science partly to his experiences with the Marist Brothers (where a certain Brother Everistus was an inspiration) and partly to an experience at Queenscliff Beach, where he was on holiday with his parents. There an "attenuated and lugubrious preacher had set up a small table in lieu of a pulpit." When the man paused in his preaching, he "clicked his fingers and an acolyte, who seemed a replica of Billy Bunter [hero of the books written by Frank Richards and of a BBC television series of the 1950s], started a record: *Eine Kleine Nachtmusik*. I stood, a congregation of one, transfixed: it was my first taste of Mozart and Fellini." The older brother of a school friend introduced him to a vast array of contemporary and classic literature, to the history of painting, and to a love of science and mathematics, while Hibberd himself plunged into music, fanatically exploring the Beethoven quartets by the time he matriculated.

He began to study pharmacy by correspondence but quickly grew tired of it and applied to study medicine at Melbourne University. He was accepted in 1959 and, although "a most erratic scholar," graduated in 1964, going on to do an internship for a year at

St. Vincent's Hospital in Melbourne. Toward the end of his medical course, Hibberd had begun writing some short stories and poetry. At the time coffee shops and terrace houses were popular venues where people read poetry and where Hibberd started to read his own verse. He put together a collection of poems that he showed to David Kendall, a literary editor and theater director. Kendall said the poems were unpublishable, but he noted a certain colloquial quality to them and suggested that Hibberd try writing drama.

After his internship, Hibberd went to work in a general practice at Mount Dandenong in the countryside outside Melbourne. Working only part-time, Hibberd had the opportunity to write, so he took Kendall's advice and wrote his first play, "The Wellington Boot." But when he showed this effort to Kendall, Kendall said it was unstageable. Furious, Hibberd stormed off and wrote another full-length play, *White with Wire Wheels* (published 1970). Kendall loved this play and in September 1967 directed it for the Melbourne University Drama Society. The production was a huge success, and Hibberd's career as a playwright was launched.

In fact, Hibberd had had several short plays already produced during 1967, all but one of them at the University of Melbourne. *Three Old Friends* (published in *Squibs* in 1984) was presented in July that year as the first play ever to be staged at La Mama Theatre in Faraday Street in the university suburb of Carlton. La Mama was a coffee shop recently set up in a former shirt factory by Betty Burstall, then wife of the movie director Tim Burstall. It was a venue for poetry, theater, and music and had been inspired by the eponymous New York venue. The following year it became the home of a newly formed theater company that later came to be known as the Australian Performing Group (APG). The core of the company was a group of Melbourne University theatricals. After a highly successful season of short plays by Hibberd (collectively called *Brainrot—An Evening of Pathology and Violence, Love and Friendship,* first performed in 1967), the group decided to work full-time in the theater, pioneering a new kind of drama that used Australian English, took Australian society as the source of its content, and adopted a fundamentally experimental approach, mixing local popular theatrical forms with new forms being explored at that time in North America and Europe.

The APG transformed Australian theater. Hibberd, by now living back in Melbourne and working as registrar in the Department of Social Medicine at St. Vincent's Hospital, was a founding member and for the next ten years supplied the scripts for some of the APG's most successful productions. The almost claustrophobic confines of the tiny La Mama space were crucial in the development of a performance style remarkable for its honesty and detail. Writing of the group of short plays performed at La Mama in 1967, Hibberd has commented that the "unadorned styles of writing, their short length and few characters, their concern with intimate rituals and claustrophobic games, made them suitable for staging in the cousinly confines of Faraday Street."

Although Hibberd has consistently experimented with theatrical form, in crucial ways, this early experience in the intimate La Mama Theatre space (and later at the nearby Pram Factory, to which the APG moved in 1970) has continued to shape Hibberd's work ever since. Although writing about the early years of the APG, Hibberd is really speaking of his own work when he says that it attempted to "amalgamate the national with the international, the comic and parodistic with the dramatic, the writers with the actors."

During this time Hibberd had met Jocelyn May, a microbiologist. She accepted a job at a hospital in London in 1967, and nine months later, in July 1968, Hibberd followed her, reading all of Marcel Proust's works on the boat to England. They were married there on 8 February 1969. Hibberd found London depressing but enjoyed some relief by visiting Ireland and doing the grand tour of Europe. Audience participation was fashionable in avant-garde theater at the time, and Hibberd saw one of its great proponents, The Living Theatre, perform in London. He did not like the experience, seeing it as a kind of audience intimidation. But the idea of audience participation intrigued him.

His solution to the problem of how to involve the audience in an authentic and nonthreatening way was to use a social ritual that the audience was familiar with and through which they could be integrated into the performance. Before leaving Melbourne he had read all of the works of Anton Chekhov and all of the works of Bertolt Brecht and so had come across Chekhov's short farce, *The Wedding* (1889), and Brecht's one-act farce, *The Bourgeois Wedding* (1919). From the former he took the idea of a cast of contrasting characters, misunderstandings, and misidentifications with a Very Important Person (VIP) who gives his imprimatur to the occasion; from the latter he took the atmosphere of uncontrolled absurdity. These ideas he combined within the ritual of a country wedding reception. Looking for a Victorian country town in which to set the play, he went to Australia House in London and consulted a map. He discovered a town with a name that had an appealing sonority—Dimboola.

Hibberd outside the Collingwood Football Gound (photograph by Brendan Hennessy)

Dimboola: A Wedding Reception Play (first published 1974) was written in London and sent back to the La Mama Company, who premiered it in July 1969. It was a hugely popular success and remains the most produced Australian play ever, adapted to local cultural norms and mounted all over the world. The play, described by Hibberd as "a balance between satire and celebration," explores what happens when two clans are brought unexpectedly together by the decision of two people to marry. The audience are guests at the reception and have the opportunity to participate by eating, drinking, and taking turns on the dance floor while the actors mingle with them.

As it turned out, it was the only play by Hibberd to employ literal audience participation, as he quickly realized the theatrical limitations of using social ritual as theatrical form. But from it grew a more sophisticated notion of audience participation that characterizes his later work, in which the audience's role is defined in terms of function rather than literal participation. This role over the years developed into a metatheatrical role in which the audience colludes (especially in the monodramas) with the performer in his/her projection of life as a complex construction of roles, the theater as a microcosm of the world, and the world itself as a metaphorical theater.

Just as *Dimboola* was an important stage in the development of Hibberd's use of ritual as a theatrical device, it also presaged thematic developments. Beneath the comic surface of his plays many such themes are dark—a cynicism about marriage, romantic love, and relations between the sexes—but offset by a celebration of "the genius of human imperfection," as he titled a later collection of poetry.

A mixture of homesickness and the sense that something exciting was happening in the Australian theater brought Hibberd back to Melbourne in December 1969. He combined working as a medical locum and preparing his short Pinteresque play *Who?* (published 1970) and a new play, *Customs and Excise* (first performed for the 1970 Festival of Perth)—a satire on prudery and censorship later retitled *Proud Flesh* (first performed 1972). Later in 1970 he collaborated with playwright John Romeril (and, indeed, with the actors), on *Marvellous Melbourne* (first performed 1970; published 1977), a knockabout musical play that drew on popular theatrical forms from nineteenth-century Victoria. It was an immense success, and later Hibberd further explored the idea of a "popular theater" in *The Les Darcy Show* (first performed 1973; published 1974) and *A Toast to Melba* (performed and published 1976), both based on the lives of two of the most iconic characters of Australia: boxer Les Darcy and opera singer Dame Nellie Melba.

In late 1971 Hibberd began writing a one-man play—a genre he later termed monodrama because it involved the characters' dramatically exploring various personae. It featured an eccentric, aging man who has turned his back on society and now lives alone in a hut in the Australian outback. Hibberd was struggling to find an alternative to naturalism, halfway through writing the play "got bored with all the heat and stuff," and put in an interval during which the character goes to bed. When he emerges, it is "apocalyptically cold" as the day nears its completion. The play was *A Stretch of the Imagination* (published 1973). Its first production in early 1972 (directed by Hibberd) had a tepid reception. But a new production later in the year (also directed by Hibberd) was a triumph, and the play is now considered one of the few Australian dramatic classics.

By the late 1970s the commercial success of *Dimboola*, together with a three-year Writer's Fellowship from the Australia Council for the Arts, enabled Hibberd to give up medicine and concentrate on writing. In 1976 he wrote *The Overcoat*, an adaptation of Gogol's short novel, which was significant for the way in which Hibberd moved away from explicitly Australian content while continuing to exploit the linguistic richness of Australian English.

His marriage to Jocelyn produced two children, Lillian Margaret "Lily" (born 1972) and James Benjamin (born 1974), but the couple divorced in 1976. On 3 January 1978 he married actress Evelyn Krape. A son, Samuel Spike, was born in 1980 and a daughter, Molly, in 1986. When Spike was five years old, he developed diabetes, and Hibberd himself was suffering from a severe lung condition. In 1985 Hibberd had returned to medicine and was working with a leading allergy specialist, Colin Little, who felt that Spike's diabetes and hyperactivity had been triggered by air pollution and recommended that the whole family leave the city. They did, moving initially to Evelyn's parents' holiday house at Mount Martha, near the coast, and later to Mount Eliza, slightly closer to the city. The move proved a great success, and Hibberd's lung condition improved dramatically, helped by his giving up cigarettes.

Marvellous Melbourne had led Hibberd to an increasing interest in the use of music. This interest was supported by the theatrical theory of Brecht, probably the single most important influence on Hibberd's dramaturgy. Music was important in *The Overcoat*, and two years later Hibberd was commissioned by the Victorian State Opera to write a piece of music theater. This work was *Sin* (first published in *Meanjin*,

Paperback cover for Hibberd's 1998 collections of poems, some of which are so colloquial that an early publisher turned them down and suggested Hibberd write plays
(Bruccoli Clark Layman Archives)

1978), in part a comic homage to Kurt Weill's *The Seven Deadly Sins* (first performed 1934). The music was written by Martin Friedl, who, with Lorraine Milne, wrote much of the music for Hibberd's plays.

By the mid 1980s Hibberd had become "a bit bogged down." He was having difficulty finishing *Odyssey of a Prostitute* (published 1985), based on a short story by Guy de Maupassant. The play went through five drafts, an unusual number for Hibberd, who normally finished a play in only one or two. The play was put away and not finished until 1984. In the meantime, Hibberd worked on a series of short plays, especially monodramas (often as vehicles for his wife, Evelyn Krape, a comic actress).

Just as suddenly as they had become successful, Hibberd's plays began to be treated with indifference as new theatrical fashions took hold in Australia. *Odyssey of a Prostitute*, commissioned by the Adelaide

Festival of the Arts, was rejected by the festival, and in 1984 Hibberd stopped writing for the theater "because of the sheer pointlessness of the activity in the Australian context, because of a sequence of shoddy productions of new plays, the mounting artistic depravity of our clique-ridden theater, the indifference to almost everything except fashion of our theater public, and lastly, because critical standards had fallen by the wayside."

The crisis with Spike, Hibberd's own disenchantment, and the fact that Evelyn (despite her own success) suddenly stopped getting any work led Hibberd to consider leaving the country to work in either Germany or Czechoslovakia. The plan was abandoned because neither Hibberd nor Evelyn wanted to be so distant from their families. But the next ten years were financially difficult, and their social life was limited by having a young boy who needed insulin injections twice a day.

Hibberd returned to medicine, specializing in immunology and clinical ecology, even writing a layman's guide to allergies, *The Great Allergy Detective Book: A Guide to the Mystery Illness* (1995). He was offered a fortnightly column in *The Age,* the principal morning broadsheet newspaper in Melbourne. Ostensibly about wine, *Grapeshots* was usually a short story with a central character and a cast of supporting characters. These columns eventually provided the basis for Hibberd's first novel, *Memoirs of an Old Bastard—Being a Portrait of a City, An Epicurean Chronicle, Fantasia and Search: A Novel* (1989). Two other novels followed in 1991 and 1992, *The Life of Riley* and *Perdita,* the first two parts of a "Melbourne trilogy."

Up until the mid 1980s Hibberd had written many short plays, including several monodramas. He returned to writing plays in the early 1990s, again with small casts. Increasingly, these plays—"some are more Brecht, some are more Samuel Beckett, some are more ritualistic"–foreground formal issues to do with structure and rhythm, so that form and content are fused (one of the most recent is about 75 percent nonverbal). Perhaps it is not surprising, therefore, that Hibberd has reconceived all the short plays as the first part of a grand musical scheme titled "Musical Parts" consisting of such forms as male and female sonatas and sonatinas, duets, trios, and quartets, culminating in a grand symphony in which all the themes and formal explorations will be brought together.

Jack Hibberd's return to the theater has been encouraged by a close association with a gifted young director, Daniel Schlusser, who has championed Hibberd's work. Hibberd continues to pursue both medicine and writing and continues to live in the countryside outside Melbourne.

Biographies:

J. D. Hainsworth, *Hibberd* (Sydney: Methuen, 1987);

Paul McGillick, *Jack Hibberd* (Amsterdam: Rodopi, 1988);

McGillick, "The Ritual Theatre of Jack Hibberd," dissertation, Griffith University, 1997.

References:

Mikail Bakhtin, *Rabelais and His World,* translated by Helene Iswolsky (Bloomington: Indiana University Press, 1984);

Vladimir Nabokov, *Nikolai Gogol* (London: Weidenfeld & Nicolson, 1973).

Papers:

The Fryer Collection at the University of Queensland Library includes a collection of Jack Hibberd's early correspondence and manuscripts. The National Library of Australia in Canberra has a collection of later letters, manuscripts, and typescripts.

A. D. Hope

(21 July 1907 – 13 July 2000)

Ann McCulloch
Deakin University

BOOKS: *The Wandering Islands* (Sydney: Edwards & Shaw, 1955);

Poems (London: Hamilton, 1960; New York: Viking, 1962);

Australian Literature 1950–1962 (Parkville, Vic.: Melbourne University Press, 1963);

A. D. Hope, Australian Poets Series (Sydney: Angus & Robertson, 1963); reprinted as *Selected Poems,* edited by Douglas Stewart (Sydney: Angus & Robertson, 1963; Sydney & London: Angus & Robertson, 1966);

The Structure of Verse and Prose (Sydney: Australasian Medical, 1963);

The Cave and the Spring: Essays on Poetry (Adelaide: Rigby / San Francisco: Tri-Ocean Books, 1965; revised edition, Sydney: Sydney University Press, 1974);

Collected Poems: 1930–1965 (Sydney & London: Angus & Robertson, 1966; New York: Viking, 1968); revised as *Collected Poems: 1930–1970* (Sydney & London: Angus & Robertson, 1972);

New Poems: 1965–1969 (Sydney: Angus & Robertson, 1969; New York: Viking, 1970);

Dunciad Minor: An Heroick Poem (Melbourne: Melbourne University Press, 1970);

The Literary Influence of Academies, lecture delivered to the Australian Academy of the Humanities (Sydney: Sydney University Press, 1970);

A Midsummer Eve's Dream: Variations on a Theme by William Dunbar (Canberra: Australian National University Press, 1970; New York: Viking, 1970; Edinburgh: Oliver & Boyd, 1971);

Henry Kendall: A Dialogue with the Past, First Herbert Blaiklock Memorial Lecture (Sydney: University of Sydney, 1971; Surrey Hills: Wentworth Press, 1972);

Native Companions: Essays and Comments on Australian Literature, 1936–1966 (Sydney: Angus & Robertson, 1974);

Judith Wright (Melbourne & London: Oxford University Press, 1975; Melbourne & New York: Oxford University Press, 1975);

A. D. Hope, 1983 (photograph by A. T. Bolton; by permission of the National Library of Australia)

A Late Picking: Poems, 1965–1974 (Sydney: Angus & Robertson, 1975; London: Angus & Robertson, 1975);

A Book of Answers (Sydney: Angus & Robertson, 1978);

The Pack of Autolycus (Canberra & Norwalk, Conn.: Australian National University Press, 1978);

The Drifting Continent and Other Poems (Canberra: Brindabella Press, 1979);

139

The New Cratylus: Notes on the Craft of Poetry (Melbourne & New York: Oxford University Press, 1979);

Antechinas: Poems, 1975–1980 (Sydney & London: Angus & Robertson, 1981);

The Tragical History of Doctor Faustus: by Christopher Marlowe Purged and Amended by A. D. Hope (Canberra & Miami, Fla.: Australian National University Press, 1982);

Directions in Australian Poetry (Townsville, Qld.: Foundation for Australian Literary Studies, 1984);

The Age of Reason (Carlton, Vic.: Melbourne University Press, 1985);

Selected Poems, edited by Ruth Morse (Manchester, U.K.: Carcanet, 1986);

Ladies from the Sea: A Play in Three Acts (Carlton, Vic.: Melbourne University Press, 1987);

Orpheus (North Ryde, N.S.W.: Angus & Robertson, 1991);

Selected Poems, edited by David Brooks (Pymble, N.S.W.: Angus & Robertson / London: Harper-Collins, 1992);

Chance Encounters (Carlton, Vic.: Melbourne University Press, 1992);

The Scythe Honed Fine: A. D. Hope: A Celebration for His 90th Birthday (Canberra: National Library of Australia, 1997).

Collection: *Selected Poetry and Prose,* edited by David Brooks (Rushcutters Bay, N.S.W.: Halstead, 2000).

OTHER: "Standards in Australian Literature," in *Australian Literary Criticism,* edited by Graham Johnston (Melbourne: Oxford University Press, 1962), pp. 1–15;

"The Reputation of Karonline von Gundernode," in *Occasional Paper/Australian Academy of the Humanities* (Sydney: Sydney University Press for the Academy, 1972);

Henry Kendall, edited by Hope and Leonie Kramer (Melbourne: Sun, 1973);

"Randolph Stow and the Tourmaline Affair," in *The Australian Experience: Critical Essays on Australian Novels,* edited by W. S. Ramson (Canberra: Australian National University Press, 1974);

Norman Lindsay, *Siren and Satyr: The Persona; Philosophy of Norman Lindsay,* introduction by Hope (Melbourne: Sun Books, 1976).

SELECTED PERIODICAL PUBLICATIONS–
UNCOLLECTED: "The Meaning of Good" and "The Esthetic Theory of James Joyce," *Australasian Journal of Psychology and Philosophy,* 21, no. 1 (1943): 17–26, 93–114;

"The Study of English," *Melbourne Graduate,* 4, no. 1 (1953): 10–19;

"Australian Literature and the Universities," *Meanjin,* 13, no. 2 (1954): 165–169;

"The Poet's Use of Language," *Technology: The Journal of the University of New South Wales,* 21, no. 2 (1962): 15–19;

"Pushkin's Don Juan," *Melbourne Slavonic Studies,* 1 (1967): 5–10;

"Presidential Address," *English in Australia,* 5 (1967): 3–9;

"The Frontiers of Literature," *Quarterly Journal of the Library of Congress,* 27, no. 2 (1970): 99–103;

"Dostoyevsky and Nietzsche," *Melbourne Slavonic Studies,* 4 (1970): 38–45;

"Voznesensky's 'Lament for Two Unborn Poems,'" *Melbourne Slavonic Studies,* 7 (1972): 38–57;

"Poetry as Journalism," *Westerly,* 3 (1975): 59–64;

"Talking to God: The Poetry of Francis Webb," *Poetry Australia,* 56 (September 1975): 31–35.

The legacy of leading Australian poet A. D. Hope to world literature is unquestionable, comprising eleven books of poetry, seven collections of critical essays, and two plays. His writing, compelling in its originality and passion, and rigorous in its satirical edge and philosophical insights, embodies in its language both the greatness and the frailty of the human spirit. Despite the many critical works Hope wrote during his lifetime, he will be remembered best and longest as a poet.

Alec Derwent Hope was born in Cooma, New South Wales, on 21 July 1907, the first of four children of Percival (a clergyman) and Florence Ellen (Scotford) Hope. Most of his childhood was spent in rural New South Wales and in Campbell Town, Tasmania, where he was educated at home by his parents. His father began to teach him Latin (Julius Caesar's *Commentaries on the Gallic Wars* [52–51 B.C.] and passages from Livy) at the age of ten. Hope's love of Latin was cemented in his final year of high school when he studied the Latin verse of Catullus; this interest in Latin continued throughout his life. In his eighty-seventh year, in personal correspondence with Ann McCulloch, he wrote, "I am always glad that I awakened to Latin before I encountered the Romance languages and was able to 'hear' the original Latin behind them."

Hope first attended Bathurst High School, where his first poems appeared in the school literary journal, *The Burr,* in 1922–1923; it included five offerings of the then fifteen-year-old Hope–three poems and two translations of poems by Catullus. He then moved to Fort Street Boys' High School, Sydney, for his matriculation year. In 1924 Hope was awarded a scholarship to study arts at Sydney University; he accepted the scholarship after dealing with his disappointment at failing to be accepted for medicine, his first choice. Hope graduated from Sydney University in 1928 with first-class honors in English and philosophy and was awarded the university medal in both; he also studied psychology and Japanese. Since he saw poetry as engaged in a philosophical view of the world, he believed John Anderson, who arrived in the philosophy department in Hope's second year, to be "the single most important philosophical interest of my youth."

In 1928 Hope was employed by the Sydney University *Appeal* under director E. R. Holme. During this period he studied courses in Italian and Spanish. In the same year he was awarded the James King Travelling Scholarship, which allowed him to accept a place at University College, Oxford. From 1929 to 1930 Hope read English at Oxford University; his teachers for language included the novelists J. R. R. Tolkien and C. S. Lewis. Hope received a third-class honors degree, which he conceded "is Oxford's kindly way of bestowing a failure on honors students though this might have been due partly to my having offered a special subject in Gothic and failed to sit for the exam" in personal correspondence with McCulloch (1989). Hope's aim at this time at Oxford was to set the foundations for becoming a scholar in the Indo-European family of languages. Although after completing his degree he was offered minor academic posts in England, they came too late, as he had already used his return ticket to Australia.

Coming home in the years of the Great Depression meant that work was impossible to find, and Hope's father sent him off to camp on a piece of land he owned near Bungan Head on the coast, paying him the equivalent of the dole. This period was an extremely happy time for Hope, who worked on the first version of a revision of Christopher Marlowe's *Dr. Faustus* (1604), which after several revisions was finally published in 1982 in a form quite different from the original draft. After three months of camping, Hope was accepted as a trainee at the Sydney Teachers' College and worked as a tutor at St. Paul's College in the same university. Because of Hope's third-class degree from Oxford, Holme was unable to employ him on the English staff as he had originally planned to do, and in fact told Hope that he must give up the idea of an academic career. Holme did, though, give Hope a letter of introduction to the editor of *The Sydney Morning Herald*, where he was offered a job. Hope rejected the offer and always thought afterward that he "must have been crazy," as he said in personal correspondence with McCulloch (1989). He graduated from the Sydney Teachers' College in 1932; his graduation was followed by another six months of unemployment before he was

appointed a relieving (substitute) teacher around the various schools in the Sydney area. He disliked teaching, however, and eventually took a job as a psychologist, giving aptitude tests to children about to leave school and advising them on suitable careers. Simultaneously, Hope upgraded his psychology studies to honors level and commenced a master's degree in psychology, which he abandoned in recognition that he did not have the required mathematical skills to carry it through. During this period in Sydney, Hope returned to his study of Russian. He frequented an Arabian coffee shop in King's Cross (a bohemian suburb of Sydney) run by Ursula Schwallbach, who gave him regular lessons in Russian. He eventually became a boarder at this woman's house, becoming an integral part of the Russian community in Sydney and being elected to their club of Returned Soldiers, Sailors and Airmen. His contact with his Russian teacher continued over the years, and the Hopes holidayed at Pebbly Beach in the years to come, where the Schwallbachs had made their home after giving up the coffee shop. Hope's interest in Russian continued throughout his life.

Hope was finally transferred to Canberra in 1937 to Telopea Park High School, where his main role was to discover why, in spite of the superb equipment and outstanding teachers of the four trades studied there, none of the pupils had managed to pass the exams. The students were children of itinerant workers who Hope discovered did not, until his appointment, have any of the basic skills in writing, reading, and arithmetic. In 1937 he met Penelope Robinson, whom he married on 27 May 1937. Hope took a position at Sydney Teachers' College in 1938, where for the first year he was employed to teach statistics before he finally found his way into the English department in 1939. The Hopes rented an abandoned house overlooking the harbor to Cockatoo Island. After they made rudimentary repairs of this four-roomed airy house, it became, with the outbreak of World War II, a resting place for many new friends. James McAuley stayed with the Hopes, at the time having been forced to give up his teaching and become a conscripted member of the army. He was waiting for the formation of the special section of army research that he, along with Harold Stewart, joined and whose principal gift to military science, Hope noted, appears to have been the famous Ern Malley Hoax. (As a joke, in one afternoon, as Ern Malley, McAuley and Stewart wrote a book of modernist poetry, which was taken seriously and reviewed.)

The Hopes' home was in an area that was considered a military target after Japan entered the war, and in 1940, with the birth of their first child, Emily, they moved to Castle Crag, at the northern edge of the city. Hope continued in his position at the teachers' college

Penelope Hope, the poet's wife, 1983 (photograph by A. T. Bolton; by permission of the National Library of Australia)

before being appointed as a senior lecturer, Department of English, University of Melbourne, in 1945. The Hopes' two other children, twins Andrew and Geoffrey, were born in 1944. In 1951 Hope was appointed professor of English at Canberra University College, which later became the Australian National University. During the early years of his professorship, Hope, along with Thomas Inglis Moore, introduced Australian literature as a major sequence of study. Up until this time, Australian literature was taught in a piecemeal fashion: the occasional text was included in general courses on literature. In 1953 a terrible fire raged through the buildings allocated to the English department. This occurrence proved personally devastating for Hope, as he lost valuable manuscripts, including all notebooks written over the previous ten years.

As an undergraduate, Hope had published poems in *Hermes, Arts Journal, The Pauline, Australian National Review,* and *The Bulletin.* Although his first collection of poems, *The Wandering Islands,* did not appear until 1955 when Hope was in his late forties and head of the Department of English at Canberra University College,

he had by this stage established himself as a poet by his regular contributions to Australian literary journals as well as having works appear in several anthologies of Australian verse. By the time *The Wandering Islands* appeared, not only had he established a reputation as a poet but also as a rather brutal, albeit insightful, literary critic.

Hope saw himself, however, primarily as a poet. In an interview with McCulloch in 1987, he said, "poetry is not a thing you decide to do, or adopt a system or theory and proceed according to plan. It grows out of you and what you have in you," and again in another interview with McCulloch in May 1986, he said, "poetry gave me the feel of the world. . . . I was no longer alone in the light of time and circumstance." Although often characterized as being a Romantic poet, Hope was always eager to emphasize that he, unlike the Romantics, saw poetry as being more than a dream of the passions; in the same interview, he said he believed it was also "a waking statement of the dream and this statement is the work of the contemplative, intellectual energy, itself the most important of the passions which listens to and interprets the voices of the dream."

Hope saw the role of poetry as a means of creating new being. He saw the poet as an actor who entered a part and explored possible answers to those questions offered up by the human condition. Central to his vision is an ironic stance that teases the reader to submit to the provisional nature of knowledge though simultaneously affirming the relentless search for truth. He wrote on page 7 of his notebook in 1968, "When we embrace a system, a faith, a plausible explanation, we have learned to be ignorant of other possible worlds we have learned to ignore." Whether directed at love/sexuality, cosmology, the beauty and terror of the landscapes of the mind and the phenomenal world, and the creative process and literary discourse, Hope reminds people that living is an act of joy and that part of the joy is to enact the humor and irony of being human.

In his lectures, interviews, and notebooks, Hope has often been quite explicit in his disbelief in the poem as a confessional of some kind and in his view that if his poetry is in any way autobiographical, the connections between the life and the art are tenuous. Ideas and interests, he concedes, lead him to writing particular kinds of poems that reflect his interests in science, travel, archaeology, literature, the Bible, society and its ironies, and boyhood and Australia. Most of his poems can be channeled into these divisions—though necessarily flavored if not, at times, determined—by his fierce opposition to free verse, a distaste for censorship, a celebration of male sexuality, the reinvention of the ancient stories included in myth and legend, and a preference for presenting a view or argument through analogy.

The Wandering Islands includes poems that reflect some of these interests, which pervade all his books until his last, *Orpheus* (1991), in which his final selection embodies them quite deliberately. In *The Wandering Islands* these interests are signaled in such poems as "Imperial Adam" and "Lot and His Daughters" (The Bible), "Ascent into Hell" and "The House of God" (Boyhood), "Pyramis or The House of Ascent" (Archaeology), "The Brides" and "Toast for a Golden Age" (Society and Its Ironies), "Return of Persephone" and "The End of a Journey" (Reinvention of Myth), and "William Butler Yeats" (Literature). The selection of poems is introduced by Hope's "The End of a Journey," which tells the tale of Odysseus, returned to his home and looking back not only at the massacre his return brought to those who had invaded his house but back further to the adventures he had known–the sound of the sirens' songs, "the bed of Circe," and "Calypso singing in her haunted cave." The allegory is not lost to the reader. The narrator hears sweet voices mocking him and asking him

> Son of Laertes, what delusive song
> Turned your swift keel and brought you to this wreck,
> In age and disenchantment to prolong
> Stale years and chew the cud of ancient wrong,
> A castaway upon so cruel a shore.

Hope was a controversial figure in the literary world. During the 1950s and 1960s he was a hero of the antipuritanical brigade for his courageous treatment of sexuality and erotica in his poetry and his stand against censorship. Some critics, however, responded negatively to the overt sexuality in his poems. Reception to *The Wandering Islands,* though overall acclamatory in its praise of the poems, included reservations with regard to Hope's treatment of sexuality. Some critics perceived a certain strange and disquieting note when Hope dealt with the subject of sex and suggested that his erotic poems were rarely love poems. They suggested that this attitude emanated from a kind of "self-repression" and Manichaeanism. Nevertheless, McAuley–a fellow poet, critic, and a man whom Hope recognized (along with Robert Brissenden) as his closest friend–identified that the tensions apparent in Hope's treatment of sexuality were part of Hope's attempt to find a principle of transcendence, reconciliation, and grace in a world that in the Nietzschean sense had lost its God. Endemic to this view is a recognition of Hope's attempts to liberate the flesh, to celebrate its sensuality, and to remove it from condemnation as being in some way evil. Critics such as Judith Wright celebrated his satirical approach that not only entailed a "half-hysterical cocktail-party wit" but one that pre-

sented a vision of the world that was compelling and highly organized. Wright drew attention to the dualistic nature of the work, the conscious awareness in the poems of the dichotomous nature of the world, with good pitted against evil, man against woman, and the spirit against the flesh. Hope, in his autobiographical notes in personal correspondence with McCulloch (1989), said of himself that he suspected he ran on repressed rage: "I imagine that the subterranean lake of suppressed fury has served as fuel for all my occupations and interests." In the same entry he vehemently rejected an alternative view: "the dreary Freudian theory that it is the libido, kept in check, which supplies all our energies."

Forever the humorist and mindful of feminist critique of the treatment of women as femmes fatales and/or the adherence to the *vagina dentata* (the toothed vagina), he nevertheless was able to deal with the subject humorously, as with the fate of Henry Clay, the protagonist of "The Conquistador":

> I sing of the decline of Henry Clay
> Who loved a white girl of uncommon size.
> Although a small man in a little way,
> He had in him some seed of enterprise

Henry, a married man, fully aware that he is doomed before he agrees to accompany the large girl home, visualizes all that might befall him, finds perdition as he "Climbed the white mountain of unravished snow, / planted his tiny flag upon the peak." His physical impact is barely noticed by the majestic girl.

> And afterwards, it may have been in play,
> The enormous girl rolled over and squashed him flat;
> And, as she could not send him home that way,
> Used him thereafter as a bedside mat.

At the time of the publication of *The Wandering Islands,* its reception emphasized Hope's existential stance in the world balanced perhaps by an equal affirmation of being solitary:

> You cannot build bridges between the wandering islands;
> The Mind has no neighbours, and the unteachable heart
> Announces its armistices time after time, but spends,
> Its love to draw them closer and closer apart.

Alongside this response, the critique of his overt, tension-ridden sexuality seems to come more from a traditional religious context that, although not always puritanical, was nevertheless fed by a reluctance for a subversion and/or recognition of the flesh/spirit duality. The poem "Imperial Adam" was the work that drew, and continues to draw, most attention. In more-recent times, this poem, among others, has been criticized by some feminists for objectifying woman, representing her, at worst, as a mere object of desire and the cause of man's fall from grace and at best as a muse for male inspiration. The poem takes its story from the Bible, and Hope follows through the logical sequence of events as Adam is given his mate described as "man's counterpart": "He knew her by sight, he knew by heart / Her allegory of sense unsatisfied." The beauty of Eve's sensual being is unquestionable:

> The pawpaw drooped its golden breasts above
> Less generous than the honey of her flesh;
> The innocent sunlight showed the place of love;
> The dew on its dark hairs winked crisp and fresh.

Hope adds a humorous touch to this controversial poem that celebrates sexuality and dramatizes the alienation of the male when the female gives birth: "From all the beasts whose pleasant task it was / In Eden to increase and multiply / Adam had learnt the jolly deed of kind." Eve is presented as the temptress: "Sly as the snake she loosed her sinuous thighs." Not only according to the critics does the poem make woman responsible for the Fall but also within this poem presents the act of sex as "evil" as the poem ends with the line, following a description of the birth of Adam and Eve's first child, "And the first murderer lay upon the earth."

The extent to which Hope is seen as a patriarchal poet is an ongoing debate. Poems, and works such as "Advice to Young Ladies" (*Collected Poems: 1930–1965,* 1966), *A Midsummer Eve's Dream: Variations on a Theme by William Dunbar* (1970), and "Botany Bay or The Rights of Women" (*The Age of Reason,* 1985) testify to the extent that Hope explored the ontology of being female and in mostly a satirical mode dramatized his opposition to societies that have limited their range, their intellect, their passions, and their creative spirit. His erotic poetry, mostly unpublished, is essentially male when he makes no excuses for the objectification of male lust. The euphemistic "John Thomas" finds its mark in bawdy ballads; the women in these works are seen to enjoy the sexual act as much as the males. Even these poems are rarely without a satirical purpose. In "Against Dildos" he curses the dildo:

> A curse upon the Dildo
> And on its naked head;
> It stultifies the passion
> And cheats the marriage bed.

The curse is extended to all who have made the dildo have a purpose: men overcome by alcohol, the "strumpet" who performs a service rather than real play, the proud virgins, parsons who "rail at fornication," and too hasty lovers and sodomites who "cheat women of their due."

Such poems sit beside ones that draw on researched knowledge of languages; Roman, Greek, and Nordic mythology; biblical studies; poetry; philosophy; and biography that span the history of Western civilization. In *Poems,* published in 1960, Hope's interest in enacting within the poems a tribute to the whole tradition of European culture is evident. Coupled with this focus is also one on the nature of the poet's task. One of the most satisfying responses to this work can be found in Jennifer Strauss's essay "'Vision that keeps the night and saves the day': Whose is the task defined in 'An Epistle from Holofernes'?" one of seventeen essays selected by David Brooks for *The Double Looking Glass: New and Classic Essays on the Poetry of A. D. Hope* (2000). Focusing on one poem that finds its source in a biblical story, Strauss contextualizes Hope's poetry not only in terms of the most significant critics writing on Hope at that time (Brissenden, McAuley, S. L. Goldberg) but also highlights Hope's preoccupations that continued to haunt and guide his poems: the relationship between the art and the life, the strands of classicism and Romanticism, the act/ritual of love and the creation of art, the content and the form of a poem, and balancing the night (the magic and darkness of myth) and the day (contemporary culture, daily events, common tribal practices). This publication also included "Australia," which dared to define Hope's country of origin in what was largely thought to be a negative way. Australian cities were described as "five teeming sores"; the country as dry and empty, "a woman beyond her change of life"; and a land "without song, architecture, history" and populated by "monotonous tribes from Cairns to Perth." The poem ends on a positive note, however, the narrator believing that from the desert prophets might spring:

> Such savage and scarlet as no green hills dare
> Springs in that waste, some spirit which escapes
> The learned doubts, the chatter of cultured apes
> Which is called civilisation over there.

Hope regretted this poem, indicating it was the voice of a young poet returning to an Australia that offered neither employment nor means of following his vocation as a poet. He came to understand the criticism of what was termed misogynist imagery, though not agreeing with that assessment, and, more important, he came to regret the complete disregard the poem had for an indigenous culture that had existed for thousands of years prior to European invasion. *Poems* also included "The Return from the Freudian Islands," which deals with another of Hope's "prejudices," in this case his contempt for Freudian analysis, which he saw as responsible for explaining away the fears, repressions, and misguided passions reductively–bringing, in his mind, the poet to a place where there was nothing but ". . . A faint, dry sound / As first a poet buttoned on his skin." This contempt took on another guise in the poem "Private Dick" in Hope's next book of poems, *A. D. Hope* in the Australian Poets series (1963), in which the protagonist is Dick, a private investigator and/or a Freudian analyst. No one is safe from Private Dick:

> Take to Art; set up your easel–landscape painting is just
>   clean fun,
> Free from the dingiest moral measles–Ah, now he's got
>   you on the run:
> Private Dick leans over your shoulder, breathes hot pep-
>   permint down your neck:
> "Call that a tree? That's a Phallic Symbol! Boy, is that
>   psyche of yours a wreck!"

Within the story of the poem, Dick, at death, is condemned to perdition and takes on his next client, Nick himself: "Back they go through the psychic tangles, the dreams he dreamed and the beds he wet, / The games he played with his sisters' bangles, the nice little snake he kept as a pet." Dick, however, is no match for Nick, who is able to cancel Dick's file with a simple trick–"The final triumph of mind over matter."

Also in 1963, *Dunciad Minimus: An Heroic Poem* was published privately by Australian National University Press. The poem appeared again, with additional material, in 1970 as *Dunciad Minor: An Heroick Poem*. Hope's polemical casting of literary critic A. A. Phillips as the hero of *Dunciad Minor* was dictated by his own distaste for a certain kind of literary criticism. In 1972 Hope wrote in his notebook 14:

> What I ought to have said in my preface to *Dunciad Minor,* is that it is not only described as minor in deference to its great predecessors, but because that [Alexander Pope's *Dunciad* (first three books, 1728; complete poem, 1743)] was about poets and this is about a minor sort of literary men, critics. Bad writers are a disaster, bad critics only a nuisance.

Hope's fight against exponents of free verse, against most strands of modernism, and against the "corrupters of poesy" drew opposition, created great poetry/critical prose, and drew controversy. In 1964 he became president of the Australian Association for the Teaching of English, a four-year appointment. The following year, 1965, the award-winning *The Cave and the Spring: Essays on Poetry* was published. This text characteristically stirred up debate as Hope, in a series of essays, offered new views on problems in English litera-

Cover for Hope's first collection of poems (1955), published when he was already well known for the poems he had published in periodicals (Bruccoli Clark Layman Archives)

ture that he considered to have been wrongly or only partially solved in contemporary criticism. Most of these essays were controversial, whether his view on the purpose of satire in "The Discursive Mode" or "The Activists," which was prompted by Marxist attempts to get him to join in communist movements. The latter was pertinent at the time because of his refusal to join public demonstrations during the Vietnam War. His refusal was somewhat abated by his involvement in Arts Vietnam in 1968 when he read a poem that was against the horror of *all* wars, situating himself in a position that did not ally him with a particular political party.

The satirical edge in most of Hope's poetry is not directed at political atrocities. In keeping with his adoption of John Keats's "negative capability," he is disinterested in ideological concerns and instead reserves his critical eye for modernity, whether marriage ("The Brides"), mass culture ("Standardisation"), tourism ("A Letter from Rome"), or psychoanalysis ("Private Dick"). Nevertheless, to categorize Hope solely as a conservative and a traditionalist would be simplistic, particularly if such a view implies that he did not create new ways of seeing, new dances of language, and philosophical insights that preempted some contemporary theory. Hope cast his net widely and deeply when writing about his world. Some of the sources he drew on are the Bible; Greek, Roman, and Nordic mythology; European culture; the history of ideas across time and place; and thirteen languages other than English. *Collected Poems: 1930–1965* won three awards; the volume consists of a hundred or so poems, at least twenty-one of them not previously published. It includes "A Letter from Rome," which embodies many of Hope's interests and preoccupations: travel and how modernity brought with it the worst aspects of tourism; poetry written as if a letter with a specific recipient in mind; and the questioning of an Australian who was aware that his culture found its source in Europe, yet, when on European soil, remained an unsatisfied spectator:

> . . . The roots are European but the tree
> Grows to a different pattern and design;
> Where the fruit gets his flavour I'm not sure,
> From native soil or overseas manure.
>
> And the uncertainty is in our bones.
> Others may think us smug or insular;
> The voice perhaps is brash, its undertones
> Declare in us a double of what we are.
> When the divided ghost within us groans
> It must return to find its avatar.
> Though this puts things too solemnly, of course,
> Yet here am I returning to this source.

Hope has in this poem a sense of coming home. He feels somewhat like a child with a quest to find "Something once dear, long lost and left behind."

In 1969 Hope published another award-winning book, *New Poems: 1965–1969*. Having retired from his position as head of the English Department in 1967 and having been elected professor emeritus, he was now free to pursue his vocation as a poet full-time. The years ahead proved rewarding. He remained engaged in his role as educator and consultant in Australian literature. In 1970, the year that *A Midsummer Eve's Dream* and a revised edition of *Dunciad Minor* were published, Hope taught at Sweet Briar College, Virginia, in the United States.

Returning to Australia in 1972, he joined the Commonwealth Literary Fund Advisory Board, contributing his voice to the encouragement of Australian writers. *Collected Poems: 1930–1965* was reprinted in paperback edition as *Collected Poems: 1930–1970* (1972), and again in 1974 in an Angus and Robertson Classics series with the addition of poems from *New Poems:*

1965–1969 and with revised notes to Book V of *Dunciad Minor*. Hope's contribution to poetry was recognized by an award of Order of the British Empire (OBE) and an honorary degree from Australian National University. His growing popularity as a poet is evident with the reprinting of *Selected Poems* of 1963 in 1974 and 1975. *Henry Kendall: A Dialogue with the Past,* including an introduction by Hope and poems and prose selected by Leonie Kramer, was published in 1971. In this year Hope became a member of the Literature Board of the Australia Council (1973–1974) and received an honorary degree from the University of New England. In 1974 a second edition of *The Cave and the Spring* was printed, and his *Native Companions: Essays and Comments on Australian Literature, 1936–1966* (1974) was published. This book is a mixture of reviews often slightly revised or augmented with later comments, three articles that Hope termed "more or less autobiographical," and revised texts of lectures he gave in the course of his academic teaching. Hope decided to give up reviewing in 1966 because it was time-consuming and poorly paid. The reviews he chose to include in this book he saw as "having some critical theory involved or some general critical attitude beyond the particular work under review."

In 1975 *Judith Wright* and *A Late Picking: Poems, 1965–1974* were published. In writing about Wright, a close friend as well as a fellow poet, Hope decided that since an abundance of material was being written about her poetry, he would focus in this study on her intellectual development and its importance as a background to her poetry rather than making the book a commentary on the poetry itself. All of the poems in *A Late Picking* first appeared in literary journals and magazines in Australia, the United States, and Canada. *A Late Picking* continues to reflect Hope's interest in the significance and need of the ancient myths and legends ("The Sacred Way"), biblical stories ("What the Serpent Really Said"), societies and their ironies ("The Invaders"), science/cosmology ("Exercise on a Sphere," "Nu Nubile," "Palinbenesia," "O Be a Fine Girl . . ."), literature ("A Letter to David Campbell on the Birthday of W. B. Yeats, 1965" and a satirical treatment of C. P. Snow's thesis on science and the arts, "Poor Charley's Dream"), the relationship between love/sex and art ("Croesus and Lais," "Pervigilium Veneris," "Apollo and Daphne, 1"), and Australia and his boyhood ("Country Places" and "Hayfever"). Within a year of the publication of these two texts Hope received the Robert Frost Award for poetry and an honorary degree from Monash University.

In 1978 Hope again published two texts, one critical prose, *The Pack of Autolycus,* and the other a new collection of poetry, *A Book of Answers. The Pack of Autolycus* consists of what Hope selected as the best lectures he gave during his academic career, and *A Book of Answers* is a book of poems in which Hope "answers back" across time to poets who have affected him. The poems of his "Old Favourites" are reconsidered–John Donne; Andrew Marvell; John Milton; John Dryden; Alexander Pope; George Gordon, Lord Byron; John Keats; Alfred, Lord Tennyson; Robert Browning; and Gerard Manley Hopkins. Hope also speaks back to the poems of such Europeans as Heinrich Heine, Aleksei Konstantinovich Tolstoy, and Charles-Pierre Baudelaire. He also takes on some contemporaries–William Butler Yeats, Robert Graves, and T. S. Eliot. Finally, he plays havoc with his friends James McAuley, Judith Wright, Gwen Harwood, Rosemary Dobson, and David Campbell. In 1979 Hope's *The New Cratylus: Notes on the Craft of Poetry* was published. This book was Hope's attempt to argue his case for what he thought great poetry must entail and what he believed was wrong with contemporary criticism–in particular, New Criticism and Leavism. He attacks such poets as Eliot, extolling the charms and musical superiority of traditional forms and damning "Free Verse" as being formless and unmusical. In the same year, his only daughter, Emily–a painter, silversmith, and writer–died of cancer at the age of thirty-nine. In his notebooks Hope writes in the years after her death of experiencing her presence and of his and his wife's great loss.

Hope was often accused by his earliest critics of not really being an Australian poet, considering his dependence on European sources, stories, and culture. Hope argued against this view, noting that all his poems, no matter what the theme, are influenced by the phenomenal world around him for their nuances, their tone, and their music. His later collections of poetry do begin, however, to deal directly with his Australian experience. In *Antechinas: Poems, 1975–1980* (1981) many of the poems are of this ilk: "Beyond Khancoban," "Tasmanian Magpies," and "The Drifting Continent."

In 1981 Hope was made Companion of the Order of Australia. The following year was an important one for Hope: *The Tragical History of Doctor Faustus: by Christopher Marlowe Purged and Amended by A. D. Hope,* begun fifty years earlier when he returned from Oxford, was finally published. Also in 1982 he translated a selection of his own poetry into Italian as *Tre Volti Dell'Amore.* Then in 1985 *The Age of Reason* was published–a collection of poems that Brooks in *The Double Looking Glass* explains are about "reason's contexts, about its ineluctible relations with such things. Its sometimes clearly unsovereign place amongst them." Brooks notes:

Among the most entertaining poems Hope has written, the eleven verse narratives of *The Age of Reason* are about the capricious, irrational, uncanny and mythical sides of the purportedly most rational of ages–Darwin's love life, Man Friday's suicide, Dampier's record of a Dantescan vision on the isle of Aves, George III's chasing Fanny Burney through Kew Gardens, and the supernatural explanation of Sir Herschel's recovery of the planet Uranus–all presented with a view to further levels of being and explanation, the rhythms of which erupt within and subvert those of Science and Reason.

In 1987, Hope's second adventure with playwriting was rewarded with the publication of *Ladies from the Sea: A Play in Three Acts,* an amusing and instructive play that examines how Odysseus, having returned home to his loyal wife, behaves when he is visited by the lovers he met on his twenty-year journey home (Calypso, Circe, and Nausica); the play has never been performed. In 1989 Hope was made an honorary member of the American Academy and Institute of Arts and Letters. This honor was Hope's last recognition in his lifetime of his contribution to literature. The National Library of Australia holds manuscripts that outline eight further projects Hope had planned but which he thought in 1986 he would "probably never live to complete." He prepared for his death for a long time. His last book of poetry, *Orpheus,* was written consciously as his last offering. In "Intimations of Mortality" in *Orpheus* he makes a plea to his readers:

Share the carcass, spare the soul;
Leave my laurels, sense or green.
Maggot, buzzard, critic, ghoul
Pick my bones but pick them clean[.]

To a large extent the poems in this slim volume represent Hope's abiding interests and the varied poetic forms he believed in and practiced throughout his life as a poet and a philosopher. Dedicated to his wife, Penelope, who died in 1988, these poems argue by analogy his view that the poet is detached and always wears a mask, his obsession with his dream-team workers that create for him at night, his reliance on the sacred provided by mythology and biblical stories, his lifelong struggle against "modernism," his view that laughter is an essential ingredient in discursive thought and art, his fascination with science, and his love for women. Some poems of the volume also record thoughts about his death. In "Intimations of Mortality" he says,

Here's the Rubbish left behind
By careless love and reckless wit.
Burrow in and what you find
May God give you joy of it.

*Cover for Hope's controversial 1965 collection of criticism
(Thomas Cooper Library, University of South Carolina)*

ated a collection of poems that brought to final form an overview of his life's work.

Hope's notebooks in particular are a means of identifying the sources of his poems, whether experiences from life or ideas from other works. His descriptions of the sexual behavior of insects exude unforgettable images of sensual beauty, which he draws from in many poems. His argument concerning the inevitability of the poet's mask, his necessary detachment as a creator in being a spectator of life, hints perhaps at how these views reveal a personality in the act of concealing it. Despite Hope's scholarly engagement with metaphysics, mythology, psychology, and cultural movements, and despite his antagonism toward aspects of modernism and his fierce views about the need for the poet's personal detachment when entering into an argument of a poem, he always expresses an element of play and disinterested contemplation of the world. When questioned about if and how he might write an autobiographical work, Hope said he "would write it as a travel book under the title 'A Visit to Earth.' It would involve no pose or artifice, since I have always felt that detachment travellers feel, no matter how well they know and feel at home in their countries they visit. No matter how immersed in the life of a foreign country they may become, their first impressions are always from the outside looking in—and that has been my attitude to the world I live in and still is." In "Visitant," from *Orpheus,* he writes,

> Yet much that I saw became dear;
> Some few were close to my heart;
> Although it was perfectly clear
> I was a stranger here
> Standing aloof and apart.

The closest Hope came to writing any form of autobiography was in his last published work, *Chance Encounters* (1992). This work gives a brief account of his life, although its focus is on the stories of encounters and incidents in his life that retained an importance for him. These included "encounters" he had with such people as Christopher Brennan, J. R. R. Tolkien, James McAuley, jazz great Kid Orey, and F. R. Leavis, to mention but a few. Peter Ryan's "A. D. Hope: A Memoir" introduces Hope's text and is one of the finest representations of the man in his many guises as scholar, satirist, poet, innovator, and character. Hope is encapsulated in Ryan's closing line: "A great poet, a great soul and that rare bird today, 'an intellectual who is not sundered from the human race.'"

Orpheus continues to express the excitement Hope experienced throughout his life when confronted with scientific interpretations of the world. A halfhearted

The humor is unmistakably Hope, even in his statement that laughter "will be my best epitaph." Hope was fascinated with the vagaries that make up a life. In "A letter to Ann McCulloch," a poem he wrote in response to a question concerning his biography, he wrote,

> We are shaped by our choices, even those we did not
>   make
> Or which were made for us, sometimes against our will.
> Where pathways diverge, the ones that we did not take
> Mostly forgotten, serve to determine us still[.]

Hope saw living as partly composed of blind choices and noted that in looking back one sees that comparatively trivial choices have often determined one's course. In identifying persistent themes in his work, gleaned from the reading of his poems and his notebooks, one realizes that in *Orpheus,* Hope had cre-

determinist, Hope enjoyed taking on the scientists–whether physicists, astrologists, or biologists–because of their inability to accept the provisional nature of knowledge. Scientific concepts themselves often served as a source of inspiration for his work. He writes of how he has never lost sight of the "awareness of the narrowness of the bases of knowledge of the world" and the way "that what we are aware of gets in the way of what we are totally unaware of," an idea expressed in his poem "A Swallow in the House." In this poem the swallow becomes the human being who, searching in the dark for answers, for a way out of failed systems, falls stunned to the ground after crashing against glass. He writes,

Something left out, not to be reckoned with,
Not conceived by science or adumbrated in myth;
Something of which he is totally unaware
As the swallow of its undreamt nightmare, solid air[.]

Endemic also to Hope's vision is his belief in a theory he constructed on the role dreams play in his creations. The notebooks include more entries on his theory of dreams than on any other topic. Hope's theory is an alternative to Freud's, and throughout his journals, he has recorded many dreams–delighting with how he, in his dreams, is taken over

. . . by a throng
of revellers and roisterers who proceed
To invent whole theatres of improbable dreams[.]

A. D. Hope died on 13 July 2000 in Canberra. He believed that poetry was philosophical music, and his work dramatizes the ways in which a philosophical argument is best represented by analogy. He believed that all great poems include within their music an argument of some kind. His preference for analogy is in line with his distrust of arguments based on the assumption that certain facts are fundamental, elemental, and axiomatic and that, in knowledge, no other facts have to be brought into consonance with them. Hope attributed this insight to the teaching he received (when he was an undergraduate at the University of Sydney) from John Anderson. Hope's use of analogy as his preferred form of argument followed in the wake of "the dead hand of nineteenth century rationalism," which had caused the assumed basis of his thinking to be effectively removed. His nightly entries into his notebooks (1949–1988) explore a wide gamut of his views on society–whether directed at social mores, the processes of artistic creation, or the impact of technology on humans' lives. Underpinning Hope's poetry, prose, and journal writings is the ever-present ironic vision that provided him his capacity to laugh at himself and to smile at his

Dust jacket for the 1970 poem in which Hope criticized how society limits women's creativity (Bruccoli Clark Layman Archives)

relentless search for meaning while he affirmed and celebrated all that being human means.

Hope identified with the mythological figures Odysseus, Faust, and Don Juan. Indeed, many of his poems played out their stories. He enjoyed that his wife was named Penelope, who, like the mythological Penelope from the *Odyssey,* must often have felt that she was weaving a vast tapestry waiting for her spouse to return from outside adventures–in Hope's case the public world of literary activities–from the attention of those fawning at his feet and from his study in their Forrest home in Canberra, in which he was ensconced for much of their life together. She gave Hope the home that made his creations possible; she took on the work of bringing up their three children, and she loved him and sustained his self-esteem. *Orpheus* is dedicated to his wife:

For Penelope

Trees

Since you left me forever, I find my eyes
See things less clearly than they used to do
All that I view lacks the hint of surprise
That once I shared with you. . . .

Interviews:

Ann McCulloch, Adrian Barker, Tony Hood, and Paul Samuel, *The Dance of Language: The Life and Work of A. D. Hope,* Deakin University, 1996–six programmed video documentaries on A. D. Hope's life and work; includes interviews with Hope.

Bibliography:

Joy W. Hooton, *A. D. Hope* (Melbourne: Oxford University Press, 1979).

References:

Lyndy Abraham, "A. D. Hope and the Poetry of Allusion," *Australian Literary Studies,* 9, no. 2 (1979);

Barry Argyle, "The Poetry of A. D. Hope," *Journal of Commonwealth Literature,* 3 (1967): 87–96;

John Barnes, "A Question of Standards," *Meanjin,* 16, no. 3 (1957);

R. F. Brissenden, "A. D. Hope's *New Poems,*" *Southerly,* 30, no. 2 (1970);

Brissenden, "A. D. Hope's 'The Double Looking Glass': A Reading," *Australian Literary Studies,* 6, no. 4 (1974): 339–351;

Brissenden, "Hope without Bawd," review of *Collected Poems: 1930–1965* by A. D. Hope, *Comment,* 1, no. 2 (1966);

David Brooks, "*Orpheus* and *The Age of Reason,*" *Redoubt,* 13 (1992);

Brooks, ed., *The Double Looking Glass: New and Classic Essays on the Poetry of A. D. Hope* (St. Lucia: University of Queensland Press, 2000);

Vincent Buckley, "A. D. Hope: The Unknown Poet," in his *Essays in Poetry: Mainly Australian* (Melbourne: Melbourne University Press, 1957);

Buckley, "Cutting Green Hay," in his *Friendships, Movements and Cultural Conflicts in Australia's Great Decades* (Melbourne: Allen Lane/Penguin, 1983);

Buckley, "Towards an Australian Literature," *Meanjin,* 16, no. 3 (1957);

Buckley, "Utopianism and Vitalism in Australian Literature," *Quadrant,* 3, no. 2 (1959): 35–51;

Robert Darling, *A. D. Hope* (Boston: Twayne, 1997);

Donald Davie, "Australians and Others," review of *Poems* by A. D. Hope, *Spectator* (24 March 1974);

John Docker, "The Image of Woman in A. D. Hope's Poetry," in his *Australian Cultural Elites: Intellectual Traditions in Sydney and Melbourne* (Sydney: Angus & Robertson, 1974);

Docker, "Sex and Nature in Modern Poetry," *Arena,* 22 (1970);

Geoffrey Dutton, "'Intellectualised Pornography': 'Imperial Adam,' and Kenneth Slessor," *Southerly,* 49, no. 3 (1989): 383–390;

Roy Fuller, "A. D. Hope's *Collected Poems,*" *Meanjin,* 25, no. 2 (1966): 224–226;

S. L. Goldberg, "The Poet as Hero: A. D. Hope's *The Wandering Islands,*" *Meanjin,* 16, no. 2 (1957): 127–139;

Suzanne Graham, "Myth and the Poetry of A. D. Hope," *Australian Literary Studies,* 7, no. 12 (1955): 130–140;

Max Harris, "A. D. Hope: Sensuous Excitement–or Monotonous Imagery?" *Voice,* 4, no. 12 (1955);

James Harrison, "Hope's 'Agony Column,'" *Explicator,* 47, no. 3 (1987);

Kevin Hart, *A. D. Hope,* Oxford Australian Writers Series (Melbourne: Oxford University Press, 1992; New York: Oxford University Press, 1992);

H. P. Heseltine, "Paradise Within: A. D. Hope's *New Poems,*" *Meanjin,* 29, no. 4 (1970): 404–420;

Evan Jones, "The Poet in the University," *Australian Author,* 1, no. 4 (1969);

Jones, "Three Conservatives," *Bulletin* (21 October 1961);

Frank Kermode, "Poetry in Australia," *Manchester Guardian* (17 March 1961);

Bruce King, "A. D. Hope and Australian Poetry," *Sewanee Review,* 87, no. 1 (1979);

Leonie Kramer, *A. D. Hope* (Melbourne: Oxford University Press, 1979);

Peter Kuch and Paul Kavanagh, "Daytime Thoughts about the Night Shift: Alec Hope Talks to Peter Kuch and Paul Kavanagh," *Southerly,* 47, no. 2 (1956): 221–231;

Noel Macainsh, "A. D. Hope's Malthusian Muse: Lubricious Disaster," *Quadrant,* 29, no. 3 (1986);

Macainsh, "Fine Wine and Triumphant Music–A. D. Hope's Poetic," *Westerly,* 31, no. 3 (1986): 25–34;

Macainsh, "The Suburban Aristocrat: A. D. Hope and Classicism," *Meridian,* 4, no. 1 (1985);

David Malouf, "A. D. Hope's *New Cratylus,*" *Meanjin,* 39, no. 2 (1980): 150–162;

Philip Martin, "A. D. Hope, Nonconformist," *Journal of Popular Culture,* 23, no. 2 (1989);

James McAuley, "The Pyramid in the Waste: An Introduction to A. D. Hope's Poetry," *Quadrant,* 5, no. 4 (1961): 61–70;

Ann McCulloch, *A. D. Hope: The Dance of Language: An Annotated Chronology, His Life, His Work, His Views* (Geelong, Vic.: Deakin University Press, 1995);

McCulloch, Susan McKernan, Vincent Buckley, Ruth Morse, and David Brooks, *Security of Allusion*–special issue of *The Phoenix Review,* edited by Brooks (Canberra: The Phoenix Review/Bistro Editions, Australian National University, 1992);

A. L. McLeod, "Maturity in Australian Satire: The Poetry of A. D. Hope," *Modern Language Studies,* 10, no. 2 (1980);

Ross Metzger, "Alienation and Prophecy: The Grotesque in the Poetry of A. D. Hope," *Southerly,* 36, no. 3 (1976): 268–283;

Susan Moore, "A. D. Hope's 'Three Faces of Love,'" *Australian Literary Studies,* 10, no. 3 (1982): 389–391;

Ruth Morse, "Editing A. D. Hope," *Australian Literary Studies,* 12, no. 4 (1986);

Morse, "Security of Allusion: Andre Chenier and the Poetry of A. D. Hope," *Quadrant,* 32 (1988);

C. D. Narasimhaiah, "A. D. Hope: Poetry of Shocked Sensibility," *ACLAS Bulletin,* 4, no. 4 (1976);

Sheila L. Roper, "An Exhumation: A Missing Link in Modern Australian Poetry," *Southerly,* 47, no. 1 (1972);

William Jay Smith, "A. D. Hope and the Comic Vision: Four Recent Contributions," *Hollins Critic,* 9, no. 2 (1972);

Peter Steele, "Contemporary Australian poetry," *Spirit,* 36, no. 4 (1970): 44–47;

W. A. Suchting, "The Poetry of A. D. Hope: A Frame of Reference," *Meanjin,* 21, no. 2 (1962);

Andrew Taylor, "A. D. Hope: The Double Tongue of Harmony," in his *Reading Australian Poetry* (St. Lucia: University of Queensland Press, 1987);

Gaye Tennant, "A. D. Hope: Sensuous Excitement—or Monotonous Imagery?" *Voice,* 4, no. 12 (1955);

Chris Wallace-Crabbe, "Three Faces of Hope," in his *Melbourne or the Bush: Essays on Australian Literature and Society* (Sydney: Angus & Robertson, 1974);

Wallace-Crabbe, "True Tales and False Alike Work by Suggestion," *Australian Literary Studies,* 14, no. 4 (1991): 415–424;

William Walsh, "A. D. Hope," in his *A Manifold Voice: Studies in Commonwealth Literature* (London: Chatto & Windus, 1970);

Edwin Webb, "Dualities and Their Resolution in the Poetry of A. D. Hope," *Southerly,* 32, no. 3 (1972): 210–225;

James Wieland, "A. D. Hope's Latter-Day Ulysses: 'The End of a Journey' and the Literary Background," *Australian Literary Studies,* 10, no. 4 (1982): 468–477;

G. A. Wilkes, "Going Over the Terrain in a Different Way: An Alternative View of Australian Literary History," *Southerly,* 35, no. 2 (1975): 141–156;

Wilkes, "The Poetry of A. D. Hope," *Australian Quarterly,* 36, no. 1 (1964);

Fay Zwicky, "Another Side of Paradise: A. D. Hope and Judith Wright," *Southerly,* 48, no. 1 (1988): 3–21.

Papers:

Manuscripts, letters, notebooks, lectures, and other materials of A. D. Hope are held by the National Library of Australia, Canberra. Still other materials are held by the Menzies Library, Australian National University; the Fryer Memorial Library, Brisbane; the Latrobe Library, Melbourne; the Mitchell Library, Sydney; and the Baillieu Library, Melbourne University, Melbourne. Broadcasting material is held by Australian Broadcasting Commission, Archives Department, Melbourne. Further material remains in possession of the family of A. D. Hope.

John Iggulden

(12 February 1917 –   )

James Packer
Workers' Educational Association Sydney

See also the Iggulden interview in *DLB Yearbook: 2001*.

BOOKS: *Breakthrough* (London: Chapman & Hall, 1960);

The Storms of Summer (London: Chapman & Hall, 1960);

The Clouded Sky (New York: Macmillan, 1964; London: Macdonald, 1965);

Dark Stranger (New York: McGraw-Hill, 1965; London: Macdonald, 1966; Melbourne: Bolinda Press, 1991);

The Revolution of the Good, volume 1 of *The Promised Land Papers* (Sydney: Cobham, 1986);

How Things Are Wrong and How to Fix Them, volume 2 of *The Promised Land Papers* (Sydney: Cobham, 1988);

Modification of Freedom: The Fundamentals and the Practicalities of Human Association, volume 3 of *The Promised Land Papers* (Urunga, N.S.W.: Cobham, 1993);

Silent Lies (Bellingen, N.S.W.: John Iggulden, 1996); revised as *Silent Lies: A Survival Handbook into the Twenty-First Century for 1990s Students, and Others with Serious Future Concerns* (Bellingen, N.S.W.: Cobham, 1997);

Good World: A Startling Novel of the Very Near Future (Bellingen, N.S.W.: Cobham, 1998).

OTHER: *Manual of Standard Procedures,* edited by Iggulden (Melbourne: Gliding Federation of Australia, 1964);

Summer's Tales 3, edited by Iggulden (Melbourne: Macmillan / New York: St. Martin's Press, 1966);

Gliding Instructor's Handbook, edited by Iggulden (Melbourne: Gliding Federation of Australia, 1968);

The Shame of Western Port: Speculator's Dream, Environmental Nightmare, edited by Iggulden (Melbourne: Western Port and Peninsula Protection Council, 1971).

SELECTED PERIODICAL PUBLICATION–
UNCOLLECTED: Iggulden and Clem Christesen, "[obituary of] Maurice Vintner," *Australian Author,* 3, no. 4 (1971): 21–22.

John Iggulden (from the cover of Good World, *1998; Bruccoli Collection, Thomas Cooper Library, University of South Carolina)*

In the first volume of his *Promised Land* trilogy John Iggulden concisely enunciates the basis of an uncompromising program for financial and literary endeavor: "You cannot manage *anything* effectively unless you first decide on, and define, the *exact purpose* of the thing to be managed." Approximately the same sentiment is expressed by the central protagonists of Iggulden's earliest novels. This belief was only announced as a distinctly literary program, however, in the 1966 introduction to the short-story collection *Summer's Tales 3.* In this introduction, Iggulden seeks to define "the qualities and the direction of development" he hopes to see "emerging from the present transitions in the main stream of indigenous creative writing." Foremost among these qualities are "directness," "clarity of meaning," and "clear communication of recognisable human realities and experienced human situations, which are utterly basic in making a work of fiction readable, and without which the finest writing must fail to some degree in its intention."

By the time he wrote these words, Iggulden had published four novels including some clearly articulated dramatic conundrums that owed far more to analytical interest in political and existential subjects than to the instinct of a writer or to literary ambition. Paradoxically, while the way they were written was largely an outcome of the effort to get "the message across," the message itself was consistently one of confusions of motives and of the incalculable fatalities of everyday life. "Day by day," says the narrator of *The Clouded Sky* (1964) as he recounts the tale of his marriage, "we had picked our careful way, progressing as soldiers do, step by uncertain step toward that clash with their fellow beings to which they were inescapably drawn." Such passages, with their appearance of folk wisdom, mask the elaboration of a coherent philosophical viewpoint, successively broadening in each novel to make them finally representative of the literary spirit evident a quarter century earlier in the work of such Anglo-Australian novelists as Frederic Manning and Brian Penton and, by the late 1950s, in the novels of the British writer William Golding. That spirit caused the novelist to ask distinctively "existential" questions such as "Who am I?" and "How did I become what I am?" This questioning led to the opening up of a definitive space between character and action (that is, between "Who am I?" and "Who was it that did *that*?") that led in turn to the entire narrational structure of the book becoming visibly indeterminate and occasionally treacherous. For how could a narrator keep a firm grip on suppositions about himself if the story he told was designed to undermine himself (the solidity and validity of the intentions of which his self is and was made up)?

Iggulden dramatized concrete problems of human existence using the forms of the popular ("genre") novel. Although he produced work whose themes mirrored those of some of his contemporaries—Colin Johnston (the novel of identity), Peter Mathers (the novel of subversion), and David Ireland (the novel of self-alienation)—no fashion for these writers could promote a writer such as Iggulden, so insistently a "storyteller" with so little obvious interest in "fine writing." Through the 1960s and into the following decade the Australian literary novel became increasingly abstract; its new look was marked by an avoidance of dramatic resolution and melodramatic effect. The novels of writers such as Iggulden, George Turner, Morris West, and Jon Cleary not only lacked this abstractness, they also seemed to acquire the bland "international style" of best-sellers (which they were), and the criticisms they suffered were increasingly those of a supposed failure to accept Australia as a scene of experiment, or vision, or

Dust jacket for Iggulden's second novel (1960), in which the protagonist justifies murdering a man to protect a friend (Bruccoli Collection, Thomas Cooper Library, University of South Carolina)

integral truth. (The high tide of this tendency, before the countermovement of "culture studies," was the publication in 1979 of Ireland's *A Woman of the Future*.) Iggulden wrote one best-seller, *Breakthrough*, which Ian Fleming praised and which found a niche among sci-fi political thrillers of the early 1960s. His subsequent books were confused in the Australian literary mindset of the 1960s with best-sellers, even though not even *Breakthrough* was a best-seller of an orthodox type. In the wake of a faded enthusiasm for the "abstract" novel, a reevaluation of Iggulden's work is needed, as that of an ambitious writer with a determinedly original perspective on writing whose best work is no more mere "story-telling" than the work of Mathers or Ireland. The best of his writing is, like that of Mathers and Ireland, so rooted in Australian historical circumstances that it not only feeds off them but attempts to explain them; it is oriented toward the moral plight of the "rational" human being, which it probes with an intensity characteristic of the most eccentric and memorable works in the Australian canon.

John Manners ("Jack") Iggulden was born in Brighton, a bayside suburb of Melbourne, to William Alfred Iggulden and Jessica Lang Manners on 12 February 1917. William Iggulden, a New Zealander who emigrated a few years before World War I, had set up the family business, the Booster (later, Bentley) Manufacturing Company, manufacturing patented building tools invented by his half brother in New Zealand. "The family fortunes," Iggulden later wrote, "were founded upon the inventiveness of Dad and his brother," and "inventive ability was taken as the greatest of intellectual values." Iggulden was educated at Gardenvale State and Hampton High Schools, both in Melbourne, but with the family's fortunes faltering in the 1930s Great Depression, became after the age of thirteen a "willing and able autodidact," working for his father alongside a slightly older brother, William. William later fulfilled an early promise in aerodynamics and industrial design, and with his father (who died in 1967) was Iggulden's partner in the family business until his death. In this context Iggulden, at the age of fourteen, encountered David Uniapon. Uniapon, the first aboriginal to have work published in Australia, acquired the use of William Iggulden's manufacturing facilities to carve the boomerangs he sold for a living (the Igguldens were at that time in the same business), as well as developing his perpetual motion machine. "Years later, in my first novel," wrote Iggulden, "it seemed logical and right that I should use David Uniapon as my model for Australia's first aboriginal Prime Minister, 'Peter Jirapon.' In my fourth novel, Dark Stranger, intended as a literary protest against the then official policy of 'assimilation,' Peter Jirapon was a young aboriginal lawyer."

In 1932, at age fifteen, Iggulden flew a solo glider for the first time: a lifelong career as glider pilot, coincidental with his pursuit of flight as a physical art, was reflected in Iggulden's third novel, The Clouded Sky; both were ultimately inspired by the aerodynamic enthusiasms engendered by his brother's experiments with boomerangs and primitive hang gliders in the early 1930s. If gliding rather than writing was Iggulden's preferred mode of artistic expression in early adulthood, both were subordinated to the requirements of his family business, which he took over from his father at the age of twenty-three. The year was 1940, and the business had turned to war production; not for a further twenty years was Iggulden prepared to announce a fuller commitment to a writing career.

At twenty-five, in January 1942, Iggulden married Helen Carroll Schapper. The union produced a son (now deceased) and two daughters. It was also a collaborative partnership extending well beyond normal family life. Iggulden, describing his involvement in the campaign of opposition to the development of Westernport Bay twenty-five years after his marriage, forcibly spelled out

the terms of mutual dependence upon which his various activities subsequently relied.

At forty-two Iggulden became Australian Gliding Champion for 1959–1960. At forty-three he published Breakthrough (1960), a dystopian novel set in "a time when present world trends are extended," the early twenty-first century. A businessman whose keen sense of the realities of industrial life regulated his political ideals, he produced a first novel in which the political and emotional outcomes were singularly tenuous for a book that seemed essentially a Cold War thriller (even one judged "outstanding" by Ian Fleming). In fact, in its Australian context Breakthrough was something quite different. Its collage of viewpoints and genres resembles the techniques of no previous Australian novel, although its archly expressed fatalism resembles that in Eleanor Dark's Prelude to Christopher (1934), and the "Australianness" of its ideologized form of science fiction becomes immediately apparent to any reader of Barnard Eldershaw's Tomorrow and Tomorrow and Tomorrow (1947). Breakthrough was rejected by Angus and Robertson in Australia but accepted (through an English agent) by the London firm Chapman and Hall. Iggulden thus settled for the fate of many internationally published Australian writers, and in later years, of a writer whose Australian prospects depended wholly on his own publishing efforts.

In spite of the literary weaknesses of emphatic plotting and melodramatic dialogue—weaknesses that Iggulden set about overcoming not only in the course of his later writing, but over the length of the novel itself—Breakthrough had a serious intent and was ill served by the mention of "heroic character" in a publisher's blurb on its opening pages. Martin Green, the schematized individualist who throughout the novel remains its focal point, is the means by which a certain moral problem is to be resolved (the legitimacy of the killing of "enemies of human freedom"), and in his preparedness to face the essence of this problem Iggulden reveals strains and tensions within "ethical thinking" of a Nietzschean dimension. Rather than float free from the realities of ethical life (a marked tendency in utopian fiction), Iggulden devotes to those realities increasing focus; while Breakthrough begins as an overstated analysis of the relation of the individual and the state, it culminates in the moral impasse that it has actively pursued, even to the moral destruction of the character it valorizes. Unusually, the admission of this impasse is not taken as an admission of weakness (Nietzsche's "nihilism") but of a delimited strength that has achieved an equally delimited, though unquestionably positive, result. Martin Green insists that his killing of Consul Bronstein is murder and can only be accepted by people who accept murder.

Breakthrough reveals the subservience of human will to cosmic fate at the moment will seizes fate as its own vehicle. Iggulden has only admitted the influence of one other author, James Gould Cozzens; and Cozzens's theme

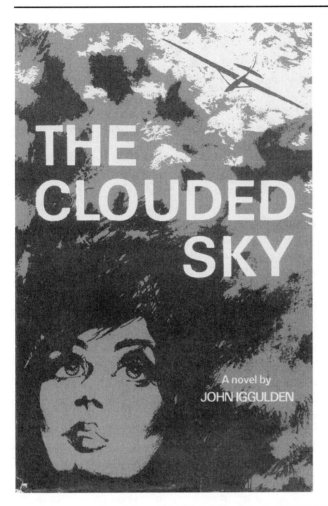

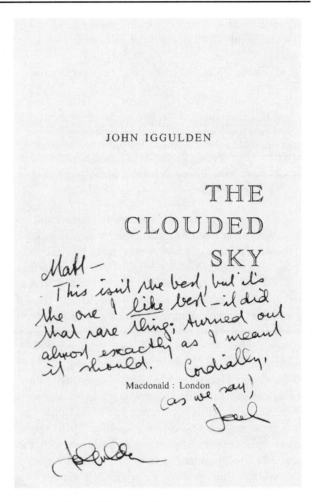

*Dust jacket and inscribed title page for the 1965 British edition of Iggulden's 1964 novel, which deals with the
author's hobby of flying gliders and is narrated by an unlikable character (Bruccoli Collection,
Thomas Cooper Library, University of South Carolina)*

of entangled compromise provides rich examples of moral analysis pertinent to the world Iggulden's characters confront. ("Victory," concludes Arthur Winner in Cozzens's *By Love Possessed* [1957], "is not in reaching certainties or solving mysteries; victory is in making do with uncertainties, in supporting mysteries.") The novels written after *Breakthrough* seek out expressions of the relation of will to fate in progressively less schematic ways; *The Storms of Summer* (1960) was published in the same year as *Breakthrough,* while *The Clouded Sky* and *Dark Stranger* were published in 1964 and 1965, respectively, after a period of intense activity during which Iggulden left Australia for the first time to compete in the World Gliding Competitions in Argentina in 1963.

At what point do human beings accept a murder? This Dostoevskian question was implicit in Norman Lindsay's *Dust or Polish?* (1950), but Australian novelists only began to use it when Iggulden wrote *Breakthrough, The Storms of Summer,* and *Dark Stranger* and David Ireland

wrote *The Chantic Bird* (1968). *The Storms of Summer* involves the killing of an Italian fisherman and appears to provide an emotional justification for acts of this sort. The fisherman had been preparing to take the life of one of his killer's mates, and the killer, Charles Desborough, the central character in the book, consequently faces the problem of "universal" morality thrown up whenever the rules of social life are shown to be the rules of force. "The point," he says, "is that sometimes you have to throw this Right and Wrong bullshit over the side. There's no argument that it was wrong to kill Domenico to save Harry if I wasn't equally prepared, if it came up, to save Domenico . . . and yet I don't care how wrong it was. I'm just glad, now, that I was there to save Harry and I'm proud that I had enough guts to do it!" Although morality is expressed in the direct terms of an action novel–terms that invariably favor an in-group against the outsider–the seed of doubt framing such anti-intellectual directness is shortly exploited, as Iggulden formulates an existential rather than

155

ideological resolution to the "beyond good or evil" motif Desborough cannot allow himself to relinquish:

> "You couldn't live like that! It doesn't even sound like you. . . ."
>
> "Of course not!" Charles agreed emphatically. "Nobody could live like that all the time. You live by the rules . . . as long as you're left to live by the rules. Only . . . sometimes you have to be ready to follow them down where the rules don't count, but you're always ready to go there if that's what they want."

The critical distaste encountered by Iggulden's two later novels was more muted than that of the earlier novels; there is evidence of a turn to acceptance by Australian critics, most notably Maurice Vintner, who, in an article for *The Sydney Morning Herald* (22 October 1966), recognized the complex existential point of both *The Clouded Sky* and *Dark Stranger*. Ritchie Harrington, the first-person protagonist of the former, is an unsympathetic narrator, a philanderer, described by Iggulden in an interview with Matthew Bruccoli in October 2001 as "bumptious, rough and generally unpleasant." Iggulden's task was to turn such a character—at a time when Australian writers such as George Johnston in *My Brother Jack* (1964) and Randolph Stow in *Merry-Go-Round in the Sea* (1965) spoke through passive narrators whose engagement with the world was largely an extension of their acts of writing—into a wholly active persona for whom self-analysis was nevertheless fundamental. On Vintner's analysis, Harrington can be properly understood only by completely discounting the first-person presentation of his dealings with the world, a necessary procedure in overcoming the preciosity of the semiautobiographical novel. He cannot be understood directly, by taking the narrative at face value. The net gain of this procedure is a possible fictional resolution of the "problem" of existence; the net loss is the weight of a reflected (or refracted) self.

Iggulden's skill as a presenter of aesthetically motivated "action" material was readily appreciated both in Australia and abroad. Alan Roberts, for example, spoke of the "vivid accounts of some six or seven flights" of gliders in *The Clouded Sky,* one of which was "a little classic, worthy of Saint-Exupery [author of *The Little Prince,* who wrote works drawing upon his experiences as a pilot before and during World War II]." In the end, however, what told against Iggulden was that each of his four novels was directed more by existential than by aesthetic purposes—that for him matters of truth weighed more heavily than authorial finesse. As Vintner remarked in his review of *Dark Stranger,* Iggulden's fourth novel exemplified "a tradesman working to capacity, stretching his imaginative powers and his techniques, reaching out further." *Dark Stranger* was one of the more successful novels of the

1960s thematizing issues of aboriginality; Iggulden shows that one can produce a dramatically complex yet coherent novel from direct rejection of all racial preferment. Yet, the book received little critical attention. Of book-length studies of Australian fiction only the highly synoptic accounts of L. J. Blake, in his *Australian Writers,* and Joseph and Joanna Jones, in their *Australian Fiction,* mention Iggulden at all: Blake gave *Dark Stranger* a single sentence; Jones ignored it completely, as did J. J. Healy in his 1978 *Literature and the Aborigine in Australia 1770–1975.*

The subject of *Dark Stranger* is, again, the question of truth in narration—in this case, the extent to which the pursuit of a "good result" justifies the corrupt strategies whereby that result is achieved. The novel focuses on the shifting meanings of "goodness" in the racial (or "racist," as Iggulden himself used the word) context of the relationship of two men, a young aboriginal lawyer and a middle-aged white public-relations consultant, seeking the acquittal of an aboriginal youth facing execution for murder. The chief concern of *Dark Stranger* is the apprehension of reality; the novel is about survival, but in Vintner's words, "there is more to this than physical survival there is the survival of ideas, of ideals, and of individual integrity." *Dark Stranger* was, in fact, about the survival of values rather than the survival of persons.

The issue of Iggulden's "stranger" (the reality of a human being's reduction to "otherness"), by contrast, is not confined to a contingency of "self" or "place," since the struggle is for a common ground on which particular types of self can have value and meaning only in terms of one another. "That's what they want," asserts the Aboriginal Peter Jirapon. "Every abo living like a white. And a lot of whites think that. It's the big new word. Assimilation. Get rid of boongs by turning them into whites." "Wanting to change others, to make them like yourself," he says later, "can be a kind of hatred. There are people who would rather have you dead, who would rather kill you, than have you stay unchanged." But this "message" cuts two ways, and the test for Jirapon is whether this view is itself anything more than an ideological rationale for (racist) nativism. Significantly, when the public-relations consultant attempts to sacrifice the truth of actual guilt or innocence to the "truth" of a racial or cultural particular interest, Jirapon turns upon him: "That is the fatal conceit which has mucked up all that your world's supposed to stand for. That's why your lives have lost their meaning and their purpose . . . because, in everything, all is expediency and compromise."

Iggulden's concern for truth in social and political relationships led him in subsequent years away from fiction to various forms of activism and the writing of works on political economy and social prognosis. His brother's death in 1970 led to a renewed commitment to the family company, which in the mid 1970s was moved from Victo-

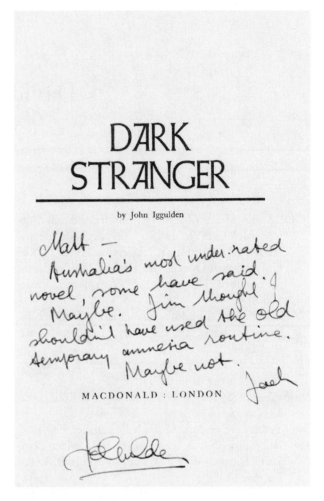

Dust jacket and inscribed title page for the 1966 British edition of Iggulden's 1965 novel, which includes a character who becomes the first Aboriginal prime minister of Australia; the inscription notes the judgment of James Gould Cozzens (Bruccoli Collection, Thomas Cooper Library, University of South Carolina)

ria to northern New South Wales. During these years, Iggulden gave some attention to "Sounds before an Echo," a memoir he had begun in the mid 1960s; its final revision, as "The Sound of the Rainbow," remains unpublished at the beginning of the twenty-first century. A further novel, *Good World: A Startling Novel of the Very Near Future,* classed by Iggulden as part of his work on social and economic issues, was published in 1998 by the firm he had set up in the 1980s to publish his trilogy of economics writings, *The Promised Land.* In 1989 the family company was split into two divisions, one of which, Lucinda Glassblowers ("Lucinda" is the proprietor of the glassblowing works in Peter Carey's Booker Prize winner, *Oscar and Lucinda* [1998]), remains a testimony to his unembarrassed and unrepentant conflation of the existential, cultural, and commercial enterprises of his unusual life.

Interview:

Matthew Bruccoli, Interview with John Iggulden, October 2001, *DLB Yearbook.*

References:

L. J. Blake, *Australian Writers* (Adelaide: Rigby, 1968), p. 179;

John Gould Cozzens, *By Love Possessed* (London: Longmans Green, 1957), p. 569;

Felicity Haynes, [review of *An Afternoon of Time, Dark Stranger,* and *The Watch Tower*], *Westerly* (Perth) (Summer 1966): 43–46;

J. J. Healy, *Literature and the Aborigine in Australia 1770–1975* (Brisbane: University of Queensland Press, 1978);

Colin Johnston, *Wildcat Falling* (Sydney: Angus & Robertson, 1965), p. 92;

Joseph Jones and Joanna Jones, *Australian Fiction* (Boston: Twayne, 1983), p. 81.

Papers:

The Thomas Cooper Library of the University of South Carolina holds a collection of John Iggulden's papers.

David Ireland

(24 August 1927 –   )

James Packer
Workers' Educational Association Sydney

BOOKS: *Image in the Clay,* prefaces by Ireland and Norman McVicker (St. Lucia: University of Queensland Press, 1964; St. Lucia & New York: University of Queensland Press, 1986; St. Lucia & London: University of Queensland Press, 1986);

The Chantic Bird (London: Heinemann, 1968; New York: Scribners, 1968; Sydney: Angus & Robertson, 1968);

The Unknown Industrial Prisoner (Sydney & London: Angus & Robertson, 1971);

The Flesheaters (Sydney & London: Angus & Robertson, 1972);

Burn (Sydney & London: Angus & Robertson, 1974);

The Glass Canoe (South Melbourne, Vic.: Macmillan, 1976; Ringwood, Vic. & Harmondsworth, U.K.: Penguin, 1982);

A Woman of the Future (New York: Braziller, 1979; Melbourne: Allen Lane, 1979; Ringwood, Vic. & Harmondsworth, U.K.: Penguin, 1979);

City of Women (Ringwood, Vic.: Allen Lane, 1981; Ringwood, Vic. & Harmondsworth, U.K.: Penguin, 1981);

Archimedes and the Seagle: A Novel (Ringwood, Vic. & London: Viking, 1984);

Bloodfather (Ringwood, Vic. & New York: Viking, 1987; London & New York: Hamilton, 1988);

The Chosen (Milson's Point, N.S.W.: Random House, 1997; London: Secker & Warburg, 1998).

Editions: *The Chantic Bird,* introduction by Julian Croft (Sydney: Angus & Robertson, 1973).

David Ireland (photograph by A. T. Bolton; by permission of the National Library of Australia)

SELECTED PERIODICAL PUBLICATIONS– UNCOLLECTED:

POETRY

"Madness," *Southerly* (Sydney), 27, no. 4 (1967): 292.

FICTION

"The Bronze Overcoat," *Bulletin* (Centenary Issue) (29 January 1980): 180–187;

"The Wild Colonial Boy," *National Times* (Sydney), 25–31 January 1981, pp. 25–27;

"Injections," *Bulletin* (Literary Supplement) (Sydney), 22–29 December 1981, pp. 172–177;

"The New Aristocrats," *Sydney Morning Herald,* 26 January 1985, pp. 33, 35;

"Vision of Lindow Man," in *Expressway,* edited by Helen Daniel (Melbourne: Penguin, 1989), pp. 68–79;

"The Stone Carnation," *Australian Book Review* (Melbourne), 144 (1992): 43–44;

"The Drover's Wife," *Australian Book Review* (Melbourne) (November 1997): 66.

NONFICTION

"Statement," *Australian Literary Studies* (Brisbane) (October 1977): 192–193;

"The Chantic Bird," *Australian Book Review* (Melbourne), 141 (1992): 31;

Extract from an early manuscript of *A Woman of the Future,* in Sue Woolfe and Kate Grenville, *Making Stories: How Ten Australian Novels Were Written* (Sydney: Allen & Unwin, 1993), pp. 136–146.

In the decade after 1979, the year *A Woman of the Future* was published, David Ireland was considered the most intriguing literary figure in Australia and its foremost novelist of ideas. *A Woman of the Future,* Ireland's complex and mischievous *The Unknown Industrial Prisoner* (1971), and his acknowledged comic masterpiece *The Glass Canoe* (1976) had each received the most prestigious literary prize in Australia, the Miles Franklin Award, not always in controversial circumstances but always with controversial outcomes. *The Unknown Industrial Prisoner* was clearly subversive in its attack upon the ownership of Australian companies and Australian lives by foreign concerns, and charges of suppression were leveled when government funding to the motion picture being made of it was cut in 1978; both *The Glass Canoe* and *A Woman of the Future* included sexual material of such directness that education officials barred the former from being studied by schoolchildren, and one of the Miles Franklin judges called the latter "literary sewage." This reputation for radicalism, however, belied Ireland's seriousness as a novelist and his fundamental literary concerns. The generation of radical critics that in the 1970s acclaimed his work for its political content became distinctly uneasy when in the late 1980s and the 1990s it failed to keep step with official doctrines of "postmodern leftism," despite Ireland's singular status as the forerunner of the distinctively postmodern Australian novel, as well as the most enduring and ambitious of its practitioners.

David Neil Ireland was born 24 August 1927 in the Sydney suburb of Lakemba to John and Lilian Ireland, a kitchen-table birth used in different ways in at least two of Ireland's novels. John Ireland was a veteran of World War I who sold insurance during the Great Depression, compromising his position within the Plymouth Brethren and teaching his son some of the deeper meanings of alienation within a religious organization. John Ireland also compromised his position as an insurance salesman by taking a moral stand on the forcible surrender of insurance policies at a time of universal economic hardship; he lost his job, not quite in the manner of the Brethren-driven, insurance-salesman

father of Ireland's first novel, *The Chantic Bird* (1968), but provoking the same incredulity, a response never entirely occluded in Ireland's earlier plays and novels.

The family moved from suburb to suburb in northern Sydney; Ireland's two years at an opportunity primary school at Artarmon and his three years at Sydney Technical High School were probably the most settled of his childhood. By the end of his third year, his father was an invalid (he had been gassed in World War I and died within a few years at the age of forty-nine), and Ireland was forced to go to work. The necessity of having to earn a living at an early age, he later claimed to Sue Woolfe and Kate Grenville, gave him his formative impulse as a writer: "I was very conscious of the other kids forging ahead: I did the Leaving Certificate about four years later, by private study. They were all going to university, and I thought: Now what can you do, where your experience, you yourself, not your formal education, makes the difference? The answer was writing." In his twenties, Ireland did little to advance this "answer" beyond speculating on narrative technique–his first substantial work, the play *Image in the Clay* (1964), was written in the first months of his thirtieth year–but the speculations and copious notes compiled through them, the "mountain I could stand on," resulted in the innovations he introduced in his earliest novels. In the 1960s many Australian novelists, most notably Peter Mathers, began to rediscover the narrative radicalism of Joseph Furphy, sporadically neglected in the years since his death in 1912. In a sense, Ireland's own narrative "unreasonableness" belonged to that movement. Certainly, both Furphy and Ireland had felt the power and significance of Laurence Sterne's *Tristram Shandy* (1759).

Image in the Clay had its origins in a 1947 encounter Ireland had, ten years before the play was written. Camped on the Murrumbidgee River in search of work, the then twenty-year-old was privy to the activities of a group of Aboriginals whom he later liberally fictionalized. (His 1963 introduction to the published work is at pains to emphasize the omissions and additions found in the play.) Consequently, he fought shy of explaining the work as a left-liberal "meliorist" or reformist tract–"my interest in aboriginals is no more than anyone else's, except that they are people"–and although "they are their own misfortune" (for "something is missing in themselves which they cannot supply"), "man is more, always more, than his circumstances." Images of value, in particular the clay image created by the main character, the Aboriginal father Gunner, were more important to the coherence of the play than either the characters' interactions with each other, their tribalism, or their illusions of the future; because these same images were pretexts for sto-

*Dust jacket for the 1973 reprint of Ireland's 1971 novel, which attacks ownership of Australian
companies by foreign concerns (Bruccoli Clark Layman Archives)*

ries told by the characters that differed from the stories told by the author in the larger work, Ireland's first work set the scene for the trademark fabulist works that followed, from the "bird" fables of his unpublished play "The Virgin of Treadmill Street" and his first novel, *The Chantic Bird,* to the fable complexes in his most recently published work, *The Chosen* (1997).

"The Virgin of Treadmill Street" is an urban comedy whose extant draft dates from 1962, two years before the publication of *Image in the Clay.* More absurdist than *Image in the Clay,* "The Virgin of Treadmill Street" is Shavian comedy with heavy reliance on the purely verbal underpinnings of human reality. This style of writing repudiates the naturalism animating *Image in the Clay,* and "The Virgin of Treadmill Street" (more than the better-known earlier play) set the tone for the bulk of Ireland's later work. The emphasis of the play does not fall upon any particular fable but upon the disintegration of reality as such under the weight of fable, of the incessant Dostoevskian blather, accusation, and innuendo one character inflicts upon another. That "The Virgin of Treadmill Street" resembles Fyodor Dostoevsky's *The Double* (1846) or *The Idiot* (1868) more than it resembles any play, comic or other-

wise (including any play of Dostoevsky's predecessor, Nikolai Vasil'evich Gogol), indicates the direction Ireland's literary efforts were already taking: between 1968 and 1997 he published ten novels.

The earliest extant draft of *The Chantic Bird* comprises a series of brief, disconnected notes written during periods of shift work on a catalytic cracker at the Shell oil refinery in southern Sydney. (The early draft, now in the Mitchell Library in Sydney, dates from July 1964 and is titled "Sixteen.") Ireland's subsequent descriptions of this drafting technique indicate his interest in producing a particular sort of novel, one whose general story line is far less important to the design of the book than the incidents recorded. "Recording," in fact, became a recurrent motif in the fiction itself: *The Chantic Bird* is the story of an author who is ostensibly killed by his subject, a story that "flattens out" to a "merely" textual level as the existential issues and life crises of the sixteen-year-old are revealed as literary artifice. The problematical character of the occasional idiosyncrasies of the narrative was apparent to critics as early as 1972, when the edition of the novel published that year was furnished with a critical introduction; what was less discernible was that in this Peter Pan parable of a boy who remains exactly the same age throughout the book was a truly fabulous element, an exploration of the structure and function of the self that emerges from a character writing fable (and feeding it into his life) rather than an author seeking psychological truth and imposing it on that same character.

Yet, in his 1992 piece "The Chantic Bird," Ireland revealed a genuinely existential (or "moral") purpose to the story; the amorality and anarchism that so upset such commentators as Nancy Keesing when the book first appeared ("Angry Rooster," Sydney *Bulletin*, 6 April 1968) was founded not upon pure stylistics, but upon the adolescent Ireland's experience of a crisis of self-control. *The Unknown Industrial Prisoner,* Ireland's next novel (drafted and massively redrafted as "Low Company" by March 1967), dwelled at length on those aspects of the same sort of crisis he encountered in his work at an oil refinery as an adult. "Puroil," the name of the oil company, reflects the "puerile" behaviors of management and men as they play out their industrial and sexual roles in an intricately psychologized series of fables, whose "overall meaning" eludes all of them, including their intermittently appearing narrator. Something of Ireland's technical approach to the novel form was captured in a passage in his later *Bloodfather* (1987), in which his autobiographical alter ego articulates his dissatisfaction with prevailing literary orthodoxies:

In English, a relief teacher referred to one of the novels they'd be grappling with as an example of a "stream of consciousness" method, and likened this to a river. But Davis Blood's own consciousness wasn't continuous, rather a succession of bits of consciousness. There were moments when he was conscious of nothing, moments that later he had no memory of. His consciousness was intermittent.

So in a "Preface" for *The Unknown Industrial Prisoner*—presented with typical idiosyncrasy near the end of the book (found in a section called "To My Reader" in the "Low Company" draft)—Ireland's narrator writes,

It has been my aim to take apart, then build up piece by piece this mosaic of one kind of human life, this galaxy of painted slides, my bleak ratio of illuminations; to remind my present age of its industrial adolescence.

Well friend, I have not succeeded in putting back together those I have taken apart, for they are split, divided, fragmented, as I am split up and divided between page and character, speech and event, intention and performance.

"The mosaic," like "consciousness," is something static, a structure rather than a flow of things. Because of his concern with multiple interaction rather than linear causation, Ireland could include any number of "fables" within his novels without the work itself being a fable or presenting an ultimate unity of meanings. Like *The Chantic Bird, The Unknown Industrial Prisoner* deprived the fabulist of his final say. (Or as Ireland said in the synopsis of the book he presented to Angus & Robertson in 1968: "no one man is in control.")

Yet, like *The Chantic Bird, The Unknown Industrial Prisoner* presented human existence as active and potent in and through the text. Ireland did not seek to emulate such writers as Alain Robbe-Grillet; he was not a formalist; he was not intent upon textual purity at the expense of the rules of representation. His synopsis of *The Unknown Industrial Prisoner* makes existential and causal claims for each of the three characters who define the directions of the book:

To one the Company is God, and when it rejects him by a casually impersonal decision, his life is finished. The second, wanting the machine of industry to work, in despair at its inefficiency, sabotages the Company in the belief that strong measures will pull it to its feet. The third is on the side of life, laughter, humanity, and joy and conducts an underground war against the Company, seducing its prisoners away from their harsh empty lives toward a legendary freedom in the Home Beautiful. . . .

By the time *The Unknown Industrial Prisoner* was finally published, Ireland had written a work for which these "social-existential" issues were even more crucial: *The Flesheaters* (1972), set in a refuge for social strays, was essentially complete in its December 1969 draft and incorporated some of the material Ireland had shed in rewriting *The Unknown Industrial Prisoner* in 1967. *The Flesheaters,* however, was less impressive and imposing than its predecessor.

The Unknown Industrial Prisoner won for Ireland the Miles Franklin Award for 1971, and his industriousness as a writer pushed him to new levels of literary commitment in the course of 1973. Ireland had married Elizabeth Morris on 29 October 1955, and when interviewed by Brian Dale at his home in Winston Hills in January 1973 he presented, with his wife and four children—Stephen (born 4 May 1957), Christine (29 July 1959), Alison (27 February 1963), and David (17 August 1970)—glimpses of a family life altogether at odds with the anomic characterizations of Australian life for which he by now had so great a reputation. By the end of the year, Ireland was living alone in central Sydney, working on the first of the two novels that are generally considered his greatest achievement. Both of these novels, *The Glass Canoe* and *A Woman of the Future,* reflect deeper values of "family" life than do his previous works (in *The Glass Canoe* the "family" of the pub, the Southern Cross, has far more social credibility than the industrial "family" of Puroil). But in real life, "the family" had been replaced by "writing": "The writer has got me. I've no other life. The program is writing me now" is the title of his *National Times* (Sydney) interview with Stuart Littlemore of May 1976 on the occasion of the publication of *The Glass Canoe.* Ireland not only moved out of Winston Hills; after *The Glass Canoe* he also moved his novels out of the peculiar sociocultural realm he had inhabited in northwestern Sydney. Ireland and his wife were divorced in 1976.

The first novel to be published after the dramatic shift in Ireland's material circumstances was a reworking of the play *Image in the Clay* into a novel. Ireland had worked on the novel, first titled "Gunner," in the first half of 1970 after drafting *The Flesheaters.* He laid out the sheets of the published play in a large year-diary and amended around them. In December 1973 the book was redrafted (the manuscript bears both the Winston Hills and the newer Elizabeth Street, Sydney, addresses), given the title *Burn,* and published in April 1974. Employing a linear narrative style uncharacteristic of his previous fiction, Ireland wrote *Burn* in the present tense in the manner of the stage directions of the original play; the general effect is that of a screenplay. It also reflected significant mutations in the Australian image of "the aboriginal" over the preceding ten years. By the mid 1960s, narrative accounts of Aboriginal consciousness allowed the Aboriginal protagonist a high degree of intellectual energy–in, for example, the satirically directed novel *Trap* by Peter Mathers or John Iggulden's morally focused *Dark Stranger,* both published in 1966. With Thomas Keneally's *The Chant of Jimmy Blacksmith* (1971) appeared a far more agressive protagonist, whose violent behavior has the apocalyptic outcomes envisaged by the "Gunner" of Ireland's own book. *Burn,* while it reaches a certain pitch of rhetorical violence uncharacteristic of any part of *Image in the Clay,* is nevertheless in all respects a quite different novel from Keneally's; its apocalyptic violence retains the rhetorical feel of its origins in a play and its origins, furthermore, in the mind of an author more concerned with the meaning of ideas than with technicolor effects. Gunner is "paranoid" in *Burn* in the way that the passive-aggressive characters of Ireland's earlier novels are paranoid–with a "paranoia" explored by Xavier Pons in his classic study of those novels. For Pons, such paranoia was a means of distorting the dramatic situations of Ireland's novels in new and fruitful ways, rather than revealing in their author any distinctive psychological tendency; at the same time, the anomie characterizing so many of Ireland's central characters is, for Pons, largely generated by their own fictionalizing, their

efforts to reduce the world to a single, centrally controlled "paranoid" order.

Burn was, however, a testing ground for the non-paranoid, nonapocalyptic violence of Ireland's great comic creation, *The Glass Canoe.* Ireland conceived the book in 1970 soon after completing *The Flesheaters,* and some discarded sections from that novel (along with one or two from *The Unknown Industrial Prisoner*) are found in the drafts. Yet, the new novel acquired a comic spirit quite different from that of its predecessor by Ireland's casting its central character as not merely ultrasensitive in the pattern of Lee Malory, the tree-hugging narrator of *The Flesheaters,* but insensitive or straightforwardly ignorant along the lines of Tom Collins in Furphy's *Such Is Life* (1903). Lines similar to the following may originally have been drafted for Lee Malory; their droll, comic character more clearly suited the narrative style of *The Glass Canoe,* in which they now found a home:

> "What religion are you?" she asked. I was charmed by her directness.
>
> "Heathen," I said seriously.
>
> "Pardon."
>
> "Heathen." I didn't smile.
>
> "What's that?"
>
> "Heathen."
>
> "Oh." (*Glass Canoe* draft, p. 391)

Ireland also spent considerable effort sketching and researching the ideological background for Alky Jack, the pub philosopher who represents perhaps Ireland's most substantial purely intellectual foil to a narrator as compared to those of his various other books (Clayton Emmett in *The Flesheaters,* for example, or Jackson Blood in *Bloodfather*). A first draft of the novel was completed in 1974 and sent for placement by the agent Curtis Brown to Douglas Stewart, an influential critic and editor who had been instrumental in the publication of *The Unknown Industrial Prisoner* five or six years before. Before outlining some dramatic faults he thought the novel had, Stewart reported that he was pleased to see that Ireland had it in him to write a novel as good.

The published version of *The Glass Canoe* differs substantially from the 1973–1974 draft as a result of Stewart's commentary. Stewart (as he wrote in the *National Times*) had wondered when reading *The Flesheaters* "whether we are not just reading the bizarre for the

Dust jacket for the British edition of Ireland's 1981 novel, about an inner city taken over by women
(Bruccoli Clark Layman Archives)

sake of the bizarre," and the original draft of *The Glass Canoe* had offered the same surrealistic, indistinct climax of its predecessor. "It makes me feel," he had written to Curtis Brown, "that after chewing my way through a good steak, suddenly it has changed to fairy floss." Stewart offered several possible endings, favoring "one last tremendous fighting fucking (pardon me) orgy." This option was the one Ireland adopted, adding a sequence of short chapters to the end of the manuscript that describe the physical destruction of the locale of the novel, the Southern Cross pub, through One Big Fight, and a final twist, of Nietzschean Eternal Return, at the last moment. The manuscript was accepted by Macmillan Australia in 1975, which proved as ruthless in taming the manuscript as Angus and Robertson had been with *The Unknown Industrial Prisoner.* "The Glass Canoe—I cut a quarter of it," Ireland told Stuart Littlemore. "When you read it you should imagine one third more deathless prose. It's all here in a special folder." The contents of that folder found their way in different directions. Of the thirty-two chapters deleted, one ("Martin Dangerfield") was reprinted as a story in the *National Times* ("The Wild Colonial Boy"), while fourteen of the larger chapters had their characters changed from men to women in order to form the basis of *City of*

Women (1981), Ireland's curious story of an inner city taken over by women, its pubs frequented by manaping feminists.

With the exception of *Burn,* Ireland's novels had thus far been set in the milieus he knew best. Northwestern Sydney is the scene of all except *The Unknown Industrial Prisoner,* which details Ireland's workplace for much of the 1960s–the Shell oil refinery–while *The Glass Canoe* is narrated by a laborer whose work is modeled on a job Ireland had subsequently taken at a golf course. Having drafted *The Glass Canoe,* Ireland began formulating a rather different sort of book, one with a central character bearing no identifiable relation to Ireland himself, in a locale almost entirely constructed from the ideological fragments previously made visible only in singular characters, such as Alky Jack or the Samurai. Ireland began compiling notes for *A Woman of the Future* in July 1974, and the sheer quantity of these notes, unequaled since the "roomful" of notes for *The Unknown Industrial Prisoner,* indicates his commitment to this highly original work. Some elements of *Burn* are found in its marked preoccupation with the "interiority" of Australia. The replacement of a "paranoid" with a "comic-ironic" perspective is largely because of *The Glass Canoe,* and it replays and inverts some central features in *The Flesheaters. A Woman of the Future* is, for all of that, unlike any novel Ireland had yet written. It was first published in the United States by George Braziller early in 1979, after Macmillan Australia declined to publish it, fearing that the confrontativeness of its sex scenes would diminish Ireland's reputation. Significant amounts of the text (up to sixty microchapters, but nothing of the sexual content) were cut for this edition, although the cuts were retained in the Penguin Australian edition of November the same year. *A Woman of the Future* won the Miles Franklin Award in controversial circumstances and in Australia has tended to be regarded as the high point of Ireland's achievement.

The novel purports to be the notes of a teenage girl, Alethea Hunt; it is chronologically arranged to cover her life to the age of seventeen and her disappearance into the interior of Australia in the midst of transforming into a leopard. She inhabits a world ("the future") where such transformations are common and indicate the "failure" of the person so transformed; Ireland is taking up a theme paradigmatic in *The Flesheaters,* although Clayton Emmett (the purveyor of will-to-power) rather than Lee Malory (the impressionable neurotic) is now the central character; "failure" is no longer localized, and a conviction of the need for "greatness" is now an existential more than an ideological premise. Alethea Hunt is a drive to "know oneself" in a way previous "strong" types, such as the Samurai and Clayton Emmett, are not, and the pathos of the book is polarized between the alternatives of existence or nonexistence, not merely the outcomes of ideological will or desire. Alethea's "consciousness," indeed, is now a central issue rather in the way that for Friedrich Nietzsche (never far below the surface of Ireland's text) will *is* consciousness; will lies at the basis of existence; that one "knows oneself" is evidence that will is supremely, not incidentally, in operation. Thus, among the key expressions in Ireland's notes is "the greatness of women"–proffered as a title for a book but also (and continually) a provocation, the dynamic of a novel whose "will" heads toward self-displacement ("failure"), but only because existence, not nonexistence, has true pathos and is worth so much effort.

The title of a different book, "The Greatness of Women" (included as such in one of Ireland's lists of his own work), possibly refers to the 1978 draft of the short novel published in 1981 as *City of Women.* The presence of the many chapters of draft material from *The Glass Canoe* in this book gives an indication of the sort of book Ireland originally intended *The Glass Canoe* to be, for *City of Women* takes the "psychological" direction Ireland sacrificed in the earlier book when he accepted Stewart's recommendations. Consequently, *City of Women* reverts to *The Flesheaters* as its ironies

become textual rather than existential, and the central character, an elderly recluse who interminably laments the loss of her younger alter ego, becomes a creature of pathology rather than of pathos. Even in "The Bronze Overcoat," a story published in early 1980, the fine balance between value destruction and existential indeterminacy is more cannily preserved. *City of Women* deals with madness even more thoroughly than *The Flesheaters* does, and nothing of the central character remains finally except the micronarrative fables by which she calls the past into existence. This curiously antiexistential turn was undoubtedly intended (Ireland recycled it fifteen years later when he rewrote "Dry Australians" as *The Chosen*), but it opened the way to misgivings over the existential validity of what Ireland was doing, even by such avowed "textualists" as Meaghan Morris, who wrote in the *Australian Financial Review* (7 August 1981): "Perhaps in an otherwise disappointing novel, David Ireland has given a strong symbolic account of what the history of male exercises in 'writing like a woman' may really be about."

The history of human exercises in writing like animals is open to critique of the same sort, but Ireland's 1984 *Archimedes and the Seagle* was as little concerned to "get right" the literary ambitions of the class of red setters (of which the Archimedes at the center of the new novel was a member) as George Orwell had been in liberating horses from pigs in *Animal Farm* (1945). Like *Animal Farm, Archimedes and the Seagle* is an animal fable with a political message, and as with Ireland's previous books, the story line comprises several discrete "fables" whose upshot, textual or existential, prove difficult to moralize in a straightforward way. Like *City of Women, Archimedes and the Seagle* is to a significant extent an exploration of the streets and lanes of the eastern edge of central Sydney, reclaiming territory (or more accurately "knowledge of territory") from humans, as *City of Women* had reclaimed it from men. The difference is that Archimedes is not "pathological"–or to return to the term used by Xavier Pons, "paranoid." His vision of beauty (the "seagle," identified as an unattainable gift or an unopposable power) is, like Alethea Hunt's "mysterious beloved," prospective, not retrospective, coextensive with exploration and knowledge, not closure, shelter, or codification. Drafted between August and October 1981, the book is not so far distant from its predecessor as their publication dates suggest; their central characters—one infinitely reclusive, one infinitely sociable—are at opposite poles: first among Ireland's "concerns of the book" seems to be that "reading & writing are good, so Teach others!!" The compilers of their fables are at respective extremes of experience.

Dust jacket for Ireland's 1984 animal fable, whose leading character, Archimedes, is a red setter
(Bruccoli Clark Layman Archives)

The 1982 appearance of Helen Daniel's study of Ireland, *Double Agent*, registered not only the level of his reputation in the wake of *A Woman of the Future*, but also the growing tendency to theoretical systemization within Australian literary criticism at the time. Daniel consolidated Ireland in a pantheon of "new Australian writers" in *Liars* (1988) and was subsequently influential in Ireland's rewriting of the book that became *The Chosen*. Her view of Ireland as a sort of antipodean John Fowles, subverting the reader with his metafictional strategies, was closer in spirit to reader-reception theory than the more heavy-going school of poststructuralism becoming dominant in Australian universities (and writing the bulk of criticism, if not the reviews). Daniel, as editor of a book of short fiction and editor of *The Australian Book Review*, published two of Ireland's stories—"Vision of Lindow Man," set in prehistoric Britain, and "The Drover's Wife," purporting to tell the true story behind Russell Drysdale's painting of that name—in those publications. When Daniel died in 2000, Ireland lost his foremost literary patron.

Ireland's prolificity as an author in part resulted from his willingness to rework the superabundant material of major works into new and slightly different novels. So *Image in the Clay* became a novel, *Burn*, and a

significant part of *The Glass Canoe* was reconfigured as *City of Women*. A danger of such large-scale reconstruction can be a loss of original energy, and Ireland's next novel, *Bloodfather*, a thoroughgoing fictionalized reworking of his own life, published in 1988, lacked the edgy vitality of *A Woman of the Future* as well as the amoral comedy of *The Glass Canoe*. If for Morris "something" (in the shape of singular intelligence) was "amiss" (or lacking) in the *City of Women*, for other Ireland admirers *Bloodfather* was too plainly a bildungsroman, "portrait of the young man as artist." "It is conventional in plot, narrative technique and style," lamented Don Anderson: "No women turn into leopards." The central character of the book, Davis Blood, is an optimized Alethea Hunt from whom the hand of the author seems never entirely missing; the "fragments" of Davis's life ultimately belong to Ireland's determination to fictionalize himself, and Davis's reflections on the nature of life lack the active chutzpah (what critics such as Anderson called "irony") that had supplied so much of the dynamic of *A Woman of the Future*.

Ireland told Helen Daniel in the early 1980s that he intended in *Bloodfather* to show people a range of things about the world they live in—openly putting the novel beyond the range of "subversive" or "counterintentional" descriptors around which Daniel had organized her own book. The claim was disingenuous, if not entirely false; what the book lacks in dramatic irony, it makes up for in the ironies of its narrative stance. At its most complex, in *Bloodfather* the present-day child, Davis Blood, is the past child, David Ireland, the subject of a novel whose author is the father, and also David Ireland, whose verbal attachment to the child is not at all misplaced rhetoric, but a "father" pinned in the headlights of the child's becoming. The subversion engineered in *Bloodfather* is more subtle than that of *The Unknown Industrial Prisoner,* but it is of the same sort. A narrator, who in this case is an autobiographer, cannot overcome the split between his own production of the child and the child's production of "the man"; the false unity of this novel lies in the apparent scrambling after a reader's "understanding," the supposed unveiling of an author's "intention" through the refraction of his past self into the present moment. Emblematic of this spirit is Davis's growing understanding of the world: "inequality, riches and poverty, lazy people and energetic, good times and bad, alternate, come and go, all the time, in wave formations." But such reflections, and in fact Davis's whole history of reflections are truly his in the very specific sense that they "amount to" what his autobiographer can now say: at no point in the novel do its words belong solely or singularly to the child, the "past," as against the man, the "present." A novel that appears to be stuck fast in narrative, overdetermined by the wordiness of its narrator, has narrative values that close attention will find increasingly elusive, and a temporal solidity that rather resembles Davis's thoughts on the place in which the whole of his life has been lived: "This slope, this valley, was like a place from which everything had gone, leaving the feeling that life had been there a moment before." As is so often true in Ireland's work, the real nature of things is comprehensively hidden.

Ireland planned *Bloodfather* to be the first book of a trilogy about Davis Blood, but the novel Ireland published ten years later (and the only one he has published since) acquired Davis as its narrator only in its greatly reconstituted final drafts. That novel, *The Chosen,* originally assembled some thinly interconnected short stories set in the town of Lost River, each story the account of a "dry Australian" and each, in the final version, refracted through the tapestry Davis has been commissioned to create for the local town council. Like *Bloodfather,* though in a more obvious way, the novel plays narrator against narrated in an attempt to find a unity for "the town," using certain apparent commonalities that when explored show few meanings of permanent value. Unlike *Bloodfather,* the novel returns to the "paranoid" mode last evident in *City of Women,* as Davis

Blood fights through the thickets of "right-thinking" imposed by his theory-driven former lover (dead, it finally turns out, in a vehicle accident). The same right-thinking was an unsubtle feature of the second published monograph to be devoted to Ireland, Ken Gelder's 1993 *Atomic Fiction*. This book assembled an array of literary-theoretical perspectives from which each of Ireland's novels could be assessed and concluded that by the standards of postmodern theory, none shaped up as the works originally applauded by critics of the 1970s and 1980s. Ireland's *The Chosen* reads in part as a response to such an approach to his work, but the "paranoia" of that novel escapes "theory" in the peculiarly indirect way *Archimedes and the Seagle* had escaped Meaghan Morris and *Bloodfather* had escaped Helen Daniel: *A Woman of the Future* had been written in something of the spirit of Lewis Carroll's *Alice in Wonderland* (1865), but these final novels have the spirit of Antoine de Sainte-Exupéry's *The Little Prince* (1943): the terms of "discourse" have been subverted by the vicissitudes (and wonderments) of actual life.

Ireland's own life underwent considerable changes over the period of the three last novels. On 7 September 1984 he married Christine Hayhoe and moved to Manly, where "The New Aristocrats" is set. In 1987 he left Sydney for Goulburn, and there and in several further country towns in New South Wales and Victoria he wrote *The Chosen*. By 1997, at the time the novel was published, he was living in Bateman's Bay on the south coast of New South Wales, where he remained before moving back to the Sydney area (Allambie Heights) in September 2002. Ireland separated from Christine in the mid 1990s, and their divorce in October 1996 has become one further aspect of his life feeding the "uncertainty principle" on which his fiction, with all its complexities and fragmentations, has always drawn.

Interviews:

Brian Dale, "David Ireland Is a Sponge Absorbing People, Words and Events for New Masterpieces," *National Times* (Sydney), 1–6 January 1973, p. 14;

Stuart Sayers, "A Title Sought and Found Its Book," *Age* (Melbourne), 12 June 1976;

Rodney Weatherall, interview and review of *The Glass Canoe,* ABC Radio 2FC (Sydney), 1 May 1977;

Janet Hawley, "Ireland's Lonely Journey," *Age* (Melbourne), 10 November 1979, p. 23;

"David Ireland Keeps His Head Down," *Age* (Melbourne), 3 June 1980, p. 11;

Sandra Hall, "Male Writer Enters the Female Mind," *Bulletin* (Sydney), 10 June 1980, p. 68;

Mark MacLeod, "David Ireland," *Kunapipi* (Aarhus, Denmark) (January 1981): 64–75;

Michele Field, "David Ireland Sees Inside Women's Heads," *Sydney Morning Herald,* 25 July 1981, p. 47;

Sheridan Hay, "An Interview with David Ireland," *Science Fiction. Review of Speculative Literature* (Sydney) (March 1982): 109–116;

Ian Chance, "Interview: David Ireland," *Words and Visions* (Adelaide), 12 (1983): 6–7;

Belinda Geise, "An Interview with David Ireland," *Notes & Furphies* (Armidale) (April 1988): 15;

Sue Woolfe and Kate Grenville, "David Ireland, *A Woman of the Future,*" in *Making Stories: How Ten Australian Novels Were Written* (Sydney: Allen & Unwin, 1993), pp. 124–135;

Susan Chenery, "A Singular Man," *Sydney Morning Herald,* 23 August 1997, pp. 42–45.

Bibliographies:

Helen Daniel, *Double Agent: David Ireland and His Work* (Melbourne: Penguin, 1982), pp. 166–170;

Ken Gelder, *Atomic Fiction: The Novels of David Ireland* (Brisbane: University of Queensland Press, 1993), pp. 113–121;

Martin Duwell, Marianne Ehrhardt, and Carol Hetherington, *The* ALS *Guide to Australian Writers: A Bibliography 1963–1995* (St. Lucia: University of Queensland Press, 1997).

References:

Don Anderson, "A Portrait of the Young Man as Artist," *Sydney Morning Herald,* 5 December 1987;

Helen Daniel, *Liars: Australian New Novelists* (Melbourne: Penguin, 1988), pp. 113–137;

J. J. Healy, *Literature and the Aborigine in Australia 1770–1975* (Brisbane: University of Queensland Press, 1978);

Van Ikin, "David Ireland's Australia," *Quadrant* (Sydney) (May 1980): 68–69;

Xavier Pons, "Paranoia as a Way of Life," *Quadrant* (Sydney) (January–February 1982): 96–103.

Papers:

David Ireland's unpublished papers are located in the Mitchell Library, Sydney.

Colin Johnson
(Mudrooroo)
(21 August 1938 –   )

Maureen Clark
University of Wollongong

BOOKS: *Wild Cat Falling* (Sydney: Angus & Robertson, 1965; Harmondsworth, U.K.: Penguin, 1966);

Long Live Sandawara (Melbourne: Quartet Books, 1979);

Before the Invasion: Aboriginal Life to 1788, by Johnson, Colin Bourke, and Isobel White (Melbourne & London: Oxford University Press, 1980; Melbourne & New York: Oxford University Press, 1980);

Doctor Wooreddy's Prescription for Enduring the Ending of the World (Melbourne: Hyland House, 1983; New York: Ballantine, 1983);

The Song Circle of Jacky: And Selected Poems (Melbourne: Hyland House, 1986);

Dalwurra: The Black Bittern, A Poem Cycle, by Colin Johnson (Mudrooroo Narogin), edited by Veronica Brady and Susan Miller (Nedlands: Centre for Studies in Australian Literature, University of Western Australia, 1988);

Doin Wildcat: A Novel Koori Script As Constructed by Mudrooroo Narogin, as Narogin (Melbourne: Hyland House, 1988);

Writing from the Fringe: A Study of Modern Aboriginal Literature in Australia, as Mudrooroo Narogin (South Yarra, Vic.: Hyland House, 1990); revised as *The Indigenous Literature of Australia: Milli Milli Wangka* (South Melbourne, Vic.: Hyland House, 1997);

Master of the Ghost Dreaming: A Novel, as Mudrooroo (Sydney: Angus & Robertson, 1991);

The Garden of Gethsemane: Poems from the Lost Decade, as Mudrooroo (South Yarra, Vic.: Hyland House, 1991);

Wildcat Screaming: A Novel, as Mudrooroo (Pymble, N.S.W.: Angus & Robertson, 1992);

The Kwinkan, as Mudrooroo (Pymble, N.S.W.: Angus & Robertson, 1993);

Aboriginal Mythology: An A-Z Spanning the History of the Australian Aboriginal Peoples from the Earliest Legends to the Present Day (London: Aquarian, 1994);

Colin Johnson (Mudrooroo)—(courtesy of the author)

Us Mob: History, Culture, Struggle: An Introduction to Indigenous Australia, as Mudrooroo (Sydney & London: Angus & Robertson, 1995; Sydney & New York: Angus & Robertson, 1995);

Pacific Highway Boo-Blooz: Country Poems, as Mudrooroo (St. Lucia: University of Queensland Press, 1996);

The Undying, as Mudrooroo (Pymble, N.S.W.: Angus & Robertson, 1998);

Underground, as Mudrooroo (Pymble, N.S.W.: Angus & Robertson, 1999);

The Promised Land, as Mudrooroo (Pymble, N.S.W.: Angus & Robertson, 2000).

Edition: *Wild Cat Falling,* Imprint Classics edition, as Mudrooroo, introduction by Stephen Muecke (Pymble, N.S.W.: Angus & Robertson, 1992).

OTHER: *Struggling,* in *Paperbark: A Collection of Black Australian Writings,* edited by J. Davis, S. Muecke, M. Narogin, and A. Shoemaker (St. Lucia: University of Queensland Press, 1990), pp. 199–290;

The Mudrooroo/Müller Project: A Theatrical Casebook, edited by Gerhard Fischer, Paul Behrendt, and Brian Syron (Sydney: New South Wales University Press, 1993)–includes *The Aboriginal Protestors Confront the Declaration of the Australian Republic on 26 January 2001 with the Production of The Commission by Heiner Müller.*

Colin Johnson (also known as Mudrooroo) is one of the most enigmatic literary figures of Australia. A prolific and gifted author, his work has been influential in the development of a politics of Aboriginal writing. Johnson's craftsmanship and his theories of what constitutes "authentic," decolonizing Aboriginal writing are taught in schools and universities in many Australian states. The author's work is as well known overseas as it is in his own country and has been translated into many different languages–including Italian, German, Russian, and French. Recognized mainly for his novels–a self-conscious, postmodern form of political protest/cultural revival literature–and critical analysis, Johnson's considerable oeuvre includes plays, award-winning poetry collections, and cultural studies. Multidimensional and nonlinear, the narrative style, structure, and content of Johnson's work shifts incessantly in line with changes taking place in the Australian political climate over the passage of time. A follower of the oral tradition with a tendency to lean toward the dialogic rather than the descriptive, Johnson adopts a strategy of elusiveness in his writing. Such tactics accommodate movement in his worldview and ensure as far as possible that his artistic product avoids encapsulation within a particular category or preconceived literary framework. Nevertheless, a strong thread stretches unbroken across Johnson's life projects–his literature, his cultural-identity politics, and his academic pursuits–and that is his concern to discredit and dislodge ideologically manipulated constructs of Australian Aboriginal identity and belonging.

Colin Thomas Johnson was born on 21 August 1938, the year in which white Australia celebrated the 150th anniversary of British settlement, while black Australia mourned what it saw as the commemoration of the death of a way of life. Although officially registered in nearby Narrogin, Johnson's place of birth was the Western Australian wheat-belt town of East Cuballing. Johnson is one of an extended family of twelve children, nine of whom are matrilineal and three of whom are from the first marriage of his father, Thomas Creighton Patrick Johnson, to an Irish emigrant from Baltimore in the United States, Matilda French. Matilda died in Melbourne on 22 May 1923. Thomas married again on 25 February 1924, and his second wife, Elizabeth Barron, was Colin's mother. Elizabeth was a direct descendant of one of the first white families to arrive on the shores of Western Australia, aboard the vessel *Sulphur* in 1829. She died in Fremantle Hospital on 15 September 1989 at the age of ninety-one. Colin's father, on the other hand, was born in Sydney in 1874 to an Irish emigrant mother (Mary Gallagher from County Clare) and an emigrant father of African American descent (Thomas Creighton Johnson from North Carolina). Colin's father died in Narrogin on 7 June 1938, just six weeks before the birth of his son.

Since its inception, Johnson's writing has been haunted by a sense of belonging nowhere–of loss and abandonment born from a traumatic childhood and from teenage years spent in the welfare institutions of Australia. His work illustrates a profound consciousness of the significance of being not only an institutionalized child, but also a nonwhite child born into a racist social structure. For most of the first nine years of his life, the author lived in the small town of Beverley with his mother and just two of his siblings, the others having been given into the care of welfare institutions before he was born. In Beverley, Johnson first experienced the sense of alienation that accompanies small-town racism and that led him to the realization that he was different, or, perhaps more accurately, that he was not white. At the ages of nine and eleven respectively, like their siblings before them, both Colin and his older sister were taken into institutional care, in 1948. A younger sister, born in Beverley in 1940, remained with their mother. Little is known about Johnson's childhood relationship with his mother or about what he may have learned from her about his father, who farmed in the Highbury district of Western Australia from 1905 to 1930 and later in the Cuballing Shire until his death in 1938. An insight into this side of the Colin Johnson story, one that connects him to a hard-working but racially discriminated-against father, may be gleaned from his poem "Me Daddy," published in 1986:

Me daddy was a righteous man,
That is what me mummy told me,
Tried to build up a farm,

Tried to sell his crop–
And they said:
Hey Jacky, hey Jacky
What you trying to do,
The silo is full and yet
Cart your grain down here.
Hey Jacky, hey Jacky,
Sell us your wheat,
We'll give you sugar and tea,
Instead of white man's coin,
Which you can't count.
Hey Jacky, hey Jacky,
Give us your grain,
And when you fail,
We'll understand,
And know you can't comprehend,
That money is the boss,
In the land we took from you.

While he remained a ward of the state until his eighteenth birthday in August 1956, at the age of sixteen Johnson left the Christian Brothers' orphanage known as Clontarf Boys' Town in the Perth suburb of Waterford to take up employment in Perth. Johnson's account of coping with life while in the "care" of the Christian Brothers is revealing. As he stated in a 1993 interview with Adam Shoemaker, "the tyranny of Rome was what we had at Clontarf. We had inquisitions and so on and they tried to assert their authority by the most brutal means possible." An understanding of how Johnson learned to deal with the brutalities of Clontarf life can also be gleaned from his semi-autobiographical first novel, *Wild Cat Falling* (1965). In Johnson's hands, animosity toward his unnamed protagonist's minders is sprinkled with sexual innuendo and rebellious mockery. The narrator humorously negotiates potentially grotesque situations involving characters of authority: "The old boss is the worst of the lot. His strap doesn't hurt as much as Dickie's but he's a stupid old goat. The kids reckon a mouse once ran up his trouser leg and fell down dead." After his Clontarf experience, Johnson continued to demonstrate his anti-authoritarian disposition and as a consequence spent twelve months in Fremantle prison for the crimes of robbery and assault. Discharged in 1957, he then lived for a time in the home of the late Dame Mary Durack, an influential Australian novelist and poet, who often cared for young men such as Johnson, newly released from gaol with seemingly nowhere to go. Johnson's interest in writing was first stimulated during his stay in the Durack home, a place where artists of all descriptions constantly came and went. Subsequently, Johnson worked in Melbourne with the Motor Registration Branch of the Victorian Public Service. He also wrote and continued to mix with what he called "bohemians and beatniks and things like that . . . usually whites." Following the publi-

cation of his first and best-known novel, *Wild Cat Falling*, in 1965, Johnson traveled overseas with his first wife, Jennie Katinas, who was of Lithuanian descent. The two journeyed through Thailand and Malaysia, and then for the first time traveled to India–a country where the author later spent many years. From India, Johnson traveled to London, where he adopted the drug-taking ethos of the 1960s with apparent gusto. In an interview, the author states that while in London, he "was stoned for three months and did not see very much–you know St. Paul's and all those places people are supposed to have seen." The author again journeyed through Thailand and India before returning to Melbourne.

Wild Cat Falling was inspired by Johnson's experiences of learning how to survive both within and without public institutions in a racially structured society–a first step in a quest to find a valid philosophy of life. Heavily edited by Mary Durack, the novel includes a foreword by her that is littered with the racist discourse of the day. Nevertheless, Johnson remains steadfastly loyal to his late mentor, without whose friendship, help, and influence he believes he would never have become a writer. Critics and commentators of the day hailed *Wild Cat Falling* as both a triumph and a literary curiosity. Such observations emerged in light of what was then thought to be Johnson's unique position as the author of the first novel ever to be published by someone who identified himself as being of Aboriginal descent. While the veracity of both of these distinctions is now contested, publication of Johnson's novel at that political and historical moment marked a turning point in black Australian literature, in terms of both output and reception. The appearance of the text on mid-1960s mainstream bookshelves was an outstanding accomplishment for several reasons, but particularly as the creativity of writers from other than British/European descent was then considered to be of little value as an element of Australian literary production. However, the publication of *Wild Cat Falling* also indicated the high level of political and cultural influence of the Durack family in Western Australia as well as the reality that entry into print culture by nonwhites was held firmly in the hands of sympathetic, more powerful white patrons.

Johnson and his wife, Jennie, returned to India in 1967. Jennie spent a year with her husband in Calcutta as well as Darjeeling, where he studied Tibetan Buddhism. Johnson's decision to become a monk, however, brought about her departure for Australia, and the two subsequently divorced. Johnson spent the next seven years in India, residing mainly in Calcutta and Dar es Salaam, where he continued to study Buddhism. He lived three of those years as a monk, a cultural transition and exposure to a transcendental spirituality that is evident throughout his work. Johnson returned to Western Australia in 1974 and also traveled to the United States before going back in 1976 to Victoria, where he studied at Melbourne University, worked at the Aboriginal Research Unit at Monash University, and taught at Koorie College. While the precise date is unclear, during this time Johnson married for a second time–to Julie Whiting, a university librarian. Julie is the mother of the author's two children, a son, Kalu, born in 1985 and a daughter, Malika, born in 1988.

Not until 1979, when Johnson was forty-one, was his second novel, *Long Live Sandawara,* published–a seemingly immense gap in terms of his literary production. However, in the course of various interviews, Johnson has indicated that he never ceased to write. He refers to unpublished works he produced between 1966 and 1974 (purported to be at least six novels and one play), their manuscripts either lost or destroyed for various reasons. *Long Live Sandawara* is a savagely ironic and experimental text that attempts to bring together contemporary and historical locations in symbolic juxtaposition. The book offers a challenge to the widespread belief in the myth of Aboriginal passivity in the face of white invasion. On another level, the text also reflects Johnson's Buddhist leanings by suggesting that counterviolence is not the path that leads toward the end of suffering. Johnson reveals a yet unformed authorial sense of surety in his approach to the story of *Long Live Sandawara* by drawing heavily on *Outlaws of the Leopolds* (1952), by Ion L. Idriess. A writer of historical fiction and an exponent of the ideological production of an emerging Australian national character, Idriess wrote on the same subject as Johnson–the events surrounding the anti-invasion campaign of Aboriginal freedom fighter Sandamara (also known as Sandawara and Pigeon). Sandamara's armed rebellion, about which the majority of Australians know little, was an extended, violent colonial encounter that took place in the Kimberley ranges of Western Australia in the late nineteenth century. Johnson's failure to begin to forge a new literary tradition by embracing Aboriginal oral history as the principal source of his tale was seen by his critics as a missed opportunity to defy colonial ideology and the inherent racial prejudices informing white versions of the Australian past.

Long Live Sandawara was followed four years later by *Doctor Wooreddy's Prescription for Enduring the Ending of the World* (1983). Recognized widely as the author's "masterpiece," *Doctor Wooreddy's Prescription for Enduring the Ending of the World* is a work of historical fiction that includes many ingredients of the dramatic epic–the quest, the opponents, the conflicts, and the adventures of its many characters–while focusing on the historical

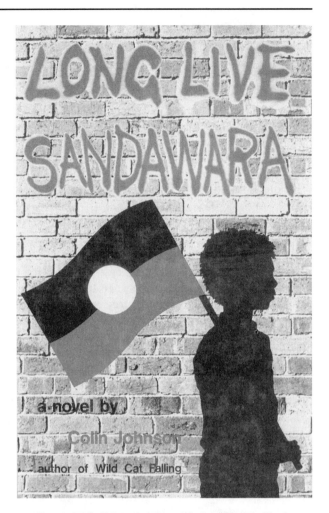

Dust jacket for Johnson's 1979 novel, about Aboriginal leader Sandawara (Bruccoli Clark Layman Archives)

period 1829 to 1842. The year 1829 identifies the appointment of George Augustus Robinson as conciliator and protector of Aborigines, the same year to which Johnson claims to have traced back his Aboriginal roots to the great Bibbulmun tribe of Western Australia. The year 1842, on the other hand, marks the symbolic death of the last Bruny Island (off the coast of Tasmania) Aboriginal male, Woorrady. *Doctor Wooreddy's Prescription for Enduring the Ending of the World* deals with one of the more catastrophic episodes of Australian recorded history, one that began in 1803–the attempted systematic extermination, as organized and directed by the early British colonial administration, of the indigenous inhabitants of Tasmania. Apparently heeding his critics, a more politically aware and culturally confident Johnson deliberately and challengingly restyles rather than rewrites a previous interpretation of what was essentially a synchronized program of conquest and dispossession. Suffused with profound ironies, the circular narrative of *Doctor Wooreddy's Prescription for*

Enduring the Ending of the World replays themes found in *Wild Cat Falling*–endings as beginnings and, perhaps more significantly, a subject that illuminates the failures of the value systems of the dominant power–the betrayal of trust.

Johnson has denied that there is any connection between the "fat old square" probation officer Robinson of his first novel and the protector, George Augustus Robinson, a central figure in *Doctor Wooreddy's Prescription for Enduring the Ending of the World*. Nevertheless, the author describes the distinctive physical features and behavioral qualities of his fictional characters in similar terms. Both are portrayed as short, overweight, untrustworthy, blustering buffoons, and, unquestionably, both representations bear an uncanny "resemblance" to Benjamin Dutrerau's 1840 painting of the actual historical figure. The appearance of Robinson, and what he has come to represent in terms of the betrayal of Aboriginal peoples by white authority generally, is not an isolated phenomenon in Johnson's work. The "relationship" is ongoing and spans a period of thirty-five years. Beginning with *Wild Cat Falling* (1965), in which the protagonist's parole officer is named Robinson, the bond is re-established in *Doctor Wooreddy's Prescription for Enduring the Ending of the World* and is revised and renewed throughout the four volumes of the series beginning with *Master of the Ghost Dreaming: A Novel* (1991). The exploits and idiosyncrasies associated with the historical Robinson are rehearsed and revised consistently throughout Johnson's project. These changes have meant that Robinson has become not simply an emblem of the colonization process against which Johnson continually struggles as a political writer, but one of his most interesting and enduring characters.

The Song Circle of Jacky and *Dalwurra: The Black Bittern,* two volumes of Johnson's poetry, were published in 1986 and 1988 respectively. The former targets the injustices of the Australian penal system and, in particular, the extraordinary number of deaths among Aboriginal people while in custody. The latter, on the other hand, takes a step forward in light of the Aboriginal peoples' proclaimed unwillingness to accept passively their ongoing oppression, and it reflects Johnson's personal sense of frustration and anger at the lack of measurable progress. The words of his long poem "Perth Stained in Blackness: A Bicentennial Gift" (later renamed "Sunlight Spreadeagles Perth in Blackness: A Bicentennial Gift") leave nothing to the imagination as to his political position. Rather, in his poem the author paints his view of Australian society clearly and viciously in grotesque terms as "a wrecked black body swarming with white termites." Johnson separated from his second wife, Julie, that same year. Again, while the

exact date is unknown, the author is believed to have married his third wife, Jacqueline Mendi, shortly after his divorce from Julie Whiting; this third union was relatively short-lived.

Published in 1988, *Doin Wildcat: A Novel Koori Script As Constructed by Mudrooroo Narogin* appeared on bookshelves some twenty-three years after *Wild Cat Falling*. The bicentennial year of Australia, 1988, links the personal event of Johnson's birth fifty years previously with the public commemoration of colonization. As had been the case in 1938, the indigenous population of Australia proclaimed 1988 a year of mourning. *Doin Wildcat* is the second volume of what is known as the Wildcat trilogy–three different, often opposing and contradictory narratives involving the same institutionalized Aboriginal figure. Despite the sketchiest of childhood history in Johnson's narratives, strong biographical links can be drawn between the author and his Wildcat character, for whom the act of writing is connected to the need/will to survive and to find a place to belong. Like its predecessor in the trilogy, *Doin Wildcat* offers some fine examples of the ironic comedy habitually exercised by Johnson in the process of transforming memory, teamed with imagination, into fiction. Johnson takes readers back to the beginning–to the location, the time, and the events of his first book–to tell the story of the scriptwriting for a motion picture based on *Wild Cat Falling*. The author uses his principal character allegorically as a way of tracing how far the Aboriginal struggle for equal rights had come since the mid 1960s and to comment on the continuing white stronghold over cultural production, whether print or movie. Primarily, the novel demonstrates Johnson's concern to raise community awareness again to the high level of Aboriginal prison conviction rates compared to their non-Aboriginal counterparts. *Doin Wildcat* emerged in a year in which a Royal Commission was formed to investigate the causes behind the continuing, disproportionately high number of deaths among Aboriginal people while held in custody in the state and territory gaols of Australia. As soon became apparent from the findings of the commission, while the appearance of change was evident, the actual distance traveled was short. In 1988 Johnson also changed his name. As a form of political protest, he became Mudrooroo Narogin, a name that later evolved into Mudrooroo Nyoongah and then became simply Mudrooroo. The name *Mudrooroo* means "paperbark" (an Australian tree) in the Bibbulmun language, the Aboriginal people or community with whom the author then identified. As a politically active writer who is also a man of color, Johnson chose the name Mudrooroo for its ambiguity and thus appropriateness in terms of his hybrid identity and cross-cultural speaking position. Mudrooroo is the name that presently appears on the covers of his books.

From 1988, Johnson's published work emerged at a greatly accelerated pace. *Writing from the Fringe: A Study of Modern Aboriginal Literature in Australia* (1990) announced the author's entry into the field of critical analysis and established him as an authority on indigenous writing. Johnson's little-known 1990 novella, *Struggling,* on the other hand, harks back to the world of disadvantaged urban Aboriginal youth expounded upon earlier in *Long Live Sandawara.* Continuing his tendency to write back to previous work, a second, much shorter bicentennial "gift" poem, renamed "Happy Birthday Australia–1988," appears in Johnson's 1991 volume of poetry, *The Garden of Gethsemane: Poems from the Lost Decade,* which in 1992 won two Western Australian Premier's Book Awards. Also published in 1991, *Master of the Ghost Dreaming* confirms the pattern of spiraling reversal now strongly evident in Johnson's writing, with a return to the time and space of Robinson in *Doctor Wooreddy's Prescription for Enduring the Ending of the World.* The revisionist trend continues in *Wildcat Screaming* (1992), the third volume of the Wildcat trilogy, with the reappearance of a now older, fully institutionalized, and still angry protagonist. Once again Johnson addresses the plight of socially excluded young Aboriginals. However, the novel reaches a new level that is a forceful indictment of the judicial practices of white Australia in the context of the early 1990s and a testament to the contemporary myth of progress toward social justice for Aboriginal people generally. Apart from the accolades Johnson received for his literature, the year 1992 proved to be a significant turning point in his life. By then the author had married his fourth wife, Jeanine Little, a Queensland academic. After forty-five years of cultural and familial displacement, in that year he was reunited with members of his biological family. As a consequence, the author stated publicly that he was now "unclear regarding his tribal connections." Nevertheless, he continued to write, publish, and identify himself as an Aboriginal person, effectively turning his back on his rediscovered family, a form of abandonment that they found hard to accept or comprehend.

Between 1992 and 1996, Johnson's published output was abundant and diverse and varied both in style and content. Significantly, it expressed anxieties about what the author saw as Australian society's disengagement as a nation in the postmodern era with the realities of homegrown political and social problems. For him, as he says in "Work Bilong Tok-Tok" (*The Mudrooroo/Muller Project,* 1993), Australia was a post of infinite posts–a kind of colonial theater "engaged in a continuing ritual, a struggle between the past and the present" in which the play of power is no harmless game. Per-

haps this position explains, at least in part, why Johnson chose to invoke a ceremonial dance scene from the imaginary world of his 1991 novel, *Master of the Ghost Dreaming,* to introduce his 1993 play, which forms the symbolic kernel of the *Mudrooroo/Müller Project: A Theatrical Casebook* (1993). Johnson's play is farcically yet symbolically titled *The Aboriginal Protestors Confront the Declaration of the Australian Republic on 26 January 2001 with the Production of The Commission by Heiner Müller.* Johnson saw this play, in which his own and Müller's *Der Auftrag* (The Commission) join together in an uneasy, collaborative mating as "a new kind of dance," a new kind of make-believe still connected to the exercise of power. Depending as it did on an imaginary link between the British invasion of Australia in 1788 and the French Revolution of 1789, the bond between the two texts was tenuous at best, particularly when one considers that the Aboriginal people of Australia have yet to enjoy their bourgeois revolution. While in the final analysis the attempted mix of two social/cultural languages proved disappointingly unsuccessful on several levels, *The Mudrooroo/Müller Project* nevertheless demonstrated the author's capacity to meet whatever literary challenge was put before him. Johnson had moved to Sydney University's Centre for Performance Studies to work on the project, which first began in 1987, the year prior to Australia's bicentennial. Finding he had achieved the ultimate, if absurd, dream of the isolated bourgeois writer when he "was escorted to the top garret of the house turned into institute" was not lost on a man who had spent most of his lifetime struggling against inner and outer exile. Johnson's novel *The Kwinkan* (meaning spiritual embodiments of lust, symbolized by the male sexual organ), was also published in 1993. An offshoot of *The Mudrooroo/Müller Project,* it too is futuristic and experimental, crossing yet another literary and geographical boundary. Narrated in retrospect, the novel is a satire of white anthropological "fact"-gathering methods. A first for Johnson, the plot moves beyond the borders of Australia to Polynesia. *The Kwinkan* was soon followed by *Aboriginal Mythology: An A-Z Spanning the History of the Australian Aboriginal Peoples from the Earliest Legends to the Present Day* (1994), *Us Mob: History, Culture, Struggle: An Introduction to Indigenous Australia* (1995), and a short collection of poetry, *Pacific Highway Boo-Blooz* (1996), which he dedicated to his wife, Jeanine Little.

In April 1996 Johnson was presented the prestigious Ruth Adeney Koori Award for Aboriginal writing for his cultural study, *Us Mob: History, Culture, Struggle.* Then head of Aboriginal Studies at Murdoch University in Perth, he remained a dominant figure in Aboriginal literature in Australia. While rumors had been circulating previously, in 1996 Western Australian journalist Vicki Laurie brought the controversy surrounding Johnson's claim to Aboriginal heritage out of the shadows in her now infamous article, "Identity Crisis." Laurie's article appeared in *The Australian Magazine,* a widely read publication with national circulation. It sparked an unprecedented level of public debate in the academic and literary community, one involving critics and commentators from both sides of the racial divide. The debate was widely reported in the press during 1996 and 1997 and culminated in the author's resigning his academic post and leaving his home state to take up residence in Queensland. At the most extreme level of the debate the coordinator of the Dumbartung Aboriginal Corporation, activist Robert Eggington, proposed that Johnson's work be removed "from all Australian bookshelves and pulped." Eggington's dangerous proposal, the worst kind of literary censorship, which included uncomfortable echoes of a repressive Nazi Germany when the books of "undesirable" authors were repeatedly burned, was not taken up. Eggington's call emanated from the same location previously known as Clontarf, the orphanage of the author's childhood. Johnson responded to his accusers by resigning his position at Murdoch University. After moving to Queensland, he continued to do what he does best—to write—producing in 1997 a revised edition of *Writing from the Fringe,* titled *The Indigenous Literature of Australia: Milli Milli Wangka.*

As a writer, Colin Johnson has demonstrated that he has few limitations. Where he falters, however, is in his female characters, who are sidelined, rarely fully developed, and often portrayed as social property with the capacity to reason, behave, and act self-consciously in a male-dominated world. They are often portrayed as physically and morally weak. In his writing, the place of women in the developing Aboriginal political environment is supportive at best. His last three novels—*The Undying* (1998), *Underground* (1999), and *The Promised Land* (2000)—complete his *Master of the Ghost Dreaming* series, which, in turn, has its beginnings in *Doctor Wooreddy's Prescription for Enduring the Ending of the World.* Each of these books is replete with metaphors of imperialism as a "retrograde social development, a backsliding toward barbarism." Johnson devotes atavistic metaphors to his vampiric, white female characters with ever-increasing rage. Along the way, names and themes are handed down from book to book almost as unfinished acts of remembrance.

Plagued by the ongoing controversy over his claim to Aboriginality, Johnson left Australia and returned to India in 2001. Married for the fifth time to Sangaya Magar of Nepal on 22 May 2002, he presently resides in Kathmandu, pursuing his studies and long-term interest in Buddhism. He continues to write.

References:

Ulli Beier, "The Aboriginal Novelist Who Found Buddha," *Quadrant* (September 1985): 69–75;

B. Bennett & L. Lockwood, "Colin Johnson: An Interview," *Westerly,* no. 3 (September 1975): 33–37;

Patrick Brantlinger, *Rule of Darkness: British Literature and Imperialism, 1830–1914* (Ithaca, N.Y. & London: Cornell University Press, 1988), p. 236;

Debra Jopson, "Destroy Books: Black Group," *Sydney Morning Herald,* 25 March 1997, p. 5;

Rod Moran, "Writer's Pen Draws on Many Cultural Lines," *West Australian–Big Weekend,* 7 November 1992, p. 9;

Adam Shoemaker, *Mudrooroo: A Critical Study* (Sydney: Angus & Robertson, 1993).

Papers:

A complete collection of titles by Colin Johnson (Mudrooroo) is held by the Battye Library, Perth, Western Australia.

Antigone Kefala
(28 May 1935 –   )

Brigitta Olubas
School of English, University of New South Wales

BOOKS: *The Alien* (St. Lucia, Qld.: Makar, 1973);

The First Journey: Two Short Novels (Sydney: Wild & Woolley, 1975);

Thirsty Weather (Collingwood, Vic.: Outback Press, 1978);

Alexia: A Tale of Two Cultures (Sydney: John Ferguson, 1984);

The Island (Sydney: Hale & Iremonger, 1984);

European Notebook (Sydney: Hale & Iremonger, 1988);

Absence: New and Selected Poems (Sydney: Hale & Iremonger, 1992);

Summer Visit: Three Novellas (Artarmon, N.S.W.: Giramondo, 2002)–comprises *Intimacy, Summer Visit,* and *Conversations with Mother.*

OTHER: *Multiculturalism and the Arts,* edited by Kefala (North Sydney, N.S.W.: Australia Council, 1986).

TRANSLATION: I. P. Koutsocheras, *Anthropoi dia ta dikaia tou anthropou orthotheite / Men for the Rights of Man Rise: A Poetic Manifesto* (Sydney: Alpha Books, 1974).

Antigone Kefala is often described as one of the first poets from a non-English-speaking background to make an impact on contemporary Australian poetry. Also a prose writer of some note, her writing takes up issues of language, identity, and location and can be read in the context of her background as arts administrator and her involvement in debates around the rise and demise of multicultural arts policy in Australia from the 1970s through the 1990s. Her writings and published interviews have been important in raising the issues of displacement, marginalization, equity, and access, particularly through the 1990s, a period when these issues largely dropped off the mainstream cultural agenda in Australia.

Antigone Kefala was born in Braila, Romania, on 28 May 1935. Her family had lived in Romania for three generations, her great-grandparents having

migrated there from Greece and Asia Minor. She has described her family, according to Jenny Digby, as "what could be termed the bourgeoisie." Kefala told Helen Nickas that participation in the arts was considered by the Kefala family as a normal and unremarkable part of life. The family moved to Greece in 1947, a return made difficult by the complexities and hardships of post–World War II Greece, including high unemployment. While the parents spoke Greek, the children did not, having attended Greek and French schools in Romania, and they struggled linguistically. Antigone herself originally learned Greek from her grandmother when she was very small but explains that she then "forgot it" and learned it again as an adolescent in Greece. So Greek for her was a learned language, like French and English. Kefala has commented further that even though her family background is Greek, she never wrote in Greek because she learned it later in her childhood. In Greece, the family, designated refugees from "communist countries," lived in camps run by the International Refugee Organisation (IRO). Under the auspices of the IRO they applied to migrate to Australia but were not initially accepted because of health considerations, and so the family migrated instead to New Zealand, leaving Greece for Wellington in 1951, when Antigone was sixteen years old.

The move was an enormous cultural dislocation, requiring another shift in language and the negotiation of another set of cultural reference points. Digby quotes Kefala as saying that "it utterly changed all our perceptions of ourselves, all suppositions. There were enormous problems. We had to relearn attitudes to life, to thinking. Living was difficult. Culturally, the place was quite barren–at the time. The immigrants used to sleep a lot!" Coupled with these dislocations was the class shift the family underwent, from the accomplishments of their lives in Romania and Greece to the deprivations of factory work in New Zealand. Kefala addresses these issues in various prose works, particularly in *Alexia: A Tale of Two Cultures* (1984).

Antigone Kefala (photograph by James Murdoch; from the cover for The Island, *1984; Bruccoli Clark Layman Archives)*

Kefala attended Victoria University in Wellington, obtaining a B.A. degree in 1958 and an M.A. degree in 1960. She married Robert Kerr in 1959, but the couple divorced in 1963. She worked part-time in the Department of Maori Affairs while studying French, ancient Greek, psychology, and philosophy. The student population at Wellington University at that time was largely of Anglo background. Kefala became friends with the small group of students from other language backgrounds: Indians from Fiji and a group of Polish refugees who had arrived in the early 1940s as children.

During her student years in Wellington, Kefala began to write, in English. Digby quotes Kefala: "I feel you have to live in a language to be able to write in it, and . . . I couldn't write in Romanian or Greek or French because they were languages that I had somehow passed through. English was the language I was actually living in—imperfectly!" However, she has also consistently drawn attention to the attenuation of her location in the English language, according to Digby, because of the complex ways that literary and other cultural, linguistic, psychological, and historical influences and inflections are absorbed by each person: "My approach to English is not quite an English approach. The kind of imagery that I use, the kind of vocabulary that I use, the whole texture of my language is not an English texture."

Sneja Gunew, Kefala's major critic, has extensively discussed and theorized these issues of multilingualism. Kefala has also insisted on the way that moving across

languages in one's life highlights what Gunew and others have termed the "otherness" of language—the differential positionings of individuals within a language structure, the multiplicitous nature of language, and the opacity with which it references the world. Kefala commented to Nickas that the issue of bi- or multilingualism reflects also on the predominantly monolingual Anglo-Australian culture in quite negative terms: "In Romania at that time, as I think in most parts of Europe, a second or third language was considered an intrinsic part of one's education, something that could only enhance one's understanding of other cultures, and provide direct access to valuable intellectual resources."

Kefala moved to Sydney in 1959, where she has worked as an ESL teacher, and in arts administration, as Multicultural Arts Officer at the Australia Council, the peak national arts funding organization. In 1964 she married Usher Weinrauch; they divorced in 1976. According to Digby, Kefala's experience at the Australia Council alerted her to a significant gender issue, which she also related to her own work: "in the area of multicultural arts . . . what was obvious . . . was that while everyone was being marginalised, women artists and women working in the arts had a modest definition of their own work." Kefala identifies with this perceived reluctance of non-Anglo women to claim the position of professional writer, arguing that it would also benefit male writers to take on aspects of this "modesty" as a counter to what she has characterized as the "inflated and at the same time mechanised" nature of public language, the increasing corrosion of "the complexity of language, its immediacy and personal dimension" with contemporary shifts in media and information technology. Further, she refers the polysemy of her own writing to the specific access to language accorded by her position as a migrant woman writer. In this sense her concern with issues of language extends out from an examination of her own location in terms of gender and cultural inheritances and background to broader issues of technology and arts management.

Questions of readership are important to Kefala, both in terms of the broad intellectual and cultural scene in Australia and in relation to the reception of her own writing. She commented to Digby on the low readership of poetry, saying that "one actually writes in a vacuum . . . apart from the critics I don't know what people think of it. I don't have any feedback. I don't think that the general public is reading me. . . ."

Genre and stylistic differences, themselves related to questions of cultural differences and access, have for Kefala, Nickas says, a bearing on questions of readership and access. The un-English qualities of her writing have made it difficult for her to find an audience, she feels, since her language seems foreign to Australian mainstream readers. Her prose is dense and poetically laden; also, she writes novellas rather than novels or short stories, a choice that has led to difficulties getting published in the first place, because of the preconceptions held by many publishers about particular genres.

This issue of genre is significant in that it relates to those questions of linguistic location and cultural literacy that engaged Kefala when she first began writing, and she has cited these questions several times in interviews with reference to what has been seen by reviewers as the darkness and bleakness of her poetry. She told Digby, "In English, people don't like to write seriously about death in the European sense, or the Greek sense. . . . I have been told for many, many years, and constantly, that I am not of this place." There is, for Kefala, also an issue of translation at work here, involving the continuous and engaged traversing and extending of cultural norms.

Kefala has participated in some of the key public debates on multicultural writing and the nature of the marginalization of migrant writers in Australia, both as an arts administrator and as an engaged writer and intellectual. Her stated approach to these issues, says Digby—the need for arts funding bodies to "recognise the place and needs of a large group of people who were disadvantaged because of language or cultural differences"—refutes the view of "multicultural literature" as "a creation of the marketplace." Further, she commented to Digby:

Australian society has changed, but this change I think is not reflected in the arts. The arts have

Dust jacket for the 1984 novel Kefala based on her family's experiences as immigrants to New Zealand (Bruccoli Clark Layman Archives)

remained very conservative to a great extent. They are not inclusive. The moment such an inclusion is suggested, everyone feels that "the newcomers" are taking the bread out of their mouths, so to speak, or their power. After all, power is a thing that changes. It cannot remain permanently in the same hands.

Kefala credits Gunew with raising these issues in academic and publishing contexts, and with working to accommodate these issues and an awareness of the need for pluralism within the intellectual and aesthetic contexts of Australia.

Kefala's poetry focuses on relationships with the past, with experiences of exile and loss, and with understandings of and attitudes toward death. Michelle Tsokos comments: "Kefala's poetry vibrates constantly between arbitrary beginnings and undefined endings. Movement between these polarities is seen to be characteristic of individual experience." Imagery from the natural world and from myth provides anchors for reading in these insistently introspective works. Various journeys provide structure and tension across and between individual poems and take on added metaphoric weight

*Paperback cover for Kefala's 1984 novel about a university
student in New Zealand (Bruccoli Clark
Layman Archives)*

in relation to the concern with the relations, transitions, and mediations of adult-child relations.

Kefala's fiction writing is also densely symbolic, the prose itself deeply invested in poetic modes and reference points. It shares with the poetry an ongoing concern with the constitution of the self, with loss, dislocation and unstable identity. In this sense, the theme of migration carries metaphoric weight across Kefala's prose from the 1970s to the recently republished bilingual version of *Alexia* published in 1995—*Alexia: A Tale for Advanced Children,* with a Greek translation by Helen Nickas. Experiences of estrangement, dislocation, and alienation persist in these stories of isolated, introspective individuals struggling to make sense of the complex lives and experiences with which they come into contact.

In *The First Journey* (published in *The First Journey: Two Short Novels* in 1975)—a young boy, Alexi, leaves a country town in Romania to join his brother, Tassos,

studying music in the capital. The migration in this work, then, is not across cultures; Alexi, however, remains an outsider because of "some initial foreignness in me from the beginning," an experience that characterizes even his family life. He is presented as comprising two selves; one of whom "moved and laughed, cried and was angry," while the other "undermined every effort towards an involvement." Much of Alexi's time and energy is taken up differentiating himself, not only from himself and his family but also from figures such as the artist Caragea, with whose wife, Anna, Alexi falls in love. The narrative is introspective, slow-moving, intense, and obsessive. Readers are drawn into Alexi's double world of mirrors and shadows, dreams and flights; he is increasingly traumatized by the death of Anna, which he had foreseen. The unresolved ending of the novella rests with Alexi's view of the lights of the city where he has been displaced.

Helen Nickas has remarked in *Migrant Daughters: The Female Voice in Greek-Australian Prose Fiction* (1992) that, despite the male narrator, this novella is dominated by women's worlds, and Nikos Papastergiadis has demonstrated that these characters articulate the processes of culture—of fabrication and fire. Alexi's final embrace of the city and of loss is traced against and in terms of this gendered cultural context.

The Boarding House, the second novella in *The First Journey: Two Short Novels,* also deals centrally with experiences of dislocation: after a broken marriage, a young female university graduate moves to Sydney from New Zealand in search of a new life. Central to the narrative is Melina's inability to deal with a doomed relationship: "I am waiting motionless for those unseen wounds inside me to heal. . . ." Her marriage has been troubled from the start, and Melina has left her husband to begin a new life in another city and another country. She describes this decision as a move to "the city of youth" bursting with "energy" and "determination," but in relation to this city, she says, "I feel old, eaten away by centuries of living," thus explaining the feeling of temporal disjunction because of her migration and the colonial "new world" sensibilities of Australia and New Zealand. Against Melina's darkness, depth, and gloom stands Mrs. Webster, the Sydney landlady whose relentless care and attentiveness gloss over Melina's introspection. Oppressed also in memory, Melina recalls obsessively her position in relation to traditional Greek Orthodox articulations of sex and women in moments of identification with the misogyny of the Church. In this sense, Melina's narrative is one of alienation—culturally, personally, and emotionally. In response to her growing awareness of her sense of isolation, she walks through the city, creating for herself a release.

The protagonist of *The Island* (1984), also called Melina, is also a university student, possibly the protagonist of *The Boarding House* at an earlier stage of her life. In *The Island,* cultural differences, particularly as experienced in language, are more explicitly presented, often in ironic terms, as when Melina explains to her aunt, after returning home from university one day, that "the nature of the understatement was more miraculous and more subtle than the Pindaric ode." At other times the gap between cultures is more alienating, more violently inscribed in the protagonist's experience: "I spoke. I could see from his face that he had not the faintest idea what I was saying, the meaning stopped somewhere mid-air between us, he incredulous that he will ever understand me, I incredulous that he will ever understand me. . . . I could see in his whole attitude the immense surprise at being confronted, here in his own room, at the University, by something as foreign as myself."

Against the intensity of these linguistic differences lies the calm solidity of Anglo-New Zealand bourgeois life, with its polished domestic surfaces and rigid gender demarcations. Melina's experiences of romantic love and confusion in the course of the narrative lead her instead into an internal world whose complexity alienates her from all the other characters, whatever their cultural location.

Alexia, the story of a migrant child arriving in New Zealand, is Kefala's most explicit account of the experiences and stakes of migration. Alexia's experience also crosses class barriers, with the protagonist's middle-class family, all musicians, linguistically adept and well read, all on their arrival sent to work in New Zealand factories at manual labor. Within the satiric mode of the novel, this fall from grace is depicted through fairy-tale motifs and characterizations, working toward critical portrayals of the processes and traumas of migration, the impossibilities of easy belonging, the displacements of complex lives by brutalizing labor.

In Kefala's most recent collection of prose work, *Summer Visit: Three Novellas* (2002), she continues the blurring of stylistic and genre categories as well as boundaries of location. In *Summer Visit* the protagonist returns to Greece for a visit after years of absence, a plot device allowing Kefala again to explore ideas surrounding migration, displacement, and cultural identification.

Nickas has suggested that a certain continuity is discernible across Antigone Kefala's prose works in the development of a single central psyche, traced across the experiences and narratives of the protagonists of each novella, echoing Kefala's own journey from Romania to New Zealand and Australia. While the writing itself is far from the confessional mode of autobiography, as Nickas notes, nonetheless, the reader can find value in drawing a range of critical, aesthetic, and political concerns together to articulate the meanings and experiences of migration and the ongoing reverberations of cultural differences in contemporary Australian writing.

Interviews:

Helen Nickas, interview with Kefala in Nickas's *Migrant Daughters: The Female Voice in Greek-Australian Prose Fiction* (Melbourne: Owl Publishing, 1992);

Jenny Digby, interview with Kofala published as "A Labyrinthian Linguistic Field," in her *A Woman's Voice: Conversations with Australian Poets* (St. Lucia & Portland, Ore.: University of Queensland Press, 1996), pp. 190–203.

References:

Judith Brett, "The Process of Becoming: Antigone Kefala's *The First Journey* and *The Island,*" *Meanjin,* 44, no. 1 (March 1985): 124–133;

Kathryn Buselich, "'Vast Unknown Places Within': The Landscapes of Antigone Kefala and John Millett," *Westerly* (Summer 1998): 88–99;

Anne Collett, "'In a season without languages': Translative Process in the Poetry of Ouyang Yu, Vasso Kalamaras, Ania Walwicz and Antigone Kefala," in *Land and Identity: Proceedings of the 1997 Conference Held at the University of New England, Armidale, New South Wales 27–30 September 1997,* edited by Jennifer McDonnell and Michael Deves (Armidale, N.S.W.: Association for Study of Australian Literature, 1997), pp. 232–238;

Pam Gilbert, "Postscript: Antigone Kefala and Marginalisation in Australian Literature," in her *Coming Out from Under: Contemporary Australian Women Writers* (Sydney: Pandora, 1988);

Sneja Gunew, *Framing Marginality: Multicultural Literary Studies* (Melbourne: Melbourne University Press, 1994);

Gunew, "Migrant Women Writers: Who's on Whose Margins?" *Meanjin,* 42, no. 1 (March 1983): 16–26;

Helen Nickas, *Migrant Daughters: The Female Voice in Greek-Australian Prose Fiction* (Melbourne: Owl Publishing, 1992);

Saadi Nikro, "Antigone Kefala: Translating the Migratory Self," *Southerly,* 58, no. 1 (Autumn 1998): 151–159;

Nikos Papastergiadis, "The Journeys Within: Migration and Identity in Greek-Australian Literature," in *Striking Chords: Multicultural Literary Interpretations,* edited by Gunew and Katerina O. Langley (Sydney: Allen & Unwin, 1992), pp. 149–161;

Michelle Tsokos, "Memory and Absence: The Poetry of Antigone Kefala," *Westerly,* 4 (Summer 1994): 51–60.

Thomas Keneally

(7 October 1935 –   )

Peter Pierce
James Cook University

BOOKS: *The Place at Whitton* (London: Cassell, 1964; New York: Walker, 1965);

The Fear (Melbourne: Cassell, 1965; London: Quartet, 1973); revised as *By the Line* (St. Lucia: University of Queensland Press, 1989; London: Sceptre, 1992);

Bring Larks and Heroes (Melbourne: Cassell, 1967; New York: Viking, 1968; London: Quartet, 1973);

Three Cheers for the Paraclete (Sydney: Angus & Robertson, 1968; New York: Viking, 1969);

Halloran's Little Boat (Sydney, 1968?); republished as *Halloran's Little Boat: A Play Based on the Novel Bring Larks and Heroes,* by Keneally and Kenneth Cook (Harmondsworth, U.K. & Ringwood, Vic.: Penguin, 1975);

The Survivor (Sydney: Angus & Robertson, 1969; Harmondsworth, U.K.: Penguin, 1970; New York: Viking, 1970);

A Dutiful Daughter (Sydney & London: Angus & Robertson, 1971; New York: Viking, 1971);

The Chant of Jimmie Blacksmith (Sydney & London: Angus & Robertson, 1972; New York: Viking, 1972);

Blood Red, Sister Rose (London & Sydney: Collins, 1974; New York: Viking, 1974);

Gossip from the Forest (London: Collins, 1975; San Diego: Harcourt Brace Jovanovich, 1976; Sydney: New South Wales Building Society in association with the Sydney Theatre Company, 1983);

Moses the Lawgiver (London: Collins, 1975; New York: Harper & Row, 1975);

Season in Purgatory (London: Collins, 1976; New York: Harcourt Brace Jovanovich, 1977);

A Victim of the Aurora (London: Collins, 1977; New York: Harcourt Brace Jovanovich, 1978);

Ned Kelly and the City of Bees (London: Cape, 1978; Harmondsworth, U.K. & Ringwood, Vic.: Puffin Books, 1980; New York: Godine, 1981);

Confederates (Sydney & London: Collins, 1979; New York: Harper & Row, 1980);

Passenger (London: Collins, 1979; New York: Harcourt Brace Jovanovich, 1979);

Thomas Keneally (photograph by Rob Atkins/Image Bank)

The Cut-Rate Kingdom (Sydney: Wildcat Press, 1980; London: Allen Lane, 1984);

Bullie's House (Sydney: Currency Press, 1981);

Schindler's Ark (London: Hodder & Stoughton, 1982); republished as *Schindler's List* (New York: Simon & Schuster, 1982);

Outback, text by Keneally, photographs by Gary Hansen and Mark Lang (Sydney: Hodder & Stoughton, 1983; Chicago: Rand McNally, 1984);

A Family Madness (London & Sydney: Hodder & Stoughton, 1985; New York: Simon & Schuster, 1986);

The Playmaker (London: Hodder & Stoughton, 1987; Sydney: Hodder & Stoughton, 1987; New York: Simon & Schuster, 1987);

Act of Grace, as William Coyle (London: Chatto & Windus, 1988);

Towards Asmara (London: Hodder & Stoughton, 1989); republished as *To Asmara* (New York: Warner, 1989);

Chief of Staff, as Coyle (London: Chatto & Windus, 1991);

Flying Hero Class (London: Hodder & Stoughton, 1991; New York: Warner, 1991; Sydney: Coronet, 1992);

Now and in Time to Be (Sydney: Pan Macmillan, 1991; London: Flamingo, 1992);

The Place Where Souls Are Born (London & Sydney: Hodder & Stoughton, 1992; New York: Simon & Schuster, 1992);

Woman of the Inner Sea (London & Sydney: Hodder & Stoughton, 1992; New York: Nan A. Talese/Doubleday, 1995);

Jacko (Port Melbourne, Vic.: Heinemann, 1993; London & Sydney: Hodder & Stoughton, 1994);

The Utility Player (Sydney: Pan Macmillan, 1993);

Our Republic (Port Melbourne, Vic.: Heinemann, 1993); republished as *Memoirs from a Young Republic* (London: Heinemann, 1993);

A River Town (Melbourne: Heinemann, 1995; New York: Nan A. Talese/Doubleday, 1995; London: Sceptre, 1995);

Homebush Boy (Port Melbourne, Vic.: Heinemann, 1995; London: Hodder & Stoughton, 1995);

The Great Shame: A Story of the Irish in the Old World and the New (Milson's Point, N.S.W.: Random House, 1998; London: Chatto & Windus, 1998); republished as *The Great Shame: And the Triumph of the Irish in the English-speaking World* (New York: Nan A. Talese/Doubleday, 1999);

Bettany's Book (London: Sceptre, 2000; Sydney & New York: Doubleday, 2000);

American Scoundrel: The Life of the Notorious Civil War General Dan Sickles (New York: Nan A. Talese/Doubleday, 2002; Milson's Point, N.S.W.: Random House, 2002; London: Chatto & Windus, 2002);

An Angel in Australia (Sydney & London: Doubleday, 2002); republished as *The Office of Innocence* (London: Sceptre, 2002; New York: Nan A. Talese/Doubleday, 2003);

Abraham Lincoln (London: Weidenfeld & Nicolson, 2003; New York: Lipper/Viking, 2003);

The Tyrant's Novel (Sydney: Doubleday, 2003; New York: Nan A. Talese/Doubleday, 2004).

PLAY PRODUCTIONS: *Halloran's Little Boat,* Sydney, Old Tote Theatre Company, 15 November 1966;

Childermas, Sydney, Old Tote Theatre, University of New South Wales, 1968;

An Awful Rose, Sydney, Parade Theatre, 1972;

Bullie's House, Sydney, Nimrod Theatre, 1980.

OTHER: *Here Nature Is Reversed,* in Keneally, Patsy Adam-Smith, and Robyn Davidson, *Australia: Beyond the Dreamtime* (Richmond, Vic.: Heinemann, 1987; London: BBC Books, 1987; New York: Facts on File, 1987).

Late in his fourth decade as a published author, Thomas Keneally has turned his well-honed techniques as a novelist to works of popular history. The first of them was *The Great Shame* (1998), his account of the Irish diaspora of the mid nineteenth century, especially to Australia and the United States. More recent was *American Scoundrel* (2002), his retelling of the story of the lawyer, politician, amorist, Civil War general, and much else besides, Daniel Sickles. Linking the two books is the vibrant figure of Thomas Meagher, an Irish political prisoner who escaped from Van Diemen's Land to make a new life in the United States as a Union general, governor of Montana, and finally victim of the Fenians. Keneally has always taken delight in such characters as these, real and imagined. Keneally's abiding interest in the American Civil War also generated his popular biography *Abraham Lincoln* (2003).

Since the 1960s Keneally has been one of the most absorbing and fluent of storytellers in world fiction. He is also one to whom great stories have been given. Thus, a chance encounter with the owner of a Los Angeles luggage store provided the germ of his Booker Prize–winning novel, *Schindler's Ark* (1982, published also as *Schindler's List*). His research on Meagher and a deepening interest in American history led Keneally to the extravagant life of Sickles, a man who had introduced his mistress to Queen Victoria while he was secretary to the American ambassador, James Buchanan; objected to his wife's adultery while expecting his own to be condoned; shot her lover and was acquitted on the first successful plea of temporary insanity. In *American Scoundrel* he dramatizes Sickles's controversial role at Gettysburg, where he lost a leg. Later adven-

Dust jacket for the U.S. edition of Keneally's 1968 novel, about a priest who revises the history of the Catholic Church in Australia (Richland County Public Library)

tures included an affair with the deposed queen of Spain. Sickles may be an historical figure, but the novelist takes over: Sickles is magnetic, histrionic, duplicitous, and expansive of appetite and imagination.

Thomas Keneally was born to Edmund Thomas and Elsie Coyle Keneally in Sydney on 7 October 1935, but he grew up in the north coastal region of New South Wales where both his grandfathers had come after emigrating from Ireland. This area is the setting for his novel *A River Town* (1995), the first volume of a proposed trilogy for which no other novels have been produced. In 1942 the family moved back to Sydney, to Homebush, while his father served with the Royal Australian Air Force in the Middle East. Keneally recalled this time in his early novel *The Fear* (1965, revised and republished in 1989 as *By the Line*), in his memoir *Homebush Boy* (1995), and in his novel *An Angel in Australia* (2002, also published in 2002 as *The Office of Innocence*). Educated by the Christian Brothers, Keneally entered St. Patrick's Seminary at the beachside suburb of Manly in 1952 to train for the priesthood. In 1960 he left, shortly before he was to be

ordained, suffering–like Morris West–what he called "a nervous breakdown." In 1965 he married Judith Martin, a nurse and former Sister of Charity nun. They have two daughters–Margaret, born in 1966, and Jane, born the following year.

While he began to write, Keneally supported himself in various jobs–as a builder's laborer, clerk, and schoolteacher. Keneally's first published work, the story "The Sky Burning Up above the Man," appeared pseudonymously in the *Bulletin* magazine on 23 June 1962 under the name "Bernard Coyle" (the surname was his mother's maiden name). Two years later his first novel, *The Place at Whitton* (1964), was published. A tale of murders in a monastery, it anticipated Umberto Eco's *The Name of the Rose* (1980, English translation, 1983) by sixteen years. Adrian Mitchell perceptively spoke of *The Place at Whitton* as a "lumber-room" where intimations of many of the fictional projects that Keneally later undertook could be found. Thus, his pair of Antarctic novels, *The Survivor* (1969) and *A Victim of the Aurora* (1977), were curiously foreshadowed in the description of the monastery as "a sort of polar weather station of God." The figure of Joan of Arc makes the first of her many appearances in his writing. (She is the heroine of the novel *Blood Red, Sister Rose,* 1974.) *The Place at Whitton* is also Keneally's first, halting endeavor to anatomize contemporary Australia. With the pardonable surprise of one emerging from years of cloistered life, he described "a lusty nation, healthily, sanely attached to its vices, a sporting, wenching, boozing, touring, colour-photographing, gambling nation." His analysis of Australian society gradually grew more complex, although it always remained genial. His most notable novels of present-day Australia–*A Family Madness* (1985) and *Woman of the Inner Sea* (1992)–have nonetheless received slighter critical acclaim than his historical fictions.

In 1966 Keneally was awarded a Commonwealth Literary Fund grant of $4,000 that freed him temporarily to write full-time. On 15 November of that year, his first play, *Halloran's Little Boat,* was performed (published in 1968). Commissioned by the National Institute of Dramatic Art, the play was an initial working of the material given fuller and richer shape in Keneally's third novel, *Bring Larks and Heroes* (1967). Set in a penal colony at the "world's worse end" at the close of the eighteenth century, the book was Keneally's first popular and critical success, not least in securing the first of successive Miles Franklin Awards for the best Australian novel of the year. What he crafted was a complex tale of the origins of his country, one that involved the British or Irish ancestry of the characters, the transplanting of their traditional antagonisms, religions, class divisions, and tribal memories. Now, for the first time in the southern continent, voice was given to ancestral European oaths, creeds, and betrayals.

Bring Larks and Heroes dramatizes how the official language of the British rulers was opposed by signs, gestures, and oaths—"secret muttering in Gaelic"—as the Irish "flaunted before the authorities the secrecy of their old, barbarous tongue." Keneally presented the struggle for mastery in the new world between the privileged and the underprivileged, figured in part as the contest between the written and the spoken word. At the same time he searched for an idiosyncratic idiom of his own, apt for this reimagining of national origins in a place variously described as "a Corinth of the south" and "this small parish of Hell." The historical setting of the novel—in which felon (the term that Keneally prefers to *convict*) and free, women and men, Irish and English are locked away together by a sail of seven months from the old world and its upheavals (notably the French Revolution)—allows Keneally to express a central moral intuition of his work. He holds that all destinies are entwined, however diverse the beliefs, prejudices, and allegiances of individuals.

Bring Larks and Heroes received warm and widespread critical attention. Writing in the *Australian* newspaper, on 14 October 1967, Derek Whitelock acclaimed "the long-sought great Australian novel." Keneally was awarded a $6,000 Commonwealth Literary Fellowship. His book was bracketed by the first two volumes of Manning Clark's *A History of Australia* (1962, 1968). This venturesome feat of the melodramatic imagination, whatever its defects as history, may have facilitated the acceptance of Keneally's historical vision in *Bring Larks and Heroes*. In the novel, as in Clark's work, the European settlement of Australia is regarded as a matter of surpassing social and ideological importance. Both authors were engaged by the neglected imaginative possibilities and the dramas of conscience in the early history of European Australia.

Keneally's next novel, *Three Cheers for the Paraclete* (1968), also won the Miles Franklin Award. This work, his second fictional account of the Catholic religious life in Australia, tells of a priest—Father Maitland—who has pseudonymously written a revisionist view of the historical and political appropriations of God that his church has countenanced. When discovered, by yet another of the betrayals that stud Keneally's novels, his punishment is to be placed by his bishop under an interdiction to publish no more. The terror of such a sentence for the fertile Keneally can readily be imagined.

Between 1968 and 1970 Keneally lectured in drama at the University of New England. He also continued to write plays—*Childermas* (1968), *An Awful Rose* (1972), *Bullie's House* (1980, published the next year)—in addition to writing a section of the motion picture *Libido*

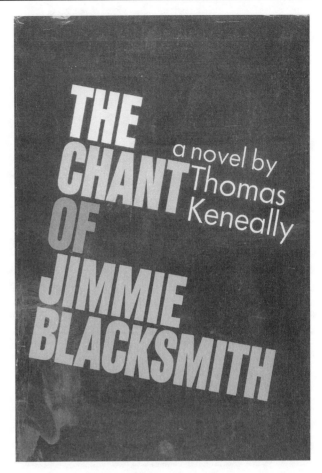

Dust jacket for the U.S. edition of Keneally's 1972 novel, in which he expresses anger about the treatment of Aborigines by white settlers (Richland County Public Library)

(1973). The time at the university furnished the "campus novel" parts of his next book, *The Survivor,* which has for its other main setting Antarctica, which Keneally had visited as a guest of the United States Navy in 1968. This novel won the Captain Cook Bicentenary Award in 1970 and was made into a television movie the following year. One of the characters "thought of Antarctica in literary terms: a prophetic landscape begging a prophet and tailored for seekings and disillusionments." Keneally found the frozen continent so congenial to his imagination that he set another novel there, *A Victim of the Aurora.* While the latter is an historical fiction, set at the beginning of the twentieth century, each interrogates the heroic elements of classic Antarctic narratives of exploration and survival; each transposes the search for the nature and identity of Australians from their country to Antarctica. And each is a deft and satisfying murder mystery, as Keneally extends his talents to another genre.

A Victim of the Aurora is in part a retrospect on Keneally's career to that point. It was his eleventh

Dust jacket for Keneally's 1976 novel, set in Yugoslavia during World War II (Bruccoli Clark Layman Archives)

angrily with the white settlers' treatment of the Australian Aborigines. He has argued that "the snake in the garden is that we have not recognised the prior sovereignty of the Aborigines." Keneally has been neither blundering, sentimental, nor too credulous in his engagement with relations between black and white Australians. Nevertheless, he became the subject of virulent, often self-interested criticism from experts in fields other than literature. For Keneally, however, the story allowed another unfettered review of matters of conscience in an Australian historical setting that still speaks urgently to the present. Nearly two decades later, he returned to Aboriginal affairs.

Flying Hero Class (1991) describes the hijacking of a plane, among whose passengers are the members of the famous Barramatjara Aboriginal dance group. Between the two novels the same mellowing of vision is discernible, the shift from alienation to affirmation, which marks the changes between another pair of his novels that are separated by two decades—*Bring Larks and Heroes* and *The Playmaker* (1987). Each of the later books is to some extent a careful and benign revision of its predecessor. Accepting at last his status as victim, Jimmie comes to see that his strategy of violent resistance is doomed. Aboriginal techniques of dealing with exploitation are subtler and more successful in *Flying Hero Class.*

One of the central procedures of Keneally's art is a probing of how such social and fictional simplifications affect and are opposed by his characters rather than the creating of stereotypes. Aware of being typecast—whether, like Jimmie, as "an honest poor bastard but he's nearly extinct"; or as a sublime tribal painter and dancer; or, to shift to the non-Aboriginal cast of these two novels, as earnest cleric, bereaved fiancé, or righteous terrorist—some of Keneally's people are virtuosos at exploiting the stereotypes that are imposed on them. Appearing to live within and up to their assigned parts, they often subvert them, suggesting a redemptive, perhaps a fundamentally comic, art. But it is one conscious of ethical responsibility. Keneally has said that "the Aboriginal issue is Australia's Ulster." Moreover, he has said that "we need some relations with their ghosts." Particularly in *Flying Hero Class,* Keneally's uncondescending act of grace toward the Aborigines is to show how, through wit, they undermine stereotypical expectations of them. (By contrast, the core of Jimmie's anguish is his refusal to live down to demeaning stereotypes.) The Aborigines are distinctive in their meticulously described history and ethnography, and at the same time they share the will to individuality of many of Keneally's other characters.

In the decade from 1972 to 1982, from *The Chant of Jimmie Blacksmith* to *Schindler's Ark,* Keneally concen-

novel—all published within a span of thirteen years. Despite the success of *The Chant of Jimmie Blacksmith* (1972), no subsequent book had won the critical favor that had been afforded to *Bring Larks and Heroes.* In his review of *A Victim of the Aurora* (*The Age,* 13 May 1978), D. J. O'Hearn said that Keneally's career was paradigmatic of the path of so much talent in Australia "from potential excellence to ineluctable mediocrity; from daring and excitement to chafing comfort; from passion to anomie." O'Hearn spoke carpingly and much too soon, but the form of his argument is significant. It is the praise of an author's early work chiefly to disparage an alleged later falling away. Keneally has from time to time been a victim of such treatment, albeit a remarkably resilient one.

After a time living in London in the early 1970s, Keneally returned to Australia. In 1972 one of his most popular and best-selling novels was published. Based on the true story of killings committed by the part-Aboriginal Governor brothers in New South Wales at the end of the nineteenth century, *The Chant of Jimmie Blacksmith* is the novel in which Keneally deals most

In the shadow of Auschwitz, a maverick German industrialist, Oskar Schindler, grew into a living legend to the Jews of Cracow – his enamelware and munitions factory a benign concentration camp, an ark of salvation.

THOMAS KENEALLY

THOMAS KENEALLY

SCHINDLER'S ARK

SCHINDLER'S ARK.

WINNER OF THE BOOKER McCONNELL PRIZE

Dust jacket for Keneally's 1982 Booker Prize novel, which was republished in the United States as
Schindler's List *(Bruccoli Clark Layman Archives)*

trated on historical fiction, and especially on war. He spent the years from 1975 through 1977 living in the United States, lecturing for a time in Connecticut. The American connection was strengthened in the mid 1980s when he became writer-in-residence at the University of California at Irvine. Later he became a Distinguished Professor for Life in the University of California system. Yet, most of the novels of this period were set in Europe. Writing principally of war and its aftermath, Keneally affirmed that war is both a monstrous and an ineradicable activity, a horror for individuals but an essential element in the making and the memories of nations.

His second novel, *The Fear,* treated the strains of home-front life and politics in Australia during World War II. His sixteenth, *A Family Madness,* dramatized the haunting, destructive legacies of that war a generation later among Belorussian immigrants to Australia. This greatest of human conflicts is the foreground of *Season in Purgatory* (1976), *The Cut-Rate Kingdom* (published first in the *Bulletin* and then by Wildcat Press, 1980), and Keneally's best-selling novel, *Schindler's Ark.* Writing

under the pseudonym "William Coyle" (a variant of his first pseudonym), Keneally produced a pair of World War II novels, *Act of Grace* (1988) and *Chief of Staff* (1991). They were written, he said, "for recreational purposes." A decade later Keneally returned to the time of World War II with *An Angel in Australia.* In Keneally's historical imagining, the crucial time period in the national past was the one he had lived through as a child—the anticipated Japanese invasion of Australia. In *An Angel in Australia* that time is the background to the crises of conscience of a young priest that echo such earlier novels as *Three Cheers for the Paraclete* while drawing on Keneally's years as a seminarian.

The Armistice that was signed in a railway car in the forest of Compiegne and that concluded World War I but ultimately helped to cause World War II is the subject of *Gossip from the Forest* (1975). From there Keneally ranged backward and forward in time. The Australian campaigns in Borneo and Vietnam are among the many narrative strands of *Passenger* (1979), a novel narrated by a fetus. The prospect of young Australians adventuring at the Boer War in the cause of the

Keneally in his study at Bilgola, circa 1987 (Graeme Kinross Smith Collection; from Peter Pierce,
Australian Melodramas, 1995; Thomas Cooper Library, University of South Carolina)

British Empire is an ironic backdrop to the hunting of
the Aborigines in *The Chant of Jimmie Blacksmith*. The
American Civil War is the business of *Confederates*
(1979), while the role of Joan of Arc in the eventual
French triumph in the Hundred Years War is the subject of *Blood Red, Sister Rose*. In *Towards Asmara* (1989,
published as *To Asmara* in New York), Keneally wrote
for the first time not only of a contemporary war—the
struggle for independence by the people of the Ethio-
pian province of Eritrea—but of one where he had been
a spectator at close quarters. He had traveled to Eritrea
in 1987 because of "the brave Eritrean People's Liberation Front" and as its partisan.

The unity within Keneally's oeuvre is most vividly illustrated in his treatments of war. Themes such as
battle and executioners, characters (notably Joan of
Arc) and motifs—"wounds" and "blood"—were present
from the start of his career. Keneally has spoken of his
work as

> a continuous and relatively homogeneous thing,
> although it can't ever *seem* to be as homogenous as the
> work of those novelists who generally write out of inti-
> mate personal experience.

His fiction quickly came to echo what had taken place
in previous novels. Thus, *Gossip from the Forest* begins at
Senlis, north of Paris, which is also one of the major
sites of its predecessor, *Blood Red, Sister Rose*.

For Keneally, war—and especially civil war—has a
central and multifaceted place in his perception of the
destiny of individuals and nations, and of how these
intersect. Keneally writes of "the monstrous nature" of
civil war in *Blood Red, Sister Rose*, in which war among
French people of different allegiances is fiercer than that
waged intermittently against the English. Civil war
rends the social fabric more bitterly; it is more shocking
because it is fought between people who share a heritage. This knowledge informs his description of the
American Civil War in *Confederates* and of World War I
for "civilization" among the nations of Europe in *Gossip
from the Forest*. A World War II novel, *Season in Purgatory*
deals with the vicious, intestine fighting of Ustachi,
Chetniks, and Partisanka, all of whom were styled
Yugoslavs after the war. Jimmie Blacksmith comes to
think of his white victims as "the first necessary casualties of war" as though he is singly to be responsible for
initiating the full-scale civil war that Australia escaped.

Keneally's concentration upon civil war is conso-
nant with the major domestic inquiry of his fiction and
with his exploration of all that divides the ostensibly
homogeneous fabric of Australian society. Sectarian disputes, resentment of more recently arrived migrants,
and loathing of minority groups are among the divisive
domestic conflicts that Keneally observes. The title metaphor of *A Family Madness* speaks not only of the belated
power of war to cause casualties, of the self-destruction

decades later of the Kabbelskis from Belorussia, but
also of tensions usually unvoiced in Australian society,
wherein this family has found a temporary lodgment.
The handling of war in Keneally's fiction is in some
measure a transposition of family romance, of savage
domestic melodrama.

The saving, not the doom, of a surrogate family is
what engrosses Keneally in *Schindler's Ark*. The Holocaust story that he was told by one of the Schindler survivors was breathtakingly unlikely. It related how a
German entrepreneur and bon vivant saved more than
a thousand Jews by sheltering them as employees in his
factory. The story accorded with crucial intuitions of
Keneally's fiction–his concern with the mysteries of
conscience, his analysis of stereotyping (here of Jews as
supposedly doomed and designated victims), and of
how stereotypes can be manipulated and resisted, as
well as surrendered to fatally. In Schindler, Keneally created
a compassionate renegade. Unlike several of Keneally's protagonists, Schindler does not surrender to coercive institutions; he subverts them from within. The hero as
lovable rogue is given fuller play in this work than in
any of Keneally's other novels.

Part of Keneally's fascination with Schindler was
this uncompelled, reckless, unquestioning generosity of
spirit. Nothing in Schindler's past had anticipated or
could explain what would "obsess, imperil and exalt
him." Nothing in what the novelist depicts of Schindler
reveals, retrospectively, the forces that energized him.
His behavior is a rare instance of good works in action,
along with the challenge to art that it represents. As
Keneally wryly remarked, "fatal human malice is the sta-
ple of narrative." Although alert to danger, Schindler was
equally indifferent to self-justification, publicity, or pos-
terity. As for the Schindler survivors, so in Keneally's
interpretation "the sum of his motives" remains impon-
derable, their rescue a blessing hardly possible to credit.

Whether *Schindler's Ark* was a novel at all bedev-
iled the Booker judges (not so, those who awarded it
the *Los Angeles Times* Fiction Prize in 1983). Only a few
years before, Keneally had been embroiled in accusa-
tions of plagiarism concerning *Season in Purgatory*. Now
he was the subject of speculation as to whether he had
written a work of nonfiction that was by definition ineligible for the prize. In the end the judges decided that
Keneally had deployed the skills of his fictive craft in
the interest of a work at once compassionate, astonishing, and surprising in its contents and compass. More
strife arose when director Steven Spielberg's version of
the novel, the Academy Award–winning motion picture
Schindler's List, was eventually released in 1994. In *Le
Monde* (3 March 1994), for instance, the self-interested
Claude Lanzmann (director of the Holocaust movie
Shoah) called Spielberg's effort "kitsch melodrama." For

*Dust jacket for U.S. edition of Keneally's 1991 book about
the hijacking of a plane carrying a dance troupe
(Richland County Public Library)*

his part, Keneally could take pleasure in the fact that no
other Booker Prize–winning novel has sold so many
copies as his. In 1994–the year the movie was
released–the novel sold 873,716 copies in Britain and
the Commonwealth alone.

Besides his American commitments, Keneally
took on various responsibilities in Australia during the
mid 1980s. From 1985 through 1988 he was a member
of the Literature Board of the Australia Council; from
1985 through 1989, president of the National Book
Council. In 1983 he had been awarded an Order of
Australia (AO) for his services to literature, while he
also acted as chairman of the Australian Society of
Authors. He began to take a more outspoken, if unfailingly cheerful, role in public life–for instance, as a television commentator during the bicentennial celebrations
in 1988 and then as a leading spokesperson for the Australian Republican Movement–an advocacy that was
responsible for one issue in his book *Our Republic* (1993).
In this period Keneally's writing spread into different
channels. He contributed to a travel book about central

Paperback cover for Keneally's 1995 memoir of his childhood during World War II (Bruccoli Clark Layman Archives)

through "southern marriages, new world associations." For all its conscientiously and sometimes bitterly maintained divisions of class and authority, the social world of the novel is sunnier and more optimistic than that of *Bring Larks and Heroes*. The characters have some of the author's hopeful beliefs about the future of Australia.

The Playmaker is Keneally's reassurance to his readers that the country that became the Commonwealth of Australia was a land of greater variety, promise, creativity, and crankiness than the hermetic version of the founding days in *Bring Larks and Heroes* had suggested. The ludic possibilities of the new world are considered in the later novel. Plays can be made with welcome rather than disastrous consequences. When Keneally resumes his interest in the material of *Bring Larks and Heroes* in *The Playmaker,* he transforms it from tragedy to comedy. This conversion has become the essence and the gift of his fictional revision of Australian history.

Throughout his career Keneally has rejoiced in the plenitude of story that national histories and his own inventions have yielded. Often they have caused him formal problems of a kind that he has rarely disciplined: how to subdue the many stories that beckon from each of his books into a consolidated narrative. Yet, these are self-imposed challenges that the author has never shirked—for instance, in his finest 1990s novel of modern Australia, *Woman of the Inner Sea,* the storytelling is riotous in pace, packed with incidents violent and slapstick; yet, the material is essentially poignant. The writer's imagination has stayed unrepentantly prodigal.

This narrative bounty is also a difficulty (for all that the author triumphs over it), as exemplified in *Bettany's Book* (2000), which appeared after *A River Town*. Certainly the result was one of the longest of his books. Indeed, *Bettany's Book* might more aptly have been titled in the plural. The novel shuttles between early colonial Australia and the 1980s. It is set in the Sudan as well as Australia. It bristles with other novels that might have been, stories not only intimated but sometimes truncated, as Keneally deals with the technical problems that he has set himself.

What connects the two historical periods of *Bettany's Book* is the force of random connections as much by blood as by chance, and their resistance to too earnest interpretation. In Keneally's cosmology, all fates are—more or less happily—linked. The plot involves a one-hit moviemaker who comes into possession of the journal of her pastoralist ancestor, Jonathan Bettany. The journal relates his struggles to establish himself as a sheep farmer in southern New South Wales, where he is troubled more by sex and conscience than by the traditional scourges of those embroiled in Australian saga

Australia, *Outback* (1983); wrote *Here Nature Is Reversed,* the first part of *Australia: Beyond the Dreamtime* (1987); and presented his responses to the Irish heritage of Australia and himself in *Now and in Time to Be* (1991). Another travel book, this one set in the American Southwest, *The Place Where Souls Are Born,* appeared in 1992.

Keneally did not neglect fiction in the late 1980s. Apart from *A Family Madness,* he also wrote his exuberant second account of the European settlement of Australia, *The Playmaker*. In it surfaced his hopeful dream that—far from entrenching antagonisms—life in the antipodes might eventually dissolve old bonds and obligations, thus enabling a renovated existence for those who had (or had to) come to live there. While the governor schemes for the rehabilitation of his charges in a world "where the person under sentence was the normal thing and to be a free man abnormal," the playmaker of the title (the officer requested to stage the first theatrical entertainment in the colony), Lieutenant Ralph Clark, ponders how freedom might be bestowed

fiction—fire, flood and drought, and Aborigines and white outlaws.

Many of the stories that Keneally has already told so memorably are instinct in *Bettany's Book*. The Australia of this novel is complicated, ultimately for its own good, by transported political agitators (in this case English rather than Irish). As has always been Keneally's way, the Aboriginal peoples are treated as humans. They are neither caricatures nor doomed to extinction; they are a perennial call to conscience and understanding. In its moral bearings this novel, like many of its forerunners, is a tale of betrayals and the reckoning of guilt. Signature events of Keneally's earlier fiction recur—for instance, a convict's damning letter and a terrible hanging. In the modern world of the novel, sectarianism endures, whatever is pretended on the surface of public life. Keneally's relish for inside knowledge of supposedly glamorous professions is at play (as it was in *Jacko,* 1993) in the portrayal of the movie industry and the plethora of acronyms for the aid organizations that distribute wealth to the Third World and never miss the chance to proselytize.

Bettany's Book includes loud echoes of previous novels. The crises of the Bettany sisters' long relationships with unexpected and unsuitable men is a keynote of the contemporary section of the novel. Keneally brings the same moral astuteness and delicacy to these attachments as he did to those of Kate Gaffney in *Woman of the Inner Sea.* The pathos and politics, nobility and corruption that he discerned in the Eritrean independence movement in *Towards Asmara* suffuses his description of the Sudan this time, and especially the treatment of the horrors of child slavery.

His 2003 work of fiction *The Tyrant's Novel* is in an unusual key—venturing nearer to satire than is usually Keneally's wont. He imagines a political refugee, housed in an Australian detention center, who writes a novel to the deadline of the tyrant from whose country he has fled. Keneally has bravely intervened in a divisive national dispute over the treatment of asylum seekers in Australia.

Keneally's achievement rests in one place on his sympathetic curiosity about sufferers past and present. He has long been sensitive to one of the most salient features of the Australian condition that can be treated in literature. The country is alert for the threat of invaders or predators, defensively hostile to alien values or to people who seem to jeopardize its comfortable homes and systems of belief; this frame of mind is the psychic temper of victims-to-be of literary melodrama. To feel that one's social and physical beings are endangered, that either assault or revelation could destroy them, is the typical anxiety of the melodramatic hero or heroine. When the source of danger and persecution is often impersonal, invisible, perhaps conjured by victims out of their own obscure needs, part of the peculiar cultural and historical conformations of Australian literary melodrama can be discerned.

No Australian writer has so acutely employed the resources of the critically rehabilitated fictional form of melodrama as has Keneally. Nor has any been so involved in a wider cultural melodrama, such as Australian literary history has long favored, for the moral absolutes that it perceives, the scapegoats it elects, and the villains whose agency it requires. Keneally has been both the diagnostician and the victim of this long-standing business. One of his characters argues that "one generation's solemnities become the melodrama of the succeeding generation and the comedy of the next." That stance positions Keneally's fiction between the historical agencies that it has so regularly addressed and the dissolution of their moral portentousness in comedy that his art has often embraced.

Thomas Keneally has also sensed that the sovereign temper of Australian culture—and not only its literary life—is now and has long been melodramatic. A primary example of the grand, unified body of his fiction, of his antipodean *comedie humaine* (human comedy), has been the attempt to comprehend and assuage the spiritual anxieties of Australians. The national melodramatist is also one of the greatest of the storytellers of the nation and the bestower of a vision of its better possibilities. Keneally has long outlasted his local critics while continuing to determine his own imaginative projects, creatively indulging his relish for all the things of the present and past worlds that his fiction might encompass.

References:

Peter Pierce, *Australian Melodramas: Thomas Keneally's Fiction* (St. Lucia: University of Queensland Press, 1995);

Peter Quartermaine, *Thomas Keneally* (London: Edward Arnold, 1991).

Papers:

The papers of Thomas Keneally from 1963 through 1972 are held by the Mitchell Library of the State Library of New South Wales, Sydney; the papers of 1967–1983 are at the National Library of Australia, Canberra.

Peter Kenna

(18 March 1930 – 29 November 1987)

Peter Fitzpatrick
Monash University

BOOKS: *The Slaughter of St. Teresa's Day* (Sydney: Currency Press, 1972; London: Eyre Methuen, 1973);

A Hard God (Sydney: Currency Press, 1974; revised, 1982);

Talk to the Moon; Listen Closely; Trespassers Will Be Prosecuted (Sydney: Currency Press, 1977);

Furtive Love (Sydney: Currency Press, 1980).

PLAY PRODUCTIONS: *The Slaughter of St. Teresa's Day,* Sydney, Elizabethan Theatre, 11 March 1959;

Talk to the Moon, London, Hampstead Theatre Club, 18 October 1963;

Trespassers Will Be Prosecuted, Sydney, Independent Theatre, 2 May 1965;

Muriel's Virtues, Sydney, Independent Theatre, 1966;

Listen Closely, Sydney, Independent Theatre, 10 May 1972;

A Hard God, Sydney, Nimrod Street Theatre, 17 August 1973;

Mates, Sydney, Nimrod Street Theatre, 1 August 1975;

The Cassidy Album (comprises *A Hard God, Furtive Love,* and *An Eager Hope*), Adelaide, Playhouse, 14 and 15 March 1978.

PRODUCED SCRIPTS: *The Emigrants,* television, by Kenna, Brian Phelan, Charles Stamp, and Keith Dewhurst, BBC/ABC, May 1976;

The Good Wife, motion picture, Laughing Kookaburra Productions, 1987.

OTHER: *Mates,* in *Drag Show,* by Kenna and Steve J. Spears (Woollahra, N.S.W.: Currency Press, 1977).

Peter Kenna (courtesy of Nicholas Pounder)

Peter Kenna was one of several Australian playwrights who came to prominence in the wake of the extraordinary success of Ray Lawler's *Summer of the Seventeenth Doll* (1955). Like the plays of Richard Beynon and Alan Seymour, other writers associated with the promising but ultimately disappointing theatrical developments of the late 1950s, Kenna's works followed the pattern that had worked so well for *Summer of the Seventeenth Doll:* tight naturalistic construction, a contemporary and distinctively Australian domestic setting, and a credible and often comic conversational style. After the encouraging response to his first professionally produced play, *The Slaughter of St. Teresa's Day* (1959; published in 1972), Kenna, like Lawler, Beynon, and Seymour, went immediately to England. While Beynon and Seymour moved away from writing for the theater to work in British television—and even Lawler, during and after his long expatriate period, struggled to meet the expectations aroused by his playwriting debut—Kenna returned to Australia to establish himself as a durable and distinctive voice in drama. In his 1978 trilogy *The Cassidy Album* (*A Hard God, Furtive Love,* and *An Eager Hope*) Kenna added to his familiar strengths of solid craftsmanship, lively characterization, and authentic dialogue a readiness to take risks—through experimental structures and the confrontation of difficult themes—that held his place in a repertoire dominated by the playwrights of the "new wave" generation.

Peter Joseph Kenna was born in Balmain, an inner suburb of Sydney, on 18 March 1930, the eleventh of thirteen children born to Agnes Horne Kenna and her carpenter husband, James O'Connor Kenna. Peter attended the Christian Brothers' School in Lewisham, although his precocious talents as a singer and actor meant that performing became the principal focus of his boyhood, particularly after he made his first professional appearance at the age of ten. He toured as a child entertainer with a concert party performing for army servicemen in Sydney during the early years of World War II and left school at fourteen, hoping to find a career in the theater. Throughout the late 1940s Kenna sustained that ambition with a succession of amateur roles and the occasional small paid opportunity as an actor and prop builder with the Genesian and Independent Theatres in Sydney, while making a living variously as a laborer in a pickle factory and a woollen mill, a packer of sheet music, and a window dresser for the department store Mark Foys.

Kenna's first substantial opportunity as an actor came through the vogue for radio serials, which provided a livelihood for most Australian actors during the early 1950s, an unpropitious period for the theater. He had continuing roles through the late 1950s and 1960s in such long-running soap operas as *Life Can Be Beautiful* and *Portia Faces Life*. With the establishment of the Australian Elizabethan Theatre Trust, Kenna was able to return in 1954 to regular work on the professional stage. He appeared as the Messenger in the trust's touring production of Euripides' *Medea*, featuring Dame Judith Anderson in the title role.

Kenna's background in acting was to prove, as it did for Lawler, a valuable preparation. Both writers offered actors developed characters and colorful dialogue; in Kenna's plays, where the dramatic conflict is characteristically realized in contending verbal styles, his work in radio might have exercised a particular, added influence. Like Lawler, too, he achieved prominence as a playwright by winning a national contest, although for Kenna the wait was longer. His twelfth play (but the first to receive a professional production), *The Slaughter of St. Teresa's Day,* won the General Motors-Holden playwrights' competition and opened on 11 March 1959 at the Elizabethan Theatre in the Newtown district of Sydney, in a production directed by Robin Lovejoy.

The context of *The Slaughter of St. Teresa's Day* looks racy enough: it is set in the Woolloomooloo neighborhood, among Sydney's urban criminal classes. Oola Maguire, the matriarchal figure at the center of the drama, has seen and tried everything that might turn a profit, but the capacity of the play to confront the mainstream theater audience was balanced by the whimsical touches of local vernacular in the dialogue and by the essentially feminized proprieties that drive the key interactions. Four shootings certainly constitute a "slaughter," but they occur between acts 2 and 3. The focus of the plot concerns Oola's relationship with her daughter, Thelma, home from school at a convent but keen to return there as a novice, and Oola's attempts to put a veil of suburban refinement over all the unsavory details of her life. The response to the play was favorable enough to lead to a television adaptation in Australia and a second stage production in England within two years. This second production persuaded Kenna to stay on and try his luck in England, where he worked as an actor and also had the second of his performed plays, *Talk to the Moon,* staged at the Hampstead Theatre Club in London in 1963.

Kenna returned to Australia in 1964, but after directing the premiere season of his play *Muriel's Virtues* (subsequently retitled *Animal Grab* for a later production) at Sydney's Independent Theatre in 1966, he went back to England for treatment of a chronic kidney condition that had become progressively worse. The illness severely constrained his work until his return to Australia in 1971, which marked the beginning of a relatively brief period that proved to be the most intensely active and significant in his career as a playwright. In 1972 *Talk to the Moon* received its Australian premiere at St. Martin's Theatre in Melbourne and was broadcast on radio; a new play, *Listen Closely,* was staged at the Independent Theatre in Sydney; and *The Slaughter of St. Teresa's Day* was given a prestigious revival at Sydney's Community Theatre. In the following year *A Hard God* premiered to great acclaim at the Nimrod Street Theatre in Sydney, and Kenna received a major Commonwealth Literature Board grant to develop the second and third parts (then provisionally titled "Unrequited Passions" and "In Captivity") of the trilogy that *A Hard God* was to engender. In 1974 *A Hard God* toured nationally under the aegis of the Australian Theatre Trust, and in 1975 *Mates* had its first performance at the Nimrod Street Theatre. The Cassidy family trilogy was completed with the productions of *Furtive Love* and *An Eager Hope* by the State Theatre Company of South Australia at the Playhouse in Adelaide on successive nights, 14 and 15 March 1978. The premiere of the third part of the trilogy also marked the first performance of *The Cassidy Album* in its entirety.

In the first few years of the 1970s, Kenna's health continued to deteriorate. In 1974 he underwent a kidney transplant, the gift of his favorite sister, Agnes Reid. The

The Slaughter of St. Teresa's Day

Currency Playtexts Series 1, No. 2

A play by Peter Kenna

*Cover for the 1973 paperback edition of Kenna's first professionally
produced play (1959), with a photograph of Gloria Dawn
as Oola Maguire in the 1972 Sydney revival
(Bruccoli Clark Layman Archives)*

operation almost certainly prolonged his life, and perhaps his productivity, but the drugs that were necessary to control the pain and to ensure the effectiveness of the new kidney created their own physical side effects and, as Nick Enright later observed in his obituary of Kenna in *The Sydney Morning Herald* (1 December 1987), "exacerbated the anxieties of a spirit that was already restless and driven."

Throughout this period, perhaps partly in response to the pain and pressure under which he was working, Kenna's plays and the determinant forces in his own life came increasingly into alignment. With the Cassidy trilogy in particular, the poignancy of his own struggle to develop a sense of his identity as an artist and a homosexual within the constrictions of suburban Irish Catholicism became an explicit focus. From the beginning, Kenna's plays had a personal dimension that distinguished his work from the social realism of the playwrights with whom he was first linked at the end of

the 1950s, and from the much less comfortable satirical and political thrust of the "new wave" writers (such as Alex Buzo, Jack Hibberd, David Williamson, and John Romeril) with whom he shared seasons in the subsidized theater of the 1970s. Kenna was the first, and remains the most significant, writer to dramatize the Irish Catholic influence on Australian culture. While several writers have dealt with the social importance of this influence as an agent of political activism and moral conformity, few have matched Kenna's depiction of its power at the individual and familial level.

The Slaughter of St. Teresa's Day, despite its setting in the Sydney underworld and the consequent impression that it comes from the perspective of a fascinated outsider, anticipates the themes that emerge with a more obvious emotional investment in Kenna's later work. Oola may be a spectacular sinner, but she remains a devout one. Her small shrine to St. Teresa is the most distinctive feature of the set. The power of her perversely respectable morality over all the people she deals with is unquestioned, no matter how hardened or homicidal they may be. Oola is the first in a formidable line of matriarchs in Kenna's plays. In criminal circles, as in more respectable ones and in the Catholic Church, men may hold all the nominal trappings of power, but the mother figures in Kenna's works exercise power, by force of will or intellect, where it counts. Thus, the men who are invited to her party on St. Teresa's Day meekly accept her decree that there should be "No grog and ironmongery parked in the hall," and the cosy tastelessness of the decor conforms to feminine stereotype in its profusion of flowers and little ornaments that proclaim, according to a stage direction, "a heart wallowing dangerously in irrepressible nostalgia." The sustained conflicts that occur are those in which Oola tries to protect Thelma from the details of her mother's sordid past and disreputable present, and Oola's Auntie Essie tries to organize her. Men come and go, some die, some leave, but even the loss of her lover, Charlie, is not much more than a sentimental distraction from the enduring issues of Oola's life.

Powerful women control the emotional agenda in most of Kenna's plays. Sometimes their influence is oppressive, as in the case of Florrie Heath in *Talk to the Moon,* Lila Jackson in *Listen Closely,* and Monica and Sophie Cassidy in *A Hard God.* Sometimes it is benign, as with Aggie Cassidy, whose marriage to Dan is the only loving one in Kenna's plays. Aggie, who bears the name of the two women who were most important in the playwright's life—his mother and his sister—has a kind of commonsense saintliness that is at the compassionate heart of *A Hard God.* But the effect of the presence of these strong women is always to shrink their husbands conversationally: Jack Heath in *Talk to the Moon* retreats into savage silence with his crystal set, Jacko Jackson in *Listen Closely* tries to hide, and even Dan's gentle wisdom turns to conciliatory blandness. The men are articulate enough at other times, and Martin Cassidy's philosophizing and Paddy Cassidy's blarney steal the stage in *A Hard God* when their wives are not there. Paddy Maguire, Oola's uncle, presents a virtuoso monologue in *The Slaughter of St. Teresa's Day* that is one of the most sustained examples of Irish performance in the theater–his wife having stayed away from Oola's party on principle. But the chances for the male raconteur to possess the stage in these suburban matriarchies are rare. In the Australian theater of the 1970s, where the coarse humor of the "ocker" male (a rough, uncultivated Australian) was the dominant voice, Kenna's creation of a succession of strong roles for women struck a distinctive note.

Even the most destructive of Kenna's matriarchs are more than simply monstrous caricatures, though. Monica's morbid religiosity and the unseen Sophie's contemptuous self-indulgence seem almost pathological, but the others are partly victims of the largeness of their personalities in conjunction with the narrowness of their spheres. Florrie has nothing on which to impose her formidable intelligence other than the belittling of her husband and the manipulation of her children, and all the women would assent to the grim challenge that Lila defines to her son's hapless girlfriend as woman's timeless obligation: "Somebody's got to win, and for the sake of civilisation it better be us." While the pressure of maternal influence in Kenna's works has all the hallmarks of painful intimate experience, it is presented with elements of understanding and compassion that give a strong impression of having been part of that personal story, too. The sense that terrible things can be survived and forgiven, overlaid by often-explicit retrospection, provides room for the comic dimension that appears in all of Kenna's plays, even in the anguished material of *A Hard God.*

The recurrent battleground in Kenna's works is the conflict between generations; the adult relationships were all fought out years before the action of the plays. The focus of the battle is the sexual maturing of the child and the implications of this process for the child's definition of identity. None of the characters at issue is unusually complex, and few are particularly interesting in themselves. But the decisions that they make or defer are critical to Kenna's most consuming subject, the loss of innocence and the awakening or perversion of passionate feeling.

There is a marked pattern in the presentation of the children in question. Sixteen-year-old Thelma dreams of being a nun and is seduced by the cynical flattery of Horrie Darcel, a ne'er-do-well mate of Charlie's. Shocked by the carnage and deception that she sees on St. Teresa's Day, she is in a state of utter confusion at the

Kenna in 1973 (photograph by Stuart MacGladrie, Sydney Morning Herald; *from the paperback cover for* A Hard God, *1974; Bruccoli Clark Layman Archives)*

end of *The Slaughter of St. Teresa's Day.* Lily Heath, also sixteen, is a tomboy playing children's games at the start of *Talk to the Moon,* becomes infatuated with her older sister's much older boyfriend, and ends up a few months later a pregnant wife whose husband already finds her an encumbrance. Joe Cassidy is a sensitive sixteen-year-old, "intense and desperate to be liked," who finds in his romantic friendship with Jack an obsessive love that runs counter to the teachings of his church and the values of his parents, a love that cannot survive the self-loathing and ambivalence in Jack's feelings.

Leonard Heath at thirteen is an early prototype for Joe, eager to win his mother's judicious approval and forced into behaving secretively. When he furtively lights a cigarette after leaving the house, there is a suggestion of other adolescent choices to come that Florrie would not approve. That issue is not explicit for the schoolboy in the two-actor *Trespassers Will Be Prosecuted* (1965), either, but his dealings with the old man suggest the way in which all his attitudes are provisional and underline his vulnerability. Even in the comedy *Listen Closely* the action turns on sexual rites of passage. Henry Jackson is eighteen and no longer a virgin, but he has much to learn on his eighteenth birthday, caught between Lila's determination that her son should learn none of it and his father, Jacko's, plans for Henry's initiation into manhood by drinking beer until he falls into the

Tony Sheldon as Joe and Andrew Sharp as Jack in the first production of Kenna's A Hard God, *Sydney, 1973 (photograph by Anthony Horler)*

arms of Flora Meadows, the local barmaid who happily introduces all the local lads to the joys of sex. Henry ends the play knowing somewhat more than Kenna's other ingenues but no less confused about what to do with the things he has discovered.

The change in the gender of the character in transition—from the naive girls of Kenna's early plays to the troubled, solitary boys conscious of being different from their peers—reflects the increasingly personal emphasis of the plays. The suppressions, denials, humiliations, and fears that were inescapably part of the experience of growing up gay in a culture that regarded homosexuality not only as an aberration but also as a mortal sin are presented most powerfully and explicitly in the Cassidy family trilogy. The fact that the imaginative material that lay behind *A Hard God* could not be confined to a single play seems in itself an indicator of the strength of the feelings involved.

The question of intimate self-reference in the later plays has become a key issue in critical assessments of the enduring value of Kenna's work. For Katharine Brisbane the assumption that the character of Joe Cassidy is "a portrait of Peter himself" is the premise for an argument that Kenna represents a uniquely brave and unsparing personal voice in Australian theater; autobiographical

candor becomes the measure for a model of theatrical truth. For Bruce Parr, whose reassessment of *The Cassidy Album* in the context of depictions of homosexual love and sex in the Australian theater rests on the analytical representativeness of the trilogy, the personal connection provides a far too convenient way of marginalizing Kenna's vision as another version of histrionic self-indulgence. Baring a troubled soul, from this perspective, guarantees a sequential process of conscientious sympathy and patronizing dismissal.

There is no denying the points of connection, though, and Kenna made no attempt to disguise them. In the course of an Australian Broadcasting Corporation (ABC) radio discussion (14 June 1976) of Ron Blair's *The Christian Brother* (1976), he observed that "You only write two or three plays in your life which you write out of your veins"; Kenna's three constitute the trilogy. He described *A Hard God* as "a tribute to my parents. . . . I hope the play says too: 'Forgive me for not caring earlier.'" The one member of the fictional Cassidy family whose origins did not lie in the factual Kenna family was Sophie, Paddy's murderous wife, who is never seen in the play. Kenna explained that "I did not bring Sophie on because I had never actually met her."

This personal emphasis seems confirmed by Kenna's choices of thematic and emotional focus. The critically controversial split structure of the play, with its dislocation of narrative between Joe's life outside the family home and the relationships among the older generation within it, is symptomatic. But in *A Hard God* he quite deliberately avoids the potential richness of the stereotypical clash between Joe's feelings and his religion. All the pressure in Joe's dialogues with Jack stems from the anxiety of how much to give or withhold of the self, and whether the lover is male or female seems to be presented as largely irrelevant to that process of self-discovery. While the avoidance of cliché is hardly in itself an assurance of personal directness, in this case it does feel as though Kenna shares the urgency of Joe's feelings. The two other plays of the trilogy seem to confirm this impression. Joe is the central character in both, and his progress through adulthood is quite explicitly reminiscent of Kenna's. In *Furtive Love* Joe is a young playwright on tour with the trust; in *An Eager Hope* he is suffering from renal failure, clinging to control of his script until he is finally forced to enter a hospital. The links in the trilogy with Kenna's own life are developed further through the important contributions of his close friend the Sydney actress and cabaret performer Gloria Dawn, who played the role of Oola in the 1972 revival of *The Slaughter of St. Teresa's Day* and Aggie in the premiere season of *A Hard God* in the following year. The roles of Doris the trouper in *Furtive Love* and the elderly Aggie in *An Eager Hope* were written for her, though Dawn's own serious illness prevented her from playing either part; the material about Doris's life as a child performer was heavily indebted to her experiences.

Kenna's productivity during the second half of the 1970s suggested that his sister's gift of a kidney had given him a new lease on life in a creative as well as a literal sense. *Mates,* his witty but poignant piece juxtaposing the drag performer Sylvia with Perce, an Old Australian battler who has struggled to reach success despite a lifetime of disadvantage, was staged in London in 1976, and the playwright's recuperation was sufficiently advanced to enable him to attend the premiere. He began work on several new projects, including the television miniseries *The Emigrants,* which was broadcast as a BBC/ABC coproduction in May 1976. In 1979 Kenna completed a screenplay, "The Umbrella Woman," which was scheduled for filming the following year but was not actually produced until 1987. He started work on a biography of his brother, a tent boxer (a boxer who toured with an itinerant troupe) between the wars. Kenna was elected to the stage subcommittee established in 1979 by the Australian Writers' Guild in order to improve the conditions under which playwrights worked in the theater industry. Most conspicuously, *The Cassidy Album* premiered at the 1978 Adelaide Festival with all the trappings of a great occasion. Like the staging in 1978 of Lawler's *The Doll Trilogy* (*Summer of the Seventeenth Doll, Kid Stakes* [1975], and *Other Times* [1976]), if somewhat more modestly, the event was represented symbolically as marking a coming of age for the Australian theater and as a celebration of the homecoming of a distinguished contributor to its newly discovered history.

These signs of renewed energy and high achievement were partly delusory, however. Kenna's stay in London was cut short by ominous postoperative complications. Two new plays, "Buffalo Grass" and an adaptation of Jules Romains's country farce *Doctor Knock* (1923), were shelved, uncompleted. The biography was abandoned. The filming of "The Umbrella Woman" was delayed and then set aside. When the movie was finally released in February 1987, under the title *The Good Wife,* the distinguished cast (including Rachel Ward, Sam Neill, and Bryan Brown in starring roles) was not enough to impress critics and audiences. The failure of *The Good Wife* was a disappointing preoccupation of Kenna's last months. Even the reception of *The Cassidy Album* in 1978 proved a disappointment. *Furtive Love* and *An Eager Hope* were compared unfavorably with *A Hard God,* and the majority of reviewers found the candor of Kenna's treatment of homosexual relationships problematic. As his health deteriorated throughout the 1980s, it became increasingly improbable that there would be new projects or that old ones would come to completion;

Kenna's response to this situation moved between a bitterly sardonic acceptance and a passionate resistance.

For the last decade of his life Kenna lived in Rozelle, a short distance from the house in which he had grown up. He died on 29 November 1987, and his funeral service was conducted at the Church of St. Augustine in Balmain, where he had been baptized. As these facts suggest, Kenna's homecoming was more specific and profound than is characteristic of the familiar trope of Australian expatriatism. It represented not only a renewed identification with the culture of his country but also a coming to terms with the forces of class, locality, and religious belief that had shaped him. The pattern of Kenna's own choices and the major achievements of his creative career both suggest that his return to his roots was a journey of self-discovery.

Interview:
Suzanne Hayes, *Peter Kenna,* tape recording, Adelaide College of TAFE Educational Media Unit, 1978.

References:
Frank Bladwell, "Peter Kenna's *A Hard God,*" *Southerly,* 39 (1979): 155–171;

Katharine Brisbane, "The Battler, the Larrikin and the Ocker," *Commonwealth Essays and Studies,* 11 (Autumn 1988): 13–21;

Dennis Carroll, *Australian Contemporary Drama, 1909–1982: A Critical Introduction* (New York: Peter Lang, 1985);

Peter Fitzpatrick, *After "The Doll": Australian Drama since 1955* (Melbourne: Edward Arnold, 1979);

Peter Holloway, ed., *Contemporary Australian Drama: Perspectives since 1955* (Sydney: Currency Press, 1981);

John McCallum, "Peter Kenna and the Search for Intimacy," *Meanjin,* 37 (1978): 317–323;

Bruce Parr, "Peter Kenna's *The Cassidy Album:* A Call for Re-viewing," *Australasian Drama Studies,* 24 (April 1994): 77–98;

Elizabeth Webby, *Modern Australian Plays* (South Melbourne: Sydney University Press, 1990).

Papers:
Several of Peter Kenna's plays, all of which predate *The Slaughter of St. Teresa's Day,* have never been published or professionally performed. Nine are extant in manuscript form in the Eunice Hanger Collection, University of Queensland, and the Australian National Library: "A Tiny Shade," "A Place at the Table," "The Littlest Nation," "Miss Rosalie Adorable," "Sixty to Rocky," "The Landladies," "The Fair Sister," "Before the Carnival," and "Burden of Shadows."

C. J. Koch
(16 July 1932 –)

C. A. Cranston
University of Tasmania

BOOKS: *The Boys in the Island* (London: Hamilton, 1958; revised edition, Sydney: Angus & Robertson, 1974; revised again, North Ryde, N.S.W.: Angus & Robertson, 1987);

Across the Sea Wall (London: Heinemann, 1965; revised edition, London & Sydney: Angus & Robertson, 1982; revised again, Sydney: Angus & Robertson, 1990);

The Year of Living Dangerously (London: Joseph, 1978; West Melbourne: Thomas Nelson, 1978; New York: St. Martin's Press, 1979);

Chinese Journey, by Koch and Nicholas Hasluck (Fremantle, N.S.W.: Fremantle Arts Centre Press, 1985);

The Doubleman (London: Chatto & Windus, 1985; New York: McGraw-Hill, 1986; revised edition, Pymble, N.S.W.: Angus & Robertson, 1992; London: Vintage, 1996);

Crossing the Gap: A Novelist's Essays (London: Chatto & Windus, 1987; Pymble, N.S.W.: Angus & Robertson, 1993); republished as *Crossing the Gap: Memories and Reflections* (Milson's Point, N.S.W.: Vintage, 2000);

Highways to a War (Port Melbourne, Vic.: Heinemann, 1995; London: Heinemann, 1995; New York: Viking, 1995);

Out of Ireland: Volume Two of Beware of the Past (Sydney: Doubleday, 1999);

The Many-Coloured Land: A Return to Ireland (Sydney: Pan Macmillan, 2002; London: Picador, 2003).

PRODUCED SCRIPT: *The Year of Living Dangerously*, motion picture, by Koch, Peter Weir, and David Williamson, M-G-M, 1982.

OTHER: "Shelly Beach," in *The Penguin Book of Australian Verse* (Harmondsworth, U.K.: Penguin, 1958), pp. 292–293;

"Grand Trunk Express," in *Modern Australian Writing*, edited by Geoffrey Dutton (London: Collins, 1966), pp. 289–296;

C. J. Koch (photograph by Jerry Bauer; from the cover of the U.S. edition of Highways to a War, *1995; Richland County Public Library)*

"The Radio Men," extract from *The Doubleman*, in *The Oxford Anthology of Australian Literature*, edited by Leonie Kramer and Adrian Mitchell (Melbourne: Oxford University Press, 1985), pp. 474–482;

"The Lost Child," extract from *The Boys in the Island*, in *The Macmillan Anthology of Australian Literature*, edited by Ken Goodwin and Alan Lawson (South Melbourne: Macmillan, 1990), pp. 555–557;

"Maybe It's Because I'm a Londoner," from *Crossing the Gap*; retitled "London, Late 1950s," in *Changing Places: Australian Writers in Europe*, edited by Laurie Hergenhan and Irmtraud Petersson (St. Lucia: University of Queensland Press, 1994), pp. 164–170;

"Shelly Beach" and "The Boy Who Dreamed the Country Night," in *The New Oxford Book of Australian Verse,* edited by Les Murray (Oxford: Oxford University Press, 1996), pp. 271–273.

SELECTED PERIODICAL PUBLICATIONS–UNCOLLECTED: "Half-Heard," *Bulletin* (10 January 1951): 4;

"Lutana Rise," *Bulletin* (22 August 1951): 12;

"Tides in Tasmania," *Bulletin* (28 April 1952): 12;

"Winter Midday," *Bulletin* (25 June 1952): 17;

"Saturday Songs: Morning," and "Saturday Songs: Noon-Day," *Bulletin* (3 December 1952): 12;

"Song for the Country Girl," *Bulletin* (26 May 1954): 13;

"The Name," *Southerly,* 18, no. 3 (1957): 153–154;

"Love Present, Love Past," *Southerly,* 19, no. 2 (1958): 81–82;

"The De Facto Wife," *Southerly,* 20, no. 2 (1959): 86.

C. J. Koch began writing poetry, then novels. Koch sees the novel as an evolution of the narrative poem–providing scope yet retaining myth, metaphor, symbolic patterns, and, as he said in "The Novel as Narrative Poem" (*Crossing the Gap: A Novelist's Essays,* 1987), presenting a "landscape of experience; the full nature of the soul's journey." In this belief he was compared with Patrick White and Randolph Stow and the move away from bush realism. Koch cites Graham Greene and the notion that "writers draw constantly on childhood, even when they are not writing about it." A general thematic concern is with spiritual health in an unpredictable world, in which "devotion to illusion and obsession with the past" lead to psychic ill health. Protagonists experience physical and cultural disinheritance as a consequence of a colonial heritage in which bodies inhabit landscapes out of keeping with the cultural myths that feed the mind. A Catholic nonpracticing believer, Koch credits Catholicism with creating an ambiguous predisposition to explore mystical "Other worlds," primarily fairyland. Part of the emotional maturity of his male characters lies in their capacity to access spiritual health and express compassion for flawed individuals. Dualistic aspects of the divided self, along with the idea that white Australians are inheritors of European, Greco-Roman, and Asian ancestral myths, are evident in his second novel, *Across the Sea Wall* (1965), and inform subsequent novels.

Koch's major characters are predominantly male and middle-class, bent on escape to somewhere. Each is psychically split, and each, knowingly or unknowingly, experiences a moral disequilibrium between the dualities of the dark and the light sides of being–illusion and reality. A major motif is doubleness. Duality is embod-ied in the relationship between character pairs and the split protagonist. Koch's Irish background gives expression to this duality through the Celtic myths of the shadowy double man; his German background provides a literary parallel in the doppelgänger. "History is a story, and we are in that story," says Koch, signaling the interplay between fact and form that emerges in later novels. Geography, too, is a shaping power in personality, and Koch's birthplace, Tasmania, provides the setting for many of his works as well as an aspect of doubleness. Geography and history intersect in the dual naming of the island (Van Diemen's Land, then Tasmania) and in its dual construction as penal colony and paradise.

Christopher John Koch was born in Hobart, Tasmania, on 16 July 1932, and now lives in Sydney, New South Wales. A fifth-generation Australian, Koch is of German, Irish, and English descent. His great-great-grandmother, Jane Devereux, an Anglo-Irish woman from County Clare, migrated to Van Diemen's Land in the 1840s. Another great-great-grandmother, Margaret O'Meara, was transported from Tipperary to the penal colony in 1845. (Their stories are told in *The Many-Coloured Land,* 2002.) Koch's great-grandfather, Johann Koch, was a Lutheran and the architect for some of the noted public and private buildings in Melbourne; Koch's grandfather moved to Tasmania and became Hobart city architect. Koch's father, John Athol Burton Koch, was an Anglican and an accountant, and his Catholic mother, Phyllis Myra (Hurburgh) Koch, was the great-granddaughter of Captain James Hurburgh, who settled in Van Diemen's Land in 1837. Koch's brother, Philip, was born in 1935, and his sister, Susan, in 1945. The family lived at 1A Bay Road, Newtown, until 1945, when John Koch built a house at 192 Lenah Valley Road. Koch attended Clemes College, Hobart, a Quaker school that his father and uncle once attended. His uncle, Gordon Hurburgh, served in the AIF on the Kokoda Trail, New Guinea, during World War II. The young Koch spent summers on the "Hermitage," a hops farm run by relatives, at Molesworth in the Derwent Valley. The farm is portrayed as "Clare" in *Highways to a War* (1995) and *Out of Ireland: Volume Two of Beware of the Past* (1999). Koch spent much of his childhood at his grandfather's house, 15 Stoke Street, which provides the setting for the Miller house in *The Doubleman* (1985). Clemes College introduced Koch to Lewis Carroll's *Alice's Adventures in Wonderland* (1865) and Rudyard Kipling's *The Jungle Book* (1894), beginning Koch's preoccupation with Other worlds and colonization. At eight, Koch began drawing cartoons in the hopes of becoming a comic-strip artist. He spent six months at Bowen Road State School before moving to St. Virgil's Christian Brothers' College. At twelve, when he contracted measles, his father read Kipling's *Kim* (1901) to him, deepening the literary image of India and the Raj that later frames the journey for characters in *Across the Sea Wall.*

In 1941 Koch experienced World War II through radio and the boy's paper *Chums,* which he read at age nine. The literary world of Thomas Hardy, Kenneth Grahame, Charles Dickens, and Beatrix Potter created an imaginary and unattainable "Home," as colonial Australians called England. Koch could only know colonial England as history and geography at "second-hand," a word he uses to indicate the unachievable world longed for by the disinherited mind.

At fourteen, Koch left St. Virgil's and entered Hobart State High School, where he failed most subjects except English and history. At fifteen he went to work at Fuller's Bookshop ("Varley's Bookshop" in *The Doubleman*). There he discovered the works of James Joyce, Fyodor Dostoevsky, D. H. Lawrence, and Thomas Wolfe. He read *Tonio Kröger* (1902) by Nobel laureate Thomas Mann and was drawn to the relationship between the middle-class outsider figure and the spiritual. His interest in reading, rather than selling, books cost him his job, and he apprenticed as a press artist and cartoonist to the Hobart *Mercury.*

At sixteen he declared himself a writer and an agnostic, a move that warranted a fruitless home visit from the dean of Hobart. Speaking of his feelings at this time, Koch says, "The feelings of that age are not just about girls—for me, anyway, the discovery of nature was just as intense." The comment links two central preoccupations: the idealization of the female and the idealization of the land. Both female and place become sites for discovery and knowledge in a coming-of-age for male characters, or what Michael Hulse calls "a fiction of initiation." Koch became interested in drinking and the turf culture, saying a bookie's winnings enabled his return to Hobart State High School to complete his leaving and matriculation years.

At Hobart High School he met Neil Davis, one of the models for the character Mike Langford in *Highways to a War.* He and school friend Vivian Smith were inspired by John Keats and William Wordsworth and began writing verse. In 1951 Koch published "Half-Heard" and "Lutana Rise" in *The Bulletin,* which was then under the editorship of Douglas Stewart. That same year he enrolled at the University of Tasmania and became an unwitting focus of attention when a proposal to relax matriculation standards polarized parties. The issue was whether or not Koch satisfied requirements. The chancellor, Sir John Morris, faced criticism for intervening on Koch's behalf. Koch continued to attract attention as a self-styled anarchist, disliking royalists and the then Australian prime minister, Robert

Menzies. Koch was part of an anarchist group including fellow writer James McQueen that disrupted a session of the Tasmanian Parliament. McQueen strung up an effigy in protest against Queen Elizabeth's visit in 1952. That year in *The Bulletin,* Koch published "Winter Midday," "Saturday Songs: Morning," "Saturday Songs: Noon-Day," and "Tides in Tasmania" and contributed poetry to the University of Tasmania literary magazine, *Platypus,* which he and Vivian Smith edited. In 1954 Koch published "Song for the Country Girl" and "The Boy Who Dreamed the Country Night" in *The Bulletin.* Koch graduated with a bachelor of arts (honors) degree that same year. He claims that his political activities earned him an Australian Security Intelligence Organisation (ASIO) file and admits being interested briefly in the Australian Communist Party, until youthful idealism was challenged by his reading and by the experience of meeting postwar European refugees from satellite countries of the Soviet Union.

In 1955 Koch sailed to England aboard the *Surriento,* a refitted American Liberty ship. Accompanied by Robert Brain, he left from Melbourne, stopped at Jakarta, and then Colombo, where he, Brain, and a Sikh friend traveled from Ceylon to the Himalayas and as second-class passengers on the Grand Trunk Express from Madras to New Delhi. Koch's experience as a sahib in a country bearing strong echoes of its colonial masters provides the background for his second novel, *Across the Sea Wall.* The geographical experience was supplemented by Koch's reading the Bhagavad Gita (circa second to fifth centuries B.C.) back onboard ship. Koch and Brain disembarked at Genoa, hitchhiking through Italy, Germany, Greece, Holland, and then London. Koch's literary illusion of Home as a "kingdom of Faery" in "Maybe It's Because I'm a Londoner" (*Crossing the Gap*) was once again tempered by experience as he encountered a war-damaged Britain. Koch lived in London for two years, busing tables at a Lyons Corner House while living in a bed-sitter in Ladbroke Square, Notting Hill Gate. He returned to London and addressed envelopes at the Hearts of Oak insurance agency, took a clerical job at Broken Hill Proprietary (BHP), taught school, and completed the manuscript for his first novel, *The Boys in the Island* (1958).

In 1957 Australian citizens were considered British subjects under the Commonwealth system. Koch received National Service call-up papers. He returned to Australia and joined the Australian Broadcasting Corporation (ABC) in Sydney as a radio producer in Schools Broadcasts. The ABC employed Koch despite being advised by ASIO that he was a supposed radical, based on his university exploits. That year "The Name" appeared in *Southerly,* followed by "Love Present, Love Past" in 1958. "Shelly Beach" was anthologized in *The Penguin Book of Australian Verse* (1958), co-edited by poet Kenneth Slessor, who became an advocate of Koch's work. Koch began reviewing the work of fellow Australian writers. In 1958 *Southerly* published "Nineteenth-Century Ghosts," a review of *Sandy's Selection & Back at Our Selection* (1904, 1906) by "Steel Rudd" (Arthur Hoey Davis), and "Marxist Variety," a review of Frederick Bert Vickers's *Though Poppies Grow* (1958).

Although Koch began by writing verse, he always wanted to be a novelist. His first novel, *The Boys in the Island,* began as a cycle of prose poems. (A fragment appeared in *The Bulletin* as "The Boy Who Dreamed the Country Night.") In this roman à clef, Koch's preoccupation with the power of illusion to prescript life is signaled in the epigraph from Keats: "Only the dreamer venoms all his days" (from *The Fall of Hyperion: A Dream,* 1819). Protagonist and narrator Francis Cullen seeks love and adventure in an attempt to escape the physical and metaphysical isolation that is a consequence of his colonial heritage, in which bodies inhabit a geography and climate out of keeping with northern cultural myths that feed the temperament of the mind. The setting, Hobart during World War II, provides the framework for the battle common to Koch's characters, which is the illusion that life happens elsewhere. Cullen (nicknamed "Dreamy") finds himself repeating his final school year. Koch's protagonists are slow learners, repeating tasks and mistakes, and sentenced to utterances within syntaxes constructed by the British Empire. Cullen's private utterances (as opposed to the public utterances of later characters, who are journalists of one sort or another) reveal Edenic readings of suburban landscapes, such as Lutana Rise, which Cullen imagines as "the edge of a dream-country." This invention proves unsustainable when Cullen steps into his own narrative construction of Lutana Rise. He is confronted with the sour reality of the landscape and of his sweetheart, Heather Miles. Cullen's narrative path (or knowledge of adulthood and sexuality) becomes a series of experiential shocks in which illusion comes hard up against reality. Driven by boredom, beneath which lies an undercurrent of violence–"the boy was waiting for everything to happen: an event of love and adventure, hidden like a bomb in certain streets, or beyond the blue barrier of the hills to the east"–Cullen escapes to the mainland, which he imagines as the Otherland. Koch's use of the term signifies "a region of the imagination that doesn't exist in the world," as described by Hulse (*Quadrant,* June 1985). The myth of "Melbourne" is destroyed as Cullen confronts the bitter irony of the illusion that life happens elsewhere. After the suicide of his friend Shane Noonan (whose dream of adventure is the Otherland of Sydney) and after a car

Paperback cover for the 1987 Australian edition of Koch's first novel, written in 1958 (Bruccoli Clark Layman Archives)

wreck in which another friend dies, Cullen rejects the tedium exemplified by his criminal-underworld suburban friends, who hunt and feed on the weak. He returns to the island. Though the book was reviewed unenthusiastically in London by *The Times Literary Supplement* (23 January 1959), the review was sensitive to its thematic concerns, such as the conflict between expectations and experience, and disillusionment with females and place, ideas more fully developed in later novels.

In 1959 Koch, having left ABC, worked at the State Archives of Tasmania for eight months, continuing to write poetry and reviews. In 1960 Koch and Stow won a Writing Fellowship to Stanford University in California. (Stow did not go.) Also in 1960, Koch married Irene Vilnonis, a Lithuanian pianist who had fled with her parents in June 1941 after the fall of the Baltic to the U.S.S.R. The Koches moved to Nob Hill, San Francisco, that autumn. Koch studied under critic and Viking Press editor Malcolm Cowley, who encouraged Koch's work in progress, *Across the Sea Wall.* The book was offered to Viking Press but rejected, signaling the last time Koch attempted to produce a work quickly. Frank O'Connor (Michael Francis O'Donovan) also taught the class, which included counterculture writers Ken Kesey, Gurney Norman, Larry McMurtry, and fantasy writer Peter S. Beagle. Kesey's parties at Perry Lane, Palo Alto, introduced the Koches to folk revival, drug culture, and the sexual revolution. At this time, at the age of twenty-eight, Koch returned to Catholicism after rereading the New Testament "like a novel," as he said in *The Age* (14 June 1986). He experienced Catholicism as a culture infused with a mystical system and spirituality that was being replaced by a pastiche of beliefs proposed by charismatic leaders. He cites the Jonestown (Guyana) deaths and Charles Manson murders as examples of spiritual ideologies gone wrong.

At the close of the 1960–1961 period at Stanford, Koch and his wife traveled to Milan, Italy, where their son Gareth was born in 1962. Koch taught English and completed *Across the Sea Wall*. The family returned to Australia in 1962, where Koch rejoined ABC educational radio, Sydney, staying for ten years.

In 1965 Koch published his second novel, *Across the Sea Wall* (revised in 1982). One of the first Australian nonwar fictions with Asia rather than Europe as its subject, the book demonstrates Koch's increasing interest in Australia-Asia relationships. The 1965 edition includes a first-person narrative in two parts ("The Wake" and "Over the North") and an epilogue ("The Unseen"). In concert with Koch's contention that life is a series of recurring historical events, the journey in the novel is patterned on his trip with Brain in 1955 and his reading of the journey in Kipling's *Kim*.

The narrator is twenty-nine-year-old Robert O'Brien, a Sydney clerk tempted by Jimmy Baden to choose the adventure of sailing to Europe over the responsibility of marriage. The journey is a rite of passage (as a geographical destination and as a path to sexual maturity) that O'Brien does not complete. Onboard the *Napoli,* a refitted troopship, the only battle the ship's crew witnesses is the war for ownership over the Latvian dancer Ilsa Kalnins. O'Brien is unable to cope with Ilsa's history, which includes the abandonment of her baby. He is confronted by Ilsa's manager, a homosexual named Michael Maleter, who accuses O'Brien of being unable to comprehend pain and suffering as experienced by Europeans during the war. He links O'Brien's naiveté to the geographical and historical context of Australia. He also accuses O'Brien of not understanding his own sexual orientation. The group disembark in India. O'Brien, a white male in an economically underdeveloped country, uses Ilsa's ambiguous, hermaphroditic body as a site for adventure and experience while he continues to misread Ilsa, Asia, and himself. Women and place, myth and reality fuse in

Ilsa's adoption of the dualistic goddess Kali as her talisman. Like India, Ilsa is foreign territory, and O'Brien retreats to Australia. When the couple meet in Sydney two years later, O'Brien, now a journalist, is again unable to make a commitment. Like Cullen, O'Brien exists as an embryonic character still too immature to sustain shocks that threaten his illusions. His conceptual immaturity is spelled out: he feels as though "he was walking like a child through a half-comprehended book."

In preparation for the novel, Koch reread the Bhagavad Gita, developing an interest in Hinduism and the Indo-European tradition. His reading of the work of Heinrich Zimmer, a scholar in Sanskrit and Tantric works, led him to the works of Joseph Campbell and Carl Gustav Jung. Together they provide a language describing such Western psychological concepts as archetypes, shadows, and dualism, which are rendered variously in Eastern mythology. Koch found Western rational explanations for the existence of dark forces, such as Manichaeism and Gnosticism, inadequate. He read the works of Sri Ramakrishna, a poet and devotee of the Hindu goddess Kali. She becomes a metaphor for the dual image of woman and land as nurturing and destructive forces beyond morality. Her existence as a primordial force in a living culture provides Koch with a mythology he describes in "Crossing the Gap" (*Crossing the Gap*, 1987) as "more rewarding than anything in the Greco-Roman pantheon." He studied Tantrism and read a book by Nirad C. Chaudhuri, who in *The Autobiography of an Unknown Indian* (1951) writes about cultural exile as a result of colonial aftermath. Koch's novel demonstrates a growing consciousness of links between Australia and Asia and explores the need to incorporate myths by which to interpret Australia. Although reviewed favorably in Australia by Slessor, the novel was better received in England, where the reviewer for *The Manchester Guardian Weekly* (11 March 1965) commented on the national preoccupation with identity in "the strange spirited geography of the subcontinent." A year later Koch published "Grand Trunk Express" (*Modern Australian Writing*), an extract from *Across the Sea Wall*, chapter 2, part 2.

In 1968 Koch was released from the ABC to UNESCO to advise on the introduction of educational broadcasting in Indonesia. He was drawn to Indonesia, which he describes in "Crossing the Gap" as a former colony "not just of Holland, but culturally of India and Arabia. Like Australia, it's in certain ways a country of second-hand." In Jakarta, President Sukarno was under house arrest following the attempted coup by and subsequent overthrow of the Partai Kommunist Indonesia on 30 September 1965. Koch's brother, Philip, was a correspondent in Jakarta during the coup and was

"No kingdom on earth can equal this one, which is the Gate of the World. Its countless islands, from the Moluccas to northern Sumatra, shield it from the storms of the Indian Ocean and the South China Sea. Active volcanoes form its spine, and Vishnu, its guardian god, protects it from all harm. Its children are more numerous, its women more beautiful, its soil more fertile: foreigners covet it. And most favored of all is Java...

"President Sukarno, Vishnu's incarnation, tells us in his speeches that Java's spirit is the terrible volcano Merapi, which seems to sleep, but is always ready to explode in violence."

In 1965, THE YEAR OF LIVING DANGER-OUSLY, Java's violent spirit finally erupted. And for a small group of Western newsmen, a desperate ordeal had begun.

ISBN 0-312-89623-9

The Year of Living Dangerously
C.J. Koch

The Year of Living Dangerously
A novel by C.J. Koch

St. Martin's

Dust jacket for the 1979 U.S. edition of Koch's 1978 novel, set in Indonesia during 1965
(Richland County Public Library)

placed under arrest at the presidential palace. He provided Koch with advice on the lives of correspondents in Indonesia at that time. The events provide the impetus for Koch's third novel, *The Year of Living Dangerously* (1978), in which Indonesia provides the setting, and Philip provides a model for Guy Hamilton. Koch left the ABC in 1972, returned to Tasmania to resume writing, and taught history and English for the university through adult education. The revised edition of *The Boys in the Island* was published in 1974. Koch left for Europe, Germany, and England in 1975 and 1976, where he completed *The Year of Living Dangerously*. The family returned to Hill Street, Launceston, in 1976. An extract, "The Wayang Show," appeared in *Quadrant* in October 1977. The *wayang kulit* (Javanese shadow-puppet plays) provides the literary architecture on which Koch explores the shadows and substances embedded in postcolonial societies. The form facilitates the correspondences between Asian and European myth and the shadows and archetypes of Jungian psychology. References to the Bhagavad Gita, the Mahabharatha, and the Bible evoke a multiplicity of myths and recurrent patterns in Indian, Indonesian, and Christian beliefs.

The Year of Living Dangerously fuses art (the *wayang kulit*) and history (Jakarta under Sukarno). The title derives from Sukarno's prophetic naming of 1965 as "A year of living dangerously" ("Tahun vivere pericoloso") during his Independence Day speech. The symbolic tension between the *wayang* of the Left and the *wayang* of the Right is frequently employed as a parable in Indonesian politics, and in the novel the politics of Marxism and Islam find expression in the aesthetics of left and right tensions. The *wayang* provides an extended metaphor of lives enacting eternal struggles within repeating patterns that are brought to life by a puppeteer—whether literary, political, or religious. Koch states in the title essay in *Crossing the Gap* that the concern of the book is to portray "a man of double nature: a man between cultures and beliefs." Since he is both Hindu and Muslim, aristocratic and socialist, Sukarno is a man of dualities; Hamilton, born in Singapore, is English Australian; his cameraman, Billy Kwan, is Chinese Australian. The concern for image and reality is expressed through their occupation, which is to transform the Indonesian struggle into images, or a motion picture. Kwan, an achondroplastic dwarf, experiences disillusionment with his split protagonist, Hamilton, described as a "giant" and a "knight." Attitudes toward Asia are reflected in commitment to women. Hamilton is slow to learn in his relationship with Jill Bryant, a British embassy secretary, pregnant with their child, whose confidentiality he betrays in the interest of his career. Hamilton's capacity to exploit is magnified in journalist characters such as the pedophile Wally O'Sullivan. Kwan demonstrates moral maturity in his actions toward the beggar Ibu ("mother" in Indonesian) and her child. His fateful ideological restlessness leads him from established belief systems to his final illusion that the charismatic flesh-and-blood Sukarno is a savior of the people. After Kwan's suicidal protest against Sukarno, the narrator, a journalist named Cookie ("R.J.C."), retrieves Kwan's memoirs and reconstructs the narrative. The conceit of finding documents that purport to be fact, the interweaving of public and private histories, and the device of the bystander narrator living vicariously through the stories of others, compound the distinction between illusion and reality. The pattern repeats in *Highways to a War* in 1995 and *Out of Ireland* in 1999, novels also concerned with political ideology and the heroic lost cause. The central character's masculine and cultural maturation is more developed in this novel. Hamilton's final reading of the female is less censorious than earlier, and he is more accepting of the human flaws that constitute the shadow in art and politics *(wayang)*, myth and women (Kali), and Jungian psychology. Hamilton's comment that "Europe would never be his. He would always be a temporary resident; in the end, the other hemisphere would claim him" indicates his weakening enthrallment with the image of England and Europe and a shift toward identifying inevitably with his own geographical place.

The reception at home and abroad was positive. In 1978 the novel won *The Age* (Melbourne) Book of the Year Award; and in 1979, the National Book Council Award for Australian Literature. In 1982 M-G-M produced a movie based on the novel. The novel began as "The Dwarf of Melbourne" but was discarded except for the character of Billy Kwan.

Koch served on the Literature Board of the Australia Council in 1980 and left Tasmania for Sydney. Both provide settings for his fourth novel, *The Doubleman,* published in 1985. An extract, "The Radio Men," appeared in *The Bulletin* and was anthologized in *The Oxford Anthology of Australian Literature* (1985). Koch was invited to Writers' Week, Adelaide, and his talk was published in *The Tasmanian Review* (1980) as "Literature and Cultural Identity: An Australian Writer Speaks." The article articulates a change from identifying with Australian culture as rooted in a European source to an assertion that it is "fundamentally different." Koch defends his original position as in part generational and

geographical; his generation of Australians were considered British subjects, and the island state of Tasmania duplicated aspects of a second England climatically apart from the Australian continent. His term "a pathos of absence" describes a consciousness disenfranchised from the landscape.

Koch and Nicholas Hasluck visited China in 1981 as part of the first official delegation of Australian writers to enter China. On the invitation of the Chinese Writers' Association, the two traveled from Hong Kong to Peking, Shanghai, Hefei, and Hangzhou. They met writers and translators jailed by the Red Guards during the Cultural Revolution, who formed part of the "Literature of the Wounded," a subgenre dealing with suffering under the Gang of Four. The trip resulted in Koch's "Report on a Proposal that the Federal Government Assist Australian Publishers to Market Books in Asia" (*Quadrant,* November 1982).

In the January-February 1981 issue of *Quadrant,* Koch published the essay "Crossing the Gap: Asia and the Australian Imagination," the title used for his essay collection published in 1987. The 1982 revised edition of *Across the Sea Wall* appeared, recast as a third-person narrative and divided into two parts, "The Wake" and "Everything for Nothing." Koch was also writing the screenplay for *The Year of Living Dangerously.* Scriptwriter Alan Sharp was dismissed from the project, which was completed by Koch, Peter Weir, and David Williamson. The screenplay was nominated for an Academy Award. Koch and his wife divorced in 1982 after twenty-two years of marriage.

Chinese Journey, a result of the 1981 China trip, was published in 1985. A type of travel narrative, Hasluck writes verse and Koch writes prose. Koch's section, "The Secret Bird: A Journey to Chairman Mao's China," explores the dualities wrought by minds and masks, which manifest themselves in his portrayal of two cities: Hong Kong, produced by "wicked" Westerners "wearing a Chinese mask," and Peking (and the People's Republic), perceived as a land of lost rural virtues in the "unhurried world of the late Middle Ages."

In 1985 Koch's "most Catholic book," *The Doubleman,* was published. Originally to have been titled "The Folksingers," this bildungsroman is set in post–World War II Tasmania and Sydney in the 1960s. The doppelgänger motif is explicit in the title, and characters shadow other characters. Richard Miller (Müller) narrates. His double name disguises his German origins. Crippled by polio, the Catholic boy's solitariness draws him into the world of art and illusion as he plays the puppeteer with a miniature puppet theater. In Hobart he meets the satanic Clive Broderick, the force behind what eventually became the Rymers, a successful folk-music group that has the power to enthrall its listeners. The group includes Miller's cousin Brian Brady and Patrick, the stepson of Deirdre Dillon—portrayed as a Catholic-Kali-Titania-Dianne figure with whom Miller is enthralled. Miller's wife, Katrin Vilde, is the singer. Katrin's status as a divorced, Estonian Displaced Person, with a quadriplegic son, reflects the profound experiential suffering of Koch's European characters in general. As a radio producer, Miller controls artistic processes and constructs the frames within which artists move but comes under threat when the group's proposed trip overseas means the possible loss of his wife to band member Darcy Burr. Burr is a Gnostic and occultist and Miller's split protagonist. Both embody the confrontation between the dualism of Augustine (in which good and evil inhabit each person) and Manichaean dualism. Once again, history and story fuse. The group is named after Thomas Rymer, a thirteenth-century poet, prophet, and historical figure said to have gained powers of prophecy from the queen of Elfland. Koch expands these ideas to include aspects of the occult, Gnosticism, and traditional Christianity. The novel closes with Miller stoned and yet able to break the hold of the dreamy Other world through the aid of Catholicism and a return to psychic health. For his subject matter Koch draws on his experience of the Stanford drug culture, his knowledge of folksingers recorded at the ABC, conversations with Keith Potger of the Seekers, and his own and his family's musical interests. Extracts were published in *The Bulletin, Mode, The Age Monthly Review, Northern Perspective,* and *Good Housekeeping* (U.K.), and as "The Bards" in *Quadrant* (April 1985). The framework pattern is signaled by the epigraph from the Scottish ballad "Tam Lin." The ballad is commensurate with the musical subject of the novel and provides an opportunity to experiment with language and lyric.

Between publications, Koch communicated with Tom Thompson of Angus and Robertson publishers on a series of literary plaques commemorating Australian writers; Koch was instrumental in saving Slessor's house (18A Billyard Avenue, Sydney) from developers. In 1986 Koch attended a conference on Asian and Australian literature at the University of Singapore on the invitation of Kirpal Singh. Singh had presented on Koch's work the year before at the Association for the Study of Australian Literature conference.

In 1987 *Crossing the Gap: A Novelist's Essays* was short-listed in Britain for the Hawthornden Prize. The eponymous essay, "Crossing the Gap" (first published in *Quadrant,* 1981), discusses influences behind *Across the Sea Wall* and *The Year of Living Dangerously.* Koch comments that "Culture is a story, and we belong to the Indo-European story." The essay demonstrates Koch's

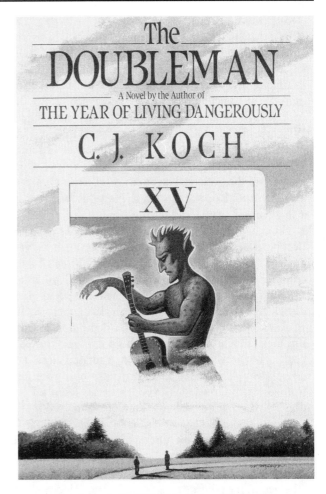

Dust jacket for the 1986 U.S. edition of Koch's 1985 novel, about a successful folk-singing group (Richland County Public Library)

interest in Hindu mythology after traveling through India in 1955. "Maybe It's Because I'm a Londoner" discusses the literature that informed Koch's initial perception then of the experience of London in 1955–1957. "California Dreaming: Hermann Hesse and the Great God Pot" concerns Koch's year at Stanford University Writing Center, 1960–1961. "The Last Novelist" examines the literary relationship between F. Scott Fitzgerald and Ernest Hemingway, stressing that Fitzgerald's superiority lies in his decency as well as in his craft; "Return to Hobart Town" reflects on a changing city. "The Lost Hemisphere" appears in altered form in *The Doubleman.* In it Koch addresses his changing attitudes regarding Australian and European cultural differences by looking at the "double strand of the European past and the Australian present" in the work of poets Les Murray, Geoffrey Lehmann, and Vivian Smith; "A Tasmanian Tone" places the beginning of quality Tasmanian writing with Young Irelander John Mitchel's *Jail Journal*

(1854); Marcus Clarke's *For the Term of His Natural Life* (1874); McQueen's "Night Run" (*Quadrant,* February 1977); and Hal Porter's *The Tilted Cross* (1961). "Mysteries" discusses the difficulties of writing as a Christian in a contemporary society preoccupied with materialistic rationalism. Koch traces New Age mysticism to the American West Coast and to his contemporaries Colin Wilson and Carlos Castaneda. Finally, "The Novel as Narrative Poem" discusses the influence of Thomas Wolfe and makes a case for the novel at a time when movies are the preferred medium.

In 1988 Koch began *Out of Ireland*. Envisioned as a single novel that would include the future *Highways to a War* and would span two centuries, it draws together European and Tasmanian narratives. Koch, however, put *Out of Ireland* aside, moved to Alfred Street, Launceston, in 1990, and began the Tasmanian-Cambodian novel *Highways to a War*. That year he received an Hon. Litt.D. from the University of Tasmania. *Across the Sea Wall* was republished and carried a dedication to Slessor, the man who supported Koch's poetry and this particular novel early in Koch's career. A revised edition of *The Doubleman* appeared in 1992 with a note of praise from Graham Greene. "Maybe It's Because I'm a Londoner" was reproduced as "London, Late 1950s" in *Changing Places: Australian Writers in Europe* (1994). In 1995 Koch received the Order of Australia (AO). He returned to Sydney to live.

That same year *Highways to a War* was published. The action moves from post–World War II and childhood gunplay in the hop fields of Tasmania, to the Vietnam and Cambodian Wars. The central character is Mike "The Lucky One" Langford, a Tasmanian who becomes a correspondent in Cambodia. His identification with the Cambodian struggle demonstrates absolute commitment to an idea that leads him to his death. Langford epitomizes character engagement with an Otherland of myth and mystery while confronting the political terror of "the others," the Viet Cong. The frame narrator, Ray Barton, is a solicitor and Langdon's boarding-school friend. Like Cookie, Barton lives vicariously, sifting through archival documents and reassembling the life of the central character. Koch's preoccupation with the merging of history and story is evident in his utilization of incidents from the life histories of Tasmanian schoolfriend Neil Davis, a combat photographer in Southeast Asia; the son of Tasmanian Errol Flynn, Sean Flynn, an actor turned freelance journalist, who disappeared in Cambodia; and British-born American war correspondent and photographer Tim Page. The Langford character is one of many who must either endure the tedium (a living death) of island life or escape and seek stimulation by seeing action (a euphemism for war and sex). The doubleness of Van Die-

men's Land–the name-changing of the island to Tasmania–signals its escape into illusion, where past atrocities remain unacknowledged. Similarly, Cambodia becomes "Kampuchea," and in 1975 the Khmer Rouge attempts erasure by restarting the world at Year Zero. Both places admit only half the story. ("Half" is a dominant modifier in Koch's work.) As Koch's oeuvre grows, male characters increasingly break through the illusion of the female; the journey is repeated but compressed in this novel, in which Langford's relationships with the Other (land and female) is completed when he returns to Cambodia to rescue Ly Keang, an embodiment of old Cambodia prior to its fall to the Khmer Rouge. Langford's crucifixion is a perversion of Catholic cosmology and a merging into legend that demonstrates Koch's interest in the "figure that undergoes apotheosis." The novel won the Miles Franklin Award in 1996.

The academic community did not receive Koch's acceptance speech as well as it did his book: he attacked postmodern literary theorists. Excerpts from the speech were published in "Fact vs Fiction: Author Strikes Back" (*The Weekend Australian*), and "Beware Bullies Who Sap Beauty from Young Writing" (*The Age*). Koch married Robin Allanah Whyte-Butler and dedicated his next book to her. In 1997 he received an Hon. D.Litt. from Macquarie University.

Out of Ireland and *Highways to a War* form the diptych titled *Beware of the Past,* a line from "Warning" by Tasmanian poet James McAuley. Raymond Barton is the narrator in both novels. The introduction to *Out of Ireland* is dated 1999; in it Barton reveals his finding of Robert Devereux's diaries (dated 1848–1851) secreted at the "Clare" farmstead. The novel ends with the "Author's Note," acknowledging the historical sources for the narrative and characters. The major character, Robert Devereux, shares the name of Koch's ancestor. The framing technique prepares for the fusion of fiction and fact in the diary entries and interspersed commentary that make up the body of the novel, which is set in Bermuda and Van Diemen's Land in the nineteenth century. Devereux is the great-grandfather of Mike Langford, and though separated by time and space, historic continuity and trace memories surface as the characters share parallel experiences. Devereux is a political journalist and lawyer. He keeps a diary tracing his transportation for sedition aboard the *Raffles*. Friends and enemies are difficult to discern. He receives preferential treatment under the care of Dr. Neville Howard, who inspires both trust and suspicion. Howard arranges the replacement of the convict attendant Long Lane with his own attendant, James Langford, following Lane's sexual indiscretion. He also recommends Devereux's removal to Van Diemen's Land when his health worsens. Devereux's reception is as a hero of the Young Ireland movement. Plans to continue Irish resistance are fractured by differing ideologies. Devereux meets Kathleen O'Rahilly, Howard's Irish Catholic convict servant. She becomes Devereux's mistress and dies from an asthma attack, leaving her child to be brought up by Bess and James Langford, now Devereux's business partners. Dante's *Inferno* (circa 1307–1321) provides the pattern upon which Devereux experiences hell in the foul Hobart Rivulet as he escapes to America, aided by Long Lane and Irish sympathizers. Devereux's doubleness is signaled in his position as a member of the Anglo-Irish ascendancy supporting the peasant rebellion; but unlike Kathleen, who is sustained by her culture and Catholicism, he is bereft of the language or knowledge of Celtic mythology. His driving force is an ideal, and that ideal lies in some Celtic Otherworld. Historical sources for Devereux include *Jail Journal,* Mitchel's record of transportation to Van Diemen's Land, and *Meagher of the Sword: His Narrative of Events in Ireland in July 1848* (1916) by fellow transportee Thomas Meagher. Margaret O'Meara, one of Koch's ancestors transported to the island, provides the inspiration for O'Rahilly. In 2000 *Out of Ireland* won the Victorian Premier's Award and the Colin Roderick Award for Australian Literature (awarded by James Cook University).

The lives of these characters take on the flesh of history in Koch's autobiographical travel narrative *The Many-Coloured Land: A Return to Ireland* (2002). The journey, undertaken in July 2000, is an attempt to occupy and meld the histories and ancestral places previously imagined as Otherworld territories. Koch traveled with Brian Mooney, a Launceston busker and folk-music artist known to Koch during his ABC days.

C. J. Koch is a writer of renown in the English-speaking world and is one of the foremost Australian writers. Though the island state of Tasmania figures in many of his novels as a place, it represents a state of mind, a "geography of the soul," and a "topography of Heaven and Hell" (*Quadrant,* 4 April 2001). Characters grapple with colonial disinheritance and psychic disease, as history and geography shape them and situate them within repeating patterns. The novels also trace journeys through relationships with women who are described by Noel Henricksen as "avatars of indigenous myth, vessels for autochthonous spiritual energies" ("On the Tides of History: Christopher Koch's Diptych," *Quadrant,* April 2001). Koch's preoccupation with mysticism and materialism is evident from his first novel, *The Boys in the Island,* to his latest, *Out of Ireland.* In each, characters attempt to escape from Tasmania into some ideal, some illusory place that the mind has partly

Dust jacket for the U.S. edition of Koch's 1995 novel, about a Tasmanian journalist in Cambodia (Richland County Public Library)

conjured in an attempt to engage in larger patterns of history.

Interviews:
Michael Hulse, "Christopher Koch in Conversation with Michael Hulse: In London," *Quadrant,* 29 (June 1985): 17–25;

Adrian Mitchell, "Christopher Koch on *The Doubleman:* A conversation with Adrian Mitchell," *Southerly,* 45, no. 2 (1985): 129–151;

"*The Boy and the Island:* Christopher Koch, Tasmanian Novelist," television script by John Muirhead, ABC, 1988;

Candida Baker, "Christopher Koch," in *Yacker 3: Australian Writers Talk about Their Work,* edited by Baker (Sydney: Pan, 1989), pp. 183–211;

Dagmar Strauss, "Christopher Koch," in *Facing Writers: Australia's Leading Writers Talk with Dagmar Strauss* (Crows Nest, N.S.W.: ABC, 1990), pp. 65–76;

Christopher Koch, Sydney, ABC, 1994;

Adrian Mitchell, "An Interview with Christopher Koch," *Australian Literary Studies,* 18 (May 1997): 67–72.

References:

Robyn Claremont, "The Novels of C. J. Koch," *Quadrant,* 24 (July 1980): 25–29;

Noel Henricksen, "On the Tides of History: Christopher Koch's Diptych," *Quadrant,* 45 (April 2001): 53–58;

Adrian Mitchell, "'Deep ancestral voices': Inner and Outer Narrative in Christopher J. Koch's *Highways to a War,*" *Australian Literary Studies,* 18 (May 1997): 4–11;

Peter Pierce, "Defection and Dislocation: The Fiction of Christopher Koch," *Westerly,* 35 (June 1990): 47–55;

Xavier Pons, "Oedipus in the Tropics: A Psychoanalytical Interpretation of C. J. Koch's *The Year of Living Dangerously,*" in *Colonisations,* edited by Pons and Marcienne Rocard (Toulouse: Université de Toulouse–Le Mirail, 1985), pp. 109–117;

Paul Sharrad, "Living Dangerously: Christopher Koch and Cultural Tradition," *Quadrant,* 29 (September 1985): 64–68;

John Thieme, "Re-mapping the Australian Psyche: The Asian Novels of C. J. Koch," *Southerly,* 4 (December 1987): 451–461.

Papers:

Collections of C. J. Koch's manuscripts and correspondence from 1952 through 1982 are in the National Library of Australia, Manuscript Section.

Ray Lawler
(23 May 1921 –)

Peter Fitzpatrick
Monash University

BOOKS: *Summer of the Seventeenth Doll* (London & Sydney: Angus & Robertson, 1957; New York: Random House, 1957);

The Piccadilly Bushman (London & Sydney: Angus & Robertson, 1961; revised edition, Sydney: Currency Press in association with Playbox Theatre Centre, Monash University, 1998);

The Doll Trilogy, comprising *Kid Stakes, Other Times,* and *Summer of the Seventeenth Doll* (Sydney: Currency Press, 1978; revised, 1985).

PLAY PRODUCTIONS: *Hal's Belles,* Melbourne, Melbourne Repertory Theatre, 1945;

Cradle of Thunder, Melbourne, Princess Theatre, 1949;

Summer of the Seventeenth Doll, Melbourne, Union Theatre, 1955;

The Piccadilly Bushman, Sydney, Theatre Royal, 1959;

The Unshaven Cheek, Edinburgh, Scotland, Edinburgh Festival, 1963;

A Breach in the Wall, Canterbury, Kent, 1970;

The Man Who Shot the Albatross, Melbourne, Princess Theatre, 1972;

Kid Stakes, Melbourne, Russell Street Theatre, 1975;

Other Times, Melbourne, Russell Street Theatre, 1976;

Godsend, Melbourne, Athenaeum Theatre, 1982.

PRODUCED SCRIPTS: *A Breach in the Wall,* television, 1967;

Sinister Street, television, serial, adapted from the novel by Compton Mackenzie, 1968;

Cousin Bette, television, serial, adapted from the novel by Balzac, 1971;

The Visitors, television, serial, adapted from the novel by Mary McMinnies, 1972;

Two Women, television, serial, adapted from the novel by Alberto Moravia, 1972;

Mrs. Palfrey at the Claremont, television, adapted from the novel by Elizabeth Taylor, 1973;

After the Party, television, adapted from the story by W. Somerset Maugham, 1974;

Seeking the Bubbles, television, *The Love School,* 1975;

Ray Lawler at the Victorian State Library, 1986 (from Candida Baker, Yacker 2: Australian Writers Talk about Their Work, *1987; Mount Holyoke College Library)*

True Patriots All, television, 1975;

Husband to Mrs. Fitzherbert, television, 1975.

The enthusiasm that greeted the appearance of *Summer of the Seventeenth Doll* (published, 1957) at the Melbourne Union Theatre in 1955 had a familiar ring to it; the Australian theater was occasionally inclined to hail the arrival of the major work that most commentators agreed that it lacked. But this time proved to be different. The status of the play was confirmed by an international tour and by the critical response it received. When *The London Star* (1 May 1957) pronounced that "It's taken a long time but the kangaroos must be smiling today," it was hardly exaggerating at all.

For Ray Lawler, the relatively unknown Melbourne actor who had written the play, the success of "The Doll" established a career and a status that would last for the rest of his life. But in another sense, the mythic scale of that success was a mixed blessing, placing on his subsequent work a set of expectations and on his private life a range of pressures that he inevitably came to resent.

Raymond Evenor Lawler was born on 23 May 1921 in the working-class Melbourne suburb of Footscray. He was the second of Bill and Ethel Lawler's eight children. His childhood appears to have been happy enough, but from early on, certain circumstances and characteristics made him something of an odd man out: burns, illnesses, and a permanently damaged foot that ruled him out of the sporting activities so central to his culture; his determined refusal to take up a trade apprenticeship, contrary to his father's wishes; and his delight in telling terrifying ghost stories to other children on his street. Still, he conformed to cultural expectations in most respects. He realized that he should leave school as early as he reasonably could (at thirteen), especially in the tough economic times of a lingering Depression. Not having started at school until he was nearly seven, Lawler observed in a 1971 recorded interview with Hazel de Berg, "I didn't really have very much of an education at all." He took a job at a local foundry and remained there for ten years. Throughout that period, however, he suppressed his incipient interest in the theater as something not quite proper for a man: "Somehow I've always had a slight sense of shame about the business" (*The Melbourne Age,* 17 September 1977).

Still, he overcame those inhibitions. At eighteen, following his rejection for military service on medical grounds, he began taking acting classes in the evenings at the Stage Door, a training center for Melbourne performers, and at the same time, as he said in an interview with de Berg, started writing short plays and skits, "sophisticated stuff set in unreal scenes" that was as far removed as possible from his days in the foundry. His first three-act play, *Hal's Belles,* a comedy based loosely on the life of King Harold of England, was staged in 1945 by the Melbourne Theatre Repertory Company in Middle Park, with Frank Thring in the title role. The run was well received, and entrepreneurial giant J. C. Williamson Limited took a three-year option (which it never exercised) on the script. Lawler was sufficiently encouraged to resign from the foundry and commit himself wholeheartedly to the theater. After "a couple of lean years," according to the de Berg interview, he left Melbourne in 1948 and spent a year as writer and

straight man with the American comedian Will Mahoney in continuous fortnightly change variety shows at the Cremorne Theatre in Brisbane. It was still a long way south of the canefields that provided an imaginative framework for *Summer of the Seventeenth Doll,* but it was as near to them as Lawler ever came.

Back in Melbourne the following year and working at the National Theatre, Lawler wrote the first drafts of *Summer of the Seventeenth Doll.* He also completed a drama about English settlers in Australia, *Cradle of Thunder,* which played at the Princess Theatre of Melbourne in 1949, and another work, "The Resignation" (never published or performed), which Lawler described as an "emotional outburst" (*The London Observer,* 8 September 1957) about the frustrations of trying to get Australian plays onto the stage. His work shifted during this period as reflected in the two pantomimes based on the Australian comic-strip character Ginger Meggs in 1952 and 1953, culminating in *Summer of the Seventeenth Doll;* these works were a return to something like the culture in which he had grown up and different from the models of English comedy in which he had sought to deny his background. *Cradle of Thunder,* despite winning the National Theatre Movement's Jubilee Play Award, disappeared, like "The Resignation," without a trace.

In several ways *Summer of the Seventeenth Doll* represented a coming together of strands of Lawler's past experience. The working-class Melbourne culture whose idiom and attitudes he knew so well was overlaid with the more exotic mythology of the far north, which he had briefly glimpsed; in the characters of Roo and Barney were elements of a couple of cane cutters who had hung around the stage door at the Cremorne. The play was also the product of another significant conjunction. For several decades Australian drama had sought its images of cultural distinctiveness in the outback, a location to challenge the resources of any conventional stage and seemingly inimical to the prevalent mode of naturalism. In bringing his cane cutters south for the "lay-off" season, Lawler was able to place them and the values they represented within the domestic frame of the realist proscenium stage and to leave the iconography of the north to the dialogue and the imaginations of the audience; in so doing, he established a strong thematic juxtaposition between their exclusively male world and the exclusively female one that waited for them in Melbourne.

The core of the plot was daring for its time. Roo and Barney come to Melbourne not only for love (the sixteen summers they have spent with Olive and Nancy respectively constitute a kind of firm commitment, even if it is only for half a year), but also—as the replacement of Nancy in the house by Pearl, Barney's new companion, makes clear—for sex. But the form of the play—fixed-set, three-act naturalism—was conservative enough and even, in the year of *Waiting for Godot* (1952), a little backward-looking; in this respect it perfectly matches the cultural milieu in which the action is set. The inner suburban neighborhood in which Olive lives with her mother, Emma, shows no sign of the waves of postwar emigration from Europe that had already begun to change and complicate the character of urban Australia; Barney and Roo are representative of a dying breed, in terms not only of the rapid disappearance of the cane cutter in the face of technological developments but also, more significantly, the increasingly problematic status of the bushman hero as the mythic embodiment of Australian national identity. The characters, too, look back; the keenly felt absence of Nancy, the woman the audience never meets but who had been the life of the party for the previous sixteen summers, is a recurring element of that preoccupation with things past. Part of the powerful appeal of *Summer of the Seventeenth Doll* to critics and audiences lay in a recognition of the familiar that was rooted in nostalgia; perhaps the definition of agreed cultural realities is always a matter of capturing something that has passed. Lawler's play has appealed even more strongly to that sentiment in its recent periodic revivals. It seems guaranteed to have a permanent place both in the repertoire of the major theater companies and in the proprietorial affections of their audiences.

Summer of the Seventeenth Doll has all the substantial virtues of the enduring, naturalistic three-act play—in its firmly grounded sense of place, its strong and knowable characters, and its appeal to a mature reflectiveness about the central hopes and disappointments of life. In one sense, its logic is inexorable. The seventeenth summer is bound to be the last, despite the genuine feeling between Olive and Roo and the determined efforts of everyone to make the best of a lay-off without Nancy. The summer is doomed not only for the reason that most of them come to recognize, that Pearl is such a poor substitute for Nancy; as Emma sees and Roo begins vaguely to understand, a relationship built on such fragile and even delusory foundations, and so dependent on youth and strength and irresponsibility, cannot last because it cannot change. Roo's reaction is to try to adjust by proposing to Olive and by trying to hold down a laboring job in the city; Olive rejects him, with the violent anguish of any child whose kewpie doll or dream has been snatched away from her. The dolls, one for each summer that they have been together, are the source of all the brightness and exoticism in an otherwise drab and uninspiring suburban house; when, after Olive's rejection, Roo, in "a baffled, insensate rage," smashes all the dolls, he strips the room back to

the grim hopelessness of the everyday world that terrifies her. Of all of them, she is the one who has most mythologized the lay-off, treasuring the sense that she is so much luckier than other women waiting for their "soft city blokes" to come home, looking forward to the precious summer when Roo and Barney come down to Melbourne like "two eagles flyin' down out of the sun." Her clothes, her manner, and—right to the end—her refusal to see the truth, all reflect Olive's fear of growing up, of which the collection of kewpie dolls is both a symptom and a metaphor.

The men share her blindness as well as some of her fantasy; Barney is touchy about his inexplicable recent failures with women that threaten his reputation as "Cassa [Casanova] of the North," and Roo partly believes the fiction that his declining physical powers are merely the result of a passing back strain. All are held within a sustained dramatic irony, which persists to the end when the two mates stumble out into the world, the little man reassuring the big one that the emptiness in front of them is just the perpetual promise of a world in which the sky is the limit: "there's a whole bloody country out there—wide open before us." The play has sometimes been seen as a parable of the unexamined life and a critique of a culture in which the hedonistic moment seems often to preclude moral reflection, spiritual growth, and even the acquiring of wisdom. But the irony is complex, and part of the strength of Lawler's writing rests in his capacity to show fairly the world as it looks to his characters. Emma articulates one aspect of the complexity when she acknowledges to Roo, "It could have been worse. Seventeen years is seventeen years"; Nancy, too, having pulled out of the lay-off arrangement to marry "that book bloke," might be said to have managed something like the best of both worlds. Choices based on self-delusion are not necessarily so pernicious when they can work so pleasantly for a while.

Finally, though, the refusal or inability to deal with change is exposed as a moral as well as a practical failure. The cost is clear, especially to Olive, for whom the dolls are not only tokens of immaturity but surrogates for the children she will never have. The commonsensical critical stance to which the audience is persuaded does not preclude a sense of the poignancy of the situation or of the painfulness of Roo's final destruction of the pathetic souvenirs of their life together.

The circumstances of the premiere of the play in Melbourne underlined the improbably good fortune that was necessary at the time in order to bring a new Australian play to production. *Summer of the Seventeenth Doll* had shared first prize with Oriel Gray's *The Torrents* (first performed, 1956; first published, 1988) in a new competition for local writers established by the Play-

Dust jacket for the 1957 book publication of Lawler's 1955 play,
about two cane cutters who spend the summer lay-off season in
Melbourne, following the same pattern for sixteen years
(Bruccoli Clark Layman Archives)

dual perspective as playwright and performer on the progress of the play.

Other important events in his life were intertwined with the successful progress of *Summer of the Seventeenth Doll*. Lawler became engaged to Jacklyn Kelleher, who played the role of Bubba in the original company, and married her in the course of the subsequent national tour; their twin sons, Adam and Martin, were born in 1957, two weeks after the play opened in London. The reviews of the London production were mostly positive, though Harold Hobson in *The London Sunday Times* found the conversational idiom "dull, flat and unrevealing"; other commentators found the quaintness of the vernacular a source of fascination. But for all the emphasis on the distinctive Australian-ness of the piece, the warmth of the response confirmed the cultural portability (if not "universality") of its themes. The London run ended after eight months, in December 1957, its success confirmed by *The Evening Standard* Award for Best New Play in that year.

Lawler complained of feeling homesick, and in a *London Daily Mirror* interview of 21 November 1957 said, "I'm dying to hear some direct Australian speech again—even if it is only someone telling me my plays are lousy and he could do ten times better himself except he has to go to the races that afternoon." The ambivalence about his own culture, with its habit of reflexive disparagement and its defiant philistinism, which is implicit in that remark, was soon after compounded by Lawler's realization of his disadvantageous tax situation should he return home. Lawler had placed a small bag of Australian dirt under Jacklyn's pillow when she was giving birth to their boys in order to ensure that they were born on Australian soil (*The London Daily Telegraph*, 15 May 1957), but in fact, he was to remain an expatriate and his sons were not to see that spiritual home for nearly fifteen years.

Lawler lived first in London, then for a time in Denmark, and finally moved to Ireland in 1965, where he remained until returning to Australia with his family in 1975. He briefly revisited Australia in 1971, for the staging by the Melbourne Theatre Company (MTC, the new name for Sumner's UTRC) of his historical play *The Man Who Shot the Albatross* (first performed, 1972). Otherwise, Lawler seemed entrenched as one of a long line of distinguished Australian expatriates; it came as a pleasant shock to most followers of Australian theater when he accepted Sumner's invitation to come back to Melbourne to write, advise, and direct for the MTC as its associate director.

Summer of the Seventeenth Doll had established a strong reputation for its author in London, and although in the period between its closure and his homecoming in 1975 he wrote four more plays, he was

wrights' Advisory Board in 1954. The award carried no guarantee of production; although it was staged in the following year, *The Torrents* remained unperformed for decades to come.

Lawler had accepted a position as acting director of the Union Theatre Repertory Company (UTRC), based at Melbourne University, in the absence of its founding director, John Sumner. When he invited Sumner to return for a guest production in the 1955 season, Sumner proposed doing Lawler's play. Lawler at first opposed the suggestion, partly because of a possible conflict of interest and partly because he was concerned about the financial viability of the project. When those objections were overcome, he was similarly reluctant to take part in the production and only agreed to accept the role of Barney when it became apparent that no other suitable contender for the role was available. For that Melbourne season and the subsequent national and international tours of the play, Lawler had a rare

most active in the area of television screenplays. Most of these were adapted from novels and short stories, including several serials, though four of his fifteen script credits were for original teleplays (*A Breach in the Wall* in 1967, and *Seeking the Bubbles, True Patriots All* and *Husband to Mrs. Fitzherbert* in 1975). The knowledge of the playwright's craft that Lawler demonstrated in *Summer of the Seventeenth Doll* made him well suited to the professional challenges of adaptation and of writing to deadlines and, occasionally, to formulas.

The first of the four stage plays during the time abroad was, fittingly, a play about the experience of expatriatism, *The Piccadilly Bushman* (published, 1961; revised, 1998), begun in London, completed in Denmark, and first staged in Sydney in 1959. It is about the return of Alec Ritchie, an unlikable and Anglophile Australian expatriate actor, to the home country that he despises, and it turns on two actions: Alec's relationship with his estranged wife, Meg, a country girl from Yanngoola who drinks heavily and picks up strange men as consolation for her husband's embarrassment about her Australian-ness; and his treatment of the aggressively Australian novelist O'Shea, whose book has been doctored for international consumption in the motion picture that Alec has come "home" to make. The conflict remains unresolved, and Alec is left lamenting that he is a man who belongs nowhere—the "Expatriate—the man who can never accept his own country, and finds that the country he hankers after never accepts him."

Though the characters of *The Piccadilly Bushman* are much more reflective and articulate about their lives than their predecessors in *Summer of the Seventeenth Doll*, their conflicts lack the power to engage an audience that marked the earlier play. That inability is partly a consequence of the inescapable sense that the problem is peculiar to the playwright himself, its lack of resolution a reflection of his own ambivalence; it is partly a product of a lack of depth and charm in the participants in the debate. Though the reception for the Sydney season was appreciative, it was tinged with some disappointment. Lawler's new play had been eagerly awaited, but *Summer of the Seventeenth Doll* was a hard act to follow. This play was less inclusive and more didactic in spirit; in the conspicuous absence of its author, moreover, an audience could read some of that distaste for the culture he came from that is expressed by Alec Ritchie.

Lawler distanced himself in interviews from both the insulting condescension of Ritchie and the proud parochialism of O'Shea. Doubtless, a little of the author could be found in each of them. Certainly, the experience of the Sydney production, with a troubled preparation followed by a rather tepid response, confirmed in him the sense that he was already somewhat out of touch with his own country, and it may have contrib-

uted to the acerbic edge of Alec's cultural critique. Lawler had experienced already something of the manipulative misrepresentation to which O'Shea is sensitive. He had retreated from the stream of "polite people" who were eager to see him as a colonial novelty (*The Daily Mirror,* 21 November 1957) only to run into the grossly insensitive American adaptations of *Summer of the Seventeenth Doll* for its Broadway season in 1958 and for its appearance as a movie in the following year.

The Broadway version significantly disfigured the script in the interests of appealing to an American audience, an accessibility that was never achieved; the season closed, after playing to mixed reviews and small and unresponsive houses for just twenty-nine performances. The motion picture was a travesty of the original play, relocating the action from Melbourne to Sydney in order to take advantage of the beauties of Sydney Harbour and the iconic status of its bridge, and altering the ending to encourage the notion that Roo might "get the girl" after all; it cast an American, Ernest Borgnine, as Roo, and an Englishman, John Mills, as Barney, while Anne Baxter and Angela Lansbury were an improbable pair of Sydney barmaids. Renamed *Season of Passion* (1959) for its United States release, the movie seemed to do precisely what O'Shea in *The Piccadilly Bushman* claimed was done by the British in making a movie of his novel: "Much more important to show us as the old country likes to think we are, are? Coarse lovable larrikins roaming around in the great outdoors with not a complexity within ten thousand miles." Lawler refused to watch it and still has not done so.

The Unshaven Cheek, which played at the Edinburgh festival in 1963, revisited the theme of cultural displacement; it was set in contemporary Australia, and focused on an expatriate Englishman's efforts to come to terms with his uncertain sense of home and with the changing values of modern life. The play was not a success; again its explicit moral seriousness was a problem, the *London Daily Express* (23 August 1963) complaining that it moved "like a slow lizard on the torturing rocks of conscience." Lawler decided to abandon plans for a London transfer and eventually declined to make the play available for revival, on the grounds that it was too close to the experience of his family and dealt with an Australia that no longer existed. *A Breach in the Wall,* a 1970 adaptation of his 1967 television play of the same name, was on safer ground. Its concern with issues of spiritual meaning and conscience through the life of Thomas á Becket was personal enough, reflecting the increasing seriousness of Lawler's engagement with the Catholicism he had finally embraced in 1965, having gone through the motions of a Catholic marriage to Jacklyn eight years earlier; but the location of the action of the play, in its performance venue at Canterbury, was remote from the cultural influences he had left behind and with which he continued to struggle. It was of the world that he and Jacklyn had settled into in Kent, as active members of the British brass-rubbing society; but it was a world in which he still felt, as he remarked in the 1971 de Berg interview, "an interloper."

The play that first brought Lawler back to Australia, *The Man Who Shot the Albatross,* was certainly a return to Australian themes. But the subject was historical, and the central debate between Governor William Bligh and the entrepreneurial pastoralist John Macarthur was couched in an idiom more redolent of Canterbury or Edinburgh than of Parramatta. Its mode and its controversies marked it out as a period piece, and while the reviews were suitably respectful, they were marked by a strong sense that Lawler's work had become a little peripheral in an Australian theatrical world that was in the middle of its most recent—and most vaunted—New Wave, in which confronting contemporary themes were dramatized in a vernacular far cruder than any language used by Roo or Barney.

Lawler found Australia much changed and confessed in his interview with de Berg that he felt that he had returned as "an exile, in the same way, now I look back on it, that I became an exile from my family when I was a child in hospital." He had hoped, nonetheless, that his return might lead to some openings in direction, but in the wake of the polite but disappointing reaction to *The Man Who Shot the Albatross* he returned to County Wicklow without any real expectation of going back to Australia again.

In 1975, however, John Sumner, whose influence had been decisive at several points in Lawler's career, intervened again, with his invitation to fill a senior role with the Melbourne Theatre Company. Lawler had already been working on *Kid Stakes* (first performed, 1975; first published, 1978), a play about the characters of *Summer of the Seventeenth Doll* in the first of their summers. It was an extraordinary concept; even in cinema, the prequel is a rare species. But for Lawler the play represented an opportunity to write about a wartime Australia that he still remembered with great immediacy, as well as to embody the character of Nancy, who had been such a lively and powerful absent friend in *Summer of the Seventeenth Doll.* At some point in the process of his repatriation, he conceived a third play involving the same people, *Other Times* (first performed, 1976; first published, 1978), which dealt with the emerging tensions of the eighth summer. Neither play quite stands up satisfactorily on its own, and inevitably both tease out into explicit action issues that are part of the subtextual density and skillful exposition of *Summer of the Seventeenth Doll.* Moreover, the "survivors"—Olive,

Roo, and Barney—remain fixed in their later public selves, waiting for the seventeenth summer and the revelations of vulnerability that it will bring. But both plays cleverly exploit the ambivalence of Nancy, who is smarter than the rest of the characters, and *Kid Stakes* particularly gives a credible sense of a long lost and apparently more innocent Australia.

The prodigal had returned, and the performances in 1977 of the newly constituted *Doll Trilogy* (published, 1978) became occasions to pay homage. In Melbourne the plays were presented in sequence, all in a day; the atmosphere suggested a hometown Bayreuth. The critics shared, for the most part, in the spirit of almost sacramental celebration. Katharine Brisbane, writing in *The Bulletin* (19 March 1977), summarized the public's feelings:

> At 55, Ray Lawler has ended the painful, long road home. From now on, whether or not he writes another play, there will no longer be the need to compete. His place as a dramatist is affirmed, and that, in our 200-year history of youthful hopes and defeated old age, has never happened before to one of our playwrights.

The intention was to praise Lawler, not to bury him, but inevitably the effect of adulation of this kind confirmed Lawler's position as elder statesman and therefore a man of the past. The historical perspective was crucial to the establishment of an Australian theatrical canon; halls of fame are confirmations of cultural values. However, eulogies can often sound like elegies, and the reception of the trilogy (as well as that the playwright felt moved to write it) underlined the difficulties of moving creatively forward from a spectacular early success. When asked by an unnamed reporter in an interview for *The Age* (31 December 1980) about the destructive influence on his later career of the mythic triumph of *Summer of the Seventeenth Doll,* Lawler accepted the applicability of the albatross metaphor with a typical wry humility. He observed that the fame of the play "is something that just hangs around my neck quite nicely. Besides, it gives people something to hook on to."

Not all the critics greeted the trilogy with the requisite reverence. Brian Hoad's review in *The Bulletin* (14 May 1985) of one of its revivals was headed "A classic transformed into soap," while the playwright Jack Hibberd went still further, challenging in an article in *Meanjin* (March 1977) the status not only of the recent prequels but of their much acclaimed progenitor. He saw the making of the trilogy as "a curious and retrograde act" and Lawler as a prisoner first of naturalistic form and subsequently of the disabilities caused by early success and prolonged exile from his own culture.

Hibberd had his own agenda, as the proponent of a popular theater that had little time for the realistic sets and psychologies in which Lawler wrote with such assurance. But his dissenting voice is an important one, as Lawler himself would acknowledge, and Hibberd's closing prediction, "The immediate future of Ray Lawler almost certainly lies in the past," had its measure of accuracy.

Certainly, after the euphoria of the trilogy subsided, Lawler found himself unable to write the play about contemporary Australia that he kept intending to produce. He spent a good deal of time revisiting old territory. In 1982 he revised *A Breach in the Wall* for the Melbourne Theatre Company as *Godsend,* developing the device of direct address effectively to explore a range of religious motive. Between 1983 and 1985 he extensively revised the trilogy, and in 1998 he produced a partially rewritten version of *The Piccadilly Bushman* with the Melbourne Playbox Theatre Company. But several proposed revisitings did not come to fruition. In an interview for the *Weekend Australian Magazine* (14–15 July 1984) about the reworking of the trilogy, he spoke of his desire to "have another lash at *The Man Who Shot the Albatross.*" In 1990 he began preliminary work on a new screenplay for a movie that did not eventuate; from 1988 he was also working on a commissioned adaptation of Henry Handel Richardson's novel, *The Fortunes of Richard Mahoney* (1917–1929), but that project, too, remained incomplete. When *Summer of the Seventeenth Doll* was adapted as an opera by Richard Mills in 1996, the libretto was the work of novelist Peter Goldsworthy.

Ray Lawler is an important figure in Australian literary and theatrical history for more than his writing the best-known play in Australian culture. He also represents, with unusual clarity, the plight of the expatriate artist. Australians of earlier generations were conventionally torn about the location of "home"; even those who never visited England in their lives had an odd propensity to see it as the place to which they truly belonged. For the many Australian writers, artists, and performers who spent most of their careers overseas, especially in Britain, the issue of affiliation was a slightly more complex one. Mostly, they were less inclined to the routine identification with the "Old Country" and rather more insistent on their identity as Australians; on the other hand, they tended to be absent for longer than the average citizen. Lawler, whose one major work was so steeped in his intimate knowledge of the culture he came from, missed almost a generation of constant change, and no doubt that loss of contact proved a creative limitation. After nearly two decades of living as an outsider in other places, Lawler on his return felt and spoke like an outsider in his own place. This circumstance meant that *Summer of the Seventeenth Doll,* though it might have spin-offs, could have no genuine successor.

Interviews:

Interview with Hazel de Berg, National Library of Australia Oral History holdings, 1971;

"Interview: Ray Lawler Talks to Alrene Sykes," *Australasian Drama Studies,* 3, no. 2 (1985): 21–31;

Candida Baker, *Yacker 2: Australian Writers Talk about Their Work* (Woollahra, N.S.W.: Pan, 1987), pp. 144–171.

References:

John Dominic O'Grady, "The Coming of Age: An Account of Ray Lawler and *Summer of the Seventeenth Doll,*" M.A. thesis, University of Sydney, 1993;

Jennifer Palmer, ed., *Contemporary Australian Playwrights* (Adelaide: Adelaide University Union Press, 1979).

David Malouf

(20 March 1934 –   )

Brigid Rooney
University of Sydney

BOOKS: *Bicycle and Other Poems* (St. Lucia: University of Queensland Press, 1970); republished as *The Year of the Foxes and Other Poems* (New York: Braziller, 1979);

Relative Freedom: The Tempest (Sydney: English Association, 1973);

Neighbours in a Thicket: Poems (St. Lucia: University of Queensland Press, 1974);

Johnno (St. Lucia: University of Queensland Press, 1975; Ringwood, Vic. & Harmondsworth, U.K.: Penguin, 1976; New York: Braziller, 1978);

Poems 1975–1976 (Sydney: Prism, 1976);

An Imaginary Life: A Novel (New York: Braziller, 1978; London: Chatto & Windus, 1978; Sydney: Pan, 1980);

New Currents in Australian Writing, by Malouf, Katharine Brisbane, and R. F. Brissenden (Sydney: Angus & Robertson, 1978);

First Things Last: Poems (St. Lucia: University of Queensland Press, 1980; London: Chatto & Windus, 1981);

Wild Lemons: Poems (London & Sydney: Angus & Robertson, 1980);

Child's Play; The Bread of Time to Come: Two Novellas (New York: Braziller, 1981); *The Bread of Time to Come* republished as *Fly Away Peter* (London: Chatto & Windus, 1982; Ringwood, Vic. & Harmondsworth, U.K.: Penguin, 1983);

Selected Poems (London & Sydney: Angus & Robertson, 1981);

Child's Play; With Eustace and The Prowler (London: Chatto & Windus, 1982; Ringwood, Vic. & New York: Penguin, 1983);

Harland's Half Acre (London: Chatto & Windus, 1984; New York: Knopf, 1984; Ringwood, Vic.: Penguin, 1985);

Antipodes: Stories (London: Chatto & Windus, 1985; Harmondsworth, U.K. & Ringwood, Vic.: Penguin, 1986);

12 Edmonstone Street (London: Chatto & Windus, 1985; Ringwood, Vic.: Penguin, 1986);

David Malouf (from Ivor Indyk, David Malouf, *1993)*

Blood Relations (Sydney: Currency Press, 1988);

The Great World (London: Chatto & Windus, 1990; New York: Pantheon, 1990; Sydney: Picador, 1991);

Poems 1959–1989 (St. Lucia: University of Queensland Press, 1992); republished as *Selected Poems, 1959–1989* (London: Chatto & Windus / Sydney: Random House, 1994);

Bicycle: A Poem (Sydney: Thinking Fisherman, 1993);

Remembering Babylon (Milson's Point, N.S.W.: Random House, 1993; New York: Pantheon, 1993);

The Conversations at Curlow Creek (Milson's Point, N.S.W.: Random House, 1996; London: Chatto & Windus, 1996; New York: Pantheon, 1996);

A Spirit of Play: The Making of Australian Consciousness (Sydney: ABC Books for the Australian Broadcasting Corporation, 1998);

214

Untold Tales (Sydney: Paper Bark Press, 1999);

Dream Stuff (London: Chatto & Windus, 2000; New York: Pantheon, 2000).

Collection: *David Malouf: Johnno, Short Stories, Poems, Essays, and Interview,* edited by James Tulip (St. Lucia: University of Queensland Press, 1990).

OTHER: *Four Poets: David Malouf, Don Maynard, Judith Green, Rodney Hall* (Melbourne: Cheshire, 1962)– includes "Interiors" by Malouf;

Gesture of a Hand, edited by Malouf (Artarmon, N.S.W.: Holt, Rinehart & Winston, 1975);

Charlotte Brontë, *Jane Eyre,* introduction by Malouf (Oxford, U.K. & New York: Oxford University Press, 1999);

Robert Adamson, *Mulberry Leaves: New & Selected Poems 1970–2001,* edited by Chris Edwards, foreword by Malouf (St. Leonards, N.S.W.: Australian Humanities Research Foundation [AHRF], 2001).

David Malouf enjoys a distinguished reputation, nationally and internationally, as a writer whose lyrical mappings of identity, place, and the body also bear upon questions of belonging and national identity. Crossing successfully from poetry to prose fiction in 1975, Malouf has continued to write in a wide variety of forms and genres. He is author, to date, of at least six volumes of poetry, several editions of selected poems, six novels, two novellas, three short-story collections, many autobiographical and prose nonfiction publications, a series of libretti for opera, and an original play. While this range demonstrates unusual versatility, Malouf's writing also exhibits remarkable consistency in approach, preoccupation, and style. On the shortlist for the Booker Prize in 1993 for *Remembering Babylon* (1993), Malouf has been the recipient of many prestigious awards for fiction, poetry, and drama. These include the 1974 Australian Literature Society Gold Medal and the 1974 Grace Leven Poetry Prize, for *Neighbours in a Thicket: Poems* (1974); the New South Wales Premier's Literary Awards, in 1979 for *An Imaginary Life: A Novel* (1978) and in 1987 for *Blood Relations* (1988); the 1983 *Age* Book of the Year and the 1983 Australian Literature Society Gold Medal, for *Fly Away Peter* (1982); the Best Book of the Region Award, the Commonwealth Writers' Prize (Southeast Asia and South Pacific Region), the Miles Franklin Award, and the Prix Femina Prize (France) for *The Great World* (1990) in 1991; and the 1994 *Los Angeles Times* Book Prize, the 1994 Commonwealth Writers' Prize (Southeast Asia and South Pacific Region), the 1995 Prix Baudelaire (France), and the 1996 IMPAC Dublin Literary Award for *Remembering Babylon.*

Born in Brisbane on 20 March 1934 into a family of mixed British and Lebanese ancestry, Malouf's writing does not explicitly treat issues of ethnic minority or difference, instead drawing upon European heritage in ways that engage primarily with the (white) mainstream of Australian literary culture. As Bob Hodge and Vijay Mishra point out, for Malouf "Australia is not the place of exile; it is in fact the place of return." Educated at Brisbane Grammar School, Malouf graduated with honors from the University of Queensland before departing for England, where he worked as a teacher from 1959 to 1968. On his return to Australia, Malouf took up a teaching post in the Department of English at the University of Sydney. During this decade Malouf not only developed an increasingly sophisticated body of poetry but also made his mark as a novelist with the publication of *Johnno* in 1975. Reviewers heralded this first novel as an innovative contribution to Australian writing, and thereafter Malouf's novels evolved in confidence, breadth, and complexity, ultimately earning him an international readership and reputation. On winning a three-year fellowship from the Literature Board of the Australia Council in 1978, Malouf retired from teaching to commit himself full-time to writing. Living alternately in Tuscany and Sydney, Malouf has been able to harness his expatriate experience to situate Australian writing in an international frame, promoting the imaginative transformation and interpenetration of both Australian and European meanings. In the words of Martin Leer, Malouf "sees Australia as producing 'critical variants of Europe': it is 'Europe translated.'"

Though his fiction has made a greater public impact, Malouf's poetry displays an artistry considered by some (particularly his fellow poets) to source–if not eclipse–his prose writings. For Ivor Indyk, Malouf "remains a poet, writing in the medium of prose." Malouf's first significant mark as a poet was as one of the contributors to *Four Poets: David Malouf, Don Maynard, Judith Green* (later known as Judith Rodriguez), *Rodney Hall* (1962), a collection showcasing the work of newcomers to the field. Three volumes of poetry that followed–*Bicycle and Other Poems* (1970), *Neighbours in a Thicket,* and *Poems 1975–1976* (1976)–attracted considerable critical interest, establishing Malouf's as a distinctive new voice in Australian poetry.

From the outset, Malouf's poetic voice has been infused by a sense of immediacy, an intimacy of address, and, as Dennis Haskell observes, an emphasis on "presentation of the self." A critical moment in Malouf's poetry–signaling the development of a characteristic approach–occurs in his much anthologized poem "An Ordinary Evening at Hamilton" (1974):

The garden shifts indoors, the house lets fall
its lamp light, opens
windows in the earth

The commingling of house and garden relays an encounter–described by Vivian Smith as "the opening out of the individual consciousness to merge with a landscape, a past, another consciousness; a moment which becomes one of self-recognition, of which the poem is the voice"–that recurs throughout Malouf's writing. In both his poetry and his prose, attention is frequently drawn to the space of boundaries, in which the encounter between such pairs as self and other, animal and human, sea and land, nature and culture is negotiated. For Malouf, such encounters on the boundary–a place of meeting or crossing into otherness–can dissolve and transform being. The crossing of consciousness into difference is arrestingly realized in the sensuous sequence "The Crab Feast I–X," from Malouf's highly praised collection *First Things Last: Poems* (1980):

Bent over you I dip my hand

in the bowl, I shake my cuffs, out in the open
and lost. Deep down
I am with you in the dark. The secret flesh of
My tongue enters a claw.

Observing both the gravity and inventiveness of his poems–their often "anecdotal starting point" and their "sense of intellectual searching"–Thomas W. Shapcott, in "The Evidence of Anecdote: Some Perspectives on the Poetry of David Malouf" in *Provisional Maps* (1994), argues that "process is centre-stage in Malouf's poetic world." These qualities are amply illustrated in "The Crab Feast I–X" and indeed in poems such as "Adrift," which recalls the lonely and bereft mother in old age, or "This Day, Under My Hand," with its vivid image of

The cold Pacific banging
an open gate. Australia
hitched like a watertank
to the back verandah, all night
tugging at our sleep.

Malouf's poems sometimes prefigure his fiction, especially in their recourse to meditation and the resources of memory. As Philip Nielsen points out, "The Judas Touch," an early poem dedicated to "John Milliner: drowned February 1962," foreshadows Malouf's first novel, *Johnno*. Likewise, Laurie Hergenhan shows how elements of "The Year of the Foxes" prefigure elements of Malouf's later fiction.

Malouf's novels, however, do not merely repeat the preoccupations of his poetry in another form but also experiment with the novel as form, playing with its temporal constraints and possibilities. The intimacy of the poet's voice is modulated by and contends with the linear drive of narrative. Through the novels, Malouf explores intimate personal terrain in ways that refract and dramatize questions of Australian history and national identity. Andrew Taylor in "The Great World, History, and Two or One" (collected in *Provisional Maps*) notes the imaginative scope of Malouf's fictional mappings of Australian history: "two hundred years of Australian history are covered almost continuously by Malouf's fiction, something not found in any other Australian novelist." Yet, Malouf's exploration of monumental or emblematic episodes in Australian history, in World Wars I and II, for example, is never directed by a strongly "historical" focus but proceeds by means of subjective experience and encounter. The linear thrust of history is interrupted and slowed by the personal experience of time and the expansion outward of the space of narration. That this strategy is conscious is evident in Malouf's typically lucid account to Helen Daniel of how he seeks to harness the narrative process in his 1996 novel, *The Conversations at Curlow Creek*:

I'm aware of the number of times I really want to use the novel to stop time, to slow things up. You can slow up the narrative so that a second is something that can be explored maybe over pages. I like that play between movement and stillness in the novel.

In Malouf's novels, recurring scenarios cumulatively produce an elaborate network of ideas. These thoughts include, for instance, the narrated recollection of place (particularly of domestic interiors); the playing out of a dynamic between male alter egos or twinned characters (such male dyads are often triangulated by the inclusion of a third, female character); exploration of the figure or role of the artist–for example, Dante, Frank Harland, Imogen Harcourt, Ovid, and the unnamed "Great Man of Letters" in *Child's Play* (1981); and the juxtapositioning of Australia and Europe. *Johnno, The Conversations at Curlow Creek,* and *The Great World* all feature triangulated relations between central characters (the bonds between two men, partly in relation to a woman). Whereas *Fly Away Peter* and *The Great World* invoke the mythology of the Australian digger, *Child's Play, An Imaginary Life,* and *Harland's Half Acre* (1984) explore the writer- or artist-figure's response to exile and belonging. *An Imaginary Life,* like *Remembering Babylon,* plays upon the frontier space of empire, raising questions via an encounter with a hybrid being in the shape of the feral (lost or returned) child.

The evocation of wartime Brisbane in Malouf's first novel, *Johnno,* sparked excitement among critics about the potential for regionally focused Australian writing. In *Johnno,* Brisbane is both "the most ordinary place in the world" and timeless or mythological, standing in for that more elusively expansive geopolitical entity, Australia, "a place too big to hold in the mind." Likewise, the brevity and apparent stylistic simplicity of the novel belie its sophisticated organization and the play of ironies generated through the dynamic between its circumspect narrator, Dante, and his wayward and charismatic boyhood friend, Johnno. Dante's musing upon an old school photograph is an early instance of Malouf's recurring use of *ekphrasis,* a literary device involving the detailed written representation of a visual text such as a photograph or painting. Dante's meditation on the photograph initiates his retrospective tale, in which energies seemingly focused on Johnno frequently divert toward the narrator's own processes of creating meaning. Johnno himself functions, alternately, as a prototypical masculine adventurer–"our very own Tamberlaine and Al Capone"–and as a foil to Dante himself, as a marker pointing back to the narrator's "hypocritical niceness." The dynamic between Dante and Johnno unfolds through space as well as time, moving from adolescent adventure in Brisbane, to Johnno's departure for Africa, then Europe, followed by Dante, until their successive returns to Australia, where their separate yet linked destinies are played out in evasion, suicide, and regret. For Hodge and Mishra, "Johnno becomes, for Dante, both his uncanny mirror image and the shadow he also pursues." As Leigh Dale and Helen Gilbert argue, the ambiguities of the text tend to veil its dissidence, deferring absolute answers about the otherwise erotic dimensions of the relationship between the two men. The invocation of the epic poet Dante, moreover, introduces a significantly metafictional layer to the narrative: Dante's "survivor guilt" over Johnno coalesces with the guilty dilemma of the artist who, as Nielsen argues, must exploit "personal relationships for his own aesthetic ends."

In *An Imaginary Life,* Malouf broke new ground while continuing to refine and elaborate themes introduced in *Johnno.* Narrated by Ovid, the Roman poet exiled in old age to a remote northern outpost of empire, *An Imaginary Life* has been taken up by many readers as a meditation upon the writer's antipodean and (post)colonial positioning, and upon questions of exile and belonging. Flung out from the imperial center where distinctions between civilization and nature are tenuous, Ovid engages in a quest for meaning that brings him to the edges of selfhood, language, and existence. Encoun-

Dust jacket for Malouf's 1974 poetry collection, winner of the
Australian Literature Society Gold Medal and the Grace
Leven Poetry Prize (Bruccoli Clark Layman Archives)

tering the mystery of a boy brought up by wolves (mythically central to imperial Roman identity), Ovid entices the boy into the village, seeking to render him tractable to human society and language. Suffering the sudden ravages of illness, however, the villagers become superstitiously fearful, and Ovid and the boy depart, traveling beyond this last outpost into an arctic wilderness. Roles reverse, and the boy becomes Ovid's protector as he journeys toward the culmination of his quest, which is also the moment of his death. Malouf's novel–meditating upon language, spiritual and aesthetic being, and the body's experience of change–converses in imaginative and metafictional terms with the ancient Roman poet of *Metamorphoses* (completed, A.D. 8):

Our bodies are not final. We are moving, all of us, in our common humankind, through the forms we love so deeply in each other's darkness. Slowly, and with pain, over centuries, we each move an infinitesimal space towards it. We are creating the lineaments of some final man, for whose delight we have prepared a landscape, and who can only be god.

Published in seven languages, this novel is arguably the most widely known and admired of Malouf's oeuvre (with the possible exception of *Remembering Babylon,* which bears many resemblances to *An Imaginary Life*). Both when it was first published and during the intervening years, the novel has attracted a great deal of critical attention, particularly as a text about the (post)colonial condition. For Gareth Griffiths, for example, *An Imaginary Life* suggests how texts can be "effectively open to the full complexity of the condition of post-colonial societies and the problems these societies now exhibit."

Malouf next embarked on a series of novellas and short stories. Though first published in 1981 with *Child's Play,* the novella *The Bread of Time to Come* was republished separately in 1982 under the title *Fly Away Peter,* while *Child's Play* was republished in 1982 with two short stories—"Eustace" and "The Prowler." Although in some ways entailing a strikingly different scenario, *Child's Play* is unmistakably continuous with Malouf's previous fiction. As in both previous novels, a palpably metafictional element attends the dramatization of individual power and destiny in this novella—writing and death, and art and terrorism. The narrator of *Child's Play* belongs to a terrorist cell located in a provincial Italian town; his assignment involves the assassination, for reasons unspecified, of an elderly, preeminent Italian writer—the unnamed "Great Man of Letters" in the novel, whose work-in-progress bears the title "Child's Play." As he prepares for his mission, the narrator is drawn into a quasi-oedipal struggle over the question of who determines and controls meaning, narrative, and destiny—in other words, over "authorship." The terrorist's plot, seeking dominion over its target, is caught within the larger design of the great writer's text: "But I should confess that if, through long sessions of study, I have begun to understand him a little, to observe, that is, the dangers that are inherent in the very nature of his 'trick,' he has also, and so long ago that it quite scares me, both understood and accounted for me." A *mis-en-abyme* (an infinitely regressing image) opens in the shuttle among the three "author" figures—the terrorist, the writer, and Malouf himself. Other familiar elements from the previous novel that recur in *Child's Play* include its use of retrospective narration; the twinning or doubling of characters, in the relationship between the narrator and his dead older brother; and *ekphrasis* in the narrator's use of photographs to familiarize himself with the appointed scene of death, a device that occasions a meditation on issues of narrative, time,

destiny, and meaning. The ambiguous ending of the novella has been regarded as only a "qualified success," according to Nielsen, although it has also been read as a deliberate refutation of Roland Barthes's "death of the author," according to Stephen Woods. Walking "under the early blossoms" of an apple orchard, the narrator is either escaping into safety or encountering extinction. Though its significance remains opaque, this conclusion recalls the merging of self and landscape in Ovid's sublime death in *An Imaginary Life.*

In *Fly Away Peter,* Jim Saddler, humble rural worker, and Ashley Crowther, heir to a Queensland coastal property, are the mirroring couple whose differentiated class positioning both materially shapes their destinies during World War I and represents male bonding as something capable of transcending class difference. The approach the novel takes to the genesis of the Anzac legend, however, seems less concerned with history than with metaphysical themes—of self in process; self in response to others; and self in relation to landscape, destiny, and time. Educated in progressive land-management theories in England, Ashley observes Jim's practical knowledge of the swampland on his Queensland property and immediately employs him to record its migratory-bird life. Ashley recognizes that Jim's intimate knowledge gives him a claim over the land: "Such claims were ancient and deep. They lay in Jim's knowledge of every blade of grass and drop of water in the swamp, of every bird's foot that was set down there—in his having, most of all, the names for things and in that way possessing them." Although the narrative seems to efface the claims of indigenous people, Malouf's focus on belonging through knowledge and naming augurs the development, in his later fiction, of a more complex encounter with frontier history. New, twentieth-century technologies—plane and camera—enter the plot as ambivalent signs of the progress of modernity and of impending war. English freelance photographer Imogen Harcourt, a mature professional woman working in close partnership with Jim, triangulates the male pairing. Migratory patterns of birds prefigure the absurdity of young men's flight to their deaths on the Western Front, the terms of which are graphically and powerfully depicted in the contrasting second half of the novel. The cruelties that then unfold are resolved, momentarily, and in the consolation a grieving Imogen takes from her vision of a surfer an image that positively fuses human technology with nature.

A more lengthy and historically detailed novel, *Harland's Half Acre,* came next, featuring—like earlier works—Brisbane and rural Queensland settings, and a dually focused narration. In some sequences a third-person narrator recounts episodes in the life and career of Frank Harland, a landscape artist, son of a charismatic battler and widower, Clem. The significance of exile and belonging in the genesis of Australian art is dramatized in Frank's movements through time and space, from his early removal from the family home after his mother's death, his return to family and his efforts to guide his motherless siblings and his nephew, to his final, Ovid-like death on Bribie Island. An itinerant worker during the Great Depression years, Frank drifts in space even as his landscape paintings mature, finally reaching a wider public. The recounting of Frank Harland's life is interwoven with the first-person narrative of Phil Vernon, whose family life in Brisbane, seemingly tangential, eventually intertwines with Frank's life, leading to Phil's role as intermediary between artist and public. As a child, Phil mediates between his partially estranged grandparents, and later, between Frank and his temperamental nephew and heir, Gerald. Like Dante in *Johnno,* Phil is a surrogate for the writer, functioning as witness to events. Yet, as lawyer and family friend, he is torn between the need for professional impartiality and the demands of personal involvement. The *ekphrastic* device of the photo as trigger for narration, previously employed in both *Johnno* and *Child's Play,* recurs in a seminal scene in which the young Phil first encounters Frank's landscape paintings and finds himself primally caught by the portrait of a local woman who murdered her partner, a European immigrant. The darkness of European history is here, and elsewhere in the narrative, transplanted into Australian contexts, reversing clichés about Australian innocence in contrast to European experience. Likewise, Frank Harland's "half acre" is more than a modest slice of Australian ground; Frank's mental landscapes and artistic journey essay new strategies for making and thereby belonging to Australia.

Malouf's next published work was *Antipodes* (1985), a collection of short stories, which was followed by an autobiographical memoir, *12 Edmonstone Street* (1985). Shapcott in "The Evidence of Anecdote: Some Perspectives on the Poetry of David Malouf" describes these works, in which Malouf vividly recalls the contours of his childhood home and his encounters with Tuscany and India, as "autobiographical prose interiors." Gillian Whitlock in "The Child in the (Queensland) House: David Malouf and Regional Writing" (in *Provisional Maps*), discussing the regionally inflected exploration in the title story of the "Queenslander" (a wooden bungalow on stilts), observes how the narrative proceeds by means of its "spacial contiguities rather than a sequence of events": "Gradually this child-in-the-house narrative makes its way from verandah, through the rooms and down to 'under the house,'

Paperback cover for Malouf's 1980 collection of poems, many of which deal with inner self and outer world (Bruccoli Clark Layman Archives)

a space that Malouf mythologizes as a forest, as dark as anything in Grimm."

During the late 1980s Malouf turned his hand to writing for the stage. As well as a highly acclaimed libretto written for Richard Meale's opera *Voss* (1986), based on Patrick White's novel, Malouf also published his first and, to date, only original play. *Blood Relations* was Malouf's reworking of William Shakespeare's *The Tempest* (first performed, 1613; first published, 1623) and was first staged by the Sydney Theatre Company in 1987. Set at Christmastime in a family home on the tropical coast of northwestern Australia, the drama concerns the unearthing of the father's past and the transformations that this process brings. Dale and Gilbert observe that the play deploys "the edge" as a "place of negotiation," "a political space where Prospero's dream of a 'prosperous' island state, where the colonizer acts as 'husbandman' to a bountiful new world, is thwarted." Since then Malouf has produced three further librettos for contemporary opera, including Richard Meale's opera *Mer de Glace* (1991), an adaptation of Mary Shelley's *Frankenstein* (1818); Michael Berkeley's first opera, *Baa Baa Black Sheep* (1993), based on episodes from Kipling's *The Jungle Book* (1894); and most recently Berkeley's opera *Jane Eyre* (2000), based on Charlotte Brontë's novel. Annie Patrick observes that Malouf's contribution to each libretto extends beyond mere adaptation into creation of "operatic counter-parts which not only demonstrate his ability to write for voice and the stage–[but also] his collaborative skills with a composer."

The Great World was Malouf's next full-length novel and his most detailed and expansive yet. This novel, as Nielsen remarks, offers no radical departures from Malouf's earlier work but rather consolidates and extends familiar themes and approaches. Realist and historical in genre, but often ruminative and lyrical as was the earlier fiction, *The Great World* spans a seventy-year period, focusing on Australians affected–individually and collectively–by their experiences of World War II. Among other memorable episodes, the novel depicts in harrowing terms the ordeal suffered by Australian prisoners of war at the notorious Changi camp and on the Thai/Burma railway. The title of the book refers to an abandoned theme park, "the Great World," used as makeshift quarters for a contingent of prisoners working on the Singapore docks. Thus, juxtaposing the imagined expansiveness of the world with its cruel foreshortening through war and imprisonment, "the Great World" also alludes to the shifting perspectives of its protagonists–their expectations and experiences of the wider world. Narrative focus is shared between complementary male characters, ne'er-do-well Digger Keen and self-made businessman Vic Currant, whose friendship begins in the camp in Malaya and whose destinies and personal lives thereafter entwine. Malouf's exploration, via the evolving relationship between Digger and Vic, of the ethos of mastership–that quintessentially masculine virtue associated with the Anzac legend–sympathetically rewrites this period of Australian history in personal and ironic but also mythic terms. Though a few reviews were less enthusiastic–for example, Gerard Windsor's in the *Australian Book Review* (April 1990)–most concurred with A. P. Riemer's view in *The Sydney Morning Herald* (17 February 1990) that this was "a masterly novel, a deeply satisfying work of art."

In the multiple-award-winning *Remembering Babylon*, Malouf returns to the motif of the *enfant sauvage* (wild child) first treated in *An Imaginary Life,* reversing its narrative movement. Based on an account of British sailor James (Jemmy) Merrill, who was shipwrecked in 1846 and who lived for many years with an Aboriginal tribe before returning to white settlement, Malouf's

novel rewrites the imperial first-contact story of Daniel Defoe's *Robinson Crusoe* (1719). It also rewrites colonial captivity narratives, such as that of Eliza Framer, a British woman shipwrecked in 1836 on Fraser Island, off Queensland, on which White's novel *A Fringe of Leaves* (1976) was based. In mid Queensland in the 1850s (during one of the bloodiest phases of colonization), castaway ship boy Gemmy Fairley, having been rescued and nurtured by an Aboriginal tribe for sixteen years, finally returns to white society. Hovering on the fence line–the literal and symbolic perimeter of the colony– Gemmy "surrenders" to a small group of children who then mediate his encounter with the adults. With his damaged body ("smudged appearance" and "baffled, half-expectant look of a mongrel that had been whipped"), strange behavior, broken English, and obscure history, Gemmy represents a highly threatening state of being between two statuses, or liminality. As the "white blackfellow" he was "a parody of a white man," an "imitation gone wrong." Gemmy had also puzzled the Aborigines, who saw him as "half-child, half sea-calf," like Caliban in *The Tempest*. To the white settlers, Gemmy dangerously embodies that which daily eats at their security–proximity to a vast, unchartered country and to its feared Aboriginal inhabitants: "Out here the very ground under their feet was strange. It had never been ploughed." Taken in by the McIvors, Gemmy's closest link is with the children who first encountered him–Lachlan Beattie and Janet McIvor– and the narrative relays their stories, along with the varied reactions of the small community. Though widely reviewed in glowing terms, Malouf's novel also sparked a contentious critical debate about its politics. Published in the very year in which the Australian High Court replaced the legal doctrine of *terra nullius* (a legal concept meaning "the land belonging to no one" used by the British to deny the claims of the indigenous people of Australia to their native land) with that of native title (in the case of *Mabo* vs *Queensland,* No. 2), *Remembering Babylon* has been criticized for authenticating white experience and history at the expense of Aboriginal bodies, experience, and history (as Germaine Greer, Suvendrini Perera, and Garry Kinnane discuss). Others, such as Bill Ashcroft, counter this charge with the argument that the novel is subversive, representing "the very different, transformative oppositionality of post-colonial discourse" (see also Lee Spinks and Penelope Ingram).

Reception of Malouf's next novel, *The Conversations at Curlow Creek,* has generally been positive. Anthony J. Hassall praises its "passionate, poetic reimaginings" of competing versions of colonial Australia. Although replete with patterns familiar from Malouf's previous work, in this novel the representation of the violence of colonial history is arguably more direct than that of *Remembering Babylon*. The story, set in Australia in 1827, concerns the impending execution of Irish rebel and colonial bushranger Daniel Carney, who–among other crimes–has fostered insurrection against the British by local Aboriginal tribes. Also of Irish background, Michael Adair, the officer posted to supervise this execution, passes the night in the hut with the imprisoned man, while the three troopers and Aboriginal tracker who captured Carney make their camp outside the hut. Adair's recollections of his boyhood past compose much of the narrative. Adopted into a wealthy Irish family, Adair had formed a close but rivalrous bond with his foster brother, Fergus Connellan, whose identity merges during the narrative with that of Carney, the condemned man. Rivalry between the adopted brothers is complicated by the presence of a young woman, Virgilia, who was tutored alongside them. Virgilia secretly loves Fergus, while Adair secretly loves Virgilia. In contrast to the austere and conservative Adair, who is overly conscious of his lesser place in the world, Fergus is a romantic idealist who, refusing his inheritance, leaves Ireland for Australia in search of a more just society. Adair's guilt over this uneasy past oppresses him; so, too, the specter of colonial violence–in a moment of confrontation–haunts the troopers' fireside conversation outside the hut. Reconciliation, for Adair, is finally figured in two sacramental movements: in a baptismal moment when the condemned man, prior to his hanging, is permitted to wash himself in the stream, and, in the final moment of the narrative, as Adair breaks his nightlong fast: "He chews as he walks on, his saliva mixing with [the bread's] sugars and driving new light into his heart, refreshing his mouth like common speech." The narrative thus repeats a gesture familiar in Malouf's writing, moving through encounter with difference toward transformation, reconciliation, and transcendence.

As well as the less widely distributed *Untold Tales* (1999), Malouf has published two volumes of short stories–*Antipodes* and *Dream Stuff* (2000)–which show both diversity of content and thematic coherence. In *Antipodes,* which, despite positive reviews, has subsequently received little critical attention, the geographic opposition of Australian and European perspectives is, as James Tulip suggests, one of a series of dramatic oppositions across a range of stories in which the romance of distance is set against the pleasures of the everyday. "Southern Skies" treats these themes, for example, through the narrator's recollections of the Professor–an esteemed family friend whose "Old Country" manners and erudition at first annoy the young male narrator, who seeks assimilation with contemporary Australia; later the Professor draws him across the threshold into

Paperback cover for the 1981 collection that includes poems relating to Malouf's novels (Bruccoli Clark Layman Archives)

a different experience of romance, vulnerability, and desire. Suburban and familial perspectives–in stories such as "The Empty Lunch-Tin" and "Bad Blood"–delicately explore the unexpected in everyday relationships. The stories in *Dream Stuff,* set entirely in Australia, are linked unobtrusively by the motif of dreaming. "Jacko's Reach," for example, concerns how the one remaining plot of wilderness in a suburb, finally resumed for development, lingers in the imagination; and the youthful narrator of "Closer" dreams of reconciling, across the closed boundary of a Pentecostal home, with the uncle whose annual visits to the property's perimeter are studiously ignored by his family. In this collection, Peter Pierce detects an increasing sense of "skepticism about the reality of the social world," since its various stories speak "of haunting, of vanishing, of desperate attempts to put down roots and unavailing efforts to escape them–of the impact of war and of the conflicts within families."

As well as being an Australian writer of undoubted eminence and achievement, Malouf is a formidable commentator upon his own work and an eloquent exponent in the public domain of his views, particularly of the role of the writer in contemporary Australia. In addition to his creative works, Malouf has also produced many lectures, opinion pieces, essays, and interviews. During his 1998 ABC Boyer Lecture series (published as *A Spirit of Play: The Making of Australian Consciousness* [1998]), Malouf reiterates his vision of a necessarily dynamic relationship between contemporary Australians and the land:

> We are the makers, among much else, of landscapes. We remake the land in our own image so that it comes in time to reflect both the industry and the imagination of its makers, and gives us back, in working land, but also in the idealized version of landscape that is a park or garden, an image both of our human nature and our power. Such making is also a rich form of possession.

Malouf's own writing, compellingly for some readers but problematically for others, testifies to this observation. Concerned about distinguishing his sense of "making" from negative modes of colonization, Malouf advocates "a convergence of indigenous and non-indigenous understanding, a collective spiritual consciousness that will be the true form of reconciliation" in Australia. Malouf's writing maps encounters between self and other, tensions between exile and home, and relations between the individual and history–issues holding particular resonance for contemporary Australians. The transformations that, in Malouf's writing, are deployed to resolve these encounters–via death in the landscape, absorption into the other, experience of the limitless body, and immersion in the sacred–suggest the writer's belief in the efficacy and relevance of art, not merely as a powerful mode of expression, but also as a strategy of belonging.

References:

Bill Ashcroft, *Post-Colonial Transformation* (London & New York: Routledge, 2001);

Julie Carr, "The White Black Fellow," review of David Malouf's *Remembering Babylon, In Island,* 56 (Spring 1993): 71–72;

Helen Daniel, "Interview with David Malouf," *Australian Humanities Review* (September 1996) <http://www.lib.latrobe.edu.au/AHR/archive/Issue-Sept-1996/intermal.html>;

Germaine Greer, "Malouf's Objectionable Whitewash," *Age,* 3 November 1993, p. 11;

Gareth Griffiths, "*An Imaginary Life:* The Post-Colonial Text as Transformative Representation," *Commonwealth,* 16, no. 2 (1993): 61–69;

Anthony J. Hassall, "The Wild Colonial Boy–The Making of Colonial Legends in David Malouf's *The Conversations at Curlow Creek,*" *Antipodes,* 14, no. 2 (December 2000): 145–148;

Laurie Hergenhan, "Discoveries and Transformations: Aspects of David Malouf's Work," *Australian Literary Studies,* 11, no. 3 (1984): 328–341;

Bob Hodge and Vijay Mishra, *The Dark Side of the Dream: Australian Literature and the Postcolonial Mind* (North Sydney, N.S.W.: Allen & Unwin, 1990);

Ivor Indyk, ed., *David Malouf: A Celebration* (Canberra, A.C.T.: National Library of Australia, 2001);

Penelope Ingram, "Racializing Babylon: Settler Whiteness and the 'New Racism,'" *New Literary History,* 32, no. 1 (2001): 157–176;

Garry Kinnane, "Mutable Identity and the Postmodern," *Meanjin,* 57, no. 2 (1998): 405–417;

Martin Leer, "Imagined Counterpart: Outlining a Conceptual Literary Geography of Australia," *European Perspectives: Contemporary Essays on Australian Literature–Australian Literary Studies,* special issue, 15, no. 2 (1991): 1–13;

Amanda Nettelbeck, ed., *Provisional Maps: Critical Essays on David Malouf* (Nedlands, W.A.: Centre for Studies in Australian Literature, 1994);

Philip Nielsen, *Imagined Lives: A Study of David Malouf* (St. Lucia: University of Queensland Press, 1996);

Suvendrini Perera, "Unspeakable Bodies: Representing the Aboriginal in Australian Critical Discourse," *Meridian,* 13, no. 1 (1994): 15–26;

Peter Pierce, "What Dreams May Come: David Malouf's Dream Stuff," *World Literature Today,* 74, no. 4 (Autumn 2000): 750–757;

Lee Spinks, "Allegory, Space, Colonialism: *Remembering Babylon* and the Production of Colonial History," *Australian Literary Studies,* 17, no. 2 (1995): 166–174;

Stephen Woods, "David Malouf's *Child's Play* and the Death of the Author," *Australian Literary Studies,* 13, no. 3 (May 1988): 322–333.

Papers:

The two main archives for the manuscripts of David Malouf are the National Library of Australia in Canberra, which holds papers from the period 1967–1977, including drafts of *Johnno* and *An Imaginary Life,* and the University of Queensland Library, which holds papers from the period 1977–1981, including drafts of *Child's Play, Fly Away Peter,* and *An Imaginary Life.*

Frank Moorhouse

(21 December 1938 –   )

Alan Lawson
University of Queensland

BOOKS: *Futility and Other Animals: A Discontinuous Narrative* (Sydney: Gareth Powell, 1969; revised edition, London & Sydney: Angus & Robertson, 1977);

The Americans, Baby: A Discontinuous Narrative of Stories and Fragments (Sydney & London: Angus & Robertson, 1972);

The Illegal Relatives (Sydney, 1973);

The Electrical Experience: A Discontinuous Narrative (Sydney: Angus & Robertson, 1974; revised, 1980);

Conference-Ville (London & Sydney: Angus & Robertson, 1976);

Tales of Mystery and Romance (London: Angus & Robertson, 1977; London & Sydney: Angus & Robertson, 1980);

The Everlasting Secret Family and Other Secrets (London & Sydney: Angus & Robertson, 1980);

Selected Stories (Sydney & London: Angus & Robertson, 1982); republished as *The Coca-Cola Kid* (Sydney: Angus & Robertson, 1985);

Room Service: Comic Writings (Ringwood, Vic.: Viking, 1985);

Forty-Seventeen (Ringwood, Vic.: Viking-Penguin, 1988; London: Faber & Faber, 1988; New York: Harcourt Brace Jovanovich, 1989);

Lateshows (Sydney: Pan Macmillan, 1990; London: Faber & Faber, 1988);

Grand Days (Sydney: Macmillan, 1993; London: Pan Macmillan, 1993);

Loose Living (Sydney: Pan Macmillan, 1995);

Dark Palace: The Companion Novel to Grand Days (Milson's Point, N.S.W.: Random House, 2000; London: Vintage, 2001);

The Inspector-General of Misconception: The Ultimate Compendium to Sorting Things Out (Sydney: Random House, 2002; Milson's Point, N.S.W. & London: Vintage, 2002).

PRODUCED SCRIPTS: *Between Wars,* motion picture, Edgecliff Films in association with McElroy & McElroy & T&M Films, 1974;

Frank Moorhouse (photograph by Reece Scannell from the dust jacket for Grand Days, *1994; Bruccoli Clark Layman Archives)*

The Girl Who Met Simone de Beauvoir in Paris, motion picture, Australian Film and Television School, 1980;

Who Killed Baby Azaria? television, Network 10, 1983;

Conferenceville, television, Australian Broadcasting Corporation, 1984;

The Coca-Cola Kid, motion picture, Grand Bay Films International, 1985;

The Everlasting Family Secret, motion picture, International Film Management, 1988.

OTHER: *Coast to Coast: Australian Stories 1973,* edited by Moorhouse (Sydney: Angus & Robertson, 1973);

Days of Wine and Rage (Ringwood, Vic.: Penguin, 1980);

The State of the Art: The Mood of Contemporary Australia in Short Stories, edited by Moorhouse (Ringwood, Vic.: Penguin, 1983);

A Steele Rudd Selection: The Best Dad and Dave Stories with Other Rudd Classics, edited by Moorhouse (St. Lucia: University of Queensland Press, 1986);

Fictions 88, edited by Moorhouse (Crows Nest, N.S.W.: ABC Enterprises for The Australian Broadcasting Corporation, 1988).

SELECTED PERIODICAL PUBLICATIONS–
UNCOLLECTED:
FICTION
"The Drover's Wife," *Bulletin,* 1988.
NONFICTION
"What Happened to the Short Story?" New Writing in Australia, Special Issue of *Australian Literary Studies,* 8 (1977): 179–182;

"Author's Statement," *Australian Literary Studies,* 8 (1977): 189–191;

"Childhood Reading without a Library," *Educational Magazine,* 35, no. 5 (1978): 102–105;

"Author's Statement," *Australian Literary Studies,* 10 (1981): 222–223;

"The Cringe: New Variants of the Virus," *Sydney Morning Herald,* 28 September 1995, p. 19.

If one were to seek a representative figure around whom to write an account of the writer's role in Australia during the last half of the twentieth century, few would be better choices than Frank Moorhouse. Moorhouse and his career have been exemplary of a shift in the way the profession of letters has evolved in Australia during that period. He has also actively accepted the professional and personal responsibility to participate in–as well as to chronicle and critique–the evolution of the profession and the evolution of the institutional forms, social practices, and public discourses in which it is embedded. He has been involved in several of the literary controversies through which some of the central anxieties of the cultural politics of the era have been brought to light. His work has evolved in some ways that might have been unexpected at an early stage of his writing career, but in retrospect his oeuvre seems to cohere quite remarkably to his core preoccupations with how one might be Australian in times of great social, political, and cultural changes wrought by international forces. His writing is "about" Australia in the way, perhaps, that Henry James's writing was "about" America: it is about the increasingly "complex fate" of being Australian in relation to world politics between the wars (as expressed in *Grand Days* [1993] and *Dark Palace: The Companion Novel to Grand Days* [2000]), the emergence of modern production methods in small

enterprises and the spread of United States entrepreneurship (*The Electrical Experience: A Discontinuous Narrative* [1974]), the transmission of ideas from the post-Beat generation of United States writers to Australian culture (*The Americans, Baby: A Discontinuous Narrative of Stories and Fragments* [1972]), generational change magnified by globalized culture (*The Everlasting Secret Family and Other Secrets* [1980]), *Tales of Mystery and Romance* [1977], and *Forty-Seventeen* [1988]), new modes of communication and institutional organization (*Conference-Ville* [1976], *Tales of Mystery and Romance, Grand Days, Lateshows* [1990], *Dark Palace,* and *The Inspector-General of Misconception: The Ultimate Compendium to Sorting Things Out* [2002]). Underlying all these themes is a fascination with the ways in which changing social, linguistic, political, and organizational structures and arrangements have disturbing and intriguing effects on the codes of social practice–what Jane Austen called "manners" and Moorhouse calls "protocols" or "aesthetics" (and sometimes etiquette) and often analyzes as rituals. What about new behaviors, he asks, is meaningful, significant, and symbolic of new social relations as the "codes change to fit different times" (*Yacker 3,* 1989)? These characteristics are what tie together his oeuvre from *Futility and Other Animals: A Discontinuous Narrative* (1969) to *Grand Days* and from *Dark Palace* to *The Inspector-General of Misconception.*

Frank Thomas Moorhouse was born on 21 December 1938 in Nowra, a town one hundred miles south of Sydney on the Shoalhaven River near the southern New South Wales coast. Timber-getting, dairy productions, fishing, and tourism have been the economic bases of the region since the first white settlement there in the 1820s. The third son of older parents, Frank Osborne and Purth (Cutts) Moorhouse, both in business, Moorhouse was educated locally at Nowra High School and at Wollongong Junior Technical High School before marrying Wendy Halloway in 1959 (they were divorced in 1979) and moving to Sydney in the mid 1950s to study at Sydney Technical College. Before becoming a full-time fiction writer in the 1970s, he worked as a journalist, starting as a cadet reporter on *The Sydney Daily Telegraph* from 1956 through 1959. His other early placements include a period in the 1960s in the mid southwest of New South Wales, where his jobs included periods as a journalist on *The Wagga Wagga Daily Advertiser* and *Riverina Express,* and as editor of the *Australian Worker* (Sydney), *The Lockhart Review,* and *The Boorowa News* (serving a town and cattle region two hundred miles southwest of Sydney). This period was followed by a few years back in Sydney from 1967 until 1969 as a reporter and also subeditor for the Australian Broadcasting Commission. Later he became a writer and columnist for *The Bulletin,* the *Inde-*

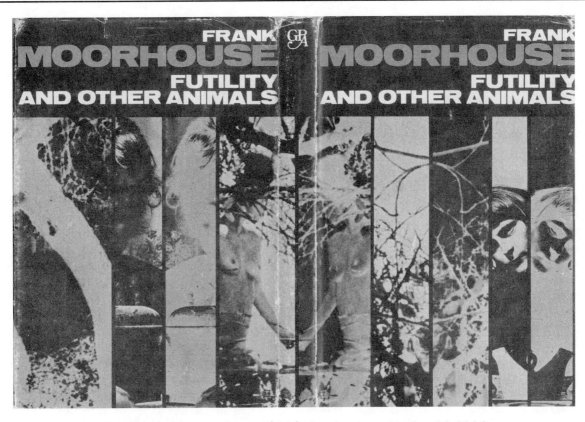

Dust jacket for Moorhouse's first novel (1969), about the writers and intellectuals he labeled
"a modern, urban tribe" (Bruccoli Clark Layman Archives)

pendent Monthly (Sydney), the *Sydney Review,* and the *Adelaide Review,* magazines located at various points on the political spectrum.

His extensive associations with small and alternative magazines include being a founding editor of both *City Voices* in 1966 and *Tabloid Story* from 1973 to 1975. *City Voices* was a new inner-city magazine modeled loosely on the New York magazine *Village Voice; Tabloid Story* was an important and innovative magazine that strongly influenced the emergence and acceptance of more experimental short prose writing in Australia in the early 1970s. Its most remarkable innovation was to publish itself as a "parasite" on other well-established journals. All of its issues appeared as supplements to student newspapers, but others appeared within the covers of mainstream mass-circulation periodicals such as *The Bulletin,* the *National Times,* the *Australian Book Review,* and even the Qantas in-flight magazine, *QV. Tabloid Story* probably did more than any other publishing phenomenon to bring the "new writing" and its writers to a broader public. The writing to which it gave space was often novel in terms of its form and technique: it included fabulist, frequently confessional, imagist, process narrative ("writing about writing"), playful, and

even surreal prose. But the content of the "new" fiction also singled it out for special attention. It often took the form of pseudodocumentary accounts of the so-called new or alternate lifestyles of the early 1970s and focused on *épater le bourgeois* (shocking the middle class) depictions of sex and drugs. The motivations were manifold, but among them were certainly strong cultural and political reactions to what were then extremely repressive censorship regulations in Australia.

Moorhouse also took on a role as a public defender of his profession. He was a contributor to *Thor* and *Thorunka* in the late 1960s when these student magazines actively and often spectacularly challenged Australian censorship laws; he found in the late 1960s that most of his work was rejected by literary magazines because of its language or material. In the early 1970s he and a group of colleagues prepared a publication–*The Illegal Relatives* (1973)–to challenge the censorship laws, but the protest lost its purpose when the government abolished censorship, and Moorhouse withdrew; the printer, however, decided to go ahead with the publication, and it appeared without the approval of the writer. The three stories in it–"Watch Town," "The

Oracular Stories," and "Alter Ego Interpretation"—all appeared in revised form in *Tales of Mystery and Romance*. In the 1970s Moorhouse and Judith Wright, the senior Australian poet, participated in a well-publicized legal challenge to the unfettered photocopying of writers' works by schools and universities. Their efforts resulted in changes to the copyright law and ultimately to the creation of the Copyright Agency Limited in 1988, through which copying institutions paid a fee to the copyright holders whose work they copied. He has been active in the profession of letters in many other roles. He has been a union organizer for the Australian Journalists' Association and a member of the Ethics Review Committee of the Media Alliance. He has served as president and as a councillor of the Australian Society of Authors, chairperson and vice chairperson of the Australian Copyright Council, director of the Copyright Agency Limited, and councillor of the Australian Press Council.

The most formal expression of his sense of responsibility to participate in as well as to chronicle and critique the evolution of the institutional forms of contemporary social practices and their public discourses is his edited collection of writing of and about the 1970s, *Days of Wine and Rage* (1980). It is a collection of pieces that captures the spirit and the major themes of that decade, arguably the most important decade of the latter half of the twentieth century in terms of its impact on cultural, social, and political changes in Australia. It includes chapters (linked collections of his own and other people's writings) about the emergence of the new wave of Australian playwriting; the major revolution in Australian literary publishing and what could for the first time in many decades be credibly called "the literary life" in Australia; the Vietnam War; the new nationalism in politics and the emergence of the modern republican movement; sexual liberation; censorship; the new wave of Australian cinema; the emergence of a modern popular environmental movement; and feminism, Marxism, and the development of a leftist critical perspective in public life. In the preface, Moorhouse also acknowledges that it is a "homage to Sydney, where I had lived for twenty years. More particularly to the Sydney 'community of ideas and arts' which had nurtured me creatively, supported me financially, and sometimes protected me." It also includes a valuable "Events of the Decade" chronological table.

Moorhouse has been associated with a variety of semiformal leftist and progressive humanist social organizations (particularly in Sydney). He was, from early in his adult life, an administrator and tutor with the Workers' Educational Association, associated with the Sydney "Push," and with the Sydney Libertarian Movement (principally influenced by the Sydney philosopher

John Anderson). "Push," though essentially never a formal association, bonded around anti-authoritarian but nonactivist positions and was overtly nonconformist. These groups were loose associations of "freethinkers," dedicated to public and private critique and to free enquiry, suspicious of formal political affiliations, yet gregariously prone to affiliation in their pursuit of social and intellectual group activity.

In an interview with Candida Baker in the third book in her *Yacker* series of interviews with Australian writers, Moorhouse speaks of his ethical opposition to the separation of his public and private lives. Although his position is important, it does not mean that Moorhouse the private individual, Moorhouse the writer, and the "I" of the writing are collapsible into one another or are identical. What it does mean is that an ongoing dialogue exists between the life and all of the continually evolving public utterances in journalism, fiction, opinion pieces, interviews, festival appearances, radio talks, conference participation, and formal and informal teaching situations. At the base is actually an extraordinarily strong sense of public responsibility from which there is no cloistered refuge. The lives from his parents' generation he is especially interested in exploring are those of people who take their social responsibilities seriously and take them into various forms of formal public engagement: Edith Campbell Berry (in *Grand Days* and *Dark Palace*) and George McDowell (in *The Electrical Experience*).

Moorhouse has been invited to literary and other conferences and festivals more often than almost any of his contemporaries. He is a highly proficient public performer, not only when reading from his work but also in "working" the conference—networking and contributing to public and semiformal discussions; facilitating the participation of newer and less-experienced delegates; and attuning himself to the rituals, ceremonies, and trivial but sustaining formalities of such events. While a popular writer and one who frequently appears on the reading lists of contemporary writing courses, Moorhouse has not won as many awards and honors as might have been expected. But his honors do include second prize in the Westerly Short Story Competition for "One Night in Bed" (1960); the Banjo Paterson Short Story Prize for "Walking Out" (1964); the Grenfell Henry Lawson Award (prose) for "The Coca-Cola Kid" (1970); the 1975 National Book Council Award for *The Electrical Experience;* the Order of Australia (AM) in 1985 for his services to literature; the Australian Literature Society Gold Medal and the *Age* Book of the Year Award for *Forty-Seventeen* (1988); the National Fiction Award for *Grand Days* (1994); and the Miles Franklin Award for *Dark Palace* (2001). He has been a Senior Fulbright fellow to the United States (1994); a Woodrow Wilson scholar (1994); an Australia Council Creative Arts fellow (1990–1993); a Colonel Johnston Scholar, University of Sydney (1995–1996); and writer-in-residence, King's College, Cambridge, U.K. (1999).

The critical response to Moorhouse and his work has been loosely organized around three themes. The first focuses on him as a representative of the "new" fiction of the 1970s, as an advocate of short imaginative prose fiction, and as the preeminent (contemporary) practitioner and theorist of the discontinuous narrative. This association is curious because of the odd links he has with some of the roots of traditional Australian fiction. The term "discontinuous narrative" is indeed a useful one and appears to be a Moorhouse neologism. Moorhouse has explained the term many times, but a particularly clear statement appears in a 1977 interview with Jim Davidson, then editor of the quarterly journal *Meanjin*:

> . . . when I felt that I had passed through [my] apprenticeship, and was starting to write stories which (looking back on it) were departures from the essentially social realist type of story of the time, I found . . . that the stories were clustering. I wasn't writing a novel, but one story suggested the next. I was writing about one locality or one group of people, and even though the connections were often oblique, tangential, and at first not altogether perceived by me, they were real and growing. I wasn't quite sure whether it was proper to have stories referring back to others. . . . But by then I knew they were clustering and I knew they were related, and by 1968 or 1969 I'd started to call it a discontinuous narrative.

In the "New Writing" special issue of *Australian Literary Studies* that same year, he described the thematic aspects of it this way:

> . . . it now seems that my work grows in clusters of stories which make fragmented perceptions of characters and situations. The discontinuous narrative appears to relate to my preoccupations with the accidental, the unintended consequence, the non-rational factors of human conduct and behavior. The clusters form larger unities of book length . . . and the books themselves have interconnections not only in theme but in character and situations.

As Moorhouse himself came to recognize, this kind of writing was not "improper," although it was, for the period, unconventional. Moorhouse distinguished his own practice from the Australian social realist tradition, but as some critics have noted, the writer who has often been claimed as the font of that tradition, Henry Lawson, can now be seen as a practitioner of the discontinuous narrative as well. But it was possible to see in

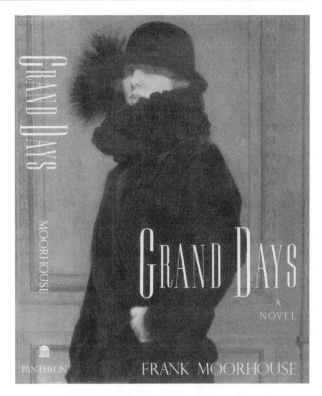

Dust jacket for the 1994 Australian edition of Moorhouse's 1993 novel, set in Geneva between the world wars (Bruccoli Clark Layman Archives)

Moorhouse's work of the 1970s in particular a new formation of writing that did, as he suggests, capture the experience of fragmentation and reconnection that characterized a generation and a culture that was losing faith in coherent and complete narratives told from a consistent point of view. Such volumes are constructed upon principles other than narrative–tone, mood, and character–and to call them "discontinuous" is to indicate that the volume proceeds along multiple trajectories of organization. As a precursor, then, of some of the literary forms of postmodernism and as a representative of a kind of fiction writing practiced by some of his national and international contemporaries, Moorhouse and the discontinuous narrative were not only a recognizable phenomenon but also a useful analytical and explanatory strategy.

Closely related to that strand of his reputation as a representative of the "new" fiction is his "role" as representative figure of a group of writers collected in and around the inner Sydney suburb of Balmain, a group (Michael Wilding is the other writer most persistently associated with this group) known–almost equally at times–for experimental writing and experimental living. This assessment focuses on content rather than form–it concentrates on Moorhouse as a chronicler and a representative of a period, a place, and a set of social and sexual practices. More recently, it has evolved into an analysis of his depiction of sexuality and of gender. Linzi Murrie and Stephen Kirby have developed the most extended analyses of this kind. Murrie argues that Moorhouse is the first major writer in Australia to move beyond narrow representations of male sexualities. Moorhouse, he writes, "challenges central tenets of patriarchal ideology by locating homosexuality in heterosexual society, and by posing a continuum between male homosocial relations and homosexuality." The limiting condition of Moorhouse's sexual radicalism, though, according to Murrie, is that he does not deal satisfactorily with that other significant element of male sexuality, homophobia. According to Murrie, Moorhouse locates homophobia solely in his female characters, losing the opportunity to investigate its major role in policing the boundaries of male sexual behavior. The identification of Moorhouse and such colleagues as Wilding, David Williamson, Murray Bail, and Peter Carey as the Balmain Writers was a phenomenon of fairly temporary historical interest in an empirical sense. Apart from living there for variously short periods in the early 1970s, they shared an enthusiasm for the publicly lived literary life, an iconoclastic predisposition, and a ready identification in the minds of some reviewers and critics with the "new." Not all of them were formally innovative, but they did come to represent a break with what had been perceived as a long tradition of writing in Australia in each of their genres. Not surprisingly, this identification depended to some extent on a misrepresentation of the conservatism of the preceding generation(s) of writers, and in particular an underestimation of their formal and informal experiments. Nevertheless, the characterization of a generation of writers as innovative in cultural forms was absolutely necessary in a country that had recently embraced the "new" on a large scale by electing the first progressive, liberal-democratic government in twenty-four years. The new Labor government headed by Gough Whitlam was elected in November 1972 with the public support of large numbers of writers and intellectuals. The public funding for culture—which had actually begun to grow during the rule of the Liberal prime minister John Gorton—increased dramatically; the growth in the number, quality, and public acceptance of Australian movies, plays, and novels was apparently unprecedented, and a discourse of the "new" was an essential accompaniment to this increase.

The language and the subject matter of the "new" fiction produced conservative and excessively cautious reactions among editors (perhaps even more than among readers). But the bringing to book of a new demographic group, an emerging social formation, was not in itself a radical act, even though its form may sometimes have made it seem so. The depiction of new demographics and their dialects has been one of the central preoccupations of short fiction since the sixteenth century. Like the late-nineteenth- and early-twentieth-century short-fiction writer Lawson (with whom Moorhouse's work shares some parallels), Moorhouse is a chronicler not only of emergent social formations but also of those that are passing. Indeed, the effect of the discontinuities is to emphasize the backward-looking narrative by disrupting the forward movement of chronology.

Moorhouse's ongoing fascination with his parents' generation is remarkable considering that his reputation, his early reputation certainly, was built as an eager chronicler of the absolutely contemporary. The intergenerational theme, however, is a strong one and emerges most often in a concern for moments of observable social transition when one set of beliefs, practices, and language ("dialect") starts to be overtaken by its successor. But his fascination is not solely with the emergent but also with the more powerful idea that "we are a walking archive," that "our lives, or parts of our lives, are formed before we are born" *(Yacker 3)*. The movie script *Between Wars* (1974)—which starred Corin Redgrave, Judy Morris, Arthur Dignam, and Martin Vaughan—traces the life of Edward Trenbow and his family from World War I, when he was a military doctor, through his discovery of the work of Freud, his bringing of "new" ideas to Australian medical practice, and the responses they evoke in a small country town and in Sydney. The struggle with well-intentioned conservatism, alienation, and bigotry follows him through a range of situations that prefigure the modern Australia of Moorhouse's own generation. Trenbow is also a character in *The Electrical Experience,* in which he and George McDowell represent the two kinds of "new"—the intellectual and the commercial. Moorhouse's most recent major fictional works, the huge novels *Grand Days* and *Dark Palace,* set mainly in Geneva between 1920 and 1946, deal with the world's greatest experiment in search of universal good intentions, ethical behavior, and world citizenship—the League of Nations. The central character of the book, Edith Campbell Berry (first met in *Forty-Seventeen*), also comes from one of those same small southern New South Wales country towns as T. George McDowell and Edward Trenbow. In Europe she, too, encounters "new" thought in such domains as politics, international relations, gender relations, sexuality, social organization, aesthetics, philosophy, and psychology and tries to explain it to her visiting compatriots and family.

Moorhouse's books of the early to mid 1970s—*The Americans, Baby, The Electrical Experience,* and *Tales of*

Mystery and Romance—were considered exemplary of this trend toward "the new." They were variously, formally innovative and iconoclastic, and, in a confessional way, personal and revelatory of the presumed lifestyle of the writer. These Moorhouse works are the most readily identified with the "new Australian writing." *The Americans, Baby* and *Tales of Mystery and Romance* were most directly concerned with what he referred to in the preface to *Futility and Other Animals* as "a modern, urban tribe." In each book, the majority of the stories are set in inner Sydney; they concern characters who are part of a loose community of writers and intellectuals, the "new" class; they are of varied geographical, employment, and class backgrounds; and their lives intersect in ways that seem random. But there is in each (and especially collectively) an emerging sense of a larger picture of social change and of the lives it affects. *The Electrical Experience* and *The Americans, Baby* are, in a formal sense, the most innovative. They include many "non-text" elements—such as photographs of soft-drink manufacturing equipment, recipes, the declaration from the St. Louis Rotary Convention, and many typographical changes.

Lateshows is divided into three long sections, each concerned with the protocols of contemporary life: "The Club: Contemporary Protocol," "The Movie: Working with Makavejev," and "The Cabaret: Cabaret Voltaire." "The Club" is the most typical of Moorhouse in midcareer. It canvasses the changing protocols that help readers deal with such things as "the sight of a former mistress breastfeeding," "literary quotations," the "book launch," "food," and "detective fiction." "The Movie" is, in its own words, "about how the flow of life is made into stories, how stories become motion pictures, how the making of stories and movies itself becomes stories, and how stories become the flow of life." It is both a chronicle of the literary life of a decade and a process narrative, a story about the making of stories. *Loose Living* (1995) is a satiric fantasy, a loose comic narrative of a young Australian writer abroad encountering the culinary, cultural, and sexual sophistication of Europe. These two books share with the earlier *Conference-Ville*, with some parts of *Tales of Mystery and Romance*, and with the 2002 novel *The Inspector-General of Misconception*, Moorhouse's characteristic interest in the protocols of contemporary life, the new rituals—those practices that are in the process of becoming traditions and those practices that mark the new manifestations of intense meaning in a culture that no longer finds those moments of significance in the cultural practices of its predecessors.

As a representative of "the new" and in keeping with his acceptance of the public responsibility of the professional writer to be involved in the issues of his

Moorhouse speaking at the Australian Food and Wine Writers Festival, 1997 (photograph by Michael Kluvanek; by permission of the National Library of Australia)

profession and the culture it serves, he has found himself frequently involved in public controversies. The most scandalous was that surrounding the 1994 Miles Franklin Award—Moorhouse's *Grand Days* (along with novels by Elizabeth Jolley and Maurilia Meehan) was ruled ineligible for the award in that year on the grounds that it did not meet one of the core conditions of Franklin's bequest, that it be awarded to a literary work that presents "Australian life in any of its phases." Moorhouse publicly contemplated legal action and gave several public talks in which he contended with the decision of the judges and analyzed it as an apparent recurrence of the virus of parochialism, a return to what A. A. Phillips had in the late 1940s diagnosed as the "cultural cringe."

The following year, the prize was awarded to *The Hand that Signed the Paper* (1994) by Helen Darville (writing as Helen Demidenko), and the prize was mired in even deeper controversy. Darville's book was a first novel, set largely in the Ukraine, written from the point of view of a young Ukrainian-Australian woman (an identity Darville herself had publicly proclaimed) but that included some passages and some historical interpretations that some readers found anti-Semitic. Subsequently, Darville was forced to renounce the claims of

Ukrainian ethnicity and to deal with some allegations of plagiarism. The Miles Franklin judging panel was also embarrassed by the events because their citation for the "Demidenko" win had praised its multicultural "authenticity."

These twin controversies focused attention yet again onto a phenomenon that many thought had been well-consigned to the historical archive, an anxiety about what might be permitted to constitute "Australianness." It is closely related to a peculiar dismay in public reactions to expatriates, to Australians (restricted almost exclusively, however, to those in the arts) who choose, for a variety of reasons, to live abroad for at least part of their working lives. It was a persistent element in the reaction to Patrick White and to Christina Stead (though not, oddly, to Franklin, who spent more than twenty years outside Australia).

The issue had flourished briefly in the late 1960s, provoked by the withdrawal of the *Encyclopedia Britannica* Award to the expatriate novelist Christina Stead in 1967 because she was no longer considered Australian. A confused reaction followed in 1968 when the same prize was awarded to the New Zealand–born writer Douglas Stewart. Most commentators thought that the controversy had been sufficient to lay to rest this literary conundrum about where to set the boundaries of an Australian book. The decision of the Miles Franklin judges to exclude *Grand Days* really was extraordinary: one of the most recurrent motifs in the novels is the character Edith Campbell Berry's concern with how to be an Australian (a citizen and the product of a nation) while working in and for an overtly internationalist and internationalizing organization, the League. To some extent, she represents the constitutionally young Australia in its attempt to find a place for itself in an international environment. That this searching occurs in the direct wake of World War I, when Australian men had ventured into dangerous international domains, is no accident. Edith is a young woman from Jasper's Brush in southern New South Wales who is recruited to join the League in the 1920s, and she conscientiously strives to be an "internationalist." When George McDowell visits her, he says that he had regarded her as "the first internationalist from the south coast. Maybe the first from New South Wales." Her concern with nationality also manifests itself in her concern for her Australian manners, in speculating about her particularly Australian contribution to the League, her mentorship by John Latham (the Australian minister for external affairs and, for a time, the senior Australian official delegate at the League), visits by Australians, and correspondence with friends and family. As Moorhouse explained with some exasperation in one of the pieces he wrote after the controversy, "The deeper irony is that the book is also about borders and the crossing of borders and the meaning of borders, national and other, and identity."

Moorhouse himself spent most of the 1990s living outside Australia. His principal reason for leaving was to do the research for his two novels on the League of Nations, *Grand Days* and *Dark Palace*. He lived for the bulk of that time in Geneva, working in the remarkably underresearched but extraordinarily comprehensive League Archives in the Rockefeller Library there, but he also spent time in France (where he lived for a couple of periods of about two years each in Besançon); in England where he did research in Oxford and London and spent a year as writer-in-residence at King's College, Cambridge (1999); and in Washington, D.C.. He also worked as a correspondent and visited the multinational peacekeeping force in the Sinai in 1982, Lebanon during the siege of Beirut, and Geneva during the negotiating of the Nuclear Nonproliferation Treaty in 1986.

Frank Moorhouse's training in research when he was a journalist is still evident in his writing but is much more than a passion for detail or for chronicling events. What continues to characterize his work is his commitment to drawing out the significance of detail, the patterns of behavior, and even the ideology to which those details contribute.

Interviews:

Jim Davidson, "Frank Moorhouse," *Meanjin,* 36 (1977): 156–171; reprinted in Davidson, ed., *Sideways from the Page* (Melbourne: Fontana, 1983), pp. 11–33;

Winifred Belmont, "Frank Moorhouse: An Interview," *Notes & Furphies,* 7 (1981): 1–4;

Graeme Kinross Smith, "Liberating Acts: Frank Moorhouse, His Life, His Narratives," *Southerly,* 46 (1986): 391–423;

Candida Baker, "Frank Moorhouse," in *Yacker 3: Australian Writers Talk about Their Work,* edited by Baker (Sydney: Picador, 1989), pp. 212–235;

Ray Willbanks, "Frank Moorhouse," in his *Speaking Volumes: Australian Writers and Their Work* (Ringwood, Vic.: Penguin, 1991), pp. 158–170.

References:

Don Anderson, "Frank Moorhouse's Discontinuities," *Southerly,* 36 (1976): 26–38;

Bruce Bennett, "Frank Moorhouse and the New Journalism," *Overland,* 70 (1978): 6–10;

Nicholas Birns, "Beyond Disillusionment: Frank Moorhouse's *Grand Days* and Post-Colonial Idealism," *Westerly,* 40, no. 1 (1995): 67–71;

Chelva Kanagayakam, "Form and Meaning in the Short Stories of Frank Moorhouse," *World Literature Written in English,* 25, no. 1 (1985): 67–76;

Brian Kiernan, "Frank Moorhouse: A Retrospective," *Modern Fiction Studies,* 27 (1981): 73–94;

Stephen Kirby, "Homosocial Desire and Homosexual Panic in the Fiction of David Malouf and Frank Moorhouse," *Meanjin,* 46 (1987): 385–393;

Humphrey McQueen, "The Thinker from the Push: Frank Moorhouse," in his *Gallipoli to Petrov* (Sydney & Boston: Allen & Unwin, 1984), pp. 101–106;

Linzi Murrie, "Changing Masculinities: Disruption and Anxiety in Contemporary Australian Writing," *Journal of Australian Studies,* 56 (1998): 169–179;

William Pope, "Frank Moorhouse's *Tales of Mystery and Romance:* A Study in Narrative Method," *Southerly,* 42 (1982): 412–423;

Peter Quartermaine, "Cultural Correspondence: Frank Moorhouse's *Forty-Seventeen,*" *Australian Studies,* 6 (1992): 60–67;

Gay Raines, "The Short Story Cycles of Frank Moorhouse," *Australian Literary Studies,* 14 (1990): 425–435;

Bruce Clunies Ross, "Laszlo's Testament or Structuring the Past and Sketching the Present in Contemporary Short Fiction, Mainly Australian," *Kunapipi,* 1, no. 2 (1979): 110–123;

Ross, "Some Developments in Short Fiction, 1969–1980," *Australian Literary Studies,* 10 (1981): 165–180;

Tim Rowse, "The Pluralism of Frank Moorhouse," in *Nellie Melba, Ginger Meggs, and Friends: Essays in Australian Cultural History,* edited by Susan Dermody, John Docker, and Drusilla Modjeska (Malmsbury, Vic.: Kibble Books, 1982), pp. 250–267;

Elizabeth Webby, "Australian Short Fiction from *While the Billy Boils* to *The Everlasting Secret Family,*" *Australian Literary Studies,* 10 (1981): 147–164.

Papers:

The largest collection of Frank Moorhouse's manuscripts and other papers is held in the Fryer Memorial Library at the University of Queensland; a smaller collection of earlier material is held in the National Library of Australia in Canberra.

Gerald Murnane

(25 February 1939 –   )

Imre Salusinszky

BOOKS: *Tamarisk Row* (Melbourne: Heinemann, 1974;
London: Angus & Robertson, 1977);
A Lifetime on Clouds (Melbourne: Heinemann, 1976);
The Plains (Melbourne: Norstrilia, 1982; Ringwood,
Vic. & Harmondsworth, U.K.: Penguin, 1984;
New York: Braziller, 1985);
Landscape with Landscape (Carlton, Vic.: Norstrilia, 1985;
Ringwood, Vic. & New York: Penguin, 1987);
Inland (Richmond, Vic.: Heinemann, 1988; London:
Faber & Faber, 1989);
Velvet Waters (South Yarra, Vic.: McPhee Gribble,
1990);
Emerald Blue (South Yarra, Vic.: McPhee Gribble,
1995).

OTHER: *The Temperament of Generations: Fifty Years of
Writing in Meanjin,* edited by Murnane, Jenny Lee,
and Philip Mead (Carlton, Vic.: Meanjin & Melbourne University Press, 1990).

SELECTED PERIODICAL PUBLICATION–
UNCOLLECTED: "The Breathing Author," *HEAT,*
new series 3 (2002): 9–31.

Gerald Murnane (from the dust jacket for Landscape with
Landscape, *1985; Bruccoli Clark Layman Archives)*

Gerald Murnane is widely regarded as one of the
most unusual and original Australian writers of the late
twentieth and early twenty-first centuries. The view of
many of those who have taken up the challenge of
interpreting his work is that, in its treatment of certain
subjects, including interpretation itself, his themes
closely parallel the continental philosophy of the mid
and late twentieth century–a body of writing in which
Murnane appears to have no interest. While he certainly sits outside the Australian prose tradition that
Patrick White characterized as "dreary, dun-coloured"
realism, neither does he fit comfortably alongside colorful "fabulist" contemporaries such as Peter Carey and
Murray Bail. Indeed, the term that Murnane himself
has repeatedly used to characterize his mature work–
true fiction–seems to gesture beyond realism, perhaps
even in the direction of naturalism. That suggestion

would astonish most of his readers, at least upon initial
contact with his work. What most readers do discover
immediately about Murnane's writing, however, is that
it is serious and difficult.

The son of Reginald and Gwenneth Murnane,
Gerald Murnane was born on 25 February 1939 in
Coburg, Melbourne, not far from Pentridge Prison,
where Reginald Murnane then worked as a warder.
Between 1939 and 1959, when Gerald Murnane left his
parents' home permanently, he and his family lived at
twenty different addresses. These disruptions were the
result of Reginald Murnane's reckless betting on race-
horses, which left the family's finances in disarray. One
year of Murnane's childhood was spent in the Western

District of Victoria, where Reginald Murnane, the eldest son of a prosperous dairy farmer, had grown up. A good deal of Murnane's fiction is set in this area and picks up his family's connections with it.

An outstanding student at De La Salle College in the Melbourne suburb of Malvern, Murnane, after finishing high school in 1957, entered the Passionist Fathers' seminary in Sydney to train for the priesthood. After only three months, however, he returned to his parents' home in Melbourne and over the next two years trained as a primary-school teacher at Toorak Teachers' College. There he met Catherine Lancaster, whom he married on 14 May 1966. Murnane worked as a teacher at various Melbourne primary schools between 1960 and 1969. In the late 1960s, going to school part-time, he completed a bachelor of arts degree at the University of Melbourne. The Murnanes had a son, Giles Francis, on 16 January 1969, followed by twin sons, Gavin Edric and Martin Bevis, on 29 May 1970.

Murnane had begun to write poetry in secondary school, and although he continued to write poetry sporadically into his thirties, in 1962 he began work on a long novel. He never completed the novel, but from this time on his ambition shifted principally to prose fiction. Ultimately, the period he and his family spent in the northern Victorian city of Bendigo, between 1944 and 1948, furnished the material for Murnane's first published novel, the semi-autobiographical *Tamarisk Row* (1974).

Set in 1946 and 1947 and presented in ninety-six subtitled sections, the novel tells the story of Clement Killeaton, a nine-year-old Catholic boy growing up in the provincial city of "Bassett." Clement's mother, Jean, originally a Protestant, is kind but emotionally distant from her son. His father, Augustine, the focus of Clement's interest and that of the novel, is an obsessive gambler who becomes involved in a series of dramatic betting "plunges" that throw the family into debt and finally oblige them to flee Bassett. While the novel covers much of the standard terrain of the bildungsroman, including the feverish misunderstandings of juvenile sexuality, it is all unusually internalized. This effect is created by a seamless sliding between the real events in Clement's life and the fantasies he weaves out of them, and by a reticence toward the rendering of direct speech. (Murnane's mature work eschews dialogue altogether.)

Among many extraordinary features, one that stands out is the extent to which *Tamarisk Row* introduces the images that occupy Murnane's interest throughout the rest of his writing. Examples include exiles, monks, and gypsies; poorly treated young women, often associated with bodies of water; and

"America" as the name for an eroticized and romanticized imaginary world. Murnane's fiction appears to have a limited number of underlying registers or "keys" that can generate sets of associated images in different contexts. In *Tamarisk Row,* for example, the impacted grid of Bassett's suburban streets is associated with the wire lattice that divides priest and confessor and with the netting of an aviary near Clement's home. Subsequently, in Murnane's work, this image of a separating grille appears in versions as distinct as the cross-hatched appearance of storm clouds that threaten to keep a son from returning home to his father. A task for the criticism of the future will be to crack the "code" of these registers and reveal the outlines of Murnane's private mythology.

The central theme in *Tamarisk Row* that looks forward to the rest of Murnane's work is horse racing. In a talk called "The Breathing Author," which Murnane delivered to an international group of scholars who gathered to discuss his work in Newcastle in 2001, he said, "Someone has written that all art aspires to the condition of music. My experience is that all art, including all music, aspires to the condition of horse-racing." Horse racing not only dominates Clement Killeaton's external world, in the sense that it is ruining his family, but also his interior world: he imagines a stud farm called Tamarisk Row, from which the novel derives its name, and the story culminates with the running of an imaginary race called the Gold Cup. For Clement's imagination, racing is a bottomless reservoir of metaphors, symbols, and images, and the case is not much different with Clement's creator. One ironic register of the racing metaphor that Murnane's work explores is that, while readers may enjoy a kind of overarching perspective upon the horses and jockeys as they follow their allotted course, or indeed upon the characters in a story as they follow their courses, the readers of a piece of fiction themselves may be vulnerable to the same kind of gaze, falling upon them from a still larger context.

Tamarisk Row was warmly received by reviewers and was runner-up for *The Age* Book of the Year Award in 1974. Writing in *The Australian* (26 October 1974), Carl Harrison-Ford suggested that the great strength of the novel lay in its "dense, packed, integrated style that at times takes on the intensity of the best lyric poetry." In *The Age* (19 October 1974), Brian Kiernan described *Tamarisk Row* as "the most promising first novel here for a long time" and compared Murnane with such Irish Australian writers as Thomas Keneally, Peter Kenna, and Barry Oakley. (The literary comparison had some force, but Murnane's ancestry is almost wholly English.) In *Nation Review* (25 October 1974), John Tittensor, who became Murnane's most important early

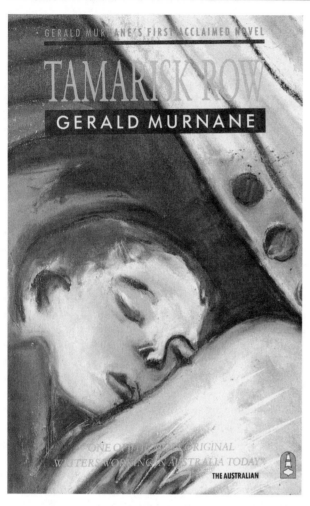

Paperback cover (1988) for Murnane's semi-autobiographical first book (1974), about a boy growing up in an Australian provincial city (Bruccoli Clark Layman Archives)

tells the story of Adrian Sherd, a student at a Catholic boys' high school in Melbourne. Adrian starts off among a bad crowd of unrepentant masturbators, and his own autoerotic fantasies transport him nightly to America, where he copulates with armies of female movie stars. In the second half of the book, as Adrian dreams of two roads away from his fallen existence—via romantic love and marriage, or a religious vocation—darker ironies and some of Murnane's characteristic themes emerge. Adrian imagines an entire "lifetime on clouds" with a pretty girl called Denise McNamara, whom he sees each day on the train, but with whom he never actually exchanges a word. Meanwhile, the search for spiritual meaning (in a tendency that mimics the complicated system the Catholic Church has set up for exacting penance from sinners) keeps collapsing into repetitive, mechanical, or even random patterns of action that have no meaning in themselves.

As social comedy, *A Lifetime on Clouds* has always been vulnerable to becoming dated, and it remains, probably unjustly, the least discussed of Murnane's books. Some reviewers were disappointed by the novel, some of them suggesting that the ending (in which Adrian has become a priest advising other troubled young men, but only in his imagination) was a letdown. Harrison-Ford argued in *Meanjin* (July 1977) that *A Lifetime on Clouds* was "not a patch" on *Tamarisk Row* "in terms of subtlety, range or insights into character." Other reviewers, however, received the book warmly, with the poet Les Murray (in the *Sydney Morning Herald* [19 February 1977]), declaring it superior to Philip Roth's *Portnoy's Complaint* (1969): "*A Lifetime on Clouds* delighted me; I was particularly admiring of the author's unfailing ability to say just enough and no more, and of the book's quiet, dryly affectionate tone."

In terms of disruptions, the second half of Murnane's life has been the opposite of the first: he and his wife have lived quietly in the same house in suburban Melbourne for more than thirty years. (His dislike of travel is legendary, and he has never flown in an airplane.) Murnane left primary teaching in 1969 and, until late 1973, worked as an editor in the Publications Branch of the Education Department, eventually rising to become second in charge of the branch. He spent the rest of the 1970s writing and caring for his young sons while his wife worked. He also worked occasionally as a freelance editor and, following the publication of *Tamarisk Row,* was supported for a time by grants from the Australia Council. In 1980 Murnane became a teacher of fiction writing at Prahran College of Advanced Education (later Victoria College, later still a campus of Deakin University). He was an influential teacher, and several of his students, including Christopher Cyrill and Tim Richards, have gone on to become published

supporter, called *Tamarisk Row* "the best novel to come out of Australia for many years." In *Nation Review* for 22 August 1975, Tittensor lamented that *Tamarisk Row* had not sold out its first printing: "Confronted with the opportunity to participate in something unique in its beauty and intensity, Australia lacks the judgement and the courage to commit itself." The comment anticipates what became a feature of Murnane's reception, that while his work has attracted a significant body of devoted readers, it has not achieved a mass audience.

Murnane followed *Tamarisk Row* with a novel of Catholic adolescence that is as close as anything he has done to social comedy. Indeed, *A Lifetime on Clouds* (1976) is a reminder that at the heart of Murnane's work is a comic vision, albeit an ironic one, in which the human need for meaning and relationship is constantly frustrated. (Thomas Hardy, whose name has become identified with just such a vision, is one of Murnane's favorite writers.) Set in 1953, *A Lifetime on Clouds*

authors whose work bears the imprint of Murnane's teaching as well as of his preoccupations and style. In addition, the situation of the writing teacher, required to demonstrate his own theory and practice to novices, became a recurrent source of interest to Murnane both in his fiction and in the essays that increasingly supplemented it. His fifteen years as a busy writing teacher turned out to be, unexpectedly perhaps, the most fertile of his career.

Through the late 1970s and early 1980s, Murnane worked on a vast and complex novel that he was finally unable to resolve to his own satisfaction. On the advice of a sympathetic publisher, he excised a thirty-thousand-word portion of the book, a fantasy about a journey to an imagined zone called Inner Australia, and allowed it to be published by itself. A miniepic in the tradition of Samuel Johnson's *Rasselas* (1759) and Jonathan Swift's *Tale of a Tub* (1704), *The Plains* (1982) surprised and delighted everyone and shaped the rest of Murnane's career. It remains easily his most discussed book and has been published in six different editions in Australia and the United States. According to Barry Oakley, reviewing *The Plains* in the *Sydney Morning Herald* (6 November 1982), Murnane had produced "a piece of writing so remarkably sustained that it is a subject for meditation rather than mere reading." As Oakley's comment implies, *The Plains* hovers somewhere between conventional fiction and philosophical writing. The novel is shaped much like the rolling grasslands in which it is set, which have seemingly drifted from the Western District of Victoria further inland: against the vast horizons of the story, individual features do not admit of easy definition, while the climaxes of action and feeling are less like mountain peaks than gently marked undulations.

The narrator of *The Plains* is an intellectual, a moviemaker who journeys from philistine Outer Australia to the plains, where a vibrant culture based upon a system of patronage flourishes. The patrons are the wealthy landowners, and on their vast estates they harbor a veritable army of artists, heraldists, philosophers, writers, and historians of design. What they value most from these "clients" is abstruse speculation regarding their relationship toward the beloved plains. The narrative is divided into three parts. In the first part, the moviemaker thinks back to his arrival on the plains twenty years earlier; he gives an account of the long-standing philosophical dispute between the Haremen and the Horizonites, of his successful interview for a tenured position on the plains, of his early years in his patron's mansion, and of his failed attempts to communicate with that man's daughter. The second part is a preliminary note on the narrator's movie project, written by him after ten years on the plains;

this section, set almost entirely inside the library of the mansion, is a meditation on the various theories of time that have prevailed upon the plains, accompanied by a series of speculations about his patron's wife and how he might open a line of communication to her. The final section returns to the present (though not to the reader's present: many of the objects and customs described in the book have a 1950s feel). The narrator is still tinkering with notes for the script for his movie, *The Interior*. He describes the occasional outdoor "scenes" organized by the landowner, together with the landowner's views concerning the visible and the invisible. The story concludes at one of these "scenes," as the landowner-patron prepares to photograph his client, at the same moment that the client prepares to photograph his own eye. The conclusion indicates two of the central themes of the book: the nature of visual perception and the question of what constitutes "inner" and "outer" consciousness.

The Plains presents the archetypal scene in Murnane's fiction: a man wants to get closer to a woman by writing to her; but writing, because it refuses to yield any stable interpretation, only increases the distance between them. Hilarious in its own solemn way, the book also wittily reverses conventional notions about the "Australian identity." In this work the famous taciturnity of rural people, usually associated with grim practicality, turns out to be merely a convenient mask for philosophical and artistic speculation.

The ironic humor in *The Plains* is deepened and extended in the six long, interconnected stories that make up Murnane's next book, *Landscape with Landscape* (1985). In "Landscape with Freckled Woman," a writer sits surrounded by nine women, having just joined their committee. The story consists of his thoughts during the meeting: about the freckled woman sitting across from him; about how he might explain to her about his past and the private "landscapes" that shape his writing; about what he might in turn learn from her; and about the way that fiction and reality would already be hopelessly intermeshed in any relation they might attempt to establish. "Sipping the Essence" tells of the friendship between the narrator and Kelvin Durkin; it concerns the sexual and emotional sacrifices made by a man with a romantic view of poetry and life versus the mundane, physical view represented by his friend. Like much of Murnane's fiction, the story emphasizes the contrast between a monastic, isolated existence and the fully engaged life.

In "The Battle of Acosta Nu" (arguably Murnane's most sustained accomplishment), a Melbourne man believes that he is actually living in Paraguay and that he is an exiled descendant of the Australian settlers who founded a New Australia there in 1893. His belief

Dust jacket for Murnane's 1985 collection of interconnected stories (Bruccoli Clark Layman Archives)

in his innate "Australianness" sets him apart from everyone, even his family. His son's death as an indirect result of his delusion causes him simply to reverse its terms, not to abandon it: he is now the true Paraguayan, while all those around him are the exiles. In "A Quieter Place than Clun," a twenty-three-year-old Catholic man, losing his faith, considers a series of possible replacements–including the psyche, the imagination, and the nervous system–for the idea of his soul. As in "Landscape with Freckled Woman," his interest in private landscapes keeps him apart from others. The narrator of "Charlie Alcock's Cock" does marry, but his longing for hidden vistas–this time parts of a vast secret Melbourne–prevents real intimacy with others. His life of gradual withdrawal from the world moves him in the opposite direction from his cousin, who is a priest. "Landscape with Artist" consists of three interwoven scenes, set in 1960, 1970, and 1980. Its descriptions of "Harp Gully" are a hilarious satire on the bohemians who gathered in the semirural Melbourne suburb of Eltham of the 1960s and 1970s: the narrator

knows that their version of the artistic life is false, but his own drive to avoid what is "merely modish" threatens to silence him completely.

All six stories, then, concern a young, or youngish, man living in Melbourne and trying to become a writer; they bear the same allegorical relation to Murnane's life in the 1960s and early 1970s as *Tamarisk Row* and *A Lifetime on Clouds* did to the 1940s and 1950s, respectively. Another connecting thread between the stories is the theme of loneliness and the link between it and the writerly vocation. Many reviewers of *Landscape with Landscape* welcomed the more familiar settings in which similar themes to those in *The Plains* were being played out. Helen Daniel suggested in *The Age* (22 June 1985) that the two books, taken together, "bring Murnane to the forefront of Australian writers."

The setting of Murnane's next book, the last book of his that could be called a novel, and his most difficult, is anything but familiar. In *Inland* (1988), two parallel narrators, speaking from distant "native districts," imagine each other into existence, apparently in order to communicate a story that each finds too painful to speak of directly. The first narrator addresses the reader from Szolnok County, on the Great Plain of Hungary; the second, from "Melbourne County" (the latter is placed in America, but the demographic details are specifically those of Melbourne). The Hungarian narrator believes, at first, that his pages will be edited by Anne Kristaly Gunnarsen, the editor of *Hinterland,* a journal of grassland studies published at the Calvin O. Dahlberg Institute of Prairie Studies in South Dakota. Later, he comes to believe that his correspondence with her is being intercepted by her husband: this belief develops into a series of meditations on the mediated and uncertain relations between readers and writers. The Hungarian narrator writes mysteriously about a young girl drowned in a well; the reader learns eventually that this detail, and other aspects of *Inland,* derive from a book about the Hungarian peasantry by Gyula Illyes. The man in Melbourne County, taking up the narrative, thinks obsessively about the harm he once did to another young girl–his childhood sweetheart, toward whom he behaved thoughtlessly thirty years earlier. Both narrators now seem to seek a reunion with a lost beloved and to seek it through the act of writing. On every page the story reverberates with images of young life and young love cut off prematurely, and in its final paragraph, *Inland* merges completely with one of the most powerful earlier treatments of the same theme, Emily Brontë's *Wuthering Heights* (1847).

Critics who thought that Murnane avoided looking at the world around him and indulged difficulty for its own sake had a field day with *Inland.* In the *Sydney Morning Herald* (16 April 1988) Peter Pierce lamented the absence of "social life" or "history" in the book and suggested that it "lies in wait" for critical sponsors, rather than readers. Even Peter Craven, one of Murnane's most influential supporters, described *Inland* in *The Australian* (10 March 1988) as "a book that you suffer through, even though it is short." But he added, "The rewards when they come are like rain after a heatwave or the moment when winter shifts into spring."

The real relief from the difficulty and seriousness of *Inland,* however, was Murnane's next book, *Velvet Waters* (1990), a collection of eleven highly accessible stories, all of them, apart from the title story, published in magazines during the 1980s. Welcomed even by some of Murnane's earlier detractors, these touching and funny stories do incorporate the "social world," including such themes as courtship, parenthood, and friendship. In the title piece, for example, a series of scenes from the early 1960s is set against scenes from the late 1980s. The story concerns two male friends and their wives, and the scenes set in the 1960s are a poignantly humorous evocation of the courting rituals

of young Catholic couples at that time. "When the Mice Failed to Arrive" evokes the narrator's concern for his asthmatic son, while "Stream System" touches on his unexpressed feelings toward his intellectually disadvantaged brother. In each story, however, these personal subjects are linked to more wide-ranging concerns about conflicting perspectives, solipsism, and the mental maps people impose upon the world.

Velvet Waters was followed by *Emerald Blue* (1995), another collection of stories, which are more difficult. These pieces swing back toward Murnane's more deductive, philosophical style of writing, indicated by repeated phrases such as "the man mentioned in the previous paragraph." Such stylistic traits have troubled some readers. They seem calculated to remind the reader that the setting of Murnane's fiction is not an agreed-upon external world but the place he described in *Landscape with Landscape* as "the space between myself and the nearest woman or man who seemed real to me."

In his more recent fiction and essays, and as part of the effort to expound on the term *true fiction* (usually to an imaginary female writing student), Murnane has revealed that imagistic threads and patterns, one of the most prominent features of his work, are consciously employed in the writing of his fiction (making him the only living Australian writer of whom it may plausibly be claimed that he has invented an original fictional method). In the first story of *Emerald Blue,* "In Far Fields," the narrator tells the female student that his mind consists only of feelings and images; that a diagram of his mind would resemble a vast map "with images for its small towns and with feelings for the roads through the grassy countryside between the towns"; and that his writing is a systematic tracing of this map, a moving from image to connected image, a journey and a search. (In *Velvet Waters,* the same method is indicated by the term *stream system.*)

That Murnane has chosen to publish less since the mid 1990s might indicate that his own search, or at least the part of it that could be prosecuted through fiction, has reached a pause, even a conclusion. (He retired from teaching in 1995 and spent more time pursuing various interests, which include horse racing and learning Hungarian, as well as writing projects that he has no intention of publishing.) While Murnane's stories gently ridicule those who write simply in order to be considered "writers," the genuine writers in his work write because, quite simply, they have to; furthermore, they experience this need as a burden and as an enforced drawing away from life. The narrator of *Inland* says, "These words rest lightly on my page, but this heaviness pressing on me is perhaps the weight of all the words I have still not written. And the heaviness

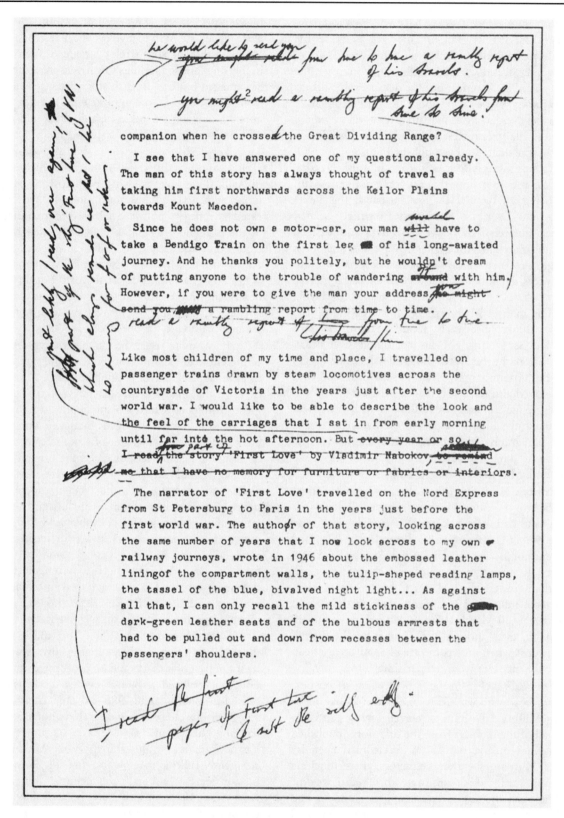

companion when he crossed the Great Dividing Range?

I see that I have answered one of my questions already. The man of this story has always thought of travel as taking him first northwards across the Keilor Plains towards Mount Macedon.

Since he does not own a motor-car, our man will have to take a Bendigo train on the first leg of his long-awaited journey. And he thanks you politely, but he wouldn't dream of putting anyone to the trouble of wandering around with him. However, if you were to give the man your address, he might send you a rambling report from time to time.

Like most children of my time and place, I travelled on passenger trains drawn by steam locomotives across the countryside of Victoria in the years just after the second world war. I would like to be able to describe the look and the feel of the carriages that I sat in from early morning until far into the hot afternoon. But every year or so I read the story 'First Love' by Vladimir Nabokov, to remind me that I have no memory for furniture or fabrics or interiors.

The narrator of 'First Love' travelled on the Nord Express from St Petersburg to Paris in the years just before the first world war. The author of that story, looking across the same number of years that I now look across to my own railway journeys, wrote in 1946 about the embossed leather lining of the compartment walls, the tulip-shaped reading lamps, the tassel of the blue, bivalved night light... As against all that, I can only recall the mild stickiness of the green dark-green leather seats and of the bulbous armrests that had to be pulled out and down from recesses between the passengers' shoulders.

Page from the revised typescript for Murnane's short story "First Love" (from Candida Baker, Yacker 2: Australian Writers Talk about Their Work, *1987; Mount Holyoke College Library)*

pressing on me is what first urged me to write." Undertaking a search that, although arduous, cannot be avoided has also been the experience reported by many spiritual seekers. The suggestion that Murnane may fruitfully be considered among their company was a possibility he hinted at in his talk "The Breathing Author":

> More than forty years ago I ceased to be a believing Catholic, but I have never been able to think of the visible world, the so called real world . . . as the *only* world. I might go further and say that the notion of this being the only world seems to me hardly less preposterous than the notions imparted to me as a child by my Catholic parents and teachers and ministers of religion. . . . I might go even further yet and say that I have lighted on what I consider sound evidence for these beliefs of mine. . . . a writer of fiction might disturb a group of scholars less by confessing to some unsavoury sexual proclivity than by announcing his belief in an afterlife and claiming to have seen evidence for his belief.

> Anyone reading through my archives after my death will find detailed notes on the matters alluded to . . . but no one should expect to receive after my death any message from the Other Side. One life as a writer will have been enough.

While Gerald Murnane has never been a popular writer, his critical reputation has continued to grow steadily through the last decade. He is the subject of a monograph in the "Australian Writers" series of Oxford University Press, and a special issue of the journal *Southerly* has been devoted to his work. Murnane has probably aroused as much serious scholarly interest overseas as any living Australian prose writer, and Ph.D. theses have been written about him in Canada, Germany, and Sweden (where his reputation is particularly strong). An Italian translation of *Velvet Waters* has been published, as well as a Swedish translation of *Inland*. In 1999 Murnane was the recipient of the prestigious Patrick White Literary Award.

References:

Imre Salusinszky, *Gerald Murnane* (Melbourne: Oxford University Press, 1993);

Southerly, special issue on Murnane, 55, no. 3 (1995)–includes a long interview with Murnane, an uncollected story ("The White Cattle of Uppington"), and critical essays by Don Anderson, Nicholas Birns, and Dominique Hecq.

Les Murray

(17 October 1938 –)

Peter F. Alexander
University of New South Wales

BOOKS: *The Ilex Tree,* by Murray and Geoffrey Lehmann (Canberra: Australia National University Press, 1965);

The Weatherboard Cathedral (Sydney: Angus & Robertson, 1969);

Poems against Economics (Sydney: Angus & Robertson, 1972; London: Angus & Robertson, 1972);

Lunch & Counter Lunch (Sydney: Angus & Robertson, 1974);

Selected Poems: The Vernacular Republic (Sydney: Angus & Robertson, 1976; London: Angus & Robertson, 1976); revised and republished as *The Vernacular Republic: Poems 1961–1981* (Sydney: Angus & Robertson, 1982; Edinburgh: Canongate, 1982; New York: Persea Books, 1982; enlarged and revised, Sydney: Angus & Robertson, 1988; London: Angus & Robertson, 1988);

Ethnic Radio (London: Angus & Robertson, 1977; Sydney: Angus & Robertson, 1978);

The Peasant Mandarin: Prose Pieces (St. Lucia: University of Queensland Press, 1978);

The Boys Who Stole the Funeral: A Novel Sequence (Sydney: Angus & Robertson, 1979; London: Angus & Robertson, 1980; New York: Farrar, Straus & Giroux, 1991);

Equanimities (Copenhagen: Razorback Press, 1982);

The People's Otherworld (North Ryde, N.S.W.: Angus & Robertson, 1983; London: Angus & Robertson, 1983);

Persistence in Folly: Selected Prose Writings (London & Sydney: Angus & Robertson, 1984);

The Australian Year: The Chronicle of Our Seasons and Celebrations, text by Murray, photographs by Peter Solness and others (North Ryde, N.S.W.: Angus & Robertson, 1985; London: Angus & Robertson, 1985);

Selected Poems (Manchester, U.K.: Carcanet, 1986);

The Daylight Moon (North Ryde, N.S.W. & London: Angus & Robertson, 1987; New York: Persea Books, 1988);

Les Murray (photograph by Valerie Murray; from dust jacket for Conscious & Verbal, *2001; Bruccoli Clark Layman Archives)*

The Idyll Wheel: Cycle of a Year at Bunyah, NSW, April 1986–April 1987 (Canberra: Officina Brindabella, 1989);

Blocks and Tackles: Articles and Essays 1982 to 1990 (North Ryde, N.S.W.: Angus & Robertson, 1990);

Dog Fox Field (North Ryde, N.S.W.: Angus & Robertson, 1990; Manchester, U.K.: Carcanet, 1991; New York: Farrar, Straus & Giroux, 1992);

Collected Poems (Sydney: Angus & Robertson, 1991; Manchester, U.K.: Carcanet, 1991; revised and

---

enlarged, North Ryde, N.S.W. & London: Angus & Robertson, 1991); republished as *The Rabbiter's Bounty: Collected Poems* (New York: Farrar, Straus & Giroux, 1991);

The Paperbark Tree: Selected Prose (Manchester, U.K.: Carcanet, 1992);

Translations from the Natural World (Paddington, N.S.W.: Isabella Press, 1992; Manchester, U.K.: Carcanet, 1993; New York: Farrar, Straus & Giroux, 1994);

Subhuman Redneck Poems (Manchester, U.K.: Carcanet, 1993; Pott's Point, N.S.W.: Duffy & Snellgrove, 1996; New York: Farrar, Straus & Giroux, 1997);

Killing the Black Dog, edited by Christine Alexander (Annandale, N.S.W.: Federation Press, 1997);

A Working Forest (Pott's Point, N.S.W.: Duffy & Snellgrove, 1997);

New Selected Poems (Sydney: Duffy & Snellgrove, 1998);

Fredy Neptune (Sydney: Duffy & Snellgrove, 1998; Manchester, U.K.: Carcanet, 1998; New York: Farrar, Straus & Giroux, 1999);

Conscious & Verbal (Manchester, U.K.: Carcanet, 1999; Pott's Point, N.S.W.: Duffy & Snellgrove, 2000; New York: Farrar, Straus & Giroux, 2001);

The Quality of Sprawl: Thoughts about Australia (Pott's Point, N.S.W.: Duffy & Snellgrove, 1999);

Learning Human: Selected Poems (New York: Farrar, Straus & Giroux, 2000; Manchester, U.K.: Carcanet, 2001);

The Full Dress (Canberra: National Gallery of Australia, 2002);

New Collected Poems (Sydney: Duffy & Snellgrove, 2002; Manchester, U.K.: Carcanet, 2003);

Poems the Size of Photographs (Sydney: Duffy & Snellgrove, 2002; Manchester, U.K.: Carcanet, 2002).

OTHER: *The New Oxford Book of Australian Verse* (Melbourne: Oxford University Press, 1986; expanded edition, Oxford & Melbourne: Oxford University Press, 1991);

Anthology of Australian Religious Poetry (Blackburn, Vic.: Collins Dove, 1986; revised, 1991);

A. B. Paterson Selected Poems (Sydney: Collins/Angus & Robertson, 1992);

Fivefathers: Five Australian Poets of the Pre-Academic Era, edited by Murray (Manchester, U.K.: Carcanet, 1994).

Les Murray is an outstanding Australian poet of his generation and one of the foremost Australian literary critics. The author of seventeen volumes of verse, five books of literary essays, and many influential editions, he has for decades helped to shape the Australian literary landscape and has been one of the most authoritative literary voices in national debates of many kinds.

Leslie Allan Murray was born on 17 October 1938 in Nabiac, on the central coast of New South Wales, to Miriam (née Arnall) and Cecil Murray and was baptized in a Free Presbyterian ceremony at Bunyah, the village near which his parents farmed. Miriam had trained as a nurse in Newcastle, the nearest big city; Cecil Murray was a struggling dairy farmer whose 150 acres were owned by his domineering father. Murray was raised in a family home that was little more than a shed, with wooden walls, iron roof, and only three internal rooms. The boy slept on the verandah. His childhood was devoid of luxuries and had few comforts.

Although his father was nearly illiterate, Les Murray learned to read at the age of four and thereafter was educated by his proud mother with the aid of a Sydney correspondence school until the boy turned nine, when he went to a local rural school at Bulby Brush.

He began his high-school career in 1951, but it was interrupted by the traumatic event that he later came to feel ended his childhood: his mother died of an ectopic pregnancy in April 1951, when Murray was twelve. The local doctor refused to send an ambulance without knowing what was wrong with the patient, and Cecil Murray obstinately refused to say; during the hours of delay Miriam hemorrhaged steadily, and she died after some days in the hospital.

Cecil Murray suffered a nervous breakdown and ceased to care for the farm, himself, or his son. In the agony of his grief Cecil accused his son of having "killed Mummy": Les Murray's birth had been a difficult one, and his father attributed Miriam's death to injuries she had suffered twelve years before. Though there is no medical evidence to support this account, the boy believed his father and suffered severe and lasting trauma. He did not return to school until 1952, and then he dropped out again after a year; he lived with his slowly recovering father in considerable squalor, spending his days out with a rifle, killing rabbits or reading on his own.

From 1955 through 1956 he attended Taree High School, where he did well academically but felt himself shunned and mocked by his fellow pupils, particularly the girls, whom he longed to impress. His weightlifter's build and great strength saved him from physical bullying, but he felt socially ostracized for two years and carried the psychological scars of this experience for life. Some of his most vivid poems focus on his experience of group cruelty, among them "A Torturer's Apprenticeship" (published in *Dog Fox Field,* 1990) and "Burning Want" (published in *Subhuman Redneck Poems,* 1993). In his last year at school he began writing his first poems.

In 1957 he entered Sydney University with a Commonwealth Scholarship. There he edited the student publication *honi soit* and later the journal *Arna,* activities

Murray at his farm near Bunyah (Graeme Kinross Smith Collection; from Peter Pierce, Oxford Literary Guide to Australia, *1987; Thomas Cooper Library, University of South Carolina)*

that brought him attention from a group that included Clive James, Germaine Greer, Robert Hughes, Bruce Beresford, Bob Ellis, Mary Gaudron, Michael Kirby, John Bell, Richard Wherrett, Geoffrey Lehmann, Richard Butler, Mungo MacCallum, Richard Walsh, Colin Mackerras, and Laurie Oakes, together with others who never became well known but whom Murray respected and from whom he learned.

He paid little attention to lectures, set assignments, or examinations and instead focused on reading the contents of Fisher Library. He had already begun studying German in his spare time as a schoolboy; at Sydney University he added Chinese, Spanish, and Italian. He revealed an astonishing gift for languages, and before he was twenty-five he could read more than a dozen, mostly Western European, languages.

His output of poems, many of them published in student papers, was steady and of a quality that impressed his fellows. He was an increasingly prominent figure in the literary life of the university.

By the end of 1959, however, he had begun to sink into a depression connected with his mother's death and his own feelings of isolation, and from which he was slow to emerge. He lost his scholarship, ceased to live in rented accommodation, and instead took to sleeping rough on building sites or in parks. In 1961 he dropped out of Sydney University and hitchhiked around Australia, skeletally thin and living from hand to mouth.

He was saved from what might have been complete dissolution by the partial lifting of his depression, which made possible his return to the university in 1962, but more importantly by meeting and falling in love with a fellow student, Valerie Gina Morelli, the beautiful daughter of Swiss-Hungarian immigrants. Murray proposed to her on Anzac Day 1962, and they were married in a Roman Catholic ceremony on 29 September 1962. Murray was baptized a Catholic in 1964. He had found emotional and spiritual stability at last, and it proved permanent in spite of intermittent depression.

Murray gained a position with the Australian National University in Canberra, acting as a translator of Western European languages, a position that required the ability to translate, at sight, everything from Dutch to

Portuguese. Those who worked with him were astonished at his linguistic range and fluency.

His output of verse continued uninterrupted by his work for the Australian National University, and in 1965, nearly coinciding with the birth of the first of his five children (three sons and two daughters), he published *The Ilex Tree,* a book of poetry written jointly with Lehmann. The volume was well received by the critics and won the Grace Leven Prize for poetry, thus bringing Murray the attention and friendship of established poets such as Kenneth Slessor and Judith Wright. Douglas Stewart asked Murray to let Angus and Robertson have his next volume, thus beginning a long association between Murray and the chief publisher of Australian poetry.

In 1967 Murray resigned his sought-after job at the Australian National University and moved his growing family to Britain for more than a year, supported by his first Commonwealth Literary Fellowship. On their return to Sydney in 1968, Murray began the first of a long series of temporary jobs, ranging from a clerkship in the prime minister's office to laboring on the railways; by 1971 he had sufficient confidence in his own ability to earn money from poetry and in Valerie's income from teaching to declare himself henceforth a freelance author.

He made good use of his new freedom. From this point on the flow of his poetic publications was copious and rapid. In 1972 *Poems against Economics* confirmed his growing reputation but received mixed reviews. By the time of its publication, with two volumes already behind him, he had been typecast, both by his supporters and by critics: he was the poet of the countryside in subject matter and a conservative in style, straightforward and accessible. *Poems against Economics* unsettled both those views, and the critics showed their bewilderment.

The volume consisted of three sections: the Cook Prize–winning "Seven Points for an Imperilled Star," which subtly raised a range of questions as to what kind of country Australia was, and where it should be going; "Juggernaut's Little Scrapbook," which was a satire; and "Walking to the Cattle-Place," a complex and learned series of meditations on the significance of the cow culture in which Murray had been raised and which drew on his curious and varied knowledge about other cattle cultures, ranging from Celt to Sanskrit to Zulu. He was putting forward alternative values to those of the bureaucratic bean counters and doing so with serious intent, and the volume had a complex thematic unity, the individual poems of his previous volumes giving way to a unified volume (in which the poems are related to each other and form a coherent whole).

Some critics were unsettled by this new direction. "There have been no great technical innovations at any stage of his career," the journal *New Poetry* grumbled,

"and at times Murray's poems have tended to ramble." From *New Poetry,* which regarded technical innovation as equivalent to poetic excellence, this criticism was a severe condemnation. In fact, in the new volume Murray was experimenting with a new form of long, meditative poem, one that moves repeatedly from startling observation to new understanding in a series of ascending pulses, slow to make its point but richly repaying openness and thought on the part of the reader. He made this form his own, though *New Poetry* did not notice. This criticism was the first from the group of poets that had formed around one of Murray's poetic rivals and for which *New Poetry* was a mouthpiece; it was not the last.

The resulting attention did him no harm. The Commonwealth Literary Fund sent him on a lecture tour of Western Australia, a gratifying experience for someone who had been a struggling university student only a short time before. Hereafter, the Literary Fund and its successor, the Literature Board of the Australia Council, supported Murray generously over many years and were amply rewarded with the quality of his writing.

The establishment of the Literature Board owed something to Murray's own persuasive writing on the subject of government support for writers, for by 1970 he had begun publishing the first of a long series of thoughtful essays on major public issues, and over the years he became a commanding voice in Australia's energetic cultural debates. He also established a reputation as a widely read and generous reviewer of contemporary Australian literature. His essays appeared in major newspapers and such journals as *Quadrant,* and Murray collected them in his five volumes of essays, beginning with *The Peasant Mandarin: Prose Pieces* in 1978.

He then embarked on another career, as one of Australia's leading literary editors, when he took over the direction of the journal *Poetry Australia* in 1973; he continued to edit it until 1980 and from 1978 extended his influence by becoming the sole poetry reader for Angus and Robertson. He added to that task the literary editorship of *Quadrant* from 1989. His editing work, particularly that for *Poetry Australia,* plunged him into the center of the "poetry wars" that so enlivened the Australian literary scene during the 1970s and 1980s, and he was an energetic, joyful, and partisan contributor to the struggle.

In 1974 he published *Lunch & Counter Lunch,* again to divided critical responses. In *Poetry Australia* (December 1975), David Malouf described the new volume as "of astonishing dexterity and scope" and added boldly: "There is no doubt about Murray's stature. He is a powerful poet, with all the gifts, one might want to assert, of a potentially great one." Other critics implied that Murray's work was becoming too predictable. Overall the response was positive, however, and the

*Cover for the 1996 paperback edition of Murray's 1993
collection of poems, a popular and critical success
(Bruccoli Clark Layman Archives)*

volume won the National Book Council Award the following year.

By 1976 Murray's poetic achievement was recognized in the first of his volumes of selected verse, *Selected Poems: The Vernacular Republic,* which he republished with additions several times in the next decade. It was early in 1976, too, that he wrote an extraordinary cycle of poems, "The Buladelah-Taree Holiday-Song Cycle," in which he drew on the oldest verbal manifestations of Australian rural culture, Aboriginal oral poetry. During his planning of the ill-fated volume of Aboriginal poetry he had read and greatly admired Ronald M. Berndt's translations of the Wonguri-Mandjikai Moon-Bone Cycle of poems from Arnhem Land. Around Christmas 1975, on a trip to Bunyah, he had conceived of writing a cycle of poems in the style and meter of Berndt's translation. He later described the process of composition in an essay collected in *Persistence in Folly* (1984) he called "The Human Hair-Thread":

As I thought about it, I realised it would be necessary to incorporate in it elements from all three main Australian cultures, Aboriginal, rural and urban. But I would arrange them in their order of distinctiveness, with the senior culture setting the tone and controlling the movement of the poem. What I was after was an enactment of a longed-for fusion of all three cultures. . . . The poem would necessarily celebrate my own spirit country.

Murray focused the book on the annual holiday migration of families to the bush or the sea, "going back to their ancestral places in a kind of unacknowledged spiritual walkabout"–as he put it in an essay, "looking for their country in order to draw sustenance from it. Or newcomers looking for the real Australia." He wrote the poem in thirteen sections, as in the Moon-Bone Cycle, producing it in two bursts about a month apart, the hiatus coming between sections 6 and 7.

The Jindyworobak poets of the 1940s had been mocked for the thinness of their understanding of Aboriginal culture, and Murray was taking a great risk with this daringly experimental poem: critics were waiting to accuse him of cultural arrogance, or ignorance, or daring to speak for Aboriginal people. That he brought it off triumphantly is a tribute not just to his powers as a poet but also to his deep knowledge of Aboriginal culture and to his refusal to admit the inevitability of cultural apartheid in Australia.

Malouf, lecturing on Caliban's naming magic in 1973, remarked on "the extraordinary way our own Aborigines have possessed the land in their minds, through folkstories, taboos, song cycles, and made it part of the fabric of their living as we never can." Murray, always opposed to the division of Australians, always on the lookout for convergence, riposted crisply in "The Human Hair-Thread": "We can, and some of us do, possess the land imaginatively in very much the Aboriginal way," and his poem richly demonstrated what he meant:

It is good to come out after driving and walk on bare
    grass;
walking out, looking all around, relearning that country.
Looking out for snakes, and looking out for rabbits as
    well;
going into the shade of myrtles to try their cupped climate,
    swinging by one hand around them,
in that country of the Holiday . . .
stepping behind trees to the dam, as if you had a gun,
to that place of the Wood Duck,
to that place of the Wood Duck's Nest,
proving you can still do it; looking at the duck who hasn't
    seen you,
the mother duck who'd run Catch Me (broken wing) I'm
    Fatter (broken wing), having hissed to her children.

Like all of Murray's work, the poem cycle is a magical naming and evocation that gives everyone who reads it the sense of being possessed by this land that he rejoiced in. The cycle concludes with a subtle evocation of Australian spirituality, the word "holiday" reverting to its original meaning, in poetry so simple that the reader cannot see how it is done, but so effective as to suspend the breath:

> People go outside and look at the stars, and at the melon-rind moon,
> the Scorpion going down into the mountains, over there towards Waukivory, sinking into the tree-line,
> in the time of the Rockmelons, and of the Holiday . . .
> the Cross is rising on his elbow, above the glow of the horizon;
> carrying a small star in his pocket, he reclines there brilliantly,
> above the Alum Mountain, and the lakes threaded on the Myall River, and above the Holiday.

In 1976 Murray was awarded a three-year Literature Board Senior Fellowship, and the next year he traveled to Rotterdam as an Australian representative at the Poetry International conference. Thereafter he frequently visited Europe, either to attend poetry gatherings or to undertake lecture tours and readings of his own work. These annual tours, which he gradually extended to include the United States, helped bring him to the attention of an international public, as well as supplying an important part of his income.

Ethnic Radio, published in 1977, was the first of Murray's volumes to pay close attention to the growing non-Anglo-Celtic section of the Australian population, that section of which his wife Valerie was a part. He also had an increasingly keen interest in Aboriginal Australians: one of his aunts had married an Aboriginal, and Murray kept contact with the Aboriginal side of his family and studied surviving lore. He had for some years been attracted to the idea of writing a truly long narrative poem. Declining to call it an epic, he published *The Boys Who Stole the Funeral* as a "verse novel" in 1979. In it he shows his passionate interest in and support for poor rural folk, both white and Aboriginal, and his wish for cultural confluence and mutual enrichment.

In 140 sonnets, formal or irregular, Murray tells the story of two city boys, Kevin Forbutt and Cameron Reeby, who steal the body of Forbutt's great-uncle from a funeral parlor and take it to the country in fulfillment of the uncle's wish to be buried in his hometown, an echo of the importance many Aboriginal people attach to returning the remains of a dead person to his or her spirit country. The poem continues Murray's examination of the Boeotian-Athenian divide, but it also examines such issues as the impact of feminism and the need to rethink masculinity, as well as the role of Aboriginal culture in defining what is Australian.

Murray considered that the traditional idea of the masculine had reached a crisis point: as he told one British critic in a private letter in 1983, *The Boys Who Stole the Funeral* is structured by the view that

> men have collapsed, are baffled, not knowing, after the collapse of the military idea-and-culture, what to do next; I don't know whether this collapse of the traditionally masculine is a cause or a symptom of the queer stoppage I feel in our world down beneath all the furious playing of variations on things long known . . . the ageing trendies furiously defending the year 1968 and the mandarinate of mere style it seemed to promise. . . .

And feminism was a corollary of this crisis. Murray looked at feminism chiefly through the figure of Noeline Kampff, a two-dimensional caricature of the feminists he met, mainly on university campuses, in the late 1970s. During this period certain campus feminists felt the need to try to sound like men. Noeline Kampff speaks entirely in clichés and curses, expresses confused hatred and despair, and pours a bucket of blood over Reeby in a symbolic abortion or human-sacrifice scene: by creating her, Murray offered himself as a target for feminists on the lookout for one, and the offer was accepted gleefully.

For years he was hounded on campuses by demonstrators who disrupted his talks with angry speeches masquerading as questions and who on the campus of the University of New South Wales, in 1983, displayed posters attacking him, wrote obscene comments in lipstick in the male staff toilet he used, and sent him anonymous envelopes of excrement. He had had similar though less extreme experiences at Newcastle University the year before.

By contrast, the reviews he got were mostly respectful, but reviewers in Australia wrote few thorough-going encomiums, and a groundswell of negative comment arose. This response strongly contrasted with the enthusiastic overseas reception of the volume when it was published in Great Britain and America. What Murray termed "a strong whispering campaign" also arose against *The Boys Who Stole the Funeral.*

Murray should have been able to take pride in the achievement of the volume. His infectious pleasure in language is evident everywhere in it. Samuel Johnson remarked disapprovingly of William Shakespeare that he could not resist a pun; the same is true of Murray. He also spins surprising and inevitable images endlessly, apparently effortlessly; by this stage in his career he was in complete control of his art, using rhyme and conventional stanzaic forms as easily as free verse. The freshness of his observation and his ability to convey vivid images is evident everywhere: from the description of a jet fighter that "floats up the valley / with a sound like a long plunger rising / in a sonorous tube, and slams over" (poem 104), to a compelling evocation of the obscene challenge posed by a motorcycle gang, urban violence personified, or the description of someone sinking into sleep and being jolted half-awake by "that abyssal start / sheer drop, that is said to come / from the heart shifting speeds"–an experience that, although universal, had not been described before.

This volume, which, in spite of negative criticism, won him the Grace Leven Prize, involved him in an intense correspondence with Judith Wright, who accused him of appropriating and misusing Aboriginal culture. Murray rebutted this charge tactfully and effectively, thus maintaining his friendship with Wright to the end of her life.

In 1982 he produced what he called a "chapbook," a brief poetic pamphlet titled *Equanimities,* published in Copenhagen, and in 1983 he published another volume of verse, *The People's Otherworld,* winning the National Book Council Prize. His books from 1976 onward were routinely published overseas following their Australian appearances: Persea in New York and Carcanet in the United Kingdom had become his publishers along with Angus and Robertson in Australia.

He was by now also a regular and honored guest on Australian campuses: he was poet-in-residence for the first time, at the University of New England in 1978, and followed this honor with many more such residences, at the University of New South Wales, the University of Sydney, Stirling University, and other institutions in Australia and the United Kingdom.

The second of his volumes of essays, *Persistence in Folly: Selected Prose Writings,* was published in 1984, confirming his status as a critic and arbiter of taste. The following year he collaborated in the production of a glossy coffee-table book, *The Australian Year: The Chronicle of Our Seasons and Celebrations,* which he filled with poetic prose descriptions of the natural landscapes he loved.

He followed up this demonstration that he was still a countryman at heart by moving, at the end of 1985, from the Chatswood house in Sydney in which he had lived since 1971 to forty acres of land he had bought in his ancestral valley near Bunyah, on which he built a small house within sight of the spot on which he had been brought up. This residence became his permanent home, a clear announcement that for all his literary success and his international travels, he remained rooted in the soil from which his poetry derived its strength.

His publication of volumes of poetry seemed to accelerate further after his move back to the bush. *The Daylight Moon* appeared in 1987, winning a National Poetry Award, and *The Idyll Wheel: Cycle of a Year at Bunyah, NSW, April 1986–April 1987,* published in 1989, announced to the world in its title and its rejoicing subject matter that he had come home. During these years back in Bunyah he was also editing actively, producing *The New Oxford Book of Australian Verse* (1986) and an *Anthology of Australian Religious Poetry* (1986). Both of these volumes showed the catholicity of his taste and his strong sense of what makes Australian writing distinctive.

The happiness of his home life had been clouded in 1981 by the realization that his fourth child, Alexander, was autistic. Alexander proved both a sorrow and a great joy to the Murrays, and in later years Murray wrote several deeply sensitive poems about him, among them the moving "It Permits a Portrait in Line Scan at Fifteen." Murray's volume *Dog Fox Field,* published in 1990, shows his interest in and concern for the mentally handicapped.

At a party in 1988 he met a woman who had been one of his most relentless persecutors while they were both teenagers at Taree High School. She jokingly used one of the insulting names that had been fastened on him then, "Bottom," and the whole of that terrible time following his mother's death came back to him with a rush. Within hours he was deep in depression again, and this time what he called "the black dog" hung on for years. Even at his worst, though, he was able to continue to write poetry and to travel to poetry gatherings in countries as diverse as India, Israel, France, and Japan. But many friends and acquaintances, knowing nothing about his psychological state, were puzzled or offended by sharp letters or apparently rude responses at this time. His position as poetry reader for Angus and Robertson came to an end in 1990, partly because of this psychological stress.

But even as lines of communication with his fellow humans became difficult, he embarked on the writing of a series of poems showing extraordinary empathy with birds, insects, and animals, which in 1992 he published to great acclaim as *Translations from the Natural World.* The reception of the volume had been triumphant, winning both the New South Wales Premier Prize and the Victoria Premier Prize for 1993, and the National Book Council Banjo Award, though Murray's illness made him convinced that Australian newspapers were deliberately ignoring his achievements. The new book, though, was particularly well received in Britain, where Murray's effortless empathy with animals seemed to strike a particularly welcome chord. Henceforth, his regular reading tours of the United Kingdom were often great successes, contributing largely to his insecure annual income.

His depression ended with a dramatic physical illness in July 1996, when he was rushed to a hospital in Newcastle with a liver abscess from which he nearly

Dust jacket for the 2001 U.S. edition of Murray's 1999 book about the neglected aspects of daily life (Bruccoli Clark Layman Archives)

died. After many days in a coma he regained consciousness to find a mountain of sympathetic mail, and the depression gone. Partly because of the amount of press coverage his illness received, his latest volume, *Subhuman Redneck Poems,* became a poetry best-seller.

Publicity much more pleasant to him came with the Australian publication of this defiantly titled volume, a month after he left the hospital. The cover illustration was a photograph by Graham McCarter of Cecil Murray in the overgrown garden of the Bunyah house, wearing his bush hat and holding his violin and bow, the image of a rugged redneck musician. Many of the poems spoke for Cecil and for Murray's people, the rural poor, against those who would patronize and suppress them; perhaps 10 percent of the poems in the volume, as a result, were passionately indignant.

Murray's *saeva indignatio* (savage indignation) in defense of the "redneck," the poor, the common man, was as vital and energizing to him as William Butler Yeats's use of the occult was to the Irish poet. The bulk of the book was made up of poems as strong as any Mur-

ray had written: he was clearly a poet at the height of his powers. Perhaps above all, the sense of suffering endured, accepted, and overcome was what gave the volume much of its force. Murray remained what he had been from the start of his career, one of the best nature poets in the language, as in "Dead Trees in the Dam":

Odd mornings, it's been all bloodflag
and rifle green: a stopped-motion shrapnel
of kingparrots. Smithereens when they freaked.
Rarely, it's weed ducks, whose children
will float among the pillars. In daytime
magpies sidestep up wood to jag pinnacles
and the big blow-in cuckoo crying
Alarm, Alarm on the wing is not let light.
This hours after dynastic charts of high
profile ibis have rowed away to beat
the paddocks. Which, however green, are
always watercolour, and on brown paper.

His description of two deaf women signing to one another, too, has a magical rightness to it, particularly in the imagist connection with Chinese calligraphy:

Two women were characters, continually
rewriting themselves, in turn, with their hands
mostly, but with face and torso too
and very fast, fluttering like the gestures
above a busy street in Shanghai.

He could produce repeatedly the same deadly accurate
bounce and stab, transfixing images like a bird, unerr-
ingly, as in "Comete," with its description of a woman's
long hair:

Uphill in Melbourne on a beautiful day
a woman was walking ahead of her hair.
Like teak oiled soft to fracture and sway
It hung to her heels and seconded her
As a pencilled retinue, an unscrolling title
To ploughland, edged with ripe rows of dress,
a sheathed wing that couldn't fly her at all,
only itself, loosely, and her spirits.
                                        A largesse
of life and self, brushed all calm and out,
its abstracted attempts on her mouth weren't seen,
nor its showering, its tenting. Just the detail
that swam in its flow-lines, glossing about—
as she paced on, comet-like, face to the sun.

Subhuman Redneck Poems was a great critical success. It won
Murray the premier British poetry award, the T. S. Eliot
Prize, worth £5,000, and television news helicopters
thwacked the skies above the Forty Acres and floated
down into the paddocks around the little weatherboard
house as journalists competed for interviews. Murray's
neighbors, to whom helicopters usually meant a medical
emergency or police aerial-spotting for marijuana, were
tremendously impressed.

What pleased Murray even more was that the volume became a great popular success, selling more than
ten thousand copies in Australia, an astonishing figure
for a book of poetry in a country of only eighteen million
people. Australians had proved again that they were willing to identify with his sometimes lonely struggle against
literary and political fashion.

The epic narrative poem *Fredy Neptune,* which Murray had been writing since 1991 and which he published
in sections, was completed in 1998 and published in full;
it was recognized immediately as one of his greatest
achievements. His reputation continued to grow both
nationally and internationally. In 1994 he was nominated
for the chair of poetry at Oxford, though he was defeated

in the ballot; many movies about his writing were made,
in which he enjoyed appearing; he won the German
Petrarch Prize in 1995 and the Queen's Gold Medal for
poetry (as a direct response to the publication of *Fredy
Neptune*) in 1999. When Poet Laureate Ted Hughes died
in 1998, Murray's name was one of the first proposed in
the British press for the laureateship, and though he
declined to let his name go forward, he was pleased by
the compliment.

Les Murray continues to write, travel, and comment on national affairs as actively as ever. With each
new volume of verse his reputation grows. Although anything approaching a final judgment on his work cannot
be made yet, clearly he is one of the major poets writing
in English at the end of the twentieth century and in the
first years of the twenty-first century.

Interview:

Janette Turner Hospital, "Interview with Les Murray,"
    Dictionary of Literary Biography Yearbook: 2001, pp.
    284–291.

References:

Peter F. Alexander, *Les Murray: A Life in Progress* (Mel-
    bourne: Oxford University Press, 2000);

Lawrence Bourke, *A Vivid Steady State: Les Murray and
    Australian Poetry* (Sydney: New South Wales Uni-
    versity Press and New Endeavour Press, 1992);

Carmel Gaffney, ed., *Counterbalancing Light: Essays on the
    Poetry of Les Murray* (Armidale: Kardoorair Press,
    1997);

Steven Matthews, *Les Murray* (Manchester: Manchester
    University Press, 2002);

Penelope Nelson, *Notes on the Poetry of Les A. Murray* (Syd-
    ney: Eyre Methuen, 1978);

Bruce Clunies Ross, ed., *Poetry of Les Murray: Critical
    Essays* (Brisbane: University of Queensland Press,
    2002);

Anurag Sharma, *A Dimension of the Angel* (Jaipur: Bohra
    Prakshan, 1997).

Papers:

Les Murray's papers, 1951–1996, including his correspondence and drafts of most of his poems, are held by
the National Library of Australia, Canberra. Access is
restricted until the author's death.

Oodgeroo of the Tribe Noonuccal
(Kath Walker)
(3 November 1920 – 16 September 1993)

Anne Brewster
University of New South Wales

BOOKS: *We Are Going,* as Kath Walker (Brisbane: Jacaranda Press, 1964; New York: Citadel, 1965);

The Dawn Is at Hand, as Walker (Brisbane: Jacaranda Press, 1966);

My People, as Walker (Milton: Jacaranda Press, 1970); revised as *My People: A Kath Walker Collection* (Milton: Jacaranda Press, 1981); revised as *My People* (Milton: Jacaranda Press, 1990); republished as *The Dawn Is at Hand: Selected Poems,* introduction by Malcolm Williamson (London & New York: Marion Boyars, 1991);

Stradbroke Dreamtime, as Walker, illustrated by Dennis Schapel (Sydney: Angus & Robertson, 1972); revised, illustrated by Lorraine Hannay (London & Sydney: Angus & Robertson, 1982); as Oodgeroo, revised, illustrated by Bronwyn Bancroft (Pymble: Angus & Robertson, 1993); republished as *Dreamtime: Aboriginal Stories by Oodgeroo* (New York: Lothrop, Lee & Shepard, 1994);

Father Sky and Mother Earth, as Walker, illustrated by Walker (Brisbane: Jacaranda Press, 1981);

Kath Walker in China, as Walker, Mandarin translation by Gu Zixin (Brisbane: Jacaranda Press/International Culture Publishing, 1988);

Australia's Unwritten History: More Legends of Our Land, as Oodgeroo (Sydney: Harcourt Brace Jovanovich, 1992).

SELECTED BROADSIDE: *Towards a Global Village in the Southern Hemisphere,* as Oodgeroo (Nathan: Institute for Cultural Policy Studies, Division of Humanities, Griffith University, 1989).

RECORDINGS: "Kath Walker Reading from Her Poems and Short Stories with Comment," read by Walker, two stories from *Stradbroke Dreamtime* and twenty-six poems from *My People,* Washington, D.C., Archive of Recorded Poetry and Literature, Library of Congress, 12503, 1978;

Oodgeroo (from Adam Shoemaker, ed., Oodgeroo: A Tribute, *1994; Bruccoli Clark Layman Archives)*

Festival Poets, readings by Oodgeroo and Peter Goldsworthy, Sydney, Australian Broadcasting Corporation, 1984.

OTHER: *Land Rights (Makarrata),* illustrated by Oodgeroo (as Walker), poster (Queensland, 1981);

The Rainbow Serpent, by Oodgeroo and Kabul Oodgeroo Noonuccal (Canberra: Australian Government Publishing Service, 1988);

The Spirit of Australia, text by Oodgeroo and Paul Cliff, photography by Reg Morrison (Silverwater: Golden Press, 1989);

Australian Legends and Landscapes, edited by Oodgeroo, photography by Morrison (Milson's Point: Random House Australia, 1990).

SELECTED PERIODICAL PUBLICATION–
UNCOLLECTED: "Aboriginal Literature," *Identity,* 2 (January 1975): 39–40.

Kath Walker, known as Oodgeroo of the Tribe Noonuccal from 1988 onward, was a formative figure in the field of contemporary Australian indigenous literature in English. *We Are Going* (1964) was the first book of poetry by an indigenous Australian to be published in the country. It was an overnight success and a landmark in giving indigenous people a presence and voice in the fields of both Australian literature and the political activism and reform that characterized the 1960s. The popularity of *We Are Going* was a clear indication of the importance of print as a medium for facilitating the development of a national or pan-Aboriginal consciousness at this crucial historical juncture.

A charismatic orator, speaker, storyteller, and educator, Walker played a central role in the agitation for reform that led to the groundbreaking 1967 referendum that gave constitutional recognition to Aborigines. Even after she had developed a high profile both nationally and internationally, Walker worked tirelessly as a community activist at the grassroots level, primarily from her base at North Stradbroke Island (Minjerriba), Queensland, where she was a custodian of Noonuccal tribal lands.

Walker was born Kathleen Jean Mary Ruska on 3 November 1920 on North Stradbroke Island. Her paternal family belonged to the Noonuccal people of the Yuggera tribal group. Gonzales, a Spaniard who took a Noonuccal mate, was Walker's great-grandfather. His daughter married a German, Captain Frederic Ruska, and their son was Walker's father, Edward "Ted" Ruska. Ted's mother died when her children were still young, and they were brought up by Noonuccal people, from whom he learned fishing and hunting. He had a happy childhood and grew up with a sense of pride in his Aboriginal heritage. Ted Ruska worked for the government on an Aboriginal workforce that built roads and loaded and unloaded supply ships, for which he received a small wage and rations for his family. Although he was exempted from the Queensland Acts, he was classified as an Aboriginal person when it came to payment. He fought for and received a higher payment for Aboriginal people not covered by the acts.

Kath Ruska's mother, Lucy McCullough Ruska, was born of a Scottish father, Alexander McCullough, and an Aboriginal mother, Minnie, who worked at Marion Downs Station in central Queensland. Lucy's father died when she was young, and she was taken from her mother and raised in a Catholic children's home in Brisbane. She later worked as a housemaid at a station near Boulia. Kath's mother always resented not being taught to read and write, and she was anxious that her children learn to do so.

Kath was one of seven children and the third daughter born to the Ruskas. She had a happy childhood with her siblings, playing in the bush, fishing, and sailing. She attended Dunwich State School on North Stradbroke Island until 1933, when she was thirteen. Most Aboriginal girls who lived in missions and reserves were sent out at this age to perform domestic work. Kath also left school and took up work as a live-in domestic servant. As her biographer, Kathie Cochrane, notes in *Oodgeroo* (1994), the first family she lived with was that of Herbert McAllister in the Brisbane suburb of Coorparoo. She was paid 2s. 6d. per week, with board and lodging. She worked in several households for the next ten years, and the highest weekly wage she received was 13s. 6d. (The average weekly wage for white women in domestic service at this time was between 15s. and £1.) When she was sixteen, she applied for training as a nurse but was rejected because she was Aboriginal.

Australia entered World War II in 1939. In 1941, when Ruska was almost twenty-one, she decided to enlist in the Australian Women's Army Service (AWAS), hoping to learn some new skills and gain an alternative means of employment. Sent to Chermside to train in switchboard operation, she was soon promoted to corporal and put in charge of training beginners. She later worked in the AWAS pay office.

In 1942 Kath Ruska married Bruce Raymond Walker, a descendant of the Logan and Albert River Aboriginal people. They had known each other since childhood; he had relations on North Stradbroke Island and had often visited there. The couple received a loan from a friend and bought a house in the Buranda district of Brisbane that they came to own, something that was unusual for Aboriginal people at that time. In the mid 1940s the Walkers became interested in the Communist Party of Australia (CPA), as it was the one political party at the time that did not subscribe to the White Australia policy, and they attended party classes. It is often said that Walker learned many of her strategic and political skills from her Communist colleagues in the 1940s and 1950s.

In 1943 Walker was invalided out of AWAS with moderate hearing loss, which developed as a result of a

 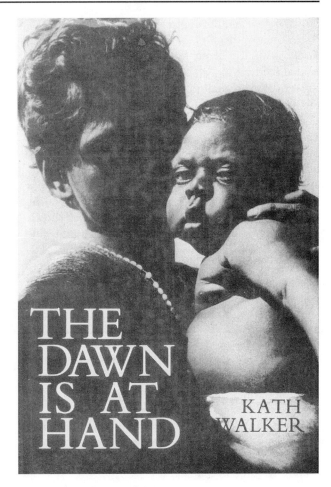

Dust jackets for Oodgeroo's first two books, published in 1964 and 1966 (Bruccoli Clark Layman Archives)

severe middle-ear infection. She consequently trained in secretarial work and bookkeeping under the army's rehabilitation program and took a shorthand and typing course at Brisbane Commercial College. She then took a position with Dandy Bacon.

The Walkers had virtually separated by 1946 when their son, Denis Bruce Walker, was born. During Denis's school years Kath Walker had to leave her job at Dandy Bacon. She reluctantly returned to domestic service with a professional family, the Cilentos. Her second son, Vivian, fathered by Raphael Cilento Jr., was born in 1953.

The decade of the 1950s was a McCarthyite period in Australia. An attempt to ban the Communist Party by federal legislation had been declared invalid by the high court. In 1954 a Brisbane branch of the Realist Writers' Group, which developed as a forum for discussing working-class literature and had close affiliations with the CPA, was established. The group also had a journal, *The Realist Writer,* of which Stephen

Murray-Smith was the editor. (It was renamed *Overland* in 1959 when Murray-Smith left the group). As John Collins, a former director of Jacaranda Press, comments, records indicate that Walker was attending meetings of this group regularly in 1959. Around this time Murray-Smith introduced Walker to the head of Jacaranda Press, Brian Clouston, who passed a manuscript of Walker's poetry on to Judith Wright, then a poetry reader for the press. She recommended publication, and Walker's first book, *We Are Going,* appeared in 1964.

Indigenous people were starting to become organized politically at this time. The inaugural meeting of the Queensland Council for the Advancement of Aborigines and Torres Strait Islanders (QCAATSI) was held in January 1958. The council consisted of individuals from churches, women's groups, the Queensland Trades and Labour Council, the Australian Labour Party (ALP), and the CPA, along with other individuals and representatives from groups concerned with human rights and the improvement of living conditions for indigenous peoples. Walker later started attending meetings of the group and in December 1961 was elected secretary.

In 1960 Walker joined the federal-level version of the QCAATSI, the FCAATSI, which had also been established in 1958. The purpose of this group was to fight for basic civil rights for Aboriginal and Torres Strait Islander people in the national arena. It consisted of representatives from various churches, trade unions, and state Aboriginal advancement organizations. The FCAATSI conference of Easter 1961, held in Queensland, was an important milestone for Walker, launching her into a life of political activism. At the fifth annual meeting of the FCAATSI in Adelaide on Easter 1962, Walker was elected Queensland secretary, a position she was to hold for the next ten years. She read her poem "Aboriginal Charter of Rights" at this meeting. In an interview with Gerry Turcotte published in *Aboriginal Culture Today* (1988) Walker described how old Aboriginal men would express themselves at public meetings through quotations from the Bible, and she said that this practice prompted her to write them "a book they could call their own." She told Turcotte that after the publication of *We Are Going* she saw one of the same old men who used to quote from the Bible reciting her poetry at a meeting, despite the fact that he could neither read nor write; he had gotten his white friends to read it to him and had memorized it.

Walker played an important role as the Queensland secretary of the FCAATSI. She later headed a delegation of the group with Faith Bandler to meet Prime Minister Robert Menzies and urge him to call a referendum on Aboriginal issues. Although they did not achieve their goal, they made a powerful impact. There is a story in general circulation that when the prime minister offered her a drink at a reception, Walker remarked, "Do you know, Mr. Menzies, that where I come from you could be gaoled for supplying alcohol to an Aborigine?"

The decade of the 1960s was a time of upheaval and change across Australia. The growing civil rights movement in America had a large impact in Australia, where a similar interest in political activism and civil rights was growing apace. Political reform of the oppressive Queensland Aborigines Preservation and Protection Acts (1939–1946) and the Department of Native Affairs (DNA) was being called for. In 1962 a petition to the federal government was circulated seeking the removal from the constitution of section 51, clause 26, and section 127. The removal of section 51, clause 26, would make the management of Aboriginal people a Commonwealth rather than a state responsibility, thus allowing for political reform of the outdated

protection laws that governed the management of indigenous people. The removal of section 127 would allow for indigenous people to be included in national censuses.

Walker made several tours around the nation with the purpose of rallying support for the petition to alter the constitution. Menzies did not agree to a referendum, but Harold Holt, who succeeded him as prime minister in 1966, called one in May 1967. Walker became the Queensland director of the campaign for changing the constitution. In the ensuing referendum more than 90 percent of Australians registered a *yes* vote.

When *We Are Going* appeared in 1964, it was an immediate success. According to Ulli Beier, it was sold out three days before the official launch. The book went through seven editions in as many months, selling more than ten thousand copies. These figures made Walker the best-selling Australian poet after C. J. Dennis. Despite this popular success and the endorsement of such major literary figures as Judith Wright, the academy initially received Walker with some reservations. The very aspects of her work that made the poetry powerful as oral performance mitigated against its classification as high art. Because of its concern with social-justice issues, Walker's verse was characterized as "protest poetry," a label that distanced it from the literary canon and that, as black commentators such as Roberta Sykes (as quoted by L. E. Scott) and Cliff Watego have pointed out, had the effect of trivializing and denigrating the work. A decade later Walker herself embraced the term with pride, characterizing her poetry in the essay "Aboriginal Literature" (1975) as "sloganistic, civil writerish, plain and simple." In a 1977 interview she told Jim Davidson that "I'm dead the day I stop protesting."

Walker was in great demand as a result of the unprecedented success of *We Are Going* and was asked to give lectures to many adult education bodies and schools in Queensland and New South Wales, both on her own writing and on Aboriginal culture and aspirations. With her strong communication skills, she developed a powerful reputation as a speaker and educator.

The Dawn Is at Hand (1966), Walker's second collection of poetry, sold seven thousand copies in two editions. The poetry in this book continued the themes of *We Are Going,* depicting in the main either dispossessed and detribalized Aborigines or an idyllic past. As a child Walker had lived in a semitraditional way, and, like many of her generation, she witnessed the passing of that lifestyle with a sense of pathos. While some commentators have suggested that Walker internalized aspects of the assimilationist period in which she lived, it is also clear that her poetry invokes the strength and

Oodgeroo at an exhibition of her drawings in Sydney, November 1985
(photograph by Branco Gaica)

continuity of Aboriginal culture and resists—often angrily—the encroachment of urban and industrial expansion and white assimilationist thinking. *The Dawn Is at Hand* won the Fellowship of Australian Writers Award and the Dame Mary Gilmore Medal in 1966 and the Jessie Litchfield Award in 1967.

In 1968 Walker moved to Holland Park, a suburb of Brisbane in the electorate of Greenslopes. In the following state election she accepted endorsement as the local ALP candidate but was unsuccessful with the voters in the district, who traditionally favored Liberal Party candidates. In 1970 she joined the advisory board of the newly established Aboriginal Aged Persons Home Trust and was elected president of the Aboriginal Publications Foundation, an organization that supported indigenous cultural activity. At this time Walker's international reputation was also growing. In 1968 she traveled to London as a delegate of the World Council of Churches at their Consultation on Racism. She was the only Aboriginal Australian (and the only female Australian) to attend.

Walker's third book, *My People* (1970), reprinted many of the poems from the first two collections along with new work. Eight thousand copies were sold in three editions. Some of the new poems, such as "Time Is Running Out," point to a rejection of the pathos in Walker's earlier poetry. Time is running out, this poem suggests, not simply for the traditional Aborigines and their way of life but also for the conservation of the land itself—a theme that was to become central to the prose writing she turned to following *My People*. No longer are Aboriginal people portrayed as helpless and frustrated; rather, these new poems are characterized by an intensified sense of protest. The same year *My People* was published, Walker became a Member of the Order of the British Empire (MBE).

By the end of the 1960s Walker's political inclinations were changing. No longer content to work within white-dominated organizations, she became involved in a new indigenous political group, the Brisbane Aboriginal and Islanders Council, and its national counterpart, the National Tribal Council (NTC; also known as the

National Aboriginal Tribal Council). The NTC was formed in 1970 as a result of the split of indigenous people, including Walker and Doug Nicholls, from the FCAATSI. In "Coalition of Black and White Australians," an unpublished paper quoted by Cochrane, Walker justified the change in her attitude: "If black Australians are to become masters of their own destiny white Australians must recognise them as capable of formulating their own policy of advancement. . . . White 'goodwill' is a shaky foundation on which to build. White Australians, if they wish, can withdraw the 'goodwill' and black Australians will then be back where they started."

Walker was elected chairwoman of the NTC, and her son Denis became one of its most prominent spokesmen. (In 1972 he withdrew from this body and formed his own militant group, the Black Panthers.) In 1971, however, Walker was informed by some young Aboriginal men in the Brisbane Tribal Council that she was considered too old to be of further service to the organization. She was deeply wounded, and her health suffered. She withdrew from the various committees with which she was involved and relocated in semi-retirement to North Stradbroke Island, which she now called by its indigenous name, Minjerriba (sometimes spelled *Minjerribah*). *The Australian* (8 June 1970) announced that she had "withdrawn from public life to her birthplace."

Thus began a new phase in Walker's life. She decided to develop an educational center on Minjerriba from which to disseminate knowledge and information about Aboriginal people and culture. She chose a place near Amity Point called Moongalba, which means "sitting down place," significant in local legend as the place where a Noonuccal tribal elder used to come to meditate when he had problems to sort out. Walker established the Noonuccal-Nughie Education and Cultural Centre, which she ran on behalf of the local Stradbroke Island Native Association and of which she was the managing director from 1972.

Although Walker was granted a twenty-five-year lease, which was later extended to her lifetime, the issue of legal title to the land remained a constant source of frustration. She initially wanted to establish a museum, library, and art gallery at the site but had inadequate support from the local council and the Queensland government regarding her requests to obtain tenure of the land. Although the government of Prime Minister Gough Whitlam promised financial help and support, it was on the proviso that the Queensland government, headed at that time by Joh Bjelke-Peterson, also give approval, which it did not. Moral support and financial assistance from prominent figures of the white community, including Wright, Manfred Cross, Nancy Cato,

and Rodney Hall, made it possible for Walker to establish Moongalba as a permanent center.

Soon, students from primary and secondary schools in Queensland and New South Wales, as well as underprivileged children for whom Walker organized holiday camps, were visiting in droves. From 1972 until her death in 1993 more than thirty thousand children visited Moongalba. Walker also continued her school visits. She was particularly interested in children; as she said in the interview with Davidson, "I'm sick and tired of talking to mentally constipated adults. It's through children that change will come, so we have them from the kindergarten stage right through to university students." Trainee teachers and tertiary students with an interest in indigenous culture also visited, as well as writers, artists, educators, politicians, and academics from all over the world.

Walker next wrote a collection of stories published as *Stradbroke Dreamtime* (1972), the first section of which consists of stories drawn from her childhood on North Stradbroke Island, and the second, stories "from the old and new dreamtime." (*Dreamtime* is the term for the mythological past of the Aborigines.) These stories announced Walker's new concern with chronicling traditional lore and devising her own ways of reading the landscape mythically. This preoccupation with the land was to dominate her prose writing from the 1970s onward, in which an exploration of indigenous spirituality and its bond with the land became a means of figuring the continuity of Aboriginal culture.

In part as a result of the high profile of Moongalba in attracting overseas visitors and the publication of her two new books, Walker traveled widely in the 1970s. In 1972 she undertook a lecture tour in New Zealand and, the following year, a trip to the University of the South Pacific in Fiji. Soon afterward she represented Australia at the International Writers' Conference in Malaysia. In 1974 she flew to Nigeria as part of a steering committee planning for the second World Black and African Festival of Arts and Culture. On her return trip the airplane in which she was traveling was commandeered in Dubai by hijackers demanding the release of Palestinian prisoners held in the Netherlands and Egypt. One passenger was shot dead by the hijackers, who initially thought Walker was Indian or Pakistani. After two days they released some of the hostages, including Walker. Two poems, "Commonplace" and "Yussef," record her thoughts on the subject.

The second World Black and African Festival of Arts and Culture took place in Lagos in January and February 1977, with Walker acting as a senior adviser. Her international travels also included attending the Papua and New Guinea Festival of Arts in 1975 as an

Australian representative and serving as poet-in-residence at Bloomsburg (Pennsylvania) State College in 1978. During this residency she also visited Lock Haven College in Lock Haven, Pennsylvania; Concorde College, in Montreal; the Institute of American Indian Arts at Santa Fe; and the University of California, Berkeley.

Despite her extensive travel, Walker's heart was still grounded in community activism, and she was deeply committed to working at the grassroots level to improve the living conditions of indigenous Australians. Having worked for a decade to establish Moongalba, in 1980 she brought the indigenous and nonindigenous people on North Stradbroke Island together to form the Community Advancement Society to address the needs of disadvantaged people on the island; she later worked to help establish other governmental agencies on the island.

In the 1980s and 1990s Walker published books of legends and drawings, including *Father Sky and Mother Earth* (1981); *The Rainbow Serpent* (1988), written with her younger son; *Australian Legends and Landscapes* (1990); and *Australia's Unwritten History: More Legends of Our Land* (1992). Beier edited a book of Walker's artwork, *Quandamooka: The Art of Kath Walker,* in 1985. Most of Walker's writing and drawings in these texts relates to her homeland of Minjerriba, but she also collected stories from elsewhere. The first three of these works in particular take up a concern with the land and environmental issues. Her lifelong commitment to reform and education is reiterated in *Australian Legends and Landscapes.*

During the 1980s Walker continued to engage in various high-profile activities. In 1983 she ran unsuccessfully as an Australian Democratic Party candidate and became a member of the Aboriginal Arts Board Council. In 1984 she was part of an Australian cultural delegation that traveled to China, a trip that proved inspiring and led to a fourth book of poetry, *Kath Walker in China,* published in 1988 with the text in both English and Mandarin. In 1985 Walker was declared Aborigine of the Year by the National Aborigines Day Observance Committee. Later that year she was involved as a script consultant for and performer in *The Fringe Dwellers,* Bruce Beresford's 1986 movie adaptation of Nene Gare's 1961 novel of the same title. In 1986 Walker traveled to Russia on invitation to attend the International Forum for a Nuclear-Free World for the Survival of Humanity.

When the Australian Bicentennary was observed in 1988, Walker felt that the celebrations were an insult to the indigenous inhabitants of Australia, and she returned her MBE by way of protest. She also decided to discard her English name for a Noonuccal one, Oodgeroo (a name suggested by Nicholls), which

Oodgeroo receiving an honorary doctorate from Deputy Chancellor J. J. W. Siganto at Queensland University of Technology, 24 September 1992 (photograph by Chris Marr)

means "paperbark," and she was known by this name from this time onward. Although she protested against the bicentennial sentiment of national celebration, she did undertake to work on an event for Expo '88, the world exposition held that year in Brisbane. The organizers of the Australian pavilion were keen to acknowledge indigenous occupation of the land, and Oodgeroo agreed to write a script for the Rainbow Serpent Theatre, *The Rainbow Serpent,* which she conceived in collaboration with her son Vivian, who had by now also taken a Noonuccal name: Kabul, the totem of the carpet snake. Kabul also directed the performance in the Australian pavilion.

Oodgeroo was honored in 1989 by a choral symphony based on *The Dawn Is at Hand,* composed by Malcolm Williamson and performed by the Queensland Symphony Orchestra and the Queensland State and Municipal Choir. She received honorary doctorates from Macquarie University in 1988, Griffith University in 1989, Monash University in 1991, and the Queensland University of Technology in 1992.

In 1990, with the establishment of the Aboriginal and Torres Strait Islander Commission (ATSIC), Oodgeroo was elected a member of the Southeast Queensland Regional Council. She worked tirelessly, attending meetings and helping people with their investigations concerning land claims. Despite these engagements, she was still committed to children's education, with her visits to schools continuing into the 1990s. In 1991 she worked with staff from the University of New South Wales to develop curricula in Aboriginal studies for trainee teachers. That same year Oodgeroo's son Kabul, one of her closest friends and confidants, died. After winning a place at the National Institute of Dramatic Art (NIDA) in Sydney in 1969, he had gone on to a productive career as a painter, actor, dancer, choreographer, model, scriptwriter, and director. His death affected his mother deeply and, according to Cochrane, contributed to her own death two years later.

Oodgeroo died on 16 September 1993. That same year a play, *One Woman's Song,* based on her early life and written by Peta Murray, was performed by the Brisbane Biennial Queensland Theatre Company, commemorating the life of a woman who was a key player in a period of crucial change in Australia and in the field of contemporary indigenous Australian literature. In an obituary tribute in the *Australian Women's Book Review* (March 1994) Ruby Langford Ginibi hailed Oodgeroo as "one of the greatest fighters for Aboriginal rights in this country."

Interviews:

Julianne Schwenke, *Kath Walker Interviewed,* recording (Brisbane, 1970s);

Jim Davidson, *Meanjin,* 36 (October 1977): 428–441;

Oscar Brand, in *Black History,* recording (Washington, D.C.: National Public Radio, 1979);

Gerry Turcotte, "Recording the Cries of the People," in *Aboriginal Culture Today,* edited by Anna Rutherford (Sydney: Dangaroo Press, 1988), pp. 17–30;

Peter Ross, *Oodgeroo Noonuccal,* video (Sydney: Australian Broadcasting Corporation, 1992).

Biography:

Kathie Cochrane, *Oodgeroo* (St. Lucia: University of Queensland Press, 1994).

References:

Ulli Beier, *Quandamooka: The Art of Kath Walker* (Bathurst: Robert Brown & Associates/Aboriginal Artists Agency, 1985);

John Collins, "A Mate in Publishing," in *Oodgeroo: A Tribute,* edited by Adam Shoemaker (St. Lucia: Australian Literary Studies/University of Queensland Press, 1994), pp. 9–23;

Ruby Langford Ginibi, "Tribute to Oodgeroo of the Noonuccal Tribe," *Australian Women's Book Review,* 6 (March 1994): 2;

L. E. Scott, "Writers from a Dying Race," *Pacific Moana Quarterly,* 4 (October 1979): 424–431;

Cliff Watego, "Aboriginal Poetry and White Criticism," in *Aboriginal Writing Today: Papers from the First National Conference of Aboriginal Writers Held in Perth, Western Australia in 1983,* edited by Jack Davis and Bob Hodge (Canberra: Australian Institute of Aboriginal Studies, 1985), pp. 75–90.

Papers:

The papers of Oodgeroo of the Tribe Noonuccal are at the Fryer Memorial Library, University of Queensland.

Peter Porter

(16 February 1929 –   )

Bruce Bennett
University of New South Wales

See also the Porter entry in *DLB 40: Poets of Great Britain and Ireland Since 1960.*

BOOKS: *Once Bitten, Twice Bitten* (London: Scorpion, 1961);

Poems Ancient and Modern (Lowestoft, U.K.: Scorpion, 1964);

A Porter Folio: New Poems (Lowestoft, U.K.: Scorpion, 1969);

The Last of England (London: Oxford University Press, 1970);

After Martial (London: Oxford University Press, 1972);

Preaching to the Converted (London: Oxford University Press, 1972);

Jonah, by Porter and Arthur Boyd (London: Secker & Warburg, 1973);

The Lady and the Unicorn, by Porter and Boyd (London: Secker & Warburg, 1975);

Living in a Calm Country (London & New York: Oxford University Press, 1975);

The Cost of Seriousness (Oxford & New York: Oxford University Press, 1978);

English Subtitles (Oxford & Melbourne: Oxford University Press, 1981; Oxford & New York: Oxford University Press, 1981);

Collected Poems (Oxford & New York: Oxford University Press, 1983);

Fast Forward (Oxford & New York: Oxford University Press, 1984);

Narcissus, by Porter and Boyd (London: Secker & Warburg, 1984);

The Automatic Oracle (Oxford & Melbourne: Oxford University Press, 1987; Oxford & New York: Oxford University Press, 1987);

Mars, by Porter and Boyd (London: Deutsch, 1988);

Possible Worlds (Oxford & New York: Oxford University Press, 1989);

A Porter Selected: Poems, 1959–1989 (Oxford & New York: Oxford University Press, 1989);

The Chair of Babel (Oxford & New York: Oxford University Press, 1992);

Peter Porter, reading Island Magazine, *London, 1981
(from Bruce Bennett,* Spirit in Exile, *1991; Thomas Cooper Library, University of South Carolina)*

Millennial Fables, Oxford Poets Series (Oxford & New York: Oxford University Press, 1994);

Dragons in Their Pleasant Palaces (Oxford & New York: Oxford University Press, 1997);

Collected Poems, 2 volumes (Oxford & New York: Oxford University Press, 1999);

Max Is Missing (London: Picador, 2001);

Saving from the Wreck: Essays on Poetry (Nottingham: Trent, 2001);

Rivers, by Porter, Sean O'Brien, and John Kinsella (Fremantle, W.A.: Fremantle Arts Centre Press, 2002).

PRODUCED SCRIPT: *Peter Porter: What I Have Written,* video, *Writers Talking,* Australian Film Institute, 1988.

RECORDING: *Peter Porter,* read by Porter, St. Lucia, University of Queensland Press, 1974.

OTHER: *Penguin Modern Poets 2* (Harmondsworth, U.K.: Penguin, 1962)–includes works by Porter;

The English Poets: From Chaucer to Edward Thomas, edited by Porter and Anthony Thwaite (London: Secker & Warburg, 1974);

The Oxford Book of Modern Australian Verse, edited by Porter (Oxford: Oxford University Press, 1996; Melbourne: Oxford University Press, 1996).

Peter Porter is often described as an Australian poet living in London. The insistence on his Australian origins may seem odd considering that he sailed to England in 1951 when he was twenty-two, and, except for visits to his homeland at different times and travels elsewhere (mainly in Europe), he has lived in London ever since. London has been an important base for the development of Porter's poetry and literary journalism, but an inherent sense of exile finds an objective correlative in the writer's sense of separation from his homeland. However, this sense of exile does not arise from a simple romantic nostalgia: a complex, ironic, and often humorous worldview emerges in Porter's poetry, marking him as one of the leading English-language poets in the world.

Peter Neville Frederick Porter was born on 16 February 1929 in Brisbane, Queensland, to William Ronald and Marion (Main) Porter. The critical event of Porter's early life was the sudden and unexpected death of his mother when he was nine years old. Nightmares, masochistic fantasies, and apprehensions of mortality haunted him. Subsequently, he constructed a paradise from fragments of his early childhood. His mother's death became the central image in a mosaic of loss. From this time, as his later poetry reveals, he felt "locked out of Paradise." The fall from grace seems to have been sudden and final. Optimism thereafter was chiefly reserved for others, though a more buoyant mood reemerged in later middle age; and throughout his work Porter's darkness of tone is often lit up with sudden apprehensions of beauty or hope, especially in encounters with music and art.

Within the framework of this understanding of Porter's life and writings to date as being informed by a sense of exile, his "journeyings," both physical and imaginative, are important markers of change. The most strikingly significant of these events are his immigration to England in 1951, his return to Australia and reconciliation with the country of his birth in 1974, and the suicide of his first wife, Jannice, the same year. Thereafter, Porter's journeyings reached a new depth of seriousness as, in the age of jet air travel and

enhanced electronic communications, he attained an influential role in the contemporary poetry scenes of both Britain and Australia.

Porter's great strength as a poet, apart from his remarkable technical adroitness with all forms of verse, is his ability to reveal the gaps between what *might be* (the dreamworld ever present in his poetry) and what *is.* His field of investigation is frequently human memory, including his own. While the roots of Porter's paradisiacal imagery are located in his family's Brisbane suburban house and garden before his mother's death, the years of his schooling were marked by frequent bouts of despair and unhappiness. After his mother died, his father, who worked in a textile warehouse in Brisbane–"a gentile in the rag trade" his son later called him in *Westerly* (March 1982)–rented out the family house and in 1939 sent his son to board at the Church of England Grammar School in Brisbane; Porter subsequently described this school in an unpublished interview with Peter Spearitt (London, 18 July 1979) as "an appalling institution modelled, miles after the event, on English public school practice of the most barbarous and outdated sort." The figurehead and chief arbiter of public school values was the headmaster. Although Porter clearly adjusted better to Toowoomba Grammar School, which he attended after the misery of "Churchie," from 1941 to 1946, he nevertheless saw a continuity there of English public-school attitudes.

In spite of his problems with schools agreement, Porter seems to have gained greatly from his studies in them as well as from the omnivorous reading he did outside the classroom. He preferred William Shakespeare to sport and found in the former a world of imaginative possibility. In 1945 and 1946 Porter won literary prizes at Toowoomba Grammar School. The wide range of his reading, which continued into adulthood, was evident in a composition written when he was seventeen on the topic "Great Men I Should Have Liked to Meet." Porter's dinner companions, with whom he conversed easily and wittily in his essay, were Themistocles, Hannibal, St. Francis of Assisi, Voltaire, Fyodor Dostoevsky, and Oscar Wilde.

After leaving school Porter worked in 1947 and 1948 as a reporter for the Brisbane daily newspaper, *The Courier Mail.* After being fired for not chasing stories hard enough, his next job was in a textile warehouse, but he had no interest in repeating his father's career. During these post–World War II years in Brisbane, Porter was a loner, drifting through the hot and humid summers of the city into which he had been born and imagining himself elsewhere. In one of hundreds of unpublished poems from this period, he pictured himself as "the summer hermit / In the sunburnt cave."

Porter's literary career commenced in England, but the intensity of his imaginative recuperations of his first twenty-two years in Australia is testimony to a recurrent desire to reconcile himself with that basically unhappy, formative period of his life (Spearitt interview). On the voyage from Australia, Porter met Jill Neville, a young woman from Sydney who later described their shipboard romance in her first novel, *Fall-Girl* (1965). Their love affair persisted in London through periods of pleasure, anguish, and misery, and she was the subject addressed in many unpublished love poems of the early 1950s. Porter developed a reputation among the young Australian expatriates in London as a brilliant talker. Neville described him as "an aficionado of the brilliant monologue. . . . He was full of an incredibly wild, almost Oscar Wildean humour." Sex and politics mixed uneasily in his life at this time of casual jobs, attempted hedonism, and deep anxiety about his own worth. After two suicide attempts and a nervous breakdown in 1954, Porter set sail for Australia but soon realized that an Australian "home" was not the answer to his problems. On his return to London ten months later, he determined to make his career there and did not revisit Australia until twenty years later.

Porter's apprenticeship as a writer in London lasted for a decade, culminating in the publication in 1961 of his first book of poems, *Once Bitten, Twice Bitten*. A major basis for this breakthrough into publication was provided by Porter's meetings with "the Group," commencing in 1955, while he was working as a cost clerk in a building firm in Baker Street. Philip Hobsbaum had convened regular meetings with writers at Cambridge University since 1952, in which the rigorous New Critical procedures of F. R. Leavis were applied to the work of young writers. When Hobsbaum moved to London in 1955, he started up similar meetings there and invited some of the aspiring younger poets, including Porter, to attend. Porter was a regular attendee from 1955 to 1965. He was grateful for his acceptance by the Group and made a substantial contribution to its meetings. He is the major talent and the most successful poet to emerge from those meetings in the 1950s and early 1960s, although George MacBeth, Peter Redgrove, and Martin Bell also developed original and distinctive poetic voices.

The Group poets have sometimes been likened to such poets of the "Movement" as D. J. Enright, Elizabeth Jennings, Kingsley Amis, Philip Larkin, and John Wain. Insofar as Group poets also reacted against the neo-Romantics of the 1940s—for example, Dylan Thomas, George Barker, and Lawrence Durrell—they shared a common enemy with poets of the Movement. However, the low-key, ironic realism characteristic of Movement poets was fractured by Group poets such as Porter and MacBeth who, in their early work especially, bore traces of the Angry Young Men of the Lon-

Porter, age nine, with his mother in Martha Place, Sydney, 1938 (from Bruce Bennett, Spirit in Exile, *1991; Thomas Cooper Library, University of South Carolina)*

don theater scene of this time, including John Osborne and Arnold Wesker. Porter and MacBeth became adept at the verse monologue that rages and rails at the injustices and absurdities of society while maintaining an ironic and critical perspective on the writer's own standpoint. Porter was also developing an elusive but distinctive strain of lyricism that surfaced occasionally and surprisingly from unlikely terrain.

Porter's first volume of poems, *Once Bitten, Twice Bitten,* was published by the little-known Scorpion Press in an edition of five hundred copies in 1961. Prior to publication of this book of forty-two poems when Porter was thirty-two years old, only eight of his poems had previously appeared in print in England. In this context Porter seems a late developer, but he had been writing personal forms of verse (for example, lyrics, elegies, and sonnets) prolifically since his late teens. When he did break into the British publishing scene, he was perceived as a "social" poet. At least reviewers of *Once Bitten, Twice Bitten* preferred to see the book that way, in spite of the strongly personal element in many poems.

Porter with his wife, Jannice, and daughter Katherine, Charmouth, Dorset, 1966 (from Bruce Bennett,
Spirit in Exile, *1991; Thomas Cooper Library, University of South Carolina)*

Porter's first book found greater favor with reviewers from the political left than from the right. *The Guardian* reviewer, for example, found the book "energetic, witty, skilful and serious" (17 March 1961), while *The Daily Telegraph* reviewer could see only distasteful surfaces: "King's Road character sketches, coffee bars, drunken parties, jeans and sweaters" (March 1961). Al Alvarez, who later included Porter in the second edition of his influential anthology *The New Poetry* (1966), observed that Porter came across in his first book as "an Australian [who] writes [a] tough, aggressive, prize-fighter verse." Porter's Australian-ness (if not always his prizefighter qualities) remained an important element in British readers' perceptions of him.

The title of Porter's first book, *Once Bitten, Twice Bitten,* expressed its author's perception at this time that the obsessive personality does not learn from experience but goes on making the same mistakes. Porter's personae in his first book are often desperate, haunted figures who mask their desperation in irony and sophistication.

Porter was working in advertising from 1959 to 1968, at which he claims to have been unsuccessful. Nevertheless, the experiences provided him with a critical understanding of commercial activity in one of the major metropolises of the world. Porter perhaps pro-

tested too much when (in a 21 September 1976 unpublished interview with Peter Ryan, London) he remarked that advertising had no direct bearing on his poetry: "and if in fact some people see signs of brashness, journalism, jumping to conclusions, etc. in my writing I can assure them it was there long before I had anything to do with copywriting." Yet, the depth of detailed observation in early poems such as "Made in Heaven" or "Lament for a Proprietor" indicates that much had been learned from London advertising in the "Swinging Sixties."

While Porter's London is the immediate milieu of the most striking poems in *Once Bitten, Twice Bitten,* several poems call up aspects of his Australian inheritance. After almost a decade of living in London, Australia seemed to offer a slower, simpler way of life. The poem "Tobias and the Angel" tries to come to terms with the distance of a son from his father through the imagery of a painting attributed to Andrea del Verrocchio that Porter had seen in one of his favorite London haunts, the National Gallery. The much anthologized poem "Phar Lap in the Melbourne Museum" offers a more ironic view of Australia, as a country that made a national hero of a race horse: "The democratic hero full of guile, / Noble, handsome, gentle Houyhnhnm." At the end this poem broadens its range of reference to suggest an ambivalent irony and affection for the poet's country-men and women:

> It is Australian innocence to love
> The naturally excessive and be proud
> Of a thoroughbred bay gelding who ran fast.

Porter's first volume of poems, *Once Bitten, Twice Bitten,* had achieved widespread notice, but his inclusion in *Penguin Modern Poets 2* in 1962 (with Kingsley Amis and Dom Moraes) rapidly established him as a poet of great promise on the British publishing scene. One of Porter's poems in that book, "Your Attention Please," achieved notoriety when it was broadcast on BBC radio and caused a similar alarm to that of Orson Welles's infamous Martian invasion broadcast in 1938. Listeners who attended closely to the poem would have detected a distinctly Porterian irony in the use of official language. Indeed, the poem can be read as a spoof on officialese and the easily aroused prejudices and fears of the Cold War period. Porter the "social poet" was entering the public arena.

At the same time, Porter was writing quieter, more introspective poems, and he acknowledged from London the ghosts of his Australian past in the poem "Ghosts" (1962, 1963). The central figure in this poem is the poet's mother, who remained an obsessive figure in his imagination. The poet generalizes his parents in terms of the cities they have inhabited, Sydney (in his mother's case) and Brisbane (where his father's family had lived). He presents contrasting temperaments in his parents: his mother's side of the family is more alive and mercurial, but she marries out of lively, brash, energetic Sydney into a deadened, colonial Brisbane. This mythology of the contrasting temperaments of two Australian cities is based on observation and experience but also on a desire to see personal and local experience as more than itself, as part of an interactive world nexus.

Porter married Shirley Jannice Henry, a nurse, in 1961. She was "on the rebound" from another relationship, and so was Porter. Their thirteen-year marriage had its share of misery, but there were also good times, especially raising two daughters, Katherine, born in 1962, and Jane, born in 1965. Some of Porter's most touching poems of the later 1960s arise from domestic settings and involve children's perspectives on the world. But his book of the early 1960s, *Poems Ancient and Modern* (1964), is firmly ensconced in the more public discourses of history and religion.

The history in which Porter was most interested was that of Europe. After he and Jannice had visited Vienna in 1963, he wrote the poem "Vienna," which reveals the powerful hold an idea of Europe was devel-

oping in his imagination. It is significant that Porter's first European holiday was to the world capital of music, the city with which the names of Joseph Haydn, Wolfgang Amadeus Mozart, Ludwig von Beethoven, Franz Peter Schubert, Johannes Brahms, and, more recently, Alban Berg and Arnold Franz Walter Schoenberg, have been associated. What appealed to Porter in this personal reimagining of Vienna was the idea of an imperial city without an empire. He was attracted there, as in London, to a metropolis that no longer wields the power it once had. In decay, it could flourish as a center of art. One "spade / Bearded patriarch" who is called up by this poem is Sigmund Freud; another is Georg Trakl, whose wartime and personal torments make him, for Porter, Austria's preeminent elegist of decay and death. Vienna, in Porter's hands, is the symbolic center of anxiety and neuroticism.

When, in another "historical" poem in *Poems Ancient and Modern,* "Sydney Cove, 1788," Porter revisited the European founding of Australia, he again tapped into this vein of anxiety in a surrealist manner. The convict settlement of Australia was reimagined with disturbing clarity. By contrast with Porter's Vienna, however, his Sydney Cove offers a note of hope. The convict beginnings of Australia, according to Porter, have a paradoxical advantage over the settlement of America by pilgrims. Since Australia was born "in horror, not in hope," its progress could only be an improvement, while America "has watched its dream of hope disintegrate into corruption and inanition" (unpublished letter from Porter to Bruce Bennett, 13 February 1986).

Alongside his work in advertising companies and writing poetry, Porter was developing an increasing reputation as a literary journalist in London through the 1960s. In time, he became a reviewer and commentator for quality newspapers and magazines, including the *New Statesman, The Guardian,* and *TLS: The Times Literary Supplement.* A demand for his work was building also on British Broadcasting Corporation (BBC) radio. Porter's wide reading and conversational skills were finding further outlets and a wider audience. He was invited to give public readings and was developing a reputation as a commentator and critic of contemporary culture. In this context, he took the courageous step in 1968 of becoming a full-time freelance writer.

Domestic life and music are major streams in Porter's third book of poems, *A Porter Folio: New Poems* (1969). The book opens with a jaunty elegy, "The Last of the Dinosaurs," which sets the tone for later "cat" poems by Porter. While dealing with adult concerns—the evolution of the species, aging, the desire to leave a footprint in history—the language and tone of the poem are reminders that during this time Porter was reading stories to his two young daughters. In "Seahorses," Por-

*Paperback cover for the 1972 book in which Porter questioned
the bases of existence (Bruccoli Clark Layman Archives)*

had two children born in England. He was reconsidering his origins and identity. The title poem of the book, "The Last of England," projects mixed messages. England is a country of "haunted tenses," and "exiled seas" fill its bays. Yet, something in its past, in the memory of England, attracts him: it is the vision of a liberal England speaking to the writer from the graveyards of that country, especially from Highgate cemetery. The idea of England for Porter, as for T. S. Eliot before him, principally includes the dead with whom he can converse through the incomparable medium of the English language. But the difference is that whereas Eliot sought a classical and royalist tradition, Porter found his principal allegiance with liberals and republicans. The other major attraction for Porter was a developing idea of Europe. In the ode "Europe" Porter tries to register the chaos of contending impressions conveyed by his interest in that continent. Nothing in Porter's Europe is "common or unified." In the manner of W. H. Auden and Wallace Stevens, Porter creates a fiction of history, a dream-like "place / Of skulls, looking history in the face."

Alongside this fascinated observer of the play of history in *The Last of England,* however, was another persona: the disappointed husband. On a lighter note, Porter played a variation on George Gordon, Lord Byron, in his poem "On This Day I Complete My Fortieth Year"; but the lightheartedness serves chiefly to intensify a "divisive music" as he piles on "fuel for the dark."

The early 1970s may be seen as Porter's Sturm und Drang period. A witty and often acerbic tone informs his observations of the Swinging Sixties and early 1970s. The standpoint he adopts is that of the outsider who is alternately fascinated and dismayed by the glittering world he observes. The Roman poet Martial (born in Spain) offered a model of the colonial malcontent in the metropolis, and Porter's free translations of Martial's verse appeared in *After Martial* (1972). In the same year, Oxford University Press published *Preaching to the Converted,* which presented Porter in a rebellious mood, questioning society and the essential bases of existence. Death, not eternity, was proposed as our future: "the base is fixed: / A Grundrisse for the dead–have marble fun, / Put on your shoes and walk into the sun." In another poem, "Timor Mortis," he presents a similarly glittering but disillusioned view, ending with a mutter from Arthur Schopenhauer, the philosopher of pessimism: "Man is ridiculous; if / it weren't for his death, / he'd have no value whatever." Against such prospects, sex quickens the body if not the spirit.

The frenetic activity of Porter's early forties was also marked by a new and fruitful collaboration with one of the most outstanding artists of Australia, Arthur

ter recalls his own childhood holidays on the eastern shores of Australia: "When we were children / We would cheer to find a seahorse / Among the wrack the breakers lifted / On to the beach." A magic world of heroic adventures is conjured up.

Music explicitly enters Porter's third book in "Three Poems for Music," "St. Cecilia's Day, 1710," and "The Porter Song Book." In one of the poems for music Porter writes, "When Orpheus plays we meet Apollo, / When there's theology to swallow / We set it to music, our greatest art, / One that's both intellect and heart." In Porter's view, humans only know about the gods when they hear about them from elsewhere: in this view, words have a subservient role to music.

Porter's fourth book, *The Last of England* (1970), his first published by Oxford University Press, signifies an ambivalent attitude toward his adoptive country. At this time Porter had lived in England for almost twenty years, was married to an Englishwoman, and

Boyd, whom Porter had met in London in 1965. Boyd found Porter's language "universal ranging from humour to great tragedy . . . [combining] delicacy with strength." Boyd had never before sensed such rapport with a writer. Working separately on agreed-upon themes, the two artists did not try to illustrate each other but went their own ways; the resultant works were counterpointed rather than harmonized (unpublished letter to Bennett, 24 August 1989). The first two books emerging from this collaboration were *Jonah* (1973) and *The Lady and the Unicorn* (1975).

Porter's next book, *Living in a Calm Country* (1975), offered for the most part a disturbing calmness of mood, similar to the lull before a storm, "awaiting / the tempest, the null epicentre" ("The Storm"). The deceptively calm country in which the poet subsists in this book is not England but the writer himself, as Porter indicates in the title poem. The poem "Down Cemetery Road" sets a mood not unlike Philip Larkin's, except that Porter's imagination tends more readily to the baroque. In the difficult poem "That Depression is an Abstract" Porter gives a satiric and surreal account of a visit to a psychoanalyst in London with his wife, Jannice, and then another alone.

Two emotional storms blew up at this time for Porter. The first occurred after his return visit to Australia in 1974 (his first return in twenty years), when he met a young married woman, Sally Lehmann (McInerney), at the Adelaide Writers Festival and stayed with her and her family in Sydney. His love affair with Lehmann (who subsequently reverted to her former name, McInerney, and to whom *The Cost of Seriousness* [1978] is dedicated) revolutionized Porter's outlook on the world and Australia in particular. The poem "An Australian Garden" *(Living in a Calm Country)* captures something of the tumult of their lovemaking and his new vision of Australia. Clearly, in this setting the lovers in Porter's poem are partaking of more than casual lust. Few of Porter's other poems so unequivocally evoke "love" or "joy."

A second, and even more intense storm, with enduring consequences, occurred less than a year after Porter's return to England. In December 1974, Jannice Porter, who had been drinking heavily for some years and was in a depressed state, was found dead in the attic of her parents' house in Marlow, Buckinghamshire. She had taken sleeping tablets followed by a bottle of gin. The coroner returned an "open" verdict, but Porter himself believed that she intended her death. In a state of shock, guilt, dismay, and apprehension, he nevertheless decided to bring up his nine- and twelve-year-old daughters on his own and not to send them away as his father had done to him when his mother

died. *The Cost of Seriousness* (1978) did not appear until four years after his wife's death.

It has been Porter's most praised volume, evoking comparisons by some critics with Thomas Hardy's elegies on the death of his wife. Jannice Porter's death had opened up all the wounds of Porter's mother's early death and thereby doubly haunted his imagination. Porter's long poem "An Exequy" is perhaps the most anthologized of his poems that deal with the aftermath of his wife's death. Unlike "The Delegate," which attempts to present Jannice Porter's reflections after death in her own voice, "An Exequy" is a monologue in the poet's voice, refracted through the verse form of Bishop Henry King's early-seventeenth-century lament of the same title, written after the death of his young wife. The poem reveals the positive effect of such distancing devices in enhancing the emotional power of a poem. In such poems, the woman seems closer to the writer in death than she was in life. Porter's recognition of this paradox is evident in several poems in this and subsequent books.

As if in response to a sense of annihilation and despair, Porter took a firmer grip on place and history in some of his poems of the later 1970s. "An Angel in Blythburgh Church" and "At Ramsholt" from *The Cost of Seriousness* show this new rapport with places in the English countryside. "The Orchid in the Rock," collected in the same book, derives from a visit made by Porter and his daughters to Australia in 1975, when they visited Boyd's place in Riversdale. In this poem, the Australian environment is no longer seen by Porter as the hostile, masculine force it had seemed when he wrote early poems such as "Forefathers' View of Failure" *(Once Bitten, Twice Bitten)* or "Eat Early Earthapples" (1962, 1963).

An important source of Porter's reengagement with Australia was his ability to see the country through the aspect of art, and Boyd was clearly a major source of this recognition. Another source was Les Murray's poetry. Porter and Murray recognized each other's skills as poets and also their different standpoints. Porter saw Murray as an outstanding "home grown" talent and an Australian patriot; Porter himself was marked by a sense of exile. In one of his major "thinking aloud" poems, "On First Looking into Chapman's Hesiod" *(Living in a Calm Country)*, Porter identifies Murray as an Australian "Boeotian," at home on the land, a truth teller and message giver of country wisdom in verse. Generalizing from his experience and Murray's, Porter announces that "Some of us feel at home nowhere, / Others in one generation fuse with the land." Porter's city is an ideal, not a reality, and it sets itself sharply against Murray's use of Australian farms and farmers as a principal source of wisdom.

*Paperback cover for Porter's 1978 collection of poems,
some of which deal with his feelings after the death
of his wife (Thomas Cooper Library,
University of South Carolina)*

Porter's poem "'In the New World Happiness is Allowed'" *(The Cost of Seriousness)* is a sharp but good-natured rejoinder to Murray, whose words Porter quotes in the title. Porter's persona sharply rejects Murray's view. Porter had argued elsewhere in his verse (as in essays and interviews) that Australians' materialism was a barrier to their spiritual and cultural development. In this poem he takes issue with a tendency in Murray's writings to present a "happy" Australian temperament and outlook in contradistinction to European angst and misery. What concerned Porter was that the suffering and unhappiness (such as he had felt in his early years in Australia) of ordinary Australians and other New Worlders should be allowed as a valid element in their experience and their art. An ethic of artificially imposed happiness he considers dishonest and contrived.

The Cost of Seriousness ends with two poems that look forward to a renewal of life and happiness and

refer directly to Porter's continuing relationship with McInerney. The predominant theme of each is hope. However, after Porter's visit to Australia with his daughters in 1975, McInerney's return visit to Europe the following year, and other reunions over several more years, this relationship, though important for each, broke up, chiefly over difficulties with their respective families. Porter has never been a triumphalist Romantic poet. Temperamentally, he has been inclined to the classical restraints of form. A strong element of realism informs his outlook. Yet, powerful undercurrents of feeling are found in his poetry, and these feelings are especially evident in the poems that refer to McInerney as well as in the poems for his dead wife. In none of these poems, however, does the thinking mind give way to bare emotion: thought and feeling interact.

Following the difficult years of the late 1970s and after McInerney had moved into a new relationship, Porter himself found a regular partner in Londoner Christine Berg, who, after several years of commuting between their flats, in 1986 moved into Porter's rented apartment in Cleveland Square, London, which had been his base for two decades. The period of commuting is captured in an affectionate and relatively light-hearted poem, "Legs on Wheels," which presents Porter as having found himself again in the city of London after the years of turmoil. Fifteen years Porter's junior, Berg (who, like Porter, had two daughters from a first marriage) commenced work as a child psychologist at the Tavistock Clinic in London in 1989. She and Porter were married in 1991.

During the 1980s Porter had four new volumes of poetry published (all with Oxford University Press), a *Collected Poems* in 1983 and two further volumes in collaboration with Arthur Boyd. This decade, which corresponds with the author's fifties, was a time of increasing public recognition. During the decade Porter was working at the height of his powers as a poet and increased his engagements as a commentator on contemporary culture and writer-in-residence or visiting fellow at universities in Australia and Britain.

The titles of Porter's first two poetry books of the 1980s, *English Subtitles* (1981) and *Fast Forward* (1984), indicate the author's interest in changing modes of human interaction in an era of rapidly developing technologies for communication and jet air travel. The female protagonists of Porter's poetry and life weave in and out like returning ghosts in this volume: the figure of Jannice Porter is there in "Good Ghost, Gaunt Ghost" and "Talking to You Afterwards." She is the speaker in "Alcestis and the Poet." McInerney's influence is recognizable in "Sonata Form: The Australian Magpie," a poem that recalls the end of their relationship. Behind both these women lies the figure of the departed mother (as in the poem "Myopia"). Through these figures of women, Porter's poems establish the power of the female presence in his work and life. (His father, with whom he had had a distant but increasingly appreciative relationship, died in Brisbane in 1982.)

Porter's ninth separate volume of poems, *Fast Forward,* was published the year after his *Collected Poems* and was glibly criticized by a few newspaper reviewers as having appeared too soon, although it had been three years since *English Subtitles* was published. Dedicated to fellow Australian expatriate Clive James, *Fast Forward* may suggest the author's attempt to move rapidly from the deep preoccupations of his previous books to new poetic territory. Certainly, the new book grapples with the future tense. The title poem sets a tone: "the tape so stretched it might at any second / snap to oblivion." An image from modern technology suggests the amazing capacity of the human intelligence to land where it wants to: "Left to itself the brain, circuiting the world, / becomes a rapid deployment force / and blasts ashore on any troubled sand." The military image, and counters to it, are taken up elsewhere in the poem.

Porter's tenth poetry volume, *The Automatic Oracle,* was published in 1987, the year in which he took a position as writer-in-residence at the University of Western Australia in Perth. Such invitations pointed to a growing recognition of Porter's substantial achievement as a poet and his increasing influence on younger poets in Australia as well as in Britain. Porter's enormous technical range and his ability to think intelligently as well as to make music in verse were influencing younger poets as widely apart as Sean O'Brien in England and Philip Salom and Peter Rose in Australia. Critics occasionally compared Porter's achievements with those of Philip Larkin, Seamus Heaney, and Geoffrey Hill in Britain, and to A. D. Hope, Judith Wright, and Les Murray in Australia. *The Automatic Oracle,* dedicated to Berg, reveals a greater assurance of tone in dealing with public or private ironies than any of Porter's previous volumes of verse.

Yet, what makes Porter's "thinking verse" so fascinating is not so much his views on particular matters as the ways in which they are shaped and expressed. Porter is an outstanding phrase-maker; his wit, irony and humor are present in poem after poem, even (perhaps especially) in his most serious work. Like Byron, he jests in earnest. Although the individual artist is ultimately responsible for his or her own handiwork, mysteries of authorship remain. As Porter succinctly puts the problem in "Throw the Book at Them," "Proust could get ten thousand lines from / One night at a party and Robert Browning / knew he was in love only when he found he'd / said so on the page."

Beginning in the mid 1970s, a third country had joined England and Australia as a major source of imagery and ideas in Peter Porter's poetry. This country was Italy, which Porter visited regularly. He became fascinated with its architecture, art, and music. Several of his poems have their starting points in an Italian church or artwork (statue or painting); and Italian opera (especially works by Puccini) is a major source of inspiration. While Porter is periodically interested in the phenomenon of popular or mass culture, his real engagement is with these "high arts." He has opposed that brand of socialist thinking that restricts ordinary people's access to art galleries, opera houses, and concert halls.

Porter's eleventh volume, *Possible Worlds* (1989), features Piero della Francesca's painting *Madonna del Parto* on its cover. Porter commented in a conference in Florence in 1989 on his sense of "possible worlds": "As Thomas Mann puts it, 'We come out of the dark and go back into the dark again.' But we find in daily life, as we live it, the revelations which Stevens calls 'stratagems of the spirit.' Thereafter we live in possible worlds and they may be centred anywhere" ("In a Trance through Paradise," University of Florence, January 1989).

Porter's possible worlds in his eleventh volume range from utopia to dystopia. In dedicating this book to English poet Gavin Ewart, Porter reminded readers of their joint excursions into satire in the 1960s. But as Ewart himself wrote in the 1980s, "The satire rings truer now, in the money-mad world of a Thatcher." Margaret Thatcher's Britain is presented in dystopian terms by Porter in poems such as "An Ingrate's England," in which he observes "the selling of the past to merchants" and the still continuing barriers of class epitomized by the upper-class accents that "drip acid rain" on those below them. The narrower forms of nationalism had been scorned by Porter since the 1960s, but his "Essay on Patriotism" posed the problem of "love of one's country" being used as a cover for wars and exclusive behavior of many kinds. In supporting groups such as PEN International and Salman Rushdie's case for freedom of expression, Porter publicly acknowledged personal freedom as an ultimate good. A major enemy of such freedoms, he warned, was the unbridled growth of capitalism. In such poems, Porter restored his credentials gained in the 1950s and 1960s as one of the Angry Young Men of his time. In his late fifties, Porter still retained an unerring eye for the follies and excesses of another "low dishonest decade," the 1980s, a decade remembered for its infamous "greed is good" credo.

Porter rediscovered the more utopian aspects of "possible worlds" chiefly in Australia. Two poems written after Porter's residency at the University of Western Australia in Perth in 1987, where he was

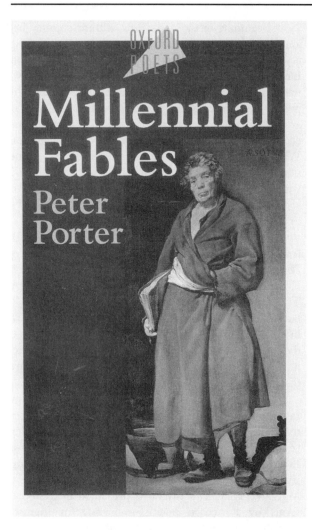

The transformational possibilities of poetry in Porter's hands are well illustrated in "The Chair of Babel," title poem of his twelfth volume, published in 1992. Porter's persona attends a surrealistic international symposium (based on a conference of psychologists in Naples that Porter attended with Berg). This poem is one of Porter's many comic and serious revisitings of the mythical Babylon, where, according to the Book of Genesis, a tower to reach heaven was begun and language was confounded. The combination of a common desire to achieve transcendence versus the actual confusions of the world continues to appeal to Porter as a source of those transformations in which his poetry excels.

Porter's two volumes of his late sixties, *Millennial Fables* (1994) and *Dragons in Their Pleasant Palaces* (1997), offer many contrasts. The first book continues some oracular portents of the coming third millennium. The second part of this volume includes sixteen poems presented as a "Homage to Robert Browning," one of the most persistent influences on Porter after Auden.

Dragons in Their Pleasant Palaces derives its epigraph and title poem from the Old Testament book of Isaiah, the first of the major prophets in both the Jewish and Christian tradition: "and the wild beasts of the islands shall cry in their desolate houses, and dragons in their pleasant palaces. . . ." But the tone and subject matter remain firmly of the late twentieth century. The rhetoric of this volume ranges from the "high" of biblical phraseology to the modern jargon of "The Internet / Pacific Rim, bi-polar wiring," often in humorous or ironic counterpoint. This book is in no sense bland, but it has a calmer, less self-lacerating tone than some earlier work. Yet, in "Anxiety's Air Miles," the poet who has "ringed the globe five times" presents himself self-deprecatingly as "a frequent flyer / Topping up his helplessness with speed" and reflects on the impersonality of time and distance, which can sometimes obliterate personal pain, love, and guilt. Such is not the case for Porter, however: "Love is the good which died / That Winter night and with its death became / The wide-winged world. . . ." For Porter, who is aware of postmodern tendencies to fragment or nullify notions of the single self, no sloughing-off of certain obsessive memories or of an old self can be allowed, despite the temptations of forgetfulness.

In *Dragons in Their Pleasant Palaces,* two poems set in Rome reinforce Porter's plangent melodies of memory, both personal and historic. "The Pines of Rome," inspired in part by Ottorino Respighi's musical score, recalls visits by the poet to his daughter Katherine in Rome. He feels at home in this city where, like the pines, "everything stays forever foreign." In "The Rose Garden on the Aventine" Porter writes an uncharacter-

accompanied by Berg, exemplify this direction in his work. "Ecstasy of Estuaries" is a lyrical celebration of the southwest coast of Australia, but it typically mixes observation and memory, recalling also for Porter the beaches of his Brisbane childhood. The lyrical force of his images relates to the writer's sense of exile from the country he has left but toward which he feels inexorably drawn. Another Western Australian poem of significance is "The Blazing Birds," an exuberant musicology of bird names and sounds. But beyond the references to particular places or times, Porter's sense of pure utopia is found in the concluding poem of *Possible Worlds,* "The Orchard in E-Flat." In this poem, Porter's love of music surmounts all other loves. In "The Orchard in E-Flat," the world is perceived as a "chord of limitless additions," which offers a space "Where the bruise of exile turns to timeless rose."

istically sustained poem of celebration. Among the decayed ruins, rubbish dumps, and traffic of an exhausted city, the roses, "killed by time, live outside time / And open, fold and blow as if the world / Were just the moment when they come in view. . . ."

Porter's seventieth birthday in 1999 was marked by several events. Oxford University Press published his two-volume *Collected Poems,* which included published work from sixteen volumes together with thirty-one new poems; Anthony Thwaite edited *Paeans for Peter Porter* (1999); and *Stand Magazine* ran a "Peter Porter at Seventy" retrospective. Porter had received honorary doctorates from the universities of Melbourne, Sydney, and Queensland and from the Loughborough University in the United Kingdom. He had won the Duff Cooper Memorial Prize for his *Collected Poems* in 1983 and the Australian Literature Society's Gold Medal in 1990. To a string of other awards in Britain and Australia was added the Queen's Gold Medal for Poetry in 2002, an honor shared only by Judith Wright and Les Murray among major Australian-born poets.

Peter Porter showed few signs of diminution in energy or output in his early seventies. Despite being knocked down by a motorcycle in a London street, he recovered and continued to write poetry and reviews, to give public performances in Europe, North America, and Australia, and to lecture at universities. With a new publisher, Picador, he produced a new volume of poetry, *Max Is Missing* (2001), which was compared favorably by reviewers with the late poetry of W. H. Auden and Thomas Hardy. The publisher's comment on the back cover of this volume is apt: "Few poets now writing share Porter's sense of the big picture, his ability to read the small event against the waxings and wanings of empire."

Interviews:

Bruce Bennett, "Peter Porter in Profile," *Westerly,* 27, no. 1 (March 1982): 45–56;

Candida Baker, "Peter Porter," in *Yacker 3: Australian Writers Talk about Their Work* (Sydney: Pan Macmillan, 1989), pp. 260–283;

Barbara Williams, "An Interview with Peter Porter," *Westerly,* 35, no. 2 (June 1990): 57–73.

Bibliography:

John R. Kaiser, *Peter Porter: A Bibliography 1954–1986* (London & New York: Mansell, 1990).

References:

Bruce Bennett, "Interior Landscapes in Peter Porter's Later Poetry," *Antipodes,* 14, no. 2 (December 2000): 93–97;

Bennett, "Peter Porter in Profile," *Westerly,* 27, no. 1 (March 1982);

Bennett, "A Porter Canon?" *Stand Magazine,* new series 1, no. 3 (September 1999): 33–41;

Bennett, *Spirit in Exile: Peter Porter and His Poetry* (Melbourne: Oxford University Press, 1991);

Alan Brownjohn, "From the Eighth Floor of the Tower: The Collected Peter Porter," *Encounter,* 358 (September–October 1983): 80–84;

Robert Gray, "Peter Porter and Australia," *Poetry Review,* 73, no. 1 (March 1983): 16–20;

Michael Hulse, "Love and Death: Nine Points of Peter Porter," *Quadrant,* 27, no. 9 (September 1983): 31–38;

Clive James, "The Boy from Brisbane," *Poetry Review,* 73, no. 1 (March 1983): 25–27; reprinted in *Snakecharmers in Texas: Essays 1980–87* (London: Cape, 1988), pp. 44–48;

Les Murray, "On Sitting Back and Thinking About Porter's Boeotia," in *The Peasant Mandarin: Prose Pieces by Les Murray* (St. Lucia: University of Queensland Press, 1978);

Christopher Pollnitz, "Peter Porter: Whether 'The World is But a Word,'" *Scripsi,* 5, no. 1 (1988): 178–208;

Peter Steele, *Peter Porter* (Melbourne: Oxford University Press, 1992);

Anthony Thwaite, ed., *Paeans for Peter Porter* (London: Bridgewater, 1999).

Papers:

The majority of Peter Porter's papers, including notebooks and manuscripts, are held at the National Library of Australia, Canberra. Some manuscripts from 1958 and 1963 are held at the British Library, London. The Lockwood Memorial Library, Buffalo, and the Lilly Library, Indiana University, also hold some papers.

Thomas W. Shapcott

(21 March 1935 –   )

Deborah Jordan
University of Queensland

BOOKS: *Time on Fire* (Brisbane: Jacaranda, 1961);

Twelve Bagatelles (Adelaide: Australian Letters, 1962);

The Mankind Thing (Brisbane: Jacaranda, 1964);

Sonnets 1960–1963 (Brisbane: Officina Donagheana, 1964);

A Taste of Salt Water: Poems (Sydney: Angus & Robertson, 1967);

Focus on Charles Blackman (St. Lucia: University of Queensland Press, 1967); revised and enlarged as *The Art of Charles Blackman* (London: Deutsch, 1990);

Fingers at Air: Experimental Poems (Ipswich, Qld.: T. W. Shapcott, 1969);

Inwards to the Sun: Poems (St. Lucia: University of Queensland Press, 1969);

The Seven Deadly Sins: Poem for the Opera (Ipswich, Qld.: Queensland Opera Company, 1970);

Interim Report: Some Poems 1970/1971 (Ipswich, Qld.: T. W. Shapcott, 1971);

Begin with Walking, Paperback Poets, no. 11 (St. Lucia: University of Queensland Press, 1972);

Two Voices: Poems, by Shapcott and Margaret Shapcott (Ipswich, Qld.: T. W. Shapcott, 1973);

Shabbytown Calendar (St. Lucia: University of Queensland Press, 1975; St. Lucia & London: University of Queensland Press, 1987);

Seventh Avenue Poems (Sydney: Angus & Robertson, 1976);

Selected Poems (St. Lucia: University of Queensland Press, 1978); revised as *Selected Poems 1956–1988* (St. Lucia & Portland, Ore.: University of Queensland Press, 1989);

Turning Full Circle (Sydney: New Poetry, 1979);

Make the Old Man Sing (Toronto: Coach House, 1980);

Flood Children (Milton, Qld.: Jacaranda, 1981);

Stump and Grape & Bopple-Nut: Prose Inventions (Brisbane: Bullion, 1981);

The Birthday Gift (St. Lucia & New York: University of Queensland Press, 1982);

Welcome!: Poems (St. Lucia & London: University of Queensland Press, 1983; St. Lucia & New York: University of Queensland Press, 1983);

Thomas W. Shapcott, 1986 (*from Candida Baker,* Yacker: Australian Writers Talk about Their Work, *1986; Paterno Library, Pennsylvania State University*)

White Stag of Exile (Melbourne: Lane, 1984; Ringwood, Vic. & New York: Penguin, 1984);

Holiday of the Ikon (Ringwood, Vic.: Puffin, 1985);

Hotel Bellevue (London: Chatto & Windus, 1986; Moorebank, N.S.W.: Black Swan, 1988);

Travel Dice (St. Lucia & London: University of Queensland Press, 1987; St. Lucia & New York: University of Queensland Press, 1987);

Limestone & Lemon Wine (London: Chatto & Windus, 1988; Moorebank, N.S.W.: Black Swan, 1990);

The Literature Board: A Brief History (St. Lucia & London: University of Queensland Press, 1988; St. Lucia & New York: University of Queensland Press, 1988);

The Search for Galina (London: Chatto & Windus, 1989; North Ryde, N.S.W.: Angus & Robertson, 1990);

Biting the Bullet: A Literary Memoir (Brookvale, N.S.W.: Simon & Schuster in association with New Endeavor, 1990);

His Master's Ghost, by Shapcott and A. R. Simpson (Ringwood, Vic.: McPhee Gribble/Penguin 1990);

In the Beginning, series 1, Pamphlet Poets, no. 6 (Canberra: National Library of Australia, 1990);

Mr Edmund, by Shapcott and Steve J. Spears (Ringwood, Vic.: McPhee Gribble/Penguin, 1990);

What You Own (North Ryde, N.S.W. & London: Collins/Angus & Robertson, 1991);

Mona's Gift (Ringwood, Vic. & New York: Viking, 1993);

The City of Home (St. Lucia: University of Queensland Press, 1995);

Theatre of Darkness: Lillian Nordica as Opera (Milson's Point, N.S.W.: Random House, 1998; Milson's Point, N.S.W. & New York: Vintage, 1998);

The Sun's Waste Is Our Energy (Cambridge: Salt, 1998);

Chekhov's Mongoose (Applecross, W.A.: Salt, 2000; Cambridge: Salt, 2000);

Twins in the Family–Interviews with Australian Twins (Melbourne: Lothian, 2001).

PRODUCED SCRIPTS: *Gilgamesh,* libretto by Shapcott, music by Colin Brumby, Adelaide, Adelaide Festival, 1968;

Five Days Lost, libretto by Shapcott, music by Brumby, Perth, Festival of Perth, 1970;

The Seven Deadly Sins, libretto by Shapcott, music by Brumby, Brisbane, Queensland Opera Company, 1970;

Celebrations & Lamentations, libretto by Shapcott, music by Brumby, Brisbane, Inter-varsity Choral Festival, 1972;

This Is the Vine, libretto by Shapcott, music by Brumby, Melbourne, International Ecumenical Congress, 1972;

Bess Song, libretto by Shapcott, music by Brumby, Sydney, Sydney Opera House, 1974;

E Tarracho, libretto by Shapcott, music by Brumby, Adelaide, Adelaide Choral Society, 1975;

Flood Valley, libretto by Shapcott, music by Brumby, Adelaide, Adelaide Festival Theatre, 1976;

Five Poems for a Vittoria Mass, libretto by Shapcott, music by Brumby, Brisbane, University of Queensland Music Society, 1978;

Orpheus Bench, libretto by Shapcott, music by Brumby, Brisbane, University of Queensland, 1979;

Three Baroque Angels, libretto by Shapcott, music by Brumby, Brisbane, Inter-varsity Choral Festival, 1979;

Stump and Grape & Bopple-Nut, words by Shapcott, music by David Watson, Brisbane, Warana Festival, 1980;

Two Voices, libretto by Shapcott, Brisbane, Cement Block Theatre, Warana Festival, 1981;

Celebration Music, libretto by Shapcott, music by Bruce Mills, Brisbane, Commonwealth Games Festival, 1982;

Singing the Sun Down, libretto by Shapcott, music by Alan John, Adelaide, Adelaide Festival closing ceremony, 1984;

Three Australian Christmas Carols, libretto by Shapcott, music by Brumby, Adelaide, Pembroke School, 1984;

The Vision and the Gap, libretto by Shapcott, music by Brumby, Brisbane, University of Queensland, 1985;

The Ghost Cave O, libretto by Shapcott, Sydney, Newtown Hall, 1986;

The Ballad of Sydney Hospital, libretto by Shapcott, music by Brumby, Sydney, Sydney University, 1988;

Inheritance, libretto by Shapcott, music by Brumby, Sydney, Presbyterian Ladies' College, 1991;

Summer Carol, libretto by Shapcott, music by Brumby, Canberra Opera Company, 1991;

Old Tom's Numerical Prophecies, libretto by Shapcott, music by Gordon Monro, Sydney, Horizons Festival of Contemporary Australian Choral Music, Sydney Philharmonic, 1992;

Carol of the Holy Innocents, words by Shapcott, music by Brumby, Grosvenor Place, N.S.W., Australian Music Centre, 1999;

Those Who Are Compelled, words by Shapcott, music by Brumby, Grosvenor Place, N.S.W., Australian Music Centre, 1999.

OTHER: *New Impulses in Australian Poetry,* edited by Shapcott and Rodney Hall (St. Lucia: University of Queensland Press, 1968);

Australian Poetry Now, edited by Shapcott (Melbourne: Sun Books, 1970);

Poets on Record, 14 titles, edited by Shapcott (St. Lucia: University of Queensland Press, 1970–1975);

Contemporary American & Australian Poetry, edited by Shapcott (St. Lucia: University of Queensland Press, 1976);

Poetry as a Creative Learning Process (Kelvin Grove, Qld.: Kelvin Grove College of Advanced Education, 1978);

Consolidation: The Second Paperback Poets Anthology, edited by Shapcott (St. Lucia, New York & Hemel Hempstead, U.K.: University of Queensland Press, 1982);

"Beware of Broken Glass: Models in a Room of Mirrors," in *The American Model: Influence and Independence in Australian Poetry,* edited by Joan Kirkby (Sydney: Hale & Iremonger, 1982), pp. 28–41;

Pamphlet Poets, series 2, 6 volumes, edited by Shapcott (Canberra: National Library of Australia, 1991);

Katica Kulakova, *Time Difference: Selected Poems of Katica Kulakova,* translated by Shapcott and Ilija Èašule (Macadonia: Zumpress, Skopje, 1998);

The Moment Made Marvellous: A Celebration of UQP Poetry, edited by Shapcott (St. Lucia: University of Queensland Press, 1998);

An Island on Land: An Anthology of Contemporary Macedonian Poetry, translated by Shapcott and Ilija Èašule (North Ryde, N.S.W.: Macquarie University Press, 1999).

Thomas W. Shapcott is acclaimed as one of the most significant poets of Australia. James Tulip in *Southerly* (March 1983) calls him a "central reflecting intelligence of his generation." A lavish writer of poems, novels, and short stories, Shapcott has also collaborated with several composers, notably Colin Brumby. He reviews widely and has edited several major volumes. He has been awarded many prestigious national and international prizes, and in 1989 he was made an Officer of the Order of Australia. His work has been translated overseas, especially in Europe.

Shapcott believes that naming "our landscape, our culture is still the most important task . . . not as a set formula, but out of inner excitement." Poets, through listening to the quiet still voice within, must share with others so they may also be part of a wider listening and remembering. As he wrote in *Biting the Bullet: A Literary Memoir* (1990), one of his most passionate personal beliefs is "that from the small, the immediate, the personal and the anecdotal, it is possible to move, through a sort of resonance, to the larger implications and perspectives."

Born on 21 March 1935, Thomas William Shapcott is a twin. His was an insulated masculine family with two other brothers—one older, the other younger. Harold Sutton Shapcott, his father, was a public-spirited accountant in Ipswich, Queensland, and of English ancestry. His mother, Dorothy Mary (née Gillespie), was of Irish, Scottish, and Spanish background. Shapcott recalls in *Chekhov's Mongoose* (2000) a miserable child-

hood when the Great Depression "led to the War, / full employment and an air-raid shelter / where our own sandpit had been." He was first educated at West Ipswich State School, then, after a stressful although brief evacuation in 1941, at Blair State School in Ipswich. Shapcott learned tolerance of varying political beliefs because many of the students' parents were communists.

Ipswich, a medium-sized mining and industrial country town, was composed in part of migrants from the 1930s; it was a town of Welsh singers and musicians. Harold Shapcott was the secretary to the Victory Eidsteddfod (Druid festival of music and art). At ten, Thomas Shapcott showed a poem to a visitor to its literary section, who encouraged his interest in technique. As a growing boy, however, Shapcott more often felt exiled from culture in its broadest sense—from poetry, literature, and music. At Ipswich Grammar School, where he became a champion swimmer, he believes he learned little. At fifteen, wanting to become a journalist, he went to business college for six months, but, as he was unable to find work afterward, he began in his father's accountancy practice. For a while he attempted to compose music, but he felt that he had failed. His love of musical composition and music, however, has remained lifelong and is evident in his writing.

In 1954, when doing compulsory National Service training, "a crucial dislocation in my comfortable middle-class world," Shapcott told Jim Davidson in an interview for *Meanjin* (April 1979), he began to write poetry seriously. Discovering the richness of contemporary and past Australian literature both delighted and angered him, for he had grown up within the alienated constructions of colonial sensibilities. Reading avidly among the poets, from Francis Webb and T. S. Eliot to Dylan Thomas, he sought out experimental writing from both Australia and America. After the publication of some of his more formal poems in 1957 and having registered as a tax agent, he set off for Sydney in 1958 to introduce himself to the literati. In 1959 he returned to Ipswich, where Margaret Hodge, his future wife, was teaching. He worked with his father (by 1961 as a partner—in Shapcott and Shapcott). On 18 April 1960 he and Hodge married. They had four children—Katherine Margaret (born 23 December 1960), Alison Jane (born 8 December 1962), Richard Thomas Lloyd (born 1 September 1966), and Isabel Marion (born 5 June 1968). Parenting "opened" his "eyes" and "enriched" his "being," he recalled in *Biting the Bullet.*

Time on Fire (1961) was well reviewed as a first book of poems and won the Grace Leven Prize for poetry in 1961. Shapcott writes about growing up in southeast Queensland, about the love for Nature, about courtship and marriage, and about the birth of a daughter. Laurie J. Clancy, in *Meanjin Quarterly* (June 1967), notes the autobiographical coherence of the poems and their "delicate intimacy." The central theme, he finds, is the destruction of the poet's hope that the things of Nature are among the symbols of earthly permanence and immortality. *The Mankind Thing* (1964) examines the same subject matter. In the long poem "Two and a Half Acres," Shapcott tells of the family's settling on the land: "we claim this hill to rebuild for our sakes / an ordered world." Reviewers concur that the volume marks the poet's increasing maturity. Clancy finds Shapcott concerned no longer with the mere celebration of the things around him but also with the attempt to assess their significance. Shapcott shows an acute consciousness of the painfulness of the poet's task and what became a hallmark of his poems–his belief in the essential ambivalence of all human response: "Loss is no more true a word than gain." Evan Jones, however, writing in the *Australian* (3 March 1965), was scathing about the personal aspects of the poems. Shapcott, as a result, became more cautious of autobiographical frankness.

From 1963 to 1968 Shapcott studied for an arts degree at the University of Queensland. Through the challenge of studying French, the use of a persona in his poems, and his involvement in musical and cultural organizations, his ambition was allowed greater scope. Recognizing his ability, Gertrude Langer, leading art critic of Brisbane, encouraged him, asking, "What is your poetic?" In 1967 Shapcott's biographical study of Charles Blackman, a figurative painter then living in Brisbane, was published. It is a riveting and innovative account of the artist's creativity; the subtext is a dialogue between author and painter. Shapcott shows his ability to focus on core ideas, the mind drawing on his poetic gifts to express a dramatic narrative and grand visioning of the ordinary–and universal–dimensions of the artist's life.

In the late 1960s a quickening in Australian poetry occurred, and the editorial conservatism began to lift. Four books of Shapcott's poems appeared in rapid succession. They indicate his incredible repertoire of form, which ranges from free verse to sestinas and sonnets, and his linguistic richness and delight in wordplay. Shapcott is a conscious and careful craftsman. *A Taste of Salt Water: Poems* (1967) is his most important book from this period. In the year of its publication Shapcott was awarded the Colin Roderick Prize for Australian literature, the Sir Thomas White Memorial Prize, and the Sidney Myer Award for poetry (which he received again in 1969). The book is wide-ranging, with an important long historical poem about Lachlan Macquarie, the early governor of New South Wales, as a father. His next volume of poetry, *Inwards to the Sun,* was published in 1969. Critics presented opposing views on

Paperback cover for Shapcott's 1972 book, which includes poems of urban Australia and the Aboriginal landscape (Bruccoli Clark Layman Archives)

Shapcott's narrative and dramatic technique at this stage. Some, such as Alec King in *Meanjin Quarterly* (June 1968), see it as a real gift; others, such as Elizabeth Marsh in *Westerly* (October 1968), call it "rough."

A major strand of Shapcott's poems continues to record the daily life of a poet. These poems about poetry are praised by Carl Harrison-Ford. Shapcott believes writing is an act of discovery. Rather than a bulletin or progress report, the poem can be a forum for the struggles with identity. Poetry is a process rather than an end product. "Where ever I go I look and see / and I clothe myself with identity," says Everyman in *The Seven Deadly Sins: Poem for the Opera* (1970). Shapcott was keenly aware of the distinction between the formal challenges of purely visual poetry and poetry meant to be spoken.

Fingers at Air: Experimental Poems (1969) begins with explorations of the spatial tensions of laying words upon a page and evolves toward the poem as sound. Harrison-Ford finds that Shapcott establishes that "through reason and example, song as a concept may precede singing." The introspection and analysis that discover this theory, the metacritical work, can also be the subject of poetry. On the other hand, in *Southerly* (30 April 1970), S. E. Lee chastises Shapcott for being diverted from his true medium, the traditional lyric. *Interim Report: Some Poems 1970/1971* (1971) includes the important Bess songs and "Miss Norah Kerrin Writes to Her Betrothed," which explores the experience of the colonial woman. As Harrison-Ford finds, Shapcott's characteristic personal style emerges, incorporating his personal and aesthetic concerns more fruitfully.

From the late 1960s Shapcott worked with Colin Brumby, who became one of the foremost composers in Australia. In 1968 Brumby set "Gilgamesh" to music; they worked together on "Five Days Lost," commissioned by the Festival of Perth for narrator and orchestra in 1969. "Bring Out Your Christmas Masks" was scored for three sopranos, tenor, baritone, mixed chorus, boys' chorus, speaker, and orchestra. *The Seven Deadly Sins* was a "noble failure," according to Roger Covell, the noted critic in *The Sydney Morning Herald* (14 April 1970), even if Shapcott was least to blame. Maria Preauer, however, in *Nation* (31 October 1970) describes it as "a timeless encounter between Everyman and the Sins," "updated with a hundred deft touches—like a mod slant to *Sloth* with obvious jibes to *O Calcutta*." The first ever Queensland opera produced by the state company, it played to packed houses for twelve nights. Shapcott and Brumby went on to produce many works, their collaboration one of the most important in Australia during the 1970s.

Shapcott also worked with other composers—such as David Watson, Bruce Mills, and Alan John—and provided the libretto and script for many gala performances, from music theater to the opening (or closing) ceremonies of the Commonwealth Games and arts festivals. Some were full-scale productions and went on interstate or overseas tours; many were specially commissioned, and others were settings for existing poems. Shapcott collaborated with the Graham Jones Kinetic Energy Dance Group on many occasions.

Receptive to the work of other contemporary poets, especially those more concerned with liveliness than rules, Shapcott has been active as an anthologist. *New Impulses in Australian Poetry,* edited with Rodney Hall in 1968, was followed two years later by *Australia Poetry Now*. A radically conceived collection of mostly unpublished work, foregrounding Michael Dransfield, *Australian Poetry Now* was reprinted by Sun Books in 1976. Dorothy Green, in the *Canberra Times* (20 February 1971), found "if there is not God's plenty of poetic qual-

ity, there is enough to excuse the editor's enthusiasm." She was more critical of gaps in the editor's scholarship—especially regarding previous poets—and his capacity to retreat "into an unassailable position" through vague generalizations.

Shapcott continued his work as an accountant throughout this period. From 1974 to 1978, working as a sole trader, he specialized in the arts. In 1972, however, a Churchill Fellowship to work on American and Australian poetry provided him "complete freedom" that enabled him to travel. He likened himself in an interview with Davidson to a "prisoner deprived not only of his bars but of his cage as well." Shapcott subsequently edited *Contemporary American & Australian Poetry* (1976), a selection intended (as he says in the introduction) to encourage the discovery of "not only each other, but oneself, and the neighbourhood of cultures."

Some poems Shapcott wrote while overseas were included in *Begin with Walking* (1972), which also includes important urban poems, notably "Brisbane Walking." "The Ghost Cave" is about a capacity to see the extraordinary ancient, rich, Aboriginal landscape rather than a barren terrain. A young white man manages to make a cultural leap with a key from his mystical experiences in Egypt. James Tulip in *Southerly* (June 1973) found that "Begin with Walking" was the most solid of all the poems in the volume. Shapcott himself, however, saw the book as a failure. On his return to Australia, Shapcott, to overcome a writer's block, sought out his origins as an act of exorcism. After working hours, he wrote about Ipswich and his past. He was traveling frequently as a foundation member of the Literature Board from 1973 to 1976 and was on the taxation advisory board of the Australia Council.

Shabbytown Calendar (1975) is Shapcott's best-known and most widely acclaimed work. Inspired by the musical structure of a series of Preludes, Interludes, and Fugues, the "calendar" of the provincial town (of Ipswich) changes from the "mango weather" of January to the "abundant sun" of November and December Christmas bells. It includes the playing off of brief poems about concrete things, people, and objects against what is once again essentially a personal discovery or meditation—that is, according to Shapcott in an interview for *Makar* in 1975, about how to work out a relationship with the past and the present. Alternating conflicting solutions are presented, leading to the underlying questions: "Can we live with the past? Can we live without a past?"

Shapcott continued to travel extensively overseas. In 1976, while in New York after a near-death experience, he decided to write full-time and sell the accountancy business—to end his "completely schizoid existence," as he described it to Davidson. He under-

FIREMENS HELMETS

short story by thomas shapcott

This brass helmet is a trophy and a put-down. Years of my
past life, if not too many years: seven. Tribute to my
egregious innocence and good nature. I was Secretary to the
Ipswich Fire Brigade Board for those seven years. I learned
almost nothing.

The dents in the helmet, by the way, actually increase its
value among collectors. Evidence of real use, real firefighting
hazards, work strain. I suppose some bloodstains on the
leather headband inside might also be counted, though leather
is not durable. Could be a minus. I'm told it is worth
several hundred dollars.

I did not receive it as a retirement gift. That had been the
custom of theBrigade, to worthy firemen. Indeed, our Fire
Chief, who kept a brilliantly polished silver helmet, even
to the blue velvet case, had long viewed the formal
presentation of his symbol of position as the fitting reward
for long years of, etcetera.

The brass helmets were disposed of before that date, and the
silver one, but not to the Chief. I was there at the carve-up,
and was allowed to select a brass hat for my own services. I
of course fought no fires. The rank and file firemen, all
seventy two of them, had for six years been using polycarbonate
helmets. They had fought hard to get those, the most efficient
headgear developed. Because staff numbers had increased greatly
in this period it was not reasonable for the old hands to
expect they would get their brass helmets. These had been put
into storage. A few had been donated - to a kindergarten, to
a Folk Museum. Impossible to satisfy everyone.

The Board, one night, after its monthly meeting and the bottle
of Chivas Regal kept in the locked Boardroom, decided to settle
the problem once and for all. The booty was to be divided.
Included in the booty was the Chief's silver helmet in its
velvet case. The Deputy Chairman called for it. The Chief
naturally was unhappy and spoke of his helmet, of its history,
of its associations and of his long care of it, of fires he had
been involved in, the big rescue at the Metropole when he had
been photographed for the papers wearing this very helmet.
But the matter had been decided. Deputy Chairman was Dudley
Leary. It was Dud who had brought out the second bottle of
Chivas Regal from the safe and had encouraged the Chairman
in his decision. It was Dud who walked out of that room
with the Chief's silver helmet.

Page from the revised typescript for "Fireman's Helmets," a short story collected in Limestone and Lemon Wine,
published in 1988 (from Candida Baker, Yacker: Australian Writers Talk about Their Work, *1986;*
Paterno Library, Pennsylvania State University)

took several writer-in-residencies. At Kelvin Grove College of Advanced Education, he produced a booklet at the end of the course. *Seventh Avenue Poems* (1976), "skinny poems" as he called them in an interview for *Artlook* (November 1979) written in New York, continued his experimentation, adapting what he had learned from his explorations into a tighter, leaner form. In 1978 he received the Canada Australia Literary Award. In 1980 he and Margaret divorced, and Shapcott went to stay in Italy.

Shapcott had always written poetry for young people; his first novel for children was *Flood Children* (1981), an exciting and visual narrative based on the disastrous 1974 floods. Also published in 1981, *Stump and Grape & Bopple-Nut: Prose Inventions*—for adults—is a collection of prose poems about a range of themes allowing free play to Shapcott's quirkiness of mind and delight in language. Shapcott references "the world without to explore the world within," finds Jim Legasse in *Westerly* (March 1982), comparing Shapcott to Søren Aabye Kierkegaard and Jean-Paul Sartre in their understanding "that objectified knowledge is always at one or more remove from the truth—Truth is subjectivity."

Shapcott's first novel for adults, *The Birthday Gift* (1982), draws in part on his own experiences as a twin. Through a series of minutely detailed vignettes set in the 1940s and 1950s, he tells the story of Ben and Benno and their search for identity and meaning. The two lives crisscross from childhood to maturity in Ipswich, Sydney, and Tuscany.

Shapcott's next novel, *White Stag of Exile* (1984), is described by Davidson in *Meanjin* (Winter 1984) as "A tour-de-force . . . a major achievement, both in the range of its concerns and insights." It is a story of Karoly Pulszky, director of the Hungarian National Gallery of Art, at the end of the nineteenth century, who was charged with embezzlement, and, while on his self-imposed exile in Australia, committed suicide. Davidson believes that in its density of writing, the depth of allusion, and the variety of experience encompassed, *White Stag of Exile* should broaden the sense of what is Australian. He calls it an "extraordinary book" in which "two elements of our cultural heritage"—the Australian and the European—are placed in juxtaposition and even integrated.

The book began when Shapcott found Pulszky's nondescript grave in the Toowong Cemetery, Brisbane. Pulszky, his parents, wife, daughter Romola, her husband, Nijinsky, and the whole network of aristocratic in-house intrigues captured Shapcott's imagination, as he pursued historical research—in Hungary and Queensland. In a set of discontinuous narratives, there are dramatic monologues, fictional documents, and real letters are interwoven with poem-inserts, which can be seen as

both the versatile author's lyric gift and a widening of the genre. Those critics who found fault found it in the structure of the novel. Shapcott abnegates the historian's responsibility, argued the reviewer in *Island Magazine* (Spring 1984), leaving the reader to judge Pulszky's actions.

White Stag of Exile is considered Shapcott's most significant novel. Peter Balaban translated the text scrupulously into Hungarian. In 1988 Shapcott was invited to Budapest for his "Day of Triumph," the grand opening of an exhibition of the artworks collected by Pulszky during his term as director of the National Gallery. *White Stag of Exile* in translation sold out in Macedonia. In 1987 Shapcott edited an anthology of Australian poetry, which was launched, in Macedonian translation, at the Struga International Poetry Festival. The following year he was awarded the prestigious Golden Wreath of the festival; the bilingual (English/Macedonian) edition of Shapcott's poems had an unprecedented sale of fifteen thousand copies. That year, 1989, Shapcott was also awarded an honorary Litt.D. by Macquarie University. In 1990 he was involved as lector in a reciprocal translation project, to work on Ilija Èašule's English translations.

In 1985 Shapcott published *Holiday of the Ikon,* a second children's book, set on the family's favorite holiday place, Stradbroke Island. *Hotel Bellevue* (1986), fifty thousand words drafted in the first ten days, was finally published in 1986 after a dozen drafts. In commenting on his methods of work, Shapcott says he has learned to trust and accept his subconscious, his "internal computer," which does a huge amount of work before he starts. *Hotel Bellevue* is set in tropical and seedy Brisbane during the notoriously conservative Belkje Peterson government. An icon of the pastoral era, Hotel Bellevue is partially demolished by developers at midnight. Boyd Kennedy, an academic catapulted from his foundering marriage, arrives on a whim to stay at his grandmother's house, now rented by a group of young people involved in the demonstrations to preserve the hotel. The alternating narrative of Marie Kennedy in Melbourne, as she struggles to understand herself and her relationships, adds to the general themes of fragmentation and violation, loss and displacement—sexual, psychic, and material—through different dimensions of time. The book was favorably reviewed. Marion Halligan, in *The Canberra Times* (6 December 1986), notes that its elaboration is elegant and finally tragic. Davidson in *Overland* (March 1987), however, claims that in comparison with *White Stag of Exile,* and despite its many virtues, it does not quite deliver.

On 13 October 1982 Shapcott married Judith Rodriguez, a well-known Australian poet and educator. In 1983 he became director of the Literature Board, a position he held until 1990. During his term of office, a period of cultural expansion in the arts, many innovative local, national, and international projects were established. Shapcott was responsible for a government report on price surveillance. *The Literature Board: A Brief History* (1988) covers the huge variety of tasks and work undertaken by the board and those beneficiaries of it and includes a wealth of factual detail and information.

Other nonfiction prose undertaken during the late 1980s includes the revision and extension of Shapcott's critical biography of Blackman as *The Art of Charles Blackman* (1990) with a further two sections tracing the artist's life and work during the 1970s and 1980s. Blackman's work, at the forefront of the international rise of Australian art, is beautifully collated by Robin Burridge. Shapcott's exposition allows readers insight into this artist. Blackman's attempt to paint pictures shaped by internal feelings and his struggle to capture the float of the intuitive subconscious into the mind parallels Shapcott's own technique. Shapcott is more poet than scholar; the inclusion of a panorama of recollections, articles, and comments by Blackman, however, lacks the freshness of his first volume.

Shapcott uses the same method of collation through a selection of essays, articles, speeches, and reviews in *Biting the Bullet: A Literary Memoir*. Rather than a developed argument, he offers instead views from "various thought-provoking angles." His section on the making of poetry is lucid and powerful. The milestones of his development as a writer, Judith Wright finds, in *Sun Herald* of Sydney (23 September 1990), are notes for an autobiography. She approves of his selection of "provocative" book reviews and believes his travel pieces are the "high point of the book." Portraits of David Malouf, Gwen Harwood, Bruce Beaver, Michael Dransfield, and Elizabeth Jolley, all well known to Shapcott, were specially scripted for the book. Shapcott is an elegant stylist, as John Hanrahan in *The Melbourne Age* (30 November 1990) notes. Even his speeches suggest his vision and courage.

While most reviews were favorable, Mark O'Connor, in *Quadrant* (May 1992), attacked Shapcott for the way he constructed himself as "self-revealer" (yet his revelations were hardly daring); "arts bureaucrat" (yet the role of the Literature Board declined); "literary figure" (yet he does not deal with major opponents); and as a "critic" (yet he is unrepresentative). Shapcott was not above the battle. Rosemary Wighton, Chairperson of the Literature Board, wrote to *Quadrant* (June 1992) in defense of Shapcott, and the correspondence became even more vituperative.

Shapcott believes poetry needs to be more widely appreciated. In his novels, poetry is often built into the narrative. In *The Search for Galina* (1989), which draws

Paperback cover for Shapcott's 1987 collection, which includes poems inspired by trips overseas (Thomas Cooper Library, University of South Carolina)

on a Russian iconography of suffering, the poems of Galina, a Russian poet exiled in Australia, are about the siege of Leningrad in 1941 to 1943. The protagonist, David Cumberland, is working on a book about the forests. Partly ironic, partly sympathetic, he is another of Shapcott's middle-aged male characters facing life challenges. An "imaginatively taunting and passionate" book, Dinny O'Hearn concludes in *Overland* (volume 116, 1989); Shapcott's search is to understand what it means to inhabit this land and survive spiritually.

Shapcott published three volumes of poetry in the 1980s, all praised for their breadth, thematic variety, and maturity. *Welcome!: Poems* (1983), concludes Ken Goodwin in *A History of Australian Literature* (1986), returns to Shapcott's most successful mode–that of the vulnerable, self-amused, self-celebrating existence in a specific locale, mostly Brisbane. *Travel Dice* (1987) includes many poems about overseas trips. Peter Porter, in *Australian Literary Studies* (October 1990), highlights key aspects of Shapcott's *Selected Poems 1956–1988* (1989): his continuous experiment with language and the resources of poetry, his comprehensive picture of modern living, his use of dramatic monologue (happiest with characters on the point of losing their freedom to be themselves), and his successful use of the satiric and the ironic:

> People who live by the open sewer
> 　　forget that it was once a shaded creek.
> People who drive the bare road between Bulima and the airport
> 　　forget it was once a shade rainforest
> People who live in development brick-veneer bungalows
> have forgotten entirely whatever was once meant by words like 'community'
> You will go far
> 　　taking us all with you.

Shapcott published many short stories during the 1980s. His first collection, *Limestone & Lemon Wine* (1988), is a patchwork of small-town (Limestone) lives in a series of interconnected stories. It is a social, economic, and emotional portrait at once ordinary and not so ordinary, with insights into the dynamics of private, family, and working lives. "Lemon Wine" is the story of Norma and Mick's dinner party to which they invite the new Italian restaurateur and his wife. Alberto saves the evening with the sharing of his recipe. Shapcott's second volume of short stories, *What You Own* (1991), has three sections—"What You Have," "What You Leave," and "What You Own." He explores the interconnections between identity, memory, and the values, especially possession, of a materialist culture.

From 1990 to 1992 Shapcott again worked as a full-time writer. In late 1992 he was appointed executive director of the National Book Council until 1997. His next novel, *Mona's Gift* (1993), tells the story of Michael's search into the life of his aunt and her passionate love affair with Ted Stephen, an army doctor during World War II. After Mona Enright dies, her nephew, Michael, is bequeathed a jumble of letters, diaries, and newspaper clippings. Michael rediscovers a younger Mona, charismatic matron of a hospital for babies, whose first erotic encounter with Stephen takes place in an elaborate terraced Japanese garden. Stephen serves on the Kokoda Trail in New Guinea. The female-male sexuality is the core of the book. Whether because of the struggle for possession, Stephen's traumatic experience in the army, or unresolved class conflicts, the relationship falters, but Mona emerges for her nephew as giving the gift of herself.

Shapcott had been fascinated by the Mosman-Cremone area of Sydney Harbour since he had lived there in 1958. When he began to write about it in 1990, the character of Mona emerged. Shapcott believes that a male writer should be able to write about women and their sexuality—despite the subject's being political. While Shapcott has used discontinuous narrative and juxtapositions of time previously, in *Mona's Gift,* through the character of Michael, speculation and imagination are allowed more scope. The book was favorably reviewed. Venero Armnanno in *Imago* (1993) finds it has an immaculate, almost seamless feel for life in Sydney, and he finds its insight into jungle warfare to be the most powerful he has read.

The City of Home (1995), Shapcott's most important collection of poems in recent years, includes eight long sequences of meditations that address different themes. "The River in Brisbane" combines a celebration of nature with a sophisticated historical sensibility—"We all shrink in the drought years, / reminded of our own poisons." Several short lyrical pieces are devoted to Itchy Park—a vivid, childhood, special place. Separate poems address the involvement of Australia in the first Gulf War, and the victory celebrations after World War II in Ipswich. Kevin Hart, in *The Age* (18 November 1995), found *The City of Home* a rich meditation on the realization that naming is both a form of appropriation and a mode of loss. The book won the New South Wales Premier's Special Award and the Wesley Michel Wright Prize for poetry.

"Music, obsession, fame and love" is the subtitle for *Theatre of Darkness: Lillian Nordica as Opera* (1998), Shapcott's reconstruction of the last months of the life of American opera singer Lillian Nordica after she was shipwrecked in the Torrens Strait and nursed with pneumonia on Thursday Island. Siegried Fomorian, the other principal character in the novel, is an obsessive phrenologist who spies on Nordica and is barely prevented from killing a two-year-old island girl to steal her skull. He casts himself bathetically in the struggle for recognition and fame in the role of Siegfried to Nordica's Brunnhilde. Nordica is a remote figure increasingly haunted by her memories. She sings for the young and naive Quetta Braun—the past made whole and potent in the present—giving form to Shapcott's credo. Katharine England, in the *Adelaide Advertiser* (7 February 1998), believes *Theatre of Darkness* is Shapcott's most accessible novel, the most relaxed and entertaining; he has jettisoned the stiffness of earlier novels without jeopardizing his experimental edge or his metaphysical underpinnings.

Shapcott is presently Professor of Creative Writing at the University of Adelaide, a position to which he was appointed in 1997. In 1998 he edited *The Moment Made Marvellous: A Celebration of UQP Poetry,* a selection of contemporary Australian poetry, marking the fiftieth anniversary of the University of Queensland Press.

From 1999 to 2000 he was the director of the Adelaide Theatre Centre. He continues his high-profile contribution to the cause of Australian literature. In 2000 he won the Patrick White Award. *Chekhov's Mongoose,* published the same year, includes more of his philosophical musings on the nature of the world, with even deeper probes into different phases of his life—especially childhood, the body, and the environment—ever stepping off from the immediate into sometimes disruption, sometimes joy. The issue of twinship was again his focus in a study of twins in Australia, *Twins in the Family—Interviews with Australian Twins* (2001).

Shapcott's continual experimentation and his breakthrough into the rawness of the immediate and of place ensures his importance in the future. The strand of Shapcott's poetry that resonates so strongly with his public—the personal chord, his contextualizing of his intimate experiences often in myths—allows readers to reframe their own experiences within a mature view of larger implications and perspectives. A "knowledge eked out of 'the essential ambivalence of human response'" is how David McCooey describes Shapcott's courageous contribution to the wider sharing and remembering.

Thomas W. Shapcott has created a corpus of work of enduring value. His individual works, with their great variation in quality, have been widely reviewed from different vantage points, yet critical overviews are still rare. While scholars are beginning to address the collaboration with Colin Brumby, Shapcott's influence on contemporary Australian poetry (and especially the rise of "New Australian Poetry" during the 1960s) extends far beyond his own creative writings through his extensive reviews, work as an editor, teacher, and judge, role in committees, and work as a public servant. His influence extends beyond the boundaries of his own country, to Europe and America.

Interviews:

Hazel de Berg, March 1974, Thomas Shapcott Collection, Fryer Library, University of Queensland;

Martin Duwell and Philip Neilsen, "An Act of Exorcism: An Interview with Thomas W. Shapcott," *Makar,* 11, no. 3 (1975): 4–16;

Jim Davidson, "Thomas Shapcott," *Meanjin Quarterly,* 38, no. 1 (April 1979): 56–68; reprinted in *Sideways from the Page* (Melbourne: Fontana, 1983), pp. 146–163;

John Allert, "Thomas Shapcott," *Artlook,* 5, no. 11 (November 1979): 3–4;

David McCooey, "An Interview with Thomas Shapcott," *Australian Literary Studies,* 18, no. 1 (May 1997): 79–84.

References:

Bruce Beaver, "Recent Poetry of Thomas Shapcott," *Scripsi,* 4, no. 4 (1987): 117–120;

Laurie J. Clancy, "The Poetry of Thomas W. Shapcott," *Meanjin Quarterly* (June 1967): 182–187;

Ken Goodwin, *A History of Australian Literature* (London: Macmillan, 1986), pp. 212–213;

Carl Harrison-Ford, "The Dance of Form: The Poetry of Thomas W. Shapcott," *Meanjin Quarterly* (September 1972): 300–307;

Igor Maver, "Thomas Shapcott's Verse from a European Perspective," *Australian Literary Studies,* 14, no. 4 (October 1990): 507–509;

David McCooey, "'What is gone is not gone': Intimations in the Poetry of Thomas Shapcott," *Australian Literary Studies,* 18, no. 1 (May 1997): 21–30;

Geoff Page, *A Reader's Guide to Contemporary Australian Poetry* (St. Lucia: University of Queensland Press, 1995), pp. 265–267;

Peter Porter, "Markers to the Millennium: Thomas Shapcott's Poetry: A Retrospective," *Australian Literary Studies,* 14, no. 4 (October 1990): 505–507.

Papers:

Thomas W. Shapcott's papers are held by the Fryer Library, University of Queensland; the National Library of Australia; and the Australian Defence Force Academy.

Peter Skrzynecki

(6 April 1945 –   )

Marcelle Freiman
Macquarie University

BOOKS: *There, Behind the Lids* (Normanhurst, N.S.W.: Lyre-Bird Writers, 1970);

Head-Waters (Sydney: Lyre-Bird Writers, 1972);

Immigrant Chronicle (St. Lucia: University of Queensland Press, 1975);

The Aviary: Poems (1975–1977) (Sydney: Edwards & Shaw, 1978);

The Polish Immigrant: Migrant Poems (1972–1982) (Brisbane: Phoenix, 1982);

The Wild Dogs: Stories (St. Lucia & London: University of Queensland Press, 1987);

The Beloved Mountain (Sydney: Hale & Iremonger, 1988);

Night Swim: Poems (1978–88) (Sydney: Hale & Iremonger, 1989);

Rock 'n' Roll Heroes (Sydney: Hale & Iremonger, 1992);

Easter Sunday (Pymble, N.S.W.: Angus & Robertson, 1993);

The Cry of the Goldfinch (Sydney & New York: Anchor, 1996);

Time's Revenge (Rose Bay, N.S.W.: Brandl & Schlesinger, 1999).

OTHER: *Joseph's Coat: An Anthology of Multicultural Writing,* edited by Skrzynecki (Sydney: Hale & Iremonger, 1985);

"Paradox of the Empty Socks (or, Slowing Down to Hurry Up)," in *Striking Chords: Multicultural Literary Interpretations,* edited by Sneja Gunew and Kateryna Longly (Sydney: Allen & Unwin, 1992), pp. 51–54;

The Breaking Line, edited by Skrzynecki (Surry Hills, N.S.W.: Galley Press Publishing, 1995);

Influence: Australian Voices, edited by Skrzynecki (Sydney: Transworld, 1997; Sydney & New York: Anchor, 1997).

SELECTED PERIODICAL PUBLICATION—
UNCOLLECTED: "Ulysses in New England: A Tribute to Judith Wright," *Southerly,* 52, no. 3 (1992): 101–106.

Peter Skrzynecki (photograph by A. T. Bolton; by permission of the National Library of Australia)

Peter Skrzynecki is best known in contemporary Australian literature for his poetry, fiction, and edited collections of multicultural writing. His main concern is with immigration and the displacements caused by the changes of place and culture, together with a close interest in the natural environment. Skrzynecki was born on 6 April 1945 in Germany, shortly before the end of World War II. His Polish-born adoptive father, Feliks

Skrzynecki, who had been in forced labor in Germany, in 1948 married Skrzynecki's mother, Kornelia Woloszczuk, a young Ukrainian woman working in Germany when war broke out. The family left Europe and, as part of the Australian postwar immigration program, arrived in Sydney in November 1949. Initially, they lived in migrant camps at Bathurst and then at the Parkes Migrant Centre, a former Air Force training base in central-western New South Wales.

In 1951 the family moved to Sydney to the working-class suburb of Regents Park, where they had purchased a home at 10 Mary Street. Both parents found work almost immediately: Skrzynecki's father worked as a laborer for the water board and his mother as a domestic worker for several families in the suburb of Strathfield. Skrzynecki attended the local Catholic school, St. Peter Chanel's, and in 1956 began school at St. Patrick's College, Strathfield, where he completed his leaving certificate in 1963. After an unsuccessful year at Sydney University in 1964, during which he first began to write poetry, he continued to write while he completed a primary teacher training course at Sydney Teachers' College in 1966.

Skrzynecki began teaching in 1967, the year his first poems were published, and his poetry began to appear in anthologies and journals, a trend that has continued throughout his career. From 1967 to 1970 he taught in small rural schools in New South Wales: at Jeogla on the New England Tablelands, Kunghur on the Tweed River, and Colo Heights in the Colo River district. At the end of this period, during which he recommenced his university studies as an "external" student at the University of New England, his first two books of poetry were published.

His first poetry collection, *There, Behind the Lids* (1970), introduces concerns dealt with throughout his later work. These poems, written while he was a primary teacher in rural New South Wales, away from his home in Sydney, articulate a sense of physical and spiritual displacement. These deeply metaphysical poems approach the natural world as a way of exploring the complexities of human existence—the mind "behind the lids," its relation to the past, and the struggle toward faith. The repetition of the image of the skull (in "The Relic" and "Wallace Stevens") symbolizes both interiority and death, and "Long after the words are written" explores the relationship of poetry, suffering, and physical mortality:

in the country of my bones,
Long after the last words are written
And the pain begins. But you will know, by then,
That the worst is over, once and for all.
Only the bare expanse of cracked plains
Stays in sight, hour by hour, until the end.

Head-Waters (1972), Skrzynecki's second collection of poems, received the Grace Leven Poetry Prize the same year it was published and continues Skrzynecki's record of his experiences during his years teaching in the country. While the detailed language and a focus on human relationship to nature show the poet's debt to D. H. Lawrence ("Snake Country" and "The Cicada Nymph"), these poems are especially local, reflecting the poet's increasing familiarity with the country, learning a "language / I was born without" ("Small school at Kunghur"). The opening sonnet, "Weeping Rock," echoes the way the first volume focused on death in nature as a way to understand the life-death cycle of human existence:

The rock's water seeped noiselessly into
The chasm from boulders and forests of gum—
Streamed, as if the years in grief had come to claim
Our presence: turn bone to rock and flesh to moss.

In "Wyatt's Creek," physical love of the land is linked to Christian iconography: "And then the crush of pebbles as a man stoops down / To drink from a creek, solitary as Christ in Gethsemane." In "Wallamumbi," dedicated to poet Judith Wright, the connection to landscape involves grafting the identity of the inheritors of the land onto the land: "how does a man choose the name / That will accompany him faithfully to the grave?" Increasingly in his writing, Skrzynecki explores the rifts in the migrant figure's inheritance of place, a theme foreshadowed in this poem, which compares his own displacement with that of the Australian generations who inherit the land:

Grandfather and father—man I never knew—
The name falls softly across the ranges
And paddocks that once were part of your flesh. . . .

Skrzynecki graduated with a B.A. degree from the University of New England in 1975, the same year that his third collection of poetry, *Immigrant Chronicle,* was published. He went on to complete postgraduate study in English literature, including an M.A. degree from the University of Sydney in 1984 and a master of letters degree from the University of New England in 1986. After twenty years of teaching in the country and in primary schools in the western and southwestern suburbs of Sydney, in 1987 Skrzynecki began teaching at Milperra College of Advanced Education, now amalgamated into the University of Western Sydney, where he is a senior lecturer.

In *Immigrant Chronicle,* Skrzynecki's style changed markedly from the dense, figurative language of his earlier work, shifting to a poetry of clarity and simplicity, using more denotative language and shorter, sparer

*Dust jacket for Skrzynecki's 1975 collection of poems about
his family's experiences as immigrant laborers
(Bruccoli Clark Layman Archives)*

poetic lines. These poems are also more overtly autobiographical. The focus on alienation and displacement now shifts to his own family. Poems such as "10 Mary Street" and "St Patrick's College" recount their lives in Sydney, while "Crossing the Red Sea" and "Migrant Hostel" reconstruct the migrants' journey and their transition to the new home, and the poems "Feliks Skrzynecki" and "Kornelia Woloszczuk" pay tribute to his parents. The migrant child's identity is created by the opportunities for education in the new English-speaking country, while the parents, identities already formed in Europe, look back to the Old World. In "Feliks Skrzynecki" he writes,

> At thirteen,
> Stumbling over tenses in Caesar's *Gallic War,*
> I forgot my first Polish word.
> He repeated it so I never forgot.
> After that, like a dumb prophet,

> Watched me pegging my tents
> Further and further south of Hadrian's Wall.

In "Appointment: north-west," as an adult measuring his gradual identification with his Australian home, he is tinged with a cold sadness:

> At first you checked thermometers
> Regularly, like a heartbeat—
> Then learnt about the weather
> From the colours of a tree.

Despite his parents' settlement in Australia, the son remains an emotional exile, a "visitor" to an Australian "past / Which isn't mine" ("In the folk museum"), finally seeing a postcard from a friend in present-day Warsaw as a "call" to remain connected with his European heritage: "A lone tree / Whispers / 'We will meet / Before you die'" ("Post card"). The condition of exile means living in a state of suspension, constantly searching, the loss of the past exerting itself on the protagonist while he simultaneously forges a new "self" in the present.

The next volume of poetry, *The Aviary: Poems (1975–1977)* (1978), continues Skrzynecki's now-established style, expanding the themes on place, the past, alienation, migration, and mutability and death. These issues are explored in meditations on the meaning of diverse histories. In the sequence on "Rookwood Cemetery" in Sydney, different sections of the cemetery are treated according to their cultural and historical identities, such as "Russian Orthodox," "Irish Settlers," "Colonial Graves," "Family Vaults," the Jewish "Martyr's Memorial," the "Ukrainian Section," and "Polish Headstones." The concern with the significance of death is less metaphysical than temporal and physical. In another volume, *The Polish Immigrant: Migrant Poems (1972–1982)* (1982), is a selection of poems on migration taken from *Immigrant Chronicle* and his previous collections, with the addition of some new poems.

Immigrant Chronicle, The Polish Immigrant, and the anthology following—*Joseph's Coat: An Anthology of Multicultural Writing* (1985)—which Skrzynecki edited, all reflect the growing interest and acceptance of Australian cultural diversity as national identity during the 1970s and 1980s and the development of a policy of multiculturalism, which received government support up to the late 1980s. *Joseph's Coat* includes a collection of English-language poetry and prose by writers who "have or have had a basic language other than English" and whose writing has been marginalized because they speak "a foreign language" and are "unwilling to sever the roots from which they grew." Most of these writers are post–World War II European migrants, but Skrzynecki also included work by Aboriginal writers.

Skrzynecki's prose fiction enables the writer to bring his poetic sensibility to the narrative form of the short story. In his first short-story collection, *The Wild Dogs: Stories* (1987), tales of childhood and growing up are set in the migrant communities of the 1950s. The naturalistic detail and realist prose of the stories relate events that often have a powerful undertow of violence within the shadowy adult world. Some stories are about the child's initiation into sadness, and others are about adults suffering loss. In the title story, "The Wild Dogs," the child is initiated too early into a world of brutality when he witnesses the shooting of a pack of dogs and a suicide during the family's initial residence at the migrant hostel. The story "Pick-and-Shovel Hero," which won the Henry Lawson Short Story Award in 1985, relates the story of a son's realization of his growing distance from his father, who works for the water board in Sydney's outer western suburbs. Yet, he recognizes the father's satisfaction in manual labor and his act of strength in shifting a heavy pipe from an injured man's leg. The story becomes a tribute, while it also notes the hard work of the migrant laborer and the difficulties he experiences because of his lack of English. The narrator is aware that he might have mythologized the father's heroism through his need to tell the story and to understand the emotional complexity of his own position.

Skrzynecki's first novel, *The Beloved Mountain*, published in 1988, is noted for its sensuous detail and a focus on the natural environment that motivates the narrative. The story is of a young migrant teacher, Dominic, who—in the context of restrictive Australian postwar attitudes toward race, sex, and religion—embarks on a relationship with an older, married woman. Set in the rain-forest area of Mount Warning in northern New South Wales, where the teacher works, and also in Sydney, his home, where his parents reside, the novel tracks a quest for a connection with place. Dominic develops an almost spiritual attachment to Mount Warning, where the novel reaches its climax. His search for moral and spiritual direction includes the Catholic Church, a relationship that becomes increasingly important in Skrzynecki's life and in his writing.

A sixth volume of poetry, *Night Swim: Poems (1978–88)* (1989) illustrates the biographical underpinning of the period of this volume, as the protagonist meditates:

> echoes of distances he crossed in thirty-three years:
> birth-place, parents, his two
> young children—
> a marriage shattering in dissolution
> like surf on a virginal
> backbone of sand

Poems about separation and divorce, parenting, and remarriage explore the period of life change, while other poems revisit the increasingly receding past. In "Migrant Centre Site" the past is like a cemetery: all are "Broken slabs of concrete / . . . pieces of brick, steel and fibro." But vividly, in "Hunting Rabbits," the memory is also a metaphor for the complex emotional vulnerability of the present:

> I could never bring myself
> to watch the animals being skinned
> and cleaned—
>   excitedly
> talking about the ones that escaped
> and how white tails bobbed among brown tussocks.
> . . . .
> But eat I did, and asked for more,
> as I learnt about the meaning of rations. . . .

Skrzynecki's second collection of short stories, *Rock 'n' Roll Heroes* (1992), deals with the autobiographical concerns of *Night Swim*. Coupled with the pain of loss is the wonder of existence in the epigraph lines from "Hercules" by Midnight Oil: "My life is a valuable thing / I want to keep it that way"; and from Thomas Traherne, *Centuries of Meditation* (1908): "all things abided eternally as they were in their proper places. Eternity was manifest in the light of day. . . ." These stories look back to childhood innocence and the beginnings of adolescence, the tensions of family and the experience of displacement. The cultural setting details life in the 1950s and 1960s, with reference to the music and popular movies of the period. In the lives of young migrant characters, most of them male, conflicts and painful memories are often resolved or spiritually affirmed.

In Skrzynecki's seventh collection of poems, *Easter Sunday* (1993), which includes a series of poems based on a heart attack he had suffered five years earlier, religious faith, strengthened in the face of physical suffering and illness, moves toward a sense of resurrection. The seven poems in the sequence "Coronary" form the core of the collection. Human vulnerability, coupled with an intensified religious spirituality, extends to the poems in the sequence "Five Lakes," poems based on paintings by five contemporary Australian artists: John Olsen, John Coburn, Charles Blackman, Brett Whiteley, and Robert Dickerson. These poems explore religious overtones in the artists' paintings or use the artwork as a point of departure for the poet's own spiritual investigations as he celebrates the spirituality of creation. Of John Coburn's "Goodbye Little Yellow Bird II," he writes,

>   the little bird's song
> ascending over ominous shadows that fell

*Paperback cover for Skrzynecki's 1987 collection of stories
about growing up in immigrant communities during
the 1950s (Thomas Cooper Library,
University of South Carolina)*

into our lives and attempted to create a disturbance:
invisible notes returning majestically
in long and trailing echoes
                        flowering
across the sky and upwards
in an ecstasy of yellow trembling.

Some poems in "Five Lakes" had previously been published in *Night Swim,* but the series is expanded in this book. The poems in *Easter Sunday* are presented as an act of thanksgiving, as attested to by the final poem, "Deo Gratias," which states plainly, "Thank you for the life I was given."

Skrzynecki's second novel, *The Cry of the Goldfinch* (1996), confronts the contradictory and complex influences that make up a personality that is both gentle and violent. The novel poses the question of whether these conflicting traits are the result of trauma and an instinct for survival, or whether they result from a deep, unidentifiable psychological cause. Wiktor Bujak is

twenty-one in 1940, deported from Poland by the Nazis to work for a German farmer, where he is witness to child sexual abuse. As a child he had both witnessed and perpetuated violence toward animals. When he migrates to Australia and settles there after the war, he has become "a man of contradictions," living an "ordinary" life of friendship, work, and gentleness, but he is also plagued by sexual fantasies that eventually erupt in a terrible betrayal of trust. In this novel Skrzynecki confronts issues of moral behavior as well as conditions of history and politics, forcing readers, finally, to make their own judgments about moral behavior and personal dysfunction.

In the following year, 1997, another anthology of Australian writing edited by Skrzynecki was published. *Influence: Australian Voices* revisits the changing face of Australian society. Twelve years after the publication of *Joseph's Coat,* which included both prose and poetry, *Influence* is a collection of short prose fiction. It includes writers born in Vietnam, India, China, South America, and the Middle East, some of whom, Skrzynecki had noted in the introduction to *Joseph's Coat,* had not made their presence felt in Australian writing at that time. Some of those published in *Influence* had been successful writers in their home countries. *Influence* also includes writing by Australian-born Anglo-Saxon writers. Unlike the earlier volume, which aimed to publish the work of writers marginalized because of their "difference," this collection is inclusive: at the editor's invitation, writers contributed to a collection of Australian fiction with the theme of "influence," a topic that reflects Skrzynecki's ongoing interests. The initial stimulus for this project was the story "The Death of a Silent Hero" by Syrian writer Chahin Baker. In this story a child's identification with family, community, and patriotism all determine the split-second decision to remain in a dangerous, war-torn situation rather than to flee. This response highlights Skrzynecki's criteria for this volume of stories, which are motivated by "decision and action or inaction, however obliquely or abstractly it is managed–whether it is in dealing with relationships or in the discoveries of self in time, place and memory."

Skrzynecki's book of poems *Time's Revenge* (1999) was published after the deaths of his parents, and after a period during which his wife, Kate, suffered a life-threatening bout of leukemia, recorded in the second sequence of the book. His father, Feliks, died in 1994, aged eighty-nine, and his mother, Kornelia, died in 1997, aged seventy-nine. Skrzynecki subsequently traveled to his birthplace in Germany, which fostered thoughts on his own origins and on the workings of time and memory; he expresses his feelings in "Birthplace":

War was still being waged
when I was born here
more than forty years ago—
though nationalities knew the end
was being liberated not far away
and the migration into the future
had already begun[.]

A trip to Ireland, also at this time, is the basis of the final sequence of poems, while the penultimate section is a set of elegiac poems.

Peter Skrzynecki has gained his reputation as Australia's "multicultural" poet. Having come to Australia at a young age and having been educated there in English, he was well placed to be received positively in the 1970s, a time of increased awareness and support for multiculturalism. As his writing is firmly based within concrete and emotional experience, one can read the conflicts, events, and concerns of his life through their record in his poetry and prose. These themes, even in his most fictional work, *The Cry of the Goldfinch,* convey experience intensely lived, the sense of cultural and temporal displacement, the search for religion, and confrontations with death throughout his life. In June 2002 he was awarded the Order of Australia Medal (OAM) for his contribution to "Australian multicultural literature, particularly as a poet." Skrzynecki is working on an autobiography.

Interview:

"Peter Skrzynecki Talks about Death and Religion, Nature and the Use of Poetry," *Australian Book Review,* no. 157 (December 1993–January 1994): 57.

References:

Marcelle Freiman, "Poems of Change: Peter Skrzynecki's *Immigrant Chronicle,*" *Metaphor,* issue no. 4 (October 2001): 67–70;

Michael J. Griffith, "Peter Skrzynecki: 'The Revelation of a Landfall Beyond Any Known Map,'" *Southerly,* 54, no. 3 (September 1994): 119–128;

Uli Krahn, "'How Nourishing Is Nature': Imaginary Possession of Landscape in Harpur and Skrzynecki," *Southerly,* 60, no. 3 (2000): 29–38.

Papers:

Peter Skrzynecki's papers and notebooks are held in the University of New England, Armidale, New South Wales; in the library of the Australian Defence Force Academy, Canberra, Australian Capital Territory; in the New South Wales State Library; and in a private collection.

Colin Thiele

(16 November 1920 –   )

Alison Halliday
Workers' Education Association, Macquarie University

BOOKS: *Progress to Denial* (Adelaide: Jindyworobak, 1945);

Splinters and Shards: Poems (Adelaide: Jindyworobak, 1945);

The Golden Lightning (Melbourne: Jindyworobak, 1951);

The State of Our State: Peeping at South Australia (Adelaide: Rigby, 195?; revised, 1961);

Man in a Landscape (Adelaide: Rigby, 1960);

The Sun on the Stubble (Adelaide: Rigby, 1961; London: White Lion, 1974);

Gloop the Gloomy Bunyip (Brisbane: Jacaranda Press, 1962); republished as *Gloop the Bunyip* (Adelaide: Rigby, 1970);

Storm Boy (Adelaide: Rigby, 1963; Chicago: Rand McNally, 1966; London: BBC, 1978);

February Dragon (Adelaide: Rigby, 1965; London: Angus & Robertson, 1966; New York: Harper & Row, 1966);

In Charcoal and Conté (Adelaide: Rigby, 1966);

The Rim of the Morning: Six Stories (Adelaide: Rigby, 1966); republished as *Storm Boy and Other Stories* (Dee Why West, N.S.W.: Rigby, 1966);

Mrs Munch and Puffing Billy (Adelaide: Rigby, 1967; London: Angus & Robertson, 1968);

Barossa Valley Sketchbook (Adelaide: Rigby, 1968; revised, 1982);

Heysen of Hahndorf (Adelaide: Rigby, 1968);

Blue Fin (Adelaide: Rigby, 1969; London: Angus & Robertson, 1969; New York: Harper & Row, 1974);

Yellow Jacket Jock (Melbourne: Cheshire, 1969);

Flash Flood (Adelaide: Rigby, 1970; London: Angus & Robertson, 1970);

Flip-Flop and Tiger Snake (Adelaide: Rigby, 1970; London: Angus & Robertson, 1971);

Labourers in the Vineyard (Adelaide: Rigby, 1970; London: Hale, 1970);

Selected Verse (Adelaide: Rigby, 1970);

Coorong (Adelaide: Rigby, 1972; London: Hale, 1972);

The Fire in the Stone (Adelaide: Rigby, 1973; New York: Harper & Row, 1974; Harmondsworth, U.K.: Puffin, 1981);

Colin Thiele (courtesy of the author)

Albatross Two (Adelaide: Rigby, 1974; London: Collins, 1975);

Fight against Albatross Two (Dee Why West, N.S.W.: Rigby, 1974);

Magpie Island (Adelaide: Rigby, 1974; London: Collins, 1974);

Range without Man: The North Flinders (Adelaide: Rigby, 1974);

Uncle Gustav's Ghosts (Adelaide: Rigby, 1974);

Grains of Mustard Seed (Adelaide: Educational Dept., South Australia, 1975);

The Little Desert (Adelaide: Rigby, 1975);

The Bight (Adelaide: Rigby, 1976);

The Hammerhead Light (Adelaide: Rigby, 1976; New York: Harper & Row, 1976; Ringwood, Vic. & Harmondsworth, U.K.: Puffin, 1983);

Heysen's Early Hahndorf (Adelaide: Rigby, 1976);

The Shadow on the Hills (Adelaide: Rigby, 1977; New York: Harper & Row, 1977);

The Sknuks (Adelaide: Rigby, 1977);

Lincoln's Place (Adelaide: Rigby, 1978);

Ballander Boy (Adelaide: Rigby, 1979);

Chadwick's Chimney (Sydney: Methuen, 1979; London: Eyre Methuen, 1980);

Maneater Man: Alf Dean, the World's Greatest Shark Hunter (Adelaide: Rigby, 1979);

River Murray Mary (Adelaide: Rigby, 1979);

The Best of Colin Thiele (Adelaide: Rigby, 1980);

Tanya and Trixie (Adelaide: Rigby, 1980);

Thiele Tales: Three Long Stories for Children (Adelaide: Rigby, 1980);

Little Tom Little (Adelaide: Rigby, 1981);

The Valley Between (Adelaide: Rigby, 1981);

The Adelaide Story (Frewville, S.A.: Peacock Publications for ADS Channel 7, 1982);

Songs for My Thongs (Adelaide: Rigby, 1982);

The Undercover Secret (Adelaide: Rigby, 1982);

Pinquo (Adelaide: Rigby, 1983);

Coorong Captive (Adelaide: Rigby, 1985);

Seashores and Shadows (Glebe, N.S.W.: McVitty, 1985);

Shadow Shark (New York: Harper & Row, 1985);

Farmer Schulz's Ducks (Glebe, N.S.W.: McVitty, 1986; New York: Harper & Row, 1988);

The Seed's Inheritance (Adelaide: Lutheran Publishing House, 1986);

South Australia Revisited, text by Thiele, illustrations by Charlotte Balfour (Adelaide: Rigby, 1986);

A Welcome to Water (Netley, S.A.: Wakefield Press in association with the Engineering and Water Supply Department, 1986);

Ranger's Territory: The Story of Frank Woorle (North Ryde, N.S.W.: Angus & Robertson, 1987);

Shatterbelt (Glebe, N.S.W.: McVitty, 1987);

The Ab Diver (Cammeray: Martin Educational, 1988);

Jodie's Journey (Glebe, N.S.W.: McVitty, 1988; New York: Harper & Row, 1990);

Danny's Egg (North Ryde, N.S.W.: Angus & Robertson, 1989);

Poems in My Luggage (Norwood, S.A.: Omnibus/Puffin, 1989);

Stories Short and Tall (Sydney & Chicago: Weldon, 1989);

Farmer Pelz's Pumpkins (Glebe, N.S.W.: McVitty, 1990);

Emma Keppler: Two Months in Her Life (Glebe, N.S.W.: McVitty, 1991);

Speedy (Norwood, S.A.: Omnibus, 1991);

Rotten Egg Paterson to the Rescue (New York: Harper-Collins, 1991);

Aftershock: The Sequel to Shatterbelt (Montville, Qld.: McVitty, 1992);

The Australian ABC (Sydney: Weldon, 1992);

The Australian Mother Goose (Chatswood, N.S.W.: Weldon, 1992);

Charlie Vet's Pet (South Melbourne, Vic.: Macmillan Australia, 1992);

The March of Mother Duck (Montville, Qld.: McVitty, 1993);

Martin's Mountain (Adelaide: Lutheran Publishing House, 1993);

Timmy (Montville, Qld.: McVitty, 1993);

The Australian Mother Goose II (Sydney: Weldon, 1994);

Gemma's Christmas Eve (Adelaide: Openbook, 1994);

Reckless Rhymes (Montville, Qld.: McVitty, 1994);

Tea for Three (Carlton, Vic.: Moondrake, 1994);

Brahminy: The Story of a Boy and a Sea Eagle (Montville, Qld.: McVitty, 1995);

High Valley (Montville, Qld.: McVitty, 1996);

The Mystery of the Black Pyramid (Montville, Qld.: McVitty, 1996);

Dangerous Secret (Montville, Qld.: McVitty, 1997);

Landslide (Port Melbourne: Lothian, 1997);

With Dew on My Boots: A Childhood Revisited (Montville, Qld.: McVitty, 1997); revised as *With Dew on My Boots and Other Footprints* (South Melbourne, Vic.: Lothian, 2002);

The Monster Fish (Norwood, S.A.: Omnibus, 1999; London: Southwood, 2001);

Wendy's Whale (Port Melbourne: Lothian, 1999);

Pannikin and Pinta (Port Melbourne: Lothian, 2000);

The Sea Caves (Port Melbourne, Vic.: Lothian, 2000);

The Cave; and The Glory of Galumph (South Melbourne, Vic.: Lothian, 2002);

Swan Song (Melbourne, Vic.: Lothian, 2002);

Sun Warm Memories: The Colin Thiele Reader (Wagga Wagga, N.S.W.: Triple D Books, 2003);

Wedgetail (South Melbourne, Vic.: Lothian, 2003).

For more than fifty years Colin Thiele has been delighting children, parents, and teachers with his stories. More than twenty of his books remain in print from a highly productive writing life, and the list continues to grow each year. The reasons for his success are his remarkable understanding of the qualities necessary for children's books, an abiding love of the Australian landscape and its people, and his recognition of the primacy of the story.

Thiele's father, Carl Wihelm Thiele, was born on 3 October 1873 in the Eudunda district north of Adelaide, South Australia. His mother, Amalie Anna Wittwer,

*Paperback cover for Thiele's first publication, winner of the 1944
W. J. Miles Competition for a patriotic poem
(Bruccoli Clark Layman Archives)*

was born in Australia on 14 January 1887. Both his parents were of German extraction and lived in an area of South Australia where many German immigrants had established a thriving rural community. Colin Milton Thiele was born on 16 November 1920 in the small town of Eudunda, South Australia, which lies about one hundred kilometers northeast of Adelaide. He was the second-youngest child in a family of three daughters and two sons. He grew up with his siblings on a farm, where, as he says in *The Story Makers* (1987), he was "surrounded by a great array of farmyard creatures, from fowls to the big draught horses." He describes his childhood as one of considerable freedom but also responsibility:

> I roamed the hills near our farm in summer and winter alike, catching rabbits and colds, watching foxes and eagles, climbing trees and going down wells. We were taught to be hardy, responsible and self-reliant, and to accept the consequences of our actions.

This farming area beyond the Barossa Valley had first been settled by migrating Germans, and Thiele, like most in the district, spoke a German-based dialect, "Barossa Deutsch," until he went to school. He has said in *The Story Makers* that although his knowledge of books and reading was limited until high school, he wrote poems and stories from an early age. His farming childhood and the experiences of living through the Great Depression are found in many of his books for children. Thiele has said that if he had not become a writer and teacher he would have been a farmer, and many of his books reflect upon the joys and difficulties of a life on the land. Thiele was educated at Adelaide University, achieving a distinguished scholastic record and graduating with a bachelor of arts degree. He was awarded a Diploma of Education at Adelaide Teachers' College immediately prior to World War II. He served in the Royal Australian Air Force during World War II and was discharged in 1945. Before the war ended, Thiele married Rhonda Gladys Gill in Adelaide on 17 March 1945, St. Patrick's Day. They had met at Adelaide University. They subsequently had two daughters—Janne Louise, born 3 August 1948, and Sandra Gwenyth, born 28 July 1954. After the war Thiele taught English in rural and urban South Australian high schools for eleven years, eventually holding the position of senior master, and he continued to write. His first poetry collection was published in 1945. His collection of poetry shows a nationalistic sensibility, through poems about war and an interest in the Australian landscape. A later collection, *Man in a Landscape* (1960), won the Grace Leven Poetry Prize in 1961. Thiele's poetry, from five earlier editions, is found in his *Selected Verse* (1970).

Thiele went on to establish a distinguished career as teacher and educator. He was the vice principal at Wattle Park Teachers College for two years and then principal from 1965 to 1972. He left briefly to take up a position as director at Murray Park College of Advanced Education in 1973 and then returned to be the director of Wattle Park Teachers Centre from 1974 to 1980. Thiele said in a 2002 interview that he has enjoyed writing part-time—"the part-time writer can walk out and hold on to the integrity of the book"—and he has followed his English teacher's advice to write about things one knows. When asked to name his hobbies at this time he commented that he was "too busy writing, reading, teaching, gardening and answering the phone to have any." Since then Thiele has continued to write and lecture and to be an integral part of the world of literature in Australia.

Thiele's collection *The Rim of the Morning: Six Stories* (1966) was found in many school textbook libraries in the 1960s and 1970s. One of the six stories, "Storm

Boy," became the best known of Thiele's works. The story of Storm Boy and his pelican, Mr. Percival, is known to thousands of children and was made into a successful movie with the help of the South Australian Film Corporation. Storm Boy lives with his father on the Coorong, a wild and wonderful part of the coast of South Australia that both birds and fisherman claim as their own: "A wild strip it is, windswept and tussocky, with the flat shallow water of the Coorong on one side and the endless slam of the Southern Ocean on the other."

Here Storm Boy spends his days collecting things brought in by the sea and playing on the beach with his pelican, his father, and an old Aboriginal friend. From this beach Mr. Percival helps to rescue a distressed ship, and on it he is shot by duck hunters because he learns to frighten away the ducks from their shotguns. The death of Mr. Percival teaches young Storm Boy some hard lessons about the fragility of life and the importance of mutual trust and respect, not only between people but also between people and those living creatures that depend upon them. With the pelican dead and no longer dependent upon Storm Boy, he decides to leave his home on the Coorong and go to school in Adelaide to learn to read and write. Growing up is a necessity, but it does not come without regrets for leaving the Coorong or awareness of loss. *Storm Boy* (1963) is a simple, poignant story but with significant ideas that are reflected in continual threads through the work of Thiele. It was awarded the Silver Pencil Award from the Netherlands.

Thiele has written only one novel for adults, *Labourers in the Vineyard* (1970) which is, like so much of his work, set in the farming and vine growing area of the Barossa Valley in South Australia. He continued to use his knowledge and love of this part of Australia in various environmental and historical prose works for adult readers, published during the 1970s, such as *The Little Desert* (1975) and *The Bight* (1976). In 1975 he also wrote a history of the South Australian Department of Education, *Grains of Mustard Seed*.

Four main themes are developed and explored in Thiele's work. First is the love of the Australian landscape, from the farming areas in South Australia where he spent his boyhood to the beautiful and treacherous coastline of the Coorong and the coastal regions near the Great Australian Bight.

Associated with these cultivated and wild settings is the idea of the ultimate importance of the natural cycles of life, including that of humans. This second theme explores the idea that life is transitory, so people should recognize the significance of the natural world beyond the span of one person's lifetime. The endurance of the natural world, from the inland deserts to the beautiful birds of the water and sea, is shown to be essentially fragile, and so people not only should work in conjunction with the natural world but also respect and care for it.

The third theme is apparent in Thiele's sensitivity to the partnership of place and people, and his work is suffused with praise for the hardworking people of the land and the fishing industry. He writes with clarity and sympathy of the struggles and hardship faced by these people and the dangers posed by the shifting sea and the cycle of seasons.

The fourth, and possibly the most significant, idea fundamental to Thiele's work is the courage of children under adversity, often in the face of conservative parents or events both natural and created that are beyond their control. For children to achieve independence is necessary, but it is often gained at considerable cost to themselves. The ultimate responsibility for life lies within each person and thus requires a recognition of what can and cannot be changed.

Thiele's books for children, from picture books to those for young adult readers, offer a sustained view of these ideas. His picture books, most notably *Pannikin and Pinta* (2000), nominated and short-listed for the 2001 Children's Book Council of Australia awards, focus on the ways in which the lives of wild creatures and children intersect. This book, illustrated by Peter Gouldthorpe, traces the journey of a family of pelicans from a shrinking Lake Eyre in the central Australian desert to a refuge on the coast. On their journey some of the pelicans die of hunger and thirst, some are shot, and some become exhausted and lost. They are also helped by the kindness of people who feed them and wish them well. The tender relationship between wild creatures and people is both dangerous and potentially rewarding for the people who are granted a special insight. However, Thiele makes plain his view that the lives of birds and people can only touch, intersect, and then move on. At the end of the story the children are told after the death of one of the pelicans:

> It was a victory in defeat. Often that is a finer thing than an easy success. . . . Sometimes the effort we make is more important than the goal we reach. It can be an inspiration that lives forever.

Similar ideas are explored in a gentler, more humourous fashion in *Farmer Schulz's Ducks* (1986) and *The March of Mother Duck* (1993). Both these books are delightfully illustrated by Mary Milton. They focus on the life of ducks on a farm and in the city and their search for water in which to survive: "The bending reed whispered and the tall rushes sighed, and the ducks were at peace where the world was wide." For

Dust jacket for the 1978 U.S. edition of Thiele's best-known story (1963), about a boy and a pelican named Mr. Percival (Richland County Public Library)

farmer Schulz's ducks "all traffic stopped every day as the farmer's 50 ducks went down to the Onkaparinga River." Not surprisingly, the unusual solutions of his youngest daughter allow the ducks to continue to reach the river *under* the busy road.

Many of Thiele's books revisit the Barossa Valley region of his childhood and are often set at the time of the Great Depression. Thiele himself recollects the hardship of these years as "a terrible time of hunger, unemployment and misery for many Australians," and in his work he usually focuses on the coming of age of young people when they are faced with personal and cultural challenges. Thiele makes considerable use of humor to show how old-fashioned attitudes are resented by younger members of a community, but he also shows the mutual respect and hard work that have enabled these small communities to survive. The children are the ones who change, leave home, and learn to face adversity with courage and determination.

Thus, growing up on a farm in 1929, Emma, in *Emma Keppler: Two Months in Her Life* (1991), is desperate to go to high school, but she has to battle her father, who thinks she should be at home learning the myriad duties necessary for the smooth running of the farm so she will make a good bride like her sister Louisa. An accidental shooting means that Emma has to think and act quickly to save a life. As a result of her actions, her brother-in-law urges her stubborn father to send her away to school where she will be a credit to the family.

She knew that things would never be the same again. No matter how often she returned home she would be a stranger. . . . Yet it was all of her own doing. She had wanted it to happen. She had really made it happen. Now she would have to carry the burden of that decision, and cope as best as she could[.]

Thiele does not present the reader with an idealized childhood. He has no illusions about the possible dangers and uncertain future for the younger generation, as shown by Emma and the other resilient children from the Borossa Valley, such as Bruno from *The Sun on the Stubble* (1961), the first of Thiele's books to reflect on this region (Bruno journeyed "down from the sunny uplands of his boyhood, to the great grey plains of adult life ahead"), and the rollicking adventures of Benno Schultz in *The Valley Between* (1981), the Australian Children's Book of the Year in 1982. Despite the hardships there is humor, as Benny realizes in *Uncle Gustav's Ghosts* (1974): "hard work and harvest, heat and light, fruitfulness and contentment."

Life on the land is mirrored in books such as *Storm Boy,* which are based on the lives of those who live on or near the sea. The tuna fishermen in Thiele's 1969 *Blue Fin* (recipient of a Highly Commended Award by the Children's Book Council of Australia), as well as the tourists and scientists, the lighthouse keepers, the visiting shark hunter of *Seashores and Shadows* (1985), and the children growing up in these isolated and sometimes dangerous places show courage and determination. Not only is Thiele realistic about the lives of these people, but he also takes a longer view:

> All around, the sea fretted and bickered against the island shore; above them the stars wheeled as impersonally as fate. In the far universe the business of earthly humans was about as important as the antics of a dust mote on the wind[.]

The problems that Thiele's young protagonists face as they grow up are often personal and irresolvable. In *Jodie's Journey* (1988) the young girl Jodie suffers continually from rheumatoid arthritis, which prevents her from riding her beloved horse. She comes to terms with her disability through surviving a bushfire and the terrible events of Ash Wednesday. She needs her courage against dangers both of the inner and of the natural world. Thiele has suffered from rheumatoid arthritis for most of his adult life, and he wrote this story in response to a letter from a young reader. *Jodie's Journey* was awarded the Australian Family Award for Children's Books. A different problem faces the young boy in *Timmy* (1993) who has lost his parents and gone to live with a friendly but childless aunt in the country. He is frightened and shy, but the fostering of a wild hare leads him to a sense of acceptance and the realization that while some problems can be shared and resolved, others cannot.

Acceptance of the world and of family or personal problems is often aided by a friendship with an older person. This person is usually someone marginalized by society but able to respond to the needs of the younger character, who may feel similarly isolated. Thus, Jenny in *The Undercover Secret* (1982) befriends old Swampy and his hobo friends against the sinister Mr. Mudge. Similarly, in *The Shadow on the Hills* (1977) young Bodo Schneider helps the mad hermit Ebenezer Blitz and his dog Elijah after an accident, and he comes to realize that the world can "be a powerful and dangerous place."

Implicated in many of these stories of young people facing adversity and growing into adulthood is a strong sense of the need for conservation and protection of the natural world against the accidents and abuse of people. Thus, in *Albatross Two* (1974), the story of a blowout on an oil rig at sea, the theme of conservation underpins the exciting story of blocking the oil and saving the rig. However, in *The Hammerhead Light* (1976) all the efforts of old Axel and Tessa to save the whimbrel bird are in vain:

> It was the cry of a man for the death of something in his heart, for a magical bond that was broken, for the spirit of a special creature that was born to high flight

Dust jacket for the U.S. edition (1990) of Thiele's 1988 novel about a young girl whose rheumatoid arthritis prevents her from riding her beloved horse (Richland County Public Library)

and the wild freedom of the earth, now nothing more than a lifeless bundle like an old shirt.

This same natural world can also be dangerous, as in the violent water spout in *Blue Fin,* which kills three men and virtually destroys the boat, and as in *Shatterbelt* (1987) and its sequel, *Aftershock* (1992), when Tracey confronts her foreknowledge of a disastrous earthquake. She nearly drowns when the town reservoir falls down and floods the town. "It makes you realise how small and unimportant we are. . . . We always think we control the world, but we're really weak and temporary. Quite ephemeral."

Thiele's concerns and themes come together in *The Fire in the Stone* (1973), which offers no future for young Ernie other than the one he must determine for himself. However, after his discovery of the opals and the rescue of his mate, the reader may appreciate that he has all the qualities necessary to survive and to succeed in this world. Although Thiele's young characters have to realize that they are involved in "a long unending struggle of man against nature, man against man, and, hardest of all, man against himself," hope is offered by going forward and by an understanding of the land where they live:

> It was a new day. The morning full of sunrise, long warm beams of it shooting clear thorough his floating body, and touching the hills with light. And there was no darkness. The plains were wide with air, the golden dust rising on the roads, the high, high arch of the sky— all were bright and brimming.

After his retirement Thiele moved to Queensland to live, where he is closer to his daughters and grandchildren, and the climate is kinder to his arthritis. He and his wife spend time traveling through Australia to appreciate the people and enjoy the country.

As well as those notable prizes mentioned above, Colin Thiele has received other awards for his work, including the Australian National Children's Book prize in 1979 and 1986. He was awarded a Fulbright fellowship to study in the United States and two Commonwealth Jubilee Literary Awards; his work, moreover, has been recognized by societies as diverse as the Mystery Crime Writers of America and the Wilderness Society. Thiele's books have been published in many other countries: the United States, Canada, the United Kingdom, South Africa, Japan, China, the Soviet Union, the Scandinavian countries, Germany, France,

Austria, the Netherlands, and Italy. In 1977 he was awarded the Companion of the Order of Australia for his services to literature and education; an honorary doctorate was conferred on him by the University of South Australia in 2000; and he received the Federation Medal in 2003. This diversity of official recognition and awards acknowledges the breadth of his subjects, the respect of his readers, and his dedication to the craft of writing.

Interview:
Leisa Scott, Interview with Colin Thiele, *Australian,* 4 May 2002, p. R3.

References:
Margaret Dunkle, ed., *The Story Makers* (Melbourne: Oxford University Press, 1987), p. 69;

Stella Lees and Pam MacIntyre, eds., "Colin Thiele," in *Oxford Companion to Australian Children's Literature* (Melbourne & Oxford: Oxford University Press in association with ALIA Press, 1993), pp. 412–413;

Maurice Saxby, *The Proof of the Puddin': Australian Children's Literature 1970–1990* (Gosford, N.S.W.: Ashton Scholastic, 1993).

Papers:
Colin Thiele's manuscript papers from 1933 through 1992, as well as interviews with him in 1964, 1974, and 1995, are held at the National Library of Australia, Canberra.

John Tranter

(29 April 1943 –   )

Martin Duwell
University of Queensland

BOOKS: *Parallax and Other Poems* (Sydney: South Head
Press, 1970);

Red Movie and Other Poems (Sydney: Angus & Robertson,
1972);

The Blast Area (St. Lucia, Qld.: Makar, 1974);

The Alphabet Murders: Notes from a Work in Progress (London: Angus & Robertson, 1976);

Crying in Early Infancy: 100 Sonnets (Brisbane: Makar,
1977);

Dazed in the Ladies Lounge (Sydney: Island, 1979);

Selected Poems (Sydney: Hale & Iremonger, 1982);

Under Berlin (St. Lucia & London: University of Queensland Press, 1988; St. Lucia & New York: University of Queensland Press, 1988);

Days in the Capital (Canberra: National Library of Australia, 1992);

The Floor of Heaven (Pymble, N.S.W.: Angus & Robertson, 1992);

At the Florida (St. Lucia & Portland, Ore.: University of Queensland Press, 1993);

Gasoline Kisses (Cambridge: Equipage, 1997);

Different Hands: Seven Stories (South Fremantle, W.A.: Folio/Fremantle Arts Centre Press, 1998);

Late Night Radio (Edinburgh: Polygon, 1998);

Blackout (Cambridge: Barque, 2000; Sydney: Vagabond, 2000);

Heart Print (Cambridge: Salt, 2001);

Ultra (Rose Bay, N.S.W.: Brandl & Schlesinger, 2001);

Borrowed Voices (Nottingham: Shoestring, 2002);

Studio Moon (Cambridge: Salt, 2003).

OTHER: *The New Australian Poetry,* edited by Tranter
(St. Lucia, Qld.: Makar, 1979);

The Tin Wash Dish: Poems from Today's Australians,
selected by Tranter (Crow's Nest, N.S.W.: ABC,
1989);

The Penguin Book of Modern Australian Poetry, edited by
Tranter and Philip Mead (Ringwood, Vic.: Penguin, 1991); reprinted as *The Bloodaxe Book of Modern Australian Poetry* (Newcastle upon Tyne:
Bloodaxe, 1994);

*John Tranter (photograph by Virginia Wallace-Crabbe;
by permission of the National Library of Australia)*

Martin Johnston: Selected Poems and Prose (St. Lucia: University of Queensland Press, 1993);

Jacket, Internet journal, edited by Tranter <http://
www.jacketmagazine.com> [accessed 8 September 2003].

John Tranter is widely recognized in Australia as, of all the major poets, the one most committed to a continual process of poetic experimentation. He is one of the older poets of the large group of writers coming to prominence in the late 1960s and, as the editor of the major anthology that collects the earlier work of that group (*The New Australian Poetry*, 1979), has had a position of authority and respect. His desire to make his own poetry continually new has led him to form strong bonds not only with contemporary American poetry but also with contemporary European and, much more surprisingly, classical poetry. He is an avant-garde poet in the sense that he has imported some of the versions of Surrealism into Australian poetry, and yet he has always been interested in poetic craft and the challenges it poses. He also remains a distinctively Australian poet; like Kenneth Slessor, he is a poet of Sydney, and the "ambient noise"–to use a phrase from a poem in *Ultra* (2001)–of that city forms a background to many of the poems. The material of many of the poems derives from his upbringing in the south of New South Wales–an essentially rural experience–or from the world of teenage high-school culture in the 1950s.

John Ernest Tranter was born in Cooma on 29 April 1943 to Frederick Aubrey (a teacher) and Anne Katherine Tranter. Tranter attended Moruya High School and Hurlstone Agricultural High School and began studies at Sydney University in 1960. His university career was interrupted at this time and not completed until 1970. He worked in the meantime at odd jobs and occasionally in the Australian Broadcasting Corporation (ABC). He lived in London from 1966 through 1967, and in Australia in the late 1960s he began both a serious journal, *Transit*, and another journal, *Free Grass*, a parody of what he considered badly written "hippie" poetry. He also edited, in 1970, *Preface to the 70s*, an anthology of new poets for the journal *Poetry Australia*. Editing has occupied some of his time throughout his career. He spent 1971 and 1972 in Singapore as a senior editor in the education division of the publisher Angus and Robertson. In 1975 he moved to Brisbane as a drama producer for the Australian Broadcasting Corporation and returned to Sydney in 1978 to continue working for the organization, including producing the weekly arts program *Radio Helicon* from 1987 through 1988.

In the late 1960s Tranter met his future wife, Lynette Grady, in London, and they were married on 2 March 1968. They had two children, both born in Singapore: Kirsten Isobel Tranter, born on 17 July 1972, and Leon Frederick Tranter, born on 10 October 1975.

Tranter's first book, *Parallax and Other Poems*, was published in 1970 as a special issue of *Poetry Australia*. Its most sympathetic reviewer was Tranter's contemporary Martin Johnston, who, in the pages of *New Poetry: Magazine of the Poetry Society of Australia*, described the poems as "verbal constructs of a fairly high order of complexity," based not on themes "so much as central images, or rather pigments." One is struck first by the extent to which these recurrent images–of trees, the city, rain, and green, for example–are framed. Readers visualize them as on a screen in a movie theater. Such conception leads to a general interest in the way that images and narratives can be structured. "The Plane," for example, has a complex organization whereby the "reality" of the flight is placed alongside and inside other realities–a family photo taped to the cockpit and what the pilot is seeing inside his brain. One also sees an emphasis on the nightmarish, on brief portraits of dysfunctionality, such as "The Non-Commercial Traveller" and "Whitey," which comprise an important strand of Tranter's later poetry. The much-anthologized "The Moment of Waking" is a triptych of nightmare images expressed in a cool and elegant rather than expressionist manner:

> Now the nights punish me with dreams
> of a harbour in Italy–you are there
> hung in the sky on broken wings
> as you always have been, dancing,
> preparing to wound me with your
> distant and terrible eyes.

Tranter's second book, *Red Movie and Other Poems* (1972), extends his first by focusing on the narratives of failed lives and the ways in which such narratives can be plotted into larger forms. The volume reminds readers that human lives are one of Tranter's most basic thematic resources. The book is carefully plotted: the central two sections are a portrait of a failed urban poet, Cronstadt, and "The Raft"–later rewritten as "Waiting for Myself to Appear" for the 1982 *Selected Poems*–which is a nightmarish, compressed bildungsroman and may have an autobiographical component. The first section of the book is a set of portraits, gradually increasing in size and complexity and introduced by a quotation from Jorge Luis Borges excusing the brevity and fragmentariness: "The composition of vast books is a laborious and impoverishing extravagance. To go on for five hundred pages developing an idea whose perfect oral exposition is possible in a few minutes!" The most important part of *Red Movie* is the final, title section. In it, fragments of lives are put together according to "field theory"–that is, they are not in themselves significant but have meaning derived from the larger interactive pattern. This approach is a form of abstraction that does not deny meaning to lives but locates that meaning in interactions rather than in the lives per se. Although the tone of the poems in *Red Movie* is one of detachment and coolness, the dominant impression is expressionist–one of lurid visual images and garish colors, as though the city forming the background to many of the lives were being seen as a distorted and badly processed film.

The next two books, *The Blast Area* (1974) and *The Alphabet Murders: Notes from a Work in Progress* (1976), were originally conceived as a single volume. The former has one section of lives; another made up of a series of poems with a central character, Peta, and an early 1960s ambience using French and popular-culture images; and a sonnet sequence, "The Poem in Love." The brilliant single poem "Mark" perhaps sums up best this early phase of Tranter's work. Although it does not process lives in ways that recall "Red Movie," it makes clear that methods of patterning lives are extremely important. The central character, Mark, has committed suicide after a long period spent in a drug-induced paranoia. His suicide-note plea "please try to bring me back" is fulfilled when "They pulled him up from the mud and dressed him up / and put him underground again." At the conclusion of the poem the narrator remembers their friendship in saner days when Mark was "elegant," but the poem concludes with a twist that makes the body of the poem a piece of testimony interrupted by a doctor's saying "I'm not interested in arty / reminiscences. . . . Find the stupid prick and bring him back." This statement obviously raises the question of the status of both character and poem: the poem is an attempt to "bring him back," though the doctor does not understand.

"The Alphabet Murders," a twenty-seven-poem search for "a possible contemporary poetry," may be Tranter's single most important poem after "Red Movie," but it stands slightly aside from the methods of these early poems and comments on them. Its dominant image is the French-derived idea of a voyage into a new mode of expression, and this voyage begins by attempting to destroy the predictable in style:

Before this complex thought begins attacking
what we had left behind—riddles, packaging—
    itself must generate enough good luck for the whole voyage.
After trunks full of shit flung overboard. . . .

On the way it mocks various accepted attitudes as to what poetry is and what it can or should do, including the Georgian ("It is English, autumn, smoky and reposed, / badgers wander across the great lawns in the evening . . ."), the lyric, the idea of poetry as originating from transformed prose, the surreal, the destructively avante-garde ("Sure we can abandon sense / and sensibility, and all the disinterred Romantics / like a wicked boy punching in a stained glass knight"), and the idea of the poem as representing a map of the heart ("the little 'heart' grows 'dark' at night / and lacking infra-red

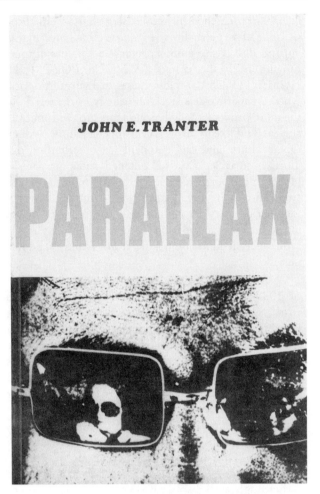

Paperback cover for Tranter's first book (1970), published as a special issue of Poetry Australia *(Bruccoli Clark Layman Archives)*

photometry and radar / we rave down along the flare path looking like / an anxious moth . . ."). But the sea cruise of the poem is paralleled by another voyage through the alimentary system, and "Zero is the shape of the volcano's orifice / as seen from above, as it is of the human's as seen from below. . . ." The poem concludes by seeing the voyage as both continuous and also, in a sense, always about to begin. The poem is likewise notable for its varieties of tone, especially for the way in which the dominant cooler tone makes way for "verbal intemperance," which has a powerful ability to animate the verse and which recurs in most of Tranter's later work.

These two books were followed two years later by *Crying in Early Infancy: 100 Sonnets* (1977) and two years after that by *Dazed in the Ladies Lounge* (1979). The sonnets of the first of these volumes all have an octet/sestet structure, though most are unrhymed. Part of the appeal of the book is its dexterity as it plays with the possible variations of the form—ranging from poems using long sentences to those using short, from those using end-stopped lines to those that are highly enjambed. It is also a book playing on varieties of tone, ranging from the comic ("FAMOUS POET JETS HOME TO USA! / How lucky to live in America, where / supermarkets stock up heavily on writers!") to the more conventionally lyrical in tone; to the comically surreal ("I'd like to throw an epileptic fit / at the Sydney Opera House and call it Rodent"); to the harder, disjunctive surreal ("Every frightened smile prepares / blood for the borrowed floor and then / morning on the street disrobe"). The sonnets were composed over a long period; they are not arranged chronologically, but inside the existing order one can detect that they represent different kinds of writing from Tranter's middle period.

Dazed in the Ladies Lounge and the *Selected Poems* of 1982 mark the end of this phase of Tranter's work. *Dazed in the Ladies Lounge* is one of his most impressive books. Of its four parts, only "The False Atlas" seems weak. The first and last sections are radically different poems dedicated to the problems of contemporary poetry itself. The first, "Rimbaud and the Modernist Heresy," is a rewriting of a long poem originally published in a journal. It is a powerful investigation of the influence of Arthur Rimbaud, focusing especially on the paradoxes that derive from the credo "One must be absolutely modern"—including the assumption that to obey this command a writer might well disobey it. The rewritten version of this poem is not quite as remorselessly engaged and solemn as the original and has something of the quality of *The Alphabet Murders* about it—not surprising, considering how close the two are in subject, if not in material. The voice of the speaker— "Sitting by the river under damp trees / I listen to the wind in the leaves / whispering hatred and loneliness"—is similar to that of an Australian apocalypse survivor, and the conclusion of the poem is as direct and powerful as anything in Tranter's work:

> Learning, where the deeply human
> is the object of a fierce knowledge,
> can reach an imitation of the style of love,
> but in that future under whose arrogant
> banner we have all laboured for our own rewards
> we shall both be gone into that
> unforgiving darkness.

The final poem of the book, "Ode to Col Joye," is one of Tranter's most successful works. It combines the mockery of existing poets with the search for a poetic method and a comic structure by invoking the search for "a John Tranter day":

> You open your eyes and realise
> it's the morning of a summer's day in Sydney
> and it's going to be—not a John Betjeman day,
> though you can hear church bells
>   faintly across Annandale,
> and not a John Forbes day, though
> the first thing you notice is your suntan lotion . . .

The main section of this book, however, "Radio Traffic," looks forward to later developments. It consists of a group of twenty-two thirty-line poems. Some are a mixture of surreal narratives such as are found in Tranter's most recent work. Others, such as "Butterfly" and "The Germ," play with the patterns of containment found throughout the work. But the best known are a group in which well-known literary/philosophical figures are associated alliteratively (in the titles at least) with Sydney pubs and other venues—"Leavis at the London" and "Enzensberger at Exiles," for example. In the first of these poems, images of an aging lecturer ("You need the money—your way of thinking's / going out of fashion, and you're growing old") are crossed with images drawn from a bombing run (evoking T. S. Eliot's "raid on the inarticulate") and a set of images from past popular culture ("It's not Humphrey Bogart—you / should have gone to Acapulco like / mother said . . . "), to brilliant effect.

Between *Dazed in the Ladies Lounge* and *Under Berlin* (1988) is a gap of nine years, although a *Selected Poems* (which includes ten new poems) was produced in 1982. *Under Berlin* and the next two books, *The Floor of Heaven* (1992) and *At the Florida* (1993), form a coherent whole within Tranter's work and include poems written in the 1980s and early 1990s. The period beginning in 1985 was one of extensive travel for Tranter, who undertook many reading tours of the United States, England, and mainland Europe. The poems of *Under Berlin* begin with portraits. As in his first two books these pictures are often of ruined lives, but the source of the ruin in this book is the natural processes of aging seen through a bleak perspective: "I see them meet, / they fight, they separate, / travel, / grow old," as one poem ("South Coast after Rain, 1960") says of an adolescent couple. The poems of the book also include a series of intense tours de force, often involving items of popular culture from the 1950s, such as "The Creature from the Black Lagoon," "High School Confidential," and "Stratocruiser," or more current technology, such as the much anthologized "Lufthansa"; two experimental narratives that lead eventually to the embedded narratives of *The Floor of Heaven;* and a twenty-two-poem sequence, "Sex Chemistry." The book also includes four epigrams in the classical mode—one for fellow poet Martin Johnston, which concludes,

From the blue Aegean

he declined to Darlinghurst, exchanging the dialect
of Callimachus and Cavafy for the meat-pie-eaters'
drab vernacular. For this indignity, a gentleman's
revenge: he wrought the vulgar tongue into
exquisite poetry.

One of the finest poems in *Under Berlin* is "Having
Completed My Fortieth Year," which is, as the notes
say, "a stanza-by-stanza reply to Peter Porter's 'On This
Day I Complete My Fortieth Year,'" itself a response to
a poem by George Gordon, Lord Byron. After a consideration of the state of poetry and the function of the
artist the poem concludes with a reference to a poetic
mentor–Porter's was W. H. Auden–in a way that
recalls "Rimbaud and the Modernist Heresy":

as I did some twenty years ago,
embarking on this yacht, this drudger's barge,
being "absolutely modern" as my mentor taught
    from the embers of his youth,

and hardly guessing then what would turn up:
these postcard views from a twinkling and distant
colony, of the twin cities: dying heart of Empire,
    sunset on the empire state.

The book *Late Night Radio,* published in the
United Kingdom in 1998, is composed of forty poems
from the sixty-five poems in *Under Berlin* together with
seven earlier ones. This combining suggests not only
the importance of *Under Berlin* but also that the volume
might best be seen as a selected group of poems from
the 1980s rather than as a conventional collection.

Between *Under Berlin* and *At the Florida,* Tranter
published an experimental set of verse-narratives, *The
Floor of Heaven.* One of the poems of *Under Berlin,* "During the War," shows evidence of being an earlier move
in the same direction. The tone of this poem is flat and
denotative, and it appears to be a recorded conversation with a retired policeman who occasionally consults
his notebooks while recalling criminal activity in New
South Wales during World War II. Nothing in
Tranter's earlier work prepares the reader for this
brisk, remorseless, "unpoetic" monologue:

I said "If you are here tonight
I will dump you, as I promised."
He replied "You're a tough Bastard.
I just drove the truck. I done nothing wrong. . . ."

The Floor of Heaven is a set of four framework narratives
loosely based on the same group-therapy workshop run
by a Dr. Masterson. But each section is a group of
inlaid narratives: the first, "Gloria," is exceptionally
complex because of the speaker's tendency to displace

Dust jacket for Tranter's 1972 book of poems that focus
on failed lives (Bruccoli Clark Layman Archives)

her narratives onto either her sister Karen or her twin,
Marjorie. The book was admiringly reviewed by both
Christopher Pollnitz and Andrew Riemer. The former
describes the way in which each narrative "is seeded
with a nightmare vignette or little constellation of nightmares. Each, as the monologist struggles to articulate
and lay to rest her (or his) trauma, enters the dark areas
of narratology–the narrator's authority seducing the
auditor's complicity"–and concludes that the brisk, flat,
narrative voice, so different from the distinctively personal dramatic utterances of characters in long poems
by Les Murray, John Scott, and Alan Wearne, is a
result of the central characters' not having a grounded
identity to form the basis of individualized speech. The
latter celebrated Tranter's assumption of the ancient
power of storytelling in poetry and comments, "almost
everywhere in these tales he strikes the appropriate balance between jokiness and gravity, between richness of
texture and flat, prosaic diction. . . ."

*Paperback cover for Tranter's 1974 book, which includes
his acclaimed poem "The Alphabet Murders"
(Bruccoli Clark Layman Archives)*

At the Florida is made up of three sections. The first group of poems re-creates the obsession with entropy which marked many of the poems of *Under Berlin*. The mode is stoic–"From ancient times // to the technical present most things decline; / only the means of oblivion improve"–and the material tends to recall adolescence, country towns, and sexual confusion. One poem, "Journey," in using the metaphor of a train journey to represent life, overwrites A. D. Hope's "Observation Car":

> . . . wondering
> why she wanted you so much, and what was the matter.
> And now she's disappeared, or what's worse, turned into
> just
>> Another bothered mum. Back
>> there in the twilight

> then, she was a pink
> breathless angel, all clumsy enthusiasm and lust.

> They hope for more, they all want something mysterious,
>> the heartbreak girls, the
>> lost lads . . .

As with so many Tranter book sections, the poems are organized in order of complexity, and the first part–after including two extended portrait poems, "The Moths" and "Opus Dei," respectively about a young teacher settling in to a routine that will eventually produce a miserable life and a minister already in that state of late-career dissolution–concludes with two intense, seminarrative poems–"Decalcomania" and "Dark Harvest." The latter begins with a storm, "thunder unrolling over the vulnerable city," and concludes with a bleak image of the poet "looking up at the thunderheads lit from below: / everything's blowing / into the future that waits for us but doesn't want us." The second section comprises longer poems, some with clear narrative bases, such as "Curriculum Vitae," and others, such as "Hot Nights," with a collocation of different voices and stories. The final section consists of thirty *haibun*–a Japanese form originally, in which poetry is mixed with prose. In Tranter's "re-engineered" *haibun,* twenty-line stanzas are followed by passages of prose of varying lengths and varying kinds of interaction with the poem. It is a return to disjunctive juxtaposition as a major poetic form in Tranter's work, although the relationships between the "halves" of each *haibun* are often difficult to read. Sometimes they operate with related scenarios, as in "Con's Café" and "Another Country," but in such later examples as "Bells Under Water" and "Quaker Clambake" the reader suspects that one of the halves is generated from the other in more complex ways.

In the late 1980s Tranter discovered a computer program that generated parodies by analyzing the frequency of letter repetition in a target text. The results are always words, but, as there is no screening for grammar or sense, the results are surreal texts, clearly in the style of the original. Tranter published a description of this program and a poem derived from Matthew Arnold's "Dover Beach," "The Buried Life," and "The Scholar Gypsy"–its author's name, Tom Haltwarden, an anagram of Arnold's name, as well as one derived from John Ashbery (Joy H. Breshan)–in a 1991 issue of the journal *Meanjin,* "Dogs in All the Unregarded Bales: Mr. Rubenking's 'BreakDown.'" This interest in the generation of textual material extends throughout Tranter's later work. Although it marks a change, it is not out of character with his interests throughout his career; it is at the most obvious level an interest in style for the "Break-Down" texts in all their meaninglessness, each eerily

Paperback cover for Tranter's 1998 collection of poems from the 1980s
(Thomas Cooper Library, University of South Carolina)

catching the voice it is based on. But early poems, such as "Red Movie," also represent a veering away from dominant interest in content to an interest in the more abstract question of how meaning derives from the organization of that content.

The 1998 collection *Different Hands: Seven Stories* is built on this letter-frequency analytical technique but extends it by producing amalgams of two selected texts. Much of the pleasure of these stories lies in the choice of the two texts to be juxtaposed: "Magic Women," for example, is a "blend" of *Little Women* and Carlos Castaneda's *Tales of Power* (1974); "Lonely Chaps" derives from Radclyffe Hall's *The Well of Loneliness* (1928) and William Earl Johns's *Biggles Defies the Swastika* (1941). But it is not a mechanical process. Tranter's introduction, describing how Allen Ginsberg's "Howl" and Laura Lee Hope's *The Bobbsey Twins on a Bicycle Trip* (1958) produced "Howling Twins," suggests that the result of the text generation was "twenty pages or so of fractured letters, words and phrases." The task of the author was not

so much to create as to uncover the "buried tale of lust, ecstacy and a lost cat" that was present in the text. "Most of the words in the final versions," he says, "are my own." The later pamphlet, *Blackout* (2000), blends three texts—William Shakespeare's *The Tempest* (circa 1611), Joan Didion's "Some Dreamers of the Golden Dream" (1968), and a chapter from Tom Wolfe's *The Electric Kool-Aid Acid Test* (1968)—by selecting words and phrases and then interleaving them, retaining the original order.

Tranter's book *Ultra* is highly structured formally in a way that recalls the one hundred sonnets or the poems of the "Radio Traffic" section of *Dazed in the Ladies Lounge:* twenty-four poems of fifty lines each follow a brief introductory poem. In a sense *Ultra* itself reads as a blend, but a blend of the earlier narratives of lives, such as are found in *Red Movie* and *The Blast Area,* again written with the radical text generating program. Some, such as "Country Matters," seem to be a mixing of several lives whereas others can be read as having a single life at the core, although they are more likely made from a group of separate narratives. Some of the poems also suggest that a Riffaterrean hypogram might generate them; "Locket," for example, includes the words "locket," "locker," "jockey," and "loser." At the same time, whatever their generative origins, they reflect consistent Tranter concerns with technology; adolescence; the city; individuals living within large, determining cultural structures; and the act of writing itself. "Globe" is a powerful statement of the frustrating power of the text:

> in the face of the inhuman demands of this print,
> that reaches out of some corner of the past—
> a grubby back room stinking of tallow—
> and orders you to stop thinking like that, now
> start thinking like this, and do the things
>
> that are inevitable, given this new
> political alignment of wish and fear . . .

It is the continual interaction of text and subject matter that lies behind Tranter's work. Each influences the other. Narratives of human lives are shaped by the structures in which they are embedded. Fragments of lyrics are re-animated by the larger poem in which they find themselves. Themes are released from blended texts after the words of the originals are analyzed and new words derived from his analysis. Many Australian poets grounded their work in an appreciation of the textual quality of poetry, but none has pursued the implications as rigorously and consistently as Tranter has. Far from being a remote aesthetician, he has at the same time remained a poet of his place—Sydney and the south coast of New South Wales—and his time.

Interviews:

Martin Duwell, *A Possible Contemporary Poetry* (St. Lucia, Qld.: Makar, 1982), pp. 15–37;

Jim Davidson, *Sideways from the Page* (Sydney: Fontana, Collins, 1983), pp. 324–345;

Barbara Williams, *In Other Words: Interviews with Australian Poets, Cross/Cultures*, 29 (Amsterdam: Rodopi, 1998), pp. 214–240, notes 278–279.

References:

David Brooks, "Feral Symbolists: Robert Adamson, John Tranter, and the Response to Rimbaud," *Australian Literary Studies,* 16 (May 1994): 280–288;

Kate Lilley, "Playing Possum: John Tranter's Poetry," *Verse,* 8 (1991): 82–89;

Lilley, "Textual Relations: John Tranter's *The Floor of Heaven,*" *Southerly,* 60 (2000): 106–114;

Lilley, "Tranter's Plots," *Australian Literary Studies,* 14 (May 1989): 41–50;

Andrew Taylor, "John Tranter: Absence in Flight," *Australian Literary Studies,* 12 (October 1986): 156–170.

Papers:

The University Library at the Australian Defence Force Academy has a manuscript collection of John Tranter's works, as does the State Library of New South Wales. The most extensive collection, including drafts of books from *The Blast Area* to *At the Florida,* is held by the National Library of Australia, Manuscript Section.

Chris Wallace-Crabbe
(6 May 1934 –)

David McCooey
Deakin University

BOOKS: *The Music of Division* (Sydney: Angus & Robertson, 1959);

Eight Metropolitan Poems (Adelaide, S.A.: Australian Letters, 1962);

In Light and Darkness (Sydney & London: Angus & Robertson, 1963);

The Rebel General (Sydney: Angus & Robertson, 1967);

Where the Wind Came: Poems (Sydney & London: Angus & Robertson, 1971);

Selected Poems (Sydney: Angus & Robertson, 1973; London: Angus & Robertson, 1973; Oxford & New York: Oxford University Press, 1995);

Act in the Noon (Warrandyte, Vic.: Cotswold Press, 1974);

Melbourne or the Bush: Essays on Australian Literature and Society (Sydney: Angus & Robertson, 1974);

The Shapes of Gallipoli (Warrandyte, Vic.: Cotswold Press, 1975);

The Foundations of Joy (Sydney: Angus & Robertson, 1976);

Toil & Spin: Two Directions in Modern Poetry (Richmond, Vic.: Hutchinson, 1979);

The Emotions Are Not Skilled Workers (Sydney: Angus & Robertson, 1980; London: Angus & Robertson, 1980);

Splinters (Adelaide: Rigby, 1981);

Three Absences in Australian Writing (Townsville, Qld.: Foundation for Australian Literary Studies, 1983);

The Amorous Cannibal, Oxford Poets Series (Oxford & New York: Oxford University Press, 1985);

I'm Deadly Serious, Oxford Poets Series (Oxford & Melbourne: Oxford University Press, 1988; Oxford & New York: Oxford University Press, 1988);

Beyond the Cringe: Australian Cultural Overconfidence? The Trevor Reese Memorial Lecture 1990 (London: Menzies Centre for Australian Studies, University of London, 1990);

Falling into Language (Melbourne & Oxford: Oxford University Press, 1990; Melbourne & New York: Oxford University Press, 1990);

Chris Wallace-Crabbe (photograph by Virginia Wallace-Crabbe; by permission of the National Library of Australia)

For Crying Out Loud, Oxford Poets Series (Oxford & New York: Oxford University Press, 1990);

Poetry and Belief, 1989 James McAuley Memorial Lecture (Hobart: University of Tasmania, 1990);

Rungs of Time, Oxford Poets Series (Oxford & Melbourne: Oxford University Press, 1993; Oxford & New York: Oxford University Press, 1993);

Apprehensions, Artist's Book, art by Bruno Leti, text by Wallace-Crabbe (Melbourne: Centre for the Development for Artists' Books, 1994);

Drawing, Artist's Book, art by Leti, text by Wallace-Crabbe (Melbourne: Centre for the Development for Artists' Books, 1994);

Phantoms in the Park, Artist's Book, art by Leti, text by Wallace-Crabbe (Melbourne: Artist, 1995);

Selected Poems 1956–1994 (Oxford & New York: Oxford University Press, 1995);

Florobiography (Sunday Garden), Artist's Book, art by Bruno Leti, text by Wallace-Crabbe (Melbourne: Artist, 1996);

The Iron Age, Artist's Book, art by Leti, text by Wallace-Crabbe (Melbourne: Artist, 1996);

The New Year, Artist's Book, art by Leti, text by Wallace-Crabbe (Melbourne & Canberra: Artist & Raphael Fodde, 1996);

Incomprehensible Picture, Artist's Book, art by Leti, text by Wallace-Crabbe (Melbourne: Artist, 1997);

The Neilson Lines Monotypes, Artist's Book, art by Leti, text by Wallace-Crabbe (Melbourne: Artist, 1998);

Timber, Artist's Book, art by Leti, Inge King, and Graham King, text by Wallace-Crabbe (Woodmere, N.Y.: Raphael Fodde, 1998);

Whirling, Oxford Poets Series (Oxford & New York: Oxford University Press, 1998);

The Alignments (One), Artist's Book, art by Leti, text by Wallace-Crabbe (Melbourne & Canberra: Edition and Artist Studio, Canberra School of Art, Australian National University, 1999);

The Alignments (Two), Artist's Book, art by Leti, text by Wallace-Crabbe (Canberra: Edition and Artist Studio, Canberra School of Art, Australian National University, 1999);

By and Large, Oxford Poets Series (Manchester, U.K.: Carcanet, 2001; Rose Bay, N.S.W.: Brandl & Schlesinger, 2001).

PLAY PRODUCTION: *Masks,* Sydney, Flashpoint Festival, 1970.

RECORDING: *Chris Wallace-Crabbe Reads from His Own Work,* Poets on Record, 10, University of Queensland Press, 1973.

OTHER: *Six Voices: Contemporary Australian Poets,* edited by Wallace-Crabbe (Sydney: Angus & Robertson, 1963; revised edition, Cremore, N.S.W.: Angus & Robertson, 1974; Westport, Conn.: Greenwood Press, 1979);

The Australian Nationalists: Modern Critical Essays, edited by Wallace-Crabbe (Melbourne & New York:

Oxford University Press, 1971; Melbourne & London: Oxford University Press, 1971);

Australian Poetry 1971, edited by Wallace-Crabbe (Sydney: Angus & Robertson, 1971);

The Golden Apples of the Sun: Twentieth Century Australian Poetry, edited by Wallace-Crabbe (Carlton, Vic. & Forest Grove, Ore.: Melbourne University Press, 1980);

"Australian Literary History," in *An Introduction to Australian Literature,* edited by C. D. Narasimhaiah (Brisbane, Qld.: Wiley, 1982);

Clubbing of the Gunfire: 101 Australian War Poems, edited by Wallace-Crabbe and Peter Pierce (Carlton, Vic.: Melbourne University Press, 1984);

"Autobiography," in *The Penguin New Literary History of Australia,* edited by Laurie Hergenhan (Ringwood, Vic.: Penguin, 1988), pp. 560–571;

Multicultural Australia: The Challenges of Change, edited by Wallace-Crabbe, David Goodman, and D. J. O'Hearn (Newham, Vic.: Scribe, 1991);

"The Escaping Landscape," in *Intruders in the Bush: The Australian Quest for Identity,* edited by John Carroll (Melbourne: Oxford University Press, 1992), pp. 155–180;

From the Republic of Conscience: An International Anthology of Poetry, edited by Kerry Flattley and Wallace-Crabbe (Flemington, Vic.: Aird in association with Amnesty International, 1992; Fredonia, N.Y.: White Pine, 1993);

"The Language of Poetry," in *The Languages of Australia,* edited by Gerhard Schulz (Canberra: Australian Academy of the Humanities, 1993), pp. 136–147;

"On the Balcony," in *Books, Death and Taxes,* edited by O'Hearn (Ringwood, Vic.: Penguin, 1995), pp. 76–81;

"Poetry and the Common Tongue," in *The Space of Poetry: Australian Essays on Contemporary Poetics,* edited by Lyn McCredden and Stephanie Trigg (Melbourne: University of Melbourne, Literary and Cultural Studies, 1996), pp. 69–80;

Approaching Australia: Papers from the Harvard Australian Studies Symposium, edited by Harold Bolitho and Wallace-Crabbe (Cambridge, Mass.: Harvard University Committee on Australian Studies, 1998);

Author! Author! Tales of Australian Literary Life, edited by Wallace-Crabbe (Melbourne & Oxford: Oxford University Press, 1998);

"Duncan Grant in New Haven," in *Seams of Light: Best Antipodean Essays,* edited by Morag Fraser (Sydney: Allen & Unwin, 1998), pp. 139–142;

The Oxford Literary History of Australia, edited by Bruce Bennett and Jennifer Strauss, associate editor, Wallace-Crabbe (Melbourne: Oxford University

Press, 1998)–includes an essay by Wallace-Crabbe titled "Poetry and Modernism," pp. 217–235;

La poésie australienne: une approche possible: le critique à l'oeuvre, edited by Simone Kadi and Wallace-Crabbe (Valenciennes, France: Presses Universitaires de Valenciennes, 2002).

TRANSLATION: *Ur Riki Samviskunnar,* edited by Wallace-Crabbe, Kerry Flattley, and Sigurdur A. Magnusson (Reykjavik, Iceland: Amnesty International, 1994).

SELECTED PERIODICAL PUBLICATIONS–UNCOLLECTED: "The Habit of Irony? Australian Poets of the Fifties," *Meanjin,* 20, no. 2 (1961): 164–174;

"Poetry in the Pop Age: Or the Battles between the Weak and the Strong," *Australian Book Review,* 144 (1992): 35–42;

"My First Love," *Age,* 29 July 1995, Extra, pp. 3, 6;

"Kit, Lost," *Southerly,* 60, no. 1 (2000): 115–119;

"Black Rock," *Meanjin,* 61, no. 1 (2002): 146–157.

Chris Wallace-Crabbe–poet, critic, and scholar–is central to contemporary Australian poetry. Originally one of the "Melbourne University poets," he was among the first (in the late 1950s) to represent Australian suburbia in poetry. His interest in Australia is coupled with a deep engagement with the wider world. He is an internationally recognized academic, and his engagement with prose poetry and American poetry took place notably early in Australia. He is also one of the few living Australian poets with an international reputation.

Wallace-Crabbe's poetry developed from ethical-formalist beginnings to include interests in politics and the self. His publications in the Oxford Poets Series, especially, are an important and accomplished body of work. Strongly attracted to the Australian vernacular and the quotidian, Wallace-Crabbe's poetry is marked by dualism. While characteristically elegiac, it also looks to the world of ideas and nature as sources of replenishment and joy.

Christopher Keith Wallace-Crabbe was born in Richmond, Melbourne, on 6 May 1934. His father, Kenneth Wallace-Crabbe, was a journalist with the *Melbourne Herald.* His mother, Phyllis Cock Passmore, was from a working-class background, had trained to be a secretary, and, according to Wallace-Crabbe in a 1996 *Australian Literary Studies (ALS)* interview, was "also, marginally, a concert pianist."

From 1935 to 1936 Wallace-Crabbe, known as Kit, traveled with his parents to Europe, where his father was a journalist. On 17 October 1938 Rollo (later

Robin) Wallace-Crabbe was born. He became a well-known artist (and also a writer). In late 1941 Kenneth Wallace-Crabbe went to war, and in 1942 his family lived briefly with his mother and sister in Black Rock, a Melbourne seaside suburb. With her husband away (at one stage "missing, believed dead"), Phyllis Wallace-Crabbe suffered from mental illness. When she and her sons returned to Melbourne, they lived in a flat in the comfortable suburb of Toorak. Wallace-Crabbe's father returned from World War II in 1946.

In a 1996 interview with David McCooey, Wallace-Crabbe described his father's Scottish family background as "middle-class bohemia, or Celtic-military bohemia." In his autobiography, *A Man's Childhood* (1997), Robin Wallace-Crabbe presents his mother as having "the power of madness" and his father as right-wing and lacking in insight. In his *ALS* interview, Chris Wallace-Crabbe is less trenchant:

> Imaginatively, my father represented the Exotic; he was orientalism, versatility, journalistic lightness. He could do anything, like Robinson Crusoe or the Swiss Family Robinson. Short concentration span, that's the secret . . . But his prolonged absence also cancelled out the conflicts inherent in the Oedipus complex. He was merely an ally: nimble, supportive, utterly unthreatening.

Both men attest to their father's vitality. As well as being a journalist and soldier, Kenneth Wallace-Crabbe, OBE (Order of the British Empire), was a handyman, amateur moviemaker and photographer, artist, publisher, author of children's stories (published) and historical fiction (unpublished), and (in his fifties) builder of his own house. He clearly affected Chris Wallace-Crabbe, who inherited his father's versatility and liking for busyness.

In 1943 Wallace-Crabbe began attending Scotch College, a large, Presbyterian private school for boys. He enjoyed the sports and the comparative liberality of the school but was not a star student. In 1950 he left school and in 1951 became junior technical officer at the Royal Mint in Melbourne. In the same year he began writing and won the Centenary Prize for best history essay in Victoria (for those under nineteen), despite having failed history in his last year at school. From September 1952 to February 1953 he undertook National Service as a wireless technician in the Royal Australian Air Force (RAAF).

In 1953 he began an arts degree part-time at the University of Melbourne while working for an electrical trades magazine. For four years he studied (mostly taking night classes) and worked–laboring in a malt house, working as a clerk at the Gas and Fuel Corporation, and laboring for a summer in an open-cut mine. In his last year at the university, 1956, he tutored in Aus-

*Paperback cover for Wallace-Crabbe's 1985 book of poems,
which attracted international attention (Thomas Cooper
Library, University of South Carolina)*

tralian history at Taylor's, a school for adult matriculation. He also won his first poetry prize, the John Masefield Prize for Poetry.

Attending the University of Melbourne began his long association with that institution. With occasional international fellowships and professorships, Wallace-Crabbe worked there for nearly forty years. As an undergraduate he studied English, French, and philosophy; met poets, such as Bruce Dawe, Jennifer Strauss, and Evan Jones; and met charismatic intellectuals, including the poet-critic Vincent Buckley and the political scientist A. F. ("Foo") Davies.

In 1957 Wallace-Crabbe married Helen Wiltshire, whom he had met in 1954. He was then a schoolteacher, teaching until late 1958 at Haileybury. In 1959 he undertook his M.A. qualifying year (honors equivalent). Peers included Germaine Greer and Barry

Humphries. Wallace-Crabbe's minor thesis was on "Syntax and Rhetoric in Yeats." That year his first child, Ben, was born and his first book was published.

The Music of Division (1959), a surprisingly mature debut, is formalistic, but its quintains and unrhymed lines show Wallace-Crabbe's early attraction to idiosyncrasy. The influence of W. B. Yeats and W. H. Auden is apparent, but Wallace-Crabbe's interest in suburbia was groundbreaking. The book is ironic, sometimes satirical. Suburbia generally figures as an inauthentic space between city and country, but in "Citizen" and in Wallace-Crabbe's second collection, *In Light and Darkness* (1963), suburbia becomes a place worthy of metaphysical speculation.

In 1960 Wallace-Crabbe became a tutor in English at the University of Melbourne, and in 1961 his daughter, Georgia, was born. That year was the first of his three as Lockie fellow in Australian literature and creative writing, a position that placed him in two new academic fields in Australia. In 1963 his *Six Voices: Contemporary Australian Poets,* an often reprinted anthology used in schools, appeared, as did his third book of poetry, *In Light and Darkness.* Imagery of light and darkness appears throughout the book. The eponymous poem, which meditates on how "we dance, into and out of the darkness / To tireless music," illustrates how early Wallace-Crabbe incorporated both realist and Romantic impulses: "But come tomorrow, we will neither be Christ nor Ghandi / But will breathe this polluted air and rejoice with the birds."

The poetry is again formalistic and ironic, though Wallace-Crabbe's formalism is more ambitious, producing a sestina, longer odic poems, and–significantly–prose poetry. Gary Catalano has credited Wallace-Crabbe with introducing the latter to Australian poetry. The less successful poems are the most ambitious, dealing with heroism and exotica. In contrast, "Melbourne" is an early, and unheroic, response to the poet's hometown: "Though much has died here, little has been born." Wallace-Crabbe's subsequent rejection of this position was a result in part of his own artistic efforts.

In 1964 Wallace-Crabbe wrote his masters thesis on the later poetry of Auden, and from 1965 through 1967 he was a Harkness fellow at Yale University. Corecipients included moviemaker Tim Burstall and composer Peter Sculthorpe, with whom Wallace-Crabbe planned to write an opera. (An unused libretto on an Aztec theme was written.) Before leaving for Yale, Wallace-Crabbe became lecturer at the University of Melbourne. While in the United States he "relearned Romanticism, and tried to understand a truly violent society" *(ALS),* experiences that deeply affected his work, most obviously in *The Rebel General* (1967), a conspicuously hard book, in which he is drawn to military themes and portentous language, as in "An Exile Broods upon Reality": "The grumbling guns are rusted now / And I forget what angel stands / With his fiery sword at the gate." An abstract quality is seen in the title poem, which meditates on the difference between idealism and personal responsibility.

More characteristic is the book's concern with landscape and metaphysics. The duality of Wallace-Crabbe's thinking was, by then, established. In "Nature, Language, the Sea: An Essay," wonder and ignorance are the conditions of existence: "For the world is wonder, is profusion, / A boundless brilliant orchard of / Sun-licked, thunder-shaken strangeness, // But nobody can claim it makes good sense." Such duality reverberates through Wallace-Crabbe's poetry.

Concern with violence continues in the long poem "Blood Is the Water," from *Where the Wind Came* (1971). Another meditation on power and responsibility, this poem involves a Latin American dictator who symbolizes the tension between personal responsibility and history. The book is more notable for its interest in language and subjectivity, twinned themes central to Wallace-Crabbe's later work. Duality is again present. While self is the source of joy, it is also—paradoxically—the source, as in "The Joker," of self-alienation: "Musketeer, / I delight in your quick spring heels, / and yet baffled in the end / I fall back / . . . You tear me apart."

The collection also shows continued interest in form, as seen in the long prose poem "Sailing to Cythera." This poem appears to be a meditation on love, but is also about human categories of meaning. One of Wallace-Crabbe's strangest pieces, it is also a reminder that his reputation as an academic at times could obscure the lyric, sometimes surreal, energy that inhabits his poems. The tag of "Melbourne University poet" (shared by Buckley, R. A. Simpson, and Evan Jones) was a description that took Wallace-Crabbe some years to leave behind.

Rather than reprint *Where the Wind Came,* Angus and Robertson published Wallace-Crabbe's *Selected Poetry* in 1973. This premature collection is mainly of interest today because of the section titled "Meditations," made up of poems from diverse sources and described in Wallace-Crabbe's preface as "a continuous landscape-of-debate . . . grandfathered by the painter J. M. W. Turner." Visual art is a major element in Wallace-Crabbe's career. It has operated thematically in his poetry—especially in *By and Large* (2001)—and Wallace-Crabbe has also written widely on Australian art; over the last decade he has collaborated with artist Bruno Leti on several artists' books that marry Wallace-Crabbe's poetry with Leti's images.

By 1971 Wallace-Crabbe was a senior lecturer. He spent most of 1973 with his family overseas while he was visiting fellow at Exeter University and visiting professor at the University of Venice, Ca Foscari. In 1974 he won the Farmer Prize for poetry, and his first book of essays, *Melbourne or the Bush: Essays on Australian Literature and Society,* was published (with essays on Australian literature and two essays on Melbourne).

From 1974 through 1976 Wallace-Crabbe was chairman of the English department at the University of Melbourne (and again from 1984 through 1985). In December 1975 he and his wife separated. He lived with Marianne Feil, and they spent most of 1977 (the year Wallace-Crabbe became reader in English) in Florence, where Wallace-Crabbe wrote and translated. In 1978 he and Marianne Feil married. They had two boys, Toby (born in 1979) and Joshua (born in 1980).

In 1979 Wallace-Crabbe's second book of essays was published. The "two directions" discussed in *Toil & Spin: Two Directions in Modern Poetry* are characterized variously as realism and symbolism, high and low poetics, and popularism and experimentation. One major concern related to Wallace-Crabbe's own poetry is the tension between writing so as "to merge or attach oneself to the external world" and writing so as to "allow the creative ego room to assert itself distinctively."

Such a tension is apparent in *The Emotions Are Not Skilled Workers* (1980). The mixing of registers and use of the Australian vernacular—which is central to Wallace-Crabbe's later style—can be seen as catering to both impulses. The extraordinary lexis (surely among Australian poets), the complicated syntax, the alliteration and internal rhyme, and the eccentric euphony of Wallace-Crabbe's poetry all suggest an intense grappling with chaos and a desire to render a poetry that is both artful and of the common tongue. Poems such as "Introspection," "Inventing a Tongue," and "Puck in January" deconstruct the divide between "serious" poetry and "light verse." Humor and intelligence are presented as coexistent.

The Emotions Are Not Skilled Workers includes Wallace-Crabbe's last and most successful sequence dealing with the bloodiness of history, "The Shapes of Gallipoli" (published separately in 1975). Mixing prose, highly rhetorical verse, and versified demotic, this poem evokes the voices of the lost. For all the interest in the mythic quality of the Anzacs, the poem is marked by immediacy, subjectivity, and the quotidian (albeit a soldier's quotidian).

Wallace-Crabbe's interest in the quotidian is seen in his only novel, *Splinters* (1981). More a series of vignettes held together by characterization than a conventional novel, this work is set in Melbourne in 1968, and the chaos of its characters' lives suggests that poli-

Paperback cover for Wallace-Crabbe's book of essays on literary criticism (Thomas Cooper Library, University of South Carolina)

tics and (more ambiguously) art are unable to order that chaos. *Splinters* is perhaps the last modernist novel, with its formal experimentation, emphasis on character over plot, and interest in representing the quotidian. But while the influence of Virginia Woolf and Katherine Mansfield is clear, so is the interest in Australian idioms and manners.

The use in the novel of the demotic, satire, and parody is supported by an almost manic narratorial cheeriness, but the lack of coherent political belief and the emphasis on the opacity of self give the work a bleakness at odds with the tone. At times this bleakness breaks through: "Underneath us all the abyss, the gap, the toothed mouthful of horror, the O."

Thanks to *The Emotions Are Not Skilled Workers*, Wallace-Crabbe was asked to submit a manuscript to Oxford University Press, and in 1985 it published *The Amorous Cannibal*, making Wallace-Crabbe one of the few Australian poets (including Les Murray and Peter Porter) to gain an international reputation. One is

tempted to see *The Amorous Cannibal* as marking Wallace-Crabbe's poetic maturity. Its interest in language could be a theory-inspired "linguistic turn"; the mixing of modes could be a new postmodern aesthetic, and the interest in Australia could be in step with the emergent nationalism of the 1980s.

In fact, these elements had been present in Wallace-Crabbe's poetry since the early 1970s. Rather, *The Amorous Cannibal* stands out more for its aesthetic strength and technical control. Martin Duwell, in his review (*Australian*, 6 January 1996) of *Selected Poems 1956–1994* (1995), argues similarly: "the great development in Wallace-Crabbe's poetry isn't really one of theme nor necessarily of mode; the obsessions seem more or less consistent. Perhaps it is really a matter of poetic intensity, of abandoning a poetry in which the tension between formal restraints and an edgy subject matter is the source of excitement and just going flat out."

"Just going flat out" is what Wallace-Crabbe does. "Eating the Future (I)," by turns slangy, lyrical, self-reflexive, and allusive, is characteristic in its risky syntax and lexis.

> Can I feel order in the whole shebang?
> Pain I experience, and blood, and phlegm,
>
> hardening of iliac and hamstring;
> but as for order–I write verse.
>
> Something is larger, like role of light at noon
> enabling turquoise, lime and cinnabar,
>
> we feel its brushy mayhap and we sing.
> I stroll abroad as Puck, wagging or winking.

The Shakespearian (or Kiplingesque) figure of Puck has featured in Wallace-Crabbe's poetry for more than twenty-five years. Sometimes a version of the poet, sometimes a postcolonial revisionist, Puck represents an aesthetic: "I lean to whatever is tousled, / windy, brownish, water-kissed, lit by irregular streaks of glinting / and, above all, out of place" ("Puck Is Not Sure About Apollo"). "Puck Disembarks" (from *For Crying Out Loud,* 1990) subverts the elegiac quality of the Australian landscape (and its history), replacing it with a history that both accepts and rejects its European heritage. Puck is chosen to disembark with the First Fleet in Sydney Cove, 1788, because he is the ur-larrikin:

> . . . the imp rises inside him, getting ready
> To rewrite Empire as larrikin culture.
>   He daubs a first graffito on
>   The commissary tent, GEORGE THE TURD.

This "first" nonindigenous mark is notably scatological and anti-authoritarian, but the Australian landscape offers consolations and a new sense of place as Puck "begins to adore / The willy-wagtail's flirting pirouettes."

Wallace-Crabbe's comedy also ranges from the philosophical to the throwaway in sequences such as "Squibs in the Nick of Time" and "The Bits and Pieces." But jokiness and the ephemeral do not preclude seriousness. As Jennifer Strauss argues, the pun in "Squibs in the Nick of Time" (in which "nick" equals "prison") suggests that humans are "prisoners in time, with only language to enable us to gain brief flashes of light and sound, and wise-cracks acting as little crackers." The switching of registers and breaking of decorum, then, often imply that comedy is imbricated with tragedy, a point made in the final poem of the collection, "A Stone Age Decadent." As Wallace-Crabbe stated in his 1990 interview with Barbara Williams: "the comic mode, in the fullest, most complicated, sense takes in enormous contradictions and essentially asserts that, given these contradictions, something goes on. I think of that as a basis for my writing: tragedy, taken far enough, ends up as comedy."

Such an aesthetic is seen in the next collection, *I'm Deadly Serious* (1988), significantly (and disturbingly) in the elegy for the poet's father, "Thermodynamics," in which scientific materialism, the consolatory power of jokes, lyricism, and philosophy all join in an agonized account of grief. Only slightly less anguished is "Intensive Care," which links language, self, and mortality, and in which the poet writes he would "like to be as funny as a real hexameter." In "Stuff Your Classical Heritage" the seriocomic mode develops Wallace-Crabbe's position on the postcolonial status of Australia, showing an ambivalence about the elegiac relationship between Australian and European culture.

In *I'm Deadly Serious* Wallace-Crabbe returns to politics, but in a less outré fashion. In "Sonnets to the Left" he employs wit in the verse form where before high rhetoric and exotic situations had dramatized the political interests. The flexibility of the form allows for several tonal changes, from the comic to the elegiac, and—as the syntactical ambiguity of the title suggests— the sequence wittily undermines Marxist, feminist, and postmodern positions (only univocally supporting Aboriginal land rights). While not a formalist as such, Wallace-Crabbe habitually writes stanzaic poetry, and— in addition to sonnets and prose poetry—he has employed such forms as the pantoum, dramatic monologue, rondo, and ballad stanza.

In November 1986 Wallace-Crabbe's eldest child died. Ben Wallace-Crabbe, who had been bassist in the alternative rock band Ed Kuepper and the Laughing Clowns, was twenty-six. Amid such personal tragedy Wallace-Crabbe's career flourished. He was awarded the Grace Leven Prize for poetry. In 1987 he won the quinquennial Dublin Prize for distinction in the arts and sciences, and he gained a Personal Chair at the University of Melbourne. From 1987 to 1988 he was visiting professor of Australian Studies at Harvard.

In 1989 he became director of the Australian Centre at the University of Melbourne (a position he held until the end of 1994). In 1990 he was awarded the 1989 FAW (Fellowship of Australian Writers) Christopher Brennan Award for a poet of sustained distinction, and from 1992 through 1996 he edited the Oxford University Press (Melbourne) Australian Writers Series, a series of monographs on Australian writers.

With the loss of his son, the elegiac nature of Wallace-Crabbe's poetry intensified, and some of his most powerful poems are elegies for his son. The first appeared in *For Crying Out Loud*. Simply called "An Elegy," it illustrates an insight of David Malouf's: "Romanticism and hard-head realism are in sharp tension in Wallace-Crabbe's poetry and the resolutions achieved are of one over the other. They are almost always affirmative in their rhetorical form but deeply ambiguous in their final meaning." "An Elegy" reveals this ambiguity in its final lines: "I wish again / it were possible to pluck my son / out of dawn's moist air / and gather him gasping back into this life." This image is strikingly like that of rebirth (as one would find in a traditional elegy), but the use of the demonstrative pronoun *this* (rather than simply *life*) ambiguously suggests both the untranscendent particularity of human existence and the possibility of "another life."

In many ways, *For Crying Out Loud* is a continuation of the previous two books. Indeed, a striking number of powerful poems around this time emphasize "the slubbing barabble of language," selfhood, mortality, dreams, and Australia. If *For Crying Out Loud* is more explicitly elegiac, then the powerfully idiosyncratic elegy for A. F. Davies, "The Life of Ideas," illustrates how Wallace-Crabbe's mixed-mode technique allows for the expression of strong emotion to be allied with intellectual rigor and liveliness.

Several poems show Wallace-Crabbe's developing interest in writing autobiographically (if not confessionally). Wallace-Crabbe's third book of essays, *Falling into Language* (1990), shows this interest to be thematic rather than accidental. The book is concerned with "how the autobiographical text replaces the gone life, with the gestures which announce its claim to liveliness, with the ambiguous personality of lyric poetry and with the self, or selves, which I am bringing into my own critical acts and arguments." The autobiography is central, rather then peripheral, to literary criticism. As such, these essays cover a wide range of biographical ground, from an account of Wallace-Crabbe's official trip to Russia in 1985 (with Thomas Shapcott and Olga

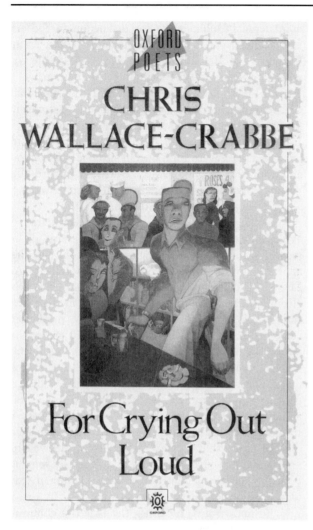

Paperback cover for the 1990 book that includes Wallace-Crabbe's elegy for his son (Thomas Cooper Library, University of South Carolina)

Masters) to reflections on a 1940s childhood and accounts of the author's dreams (a longtime obsession). The thematic unity, wide cultural range, and intellectual acumen of the essays make this book Wallace-Crabbe's most fully realized critical work.

Falling into Language provides insights into the author's perspective on his creative processes. With regard to the intellectual basis for his dualism, Wallace-Crabbe writes,

> As a poet . . . I simultaneously have a sensuous hunger to capture the world through depiction and a sceptical awareness that such depiction depends on conventions of discourse which are historically bounded; or, worse, linguistically doomed from the start. How do you write down the leaves on one small tree in your backyard? To this doubleness I tend to respond manically: over-reacting, I signal my awareness of a disabling gap by upping the ante, mixing the dictions, breaking deco-

rum, doing all that I can to syncopate readerly expectations.

Rungs of Time (1993) is the last in a quartet of books dealing primarily with self, language, and mortality. It includes Keatsian odes, such as "Like Vibrations of a Bell," and mordant jokes, such as "Medico's Song." Poems such as "Philosophical Concepts," "Drunken Concepts," and "Free Will" grapple with the "doubleness" expressed in *Falling into Language,* while the elegiac project of trying to name or conceive the dead continues, as in "Trace Elements": "Space-time is no longer their medium; / they inhabit / antipodes of the radiant fair dinkum, post-Heisenberg, transphysical, post-Planck, / taunting us with quips of antimatter."

In 1995, *Selected Poems 1956–1994* received universally favorable reviews and won *The Age* Book of the Year Award (the first poetry book to win that prize). The selection was reprinted in 1997, the year Wallace-Crabbe retired from the English department at the University of Melbourne. He became Emeritus Professor and since 1998 has been based at the Australian Centre.

Whirling (1998) is a lighter work than Wallace-Crabbe's previous Oxford collections. The fascination with the natural world (always present) is emphasized, as a test of skill to render the ever-changing yet changeless world of clouds, sea, and leaves. Despite the lighter poems, an autumnal note is present throughout the volume, in the elegies for Wallace-Crabbe's son, the evocation of "the gods," and the obsession with the passing of time.

Whirling was Wallace-Crabbe's last collection with Oxford University Press, as they canceled (amid considerable outcry) their poetry list in December 1998. Carcanet bought the "Oxford Poets" list, and Wallace-Crabbe's *By and Large* was published by Carcanet in England and Brandl & Schlesinger in Australia. In 1999 Wallace-Crabbe and his second wife separated. His partner (though they do not live together) is painter Kristin Headlam.

Wallace-Crabbe's *By and Large* includes a major sequence of forty sonnets, "Modern Times," a survey of modern politics and habits, the self, food, and important cultural references, such as one to Sigmund Freud. This bravura work brings together the reading and poetic practice of a lifetime. It ranges widely over the poet's life, from his days in the RAAF to his days at Black Rock with Aunt Violante. Wildly self-referential, the poems in the volume include quotes from other poems in the volume as well as from earlier poems. The bleak view of "modern times" in the book suggests not so much nostalgia (though this feeling may be present) as a critique of the political shift to the right in contemporary Australia. In contrast, the final poem of the collection, "New Year," is one of the most poignant versions of Wallace-Crabbe's insistent theme of loss accompanied by aesthetic renewal:

> As when the locality darkens,
> earth odours rise up
> and colour has bled away
>
> while the lit clouds yet
>   sail sweetly over us
> inhabiting a daylight of their own.

Wallace-Crabbe shows no signs of retiring from poetry or public life. Since retiring from teaching at the University of Melbourne, he has received many commissions (including one from the City of Melbourne for a millennium poem); he regularly features in literary festivals; and he continues to write arts journalism. One gets the sense that, just as it was for his family during his childhood, time is a "precious medium." This comment, from the autobiographical essay "Kit, Lost" (2000), seems particularly telling: "we lived in time like farmers in weather."

Wallace-Crabbe's artful use of the demotic is part of a desire to mix modes and break decorum; it shows Australian English as rich, not poor. The theatrical element of his work–for example, "Exit the Players" and "Spirit and Act"–is matched by an interest in the theatricality of the self, played out in a world inhabited by death and the ever-changing but changeless forms of nature. Wallace-Crabbe's description, in *Toil & Spin*, of Roethke's "strange vision of minutiae and largenesses" can equally apply to his own work.

Chris Wallace-Crabbe's poetry dramatizes an abundant engagement with the world, the self, and their transformations. His knowledge of philosophy and literary theory makes him attuned to the fragility and provisional status of "reality," but his skepticism about the uses to which such insights have been put illustrates a humanist basis to his postmodern techniques. As he writes in an unpublished piece titled "The Moi": "My short poems are nearly all about epiphanies: about what such privileged moments might reveal about 'gods,' about the Oceanic Feeling, about transcendence. Not a religious person, yet a kind of astronomical deist, I go to poetry (as to music) to walk upon a level of experience that is not materialist."

Interviews:

R. A. Simpson, Interview, *Poetry Magazine,* 3 (1966): 3–5;

Thomas Shapcott, "The Imaginative Enterprise: An Interview with Chris Wallace-Crabbe," *Makar,* 13, no. 2 (1978): 37–43;

David Carter, "Shape-Changing: An Interview with Chris Wallace-Crabbe," *Helix,* 7–8 (1981): 101–109;

Barbara Williams, "Interview with Chris Wallace-Crabbe," *Ariel,* 21, no. 2 (1990): 77–90;

David McCooey, "An Interview with Chris Wallace-Crabbe," *Australian Literary Studies,* 17, no. 4 (1996): 377–382.

References:

Gary Catalano, "Other Forms: Some Remarks on the Prose Poem," *Germinal,* 3 (1986): 62–71;

E. Adrian M. Colman, "A Modest Radiance: The Poetry of Chris Wallace-Crabbe," *Westerly,* 1 (1969): 45–51;

Dirk Den Hartog, "Self-Levelling Tall Poppies: The Authorial Self in (Male) Australian Literature," in *Australian Cultural History,* edited by S. L. Goldberg and F. B. Smith (Cambridge: Cambridge University Press, 1988), pp. 226–241;

David Malouf, "Some Volumes of Selected Poems of the 1970s," *Australian Literary Studies,* 10, no. 1 (1981): 13–21;

David McCooey, "Leisure and Grief: The Recent Poetry of Chris Wallace-Crabbe," *Australian Literary Studies,* 17, no. 4 (1996): 332–343;

McCooey, "Neither Here Nor There: Suburban Voices in Australian Poetry," in *Writing the Everyday: Australian Literature and the Limits of Suburbia,* edited by Andrew McCann (St. Lucia: University of Queensland Press, 1998), pp. 101–114;

Peter Steele, "To Move in Light: The Poetry of Chris Wallace-Crabbe," *Meanjin Quarterly,* 29, no. 2 (1970): 149–155;

Jennifer Strauss, *Stop Laughing! I'm Being Serious: Three Studies in Seriousness and Wit in Contemporary Australian Poetry* (Townsville: Foundation for Australian Literary Studies, James Cook University of North Queensland, 1990);

Andrew Zawacki, *Chris Wallace-Crabbe* (forthcoming).

Papers:

An extensive collection of Chris Wallace-Crabbe's papers is held in the Melbourne University archives (Accession Numbers: 90/146; 76/11; 100/20; 97/15). Most of this material is classified as restricted. Holdings for Kenneth Wallace-Crabbe are also available there (Accession Number 90/147). Some additional material relating to Kenneth Wallace-Crabbe is available in the MS section of the State Library of Victoria. Additional material on Chris Wallace-Crabbe is held in the National Library of Australia (ANL MS 7800 and MS 732), which also holds extensive papers on Robin Wallace-Crabbe (ANL MS 8053).

Judah Waten
(29 July 1911? – 29 July 1985)

David Carter
University of Queensland

BOOKS: *Alien Son* (Sydney: Angus & Robertson, 1952);

The Unbending (Melbourne: Australasian Book Society, 1954);

Shares in Murder (Melbourne: Australasian Book Society, 1957);

Time of Conflict (Sydney: Australasian Book Society, 1961);

Distant Land (Melbourne: Australasian Book Society, 1964; London: Angus & Robertson, 1965);

Season of Youth (Melbourne: F. W. Cheshire, 1966);

From Odessa to Odessa: The Journey of an Australian Writer (Melbourne: F. W. Cheshire, 1969);

So Far No Further (Mount Eliza, Vic.: Wren, 1971);

The Depression Years, 1929–1939 (Melbourne: F. W. Cheshire, 1971);

Bottle-O! (North Melbourne, Vic.: Cassell, 1972; London: Cassell, 1975);

Love and Rebellion (South Melbourne, Vic.: Macmillan, 1978);

Scenes of Revolutionary Life (Sydney & London: Angus & Robertson, 1982);

Judah Waten: Fiction, Memoirs, Criticism, edited by David Carter (St. Lucia & Portland, Ore.: University of Queensland Press, 1998).

OTHER: Herz Bergner, "The Boardinghouse," translated by Waten, in *Southern Stories: Poems and Paintings,* edited by Brian Fitzpatrick (Melbourne: Dolphin, 1945), pp. 68–76;

Pinchus Goldhar, "Cafe in Carlton," translated by Waten, "Reflections on Literature and Painting," and "Inspector Ryan," as Matt Turner, in *Southern Stories: Poems and Paintings,* edited by Brian Fitzpatrick (Melbourne: Dolphin, 1945), pp. 29–47, 52–58, 88–102;

Bergner, *Zwishm himi un waser,* translated by Waten as *Between Sky and Sea* (Melbourne: Dolphin, 1946);

Twenty Great Australian Stories, edited by Waten and V. G. O'Connor (Melbourne: Dolphin, 1946);

Judah Waten (from the dust jacket for Scenes of Revolutionary Life, *1982; Bruccoli Clark Layman Archives)*

Maurice Carter, *Our Street,* introduction by Waten (Melbourne, 1949);

Bergner, "The Actor," translated by Waten, *Southerly,* 18 (1957): 94–101;

Report of Literary Trends (Privately published, 1966);

Trends in Australian Literature (Privately published, 1966);

Classic Australian Short Stories, edited by Waten and Stephen Murray-Smith (Melbourne: Wren, 1974);

"Victor O'Connor's Paintings," introduction by Waten, in *Selected Paintings by Vic O'Connor 1939–1983* (Melbourne: Gryphon Gallery);

"Pinchas Goldhar," in *Australian Dictionary of Biography Volume 9: 1891–1939,* edited by Bede Nairn and Geoffrey Serle (Melbourne: Melbourne University Press, 1983), pp. 40–41.

SELECTED PERIODICAL PUBLICATIONS–
UNCOLLECTED: "Use and Beauty," *University High School Record* (December 1926): 23–24;

"Guerre dans le monde," *Nouvel Age,* 11 (November 1931): 1006–1007;

"Pinchas Goldhar," *Voice* (February 1947): 13;

"Anti-Semitism in Australia," *Unity,* 1 (March–April 1948): 4–5;

"Contemporary Jewish Literature in Australia," *Australian Jewish Historical Society Journal,* 3 (1949): 92–97;

"Bitter Freedom," *Tribune* (Sydney), 28 August 1957, p. 6; *Labour Monthly,* 39 (December 1957): 561–565;

"Howard Fast Steps into a New Camp," *Tribune* (Sydney), 21 November 1957, p. 6;

"*Quadrant:* A Voice of America," *Tribune* (Sydney), 29 January 1958, p. 6;

"The Australian Tradition and Communism," *Tribune* (Sydney), 22 October 1958, p. 7;

"How People's Culture Flourishes in USSR," *Tribune* (Sydney), 14 January 1959, p. 7;

"Literature and the Writer in the Soviet Union," *Tribune* (Sydney), 28 January 1959, p. 7;

"They Were Right to Reject *Dr. Zhivago,*" *Tribune* (Sydney), 4 February 1959, p. 7;

"The Jews in the Soviet Union," *Tribune* (Sydney), 11 March 1959, p. 6;

"What Soviet People Read," *Labour Monthly,* 41 (April 1959): 184–188;

"Professor's Book Is a Great Disappointment," *Tribune* (Sydney), 9 March 1960, p. 6;

"Socialist Realism–An Important Trend in Present Day Australian Literature," *Communist Review,* 221 (May 1960): 204–207;

"D. H. Lawrence and *Lady Chatterley's Lover,*" *Realist Writer,* 6 (May 1961): 8–9;

"Vance Palmer and His Literary Contribution," *Realist Writer,* 11 (April 1963): 22–24;

"Famous Writer Tells How He Sold Communist Press in 1926," *Guardian* (Melbourne), 18 July 1963, pp. 4–5;

"Australian Literature in 1962," *Realist Writer,* 12 (August 1963): 26–28;

"Australian Literature, 1963–1964," *Realist,* 17 (Summer 1964): 27–29;

"Coming Back to Odessa," *Communist Review,* 288 (January 1966): 17–19;

"Ehrenburg, Miller and Yevtushenko," *Age* (Melbourne), 5 February 1966, p. 21;

"Stephen Spender, the Snows and Arnold Wesker," *Age* (Melbourne), 12 February 1966, p. 22;

"Some Australians and Iris Murdoch," *Age* (Melbourne), 19 February 1966, p. 22;

"Yiddish Culture in West and East," *Labour Monthly,* 48 (August 1966): 374–379;

"Will Yiddish Culture Survive?" *Labour Monthly,* 48 (September 1966): 440–446;

"Yiddish Culture in the West," *Australian Left Review,* 3 (October 1966): 52–57;

"The Powys Brothers and Modern Symbolism," *Realist,* 30 (1968): 63–65;

"Melbourne Jewry," *Australian Book Review,* 7 (1968): 202;

"Books and the Bottle-O's Son," *Sydney Morning Herald,* 12 April 1969, p. 19;

"In Other Tongues," *Nation* (Sydney), 27 June 1970, pp. 22–23;

"Marxism and Australian Literature," *Issue,* 1 (May 1971): 8–10;

"My First Two Schools," *The Secondary Teacher* (July 1971): 19–20;

"The Jewish Contribution to Australian Society," *Age* (Melbourne), 18 August 1973, p. 12;

"Arthur Phillips: A Fellow in Literature and Humanity," *Overland,* 60 (1975): 57–59;

"Changing Camps," *Socialist* (Sydney) (October 1975): 6;

"Books that Influenced Me Deeply," *Educational Magazine,* 36 (1979): 30–32;

"Writers from Two Cultures," *Aspect,* 5 (1980): 49–55;

"My Literary Education," *Bulletin Literary Supplement* (April 1981): 24–28;

"Seventy Years," *Overland,* 86 (1981): 16–18;

"Ethnic Australia," *New Literature Review,* 12 (1983): 46–48;

"Alan Marshall–Obituary," *Australian Author,* 16 (1984): 15;

"A Writer's Youth," *Outrider,* 1 (June 1984): 114–121.

Judah Waten is best known for his short stories and novels of migrant life in twentieth-century Australia. He is generally seen as the first Australian writer to have written "from the inside" about non-English-speaking migrants and immigrant communities, and thus he is an important figure in the history of migrant or multicultural literatures in Australia. More specifically, he is a significant figure in the history of Australian Jewish writing. The collection of interrelated short stories *Alien Son* (1952), Waten's first book, which is concerned with the early experiences in Australia of a Russian Jewish immigrant family, remained in print continuously between 1952 and 1993. It has often been referred to as an "Australian classic." As a critic and commentator, Waten also wrote some of the earliest essays on migrant literature in Australia.

Waten's other claim to interest for literary historians is as a communist novelist and critic. As such, his writings and related literary activities provide a rich

*Waten in Melbourne during the 1960s (from the dust
jacket for the 1965 edition of* Distant Land,
Bruccoli Clark Layman Archives)

source of materials for understanding the complex relations between cultural nationalism and left-wing intellectual movements in Australia. His politics often made him
a controversial figure, especially in the Cold War years
of the 1950s and 1960s. A determinedly realist writer,
Waten saw himself as belonging to both the great European tradition of realism and to a specifically Australian
democratic tradition. He could also give this Australian
tradition an overtly communist inflection, aligning his
own writings and those of others on the Left with what
he saw as an emerging strand of "socialist realism," but,
more generally, Waten was happy to identify with a
broader tradition of democratic nationalism.

Waten's writings have also continued to attract
attention from critics interested in Australian autobiographical or life writing. All his best-known work has a
strong autobiographical basis, whether presented as fiction
or memoir. Much of this history is reprinted in a loosely
autobiographical sequence in *Judah Waten: Fiction, Memoirs,
Criticism* (1998), edited by David Carter.

Judah Leon Waten was born on 29 July 1911 (?) in
Odessa, Ukraine, then part of greater Russia. Waten's
birth date is uncertain because of the confusion of calen-
dars (Russian, Jewish, and Ottoman) created by his fam-

ily's circumstances at the time. His parents had left the
czarist empire to settle in Palestine, although his mother
returned to Odessa, to the Waten family, for his birth.
Some of Waten's most memorable fiction is based on the
lives and characters of his parents–for example, in the
short stories "To a Country Town" and "Mother," from
Alien Son, and in the novel *The Unbending* (1954). Nehama
Press and Solomon Waten belonged to that generation
of Eastern European Jews that produced the great modern Jewish diaspora, the same generation as the founders
of modern Israel. More than two million Jews left the
Russian Empire in the three decades before World War
I in the face of czarist repression, pogroms, and economic
deprivation. Waten's mother's family were from
Borisov, near Minsk, within the Pale of Settlement (the
territory within which Jews were compelled to live).
Nehama Press was a modern Jewish woman profoundly
affected by the political and intellectual turmoil of her
epoch. She traveled to Warsaw to obtain qualifications as
a midwife. She was a Tolstoyan idealist, an enthusiast for
contemporary Russian and Yiddish literature, and a secular Jewish nationalist sympathetic to socialism. Her family left Russia for Palestine soon after the failed 1905
revolution. Both Nehama and a brother, who also later
migrated to Australia, became involved in early Zionist
work in Palestine.

Solomon Waten appears to have been a totally different personality, and the tension between the characters
of "Mother" and "Father" in *Alien Son* and between Hannah and Solomon Kochansky in *The Unbending* produces
some of the most deeply moving–and humorous–writing
in Waten's oeuvre. Solomon Waten came from the cosmopolitan city of Odessa, a member of a family of small
merchants in the clothing trade. Odessa is memorably
described in Waten's *From Odessa to Odessa: The Journey of an
Australian Writer* (1969). A different product of modern
Jewry from his wife, Solomon appears to have been
largely without political or intellectual commitments but
had an unsettled, if optimistic, spirit. Waten described his
father as a true *luftmensch* (a "trader in air," as Waten says
in *Alien Son*).

Solomon and Nehama met in Palestine and married
in 1910. Although Nehama journeyed to Odessa for
Judah's birth, she returned to Palestine, to Jaffa, soon after.
Palestine, however, did not provide security or success for
the family. Ottoman rule was increasingly unstable and
repressive; Nehama became disillusioned with Jewish settler politics; and Solomon was probably not successful in
business. The Waten family–Solomon, Nehama, Judah,
and his baby sister, Mena–thus left Palestine for Australia,
arriving in Perth in February 1914. Nehama's brother had
arrived in Western Australia three years earlier. As the
first port of entry Perth had a growing community of Eastern European, Yiddish-speaking Jews at this time.

The Watens settled first in Perth, where a second daughter, Fanny (Hafaiga), was born, and then in Midland Junction, an important railway town on the outskirts of the city, where Solomon established a drapery shop. When the shop failed, he sold drapery from a horsedrawn cart, and then he became a "bottle-o" (collector of empty bottles), experiences that feature prominently in *Alien Son, The Unbending,* and Waten's book for children *Bottle-O!* (1972). Waten's parents spoke Russian and Yiddish–Yiddish to the children–but the children grew up speaking English among themselves. Judah went to the state school in Midland Junction and then to the Catholic Christian Brothers College in Perth. In late 1925 the Watens joined a more general movement of the Jewish immigrant community east to Melbourne, where they settled in the inner-city Carlton area, then the center of Jewish/Yiddish life in Australia. Solomon joined Nehama's brother as an unqualified traveling optician and spent long periods away from home. Nehama was unwell, after contracting typhus in Perth, and, as Waten's stories and memoirs powerfully show, she remained determinedly alienated from Australian life.

Despite relative poverty and an unsettled family situation in a succession of houses, Waten was able to attend University High School, one of the best schools in the city. His precocious political and literary interests soon became evident. He published an article on Percy Bysshe Shelley in the school magazine and debated the virtues of the soviet system. In 1926, during his last year at school, he joined the Communist Party of Australia (CPA), itself scarcely established. By 1927, aged fifteen, he could sign himself propaganda secretary of the CPA Melbourne group when inviting Australian Labor Party (ALP) official, and later ALP leader, Arthur Calwell to speak at a communist meeting on the provocative topic "Can a Labor Government Abolish the Capitalist System?" In 1928 Waten was arrested for distributing antiwar leaflets on Anzac Day (Australia's national day for the commemoration of war veterans). He was a Communist Party speaker and wrote for the Communist Party press but also had an uneasy relationship with party officials because of his "bohemian" attitudes. He stowed away to Sydney and New Zealand in the late 1920s to early 1930s period and was expelled from the party (the first of three occasions).

Waten's early contemporary literary influences included James Joyce, John Dos Passos, and American and European "proletarian" literature. In October 1930, with other radical or bohemian figures–activists, journalists, writers, artists, and students–Waten published a magazine in Melbourne called *Strife.* The magazine–a mix of libertarian, communist, and avant-garde views–was published in support of the unemployed, but most copies were seized by police at a demonstration. Waten contributed an editorial manifesto and some extremely

radical "Notes of the Month" on world events and literature ("Facts are the new literature"). These have been collected in *Judah Waten.*

In the early 1930s Waten also completed a "proletarian novel," which he called "Hunger." In March 1931 he sailed for Europe. He spent several months in Paris before moving to London, where he tried unsuccessfully to have his novel published. In Paris he moved in left-wing avant-garde circles. An excerpt from "Hunger" was published in the international magazine *Front* (and reprinted in *Judah Waten*), and another piece was published in Henri Poulaille's *Nouvel Age.* In London, Waten abandoned his literary ambitions for politics. By early 1932 he was co-editor of the *Unemployed Special,* the newspaper of the National Unemployed Workers' Movement, during the period of the great Hunger Marches. He joined the British Communist Party and was active in the League against Imperialism. In November 1932 he was arrested at a mass demonstration for inciting police not to obey lawful orders and was jailed for three months in Wormwood Scrubs. Waten published a fictional account of this period in *Scenes of Revolutionary Life* (1982).

After his release, Waten returned to Australia, in June 1933, and was soon active as a CPA speaker. His lifestyle, though, was still "bohemian." In mid 1935 he was expelled from the CPA for a second time, for "petty-bourgeois irresponsibilities." With artist Noel Counihan he left Melbourne on a long journey through Victoria and New South Wales to Brisbane. In 1939 the pair traveled to New Zealand, where they became involved in the communist and anticonscription movements; Counihan was deported in mid 1940, and Waten left soon after. Later in 1940 or early in 1941, Waten met Hyrell McKinnon Ross, a secondary-school teacher, through the communist movement. They were married in 1945. Together with Counihan and his wife, Judah and Hyrell Waten were expelled from the CPA in 1942 for advocating a government of national unity to defeat fascism. Waten worked for the Taxation Office from 1942 to 1945. Soon after the war the Watens moved to the outer Melbourne suburb of Box Hill, where they remained for the rest of Waten's life. Their daughter Alice ("Pip") was born 11 November 1947.

Waten's "second literary career" (according to his account in "My Two Literary Careers," in *Judah Waten*) began in the early 1940s. He first began to write realist short stories of working-class characters and Aborigines–"Inspector Ryan" in 1945 and "Young Combo's Day," which was awarded a prize in the 1947 *Sydney Morning Herald* story competition and survives in typescript in Waten's papers. Through the Writers' League in Melbourne he had come into contact with such figures as Frank Dalby Davison, Alan Marshall, Flora Eldershaw, and Vance and Nettie Palmer. He was one of the managers of Dolphin Publications (1945–1947), a small independent press that

Dust jacket for Waten's 1964 novel, about the experiences of Jews in his parents' generation (Bruccoli Clark Layman Archives)

published two anthologies of Australian writing plus other books of new fiction. From its formation in May 1942 he worked in an official capacity for the Jewish Council to Combat Fascism and Anti-Semitism. He was also close to a group of Yiddish writers, whose work he translated. According to Waten, the Yiddish writer Pinchas Goldhar is the person who suggested to him that he turn to his own Russian-Jewish immigrant background for his literary material.

Waten's first published story in this vein was "To a Country Town," which appeared in 1946. It became the opening story of *Alien Son*. Waten described the book as a "novel without architecture" and later, borrowing a term from the new fiction of the 1970s, as a "discontinuous narrative." Its interconnected, first-person stories are presented through a child's perception (strictly speaking, the adult-narrator's recollection of his childhood perceptions) of his Russian-Jewish parents. The stories sensitively, poignantly, and often humorously represent the unsettled immigrant lives of the family and their small community.

Although recalling Yiddish stories in some respects, Waten's stories are not nostalgic; they quietly suggest the alienation indicated in the title of the collection. The themes of the book are brought together memorably in the final story, "Mother," Waten's best-known and most anthologized piece.

Alien Son was well received within the limiting terms of the criticism of the time, which stressed its realist simplicity and autobiographical fidelity. It was read in the light of then-dominant notions of assimilation. On the strength of the published stories, Waten was awarded a Commonwealth Literary Fund (CLF) grant in November 1951 to write a novel of migrant life. *Alien Son* was also published with a CLF subsidy. Soon after the appearance of the book, at the height of Cold War anticommunism, Waten and the CLF were attacked in the Australian Parliament. Despite defending the CLF in Parliament, Prime Minister Robert Menzies ordered that all subsequent grants should be subject to security clearance as the Waten case was "scandalous and embarrassing."

Not surprisingly, Waten's first published novel, *The Unbending*, was controversial when it appeared in 1954. It was indeed a novel of migrant life. Its central characters are Solomon and Hannah Kochansky and their children, Russian-Jewish migrants to Perth in the early years of World War I. But this story is interwoven with that of political struggles over the conscription issue and the radical International Workers of the World. This dimension to the novel is historically based, as is its representation of prejudice against foreigners, which was provoked by the war, but Waten's radical sympathies are clear. Despite some subtle juxtaposing of political positions, the "political" characters are generally cruder than the superb portraits of the parents. The novel was attacked in newspaper editorials and reviews, though it also had strong defenders. Angus and Robertson, the publishers of *Alien Son,* had rejected *The Unbending* as "too political," and it was published by the recently-established left-wing Australasian Book Society (ABS). The novel has only been reprinted once, in an unreliable edition (1972), despite its including some of Waten's most deeply moving writing. Lengthy excerpts, however, are included in *Judah Waten.*

The ABS also published Waten's next two novels. *Shares in Murder* (1957) is perhaps his most surprising book, a kind of "anti-detective story" in which the climax is not, according to generic expectations, the exposure and judgment of the criminal but rather the reverse, as the chief detective accepts a bribe. *Time of Conflict* (1961) is in some ways Waten's most ambitious novel. It is certainly his most overtly communist. The novel recounts the political growth from innocence to experience, or rather from exploitation to class-consciousness, of Mick Anderson, a "typical" rural working-class youth who rises to become an important union leader and communist. The novel spans the crucial years of communist history, from the 1920s to the 1960s. Thus, it can also tell of the formative years of the communist movement through the Great Depression, unemployment struggles, the Spanish Civil War, the rise of fascism, and the Cold War. The novel is part bildungsroman, part historical novel, and part *roman à thèse* (novel with a thesis). Nothing of Waten's Russian-Jewish background is found in it, although some of the political experiences are based on Waten's own.

Outside the Communist Party press, the novel was generally seen to be crude and simplistic in its political bias. It is, nevertheless, a significant cultural document as an attempt to write the communist novel in Australia. Waten had rejoined the Communist Party in 1957, just when, following the intervention of the U.S.S.R. in Hungary, many left-wing intellectuals were leaving it. He immediately became a prominent communist man of letters, writing regularly in the party press and *Realist Writer* magazine while maintaining his links to the mainstream Australian literary world, despite occasional bitter disputes over political matters. He was active in PEN Australia and the Fellowship of Australian Writers in Melbourne.

Individual communists and left-wing associations had a considerable influence in 1950s Australia. Frank Hardy's novel *Power without Glory* appeared in 1950, and Katharine Susannah Prichard, John Morrison, and Dorothy Hewett also published important books. New Theatre and Realist Writer groups were active in all major cities. The ABS was established in 1952 and *Overland* magazine in 1954, and Waten was closely involved in both.

In 1958, together with historian Manning Clark and poet and critic James Devanney, Waten toured the U.S.S.R. as part of a Fellowship of Australian Writers delegation. The trip produced Clark's *Meeting Soviet Man* (1960), which unexpectedly became controversial thirty years later in the 1990s. Waten reviewed his close friend's book critically in the communist press. Waten himself kept notes on the trip for a book that was never written, although a series of articles on the Soviet Union appeared in communist papers. From 1962 to 1966 Waten published a column called "Literary Comment" in the Melbourne CPA newspaper, *The Guardian*.

In his next novel, *Distant Land* (1964), Waten returned to the theme of Jewish migration and to a mainstream publisher. Somewhat more distanced from his own direct experience, much of the novel is nevertheless based on typical experiences of Russian Jews of his parents' generation. Joshua and Shoshanah Kuperschmidt are born into a world of change and uncertainty, between religious and secular, Jewish and Russian, and orthodox and Zionist influences. Joshua is a musician, scholar, and idealist who becomes committed to Zionism in its early manifestations. Shoshanah is pragmatic and worldly. She urges their migration to Australia, where, to Joshua's initial humilia-

tion, they become Josh and Susan Cooper. Like Waten's own father and uncle in Australia, Joshua and his friend become unqualified traveling opticians. The novel, although focused on character studies, is also an essay on the various meanings of assimilation. Joshua is able finally to reconcile his Jewishness and his Australian life. *Distant Land* was a Readers' Book Club choice and winner of the Moomba Festival Best Australian Novel Award.

At the end of 1964, the Watens left Australia for the U.S.S.R. via India and Germany. Waten returned to his birthplace, Odessa, in March–April 1965. In May he attended International Writers' Conferences in Berlin and Weimar, along with Morrison, Hewett, Marshall, Hardy, and other Australian writers. Waten was in London and Paris later in 1965 and produced a series of profiles of writers he met and interviewed, including Yevgeny Yevtushenko, Christina Stead, Iris Murdoch, and André Maurois, for the Melbourne *Age*. The Watens returned home via Berlin and Moscow in early February 1966. Waten's return to the U.S.S.R. in 1965 through 1966 provided the basis for *From Odessa to Odessa*. On his return, Waten also wrote two pamphlets, a report on international literary trends, important in local literary circles for indicating the "thaw" in Soviet literary politics, and a study of trends in Australian literature, which emphasized an emerging socialist realist tendency. He contributed a series of articles to Jewish and left-wing periodicals in Australia and overseas on the question of the survival of Yiddish culture in the West and the East (the U.S.S.R.).

Waten's next novel, *Season of Youth* (1966), is a portrait of the artist as a young man. Although about the life of an Anglo-Australian working-class youth, it captures something of the bohemian atmosphere of Waten's own early years. A lively novel, it draws a realist message ultimately from its central character's experiences.

In the late 1960s Waten was often a controversial figure in the Jewish community because of his unwavering support for the Soviet Union and his denial of Soviet anti-Semitism. Increasing tensions on the Left following the Soviet Union's invasion of Czechoslovakia in 1968 also made his political position controversial. At the same time, Waten was a regular—and generous—reviewer for both *The Age* and *The Sydney Morning Herald* from 1967 until his death. His wife, Hyrell Waten, had taught at secondary schools in Melbourne since 1938. When she was appointed Principal of Richmond Girls' High School in 1968, she became Victoria's first female principal.

From Odessa to Odessa is part autobiography, part travel book, somewhat in the genre of the eyewitness account. It recounts Waten's journey east, through Germany into the U.S.S.R., and then his meetings with prominent Jewish figures and Russian writers such as Ilya Ehrenburg. The book underplays Waten's politics. It joins the criticism of Stalinist literary policies and practices and

Paperback cover for a 1972 edition of Waten's 1966 novel,
based partly on his experiences as a young man
(Bruccoli Clark Layman Archives)

dice. Waten was largely out of sympathy with the new radical politics and alternative cultures of the period.

Waten's next book was an assignment from F. W. Cheshire to write a volume in a series of large-format photographic history books. The text of *The Depression Years, 1929–1939* (1971) presents an intelligent, concise popular history of the Depression decade. In 1972 he returned to stories first explored in *Alien Son* in publishing *Bottle-O!* but this time in a short children's novel for "reluctant readers." *Classic Australian Short Stories* (1974) was a collaboration with Stephen Murray-Smith, editor of the nationalist literary magazine *Overland,* who, as a former communist, had had a long and sometimes troubled relationship with Waten. Both men, however, were strong supporters of a nationalist understanding of Australian literature, and this view was reflected in their anthology.

Waten was elected to the National Committee of the Communist Party in 1967, but this body represented the last significant presence in the CPA of the older generation of communists still loyal above all else to the Soviet Union. In March 1970 most of this group were removed from the National Committee. In late 1970 political disagreements led to the end of Waten's lifelong friendship with Counihan. In 1972, together with Hyrell, Waten resigned from the CPA and joined the pro-Soviet Socialist Party of Australia (SPA), of which he remained a member for the rest of his life.

In February 1973 Waten was appointed to the Literature Board of the newly created Australia Council, on which he served through 1974 under the chairmanship of Geoffrey Blainey, who became a close friend. In 1975 Waten was awarded an Australia Council Writer's Fellowship. In 1977 he was president of the Melbourne branch of PEN. In 1979 he was awarded the Australia Medal (Order of Australia).

The collection *Love and Rebellion* (1978) brought together many of Waten's short stories and memoirs written over the previous decade. Most important were autobiographical pieces, such as "A Child of War and Revolutions," and some migrant stories, such as "The Knife," which moved away from Waten's own experience and to other migrant groups (Italian in this instance).

Waten's final novel, *Scenes of Revolutionary Life,* might be read as the expression of his ambition to write an account, according to an interview by Suzanne Lunney, of "the revolutionary mind in a country [with] no revolutionary perspectives." The novel is presented as the story of Tom Graves, a recently retired left-wing union official. The bulk of the text is Tom's memoirs of his political experiences. Much of this material is based closely on Waten's own life, including his work on the

is thus aligned with the relatively liberal practices of the mid to late 1960s. The book, however, includes no critique of official policies beyond what the regime itself had countenanced, although Waten expresses disappointment that no contemporary writers had equaled the stature of the greats of Russian literature. Although some found the book biased or bland, it was generally well received in a climate in which new literary links between Australian and Russian writers were being fostered on both sides.

Waten returned to migrant themes in *So Far No Further* (1971). This book focuses on the second generation–the daughter of a Jewish family and the son of a Catholic Italian migrant family, both from conservative backgrounds, both experiencing the challenges of New Left and counterculture values in the university. Although the two young people come together, they are only able to go "so far" in overcoming inherited preju-

Dust jacket for Waten's 1982 novel, based on his experiences with the National Unemployed Workers'
Movement in London during the 1930s (Bruccoli Clark Layman Archives)

newspaper of the unemployed movement in England and his arrest and imprisonment.

From 1979 to 1985 Judah and Hyrell Waten together wrote a regular column for the newspapers of the SPA. She shared Waten's political beliefs absolutely. They were regular overseas travelers in later life. Judah Waten was working on memoirs at the time of his death on 29 July 1985 in Melbourne. Some fragments of these memoirs were published and, together with some unpublished pieces, are collected in *Judah Waten*. Posthumously, in 1985, Waten was awarded the Patrick White Award.

Waten has never been a major figure in Australian literature, but his significance as a "migrant" or "ethnic" writer, an Australian-Jewish writer, and a left-wing nationalist literary figure remains considerable. Within the limitations of the strictly realist style he adopted after abandoning his first avant-garde proletarian experiments, Waten's writing of the relations within an immigrant Russian Jewish family are subtle, poignant, and often moving.

His portraits of the alienated migrant parents, in several fictional and autobiographical versions, are especially memorable. For a writer who has often been seen as simple and straightforward, an emphasis on guilt and self-consciousness is surprisingly prominent in the stories.

Waten's memoir pieces, although less well known, are also quietly effective and, like the migrant fictions, create an unemphatic but pervasive sense of the self in history. Rather than stories of individuation or of family life alone, the histories of Waten's characters are part of larger social and cultural structures. By contrast, when he turns to more explicit political themes, this subtle sense of character tends to be lost.

Waten has continued to be an important writer for critics interested in the themes of migration, ethnicity, Jewishness, communism, and nationalism in Australian culture. Because of his own life of political and literary activism, he was a figure in which many of these threads crossed and became intertwined. *Alien Son,* at least, is likely to retain its status as an Australian "classic," but a number of Waten's other writings also deserve to be remembered and reread.

Interviews:

Hazel De Berg Tapes (Tape 92), 13 March 1960, National Library of Australia;

"*Spectrum:* Judah Waten on Commitment," interview with Tony Morphett for ABC Television, 18 December 1966 (typescript in Waten papers);

Interview with Barrett Reid, 27 February 1967, State Library of Victoria;

Interview with Suzanne Lunney, 27 May 1975, National Library of Australia.

References:

Susan Ballyn, "Judah Waten and the Jewish Immigrant Experience," in *A Passage to Somewhere Else,* edited by Doireann MacDermott and Ballyn (Barcelona: University of Barcelona, 1988), pp. 11–18;

Jack Beasley, *Journal of an Era: Notes from the Red Letter Days* (Sydney: Wedgetail Press, 1988);

Beasley, *Red Letter Days: Notes from Inside an Era* (Sydney: Australasian Book Society, 1979);

D. R. Burns, *The Directions of Australian Fiction, 1920–1974* (Melbourne: Cassell, 1974);

David Carter, "Before the Migrant Writer: Judah Waten and the Shaping of a Literary Career," in *Striking Chords: Multicultural Writing in Australia,* edited by Sneja Gunew and Kateryna Longley (Sydney: Allen & Unwin, 1992), pp. 101–110;

Carter, *A Career in Writing: Judah Waten and the Cultural Politics of a Literary Career* (Toowoomba, Qld.: Association for the Study of Australian Literature, 1997);

Carter, "'An Important Social Duty': The Brief Life of Dolphin Publications," *Publishing Studies,* 6 (Autumn 1998): 3–13;

Carter, "Mother: Excerpts from a Biography of Judah Waten," *Westerly,* 41, no. 4 (Summer 1996): 114–122;

Carter, "The Outsider with Inside Knowledge?: Migrant Writing, Assimilationism and Recent Theory," in *Australia in the World: Perceptions and Possibilities,* edited by Don Grant and Graham Seal (Perth: Black Swan Press, 1994), pp. 51–56;

Geoffrey Dutton, *The Australian Collection: Australia's Greatest Books* (North Ryde, N.S.W.: Angus & Robertson, 1985), pp. 207–210;

Dutton, *Snow on the Saltbush: The Australian Literary Experience* (Ringwood, Vic.: Penguin, 1985), pp. 173–177;

Ken Gelder and Paul Salzman, *The New Diversity: Australian Fiction 1970–1988* (Melbourne: McPhee Gribble, 1989), pp. 243–245;

Carole Gerson, "Some Patterns of Exile in Jewish Writing of the Commonwealth," *Ariel,* 13, no. 4 (1982): 103–114;

M. J. Haddock, "The Prose Fiction of Jewish Writers of Australia 1945–1969," *Australian Jewish Historical Society Journal of Proceedings,* 7, no. 7 (1974): 495–512;

John Hetherington, "Australian From Odessa," in his *Forty-Two Faces* (Melbourne: F. W. Cheshire, 1962), pp. 127–131;

Edward Hills, "Babylon: The Stories of Judah Waten," *Span,* 44 (April 1997): 50–61;

A. D. Hope, "The Sty of Circe: Judah Waten's *The Unbending,*" in *Native Companions: Essays and Comments on Australian Literature, 1936–1966* (Sydney: Angus & Robertson, 1974), pp. 277–287;

Brian Kiernan, "Memoirs of an Australian Alien Son," *Australian,* 1 April 1972, p. 14;

Graeme Kinross-Smith, *Australia's Writers* (Melbourne: Nelson, 1980), pp. 251–256;

Serge Liberman, "Australian Jewish Fiction since World War II," *Jewish Quarterly,* 31, no. 2 (1984): 38–43;

Peter Lumb and Anne Hazell, *Diversity and Division: An Annotated Bibliography of Australian Ethnic Minority Literature* (Richmond, Vic.: Hodja Educational, 1983);

David Martin, "Three Realists in Search of Reality," *Meanjin,* 18, no. 3 (1959): 305–322;

Susan McKernan, *A Question of Commitment: Australian Literature in the Twenty Years after the War* (Sydney: Allen & Unwin, 1989);

John Morrison, "Judah Waten," *Overland,* 11 (January 1958): 13–14;

Patrick O'Brien, *The Saviours: An Intellectual History of the Left in Australia* (Melbourne: Drummond, 1977), pp. 35–63;

Vance Palmer and others, "Comments on *The Unbending,*" *Meanjin,* 13, no. 3 (1954): 456–460;

Bernard Smith, *Noel Counihan: Artist and Revolutionary* (Melbourne: Oxford University Press, 1993).

Papers:

The National Library of Australia holds the Judah Waten Papers, comprising letters, manuscripts, notebooks, cuttings, and other materials. The Australian Archives holds a substantial Australian Security Intelligence Organisation file on Waten from 1928, plus Prime Minister's Department files, including Waten-Commonwealth Literary Fund material, 1954–1971.

Morris West

(26 April 1916 – 8 October 1999)

Peter Pierce
James Cook University

BOOKS: *Moon in My Pocket,* as Julian Morris (Sydney: Australasian, 1945);

Gallows on the Sand (Sydney: Angus & Robertson, 1956; London: Mayflower-Dell, 1964; New York & Toronto: Bantam, 1981);

Kundu (New York: Dell, 1956; Sydney: Angus & Robertson, 1957; London: Hamilton, 1959);

The Big Story (London: Heinemann, 1957; Melbourne: Heinemann, 1963); republished as *The Crooked Road* (New York: Morrow, 1957);

Children of the Sun (London: Heinemann, 1957); republished as *Children of the Shadows: The True Story of the Street Urchins of Naples* (New York: Morrow, 1957);

The Second Victory (London: Heinemann, 1958); republished as *Backlash* (New York: Morrow, 1958);

McCreary Moves In, as Michael East (London: Heinemann, 1958); republished as *The Concubine* (New York: Dell, 1958);

The Devil's Advocate (London: Heinemann, 1959; New York: Morrow, 1959);

The Naked Country, as East (London: Heinemann, 1960; New York: Dell, 1961);

Daughter of Silence (London: Heinemann, 1961; New York: Morrow, 1961);

Daughter of Silence: A Drama in Three Acts (London: S. French, 1962);

The Shoes of the Fisherman (London: Heinemann, 1963; New York: Morrow, 1963);

The Ambassador (London: Heinemann, 1965; New York: Morrow, 1965);

The Tower of Babel (London: Heinemann, 1968; New York: Morrow, 1968);

The Heretic: A Play in Three Acts (New York: Morrow, 1969; London: Heinemann, 1970);

Summer of the Red Wolf (London: Heinemann, 1971; New York: Morrow, 1971);

The Salamander (London: Heinemann, 1973; New York: Morrow, 1973);

Harlequin (London: Collins, 1974; New York: Morrow, 1974);

Morris West (photograph by M. Courtney-Clarke, from the dust jacket for Lazarus, *1990; Richland County Public Library)*

The Navigator (London: Collins, 1976; New York: Morrow, 1976);

Proteus (London: Collins, 1979; New York: Morrow, 1979);

The Clowns of God (London: Hodder & Stoughton, 1981; New York: Morrow, 1981);

The World Is Made of Glass (London: Hodder & Stoughton, 1983; New York: Morrow, 1983);

Cassidy (Sydney: Hodder & Stoughton, 1986; Garden City, N.Y.: Doubleday, 1986);

Masterclass (London: Hutchinson, 1988; New York: St. Martin's Press, 1988);

Lazarus (Port Melbourne: Heinemann Australia, 1990; London: Heinemann, 1990; New York: St. Martin's Press, 1990);

The Ringmaster (Port Melbourne: Heinemann Australia, 1991; London: Heinemann, 1991; New York: HarperPaperbacks, 1996);

The Lovers (Port Melbourne: Heinemann Australia, 1993; London: Heinemann, 1993; New York: D. I. Fine, 1993);

Vanishing Point (London: HarperCollins, 1996; New York: HarperPaperbacks, 1996);

A View from the Ridge: The Testimony of a Twentieth-Century Christian (Sydney: HarperCollins, 1996; London: HarperCollins, 1996; San Francisco: HarperSanFrancisco, 1996);

Images & Inscriptions, edited by Beryl Barraclough (Pymble, N.S.W.: HarperCollins, 1997);

Eminence (Sydney: HarperCollins, 1998; London: Harvill Press, 1998; New York: Harcourt Brace, 1998);

Scandal in the Assembly: A Bill of Complaints and a Proposal for Reform on the Matrimonial Laws and Tribunals of the Roman Catholic Church, by West and Robert Francis (London: Heinemann, 1970; New York: Morrow, 1970);

The Last Confession (Sydney: HarperCollins, 2000).

Collections: *The Devil's Advocate; The Second Victory; Daughter of Silence; The Salamander; The Shoes of the Fisherman* (London: Heinemann, 1977; New York: Octopus/Heinemann, 1980);

A West Quartet: Four Novels of Intrigue and High Adventure (New York: Morrow, 1981)—comprises *The Naked Country, Gallows on the Sand, The Concubine,* and *Kundu;*

The Devil's Advocate; The Salamander (London: Chancellor Press, 1992);

The Vatican Trilogy (Port Melbourne: Heinemann Australia, 1993); republished as *Three Complete Novels* (New York: Wings Books, 1993)—comprises *The Shoes of the Fisherman, The Clowns of God,* and *Lazarus.*

OTHER: Mary C. Morrison, *Let Evening Come: Reflections on Aging,* preface by West (Garden City, N.Y.: Doubleday, 1998; St. Leonards, N.S.W.: Allen & Unwin, 1998).

SELECTED PERIODICAL PUBLICATIONS—
UNCOLLECTED: "A Perception of Evil," *America,* 161 (23 December 1989): 466–469;

"The Seven Deadly Sins: Looking Back 56 Years, the Author Recalls the Beginning of the Slow Erosion of His Convictions about the Authenticity of His Own Vocation to Religious Life," *America,* 162 (28 April 1990): 422–427;

"Its Principles Will Stand, but the Church Shall Change," *National Catholic Reporter,* 29 (12 February 1993): 14;

"One Man's Voice," *Eureka Street,* 4 (August 1994): 28–32;

"Pain and Paradox of a Pope on a Mission," *National Catholic Reporter,* 31 (27 January 1995): 6;

"Doctor Newman's Toast," *Eureka Street,* 8 (December 1998): 24–28.

Like Charles Dickens, the Australian novelist Morris West died suddenly at his desk, with an unfinished manuscript before him. The date was 8 October 1999; then in his eighty-fourth year, West had published twenty-six novels and two plays. His works had been translated into twenty-seven languages and had sold more than sixty million copies. His first bestseller (and the first book in the so-called Vatican trilogy), *The Devil's Advocate* (1959), presents the investigation by Blaise Meredith—on behalf of the Catholic Church—of the claims for beatification of an Italian partisan. With this book began four decades of popular success on a scale enjoyed by no other Australian novelist. It was not, however, often complemented by critical acclaim.

The book that West left unfinished at his death is, nonetheless, hardly incomplete. *The Last Confession,* published posthumously in 2000, is the story of Giordano Bruno, sixteenth-century Dominican priest, philosopher, and foremost martyr of the Renaissance, during the last days of his life in the prison of the Holy Office in Rome, where he was a victim of the Inquisition. In answer to his own question—"who am I?"—Bruno responds, "failed priest, fugitive monk, magus with a box of conjuring tricks, prevaricator, would-be torch bearer trudging through his own darkness, garrulous in language, viperous in debate." This is the last, one guesses, of the many versions of himself that West scattered through his fiction. Bruno's life had exercised him three decades before, when he wrote the play *The Heretic: A Play in Three Acts* (1969). What West found in Bruno was a man of paradoxes, someone who believed himself to be a loyal son of the Catholic Church but found himself in persistent conflict with it.

The personal reference is clear, but West sought a wider understanding of Bruno's position. In 1996 he wrote that "the better I knew him, the more modern I found him." Even if people are no longer burned in public, torturers are still on the payroll (as West's fictions often depict). Further, "it is the illusion of our time that the nonconformist is in the ascendant, that the heretic is the hero and the revolutionary is the new redeemer." Instead, West believed, "the odd person out has never been so much at risk or so completely menaced by that conspiracy of power which we are pleased to call government." In his novels West regularly confronted and denounced the apparatus of state and private terror and the fate of prisoners of conscience and of the accidental, incidental victims of authoritarianism. This is, for instance, the theme of *Proteus* (1979), a novel in which there is no easy way to build those "bridges of benevolence" that are necessary for a civilized world. West's own travails, and his unsparing treatment of his personal failings, inclined him to such a belief.

Morris Langlo West was born on 26 April 1916 in St. Kilda, an inner Melbourne suburb. As he related in *A View from the Ridge: The Testimony of a Twentieth-Century Christian* (1996), "my family life was not happy." His parents, Clarence Langlo West and Florence Guilfoyle Hanson West, separated when he was a child. He attended the Christian Brothers' College in St. Kilda, completing his studies in 1929, when he was *dux* of the school. (His prize was presented by Archbishop Daniel Mannix, who later, in 1951, refused West's petition for a decree of nullity on his first marriage.) West became a Christian Brothers postulant at thirteen, spent the next four years in tutelage, and then took annual vows. He graduated with a bachelor of arts degree from the University of Melbourne and taught mathematics and modern languages in New South Wales and Tasmania from 1933 to 1939. Like several of his protagonists (for instance, Gil Langton in *The Ringmaster* [1991]), West was a skilled linguist. He judged himself "competent in half a dozen European languages and adequate in a few other unusual ones."

In 1939, when the time came to take his last vows, West decided not to remain within the order. In *A View from the Ridge* he recalled that "When I left the religious life, I was a man without a shadow, I had no past to which I could make reference, no future to which I could direct myself." After a brief nervous breakdown (for which he refused shock treatment) he joined the army, married for the first time, was commissioned as a lieutenant, and worked as a decryption officer posted to the Northern Territory. In 1943 West was plucked from the army by the veteran politician William Morris Hughes, becoming Hughes's private secretary and biographer. Hughes fired him after a few months, but by then West's real career had begun. His first novel, *Moon in My Pocket* (1945), the tale of a disillusioned religious, had already been published, under the pseudonym Julian Morris, and sold ten thousand copies. West did not, however, write another novel for a decade. Before the end of World War II he was

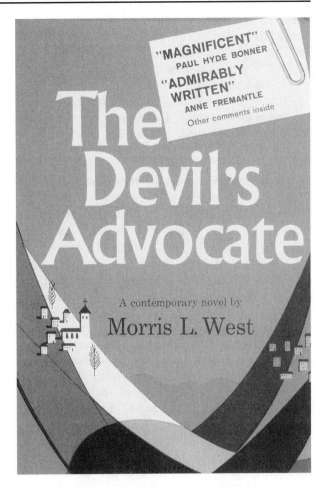

Dust jacket for West's 1959 novel, his first best-seller
(Richland County Public Library)

working as a publicity officer for a Melbourne radio station. In 1945 he founded and became managing director of Australian Radio Productions, with which he remained until 1954. The following year he left Australia with his second wife, Joyce Lawford West, whom he had married on 14 August 1952, and their first son, Christopher. West did not return to live in his native country for more than a quarter of a century.

Initially, West paid his way with a couple of potboilers, *Gallows on the Sand* and *Kundu*, both published in 1956. The following year he became the Vatican correspondent of the *Daily Mail* (London), working in Rome for seven years. This was perhaps the most fecund time of all for gathering material for his later fiction. Meanwhile, West had begun to attract wider acclaim with an angry nonfiction work, *Children of the Sun* (1957), published that same year in the United States as *Children of the Shadows: The True Story of the Street Urchins of Naples,* an account (which Eleanor

Roosevelt apparently called "one of the most moving stories I have read") of the plight of "the *scugnizzi* (spinning tops), the wild, tormented boy-children of Naples." The book is a tribute to a priest, Don Mario Borelli, who devoted his adult life to caring for these children. West said of him, "of all the men I have met, this one is most a man." The counterpart of Borelli's devotion is West's anger at a situation that he cannot remedy. *Children of the Sun* provided an early intimation of the intense but usually thwarted desire for control that torments many of West's protagonists. He writes, "I was angry with myself for becoming embroiled in the affairs of this ancient, worm-eaten, hopeless country, where men were bought and women were sold and the children were damned the moment they were begotten."

West was intrigued—and not for the last time—by what an individual could do in the face of institutional intransigence with, as he says in regard to Borelli, "faith, hope, charity and no politics." But politics always trammels the efforts of the innocent and good, or—in West's case—the passionately well-meaning. *Children of the Sun* ends with West's vain attempts to remedy the plight of the urchins. He blames "the Church of the South" and recommends immigration to Australia, the United States, Canada, or Rhodesia. Unavailingly, he writes to the American ambassador and to the Australian minister in Rome. Here was an early testing of the power that West the citizen could wield. Finding that it was not much, he instead imagined supranational, covert organizations that might bring benefits to the lives of those abandoned and seemingly without hope.

The 1959 novel *The Devil's Advocate* marked the beginning of West's impassioned inquiry into the workings, for good and ill, of the Catholic Church. In his own words, the book was "a blockbuster." A stage adaptation by Dore Schary was produced by the Theatre Guild at New York's Billy Rose Theatre in 1961. *The Shoes of the Fisherman* (1963), adapted as a movie of the same title in 1968, has been cited as an astonishing example of West's prescience about world affairs: his Kiril I is the first Polish pope, years before the elevation of John Paul II. West's hero was actually modeled on the gentle, liberating Pope John XXIII, who aroused the author's expectations for reform of the church after Vatican II. In the journal *Eureka Street* (August 1994) West wrote, "I was in Rome during the wonderful, hopeful years of the Second Vatican Council. I wrote for *Life* magazine the obituary of the man I most admired, the man for whom I felt an extraordinary deep and personal affection, the good pope John XXIII." The Pope died on 3 June 1963, the day *The Shoes of the Fisherman* was published. The Vatican trilogy, as it has come to be called in retrospect, concluded with *Lazarus* (1990), the tale of another fictional pope, Leo XIV, called to account for himself after a dire intimation of mortality that West himself had endured, a heart-bypass operation. The result is an access of forgiveness and compassion that displaces the Pope's fears.

West's more familiar, if not so famous, register lies in what have been called "moral thrillers." One of the earliest and most notable was *Daughter of Silence* (1961), which was staged as a play the following year. The epigraph of the novel is from the eighteenth-century Italian poet and dramatist Vittorio Alfieri: "Noble vengeance is the daughter of deep silence." The reader is transported to a rural idyll, the "upland valleys of Tuscany." Here, in the public square of a small village, a pale woman shoots dead a leading citizen outside his house. This is the apparently simple case that embroils a typical set of West characters—powerful but troubled people. There are usually only bit parts for the lower classes in his novels. One of the powerful ones in *Daughter of Silence* is the cynical and famous Alberto Ascolini; another is his unruly daughter, Valeria Rienzi, the wife of her father's associate Carlo Rienzi, whom she cuckolds. Unable to remain outsiders are the artist Ninette Lachaise and the London-based, Australian-born criminal psychopathologist Peter Landon. With Landon, West embarks on another probing quest into his dissatisfied self. Lachaise sees Landon with European eyes: "to us you are the new men from the New World, proof that it is possible to live without history, to start with a clean canvas in a land with new light." Perhaps, but West's canvas was not Australia.

In West's novels those who are powerful in the world's eyes find that success is always flawed and costly. Their capacity to damage others is great and often unconsidered. West writes astutely of their subtleties, deceptions, elegant tastes, and histories of betrayal. It is as though he is again in the role of Bruno—the shrewd outsider, the onlooker at court who has never been fully accepted as a courtier. This sense of displacement is the source of some of West's most compelling work. His fictional medium is melodrama, which is to say that he writes of innocent victims and their persecutors, most crucially of the threat of dispossession—loss of life, liberty, chastity, fortune, or selfhood. In *Daughter of Silence* the victim and the avenger is Anna, daughter of a woman murdered by partisans from her village for alleged collaboration with the Germans. Anna embraces the vendetta, the bloody course of action that is the mainspring of several of West's novels. Yet, those who seek to assist

*West with his son Paul in the study of his Sydney home, circa 1965 (photograph by Elizabeth Malko, from the
dust jacket for the U.S. edition of* The Ambassador, *1965; Richland County Public Library)*

Anna by controlling her become in the end, perhaps, the most damaged.

If West had predicted a Polish pope in *The Shoes of the Fisherman,* he surely admonished the Americans to stay out of Vietnam in *The Ambassador* (1965). In a preface to the novel he says something of his techniques. His fiction is "built by the time-honoured literary method of peopling an historical situation with characters constructed out of the imagination of the author." As usual, West did fieldwork, going to Saigon in October 1963, a month before the assassination in a military coup of Prime Minister Ngo Dinh Diem, on whom the character Phung Van Cung is based. The novel is told in retrospect by Maxwell Amberley, the former American ambassador to South Vietnam. Amberley remained in his post for a year after the murder of the South Vietnamese leader, the Catholic Cung, gave "more than enough [time] to absolve the Administration from any guilt in his death and the responsibility for its consequences." Now, Amberley seeks peace, if not absolution, at "the old Zen shrine of

Tenryu-ji: the Temple of the Heavenly Dragon," in Kyoto. (It is a place fondly recalled in *A View from the Ridge,* where West remembers "standing beside the pool in the monastery of Tenryu-ji while the Zen master presented me with riddles which bend the mind out of logic and into perception.")

Some time before, Amberley had been tempted away from Japan to Vietnam, notwithstanding a briefing that described the country as "a bloody, thankless mess. We call it a subversive war, but at bottom it's a civil war as well." The domino theory is also arrayed: "If South Vietnam goes, Thailand is outflanked and Singapore is threatened." The first analysis proved truer than the second. Amberley is deterred neither by the emblematic sight on his first day of a Buddhist monk incinerating himself nor by a later attempt on his life. Amberley's own thinking is mired in a well-intentioned Orientalism. Thus, he speaks of "the old, old complexity of Asia," "the vast indifference of Asia," although this opinion is more respectful than the attitudes of some of his professional compatriots.

By his own admission, Amberley is "truly the unresolved man, the man who would not gamble on the truth he saw, but tried to hedge it with opportune casuistry." It is an unqualified self-criticism, typical of the bitter evaluations of themselves that West's protagonists often privately deliver. It is Amberley, however, who asks his colleagues (years before Nixon's intervention), "Could we ourselves remove the Chinese pressure by diplomatic recognition, removal of trade embargoes and voting for her admission to the United Nations?" This speculation is a sharp instance of West's fabled prescience (or of Amberley's on his behalf). Prophecy is not the word that West would have favored. On 6 June 1994, in the Veech Lecture delivered at the State Library of New South Wales, he reminded his audience that "prophecy–the expression of care and concern in the assembly–is one of the most ancient charismata. It is, I regret to say, one of those which has fallen into disuse, has been rendered suspect and sometimes suppressed within the church." But it was suppressed neither in West's writing nor in his public utterances.

In 1965, the year in which *The Ambassador* was published, West went back to Australia after a decade away. That July he was one of the first public figures to declare opposition to Australian involvement in the war in Vietnam. In *A View from the Ridge,* West writes that he was "one of the acknowledged leaders of the first teach-in at the Australian National University against our proposed commitment to the war in Vietnam." This teach-in was among the earliest of what, from the 1980s, became regular occasions when West engaged in the public affairs of Australia, commenting gravely and eloquently on moral perfidies and speaking wisely, liberally, and often unfashionably to audiences, some of whose members might have been ill attuned to his words.

In his next novel, *The Tower of Babel* (1968), West managed an even more remarkable feat of the proleptic imagination by anticipating the complex details of the processes that were to lead Israel to launch a preemptive strike against its Arab enemies in the so-called Six-Day War of 1967. (The book was finished before and published soon after war began.) West moves from side to side of the impending conflict, from Colonel Omar Safreddin, head of Syrian Security, to the Israeli director of military intelligence, Brigadier General Jakov Barutz, and from Beirut to Jerusalem. The characters are treated with a notable evenhandedness. Although Israelis get the portentous last words–"Masada shall not fall again"–it is as if West assumes that, in the end, only God's judgment will matter.

Pivotal in *The Tower of Babel* is the Israeli spy Adom Ronen, who pretends to be Selim Fathalla, an Arab businessman based in Damascus. Barutz asks the doctor, Franz Lieberman, what it takes to engage in such undercover work. According to Lieberman, the spy needs to be "an alienated man" (such as Ronen, yet one thinks also of "the unresolved man," Amberley from *The Ambassador*), "one who is dissatisfied with the real which he has, and yet knows that the ideal to which he aspires is unattainable." It is a characterization that fits several of the troubled protagonists in West's fiction. Elsewhere in the novel, other themes recur: betrayal, torture, the subjugation of the individual to the needs of the state, and the want of compassion in those who have most need of it.

Rather than foretelling the future, *Harlequin* (1974) is a novel decidedly of its own time, with oil shocks, Richard Nixon in disgrace, the final stages of the Vietnam War, hijacks, and hostage taking. Now, "outcasts from the Fertile Crescent found that they could terrorize the world with handguns, and grenades, and plastic explosives . . . every airport in the world is an armed camp." Again, the world is the domain of the powerful but embattled. The eponymous hero is a slim, elegant, polyglot tycoon who "wears a quite prodigious learning with the offhand charm of a renaissance courtier." His second-incharge, Paul Desmond, is rougher hewn. Another of West's transplanted Australians, he is "an antipodean, eager, impulsive, apt to be harsh or simplistic in [his] judgments." As a sympathizer tells him, he is "a confused man," Amberley's cousin under the skin. On this occasion, West does less with Desmond's internal travails than with routine thriller action. *Harlequin* seems forced to a deadline that the desire for topicality has imposed.

Certainly, *Harlequin* presents West's prose at its least polished. Not for the last time in his novels, a character shivers "as if a goose had walked over his grave." Sexual activity provokes West to his most ponderous prose. Of a potential lover, Desmond admits that "I never found the talisman that would open the treasure trove of her loving." Compare this statement with Amberley in action in Honolulu–"it was a very satisfying mating for both of us"–or with the errant Valerio and Peter in *Daughter of Silence:* "passion lifted them like a wave and set them down in darkness and tumult on the tumbled sheets." Passages such as this (although few novelists do such descriptions well) have caused excessive harm to West's reputation, which ought rather to depend on the strenuousness of his moral intelligence, as well as his perspicacity about and freedom from prejudice toward the peoples of the countries where his books have been set. A hint at what would now be called globalization comes near the end of *Harlequin:* "We are, perforce, one world, mutually dependent upon complex trade patterns and the distribution of diminishing resources." The speaker is the melodramatically named villain Basil Yanko talking sense about needful compromises in the near future.

Another implacable self-made man (and also a loving family man), John Spada, is the hero of West's 1979 novel *Proteus.* As the narrative opens in Italy, West's awkward prose is perhaps apt for an ambiguous situation: "Even here in the land of his fathers he was half an alien: John Spada from New York, president of a multi-national financial empire, a merchant prince among the old nobility and the new restless commons of this city of Emperors and Popes." Spada is a kingpin of Proteus, a secret, supranational organization. The name comes from "the sea-god, shepherd and guardian of all the creatures who live in the deep." Proteus was endowed by Poseidon "with knowledge of all things, past, present and future, and with the power to change himself at will into a multitude of shapes." When Argentinian thugs kidnap and torture Spada's daughter, Proteus becomes an instrument of his vendetta, at a cost that West soberly reckons.

If his prose is far from nimble, West's mind is unfailingly agile and tough. One of his most unusual enterprises was *The World Is Made of Glass* (1983), published not long after he moved back to Australia. The novel is based on a strange episode in the career of psychologist Carl Jung, in which a woman consulted him in order to confess a murder. In *A History of Australian Literature* (1986) Ken Goodwin argues that *The World Is Made of Glass* "is of a higher order than any of his [West's] earlier works." Goodwin's praise is out of the common run of criticism of West, who has either been written out of the canon of Australian literature altogether or parochially marginalized as an expatriate or international author. Goodwin does not follow this course, although he calls West "a highly successful cosmopolitan novelist," but in a chapter whose title–"Symbolic and Social Realist Fiction"–bears little on West, he moves from him straight to another "international best-seller," Colleen McCullough. This juxtaposition implies both respect and limitation in Goodwin's evaluation of West. In the revised edition of *The Oxford Companion to Australian Literature* (1994) West is given a column that blandly summarizes his career, noting "his knack of predicting world issues and even events." The editors write that "West deals with serious, often religious themes . . . and internationally significant political events."

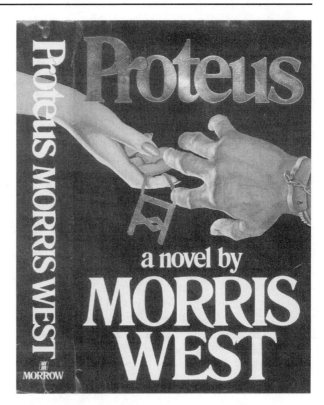

Dust jacket for West's 1979 novel, about a secret multinational organization (Richland County Public Library)

West was not without honors in the wider world, where both his literary and his humanitarian achievements have been recognized. He won the 1959 William Heinemann Award of the Royal Society and the 1960 James Tait Black Memorial Prize for *The Devil's Advocate.* Other awards include the Dag Hammarskjöld International Prize and the Brotherhood Award of the Conference of Christians and Jews. In Australia, West served as chairman of both the National Book Council and the National Library Council. In 1985 he was made a Member of the Order of Australia (AM), and the higher honor of the Award in the Order of Australia (AO) was bestowed on him in 1997. West also received honorary degrees from the University of Western Sydney; Mercy College in Dobbs Ferry, New York; the University of Santa Clara; and Australian National University.

In the 1990s West spoke often and fervently in public, wryly characterizing himself in the 1994 Veech Lecture as "an aging pilgrim, one of the elders who has been a long time on the road." In a 1998 lecture at Australian Catholic University in Sydney, West returned to what had been the training ground of the Christian Brothers. There his own training had begun on 20 December 1929, nearly seventy years before.

Now, he concluded his address by defining what he felt to be the real meaning of private conscience, "the judgment which no one else can deliver but which we make with experience and goodwill. It is the judgment which we make not always with certainty but certainly with peace of heart."

West's work was almost done. There remained *The Last Confession*. Bruno was from Nola, near Naples—"I am a child of the sun." West was looking back toward his compassionate indictment of the treatment of the urchins there in *Children of the Sun*. Bruno describes himself as if he were one of the *scugnizzi*, "a whirligig creature, now up, now down, spinning like a top . . . a monk, a priest, a scholar and fortune's fool as well." Imagining Bruno's thoughts a few days before the priest's scheduled execution, with which the unfinished novel would presumably have concluded, West gave his favorite character these last reflective words: "I still have time to choose a better moment—besides, who knows to what nightmare I might wake."

As a writer of intelligent, morally reflective popular fiction, Morris West's triumph was to find many moments when upheavals in world politics provided opportunities for his art. Even if West is never recognized as one of the greatest novelists in the canon of Australian literature, along with such writers as Christina Stead and Patrick White, his place in world literature is still significant. West's status as a best-selling author never dulled the acuity of his intelligence and ethical perception, a rare circumstance among writers.

References:

Maryanne Confoy, *Morris West: Wandering Scholar and Restless Spirit* (Canberra: Friends of the National Library, 1992);

Ken Goodwin, *A History of Australian Literature* (London: Macmillan, 1986).

Papers:

Morris West's papers are at the National Library of Australia in Canberra.

David Williamson

(24 February 1942 –)

Brian Kiernan
University of Sydney

BOOKS: *The Removalists* (Sydney: Currency Press, 1972; Sydney: Currency Press / London: Eyre Methuen, 1975);

Don's Party (Sydney: Currency Press, 1973; London: Eyre Methuen, 1975);

Three Plays: The Coming of Stork, Jugglers Three, and What If You Died Tomorrow (Sydney: Currency Press, 1974; London: Eyre Methuen, 1974); *Jugglers Three* revised as *Third World Blues* (Sydney: Currency Press, 1997);

David Williamson's The Removalists, edited by Sylvia Lawson (Sydney: Currency Press / London: Eyre Methuen, 1975);

The Department (Sydney: Currency Press, 1975; London: Eyre Methuen, 1975);

A Handful of Friends (Sydney: Currency Press, 1976);

The Club (Sydney: Currency Press, 1978);

Travelling North (Sydney: Currency Press, 1980);

The Perfectionist (Sydney: Currency Press, 1983);

Sons of Cain (Sydney: Currency Press, 1985; revised, 1988);

Collected Plays, volume 1 (Sydney: Currency Press, 1986)–includes *The Removalists, Don's Party,* and the titles previously published in *Three Plays;*

Emerald City (Sydney: Currency Press, 1987); republished as *Emerald City: A Play in Two Acts* (New York & London: S. French, 1987);

Top Silk (Sydney: Currency Press, 1989);

Siren (Sydney: Currency Press, 1991);

Money & Friends (Sydney: Currency Press, 1992; New York: Dramatists Play Service, 1997);

Brilliant Lies (Sydney: Currency Press, 1993);

Collected Plays, volume 2 (Sydney: Currency Press, 1993)–includes *The Department, A Handful of Friends, The Club,* and *Travelling North;*

Sanctuary (Sydney: Currency Press in association with Playbox Theatre Centre of Monash University, 1994);

Dead White Males (Sydney: Currency Press, 1995);

Heretic: Based on the Life of Derek Freeman (Sydney: Currency Press, 1996; Melbourne & Harmonds-

David Williamson in Birchgrove, Balmain, circa 1987
(photograph by Anthony Browell)

worth, U.K.: Penguin, 1996; Melbourne & New York: Penguin, 1996);

After the Ball (Sydney: Currency Press, 1997);

Two Plays (Sydney: Currency Press, 1999)–comprises *Corporate Vibes* and *Face to Face;*

The Great Man; Sanctuary [revised]: *Two Plays* (Sydney: Currency Press, 2000);

Two Plays (Sydney: Currency Press, 2001)–comprises *Up for Grabs* and *Corporate Vibes;* revised edition of *Up for Grabs* (London: Faber & Faber, 2002);

The Jack Manning Trilogy: Face to Face, A Conversation, Charitable Intent (Sydney: Currency Press, 2002);

Birthrights; Soulmates: Two Plays (Sydney: Currency Press, 2003).

PLAY PRODUCTIONS: *The Indecent Exposure of Anthony East,* Melbourne, Union Theatre, 16 August 1968;

The Coming of Stork, Melbourne, Café La Mama, 25 September 1970;

The Removalists, Melbourne, Café La Mama, 22 July 1971;

Don's Party, Melbourne, Pram Factory, 11 August 1971;

Jugglers Three, Melbourne, Russell Street Theatre, 17 July 1972;

What If You Died Tomorrow, Sydney, Opera House Drama Theatre, 9 October 1973;

The Department, Adelaide, The Playhouse, 15 November 1974;

A Handful of Friends, Adelaide, The Playhouse, 20 May 1976;

The Club, Melbourne, Russell Street Theatre, 24 May 1977;

Lear, Melbourne, Alexander Theatre, 28 June 1979;

Travelling North, Sydney, Nimrod Theatre, 22 August 1979;

Celluloid Heroes, Sydney, Nimrod Theatre, 2 December 1980;

The Perfectionist, Sydney, Opera House Drama Theatre, 20 July 1982;

Sons of Cain, Melbourne, Victorian Arts Centre Playhouse, 26 March 1985;

Emerald City, Sydney, Opera House Drama Theatre, 1 January 1987;

Top Silk, Sydney, York Theatre, 11 January 1989;

Siren, Sydney, Wharf Theatre; Melbourne, Atheneum, 22 March 1990;

Money & Friends, Brisbane, Suncorp Theatre, 28 November 1991;

Brilliant Lies, Brisbane, Suncorp Theatre, 29 April 1993;

Sanctuary, Melbourne, Playbox Theatre, 4 May 1994;

Dead White Males, Sydney, Opera House Drama Theatre, 9 March 1995;

Heretic, Sydney, Opera House Drama Theatre, 28 March 1996;

Third World Blues (a revised version of *Jugglers Three*), Sydney, Opera House Drama Theatre, 13 March 1997;

After the Ball, Brisbane, Suncorp Theatre, 3 July 1997;

Corporate Vibes, Sydney, Opera House Drama Theatre, 30 January 1999;

Face to Face, Sydney, Ensemble Theatre, 20 March 1999;

The Great Man, Sydney, Opera House Drama Theatre, 9 March 2000;

Up for Grabs, Sydney, Opera House Drama Theatre, 1 March 2001;

A Conversation, Sydney, Ensemble Theatre, 5 September 2001;

Charitable Intent, La Mama Theatre, 10 October 2001;

Soulmates, Sydney, Opera House Drama Theatre, 18 April 2002.

PRODUCED SCRIPTS: *Stork,* motion picture, based on Williamson's play *The Coming of Stork,* Bilcock & Copping Film Productions, Burstall & Associates, 1971;

The Family Man, motion picture segment of *Libido,* Producers and Directors Guild of Australia, 1973;

"Helen," television, *Certain Women,* Australian Broadcasting Corporation, 1973;

Petersen, motion picture, Hexagon Productions, 1974;

The Removalists, motion picture, based on Williamson's play of the same title, Margaret Fink Productions, 1975;

Eliza Fraser, motion picture, Hexagon Productions, 1976;

Don's Party, motion picture, based on Williamson's play of the same title, Double Head Productions, 1976;

The Club, motion picture, based on Williamson's play of the same title, South Australian Film Commission and New South Wales Film Commission, 1980;

The Department, television, Australian Broadcasting Corporation, 1980;

The Perfectionist, television, Channel 10 Australia, 1980;

Gallipoli, motion picture, Australian Film Commission, R & R Films, South Australian Film Commission, 1981;

Duet for Four, motion picture, Burstall Nominees, 1982;

The Year of Living Dangerously, motion picture, by Williamson, C. J. Koch, and Peter Weir, M-G-M, 1982;

Phar Lap, motion picture, 20th Century-Fox, 1983;

The Last Bastion, television, miniseries, by Williamson and Denis Whitburn, Network 10, Australia, 1984;

Travelling North, motion picture, based on Williamson's play of the same title, Australian Film Commission, Queensland Film Commission, View Pictures, 1986;

A Dangerous Life, television, miniseries based on the novel by Koch, Australian Broadcasting Corporation and HBO (U.S.), 1988;

Dog's Head Bay, television, by Williamson and Kristin Williamson, Barking Mad Television, Australian Broadcasting Corporation, 1988;

Emerald City, motion picture, based on Williamson's play of the same title, New South Wales Film Corporation, Limelight Productions, 1988;

The Four Minute Mile, television, miniseries, British Broadcasting Corporation, Australian Broadcasting Corporation, 1988;

Princess Kate, television, by Williamson and Kristin Williamson, Australian Children's Television Foundation in association with the Australian Broadcasting Corporation, 1988;
Sanctuary, motion picture, based on Williamson's play of the same title, Robin de Crespigney, 1995.

OTHER: Ortrun Zuber-Skerritt, ed., *David Williamson,* Australian Playwrights Series (Amsterdam: Rodopi, 1988)–comprises autobiographical statements, articles, and talks by Williamson.

David Williamson's career is unprecedented in the history of Australian drama. From early in the 1970s he became the single most important figure involved in the establishment of a contemporary national theater. His early plays, first performed in "alternative" little theaters, were soon attracting large audiences to their productions in commercial theaters or in local venues, performed by recently founded state theater companies traveling around the country, and then the plays moved on to London, New York, and elsewhere. Averaging a play each year since then, Williamson has maintained his preeminence among local playwrights and his public prominence. Few, if any, writers in Australia have attracted such sustained attention and controversy as he has during his long career. To many commentators, his successive plays constitute an ongoing, critical chronicle of his times, a discerning analysis of changing social attitudes and shifting ethical concerns. For them, Williamson has an "uncanny" ability to bring to the surface the anxieties prevailing "in the national psyche" at any one moment. To others, though, he is merely an entertainer, an antipodean equivalent of Neil Simon or Alan Ayckbourn. Each new play constitutes an event in the national media, with reviewers often widely divided over its merits, and with the playwright frequently joining in the dispute.

David Keith Williamson was born in Melbourne on 24 February 1942, the elder son of Edwin Keith David Williamson, a bank employee, and his wife Elvie May (née Armstrong). The family lived in the suburb of Bentleigh until 1954, when the senior Williamson became branch manager of the bank at the Victorian country town of Bairnsdale, where David attended high school. A gifted student concentrating on science subjects, Williamson enjoyed musical and sporting activities. His only adolescent concern was his ever upward growth: by sixteen he had attained his full height of 6' 7". For his final year of schooling he was sent to Melbourne, ahead of his family's return there, to attend a more academic school; but this move proved disruptive for him, and he did not sit all the required examinations. He successfully repeated the year and enrolled in mechanical engineering at the University of Melbourne in 1960. After failing his third year at Mel-

bourne, he completed his degree at the newly founded Monash University. On both campuses he edited the faculty magazines, and he was more active in student revues and more interested in writing fiction and verse than in pursuing professional qualifications.

After graduating at the end of 1964, he spent a year working at General Motors Holden and married Carol Cranby in 1965. They had met as students and were both active opponents of the war in Vietnam, Williamson becoming the inaugural president of the Youth Campaign against Conscription. In 1966 he became a lecturer in mechanical engineering at Swinburne College of Technology, Melbourne, and commenced studying part-time for a postgraduate degree in social psychology at the University of Melbourne. The Tin Alley Players, the graduate theater company of the university, became the first to produce a Williamson play, *The Indecent Exposure of Anthony East,* in August 1968. The unpublished script, the first of Williamson's "institutional" plays, genially satirizes corporatism. In the note he provided for the program, Williamson, who later described his role as "storyteller to the tribe," asserted, "We need an Australian theatre because we are not Americans, Britons, or Swedes."

He soon found that he was not alone among recent graduates who aspired to create a contemporary national theater and cinema. In Carlton, adjoining the University of Melbourne campus, the Australian Performing Group had converted a former pram factory into an alternative theater, and nearby an old loft had become the tiny Café La Mama, which, as the name indicates, had been inspired by "Off-Off-Broadway" venues. The emergence of a "new wave" of playwrights, performers, and moviemakers coincided with the coming of age of the post–World War II "baby-boomers," a generation who were better educated and more affluent than their forebears, more critical of colonialist attitudes toward the United Kingdom and the U.S.–though they were also more open to the influences of the United States "counter-culture." The alternative theater not only espoused formal and stylistic experimentation but also attempted social melioration. Its causes included feminism, anticapitalism, antiracism, anti-imperialism, and antixenophobia. The full-length plays that Williamson wrote for the Melbourne alternative theater and that launched his career are, in their varied comic-satiric modes, engaged with the challenges the Women's Movement (as it was then called) presented to traditional male attitudes.

In 1970 the first of these plays, *The Coming of Stork* (published, 1974), was produced at La Mama. It is structured in a series of scenes (a legacy from his years of writing sketches for revues) that present conflicts, especially sexual conflicts, among young male graduates sharing a house–and the same female. The outrageous comedy masks both its autobiographical basis and its serious

*Paperback cover for a 1980 edition of Williamson's 1971 play,
an absurdist satire on troubled relationships between men
and women (Bruccoli Clark Layman Archives)*

attempt to engage with the consequences of "sexual liberation." Soon after, it was produced in one of the alternative theaters in Sydney and eventually had a long run in Los Angeles. Williamson's adaptation of it to the screen as *Stork* (1971) was one of the early successes of the revitalized Australian cinema and quickly led to more commissions for movie and television scripts. In 1971 La Mama provided the venue for the first production of *The Removalists,* in which the playwright played a furniture mover (or "removalist" in Australian English). Again, troubled relationships between the sexes, and also between the police and the public, are involved, in what at first seems a comic-satiric presentation of differing attitudes toward sex and violence between social classes but shifts unexpectedly into a mode akin to absurdism or the "theatre of cruelty," as the two policemen attempting to interfere opportunistically in a domestic dispute end up bashing the husband to death.

Before *The Removalists* had finished its short run, the previously written *Don's Party* (published, 1973) opened at the Pram Factory in 1971. Employing the "found form" of a familiar social ritual, an election-night party, it presents the bored, frustrated lives of early-middle-aged suburban couples—beneficiaries, like the playwright himself, of postwar affluence and the expansion of educational opportunities. With eleven characters interacting comically and often farcically, its surface is apparently random, but it is unobtrusively shaped into a Chekhovian satire of contemporary mores as, over the course of an evening while election results are progressively announced, the revelers' hopes of a new life, politically and personally, wax and wane. Like *The Coming of Stork, Don's Party* traveled, first to Sydney, then nationally and internationally, and was adapted for the screen. Early in 1972 came the announcement that the production of *The Removalists* by the Nimrod Theatre of Sydney had won the British Drama League's George Devine Award for the most promising play, playwright, or production of the year. Never before had the award gone to a playwright outside the United Kingdom (and the subsequent London production won Williamson an award by *The Evening Standard* for most promising playwright in 1973). Almost overnight, Williamson acquired the public prominence he has retained ever since.

For many of Williamson's colleagues in the alternative theater movement, these plays were too "naturalistic"; they were not "experimental" enough (unfair in the case of *Don's Party,* which was written as a challenge to directors); or they were too equivocal in their comic exposure of male chauvinism. In responding, Williamson accepted the (inaccurate) tag of "naturalist" because he wrote from observation and experience, not in imitation of any of the then-fashionable overseas influences. Audiences, however, responded enthusiastically to his comic-satiric realism. Williamson not only made them laugh, but he also presented them with social types and situations they could readily identify, or identify with; at a time, moreover, when the Australian vernacular was still unfamiliar on stage and screen, the language rang true, even if some found it offensive. These comedies brought to audiences shocks of recognition about their society and the changes that were occurring within it.

At the end of 1972, these changes, and reactionary political attempts to resist them, culminated in the return of the first federal Labor government for nearly a quarter of a century. (*Don's Party* is set on the night of the previous election, when Labor had lost yet again.) Greatly increased funding for the arts was included in the wide-ranging agenda for social reform of the new Edward Gough Whitlam government. The Australia Council was established to administer grants, and Williamson, who the new prime minister announced was his favorite local playwright, was appointed to it. Changes had also occurred in Williamson's personal life. By this time he and Carol had two children: Rebecca, born 28 August 1969, and Matthew, born 16 December 1971. During the first production of *The Removalists* Williamson had become involved with Kristin Green (née Löfvèn), a lecturer in drama cast as the play's elder sister, who was also married with two young children, Jonathan (22 April 1966) and Felix (29 May 1969). She and Williamson began living together. In 1972 he and Carol were divorced; he and Kristin married in 1974 after her divorce was finalized. Williamson, who had just been appointed to lecture at Swinburne in social psychology instead of thermodynamics, resigned to write full time. His next play, commissioned by the Melbourne Theatre Company (MTC), the pet aversion of the local alternative theater, premiered the same year. His working title had been "Return from Vietnam," and, ambitiously, he attempted to engage with guilt at both public and personal levels, with Australian involvement in the Vietnam War and with the protagonist's desertion of his wife, pregnant with their second child, for a femme fatale. The MTC, however, objected to the strong flashback scenes set during action in Vietnam (which, like *The Removalists,* linked sexism with violence). Williamson restructured the script, introducing a farcical subplot that ran counter to his original intentions. Retitled *Jugglers Three* (first performed, 1972; first published, 1974), the play pleased reviewers and audiences.

Another commission from a major subsidized company followed. The Old Tote in Sydney was the equivalent of the MTC, and for its inaugural 1973 season at its new venue, the Drama Theatre at the Sydney Opera House, Williamson wrote *What If You Died Tomorrow* (first published, 1974). In outline, this play promised to be more overtly "autobiographical" than its predecessor—it is about the success of a doctor turned novelist who, like Williamson himself at that time, was in a new relationship—but Williamson's skills with rapid pacing, multiple interactions, and conflicting levels of dialogue resulted in a detached comedy that contrasted the values of the "now generation" with those of their parents. *What If You Died Tomorrow* was the hit of the first season at the Sydney Opera House (rescuing the company financially), and the production transferred to London. Artistic directors of state theater companies and commercial producers around the country were keen to schedule a Williamson play, preferably a new one, in their seasons. Inevitably, amid all the acclamations, there were dissenting voices: after the early plays first performed in "non-commercial" alternative theaters, Williamson was now seen as mining his personal relationships for all they were worth, which—perhaps most disappointing of all to these critics—was quite a lot. His public responses to such criticisms only

made him more newsworthy and became integral to the history of the initial reception of his plays.

His next commission came from the South Australian Theatre Company (SATC) for their 1974 season. *The Department* (published, 1975) offered Williamson's detractors only the satisfaction that he was clearly drawing on his memories of teaching in the mechanical engineering department at Swinburne. But these memories were elevated into a humorous satire of how ideals and principles are the first casualties in the struggle of any institution for power, no matter how petty the prize. Williamson later wrote other "institutional" plays—though "personal" plays were more frequent and focused immediately on familial and intimate relationships, with social, political, and moral issues in the background. *A Handful of Friends* (first published in the *Collected Plays,* volume 2 [1993]), first produced by the SATC in 1976 and later the same year by the MTC, is an example of the latter and also of Williamson's continuing technical experiments—though, because these were within realist conventions, his critics did not see them as experimental. A comedy of professional and sexual manners, *A Handful of Friends* involves its five highly articulate and self-conscious characters—a moviemaker and his actress wife, an academic and his wife, and a journalist sister—in an acrimonious release of revelations and resentments about the past.

The Club (published, 1978), commissioned by the MTC and first produced in 1977, has proved through constant revivals to be the most popular of Williamson's "institutional" plays. Set in the committee room of one of the Australian Rules football clubs in Melbourne, the play satirically reveals the self-interest and double dealing underlying the politics of any ostensibly democratic institution, whether a football club or the government of the day. The question of where power ultimately lies—a topical question at that time, following the dismissal of the Whitlam government by the governor-general—is finally resolved democratically, if ironically: the players determine to thwart the committee's plans for the players' retirement by doing what they should have been doing all along, winning games, and so gaining supporters. The Sydney production of *The Club* transferred to London; retitled *Players,* it enjoyed good runs in Washington, D.C., and on Broadway and was later made into a movie by Bruce Beresford.

Overseas productions of Williamson's plays since *The Removalists* had frequently taken him to the United Kingdom and United States. In 1978 he accepted the post of Visiting Professor of Drama at the University of Aarhus, Denmark, for a semester. On their return, the family (which included Kristen's two sons from her previous marriage and young Rory Williamson, born 22 March 1977) decided to move from Melbourne, where they had been living on the rural outskirts, to inner Sydney. Motivating factors were a more congenial climate, escape from what Williamson felt was envy-based resentment of his success in Melbourne, and convenient access to the center of theatrical, movie, and broadcasting activity. Williamson had accepted appointment to the Australian Broadcasting Corporation (though he resigned shortly after, in protest against political interference) and presidency of the Australian Writers' Guild, a position he held for an unprecedented thirteen years. He was becoming increasingly involved in his parallel career of writing for the screen, having adapted most of his plays for movie or television, and his original script for Peter Weir's *Gallipoli* (1981) and his adaptation for the same director of C. J. Koch's novel *The Year of Living Dangerously* (published, 1978; movie produced in 1982) soon brought Williamson international recognition as a screenwriter and several offers from, and visits to, Hollywood.

The move to Sydney reignited in the media the traditional rivalry between the two cities, Sydney and Melbourne, a theme Williamson playfully introduced in his next major play. *Travelling North* (first published, 1980) premiered in 1979 at the Nimrod Theatre—which had been the leading alternative theater in Sydney when Williamson's plays were first being performed. However, instead of being drawn from his own recent experience of traveling north, the characters Frances and Frank in the play were inspired by Kristin's mother and her late-life companion who, like so many other retirees, had left wintry Melbourne in search of paradise in the north, only to confront the inevitabilities of old age. These characters are affectionately presented not only to reveal this personal irony but also to suggest other ironies in the wider social and historical context. Opening around the time in which the earlier *Don's Party* is set, when hopes of an end to conservatism were temporarily dashed, the play ends on the eve of the coming to power of the Whitlam Labor government (but audiences knew that did not last long). The constant scene changes—which showed how Williamson's simultaneous writing for the screen was suggesting techniques for making drama more "accessible" for audiences in the age of television—place Frances and Frank in a variety of situations, together and apart, against this background. Cumulatively, as they move toward the moment of Frank's death, they suggest a pattern not only of inevitability but also of life as mysterious and fulfilling. The classical music specified as part of the total structure of the play in performance—for Williamson, as he has constantly insisted, a script can only be a "blueprint for performance"—invokes a dimension beyond the quotidian; and the final stage direction, that the actor playing Frank should rise from his chair at the end and join the rest of the cast in acknowledging the applause, suggests a sense of regeneration and of the continuance of life. Before leaving Melbourne, Williamson in

1979 had adapted William Shakespeare's *King Lear* (1608) for school students. With *Travelling North,* though, any Shakespearean associations are with the late comedies, not with that tragedy.

By this time Williamson's writing had drawn on a wide range of comedy, from the low and farcical, as in *The Coming of Stork,* to the high comedy of *Travelling North.* In 1980 Nimrod Theatre commissioned a play to celebrate its tenth birthday, and Williamson also burlesqued the local movie industry in a light-hearted, satirical farce, *Celluloid Heroes.* This motion picture proved an unexpected exception to his unbroken run of successes, even if that success had not been shared equally among all his plays to date; but clearly reviewers and audiences by this time expected the latest Williamson production not only to amuse them but also to engage revealingly with significant topical issues. These expectations were well met by *The Perfectionist,* first produced by the Sydney Theatre Company (STC) at the Sydney Opera House in 1982 and published in 1983. (The STC was invited to present this production to the Spoleto Festival in Charleston, South Carolina, in 1984.) A comic-satiric study of a contemporary marriage, the play engages with the impact of feminism on a middle-class, two-career couple and develops further the fluent scene and time shifts found in *Travelling North.* More than in any preceding Williamson play, the issues are fully on the surface, wittily argued by mature, intelligent, articulate characters. By now, though, various commentators opined that Williamson was satirizing too gently what he himself referred to as the "pseudo-problems" of the bourgeoisie: they were asking what had happened to the confronting style of the early plays, with their clash of various subcultures and levels of language. As if in response, his next play, *Sons of Cain* (first performed, 1985; first published, 1985), confronted the scandals then linking politicians and the police to drug trafficking and corruption in the administration of justice. Williamson has always been closely involved with the productions of his plays—attending rehearsals, previews, opening nights, progressively refining his scripts through such "workshopping" and later carefully choosing the initial director of each new play. As well as revues during the early 1970s and a production of Jack Hibberd's *Dimboola* (1969) at the Pram Factory in April 1973 in Melbourne, he had directed John Powers's *The Last of the Knucklemen* (1974) and Arthur Miller's *All My Sons* (1947) for the SATC. He decided to direct the next play himself, for the MTC in 1985 and, later that year, the STC. *Sons of Cain* combined elements reminiscent of his earlier plays for the alternative theater with others familiar from his recent comedies of manners. Something of the larger-than-life caricaturing of the earlier plays enters into the character of Kevin Cassidy, editor of an investigative weekly, while the battle between the sexes in the office of

EMERALD CITY   ①

~~SCRADDEY'S MEN~~
~~IN THE INTERIOR~~   ⌐ FIRST ROUGH DRAFT ¬
                              └   Nov '85   ┘

COLIN stands by a window gazing out. He's in
his mid thirties. A handsome, engaging man
who is   warm and open   when he's
feeling secure but,
         when he feels under attack, capable of
stinging retaliation. He's being watched by ELAINE ROSS
a woman in her fifties. She's been beautiful and
is still striking.
She's intelligent and perceptive but subject to
emotional ups & downs.
          (exalted)
COLIN : What other city in the world could offer
         a view like this?
ELAINE : Rio—but I'm prepared to believe it's the second most
         beautiful city in the world.
COLIN :   I came up here when I was a kid
         and Sydney became a place of sunshine on blue
water and forms in green water and flame trees &
         jacarandas, and I wanted to be there.
                        I should've come years
         ago, but I couldn't convince Kate. She was
         convinced that it was full of con men
         crooks and hustlers.
ELAINE : She was right.
COLIN : Come on Elaine! Melbourne has its quota
         of shysters
ELAINE : There is a difference. Money is more
          important here.
COLIN : Why more so than Melbourne?
ELAINE : You To edge yourself closer to a view.
          In Melbourne all views are equally depressing.

Page from the first draft for Williamson's 1987 play (from Candida Baker, Yacker: Australian Writers Talk
about Their Work, *1986; Paterno Library, Pennsylvania State University)*

his paper has something of the comedy of manners found in *The Perfectionist,* even if they are bad manners.

Williamson returned to this latter mode in *Emerald City* (first performed, 1987; first published, 1987) and also to satirizing the local motion-picture industry. Combining the presentation of personal, moral, sexual, and Melbourne-Sydney conflicts with this satire, the play showed again Williamson's ability to draw on his immediate experience for detached, significant comedy. Colin, the screenwriter who moves with his family from Melbourne to Sydney, is clearly a comic version of Williamson himself, and Colin's conflicts between maintaining his artistic integrity and succumbing to the lures of fame and fortune are projected from criticisms Williamson had recently received, but their implications extend beyond the personal, the topical, and the local. In *Top Silk* (first performed, 1989; first published, 1989), Williamson returned to a more straightforward realism and to the questions raised in *Sons of Cain* of how governments and the judiciary can address the drug problem, but this time in a family rather than an institutional setting. Reviewers panned the initial (commercial) production as unconvincing and melodramatic, but Williamson's large audience nationwide–many of whom had followed his career from *Don's Party* and *The Removalists* and shared his ethical concerns as well as enjoying his humor–remained loyal. Claiming that he despaired of ever pleasing the critics, Williamson announced that his next play would be totally self-indulgent and without any redeeming feature. *Siren* (first performed, 1990; first published, 1991) engages with another current public issue, the corruption associated with land development and with the more perennial personal theme of sexual fidelity, in the mode of bedroom farce, though its dominant mode is more akin to the traditional comedy of humors. As he had gleefully predicted, the reviewers hated the play, but it enjoyed unprecedented simultaneous premieres in Melbourne (a commercial production) and at the STC.

Shortly after moving to Sydney, the Williamsons had purchased a holiday house on the coast at Pearl Beach, and Williamson's next play, *Money & Friends* (first performed, 1991; first published, 1992), was set in just such a seaside hamlet. An incongruous bevy of vacationers, an environmentalist turned television star, a lawyer-developer, a surgeon, their wives, and a couple of academics are drawn together to test the competing claims of loyalty and self-interest. Like *The Perfectionist* and *Emerald City, Money & Friends* is a witty comedy of contemporary manners, this time of nouveau riche manners, with, as in *Siren,* the satiric social types extended toward the "humors," or vices, of the traditional morality play. Reviewers thought it a perfect mirror of the boom-and-bust 1980s. Its opening season at the Queensland Theatre Company (QTC) in 1991 set a new atten-

dance record (now expected by any company fortunate enough to premiere the latest Williamson play), and the production toured the other major state companies. By contrast, *Brilliant Lies* (first performed, 1993; first published, 1993) was calculatedly problematical. Coincidentally addressing at the same time as David Mamet's *Oleanna* (first performed, 1992; first published, 1993) the same theme of sexual harassment in the workplace, its national tour brought most of the critics in line with the public, who had no difficulty in enjoying both Williamson's comedies of manners and his plays confronting difficult issues. *Sanctuary* (first performed, 1994; first published, 1994), written specifically as a two-actor "chamber play" for his then favorite director, Aubrey Mellor, was a further example of the latter. In it, an idealistic student researching American involvement in atrocities around the globe aggressively confronts a former expatriate journalist, now comfortably retired, who had been a high-profile apologist for U.S. policy. The intensity of this confrontation as it mounts toward catastrophic violence is reminiscent of that in *The Removalists,* which had launched Williamson's career.

A different kind of play, as though to counter those critics who referred to his plays as formulaic, *Dead White Males* (first performed, 1995; first published, 1995) was written for a Shakespearean-sized cast. With the Bard having a walk-on part, the play satirizes the theory of deconstruction and the "political correctness" then disrupting humanities departments throughout Australia, as elsewhere. As usual, Williamson balances the not merely topical satire with comedy that extends beyond the quotable one-liners to a plea for an understanding, if resigned, recognition of the human condition. Wayne Harrison, artistic director of the STC, responded imaginatively to the classic comic affinities of the play in its first production. But when Harrison directed Williamson's next play for the company, he discovered close to opening night, with much dismay (and amid gleeful media reporting), that the playwright objected strongly to his interpretation. Williamson–seeing during rehearsal Harrison's interpretation, which introduced such icons of the 1960s as Marilyn Monroe and a yellow submarine–felt that the production was a travesty of the serious concerns of the play. With some last-minute compromises, the production went ahead. This time around, though, any sympathies the dreaded reviewers expressed were for the playwright. The idea for *Heretic: Based on the Life of Derek Freeman* (first performed, 1996; first published, 1996) grew from Williamson's receiving a complimentary letter about *Dead White Males* from Derek Freeman, Emeritus Professor of Anthropology at the Australian National University. Freeman had disputed the thesis of Margaret Mead's *Coming of Age in Samoa* (1928) and had been ostracized by the international anthropological community as a consequence.

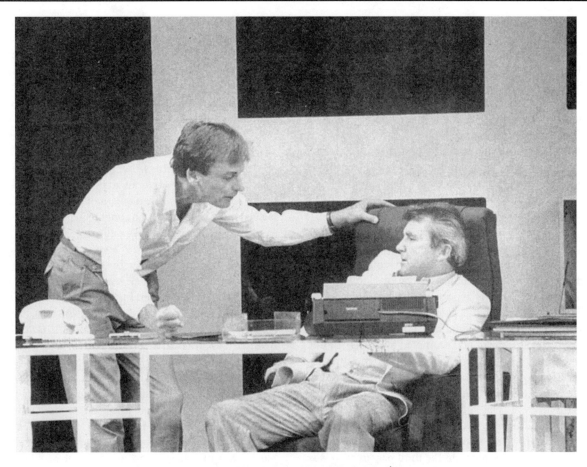

John Bell as Colin and Max Cullen as Mike in the Sydney Theatre production
of Emerald City, *January 1987 (photograph by Branco Gaica)*

Williamson identified Mead's book as a basic pretext for the sexual permissiveness of the countercultural generation he had presented, satirically and comically, in earlier plays. It had also been very influential in popularizing the extreme culturally relativistic or social constructivist denial of any common human nature that he had satirized in *Dead White Males.*

Following his much publicized falling-out with the STC, Williamson promised his next play to Robyn Nevin, who had performed in several of his plays and was now artistic director at the QTC. Having missed out on the new play, Harrison proposed that *Jugglers Three,* which he had seen when a student, be revived by the STC. When Williamson, who had been so publicly sensitive to adverse criticism in recent years, reread it, he announced that he found it a "piece of melodramatic nonsense" and reduced the farcical elements he had introduced in 1972 to ensure its production. Retitled *Third World Blues,* the play premiered in 1997 and was followed the same year by *After the Ball* at the QTC. Williamson and family had been spending increasingly frequent and extended periods on the Queensland Sunshine Coast and by this time had made it their home while retaining an apartment in central Sydney. Williamson spoke of retiring to enjoy the more relaxed lifestyle in the semitropical seaside settlement of Noosa; but as his output of plays and television scripts has not diminished, "retirement" seems to mean not feeling the need to work on even more scripts for Hollywood movies that will not be made and being free to write what most interests him.

After the Ball is a successor to *What If You Died Tomorrow, The Perfectionist,* and *Emerald City* in being, as Williamson has acknowledged, an autobiographically based, family-centered drama. A response to the death of his own mother in 1995, the play shifts between the present, when a brother and a sister review their lives while awaiting their mother's death, and scenes of their parents' courtship and marriage. The rival siblings are of the playwright's own generation, and, as they await their mother's death, they assess their different lives and different understandings of their parents, arguing about many of the cultural, political, and moral questions raised in earlier plays. This type of situation, the enthusiastic reviewers of the production agreed, was Williamson's characteristic strength—his ability to involve his audiences' hearts as well as their minds in the situations on stage.

Williamson was pleased with Nevin's production, and she directed the premiere seasons of his next two major plays, *Corporate Vibes* (published in *Two Plays,* 1999) for QTC in 1999 and, in 2000, *The Great Man* (published, 2000) for the STC, where she had become artistic director. Both plays returned to the by-now classic Williamson mode of comic satire—the first to mock the contemporary ethos of corporatism and development at any cost; the second to disclose some skeletons in the cupboard of the Labor Party, a party now in opposition, which Williamson, a lifelong but not uncritical supporter, shows as more looking back nostalgically to the past than being concerned to develop appropriate policies for the future.

As well as *Corporate Vibes,* another play premiered in 1999. Williamson's continuing interest in social psychology had made him aware of community conferencing as a technique for resolving conflicts of various kinds, many of which he had already represented in his plays. As he felt conflict was inherent to drama, to script an imagined conference based on those he had observed provided a "natural" theatrical form and promoted awareness of this process. *Face to Face* (published, 1999), with ten actors sitting in a circle participating in a workplace conference, was directed by Sandra Bates at the small Ensemble Theatre in Sydney. It was followed at the same theater in 2001 by *A Conversation* (published, 2002), in which the family of a rapist and murderer confront the parents of his victim. Later the same year, the third play in what was published in 2002 as *The Jack Manning Trilogy* (titled after the convener of each of the conferences) premiered at La Mama in Melbourne; this play presented corporate conflicts within a charitable institution. Also in 2001, *Up for Grabs* (published, 2001), a comedy satirizing the commercializing of art in the dot-com age, premiered at the STC under Gale Edwards's direction before being produced elsewhere, including London.

Throughout his career as a playwright David Williamson has been sensitive to criticisms that he is more a popular entertainer than a "serious" or "literary" artist. While he has often reacted defensively to negative reviews, he has at times also subsequently acknowledged that the play then in question did not fully realize his serious intentions in production, even if it proved popular. This issue of "serious" or "literary" versus "popular" art, which has been the subtext to the reception of his work since his debut in the Melbourne alternative theaters, is addressed directly in *Soulmates* (published, 2003), his comedy of contemporary marital, and literary, manners for the 2002 season of the STC, again directed by Edwards. However, since Williamson's preferred dramatic mode, almost without exception, is comedy, the dichotomy perceived confuses mode with matter by assuming comedy cannot be serious. Fundamental to Williamson's wide appeal to audiences is his ability to merge the serious (and also at times the literary) with the popular, understood to be entertaining and, in his case, amusing. With varying degrees of satiric intensity and—not surprisingly, considering his prolific output—with varying degrees of success, his comedies engage with ideas and issues, topical and perennial, that audiences within and beyond Australia can readily relate to.

While from the start Williamson's career as a playwright has been critically contentious, this kind of reception has by no means inhibited recognition of the centrality of his contributions to the growth of a national drama, to the Australian movie industry, and to cultural life generally. (He is a much sought-after commentator on all aspects of these areas.) As well as receiving the English awards, *The Removalists* in 1972 was voted best play and best script in any category by the Australian Writers' Guild—the first two of the eleven "Awgies" he has won to date. The others have been for *Don's Party* (1973), *The Club* (1978; also having received a Major Award), *Travelling North* (1980), and *Emerald City* (1988). *Gallipoli* was declared best original screenplay in 1981; the script for the television movie of *The Perfectionist*, best adaptation in 1986; that for *Travelling North,* the best feature film adaptation in 1987; and the same award in 1989, for *Emerald City*. His movie scripts have also won him four Australian Film Industry Awards—for *Petersen* (1974), *Don's Party* (1976), *Gallipoli* (1981), and *Travelling North* (1987)—and he has been a member of the Academy of Motion Picture Arts and Sciences (United States) since 1993. He was appointed an Officer of the Order of Australia (OA) in 1983 (having earlier, as a proudly decolonized Australian, refused an imperial order); has received several honorary doctorates; has had a theater on a Swinburne campus named for him; and in 1999 was declared a Living National Treasure.

References:

Peter Fitzpatrick, *Williamson* (North Ryde, N.S.W.: Methuen, 1987);

Brian Kiernan, *David Williamson: A Writer's Career* (Port Melbourne, Vic.: Heinemann, 1990; revised edition, Sydney: Currency Press, 1996).

Papers:

The National Library of Australia holds the bulk of David Williamson's papers, including drafts and correspondence, from 1956 through 1995. Important minor holdings are located in the Australian Group Records of the La Trobe Library, State Library of Victoria; Graeme Blundell's papers in the Australian Defence Academy Library, Duntroon, Australian Capital Territory; Betty Burstall's La Mama records in the University of Melbourne Archives; and the Currency Press correspondence files.

Patricia Wrightson
(19 June 1921 –)

Alison Halliday
Workers' Education Association, Macquarie University

BOOKS: *The Crooked Snake* (Sydney & London: Angus & Robertson, 1955);

The Bunyip Hole (Sydney & London: Angus & Robertson, 1958);

The Rocks of Honey (Sydney: Angus & Robertson, 1960; London: Angus & Robertson, 1961);

The Feather Star (London: Hutchinson, 1962; New York: Harcourt, Brace & World, 1963);

Down to Earth (London: Hutchinson, 1965; Richmond, Vic.: Hutchinson, 1965; New York: Harcourt, Brace & World, 1965);

'I Own the Racecourse!' (London: Hutchinson, 1968); republished as *A Racecourse for Andy* (New York: Harcourt, Brace & World, 1968); republished as *'I Own the Racecourse!'* (Ringwood, Vic.: Penguin, 1972);

An Older Kind of Magic (Richmond, Vic.: Hutchinson, 1972; London: Hutchinson, 1972; New York: Harcourt Brace Jovanovich, 1972);

The Nargun and the Stars (Richmond, Vic.: Hutchinson, 1973; London: Hutchinson, 1973; New York: Atheneum, 1974);

The Ice Is Coming (Richmond South, Vic.: Hutchinson, 1977; London: Hutchinson, 1977; New York: Atheneum, 1977);

The Dark Bright Water (Melbourne: Hutchinson, 1978; London: Hutchinson, 1979; New York: Atheneum, 1979);

The Human Experience of Fantasy (Sydney: Alexander Mackie College, 1978);

Night Outside (Adelaide: Rigby, 1979; New York: Atheneum, 1979);

Journey behind the Wind (Richmond, Vic.: Hutchinson, 1981; London: Hutchinson, 1981; New York: Atheneum, 1981);

The Haunted Rivers (Maclean, N.S.W.: Eighth State Press, 1983);

A Little Fear (Richmond, Vic.: Hutchinson, 1983; London: Hutchinson, 1983; New York: Atheneum, 1983);

Patricia Wrightson (photograph by Virginia Wallace-Crabbe; by permission of the National Library of Australia)

Moon-Dark (London: Hutchinson, 1987; New York: McElderry, 1988);

The Song of Wirrun (London & Melbourne: Century, 1987)—comprises *The Ice Is Coming, The Dark Bright Water,* and *Behind the Wind;*

Balyet (London & Sydney: Hutchinson, 1989; New York: McElderry, 1989);

Old, Old Ngarang (Melbourne: Nelson, 1989);

The Sugar-Gum Tree (Ringwood, Vic. & New York: Viking, 1991);

Shadows of Time (Milson's Point, N.S.W. & London: Random House, 1994);

Rattler's Place (Ringwood, Vic. & New York: Penguin Puffin, 1997);

The Wrightson List of Aboriginal Folk Figures, by Wrightson and Peter Wrightson (Milson's Point, N.S.W.: Random House, 1998);

The Water Dragons (Ringwood, Vic.: Penguin Puffin, 1999);

Great Aussie Bites (Camberwell, Vic.: Puffin, 2002)—comprises *Rattler's Place, The Sugar-Gum Tree,* and *The Water Dragons.*

OTHER: *Beneath the Sun: An Australian Collection for Children,* edited by Wrightson (Sydney: Collins, 1972; London: Collins, 1973);

Emu Stew: An Illustrated Collection of Stories and Poems for Children, edited by Wrightson (Harmondsworth, U.K. & Ringwood, Vic.: Kestrel, 1976).

Patricia Wrightson is a significant writer in Australian children's literature of the twentieth century. Her novels show a deep understanding for what it has meant to be an Australian child growing up in a country of conflicting mythologies where the wonder of the natural world may be found for every child. Her provocative and complex re-creations of Aboriginal people, their stories and beliefs, have delighted both child and adult readers.

Alice Patricia Wrightson was born 19 June 1921 at Lismore, northern New South Wales, a country town surrounded by farming land and lush rain forest. Her parents, Charles Radcliff Furlonger and Alice Dyer Furlonger, were country people born about the end of the nineteenth or the beginning of the twentieth century. Her father worked as a solicitor. Wrightson re-created this environment in the settings of her early books. She was educated in country state schools and, for a time, was a pupil of the State Correspondence School, which gives lessons by post to those children who live far away from any conventional school. She spent one year, in the middle of high school, at a boarding school, St. Catherine's College, at Stanthorpe in Queensland. She said in a 2003 telephone conversation with Alison Halliday that she was "really educated by her father in literature, philosophy and wonder." She has described herself as a lonely child isolated between two older sisters and three younger brothers. From an early age, writing school compositions was something she regarded as "her job," to be done without interference from her teachers. In the same conversation, she said that several of her teachers told her that "she would be a writer someday."

Wrightson left school after doing the Intermediate Certificate—that is, after three years of high school education. During World War II, in 1943, she married a country man and during this time her two children were born—Jennifer Mary in 1944 and Peter Radcliff in 1946. The marriage was brief, ending in divorce in 1953, and as a single parent Wrightson worked as a hospital administrator at the Bonalbo District Hospital in northern New South Wales from 1946 to 1960. During this time she began to write. Her first two books were written "deliberately and methodically" as books for children because there were so few good Australian books for children then.

Wrightson received the Australian Children's Book of the Year Award in 1956 for her first novel for children, *The Crooked Snake* (1955). Today, the adventures of these six children during the summer holidays when they form a secret society called "The Crooked Snake" may seem to be rather naive and old-fashioned. Nevertheless, this first book explores ideas and demonstrates the strengths of writing that have continued to be found in Wrightson's works. At a time when so much of the reading for Australian children was centered on British books and the lives of British children, *The Crooked Snake* is set in a specific part of Australia and concerns Australian children. That these children are clearly children of British descent is a reflection of the status quo rather than any prejudicial position. (Their teacher is reading them Kenneth Grahame's *The Wind in the Willows* [1908].) Their Australian identity is created by their interest in the immediate landscape, birds, and animals.

> It was quite different from the soaring forests of gum they had been in, where the trunks rise clear like the columns of old churches and the cool light comes through high arches of grey-green leaves. This was like being under the sea. The green boughs overhead, green vines hanging, green ferns and creepers beneath, were not the dull green of the gums but rich forest green. Dead timber was covered in thick green moss. Even the light was green except in clearer patches where the sun splashed in. The path they walked on was crunchy with dead leaves.

This passage is both an affirmation of a particular place and a celebration of its unusual qualities. The elevated register of the writing underlines not only its importance within the book but also its significance to Wrightson herself.

The "Australian-ness" of the children is also characterized by a freedom of movement during the holidays as they ride their bicycles along old stock routes and through the neighboring paddocks. Their picnics consist of steak, potatoes cooked in the coals, and hot "bitter sugary" billy tea for "the best lunch I ever had."

Dust jacket for the U.S. edition of Wrightson's 1977 novel, which won the 1978 Australian
Children's Book of the Year Award (Richland County Public Library)

Wrightson's concern for the environment is evident, as the plot centers on the younger children preventing some of the older ones from hunting in an old sanctuary. The children, the adults of the town, and the Forestry Department all acknowledge the importance of saving and protecting the wildlife and timber in this remote, and apparently forgotten, place. This combination of celebrating all (or anything) that is unique in the Australian bush with a keen eye for what identifies a particular place (Bangalow palms and bush-turkey mounds) is a thread that may be traced throughout Wrightson's work. However, these factors are not only important in themselves, for they also serve to establish the reality of the setting.

Wrightson never forgets her young readers as the ideas mentioned are included within a plausible adventure story in which the children are quickly delineated as separate individuals that are in no way idealized or simplified. Each character is created not only through brief descriptions but also through dialogue that realistically determines his or her individuality and interactions. The children's language, in small but significant ways, also identifies them as Australian, with the use of

phrases such as "carrot-headed dills" and being asked how to treat snakebite as part of their initiation ceremony. Their freedom and developing autonomy is limited, as their adventure is framed by the summer holidays, by their desire for excitement, and by the adult world of home, town, and school. Thus, ideas of an Australian childhood are layered over a close characterization of individual children.

This pattern of narrative realism within a recognizable and detailed Australian setting is continued in Wrightson's other early works. Her ideas first explored in this book set patterns that are also found in her later work and ones that continue to be developed. In 1960 Wrightson moved to Sydney, where she worked as the secretary and chief executive officer of the Sydney District Nursing Association. Her children were being educated at a boarding school in the New South Wales country town of Armidale, as there was no high school in Bonalbo. Having had several publishing successes, Wrightson then worked, from 1964, for the *School Magazine* of the New South Wales Department of Education for about ten years, the last five as editor. This influential magazine was, and still is, distributed to every primary student in the state.

Wrightson's concerns for the nature of childhood are explored further in two contrasting books from her early period. *'I Own the Racecourse!'* (1968) is a tender examination of an important event in the life of Andy, an intellectually disabled boy. Andy's secure world of playing with his friends, being the peacemaker in their arguments, and enjoying life in his town is shattered as the parameters of his own fantasy world are shown to be false. The ongoing idea that he owns the local racecourse, a belief created by those who work there so as to account for Andy's delight in that place, has unexpected repercussions when he assumes the rights of ownership. An impossible situation is defused by negotiating a "sale" of the racecourse that removes Andy's perceived responsibilities but allows him to continue to visit and enjoy the activities of the racecourse.

Childhood is shown as a time of tolerance and happiness; only with the necessary intrusion of adult perceptions are all the children made aware of the wider world. The potential of *'I Own the Racecourse!'* to be read as a political statement about disadvantaged children never overshadows the day-to-day realism of the lives of the child characters.

The Feather Star (1962) continues Wrightson's exploration of the parameters of young-adult life through the approaching adulthood of Lindy. Her friendships with her peers, her growing awareness of sexual attraction, and her desire to preserve the places and creatures where she lives are familiar ideas in Wrightson's work. This time the close observation and specific detail of the natural world occur in the coastal area of beach, sea, and rock pools. This book also touches on the relationship between a young person and an old man. These relationships across the generational divide are found often in Wrightson's work, especially with the older members of a society. While they may be outcasts or live in some isolation, they are also seen as sources of wisdom and important knowledge, especially about the natural environment in which the novel is set. The maturing of a young girl is revisited in *Balyet* (1989), but in this book the focus is on the desperate need for companionship of the Aboriginal spirit Balyet and her attempt to entrap the girl Jo. Help comes to both of them through the wise old woman Mrs. Willet.

Down to Earth (1965) is a departure from Wrightson's other early novels, but it echoes a similar position of children and childhood and an ongoing concern for precise use of setting. This novel examines how a group of inner-city children cope with an alien literally landing in their midst. Wrightson does not seem entirely comfortable in this book with the fantasy genre; the text is prefaced by a "note to readers, especially professors" in which she states that "it is not for me to explain the little details of how things happen; but to establish the main point that they do happen." The difference in the worldviews of the children and the alien allows Wrightson to make some pertinent comments about the daily life of children—what they eat and wear. More importantly, it enables her to explore notions of identification, difference, and prejudice. The book is also rather strained in having some of its humor reliant on showing the absurdities of the larger adult world. While using this perspective may be a valid form of covert criticism, a child reader may not recognize it. The most significant aspect of *Down to Earth* is that, for all its shortcomings, Wrightson does not abandon her interest in fantasy. When she uses it next, however, it appears as a function of the spiritual and mythical heritage in the lives of the Australian Aborigines.

The city setting of *Down to Earth* is revisited in *Night Outside* (1979), in which two children spend a night out on the streets searching for their missing pet budgerigar (small parrot). Their journey not only takes them through the streets made unfamiliar by darkness, but it also introduces them to some of the people who make up their local community—Ruby the bag lady, Cyril who writes "Eternity" on the pavement (based on a real character who wrote his simple message on Sydney streets for many years), and Mrs. Haitch:

> short and plump, with a face as soft and smooth as a flower and rich-red hair in heavy waves. Her eyes were brown and sharp, but when they were not looking at you they were soft. She wore tiny earrings that suddenly flashed with fire, a tight red dress and over it a wonderful shawl embroidered with faded flowers.

The lost bird is found, but more importantly the children realize that their father, despite his temper, cares deeply for them.

Wrightson's third book, *The Rocks of Honey* (1960), marks a significant change in her writing. Once again Wrightson's book is a story of three children in a bush setting, only this time the location is in a gully in the northern part of the Clarence Valley. Integrated into the children's lives are ideas about Aboriginality, the position of Aborigines in white society, and a retelling of an Aboriginal myth. The children discover a sacred axe, long spoken of in local stories, which was said to be hidden in the Rocks of Honey, an older name for the Three Sisters, three spires of sandstone rock outcrops. The central chapter of the book tells the story of the origin of the stone axe, made in mythic times by "Warrimai the Club-thrower" and then hidden in a far-off place as an act of atonement for breaking the tribal law. In the present time of the narrative Barney's new friend Eustace not only has to acknowledge the real power of the axe but also his own Aboriginal ancestry:

You want to throw the black part away and just keep the white part . . . you don't want any stone axe around you. But you better keep on knowing you got a lot of black in you and only just a little bit of white. . . . You gotta make do with the black part.

Eustace needs to understand the importance of his Aboriginality—that it will mean, for many, that he is a lesser person, but that it will also give him access to a much older and more important past. Eustace places the stone axe back into its hiding place, coming to realize that "a man is his own responsibility." Wrightson emphasizes that the autonomy of Australian adulthood will be a function of the country, for it "would fashion its people, all of them, to its own shape in its own good time." The integration of place and people, the history and stories of the Aborigines, and the impact of the traditional legends and songs of the "Dreamtime" (the Aboriginal word which describes the stories, origin and culture of the land and its people) have become an increasingly important part of Wrightson's work. However, her use of these characteristics has not been without some recent controversy. According to Clare Bradford, Wrightson is a white person speaking for Aboriginal people, and the claimed authority of some of her sources has been challenged.

Wrightson's interests in Aboriginal spirits and mythology are further explored in *An Older Kind of Magic* (1972), in which she introduces Aboriginal spirits such as the Pot-Koorak, the Nyal, and Net-Net. These are not invented spirits but rely on earlier research by such writers as George Augustus Robinson and Aldo Massola. *The Nargun and the Stars* (1973), a book that Wrightson describes as being full of "sounds and silence," returns to the implications of an association between a young Australian boy and the old spirits of the land. In 1974 this book was Wrightson's second to receive the Australian Children's Book of the Year Award. Wrightson stopped work in the mid 1970s to write full-time. Even though in recent years her characterization and use of these Aboriginal spirits have received some criticism, her recognition of Aboriginal spirits and, more importantly, her acknowledgment of the intimate and complex connections between Aborigines and the land have been significant in Australian children's literature.

The core of these ideas is seen in the three books collectively called the Wirrun trilogy. *The Ice Is Coming*, published in 1977 and also awarded the New South Wales Premier's Award, special award for ethnic writing, in 1978, was the first in the trilogy. In 1977 Wrightson was awarded an OBE (Order of the British Empire) for services to literature. The next two books in the trilogy were *The Dark Bright Water* (1978) and *Journey behind the Wind* (1981). The Wirrun trilogy traces the story of

Dust jacket for the U.S. edition of Wrightson's 1983 novel, for which she won her fourth Australian Children's Book of the Year Award (Richland County Public Library)

Wirrun, a young Aboriginal man who, through his adventures and trials, develops into Hero, Ice-Fighter, and finally Great One. In this last role he is one who can claim the whole country, and he eventually leaves his life on earth as a man to become part of the stars.

The sheer complexity of Wirrun's adventures and the problematic process of describing the development of an Aboriginal Great One within a Western mythic tradition has meant that this trilogy, for all its important intentions, may not be read as often as some of Wrightson's other works. In the third book Wirrun challenges the power of death, Wulgaru, and succeeds, but at the expense of his own mortality, as he passes into a spiritual existence and thus into the stories of the "old south land." The books are successful in three ways. The first is in showing the psychological growth of Wirrun and his gradual acceptance of his immediate Aboriginal heritage and his ancestral purpose. This development is explored most closely in *The Dark Bright Water,* when Wirrun's quest to resolve his haunting by the water spirit Yunggamurra means the loss of his close friend, Ularra. Their changing friendship, but ongoing mutual respect, is the core of this story. One aspect that makes the works successful is that the delicate and detailed descriptions of the natural world, from coastal rain forest to western desert, from sea to farming lands, literally ground the adventures of Wirrun. His power is embedded in one small special stone, but he ends up knowing, and thus being responsible for, all the land as he travels across the width of Australia:

> The tired heights circled their secret valleys, stranded rivers vanished into hidden, guarded waters. The rough old rock was wearing into soil, the trees turned their grey leaves edge on to the sun. He said soberly, "She don't give in, any rate, she creeps back another way."

The trilogy is successful finally in revisiting the fundamental ideas and responsibilities of living with others in modern Australia and on this ancient land.

Wrightson's most successful work, arguably, may be *A Little Fear* (1983), which integrates a knowledge of the land, a deep sympathy for the Aboriginal spirit being, and an appreciation of the role of the marginalized and forgotten in modern society—in this case, an old woman. For this book Wrightson won the Australian Children's Book of the Year for the fourth time, in 1984. Critics Maureen Nimon and John Foster have stated that if *A Little Fear* is a "political novel, it is also one of social realism." The clash between the land rights of old Mrs. Tucker, who has inherited the land, and those of the spirit Njimbin, who has lived there for centuries, is the central conflict: "A secret, ancient thing, small yet somehow immense and unknowable . . . all these things were in some way part of this one small thing, and this thing challenged her." That "something small and fast and tricky and ancient" is successful in driving out the old woman and reclaiming the land is not surprising. Wrightson's sympathy, however, also lies with old Mrs. Tucker. Fearing old age and an increasing loss of independence, her expulsion is tempered by reconciliation with her daughter.

Wrightson's interest in Aboriginal spirits and the Dreamtime is evident also in *The Wrightson List of Aboriginal Folk Figures,* written in collaboration with her son, Peter, and published in 1998. This work, Wrightson's only departure from fiction, forms a useful collection explaining many of the Aboriginal spirits.

Patricia Wrightson continues to write, especially for younger readers, with books such as the environmental parable *Moon-Dark* (1987) and *The Sugar-Gum Tree* (1991). These books continue her focus on ways of people living together and the necessity of understanding the physical environment:

> 'To do what is right for all of us: what else are men for?'
>
> 'To learn,' answered Keeting [the Moon spirit], 'Both to learn and to care. And they have learnt much indeed.'

As well as the four Book of the Year awards, Wrightson received the Dromkeen Medal in 1984, was selected to deliver the 1985 May Hill Arbuthnot Honor lecture (in the United States), and won the Hans Christian Andersen Medal in 1986, all for services to children's literature.

Wrightson now lives on the coast of New South Wales, where she has, according to a 2003 telephone interview, "a narrow strip of stony ridge, about a mile long and six chains wide, on which to encourage the natural growth of iron bark, stringy bark and black butt [eucalypts]" (*The Story Makers,* 1987). She describes the south slope of this ridge as her most treasured possession: "where two big figs reach each other with their branches and the silky oaks and hoop-pine spear up between them." Her latest work is for younger readers, and it continues to focus on those areas of greatest concern in all Wrightson's work: the environment, the world of the child, the necessary understanding of the Aborigines and their connections to the land, and, by implication, all that makes Australia what it is today for the child living there. As she has said, "I respond to places, people and events." These interests and a desire to reconcile all inhabitants to the ancient land of Australia are what have illuminated her work.

References:

Clare Bradford, *Reading Race: Aboriginality in Australian Children's Literature* (Victoria: Melbourne University Press, 2001);

Rosamund Dalziell, *Shameful Autobiographies* (Victoria: Melbourne University Press, 1999);

Margaret Dunkle, ed., *The Story Makers* (Melbourne: Oxford University Press, 1987), p. 77;

Aldo Massola, *Bunjil's Cave* (Melbourne: Lansdowne Press, 1968);

Maureen Nimon and John Foster, *The Adolescent Novel: Australian Perspectives* (Wagga Wagga, N.S.W.: Centre for Information Studies, Charles Sturt University, 1997), pp. 227–233;

Maurice Saxby, *The Proof of the Puddin': Australian Children's Literature 1970–1990* (Sydney: Ashton Scholastic, 1993), pp. 18, 252–453, 522–537.

Papers:

The papers of Patricia Wrightson are held in the Lu Rees Archives of Australian Children's Literature, University of Canberra.

Books for Further Reading

Adelaide, Debra. *Australian Women Writers: A Bibliographic Guide.* London: Pandora, 1988.

Beasley, Jack. *Socialism and the Novel: A Study of Australian Literature.* Sydney: Privately printed, 1957.

Bennett, Bruce. *Australian Short Fiction: A History.* St. Lucia: University of Queensland Press, 2002.

Bennett, ed. *An Australian Compass: Essays on Place and Direction in Australian Literature.* South Fremantle, W.A.: Fremantle Arts Centre Press, 1991.

Bennett and Jennifer Strauss, eds. *The Oxford Literary History of Australia.* Melbourne: Oxford University Press, 1998.

Bird, Delys, Robert Dixon, and Christopher Lee, eds. *Authority and Influence: Australian Literary Criticism 1950–2000.* St. Lucia: Queensland University Press, 2001.

Brewster, Anne. *Reading Aboriginal Woman's Autobiography.* Sydney: Sydney University Press, 1996.

Brissenden, Alan, ed. *Aspects of Australian Literature.* Nedlands: University of Western Australia Press, 1990.

Brooks, David, and Brenda Walker, eds. *Poetry and Gender: Statements and Essays in Australian Women's Poetry and Poetics.* St. Lucia: University of Queensland Press, 1989.

Brown, Cyril. *Writing for Australia: A Nationalist Tradition in Australian Literature?* Melbourne: Hawthorn Books, 1956.

Buckley, Vincent. *Cutting Green Hay: Friendships, Movements and Cultural Conflicts in Australia's Great Decades.* Melbourne: Allen Lane/Penguin, 1983.

Burgmann, Verity, and Jenny Lee, eds. *Making a Life: A People's History of Australia since 1788.* Ringwood, Vic.: McPhee Gribble/Penguin, 1988.

Burns, D. R. *The Directions of Australian Fiction 1920–1974.* Melbourne: Cassell Australia, 1975.

Cantrell, Leon, ed. *Bards, Bohemians, and Bookmen: Essays in Australian Literature.* St. Lucia: University of Queensland Press, 1976.

Carroll, Dennis. *Australian Contemporary Drama 1909–1982: A Critical Introduction.* New York: Peter Lang, 1985.

Carroll, John, ed. *Intruders in the Bush: The Australian Quest for Identity.* Melbourne: Oxford University Press, 1992.

Clancy, Laurie. *A Reader's Guide to Australian Fiction.* Melbourne: Oxford University Press, 1992.

Clark, Manning. *A History of Australia.* Carlton, Vic.: Melbourne University Press, 1962.

Clark. *A History of Australia,* volume 3. Carlton, Vic.: Melbourne University Press, 1973.

Clark. *History of Australia*. Abridged, with a Coda, by Michael Cathcart. Ringwood, Vic.: Penguin, 1995.

Clark. *A Short History of Australia*. New York: New American Library, 1963.

Colmer, John. *Australian Autobiography: The Personal Quest*. Melbourne: Oxford University Press, 1989.

Croft, Julian. *The Federal and National Impulse in Australia, 1890–1958*. Townsville, Qld.: Foundation for Australian Literary Studies, 1989.

Cromwell, Alex, ed. *From Outback to City: Changing Preoccupations in Australian Literature of the Twentieth Century*. Brooklyn: American Association of Australian Literary Studies, 1988.

Dixon, Miriam. *The Real Matilda: Women and Identity in Australia*. Ringwood, Vic.: Penguin, 1976.

Docker, John. *Australian Cultural Elites: Intellectual Traditions in Sydney and Melbourne*. Sydney: Angus & Robertson, 1974.

Docker. *In a Critical Condition*. Ringwood, Vic.: Penguin, 1984.

Dutton, Geoffrey. *Snow on the Saltbush: The Australian Literary Experience*. Ringwood, Vic.: Viking, 1984.

Dutton, ed. *The Literature of Australia*. Ringwood, Vic.: Penguin, 1964.

Duwell, Martin, Marianne Ehrhardt, and Carol Hethrington, eds. *The ALS Guide to Australian Writers: A Bibliography 1963–1995*. St. Lucia: University of Queensland Press, 1997.

Eaden, P. R. and F. H. Mares, eds. *Mapped but Not Known: The Australian Landscape of the Imagination*. Netley, S.A.: Wakefield, 1986.

Edwards, Brian, and Wenche Ommundsen, eds. *Appreciating Difference: Writing Postcolonial Literary History*. Geelong, Vic.: Deakin University Press, 1998.

Eldershaw, M. Barnard. *Essays on Australian Fiction*. Melbourne: Melbourne University Press, 1938.

Ewers, John Keith. *Creative Writing in Australia*. Melbourne: Georgian House, 1962.

Ferres, Kay, ed. *The Time to Write: Australian Women Writers 1890–1930*. Ringwood, Vic.: Penguin, 1993.

Ferrier, Carole, ed. *Gender, Politics and Fiction*. St. Lucia: University of Queensland Press, 1985.

Fitzpatrick, Peter. *After "The Doll": Australian Drama since 1955*. Melbourne: Edward Arnold, 1979.

Fotheringham, Richard. *Sport in Australian Drama*. Cambridge: Cambridge University Press, 1992.

Frost, L., ed. *No Place for a Nervous Lady: Voices from the Australian Bush*. Ringwood, Vic.: McPhee Gribble/Penguin, 1984.

Gelder, Ken, and Paul Salzman. *The New Diversity: Australian Fiction 1970–1988*. Melbourne: McPhee Gribble, 1989.

Gerster, Robin. *Big-Noting: The Heroic Theme in Australian War Writing*. Carlton, Vic.: Melbourne University Press, 1987.

Gibson, Ross. *The Diminishing Paradise: Changing Literary Perceptions of Australia*. Sydney: Sirius, 1984.

Gilbert, Kevin, ed. *Inside Black Australia*. Melbourne: Penguin, 1988.

Goodwin, Ken. *A History of Australian Literature*. Basingstoke, U.K.: Macmillan, 1986.

Green, H. M. *A History of Australian Literature*. Sydney: Angus & Robertson, 1961.

Gunew, Sneja. *Framing Marginality: Multicultural Literary Studies*. Melbourne: Melbourne University Press, 1994.

Gunew and Kateryna O. Longley, eds. *Striking Chords: Multicultural Literary Interpretations*. Sydney: Allen & Unwin, 1992.

Hadgraft, Cecil. *Australian Literature: A Critical Account to 1955*. Melbourne: Heinemann, 1960.

Harris, Margaret, and Elizabeth Webby, eds. *Reconnoitres: Essays in Australian Literature in Honour of G. A. Wilkes*. Sydney: Sydney University Press/Oxford University Press, 1992.

Head, Brian, and James Walter, eds. *Intellectual Movements and Australian Society*. Melbourne: Oxford University Press, 1988.

Healy, J. J. *Literature and the Aborigine in Australia 1770–1975*. New York: St. Martin's Press, 1979.

Hergenhan, Laurie. *Unnatural Lives: Studies in Australian Fiction about the Convicts, from James Tucker to Patrick White*. St. Lucia: University of Queensland Press, 1983.

Hergenhan, ed. *The Penguin New Literary History of Australia*. Ringwood, Vic.: Penguin, 1988.

Heseltine, Harry. *The Uncertain Self: Essays in Australian Literature and Criticism*. Melbourne: Oxford University Press, 1986.

Hodge, Bob, and Vijay Mishra, eds. *The Dark Side of the Dream: Australian Literature and the Postcolonial Mind*. Sydney: Allen & Unwin, 1991.

Holloway, Peter, ed. *Contemporary Australian Drama: Perspectives since 1955*. Sydney: Currency Press, 1981.

Hooton, Joy. *Stories of Herself When Young: Autobiographies of Childhood by Australian Women*. Melbourne: Oxford University Press, 1990.

Hope, A. D. *Australian Literature 1950–1962*. Melbourne: Melbourne University Press, 1963.

Jones, Joseph, and Johanna Jones. *Australian Fiction*. Boston: Twayne, 1983.

Kane, Paul. *Australian Poetry: Romanticism and Negativity*. Melbourne: Cambridge University Press, 1996.

Kiernan, Brian. *Images of Society and Nature: Seven Essays on Australian Novels*. Melbourne: Oxford University Press, 1971.

Kiernan. *Studies in Australian Literary History*. Sydney: Sydney Association for Studies in Society and Culture, 1997.

Kinsella, John, ed. *Landbridge: Contemporary Australian Poetry*. Fremantle, W.A.: Fremantle Arts Centre Press, 1996.

Kirkby, Joan, ed. *The American Model: Influence and Independence in Australian Poetry*. Sydney: Hale & Iremonger, 1982.

Kramer, Leonie, ed. *My Country: Australian Poetry and Short Stories, Two Hundred Years*, 2 volumes. Sydney: Lansdowne, 1985.

Kramer, ed. *The Oxford History of Australian Literature*. Melbourne: Oxford University Press, 1981.

Lock, Fred, and Alan Lawson. *Australian Literature—A Reference Guide*. Melbourne: Oxford University Press, 1977.

Lumb, Peter, and Anne Hazell. *Diversity and Division: An Annotated Bibliography of Australian Ethnic Minority Literature.* Richmond, Vic.: Hodja Educational, 1983.

Macartney, Frederick T. *A Historical Outline of Australian Literature.* Sydney: Angus & Robertson, 1957.

Macintyre, Stuart. *A Concise History of Australia.* Cambridge: Cambridge University Press, 1999.

McAuley, James. *The Personal Element in Australian Poetry.* Sydney: Angus & Robertson, 1970.

McCooey, David. *Artful Histories: Modern Australian Autobiography.* Melbourne: Cambridge University Press, 1996.

McCredden, Lyn, and Rose Lucas. *Bridgings: Readings in Australian Women's Poetry.* Melbourne: Oxford University Press, 1996.

McKernan, Susan, *A Question of Commitment: Australian Literature in the Twenty Years after the War.* Sydney: Allen & Unwin, 1989.

McLaren, John. *Australian Literature: An Historical Introduction.* Melbourne: Longman Cheshire, 1989.

McLaren. *Writing in Hope and Fear: Literature as Politics in Postwar Australia.* Cambridge: Cambridge University Press, 1996.

Mudrooroo. *The Indigenous Literature of Australia.* Melbourne: Hyland House, 1997.

Nile, Richard, ed. *The Australian Legend and Its Discontents.* St. Lucia: University of Queensland Press, 2000.

Ommundsen, Wenche, and Hazel Rowley, eds. *From a Distance: Australian Writers and Cultural Displacement.* Geelong, Vic.: Deakin University Press, 1996.

Page, Geoff. *A Reader's Guide to Contemporary Australian Poetry.* St. Lucia: University of Queensland Press, 1995.

Parsons, Philip, ed. *Companion to Theatre in Australia.* Sydney: Currency Press in association with Cambridge University Press, 1995.

Pfisterer, Susan, and Carolyn Pickett. *Playing with Ideas: Australian Women Playwrights from the Suffragettes to the Sixties.* Sydney: Currency Press, 1999.

Pfisterer, ed. *Tremendous Worlds: Australian Women's Drama 1890–1960.* Sydney: Currency Press, 1999.

Phillips, A. A. *The Australian Tradition: Studies in a Colonial Culture.* Melbourne: Longman Cheshire, 1958.

Pierce, Peter, ed. *Oxford Literary Guide to Australia.* Melbourne: Oxford University Press, 1987.

Quartermaine, Peter, ed. *Diversity Itself: Essays in Australian Arts and Culture.* Exeter: University of Exeter, 1986.

Ramson, W. S. *The Australian Experience: Critical Essays on Australian Novels.* Canberra: Australian National University Press, 1974.

Rees, Leslie. *A History of Australian Drama,* volume 1. Sydney: Angus & Robertson, 1978.

Rees. *Towards an Australian Drama.* Sydney: Angus & Robertson, 1953.

Ross, Robert L. *Australian Literary Criticism 1945–1988: An Annotated Bibliography.* New York: Garland, 1989.

Sabbioni, Jennifer, Kay Schaffer, and Sidonie Smith, eds. *Indigenous Australian Voices: A Reader.* New Brunswick: Rutgers University Press, 1998.

Schaffer, Kay. *Women and the Bush: Forces of Desire in the Australian Cultural Tradition.* Cambridge: Cambridge University Press, 1988.

Semmler, Clement, ed. *Twentieth-Century Australian Literary Criticism.* Melbourne: Oxford University Press, 1967.

Serle, Geoffrey. *From Deserts the Prophets Come: The Creative Spirit in Australia, 1788–1972.* Melbourne: Heinemann, 1973; revised edition, 1987.

Shoemaker, Adam, ed. *Black Words, White Page: Aboriginal Literature 1929–1988.* St. Lucia: Queensland University Press, 1989.

Smith, Bernard W. *Australian Painting 1788–1960.* London: Oxford University Press, 1962.

Souter, Gavin. *Company of Heralds: A Century and a Half of Australian Publishing.* Melbourne: Melbourne University Press, 1981.

Spender, Dale, ed. *The Penguin Anthology of Australian Women's Writing.* Ringwood, Vic.: Penguin, 1988.

Stephensen, P. R. *The Foundations of Culture in Australia: An Essay towards National Self-Respect,* introduction by Craig Munro, revised and enlarged edition. Sydney: Allen & Unwin, 1986.

Stewart, Douglas. *The Broad Stream: Aspects of Australian Literature.* Sydney: Angus & Robertson, 1975.

Summers, Anne. *Damned Whores and God's Police: The Colonization of Women in Australia.* Ringwood, Vic.: Penguin, 1975.

Walker, David. *Dream and Disillusion: A Search for Australian Cultural Identity.* Canberra: Australian National University Press, 1976.

Walker, Shirley, ed. *Who Is She?* St. Lucia: Queensland University Press, 1983.

Wallace-Crabbe, Chris. *Melbourne or the Bush: Essays on Australian Literature and Society.* Sydney: Angus & Robertson, 1974.

Wallace-Crabbe, ed. *The Australian Nationalists: Modern Critical Essays.* Melbourne: Oxford University Press, 1971.

Ward, Russel. *The Australian Legend.* Melbourne: Oxford University Press, 1958.

Webb, Janeen, and Andrew Enstice. *Aliens and Savages: Fiction, Politics and Prejudice in Australia.* Sydney: HarperCollins, 1998.

Webby, Elizabeth, ed. *The Cambridge Companion to Australian Literature.* Oakleigh, Vic.: Cambridge University Press, 2000.

White, Richard. *Inventing Australia: Images and Identity 1688–1980.* Sydney: Allen & Unwin, 1981.

Whitlock, Gillian, and David Carter, eds. *Images of Australia: A Reader.* St. Lucia: University of Queensland Press, 1992.

Wilde, William H., *Australian Poets and Their Work: A Reader's Guide.* Melbourne: Oxford University Press, 1996.

Wilde, Joy Hooton, and Barry Andrews, eds. *The Oxford Companion to Australian Literature*. Melbourne: Oxford University Press, 1985.

Wilding, Michael. *Studies in Classic Australian Fiction*. Sydney: Sydney Association for Studies in Society and Culture, 1997.

Wilkes, G.A. *Australian Literature: A Conspectus*. Sydney: Angus & Robertson, 1969.

Wilkes. *The Stockyard and the Croquet Lawn: Literary Evidence for Australia's Cultural Development*. Melbourne: Edward Arnold, 1981.

Wright, Judith. *Preoccupations in Australian Poetry*. Melbourne: Oxford University Press, 1965.

Contributors

Peter F. Alexander . . . . *University of New South Wales*

Bruce Bennett . . . . *University of New South Wales*

Margaret Bradstock . . . . *University of New South Wales*

Veronica Brady . . . . *University of Western Australia*

Anne Brewster . . . . *University of New South Wales*

Tom Burvill . . . . *Macquarie University*

David Carter . . . . *University of Queensland*

Maureen Clark . . . . *University of Wollongong*

Sharon Clarke . . . . *Boston University Sydney Internship Program*

C. A. Cranston . . . . *University of Tasmania*

Carmel Bendon Davis . . . . *Macquarie University*

Martin Duwell . . . . *University of Queensland*

Peter Fitzpatrick . . . . *Monash University*

Marcelle Freiman . . . . *Macquarie University*

Alison Halliday . . . . *Workers' Education Association, Macquarie University*

Anthony J. Hassall . . . . *James Cook University*

Deborah Jordan . . . . *University of Queensland*

Brian Kiernan . . . . *University of Sydney*

Alan Lawson . . . . *University of Queensland*

Susan Lever . . . . *University of New South Wales at the Australian Defence Force Academy*

Elaine Lindsay . . . .

David McCooey . . . . *Deakin University*

Ann McCulloch . . . . *Deakin University*

Paul McGillick . . . .

Brigitta Olubas . . . . *University of New South Wales*

James Packer . . . . *Workers' Educational Association Sydney*

Peter Pierce . . . . *James Cook University*

Felicity Plunkett . . . . *University of New England*

Brigid Rooney . . . . *University of Sydney*

Imre Salusinszky . . . .

Jennifer Strauss . . . . *Monash University*

Chris Wallace-Crabbe . . . . *University of Melbourne*

Cumulative Index

Dictionary of Literary Biography, Volumes 1-289
Dictionary of Literary Biography Yearbook, 1980-2002
Dictionary of Literary Biography Documentary Series, Volumes 1-19
Concise Dictionary of American Literary Biography, Volumes 1-7
Concise Dictionary of British Literary Biography, Volumes 1-8
Concise Dictionary of World Literary Biography, Volumes 1-4

Cumulative Index

DLB before number: *Dictionary of Literary Biography,* Volumes 1-289
Y before number: *Dictionary of Literary Biography Yearbook,* 1980-2002
DS before number: *Dictionary of Literary Biography Documentary Series,* Volumes 1-19
CDALB before number: *Concise Dictionary of American Literary Biography,* Volumes 1-7
CDBLB before number: *Concise Dictionary of British Literary Biography,* Volumes 1-8
CDWLB before number: *Concise Dictionary of World Literary Biography,* Volumes 1-4

D

Davis, Paxton 1925-1994 . . . . Y-89

Davis, Rebecca Harding 1831-1910 . . DLB-74, 239

Davis, Richard Harding 1864-1916
. . . . DLB-12, 23, 78, 79, 189; DS-13

Davis, Samuel Cole 1764-1809 . . . . DLB-37

Davis, Samuel Post 1850-1918 . . . . DLB-202

Davison, Frank Dalby 1893-1970 . . . . . . DLB-260

Davison, Peter 1928- DLB-5

Davydov, Denis Vasil'evich 1784-1839 . . DLB-205

Davys, Mary 1674-1732 . . . . DLB-39

Preface to *The Works of Mrs. Davys*
(1725) DLB-39

DAW Books DLB-46

Dawe, Bruce 1930- DLB-289

Dawson, Ernest 1882-1947 . . . . .DLB-140; Y-02

Dawson, Fielding 1930- DLB-130

Dawson, Sarah Morgan 1842-1909 . . . . . DLB-239

Dawson, William 1704-1752 . . . . DLB-31

Day, Angel flourished 1583-1599 . . . .DLB-167, 236

Day, Benjamin Henry 1810-1889 . . . . DLB-43

Day, Clarence 1874-1935 . . . . DLB-11

Day, Dorothy 1897-1980 . . . . DLB-29

Day, Frank Parker 1881-1950 . . . . DLB-92

Day, John circa 1574-circa 1640 . . . . DLB-62

Day, Thomas 1748-1789 . . . . DLB-39

John Day [publishing house]. DLB-170

The John Day Company DLB-46

Mahlon Day [publishing house] DLB-49

Day Lewis, C. (see Blake, Nicholas)

Dazai Osamu 1909-1948 . . . . DLB-182

Deacon, William Arthur 1890-1977 . . . . . DLB-68

Deal, Borden 1922-1985. . . . . DLB-6

de Angeli, Marguerite 1889-1987 . . . . DLB-22

De Angelis, Milo 1951- DLB-128

De Bow, J. D. B. 1820-1867 . . . . . . DLB-3, 79, 248

de Bruyn, Günter 1926- DLB-75

de Camp, L. Sprague 1907-2000 . . . . DLB-8

De Carlo, Andrea 1952- DLB-196

De Casas, Celso A. 1944- DLB-209

Dechert, Robert 1895-1975. . . . . DLB-187

Dedications, Inscriptions, and
Annotations Y-01–02

Dee, John 1527-1608 or 1609 . . . . . . DLB-136, 213

Deeping, George Warwick 1877-1950 . . . DLB-153

Defoe, Daniel
1660-1731 . . . . . . DLB-39, 95, 101; CDBLB-2

Preface to *Colonel Jack* (1722) DLB-39

Preface to *The Farther Adventures of
Robinson Crusoe* (1719) DLB-39

Preface to *Moll Flanders* (1722) DLB-39

Preface to *Robinson Crusoe* (1719) DLB-39

Preface to *Roxana* (1724) DLB-39

de Fontaine, Felix Gregory 1834-1896 . . . . DLB-43

De Forest, John William 1826-1906 . . DLB-12, 189

DeFrees, Madeline 1919- DLB-105

"The Poet's Kaleidoscope: The
Element of Surprise in the
Making of the Poem" DLB-105

DeGolyer, Everette Lee 1886-1956 . . . . . DLB-187

de Graff, Robert 1895-1981 . . . . Y-81

de Graft, Joe 1924-1978 . . . . .DLB-117

Deighton, Len 1929- DLB-87; CDBLB-8

DeJong, Meindert 1906-1991 . . . . DLB-52

Dekker, Thomas
circa 1572-1632 . . . . . DLB-62, 172; CDBLB-1

Delacorte, George T., Jr. 1894-1991. . . . . DLB-91

Delafield, E. M. 1890-1943. . . . . DLB-34

Delahaye, Guy (Guillaume Lahaise)
1888-1969 . . . . DLB-92

de la Mare, Walter 1873-1956
. . . . DLB-19, 153, 162, 255; CDBLB-6

Deland, Margaret 1857-1945 . . . . DLB-78

Delaney, Shelagh 1939- DLB-13; CDBLB-8

Delano, Amasa 1763-1823 . . . . DLB-183

Delany, Martin Robinson 1812-1885 . . . . . DLB-50

Delany, Samuel R. 1942- DLB-8, 33

de la Roche, Mazo 1879-1961. . . . . DLB-68

Delavigne, Jean François Casimir
1793-1843. DLB-192

Delbanco, Nicholas 1942- DLB-6, 234

Delblanc, Sven 1931-1992 . . . . DLB-257

Del Castillo, Ramón 1949- DLB-209

Deledda, Grazia 1871-1936. . . . . DLB-264

De León, Nephtalí 1945- DLB-82

Delfini, Antonio 1907-1963. . . . . DLB-264

Delgado, Abelardo Barrientos 1931- . . . DLB-82

Del Giudice, Daniele 1949- DLB-196

De Libero, Libero 1906-1981 . . . . DLB-114

DeLillo, Don 1936- DLB-6, 173

de Lint, Charles 1951- DLB-251

de Lisser H. G. 1878-1944 . . . . .DLB-117

Dell, Floyd 1887-1969. . . . . DLB-9

Dell Publishing Company DLB-46

delle Grazie, Marie Eugene 1864-1931. . . . DLB-81

Deloney, Thomas died 1600 . . . . DLB-167

Deloria, Ella C. 1889-1971 . . . . .DLB-175

Deloria, Vine, Jr. 1933- DLB-175

del Rey, Lester 1915-1993 . . . . DLB-8

Del Vecchio, John M. 1947- DS-9

Del'vig, Anton Antonovich 1798-1831 . . . DLB-205

de Man, Paul 1919-1983. . . . . DLB-67

DeMarinis, Rick 1934- DLB-218

Demby, William 1922- DLB-33

De Mille, James 1833-1880. . . . . DLB-99, 251

de Mille, William 1878-1955. . . . . DLB-266

Deming, Philander 1829-1915 . . . . DLB-74

Deml, Jakub 1878-1961. . . . . DLB-215

Demorest, William Jennings 1822-1895 . . . DLB-79

De Morgan, William 1839-1917 . . . . DLB-153

Demosthenes 384 B.C.-322 B.C. DLB-176

Henry Denham [publishing house]. DLB-170

Denham, Sir John 1615-1669 . . . . . . DLB-58, 126

Denison, Merrill 1893-1975 . . . . DLB-92

T. S. Denison and Company DLB-49

Dennery, Adolphe Philippe 1811-1899. . . DLB-192

Dennie, Joseph 1768-1812. . . . . . DLB-37, 43, 59, 73

Dennis, C. J. 1876-1938 . . . . DLB-260

Dennis, John 1658-1734 . . . . DLB-101

Dennis, Nigel 1912-1989 . . . . .DLB-13, 15, 233

Denslow, W. W. 1856-1915. . . . . DLB-188

Dent, J. M., and Sons DLB-112

Dent, Tom 1932-1998 . . . . DLB-38

Denton, Daniel circa 1626-1703 . . . . DLB-24

DePaola, Tomie 1934- DLB-61

De Quille, Dan 1829-1898 . . . . DLB-186

De Quincey, Thomas
1785-1859 . . . . DLB-110, 144; CDBLB-3

"Rhetoric" (1828; revised, 1859)
[excerpt]. DLB-57

"Style" (1840; revised, 1859)
[excerpt]. DLB-57

Derby, George Horatio 1823-1861. . . . . . DLB-11

J. C. Derby and Company DLB-49

Derby and Miller DLB-49

De Ricci, Seymour 1881-1942 . . . . DLB-201

Derleth, August 1909-1971 . . . . .DLB-9; DS-17

Derrida, Jacques 1930- DLB-242

The Derrydale Press. DLB-46

Derzhavin, Gavriil Romanovich
1743-1816. DLB-150

Desai, Anita 1937- DLB-271

Desaulniers, Gonzalve 1863-1934 . . . . DLB-92

Desbiens, Nicholas 1942- DLB-6, 234

Desbordes-Valmore, Marceline
1786-1859. .DLB-217

Descartes, René 1596-1650 . . . . .DLB-268

Deschamps, Emile 1791-1871 . . . . .DLB-217

Deschamps, Eustache 1340?-1404 . . . . . . DLB-208

Desbiens, Jean-Paul 1927- DLB-53

des Forêts, Louis-Rene 1918-2001 . . . . DLB-83

Desiato, Luca 1941- DLB-196

Desjardins, Marie-Catherine
(see Villedieu, Madame de)

Desnica, Vladan 1905-1967 . . . . DLB-181

Desnos, Robert 1900-1945 . . . . DLB-258

DesRochers, Alfred 1901-1978 . . . . DLB-68

Desrosiers, Léo-Paul 1896-1967 . . . . DLB-68

Dessaulles, Louis-Antoine 1819-1895. . . . . DLB-99

Dessì, Giuseppe 1909-1977 . . . . .DLB-177

Destouches, Louis-Ferdinand
(see Céline, Louis-Ferdinand)

DeSylva, Buddy 1895-1950 . . . . DLB-265

De Tabley, Lord 1835-1895 . . . . DLB-35

Deutsch, Babette 1895-1982 . . . . DLB-45

Deutsch, Niklaus Manuel (see Manuel, Niklaus)

André Deutsch Limited DLB-112

Devanny, Jean 1894-1962. . . . . DLB-260

H

Konigsburg, E. L. 1930- DLB-52

Konparu Zenchiku 1405-1468? DLB-203

Konrád, György 1933- DLB-232; CDWLB-4

Konrad von Würzburg circa 1230-1287 . .DLB-138

Konstantinov, Aleko 1863-1897. . . . . . . .DLB-147

Konwicki, Tadeusz 1926- DLB-232

Kooser, Ted 1939- DLB-105

Kopit, Arthur 1937- DLB-7

Kops, Bernard 1926?- DLB-13

Kornbluth, C. M. 1923-1958. . . . . .DLB-8

Körner, Theodor 1791-1813 . . . . .DLB-90

Kornfeld, Paul 1889-1942 . . . . .DLB-118

Korolenko, Vladimir Galaktionovich
1853-1921 .DLB-277

Kosinski, Jerzy 1933-1991 . . . . .DLB-2; Y-82

Kosmač, Ciril 1910-1980 . . . . .DLB-181

Kosovel, Srečko 1904-1926 . . . . .DLB-147

Kostrov, Ermil Ivanovich 1755-1796 . . . . .DLB-150

Kotzebue, August von 1761-1819. . . . . . . .DLB-94

Kotzwinkle, William 1938- DLB-173

Kovačić, Ante 1854-1889. . . . . .DLB-147

Kovalevskaia, Sof'ia Vasil'evna
1850-1891 .DLB-277

Kovič, Kajetan 1931- DLB-181

Kozlov, Ivan Ivanovich 1779-1840. . . . . .DLB-205

Kraf, Elaine 1946- Y-81

Kramer, Jane 1938- DLB-185

Kramer, Larry 1935- DLB-249

Kramer, Mark 1944- DLB-185

Kranjčević, Silvije Strahimir 1865-1908 . . .DLB-147

Krasko, Ivan 1876-1958 . . . . .DLB-215

Krasna, Norman 1909-1984. . . . . .DLB-26

Kraus, Hans Peter 1907-1988. . . . . .DLB-187

Kraus, Karl 1874-1936 . . . . .DLB-118

Krause, Herbert 1905-1976 . . . . .DLB-256

Krauss, Ruth 1911-1993 . . . . .DLB-52

Kreisel, Henry 1922-1991 . . . . .DLB-88

Krestovsky V.
(see Khvoshchinskaia, Nadezhda Dmitrievna)

Krestovsky, Vsevolod Vladimirovich
1839-1895 .DLB-238

Kreuder, Ernst 1903-1972 . . . . .DLB-69

Krėvė-Mickevičius, Vincas 1882-1954. . . .DLB-220

Kreymborg, Alfred 1883-1966. . . . . . .DLB-4, 54

Krieger, Murray 1923- DLB-67

Krim, Seymour 1922-1989. . . . . .DLB-16

Kripke, Saul 1940- DLB-279

Kristensen, Tom 1893-1974. . . . . .DLB-214

Kristeva, Julia 1941- DLB-242

Kritzer, Hyman W. 1918-2002 . . . . Y-02

Krivulin, Viktor Borisovich 1944-2001 . . .DLB-285

Krleža, Miroslav
1893-1981 . . . . .DLB-147; CDWLB-4

Krock, Arthur 1886-1974. . . . . .DLB-29

Kroetsch, Robert 1927- DLB-53

Kropotkin, Petr Alekseevich 1842-1921 . .DLB-277

Kross, Jaan 1920- DLB-232

Krúdy, Gyula 1878-1933 . . . . .DLB-215

Krutch, Joseph Wood
1893-1970 . . . . .DLB-63, 206, 275

Krylov, Ivan Andreevich 1769-1844 . . . . .DLB-150

Krymov, Iurii Solomonovich
(Iurii Solomonovich Beklemishev)
1908-1941 .DLB-272

Kubin, Alfred 1877-1959 . . . . .DLB-81

Kubrick, Stanley 1928-1999. . . . . .DLB-26

Kudrun circa 1230-1240 . . . . .DLB-138

Kuffstein, Hans Ludwig von 1582-1656 . .DLB-164

Kuhlmann, Quirinus 1651-1689 . . . . . . .DLB-168

Kuhn, Thomas S. 1922-1996. . . . . .DLB-279

Kuhnau, Johann 1660-1722 . . . . .DLB-168

Kukol'nik, Nestor Vasil'evich
1809-1868 .DLB-205

Kukučín, Martin
1860-1928 . . . . .DLB-215; CDWLB-4

Kumin, Maxine 1925- DLB-5

Kuncewicz, Maria 1895-1989 . . . . .DLB-215

Kundera, Milan 1929- DLB-232; CDWLB-4

Kunene, Mazisi 1930- DLB-117

Kunikida Doppo 1869-1908 . . . . .DLB-180

Kunitz, Stanley 1905- DLB-48

Kunjufu, Johari M. (see Amini, Johari M.)

Kunnert, Gunter 1929- DLB-75

Kunze, Reiner 1933- DLB-75

Kupferberg, Tuli 1923- DLB-16

Kuraev, Mikhail Nikolaevich 1939- DLB-285

Kurahashi Yumiko 1935- DLB-182

Kureishi, Hanif 1954- DLB-194, 245

Kürnberger, Ferdinand 1821-1879. . . . . .DLB-129

Kurz, Isolde 1853-1944 . . . . .DLB-66

Kusenberg, Kurt 1904-1983. . . . . .DLB-69

Kushchevsky, Ivan Afanas'evich
1847-1876. .DLB-238

Kushner, Tony 1956- DLB-228

Kuttner, Henry 1915-1958. . . . . .DLB-8

Kyd, Thomas 1558-1594 . . . . .DLB-62

Kyffin, Maurice circa 1560?-1598 . . . . . .DLB-136

Kyger, Joanne 1934- DLB-16

Kyne, Peter B. 1880-1957 . . . . .DLB-78

Kyōgoku Tamekane 1254-1332 . . . . .DLB-203

Kyrklund, Willy 1921- DLB-257

L

L. E. L. (see Landon, Letitia Elizabeth)

Laberge, Albert 1871-1960. . . . . .DLB-68

Laberge, Marie 1950- DLB-60

Labiche, Eugène 1815-1888. . . . . .DLB-192

Labrunie, Gerard (see Nerval, Gerard de)

La Bruyère, Jean de 1645-1696 . . . . .DLB-268

La Calprenède 1609?-1663 . . . . .DLB-268

La Capria, Raffaele 1922- DLB-196

Lacombe, Patrice
(see Trullier-Lacombe, Joseph Patrice)

Lacretelle, Jacques de 1888-1985. . . . . . . .DLB-65

Lacy, Ed 1911-1968. . . . . .DLB-226

Lacy, Sam 1903- DLB-171

Ladd, Joseph Brown 1764-1786 . . . . .DLB-37

La Farge, Oliver 1901-1963. . . . . .DLB-9

Lafayette, Marie-Madeleine, comtesse de
1634-1693 .DLB-268

Laffan, Mrs. R. S. de Courcy
(see Adams, Bertha Leith)

Lafferty, R. A. 1914-2002 . . . . .DLB-8

La Flesche, Francis 1857-1932 . . . . .DLB-175

La Fontaine, Jean de 1621-1695. . . . . . . .DLB-268

Laforge, Jules 1860-1887 . . . . .DLB-217

Lagerkvist, Pär 1891-1974 . . . . .DLB-259

Lagerlöf, Selma 1858-1940 . . . . .DLB-259

Lagorio, Gina 1922- DLB-196

La Guma, Alex
1925-1985 . . . . . . .DLB-117, 225; CDWLB-3

Lahaise, Guillaume (see Delahaye, Guy)

Lahontan, Louis-Armand de Lom d'Arce,
Baron de 1666-1715?. DLB-99

Laing, Kojo 1946- DLB-157

Laird, Carobeth 1895-1983 . . . . Y-82

Laird and Lee DLB-49

Lake, Paul 1951- DLB-282

Lalić, Ivan V. 1931-1996 . . . . .DLB-181

Lalić, Mihailo 1914-1992 . . . . .DLB-181

Lalonde, Michèle 1937- DLB-60

Lamantia, Philip 1927- DLB-16

Lamartine, Alphonse de 1790-1869 . . . . . .DLB-217

Lamb, Lady Caroline 1785-1828 . . . . . . .DLB-116

Lamb, Charles
1775-1834 . . . . . .DLB-93, 107, 163; CDBLB-3

Lamb, Mary 1764-1874 . . . . .DLB-163

Lambert, Angela 1940- DLB-271

Lambert, Betty 1933-1983 . . . . .DLB-60

Lamm, Donald
Goodbye, Gutenberg? A Lecture at
the New York Public Library,
18 April 1995 . . . . Y-95

Lamming, George
1927- DLB-125; CDWLB-3

La Mothe Le Vayer, François de
1588-1672 .DLB-268

L'Amour, Louis 1908-1988 . . . . . . .DLB-206; Y-80

Lampman, Archibald 1861-1899 . . . . .DLB-92

Lamson, Wolffe and Company DLB-49

Lancer Books. DLB-46

Lanchester, John 1962- DLB-267

Lander, Peter (see Cunningham, Peter)

Landesman, Jay 1919- and
Landesman, Fran 1927-. DLB-16

Landolfi, Tommaso 1908-1979 . . . . .DLB-177

Landon, Letitia Elizabeth 1802-1838. . . . . .DLB-96

Landor, Walter Savage 1775-1864. . . .DLB-93, 107

Landry, Napoléon-P. 1884-1956 . . . . .DLB-92

P

Cumulative Index

X

Y